A Guide to
Twentieth-century
Women Novelists

For Evelyn

A Guide to
Twentieth-century
Women Novelists

Kathleen Wheeler

BLACKWELL
Publishers

First published 1997

Blackwell Publishers Ltd
108 Cowley Road
Oxford OX4 1JF
UK

Blackwell Publishers Inc
238 Main Street
Cambridge, Massachusetts 02142
USA

British Library Cataloguing in Publication Data

A CIP catalogue record for this book is available from the British Library.

Library of Congress Cataloging-in-Publication Data

Wheeler, Kathleen M.
    A guide to twentieth-century women novelists / Kathleen Wheeler.
        p.   cm.
    Includes bibliographical references and index.
    ISBN 0–631–16493–6 (hc : alk. paper)
    1. English fiction—Women authors—History and criticism.
2. Women and literature—Great Britain—History—20th century.
3. Women and literature—United States—History—20th century.
4. American fiction—Women authors—History and criticism.
5. American fiction—20th century—History and criticism.
6. English fiction—20th century—History and criticism.
7. American fiction—Women authors—Bio-bibliography.   8. English
fiction—Women authors—Bio-bibliography.   9. American fiction—20th
century—Bio-bibliography.   10. English fiction—20th century—Bio-
bibliography.   I. Title.
PR888.W6W44   1996
823'.91099287—dc20   95–51085
                                                                CIP

Typeset in Ehrhardt 9$^{1}/_{2}$/11 pt
by Graphicraft Typesetters Ltd, Hong Kong
Printed in Great Britain by T.J. Press, Padstow, Cornwall

Contents

Part I New Forms of Realism and the Rise of Early Modernism, 1895–1925

CONTENTS

Part IV Further Internationalism, Diversification and Experimentation, 1970–1995

Part V Theory, Further Reading and Research

Preface

This critical guide is an introduction to the rich, varied and astonishingly large body of twentieth-century fiction by women writing in English: an 'introduction' because – as will be clear from a reading both of the four-part chronological introductions to each new period and of the conclusion in part V – many, many additional novelists are mentioned, to direct the reader beyond the one hundred-plus author entries to a further range of fascinating writers. For the field of women novelists is too rich and abundant to be encompassed, even briefly, in one book, a matter which may come as little surprise to readers already familiar with this 'hidden' literature. While each individual author entry can be consulted for biographical, bibliographical and critical information and interpretation about individual writers, the *Guide* primarily functions as a whole to give the reader a clear sense of the development of the novel in English over the last one hundred years. An effort has been made to interrelate many of these writers to their predecessors, contemporaries and successors, in order better to understand the character of the major transformations of the novel form. Concepts such as realism, regionalism, modernism, post-war literature and neo-realism, the literature of exhaustion, the *nouveau roman*, post-modernism and magic realism, as well as terms such as 'experimental' and 'conventional', as applied to narrative practice, are questioned. Rather than suggesting notions of the 'evolution' of the novel form, they are useful, instead, for focusing upon patterns of interaction between innovation and

tradition, which do not so much evolve as recur, or become emphasized, at distinct historical periods. It is evident that the twentieth-century novel by women is so varied in innovation and experimentation, as well as in its use of conventions, that such terms have a strictly limited, albeit useful, role to play in analysis.

In keeping with these two central aims – of introducing the reader to some of the variety of women novelists, and of giving the reader a clear overview of the 'development' of the twentieth-century novel – the entries on individual authors, while giving essential biographical and bibliographical information to fulfil basic reference needs, are mainly devoted to a discussion of the salient narrative forms, stylistic techniques and characteristic writerly practices of these artists. Primarily a critical and interpretative work, then, unlike the existing guides, companions and reference books available, this critical guide seeks, albeit in a very limited space, both to give the reader the flavour of individual writers and to communicate a sense of the marvellous range of nationalities and types of writing in the English language, spread across the whole of the twentieth century. By helping readers to begin to become more aware of and more informed about this vast and colourful landscape of exhilarating literature, the *Guide* may encourage exploration beyond its own all too obvious limits. Moreover, the critical and interpretative approaches of these entries vary widely, and reflect the variety of fictional writings themselves. Yet within this variety of patterns of critical practices, an effort is made to encounter the texts of these women writers as unique beings, as artifacts with a particularity in need of study. That is, an emphasis is put upon the narrative practices and techniques which these writers have developed or adapted in unique ways. Whether or not we share the views, ideas or beliefs attributed (usually mistakenly) to writers or texts, these entries show that we can still admire the passion, commitment and seriousness of purpose which the texts display.

A familiarity with a truly broad and varied range of fiction, through wide reading, makes possible a more catholic taste, and releases the pleasure of texts which otherwise might be misunderstood without contextual knowledge. Such an enlargement of appreciation, both through an increased grasp of the uniqueness of a text and through a wider experience of the varied traditions in which these art objects exist, is the critical aim of this *Guide*. In parallel, the writings of these novelists can be shown to enlarge our perceptions, enliven our sensibilities and improve our imaginative response, by widening the circumference of our experience, and by drawing our attention to the new ways in which experience can be ordered, processed and valued. New forms of consciousness emerge during these transformations of familiar modes of perception, which constitute new ways of living, writing and reading. For the selecting, forming, ordering, shaping and transforming processes of experience are the aesthetic content of every artifact. That is, works of art are the embodiments of human consciousness through which the mind realizes its protean being, as well as illuminating, and even inventing, the world of culture and nature. No gap, then, between the genuinely aesthetic and the genuinely moral is sustainable in such a critical approach: the magic of both art and criticism is in their power to make us see more imaginatively into the myriad forms of life-experience of other human beings so like, yet so fascinatingly unlike, ourselves. Both the radically experimental novel and the so-called novel of ideas challenge our perceptions of human life, if in different ways, and this challenge has inevitable and undeniable moral as well as aesthetic dimensions. The above considerations raise questions about traditional attitudes to evaluation and 'canonization', and have relevance to Harold Bloom's and others' recent controversial writings about canon.

The *Guide* is divided into four major chronological parts (a fifth part includes some concluding material of a variety of kinds). This reflects a fairly wide consensus about the 'development' of the twentieth-century novel. Each of the four chronological parts is introduced, first, by a description of some major feature of the period, then, second, by a look at some of the types of writing of the period. The third chapter in each chronological section contains the essays on individual authors.

The explosive influence of psychological writings on the first decades of the century (an influence which has continued to the present day) constitutes chapter 1, while a discussion of 'modernism' (with all the disagreements about what it is) and stream of consciousness introduces the second part. In part III on the post-war period, the gradual rise of international literatures in English by women is examined as it impinged upon issues of identity, ethnicity and colonialism, for example. Part IV is introduced by a discussion of post-structuralist theory, since many of its insights are evident in fiction both overtly and covertly. Each of these chapters concludes with a list of a dozen or so suggestions for further reading in the subject.

In the second chapter of each of the four chronological parts – that is, the chapters devoted to introducing the reader to the writers of the period – an effort is made to familiarize the reader with names of novelists which she or he may not recognize, and to identify some examples of the various forms of fictional practices characteristic of the period. Each of the individual entries that constitute the third chapters of parts I–IV, on the other hand, is introduced, in the main, by relevant if brief biographical information, and information about primary texts. The main portion of each entry is a critical and interpretative discussion of each writer's fiction. Secondary references can be found at the end of the book, in the section of the bibliography devoted to each novelist.

Entries on individual authors in parts I–IV are organized according to the date of birth of the author discussed. However, because some authors began writing late in life, their works tend to fall into the next chronological section.

On the other hand, authors who began publishing very early in life may fall into an earlier section than expected. Authors who had a very long publishing career will span two sections, so that they will be placed in one or another period according to various obvious considerations, such as when they were at the height of their reputation or influence, and so on. Occasionally, the decision will have to be somewhat arbitrary; hence, the chronological divisions should be taken merely as rough guides to a writer's practices.

Part V is made up of a chapter discussing, albeit briefly, some aspects of feminist theory which are touched upon throughout the various entries, but are treated more explicitly here. The next chapter is an effort to indicate further writers who ought to be in this *Guide*, or in a second volume, if that had only been feasible. Even in that geographically arranged chapter, it will be evident to many readers that names are missing of authors they admire and enjoy. They are missing because of the limits of any author's capacity to cover such a broad area. Finally, a chapter on research resources will, it is hoped, be useful for all readers wishing to explore this subject in greater depth. This chapter has the same geographical basis as chapter 14. The bibliography, then, is additional to and yet dependent upon the final chapter; it is a list of general books and then of anthologies (again organized geographically), followed by an extensive list of secondary criticism on each of the women novelists who have an entry in parts I–IV, and arranged alphabetically by the name of that woman writer.

Acknowledgements

Gratitude must first go to the excellently stocked English Faculty Library at Cambridge, and especially to Dr Gillian Rogers, the librarian, as well as to the University Library. Without the readily available facilities of the former, this project would not have been a feasible undertaking for a single author. Additionally, the English Faculty Office, and specifically Sandra Butler, Anne Reynolds and Helen Saunders, provided invaluable secretarial and administrative help. I also must thank the University of Alabama Library for making available, unrestrictedly for three months, their collection of American and other literature. The University of California Library at Santa Barbara also offered help for six months, in the early stages of this project. The staff at Waterstone's Bookshop gave generously of their time to help me locate books which were often very difficult to obtain, and the staff at Heffer's have also been unusually helpful in overcoming obstacles. Virago Publishers responded readily with answers to queries and with other general information.

To the publishers at Blackwell's, including Andrew McNeillie, Deborah Yuill, Alyn Shipton and Stephan Chambers, I am grateful for the time and trouble they took in the preparation of this large project. Ms Yuill and Mr McNeillie made numerous helpful suggestions in the final stages of the project. St John's College, Cambridge, provided grants and congenial surroundings in the earliest stages of the work, and Darwin College, the Master and Fellows, more recently, must be thanked for the college's wonderful study centre and other facilities. To the University of Cambridge, I owe thanks for several terms of sabbatical leave, during which the progress of this work was greatly accelerated. Without those terms of leave, it would have been quite impossible to undertake and complete this large project.

Advice and encouragement, some of it brief and occasional, some of it systematic and some going back over a decade, came from many individuals, including Lucy Adlington, Christina Baker, Suzanne Burgstaller, Cathy Clay, Diane Coleman, Diana Collecott, Sarah Colstello, Peter D'Eath, Anita Desai, Sarah Dillingham, Emma Drew, Karen Ellin, Mariko Enomoto, Netta Goldsmith, Nadine Gordimer, Catherine Hall, Gillian Hanscombe, Jenny Hodgson, Rebecca Hodgson, Jonathan Hope, Mary Ann Hughes, Claudia Johnson, Elizabeth Jones, Pippa Jones, Roseanne Kennedy, Suzanne Keys, Lola Knipe, Doris Lessing, Samantha Lewis, Esther Lightman, Pamela McCallum, Clea McEnery, Anne Malory, Elizabeth Meese, Carol Ann Michael, Ryoko Ota, John Pahl, Paulina Palmer, Suzanne Patrick, Clare Ratliff, Nicola Rehling, Suzanne Reynolds, Sue Roe, Donna Rudolph, Monica Seidl, Laura Severin, Vivian Smyers, Yaeko Sumi, Yvonne Than, Nicola Upson, Andrea Ward, Alison Wooder and Patricia Zampini.

To my mother I owe more than I can say, for her practical and secretarial help, and also for encouragement on a number of occasions during the past decade or so, when it seemed that this gigantic and often unmanageable undertaking might have quite overwhelmed one.

Alphabetical List of Authors

Kathy Acker
Ama Ata Aidoo
Margaret Atwood
Toni Cade Bambara
Marjorie Barnard
Djuna Barnes
Barbara Baynton
Elizabeth Bowen
Jane Bowles
Kay Boyle
Christine Brooke-Rose
Anita Brookner
A.S. Byatt
Hortense Calisher
Dorothy Canfield (Fisher)
Leonora Carrington
Catherine Carswell
Angela Carter
Willa Cather
Kate Chopin
Ivy Compton-Burnett
Eleanor Dark
Anita Desai
Shashi Deshpande
Jean Crook Devanny
Isak Dinesen
H.D.
Margaret Drabble
Alice Dunbar-Nelson
George Egerton
Alice Thomas Ellis
Buchi Emecheta
Louise Erdrich
Jessie Redmon Fauset
Eva Figes
Zelda Fitzgerald
Janet Frame

Miles Franklin
Mary E. Wilkins Freeman
Mavis Gallant
Jane Gardam
Martha Gellhorn
Charlotte Perkins Gilman
Ellen Glasgow
Susan Glaspell
Nadine Gordimer
Patricia Grace
Radclyffe Hall
Elizabeth Hardwick
Shirley Hazzard
Bessie Head
Winifred Holtby
Keri Hulme
Zora Neale Hurston
Rachel Ingalls
Sarah Orne Jewett
Ruth Prawer Jhabvala
Jennifer Johnston
Elizabeth Jolley
Gayl Jones
Anna Kavan
Molly Keane
A.L. Kennedy
Susan Kenney
Jamaica Kincaid
Maxine Hong Kingston
Margaret Laurence
Harper Lee
Vernon Lee
Ursula Le Guin
Rosamond Lehmann
Doris Lessing
Meridel Le Sueur
Alison Lurie

Rose Macaulay
Carson McCullers
Katherine Mansfield
Kamala Markandaya
Paule Marshall
Miriam Masoli (Tlali)
Bobbie Ann Mason
Toni Morrison
Alice Munro
Iris Murdoch
Gloria Naylor
Frances Newman
Anaïs Nin
Edna O'Brien
Kate O'Brien
Flannery O'Connor
Tillie Olsen
Cynthia Ozick
Grace Paley
Dorothy Parker
Julia M. Peterkin
Ann Petry
Jayne Anne Phillips
Katherine Anne Porter
Katharine Susannah Prichard
Barbara Pym
Ann Quin
Jean Rhys
Dorothy Richardson
Henry Handel Richardson

Michèle Roberts
Joanna Russ
Olive Schreiner
Leslie Marmon Silko
May Sinclair
Elizabeth Smart
Pauline Smith
Stevie Smith
Susan Sontag
Muriel Spark
Elizabeth Spencer
Jean Stafford
Christina Stead
Gertrude Stein
Amy Tan
Emma Tennant
Kylie Tennant
Rose Tremain
Anne Tyler
Alice Walker
Margaret Walker
Sylvia Townsend Warner
Fay Weldon
Eudora Welty
Jessamyn West
Rebecca West
Edith Wharton
Jeanette Winterson
Virginia Woolf
Anzia Yezierska
Marguerite Young

Part I

New Forms of Realism and the Rise of Early Modernism, 1895–1925

Chapter 1

The Influence of Psychological
Writings on Literature

The influence of developments in psychology and related sciences upon literature in the twentieth century are difficult to assess in detail, though they can hardly be overestimated. The proliferation of articles, reviews and books in the several decades prior to 1900 would probably astonish most students of literature, because of our preoccupation with Freud's writings and the consequences of them. As any history of psychology makes clear, however, the subject is as old as human culture, and people have speculated and written about behaviour and the human mind for thousands of years. However, following Charles Darwin's and other natural scientists' discoveries in the mid-nineteenth century, interest in behaviour and in the similarities and differences between humans and animals increased. Already, by the time of William James's *Principles of Psychology*, serialized in instalments and published in book form in 1890, there was a large body of systematic theory about psychology, which James, in the main, reacted against. Educated as he was in physiology and biology, and later philosophy, he saw the faults of the well-established atomist psychologies, which tended to view instincts as isolated from social and environmental influences. His famous 'stream of consciousness' metaphor, and all that it entailed, was received with great excitement, as was his insistence on the importance of the recent scientific formulation of the 'unconscious', which, he said, he believed to be the single most important step forwards for psychology in the last century. Later developments

included the rise of the influence of behaviourism, of which Pavlov, in the first decade of the 1900s, was the most famous expounder. Here, the influence of Darwin was also evident, if one-sided, for the shift from early theories of introspection to the observation of behaviour in concrete situations involved the study of animals in the main, and of the cognitive process of learning, though the results were sometimes tantalizingly generalizable to humans. Behaviourism forbade reference to the mind, or to reports of thoughts, feelings or intentions, because they were not publicly observable, and sought to fuse Darwinian biologism with observationalist traditions of scientific method. (Later, B.F. Skinner refined and extended these early experiments and findings.) Opposed to, or at least sceptical of, behaviourism were the purposive psychologists and the *Gestalt* psychologists. While purposive ideas, propounded by McDougall, for example, in the first decade of the 1900s, were certainly taken up by Freud later, this movement was subsumed by the powerful and long-lasting *Gestalt* theories of Wertheim and others. Again, like William James, they rejected as wholly inadequate the atomistic notions at the basis of much psychological theory, and insisted upon reconceiving human mental experience as a 'field' of sensations, rather than as a mass of elemental, atomistic units somehow put together by mysterious interaction with supernatural laws of mind. As an alternative to James's 'stream of consciousness' metaphor, the 'field' metaphor was used to explain important mental activities such as learning. Learning, it was argued, occurs not so much by means of routine, rote or repetition, or by trial and error, as the behaviourists and others had suggested; rather, *Gestalt* theorists wrote of the capacity for an individual to have insight into a learning problem by looking at the whole, at the field and the numerous inter-relationships within it – and then seeing a solution. These *Gestalt* theories had an effect upon both philosophies of education and practical school arrangements, as well as stimulating the creative artist. Moreover, for the *Gestalt* psychologist, the individual was to be understood as a part of an entire 'life-space', a social and environmental context, not observed in isolation as had been done by many psychologists. Later, R.D. Laing and Richard Reich took these insights to their logical conclusions, but already they influenced Freud in his early studies of hysteria, for example.

Freud's writings, then, were not the beginning of a tradition of sophisticated psychological systematization of theory so much as embedded in an already rich and flourishing world of active reflection, well developed theoretically by the time he learned techniques of hypnosis, for example, from Charcot, or free associative techniques of therapy from Breuer. Moreover, many of his contemporaries and closest associates were alive enough to the depth of the already-existing tradition to see Freud's contributions as only a part of the developments in recent psychologizing, albeit often central and path-breaking. Associates such as Adler and Jung, amongst others, eventually parted with Freud over issues about the nature of the unconscious, the extent of sexual influences, especially on the early development of the child's mental health, the role of the person or ego in behaviour, and so on. Other theorists, such as Melanie Klein and Piaget, took Freud's insights and developed them into vigorous and seminal studies of child psychology, while Karen Horner, Helen Deutsch and, much later, Juliet Mitchell explored the implications of Freudian and other theories for women and for feminism. Reich, on the other hand, applied Freudian insights to an understanding of social and mass psychology, while Laing worked to reveal the *Gestalt* effects of the (often illness-producing) family upon the mental health of individuals. Lacan, publishing and writing in the middle of

the century, has probably been the single most important influence on literary theorists in his 'return to Freud', and in his emphasis upon Freud's preoccupation with language and interpretation, with dreams and the unconscious as coded texts, while most recently Julia Kristeva has once again examined Freud – and Lacan's reinterpretation – for both therapy and for feminism. Contemporaneously, Michel Foucault has subjected Freudian metapsychology, and especially the theories of sexuality, to reanalysis, criticism and questioning.

While the above writers and theorists had a tremendous influence upon art and literature in the early part of the twentieth century – certainly influencing the development of surrealism and modernism, as well as other avant-garde movements – Freud's influence has continued to predominate in literary theory, whether as reinterpreted by Klein, Lacan, Mitchell and Kristeva, for example, or as influential in more accessible interpretations. Freud argued, polemically, that everything he knew was learnt from poets, writers and artists; this mutual influence explains the ease with which many of Freud's insights, emphases and metaphors are referred to literature preceding his own writings. The use of dream analysis for therapy and the splitting of the human mind into conscious/unconscious, with further splits of preconscious and subconscious, affected characterization preeminently in literature. The later postulation of the id/ego/superego trichotomy led to a considerable transformation of the literary representation of both individuals and their relationships with each other. Earlier literary motifs such as the 'double' had already established the fragmentation of the self in some individuals, but Freud established it as characteristic of the human psyche. Moreover, while artists had always used the dream, fantasy and other extraordinary states of consciousness as a means of representing the complexity of human experience, Freud articulated these complexities in a new language. These new emphases and new metaphors, along with a more systematically theoretical and generalized application, led artists to further explorations, based on these new understandings of the 'ordinariness' and normality of things which had previously been the preserve of the ill, the mad, the bad or the eccentric. Indeed, one way of describing the increasing conflict between late realist modes of writing and early modernist ones, which had been surfacing already in the pre-Freudian writings of Henry James, amongst others, was the gradual elimination of the rationality of representational social realism in favour of psychological realism, which included the irrational as part of everyday life. That is, an increased use in literary writings of the inner world as a whole, to represent reality, directly contrasted with realist descriptions of and emphases upon order, logic and externality.

The marked interest of writers in the use of the dream, fantasy, reverie, memory, interior monologue and madness, and the reporting of sensations and perceptions, thoughts and feelings, in fragmented and disorderly modes, led to the rejection of the unitary character of realism for characterization as a site of split, conflicting selves, roles and relations within the psyche as well as without. Plot and familiar, sequential time presentation were also jettisoned; interior experience took precedence over external happenings and observable events, objects, settings and so on. The Freudian idea of the timelessness of the unconscious was contrasted with the pseudo-objectivity of clock-time, thus affecting a novel's structure as well. Writers seemed to feel freer to use flashbacks and other time-disrupting techniques, including frameworks, alternative points of view, stories within stories and so on; all familiar devices, no doubt, but now made the main narrative techniques instead of a deviation from the norm of sequential, discursive, developmental unity.

Another change in literature involved experimentation with language, leading to a rejection of familiar, 'ordinary' language, that is, language used primarily to communicate some content or message, in favour of language toyed with to discover its latent resources. These resources, it was argued, are present in ordinary language and affect our communication, but are repressed or de-emphasized. The result was often a less accessible language of disrupted, fragmented syntax, swirlings of semantics, ambiguities compounded by deliberate punnings, connotations, innuendos, repetitions – but with suggestive variations – sexual insinuations, sinister hints, jokes and other devices to draw attention to the materiality of language and its self-referentiality.

Freudian insistences upon the multivalent nature of utterances encouraged artists to represent language as multilayered, through extensive use of extended metaphors, elaborate symbols and images structuring the narrative, minute particulars made intensely significant, and so on. Freud's published dream-interpretative work encouraged these techniques, and reinforced the idea that social realist and other realist literature had been concerned only with the surface of the mind; however much it had delved into the depravity of society, poverty and illness, it had always encouraged the repression of the insight that *within* the mind of every individual is the lurking power of irrationality, quiescent but wakeable.

It is probable that the impact of Freud's and others' psychological writings were strengthened by World War I. Psychoanalysis had opened up a view of the human being and of reality which was not compatible with either humanist or enlightenment emphases on a unitary subject. This subject was conceived by humanist, enlightenment thinkers as predominantly rational, capable of self-knowledge and self-control, and living in a society constantly progressing towards a better, more just human community. Freud's conception, by contrast, was of a human being only partly conscious of her or his being, only partly capable of control or knowledge, and very vulnerable to powerful, unconscious drives and forces within. The somewhat determinist element of Freudian theory, that what happens in childhood has decisive and irrevocable consequences for future possibilities of development, also added to the sinister aspects of recent theorizing. This 'new' human, profoundly sexual, violently aggressive, innately selfish, inhabited by a death instinct as strong as any life force, split into warring 'selves' and full of ambivalent impulses, and potentially irrational to an unpredictable degree, may not have been true to the complexity of Freud's theories, but became a popular view of his results. With art and science described as in part, at least, sexual fantasies or sublimations, and ethics and religion as the internalization of parental or social taboos about, usually, sex, humans were shown to contain within themselves that very 'Other' which, for thousands of years, they had been trying to destroy as if it were outside themselves. With the horrors of World War I seemingly confirming many of these notions, and with the rise of fascism definitely portraying them as reality, the impact of Freud's writing on the culture of the period was widespread and emphatic. A brief glance at some of the major metaphors in his texts suggests how these insights were thematized in the works of women novelists and were transformative of formal aspects of structure, narrative and style.

Freud's topological, depth metaphor of the conscious/unconscious (with all the intervening levels of preconscious and subconscious) was probably one of the most influential theoretical developments for literature. The ideas of hidden meanings of varying degrees of accessibility, multiple interpretation, ambiguity and interminable analysis all focused the minds of writers on textuality and language. This topological metaphor of conscious/unconscious also posited the dangerous Other inside the psyche instead of outside it, constituting a powerful critique of dualistic psychologies and mind theories, as had William James's writings. However, since the idea of the unconscious was not itself exactly new, it must have been Freud's particular characterization of it, of its relation to conscious life, and of its specific formation in childhood experience (especially sexual bodily experience) which so excited intellectuals and artists. Not only did Freud attribute to the unconscious areas of the psyche a controlling power over the conscious life and action, he also attributed to them a sexual dimension of unprecedented extent. In early publications on the dream, the psychopathology of ordinary life, and wit and jokes, he developed more fully his theories of repression, sublimation and illness. He articulated his methods for gaining access to the 'forgotten' and denied portions of human mental life, through dreams, puns, verbal slips and ambiguities, and so on. Characterizing all these developing theories of Freud's was the constant emphasis on the interpretation of language, mainly verbal language, as the primary vehicle for access to the unconscious. Indeed, Freud's description of dream analysis, for example, caught the imagination of writers and critics alike, because it seemed to offer such parallels for analysis of literary texts and creative processes. Metaphors of dream-work as involving condensation (the loading of a single word, phrase or image with multiple meanings) as well

as other metaphors of displacement and transference – which refer to the distortion and disguising of dream content in order to conceal yet simultaneously express meaning – also referred to both reading and writing.

Freud's description of other aspects of dream-work were relevant for literature too, such as the tolerance in the psyche of contradiction, the use of simultaneity for causality or other logical connections, and the pre-eminence of the relation of similarity in dreams. Similarity was represented, he explained, through techniques familiar from poetry especially, as in symbol, metaphor, simile, metonymy and other forms of condensation, such as identification of unlike things, compositions of several things or persons into one, and other devices. Thus, composite words, persons, places, objects or events will occur in dreams, as they do in art, or objects will be made to 'stand for' a person, place or event through some relevant common feature, or vice versa; interchange or the displacement of the features of one thing onto another facilitates the formation of dream content, and words are particularly serviceable according to Freud, who described words and languages generally as predestined by ambiguity.

Ultimately, all these descriptions of the dream-work were to be suggestive of ordinary language, not just literary, creative writing. Again, the abnormal or supranormal was made the norm, and this reversal is an essential feature of Freud's innovations. What the imagination does, it turned out, is simply what perception itself does at its most basic, unconscious levels. What literary language does, ordinary language does, if less systematically and intensively. What the mad-woman does is characteristic of the normal person; the degree is one of difference of intensity, rather than of kind, though it may lead to a difference in kind.

Freud also emphasized how words are often taken for things or images in dream-work, and he stressed the quality in these cases of the overdetermination or unfinishable nature of interpretation. The degree of condensation of meaning, that is, is indeterminable, with every element in a dream text being variously meaningful. However, Freud explained that, far from impeding interpretation, multiplicity facilitates the decoding of signification, which is more an unravelling of endless numbers of knots than a strict extraction of a message. Thus, a hermeneutics of interpretation usually gives way to the interminability of the decoding, due to condensation and overdetermination of elements. Freud rejected, then, the popular and well-known dream codes and dream books; for him, no dream can be interpreted according to codes, since each signifier is dependent upon a specific, individual context for meaning, however much it may draw some significance from cultural myths and other shared resources. Moreover, he attended preeminently to the dream text, that is, the 'dream' as reported by the patient in words, and to its verbal and linguistic and narrative attributes, as a reading of *The Interpretation of Dreams* confirms.

Freud's theories about the censorship of dreams by an internalized authority also fascinated writers and artists. The functions of the ego (later superego) in such work, and the nature of the material censored as well as the means, led to the systematic articulation of methods of disguise (as described immediately above) for wishes and fears, often of a sexual or taboo nature. The postulation of a censoring authority in the psyche (analogous to the narrator hidden in a text) explained the pressure which led to dream-work disguises, and was in contrast to earlier assumptions that we reveal ourselves in dreams at least, if not in life. Thus, repression and sublimation were found to be busily at work at unconscious as well as conscious levels, complicating the psyche even more, and making it still more difficult to untangle the mass of conflicting impulses of that elusive 'self'. What was the status of intention, will, self-knowledge and truth, if even the unconscious disguised itself?

The attention to language throughout Freud's early writings, whether in interpreting dream texts, linguistic curiosities such as jokes, puns and connotations, or forms of ordinary (and normal pathological linguistic) behaviour determined by reference to words expressive of wishes, offered unprecedented opportunities for influence in literature and literary criticism, as well as other arts. Many of Freud's most memorable metaphors for describing the unconscious were based not even merely on language, but on written language, on texts. In a late essay which has fascinated numerous critics, 'Note on the Mystic

Writing Pad', Freud emphasized the nature of the 'system Pcpt.-Cs [perception-consciousness]' as exemplified in this little 'toy' for children, the mystic writing pad or *Wunderblock*. Psychical content is represented by texts in the dream-work, of course, and in the writing-pad metaphor the psyche is compared to this remarkable little 'machine' for writing. Freud had made a related remark in another late essay, that 'it seems to us more appropriate to compare dreams with a system of writing than with language.' This aspect of Freud's writings is developed fully by Lacan and, later, modified by Kristeva, and it was probably this aspect which accounts for some of the impact on literature of psychological writings in the early twentieth century.

Inherent in the *Wunderblock*, for example, were the concepts of a shield or protective layer designed to diminish the force of external stimuli, and a receptor of the stimuli behind the shield which recorded traces of them. These two factors were for Freud emblematic of the relation of the perception/consciousness system and the memory/unconscious system, and their problematic dynamics. One fascinating character of the *Wunderblock* was its representation of the psyche's ability to be a constantly receptive surface for stimuli – but a surface which would not get filled up and overloaded as it conserved the indefinite, unlimited amount of traces of past stimuli for memory reconstitution (or repression). Unlike material surfaces such as paper, the *Wunderblock* constituted a design for the psyche as 'an ever-ready receptive surface *and* permanent traces of the inscriptions that have been made on it'. Moreover, Freud delighted in pointing out, the *Wunderblock* needed two hands for it to function properly, one to impress the writing on the surface, the other to raise the surface sheet and erase the text so that further writing could ensue. The erasure, of course, was only partial; traces were left on the wax block beneath the surface sheet. These 'two hands', two agencies, the one perceiving, the one erasing yet still recording, reveal the dynamic function of memory in basic perception, and of the unconscious in the conscious; neither can exist without the other. Moreover, when contextualized by Freud's later development of the idea that life and the psyche contain within themselves

7

death and quietude, or the tendency to reduce the excitation of external stimuli (as by the protective shield on the *Wunderblock*), we see a continuing rejection of essentialisms and dualisms in favour of dynamic, relational functions constituting human experience. The 'things' of experience are constructed, whether we are referring to the psyche, the personality or self, or the world – or a literary text; and they can be understood to be constructed like language, even like writing.

Not only did Freud's ideas and theories become thematized in literature and influence style and structure, then, they also provided tools both for analysing texts in interpretation and reading, and for analysing the processes of writing and creation. His theories encouraged more attention to language as a metaphor for mental processes of all kinds rather than as a mere tool or vehicle for messages, and Freud heightened awareness of the complexity inherent in ordinary, apparently simple experiences. The psyche – like a text – was interpretable, but not definitively, and language provides the emblem for its structure.

Lacan's interpretations of Freud led attention back to these emphases upon language, writing and the resulting rejection of those very essentialisms and dualisms which he felt had obscured some of Freud's best insights. Attention was redirected to Freud's articulation of the unconscious, since modern analysis had been 'forgetting' its importance, attending too much to 'helping' the ego integrate and adapt to social demands. What had been a critique of power structures had become a tool for them in oppressing individuals. By refocusing attention on the status of human discourse, as Freud had done, psychoanalysis could analyse itself and flush out some of its own authoritarianism and prejudice. By not attending enough to discourse, analysts were taking for granted not only language, but also notions of the self, the subject, the ego and the world. (Literary critics were simultaneously coming to similar conclusions about their own subject, and were seeking more insight into basic concepts, too, such as text, author, reader and reading, and so on.)

Lacan's well-known account of Freud involved his insistence that the unconscious, as formulated by Freud, has a structure, and that it is structured, moreover, like language. Indeed, the unconscious is, paradoxically, a product of language, as is the self or subject and the world. These *effects* of language are themselves best understood as having the structure of language. Along with Nietzsche, Heidegger and Saussure, Freud and Lacan rejected realist, representationalist accounts of language as meaningful by reference to some external, extra-linguistic reality (see chapter 4 for further discussion). Language is meaningful more as a system of signs interacting according to differences and other relations, involving constant displacement, translation and combination. What is important is not the imaginary referents of the signs, but their interrelations with each other. Lacan argued that Freud rejected simple hermeneutic analyses that behind every code there is a message. Lacan saw the code itself as the message, and this code/message was understood as endlessly indeterminate. Through metaphors of letters (purloined ones, for example), texts and other modes of communication, he reoriented the emphasis to the act of communication itself as an end, not as a means for some content.

Some of Lacan's central reinterpretations of Freud involved ideas about the analysis of the concept of the subject through the metaphor of the 'mirror stage', the three-fold order of the real, the imaginary and the symbolic, the phallus as signifier, and the social tie. These can only be touched upon here, but they were influences upon, and influenced by, literary writings. For example, Lacan developed Freud's idea of the split self and his rejection of any notion of unified totality or essence constituting a self. He argued that there is no direct self-awareness, and that from the outset and throughout our lives we see ourselves in the mirror of others: our concept of self is utterly saturated by otherness. This otherness disrupts the smooth, unified self-identity, displacing it from the centre or origin right at its inception. The self or psyche is better understood as a site of conflicts and a scene of writings, of traces of these disruptions involving the symbolic order – the experience of language – which brings these effects to light.

The participation in the symbolic order of language involves codes, practices and conventions, rules, regulations and taboos – laws, in short. Conflict and issues of sexuality arise, especially the mastering of the Oedipal complex; desire must be displaced onto new objects. In the process, the 'self' begins to recede or vanish into the unconscious in the face of its yawning abyss of desire within it, the *béance*, which must be repressed and distanced. Lacan introduced the concept of the phallus as a symbol of this desire, this otherness, this meaning. He described the phallus as a sign for the hyphen (hymen) suggestive of the split engendered when the child enters the symbolic order of language, where reunion with or fulfilment of this desire is impossible. For some readers of Lacan, this concept of the phallus functions effectively as a critique of a phallocentric culture, since it represents a fantasy of full presence, essence or unity never realizable. In reading both Lacan and Freud, we need to keep in mind that the conscious/unconscious distinction can be easily misunderstood. The unconscious is not some kind of animal, primordial state, preceding the conscious. The unconscious comes into being with the advent of language participation: it is the pressures of the rules, laws and conventions of this 'social tie' of language which create a split between the conscious and unconscious, and initiate desire.

Kristeva's writings have involved in part an effort to re-examine and rework some of Lacan's interpretations, particularly his 'over-emphasis', as Kristeva saw it, upon the symbolic order. She replaced his distinction between the imaginary (the pre-Oedipal realm of unity with the mother) and the symbolic (the stage of repression of desire of the mother and unity) with one between the semiotic and the symbolic, and introduced new metaphors such as the 'chora'. Much influenced by Mikhail Bakhtin as well as by Lacan, Kristeva emphasized the need to re-examine the concepts both of language and of the subject. Language is conceived as processes of signification rather than a system or structure, while the subject is reconceived as a site or position for such processes. These conceptions led to ideas of language processes as social events, essentially communal and contextual in meaning, while the subject – split, divided and multiple – speaks a heteroglossia in every utterance, depending upon the context, the recipient, or the point of view from which the utterance is heard. Kristeva's texts also relocate attention away from central structures of rationality, univocity and literality in language, towards the margins, towards multiple, ambiguous, even chaotic aspects. Ideas of the semiotic, symbolic, thetic and chora were introduced to express the signifying processes which constitute the subject, albeit a fractured, split and warring constitution which, like language itself, is in a state of constant upheaval and destabilization.

In some ways not unlike Nietzsche's concept of the Dionysiac, the chora (Greek for 'enclosed space', such as the womb) is a postulate from which the so-called thetic stage 'emerges', a stage of differentiation, self-consciousness and thus language. Only with the thetic can the chora come into consciousness, however – anterior postulate that it may be – and then it is immediately repressed. Like all repressed elements – those 'Others' – it lives a vigorous and intrusive life within the processes of signification which constitute the subject, disrupting while ordering, multiplying while unifying, and at times creating gaping holes in the (illusory) seamless, univocal rationality of surfaces. Kristeva's chora, Lacan's phallus and Derrida's trace all function as place-holders or deconstructed signifiers designed to interrogate essentialist notions, whether regarding identity (or the subject, self or knower), language, gender, truth, madness, reality or the text. The Bakhtian elements of diversity and dialogism (as well as the emphasis upon contextuality) within each individuality, whether person, concept or text, inform Kristeva's interest in individuality and particularity at every turn. Hence, criticisms of her work as 'politically unsatisfactory' suggest a failure to appreciate the social/contextual nature of the individual per se, and a misunderstanding of the import of her theories.

Michel Foucault once described Freud as he who 'more than anyone else brought the knowledge of man closer to its philological and linguistic model'. He also insisted upon the radical nature of Freud's emphasis on a continuum between normality and abnormality or madness, and the existence of abnormality and madness within the normal. Seen this way, Foucault explained, abnormality and normality are denied any essentialist meaning previously accorded to them by the 'bad blood' or inheritance theorists. They saw mental illnesses and abnormalities as other, outside, unrelated to normal mental health, instead of seeing them as an intensification or distortion by imbalance of normal processes. Foucault also seems to have shared Freud's basic scepticism resulting from the limiting function on knowledge of the concept 'unconscious', and the attendant ideas about language as making possible the construction of a known 'reality'. Foucault applied his own (Nietzschean) interest in power and its relation to knowledge, and the tendency to conceive of power only as domination instead of as 'empowerment' of individuals. He subjected psychoanalysis, madness and language to historical scrutiny, and explored some of the tendencies to ideology and mystification in order to reveal hidden power. He looked closely at the notion of the subject, at concepts of repression and sublimation, and at the central position of sexuality in Freudian metapsychology, and sought to free psychoanalytical thought from being entrapped in its own obfuscations.

To Foucault, truths – whether psychoanalytical ones or others – are never disinterested, but always used to serve political, economic and personal interests. In reasserting the relation of power to knowledge, however, Foucault argued that power needs reconceptualization into empowerment so that it can be productive, not just repressive. Thus, Foucault's writings challenge the authority of the analyst and encourage suspicion of such an unequal power relation. One of his most notable contributions to a critique of psychoanalysis was his rebuttal of accounts of the history of sexuality. He rejected the alleged repression of sexual freedom in the nineteenth century as an explanation for the rise of explicit discourses on sexuality. He implied that psychoanalysis is an example of a historical occurrence of the need human beings have felt at times to talk about sex. Psychoanalysis itself is seen as the expression of this desire to reveal our 'secrets' about the ultimate secret, sex, resulting from the historical notion that the truth about the self, the subject, is hidden in our sexuality. However suspicious we need to be about this 'truth' and its hidden power ideologies, though, Foucault still seems to encourage an interpretation of Freud which acknowledges the decentring of the concept 'subject' from an essentialist account as a rational cogito, to one of the subject as a scene of play, a site of writing out the forces of desire, discourse and domination. While

Foucault, then, subjected psychoanalysis itself to the suspicion of domination through the patriarchal analyst and other alleged truths, other theorists were trying to salvage some central elements from the sense of the failure of sexual liberation to prevent madnesses such as world wars and poverty. For the 'privileged' discourse of psychoanalysis, with its view into all other discourses and secrets of the mind and body, was unable to provide any amelioration of these horrors.

Juliet Mitchell has been one of the most determined of Freud's interpreters to counter many feminist rejections of Freudian theory as patriarchal, sexist and misogynist, which began during Freud's lifetime. With Mitchell's work, other women have similarly advocated a renewal of interest in Lacan, as well, against a current of accusations of phallocentrism. In the effort to regain psychoanalytic thought for feminist uses, Mitchell has argued that in spite of numerous objections to specific aspects or details of Freud's writings, both he and Lacan are better understood as critics of patriarchy and phallocentrism. More generally, for Mitchell, psychoanalysis is not a recommendation or a defence of patriarchal society, but the thorough analysis and exposure of such a world. Consequently, she argues, the study of psychoanalytical theories gives feminists an important set of tools, which they ignore at their peril.

For Mitchell, Freud's theoretical writings have a radical and politically subversive orientation, both in their intense interest in language and communication, and in specific theories about, first, the nature of unconscious mental life and the laws which govern its behaviour, and, second, the significance for human experience of sexuality. One of Mitchell's most insistent insights is the importance of recognizing cultural and social life as not merely sexist but patriarchally structured. Mitchell criticized numerous critics of Freud for forgetting that social structures are characterized not by a male–female opposition merely, with male domination prevailing, so much as by a father-dominated hierarchy. She rejected the former analysis as a barren social or biological dualism, which makes impossible the explanation of how the female is made both inferior and a supplement in nearly all human cultures. With the Oedipal myth of the death of the father and the institution of law, history and guilt comes, she explained, some account of the differing social roles of boys and girls, men and women.

The specific feature of patriarchal society – the law of the hypothesized prehistoric murdered father – defines the relative places of men and women in human culture and history. For Mitchell, then, it is 'fathers', not men, who have the determinant power. This power is a question neither of biology nor of sociology, but of human society itself. The overthrow of patriarchy, she argued, must be achieved by challenging the supposed naturalness of the nuclear patriarchal family. The Oedipus complex, Mitchell explained, should not be confused with the nuclear family itself, however. For there is a contradiction between the internalized law of patriarchal human culture, described by Freud as the Oedipal complex, and its embodiment in the nuclear family. This contradiction can be exploited by women for change.

Mitchell criticized Marxism for its master ideology, economics, and for its subjection of ideological analysis to economic analysis. She explained that a change to a socialist economy from capitalism would not transform patriarchy. A specific struggle against the latter – a 'cultural revolution' – is required: 'some other expression of the entry into culture than the implications for the unconscious of the exchange of women will have to be found in a non-patriarchal society.' The cultural destiny of women will no longer be made to appear misleadingly coincident with a biological capacity to produce children.

One of the most compelling dialogues with Freudian theory has come from existentialism, and specifically from Sartre, who challenged central aspects of the theory such as repression. Sartre did not accept the humanist, enlightenment accounts of human nature, since for existentialists human nature is constructed out of

acts, and is a potentiality more than an essence. He did not, however, accept Freudian theory as a whole, arguing, for example, for a concept of 'bad faith' to replace notions of repression and unconsciousness, and to restore some sense of individual will, operating albeit within a context of powerful forces, both within and without the psyche. His attack on the authoritarianism of the analyst anticipated Foucault's, and his influence on writers and critics was considerable.

Further reading

Bowie, Malcolm. *Freud, Proust, and Lacan. Theory as Fiction.* Cambridge, 1987.

Derrida, Jacques. 'Freud and the scene of writing'. In *Writing and Difference.* London, 1978.

Foucault, Michel. *A History of Sexuality. Vol. I: An Introduction.* Trans. R. Harley. New York, 1980.

Gallop, Jane. *Feminism and Psychoanalysis.* London, 1982.

Gallop, Jane. *Reading Lacan.* Ithaca, N.Y., 1985.

Grosz, Elizabeth. *Jacques Lacan: A Feminist Introduction.* London, 1990.

Hoffman, S. *Freudianism and the Literary Mind.* Baton Rouge, La., 1945.

Kofman, Sarah. *Freud and Fiction.* Cambridge, 1990.

Kristeva, Julia. *Desire in Language.* Ed. Leon Roudiez. New York, 1980.

Lacan, Jacques. *Ecrits: A Selection.* Trans. A. Sheridan. London, 1977.

Mitchell, Juliet. *Psychoanalysis and Feminism.* London, 1974.

Moi, Toril, ed. *The Kristeva Reader.* Oxford, 1986.

Sartre, Jean-Paul. *Search for a Method.* Trans. H. Barnes. New York, 1963.

Sartre, Jean-Paul. *Being and Nothingness.* Trans. H. Barnes. New York, 1956.

Wright, Elizabeth. *Psychoanalytic Criticism.* London, 1984.

Chapter 2

Introduction to Novelists, 1895–1925

I

In 'The Dehumanization of Art', Ortega y Gasset suggested that art has always sought to draw attention away from human subject matter or content. Artists have always disrupted and violated (defamiliarized) our normal perceptions and beliefs, in order to get us to attend to the art itself. The self-consciousness of art is not something especially characteristic of the twentieth century: it is characteristic of art throughout the ages. The notion persists, however, that our century has been more radically experimental and self-conscious than previous eras, regarding the novel, at least. There is probably only a degree of truth in this supposition. Moreover, the notion that the realist novel is more conventional, socio-moral and human in its concerns than so-called experimental novels is also probably true only in a superficial sense. For the realist novel was itself in the nineteenth century an avant-garde, experimental form which many readers found ugly, offensive and not art at all. Additionally, the ideologies and orthodoxies realism was supposed to underpin are just as easily deconstructed by its texts. Nothing could be more self-conscious than its extreme artifices of plot, structured unity, characterization and unnaturally factual language. It must have verged on the bizarre and the grotesque for most readers, until familiarity set in. Itself a reaction to the (then) overfamiliar but (once) remarkably innovative forms of the eighteenth and then the early

nineteenth century (*Robinson Crusoe, Tristram Shandy, Clarissa, Emma* and *Wuthering Heights,* for example), realism was eventually reacted against, as novelists began the process of defamiliarization and disruption afresh.

There are extreme, varying degrees of experimentation and innovation; words like modernism, post-modernism, experimental, *nouveau roman* and avant-garde represent defamiliarization and self-consciousness at its most systematic and overt. Yet, whenever a writer tries to write fiction, some innovation, some self-consciousness, some defamiliarization is always present, or else the result is not fiction. (As Jorge Luis Borges joked, copying *Don Quixote* word for word today would still produce something new and different from Cervantes's book.) The antithesis between modernism and realism, post-modernism and neo-realism, or experimental and conventional novels is an unfortunate set of dualities, which has come to represent a difference in kind rather than one of degree. Some novels more overtly and systematically than others draw attention away from familiarly human content and normal perceptions, towards art itself and its artifices or practices. It is another notion of the present age that the novel or narrative fiction has some special affinity with realism or with 'humanized' art. Yet, the twentieth century has shown beyond a doubt that the novel also has a special affinity with modernism, post-modernism or 'dehumanized art'. And what trait is more human than self-consciousness? What is more dehumanized than cold objectivity? The experiments of our century may look wild and dehumanized to us, but so did the works of Balzac, Zola, Flaubert and Maupassant to their early readers, as contemporary reactions and protestations show. Realism was so self-conscious of its own artifices that it defamiliarized practices readers had taken for granted and destroyed the distance needed to keep up the aesthetic illusion, shattering that illusion with its dehumanizing, microscopic vision applied to everything.

There is no question of a choice, no inherent conflict, that is, between realisms (or conventional, traditional forms) and experimentation. There is only a distinction between the more and the less familiar, or the more or less experimental, and even that is relative and historical. Not only did traditional/conventional novel forms once seem completely new and even dehumanized; the very concept of prose fiction was at first looked upon as an immoral and decadent debasement of the drama and poetry, a ridiculous and unworthy artifice, a non-art. Familiarity blinds us to the newness and arbitrariness of what is now taken as given. All novels have traces and strands of previous and contemporary traditions of fiction, but their use of fictional artifices and narrative practices varies. In seeking to read imaginatively and pleasurably we try to gain a purchase on a text, by discovering patterns and naming practices for the sake of better intimacy with the text's particularity. Such an intimacy is of course arrived at only by a comparison and contrast of fictional elements identifiable from the surrounding and preceding traditions. The vast array of types of vigorous and pleasurable fiction shows that while it may be helpful to make relative groupings of novels and narrative practices into types, we need not create hierarchies. We need not choose between different types or degrees of innovation, experiment or defamiliarization, since vigour and excellence are evident across the spectrum of divergences from today's 'norms'. Regardless, then, of one's temperamental preferences for experiment or tradition, originality cannot simply be equated either with overt, radical experimentation or with the 'socio-moral' novel form at its best. If we put behind us these misconceptions, the fiction of the twentieth century will be a source of both instruction and delight in all its various forms, from 'dehumanized' to 'humanized' art – for what is one thing today will often be the other tomorrow.

II

The gradual shift in the predominant character of the novel from modes of realism developed by the late nineteenth century to something different is evident from Henry James's novels alone, though Emily Dickinson's astonishingly innovative poetry should also alert us to how early reformulations in conceptions about literary practices generally were occurring. One of the earliest indications of a fairly radical transformation of interest from the nineteenth-century experiments of realism, naturalism, regionalism and later forms (such as those of Thomas Hardy; George Meredith anticipates the new) was the explosion in painting of an explicit emphasis upon attending to *processes* of perception and creation in overtly distorting, abstracting modes, as exemplified in the post-impressionism of van Gogh, Cézanne and others. This involved a gradual refocusing of realist attitudes away from notions of verisimilitude, that is, away from treating objects (whether things, people, society, ideas, etc.) as already constituted and essentially natural realities to be accurately represented in art or illuminated more clearly by art. Rather, objects and the world began to be emphasized anew as a cultural construct, and art was seen as capable of revealing more immediately the mental/cultural processes of perception, organization and unification which lead to such a construct. Post-impressionists also discovered that by making the processes of perception an overt and emphatic subject matter (they had always been covert) of their art, they could see and perceive those old 'things' or objects in new ways, thereby anticipating Russian formalism. The shift from an emphasis upon objects and products to one upon activities and processes involved a change back to much earlier artistic practices in literature and in painting, which drew attention to their own processes and practices (as in Shakespeare, Cervantes, Defoe and Sterne).

The theories and paintings of such artists as van Gogh and Cézanne reveal a profound commitment to revitalizing art by this change in emphasis and in practices from predominant nineteenth-century forms, from emphasis upon content to a corrective re-emphasis on artistic methods and formalities as congruent with subject matter. The reawakening in the 1880s and 1890s to an increased interest in practical innovations and experimentation with method and materials is probably a symptom of the complacency which had set in, in the last part of the nineteenth century, about its familiar styles and forms, which had served the century so well, but which were beginning to inhibit fresh response, new experiences and new ways of writing, painting and living. While it is sometimes said by critics that artists and writers moved from a more 'discursive' art to an 'imagistic' art, this is only one (misleading) way of describing changing interests and methods. For an overemphasis upon the image as the new substitute for the object or product obscures the fact that writers and painters were attending more overtly not to the results of mentality but to its processes. Along with Henry James and Emily Dickinson, Gertrude Stein was one of the earliest and most radical of experimentalists, and her interest in and personal connections with the painters of the period is hardly incidental to her extraordinarily innovative writing. Nor is William James's influence on her to be underestimated.

Ironically, one of Stein's central techniques was also one of the main characteristics of early realism, namely, a stripped-down, denuded language freed of the phoney artifices of some earlier prose and poetry. Yet she never fell into the illusion, as did the readers of realists, that such a language was a transparent medium of reality or that language was basically literal and non-metaphorical. Edith Wharton was later to remark that all language is stylized, from the most familiar and conventional to the most eccentric and innovative. Both imagism and symbolism, and later surrealism, could be said to provide less radical alternatives to realism and the other established, authoritative forms, because of a less intense interest in process over product. Stein was also fortunate in having had the enlivening effects of William James's insights into psychology and philosophy to help her break out of the mesmerizing effects of traditional philosophizing, with its eye fixed on fixities, products and eternals. James, like the post-impressionists,

turned Stein's attention towards the activities and constructive exercises of the human mind as the object of philosophy, instead of gazing upon ultimates and unchanging being. In *Principles of Psychology*, James had introduced the concept of a 'stream of consciousness' (see above for further elucidation), which the faculties of the mind rudder and curb, select and organize for specific survival and pleasure purposes. This Nietzschean emphasis on art understood as the momentary embodiment of creative processes, structured by acts of the mind itself, prepared Stein to appreciate the genius of post-impressionist painters, and established her as probably the earliest and most innovative of the post-realist writers, except for Emily Dickinson.

The developments in the philosophy of Charles Sanders Peirce and William James also turned a more sophisticated attention to language, which became a hallmark of Stein's writing, as it had been in a different way in Henry James's. The return to an increased, articulate awareness of the role of language in thought and feeling, and in the construction of experience and reality (characteristic of early seventeenth- and late eighteenth-century literature, for example), meant that language could not be treated as merely the vehicle or form of an already constituted consciousness. It was seen as the character and constructive means of consciousness itself, as it had been in Shakespeare, for instance. Language, then, became once again a central and overt subject matter of fiction, as the modernist experiments of Virginia Woolf, James Joyce, Samuel Beckett, Dorothy Richardson, William Faulkner, Joseph Conrad, Stevie Smith and D.H. Lawrence, amongst others, made evident. Interacting with these earlier developments were the earth-shattering revelations of Freud (discussed above) and Jung, which had an incalculable effect upon the literature of the period and of later literary movements, such as surrealism, right through the twentieth century. Freud's Nietzschean insistence that language is not only expressive but also formative of the characteristic structures of human consciousness, and his systematic analysis of language forms such as metonymy, metaphor, pun and symbol, led him to expound more openly than before the centrality of desire, sexuality, and the unconscious in our everyday, conscious lives. He too, like the post-impressionists and William James, redirected attention to processes of perception and described them in terms which had particular resonance for an understanding of literary practices. Freud showed that our most basic mental processes involve condensation and displacement, for example; he saw metaphors and other figures of speech as the very character of language, as he had learnt from Nietzsche and the Greek tragedians. He reiterated the Shakespearean and Romantic aesthetic attitude that we do not so much describe as interpret and construct reality out of linguistic formations (see chapter 1).

III

Writers in the early part of the century, such as May Sinclair, Catherine Carswell, Olive Schreiner, Gertrude Stein and Dorothy Richardson, most overtly expressed in their writings the influences of Freud, Jung, Havelock-Ellis and other theorists of the unconscious and sexuality. Sinclair's most acclaimed novel, *Mary Olivier: A Life*, is a remarkably successful early modernist experiment in the artistic transformation of Freudian insights into the role in our lives of repression, obsession and sublimation, while the novel shows Sinclair's fluency in German philosophy and literature generally. Both she and Richardson, in *Pilgrimage* (thirteen volumes), experimented with innovations in, for example, narrative time, plot, revelation of external events through the interiority of consciousness, and a challenge to familiar content, as thoughts, feelings and the language in which they are conveyed become the primary subject matter. Further, Olive Schreiner drew extensively on the dream, fantasy, myth and the distortion of memory to structure her novels and stories, expressing future Freudian revelations about the unconscious, desire and sexuality as inextricable elements of art, morality and religion. Meanwhile, in 'The Yellow Wallpaper', Charlotte Perkins Gilman fused the recent psychological insights from Austria and America into a scathing indictment of sexism. Through the discourse of a woman being driven mad by a 'rest cure', Gilman toyed with the reader's perspective, and by means of the metaphor of the 'woman in the wallpaper', objectivity was shattered and sanity

exposed as a cultural construct, designed to obstruct disobedience or rebellion from tyranny.

A few years later, Kate Chopin's *Awakening* burst upon a puritanical reading scene, leaving its readers outraged and shaken by its attack on realism, authority and decorum. It probably destroyed the author's career and health. Catherine Carswell also rejected repressive sexist forms of thought, language and literature. She absorbed D.H. Lawrence's liberating attitude both to sexuality (but without its dehumanizing aspect, which Mansfield later criticized) and to fulfilment in sex for women as well as men. Carswell also recognized the importance of his modernist experiments, especially regarding non-realist building of characterization, sensibility and thematics.

While not modernist in the same ways as such writers as Gilman, Stein, Richardson and Sinclair (with their stream of consciousness, foregrounding of language, non-objective experimental points of view, innovative thematics, and stylistic disruptions, as well as narrative-time deconstructions), Chopin and her near contemporaries, Sarah Orne Jewett, Edith Wharton, Willa Cather, Barbara Baynton, Miles Franklin and others were moving, in their separate and distinct ways, out of realism and beyond its (eventual) authoritarianism of alleged objectivity, neutrality, descriptive and representative accuracy, and so on. As the entries on these writers indicate in some detail, not only were their texts innovative in theme in championing the New Woman, the authority of women's experience, and women's rights to contraception, enjoyable sex, paid work and careers, independence from male domination at home or at work, to vote, to think, to educate themselves, and not to bear children. Each of these writers not only challenged old images of women; they also contributed decisively to a literary evolution into symbolism, imagism and, eventually, full modernism, as well as other innovations. They did this either through ironizing and parodying realism, or through establishing subjective narrative points of view as legitimate, or through foregrounding language and story-telling as constitutive of experience, rather than merely representing it. Willa Cather and Sarah Orne Jewett, for example, frequently revised the ancient convention of framing narration, as did Conrad, thereby 'framing' the reader, too. Chopin and Baynton developed new imagery, symbols and allegories appropriate for their new insights and experiences, while Edith Wharton used realism against itself and, by means of irony, questioned the whole social and literary edifice on which her texts appeared to rest.

Thus, it would be erroneous to underplay the anti-realist and other experimental gestures of Wharton, Chopin, Cather, Glasgow, Jewett, Franklin and others. These less modernist, perhaps, but still experimental, anti-realist writers contributed to the progression of the novel into modernism just as surely as did the more overtly, stylistically innovative experimentalists. For example, Wharton was profoundly influenced by Henry James's pre-modernist aesthetics, and while both of them saw the importance for the progress of literature of the reaction in the 1890s towards *fin de siècle* 'art for art's sake' aesthetics and symbolists' ideas, they never lost sight of the inalienable interdependence of art and morality, art and politics, or art and reality. Henry James's so-called formalism is, more properly understood, the redressing of an imbalance that had occurred by the 1890s, with the overemphasis upon familiar realist notions about verisimilitude and representation of content through plot, characterization, and detailed description of environment and setting.

Still, one would not want to give the impression that the literature of the period of transition, from the tired realism of the 1880s onwards to the first flowerings of modernism, was somehow fairly homogeneous. On the contrary, the entries which follow this introduction reveal a diversity so great as to make us question yet again the use of historical terms or single descriptions of a period, except as the roughest of guidelines for prevailing or dominant tendencies. From the clarity and economy of Jewett's 'regional stories' of New England, which, repeatedly, are told through recursive embedding of tales within tales, to the lushness and colour, symbolism and imagery of Chopin's southern mockery of realism; from Mary Wilkins Freeman's regional character studies and supernaturalist fiction to Barbara Baynton's strikingly effective fusions of stylistic purity with gruesome details of slaughterhouses and other atrocities in Australia; from Vernon Lee's richly

textured, allusive tapestries – those densely 'literary' stories – to Henry Handel Richardson's novelistic *tours de force* – her character studies of passion and obsession – and Dorothy Canfield (Fisher)'s restrained, scrupulous psychological portraits of women striving to combine work and love; from Margaretta Deland's sophisticated, ironic anticipations (albeit in a kinder mode) of Ivy Compton-Burnett's play-novels, to Alice Dunbar-Nelson's or Miles Franklin's straight-talking combinations of humour and pathos, this period is as richly diverse as it was profoundly revitalizing of the novel form. It provided the narrative innovations, stylistic liberties and thematic revolutions which made revitalization of the novel possible. It reminded writers that realism and other traditional forms of the novel are not a neutral reflection of the 'real' world – and therefore the authoritative version – but only one way of imagining society, the world and, above all, literature or art itself.

With this breaking out into new forms of expression inspired by eighteenth- and early nineteenth-century pre-realist techniques (often akin to post-modernist devices), the century was launched into its now already ninety-five-year-long reappraisal of the centrality of language in experience and art. Other changes included the interrogation of fiction (and of reading and writing) as its own covert or overt thematics, so familiar in earlier literatures; the acceptance of desire, sexuality and the erotic as part of moral-aesthetic experience; and the deepened understanding that the processes of perception and consciousness are themselves the materials and the formal structures of both art and human experience.

IV

Some of the most characteristic innovations of the best-known experimentalists, the early modernists, can be focused through the formal techniques of stream of consciousness (see chapter 4 below), which Henry James had initiated, William James had 'named', and Gertrude Stein had thoroughly developed into astonishing forms, from the more accessible *Three Lives* and *Blood on the Dining Room Floor* to *The Making of*

Americans. May Sinclair and Dorothy Richardson, along with Rebecca West in *The Return of the Soldier*, H.D. in *Hermione*, and sporadically Gilman, Vita Sackville-West, in *All Passion Spent* and others, initially developed this stream of consciousness technique into early forms, each in her own unique way. Katherine Mansfield's 'free indirect style' was an example of a slightly different technique. In its most typically modernist form, the stream of consciousness fiction involved extreme disruption of syntax, long, meditative sentences running into paragraphs (see William Faulkner's story 'The Bear' for probably the longest example of one sentence in the short story – some twelve or thirteen pages!), logical and causal disorder, and even at times virtual incomprehensibility. Mansfield, however, avoided emphasis on disruptive syntax in favour of a more accessible style, which, nevertheless, achieved an interiority and intimacy between reader and characters without resorting to 'streamy' styles of linguistic disruption. All these authors sought a kind of 'psychological realism' rather than the social, historical or documentary realism of the nineteenth-century authors. As Flannery O'Connor was to complain fifty years later, social realism was, arguably, mere surface realism of notional facts, whereas she was after a 'realism of depths'. This 'psychological realism' of the early initiators of stream of consciousness experiments led to an effort to avoid imposing artificial order upon their texts, artificial patterns or unities or structures or logic, as Jean Rhys was later to explain. Hence came the deliberate rejection of the carefully plotted realist order, that familiar structural development through a distinct story-line, or a too-overt, causally developed thematics, as false to life. Ambiguity and indeterminacy, both of the plot, shape or unity and of the theme, story or content, became central techniques, or even deliberate 'conventions'.

Other results of early modernism, not unknown in late realists' texts, were a de-emphasizing of presentation of unified characters in specified relationships with each other and the surrounding world. Characters in the texts of Mansfield, May Sinclair and Dorothy Richardson, for example, were presented to the reader from the inside of their own consciousness, rather than from an external or omniscient point of view which made them look, in realist and conventional narratives, like definite, unified identities of relatively knowable types. The reader was, instead, given a character's processes of thinking and feeling in a jumbled, disorganized, non-logical way; memory, fantasy, immediate perception, contradictory feelings and thoughts, meditations, desires – all were interwoven into a fabric of interiority which had the result of presenting consciousness more 'realistically', as well as showing it to be saturated by the unconscious. Hence, it was represented as multilayered, non-linear, non-logical, and endlessly indeterminate in meaning. A single character often began to look, in an early modernist text by Gertrude Stein or May Sinclair, or even in Kate Chopin and Willa Cather, like a loosely connected construct with several selves at war with each other. And the boundary between self and world was dissolved, especially in Mansfield, Richardson, Sinclair and H.D. (Later, in high modernism, characters would be shown not only merging into the world around them, not only dissolving into multiple selves within; they would be flowing into each other. Their identities would no longer be portrayed as completely distinct from each other.) This dissolution both affected the mode of narration and was affected by it. In this flux of people, with dissolving boundaries, subjective, limited and alternating points of view were devised in Richardson, especially, but also in Mansfield and Rebecca West, which further confused definites and certainties. A different story or plot or meaning emerged, depending upon the point of view from which things were observed.

Already, then, dissolution of realist plot, theme, narrative-time sequences, developmental structure and distinct, unified character was taking place in the very early twentieth century. In addition, stylistic lushness and relative ambiguity, materiality of language, and an attention to processes and interiorities over products were some of the major characteristics even of 'late realists', not only early modernists of this and the next period. Another major characteristic (learned from earlier centuries prior to nineteenth-century realism) was a marked and often overt self-consciousness about writing and creativity, which was frequently embedded into the texts of late realists. While less overt than in early modernists, self-consciousness was also evident in those innovators such as Chopin, Wharton, Cather and Jewett, for example. This self-referentiality added a rich dimension of meaning to the texts, as long, extended analogies and metaphors of the writing and reading of fiction were woven into the thematics as early as Henry James. While it was the later high modernism of the next period which tended to be characterized most decisively by various forms of stream of consciousness disruption (described in more detail in chapter 4), there were, then, these other types of experimentation and originality, which constituted a definite reaction against realism.

For example, Edith Wharton used irony, systematic reversals of art–reality relations, relative point of view and extreme ambiguity, along with explosive thematics, to overturn realist narrative conventions. Willa Cather took a different tack; she orchestrated novellas within novels and stories within stories 'in the best Spanish manner', used constant self-referential thematics, emphasized point of view as subjective, and also created nature–art analogies to break out of realist representations. Cather too made it a practice to strip away the documentary, cram-jammed enumeration of facts, and sought 'condensation'. Kate Chopin, on the other hand, adopted powerful symbolic imagery, lush sensuousness in style, and structural fragmentation, along with hidden subtexts, arbitrariness of endings and a mocking irony of objectivity. Other writers like Ivy Compton-Burnett and Anzia Yezierska used an almost exclusive emphasis upon dramatic devices of dialogue and juxtaposition of scenes in unusual ways to escape realist confines. Carswell, Schreiner and Sinclair sought to break out of realism through explicit use of Freudian language and ideas. All these methods were taken up and exploited by the next generation of both high modernists and other experimenters.

Chapter 3

Individual Authors, 1895–1925

Sarah Orne Jewett 1849–1909

Sarah Orne Jewett was born, and lived most of her life, in South Berwick, Maine, the daughter of a physician father who encouraged her reading and writing, and who took her with him on his horseback journeys to visit ill patients. The innumerable and often lengthy journeys through the splendid Maine landscape gave Jewett intimate views of the domestic lives of many villages in the now decaying – but once prosperous – shipbuilding, fishing, seafaring area of Maine. Her 'sketches' or 'papers', as she referred to her elegiac, lyrical meditations on the lives of lonely farmers and once-active coastal villages, have little plot, drama or conflict, but are finely structured instead by precisely that experience of her own youth, the visit, and the narratives of present and past that the visitors told each other. Even visits within visits occur, as visitors narrate past visits and recreate their experiences in storytelling of the most fundamental kind. Moreover, her stories are populated primarily by mature or elderly women; most of her characters are in fact over 60, and while many show a deepened awareness of life-experiences, Jewett never romanticized or idealized the state of old age, especially when combined with the relative poverty of this decaying natural world of southern Maine.

Jewett, a friend of Willa Cather's and an influence, through her, on American fiction, was herself deeply impressed by the commitment of Harriet Beecher Stowe to depicting the lives of ordinary, often poor, small-town people, in

the context of a carefully described locale. She learned to use the harshness of the climate and relentlessly rocky landscape of this part of New England to help create, as well, the moral and psychological atmosphere of her villages, struggling against the long winters and infertile, unyielding land, and in the process becoming, like it, enduring and determined. Her patient, reticent heroines, living circumscribed but nevertheless rich lives in these tiny New England towns, are often portrayed as strong, individualistic women of great character and dignity. Indeed, in most of her stories, the women are the active beings, doing not only domestic work – from cooking and making candles to making shoes and clothes – but farm labour, dairy work and looking after chickens, pigs and so on. The men, cut off from their seafaring or fishing lives, do very little, and are often portrayed as demanding, spoiled and selfish. Many of the stories also meditate either directly or implicitly upon the waste of human talent and intelligence, as in the following lines, in the words of the writer-narrator of *The Country of the Pointed Firs* (Boston, 1896, 1968, 1981): 'It was not the first time that I was full of wonder at the waste of human ability in this world, as a botanist wonders at the wastefulness of nature, the thousand seeds that die, the unused provisions of every sort.'

Her first published story, 'Jenny Garrow's Lovers', in a minor journal in 1868, was quickly followed by the *Atlantic Monthly* publication in the next year of 'Mr Bruce'. Other stories followed, such as 'The Shore House', her first Maine story, in 1873 in the *Atlantic Monthly*, until the collection *Deephaven* (Boston, 1877), which gained Jewett considerable notice. She then turned to novels, and produced an almost auto-biographical story of the psychological conflict of a young woman who wants to become a doctor, and the obstacles, such as marriage, which she has to find a means of avoiding in order to realize her dream of her chosen profession. After this novel, *A Country Doctor* (Boston, 1884), Jewett published a romance, *A Marsh Island* (Boston, 1885), the story of a painter and a farmer's daughter. Other collections of stories, *A White Heron* (Boston, 1886), *The King of Folly Island* (Boston, 1888) and *A Native of Winby* (Boston, 1893), preceded the publication of what is generally considered to be not only her finest work but one which ranks, according to Willa Cather, with *The Scarlet Letter* and *Huckleberry Finn*, namely, *The Country of the Pointed Firs* (Boston, 1896). Other stories, writings for children and adolescents, verses and a historical novel, *The Tory Lover* (Boston, 1901), set during the American revolution, concluded her writing career, cut short by an accident at age 51, which left her unable to continue her work. She died aged 60 of a cerebral haemorrhage.

Jewett had little formal secondary education, but her father had introduced her early to a life of reading and writing; neither she nor her sister Mary were ever pressured to marry, and financial independence made possible greater emotional independence. While she spent most of her life with her sister in South Berwick, after 1881 she began spending months of each year in the Boston household of her friend Annie Fields, and in her summer cottage. There, she came to know William Dean Howells, Lowell, Whittier, and others of the Boston literary circle. Her friendship with Willa Cather led to much admiration and influence, and to letters, which are published in *Sarah Orne Jewett: Letters*, ed. R. Cary (Waterville, Maine, 1956). Cather also wrote a deeply respectful preface to the 1925 edition of *The Best Stories of Sarah Orne Jewett* (Boston). Cather's appreciation of Jewett is expressed in unambiguous terms; she spoke of her stories as 'flawless examples of literary art', and noted the fine artistic design of each of these plotless stories: 'every line is designed for one purpose,

. . . everything about it furthers that purpose, so that it has an organic, living simplicity and directness.' Cather identified in her preface several of Jewett's strengths; she wrote of Jewett's marvellous ear for the native speech of the local people, which enriches her pages, and of her use of dialogue, both direct and reported, as a central structuring element. Jewett's eye for the beauty of the rugged, stubborn rural landscape is also praised, and Cather identified an exquisite tact and a gentle humour as giving her narrative an integrity and direct appeal. But what she most valued about Jewett's stories was their fresh vitality; they are 'living things caught in the open with light and freedom and air-spaces about them. They melt into the land and the life of the land until they are not stories at all, but life itself.' Cather also beautifully captured the effect of Jewett's best stories, especially those in *Country of the Pointed Firs*, when she described them as lingering in the reader's mind, leaving an 'intangible residuum', a cadence unique and individual.

Country of the Pointed Firs is a set of twenty-one linked sketches set in the poverty, hardship and old age of rural, small-town villagers, yet in the context of the wild landscape of this enduring country. These poignant stories are elegies to a dying community, echoes of whose previous prosperity can be heard throughout. The un-named narrator of these stories, who is staying for the summer in Dunnet Landing to write without the interruptions of city life, provides the framework for the designs. The visits of various villagers to the narrator and to each other – with the narrator accompanying – as well as a large reunion of the older community, constitute the 'action', when the narrator is not describing life in the village directly. *The Country of the Pointed Firs* is, then, an experiment in genre and, like a number of late nineteenth-century texts, was already rejecting the structuring devices of realism, as well as aspects of its stylistic dogma and thematic concerns. Jewett's thematic concerns are primarily with the world of elderly women, especially one Mrs Almira Todd, whom the narrator describes as 'landlady, herb-gatherer, and rustic philosopher'. Men are in the main excluded, not only from the journey to 'Green Island'; they hardly appear except nearly to capsize the boat, or the story: 'We don't want to carry no men folks havin' to be considered every minute an' takin' up all our time. No, you let me do; we'll just slip out . . . by ourselves.' And so she does, as in nearly all of Jewett's stories, which show women capable of doing almost anything, and usually more ably than the men, who offer advice and criticism all too readily.

Women are portrayed by Jewett as having a strong sense of identity precisely through their work, whether domestic, agricultural or fishing. They achieve a meaningful place in their small communities which is never questioned; but Jewett also portrayed the ill and disabled, and their dependence on the good will of other women to make their lives more bearable than the meagre, stingy arrangements that the village 'welfare' would allow. The value of the large family group and the close community is explored, but Jewett does not neglect the oppressiveness of such a closely knit communal life. All these larger themes are portrayed only indirectly, however, through the most trivial and minute of daily occurrences or the narrative of a past minor event. Jewett had the insight to intuit the deeper meanings of what she observed in this apparently insignificant everyday life, and she drew out the history, attitudes and unique character of these individuals.

Kate Chopin 1851–1904

Kate Chopin was a well-known and widely admired local colourist in her own time, until the publication of her infamous novel, *The Awakening*, in 1899 (Chicago and New York). She was born in St Louis, Missouri, in 1851, and lived in New Orleans with her husband and six children after 1870, returning to St Louis around 1884, as a widow, to take up a serious writing career. She allegedly fashioned her first novel, *At Fault* (St Louis, 1890), after *Jane Eyre*, destroyed her second novel manuscript, 'Young Doctor Gosse', and made her name instead with wide publication of her short stories, *Bayou Folk* (Boston, 1894) and *A Night in Acadia* (Chicago, 1897), receiving considerable critical acclaim until the insanely hostile reaction to *The Awakening*, and her publishers' consequent refusal to publish her third collection of short stories. Five years later,

she died of a brain haemorrhage, and only sixty years later, with the 1969 Per Seyersted edition of *The Complete Works* (Baton Rouge, La.), did her writing come again into circulation.

Chopin, brought up by a French Creole mother and a successful Irish immigrant father, was an accomplished pianist and avid reader of Darwin, Huxley and other Victorian thinkers, as well as French realists and naturalists, especially Maupassant. Her controversial thematic interest in the sexual, financial and emotional independence of women has tended to distract critical attention away from the fine detail of her style. Like Maupassant, Chopin cultivated a clarity and understatement complemented by an ironic, detached undertone, or sometimes even an overtly ironic narrative stance. This tone was designed to criticize indirectly double standards and prejudices in society and in literature, particularly those that functioned to exclude women from male preserves. European realism, that 'poison of Europe', at first helped Chopin to find a way out of the sentimental idealization of marriage, family and romance characteristic of many authors, whether male or female. Gradually, however, she came to feel that realism was too restrictive and prescriptive, interfering – in part due to its ideological notions about neutrality, objectivity and factual, detailed truth – with individuality and imagination. Not only is her style in *The Awakening* a testimony to this advance beyond realism; the struggle out of realist conventions is allegorized thematically in the novel as a woman's and a female artist's struggle for her own identity and self-development in her terms, and not in male social or realist terms.

Chopin's style is intensely symbolic and its imagery rich in erotic and sensual overtones. Her use of light and warmth as metaphors for the imagination, her painterly use of brilliant colouring, her lush visual settings, all renounce the preoccupation of realism with selected details that focus often on the ugly and distasteful. Chopin mingled portrayals of poverty and the humdrum of ordinary, everyday life with colour and beauty in a way that does not idealize poverty or the familiar, but shows its mixed character. *The Awakening* depicts a network of interwoven symbols and images threaded with a subtle but powerful ironic undertone. This irony is strengthened further by gestures of Sophoclean ironic prognostication studded throughout the novel, which add to its tight unity and rich texture. Chopin's novel involves several thematic, interrelated levels of meaning which constitute a unified challenge to patriarchal tradition and authority, both in the social realm and in the literary realm. That is, Edna Pontellier, the heroine, struggles overtly at the surface level against imprisoning social conventions, while a carefully designed subtext shows a metaphorical drama of the woman-artist fighting against imprisoning literary forms, decorous thematics and realistic style. A third thematic level suggests the struggle of the human spirit (both male and female) against the constraints of fear, convention and mediocrity, which cripple imagination, creativity and individuality in the name of conformity and propriety. Finally, symbolic, metaphoric and allegorical gestures in the text lead the reader to a thematic level which portrays these conflicts as not only between an individual and society. They are shown to go on in the psyche of the individual, as she or he struggles with powerful unconscious forces which can defeat fulfilment if they are not engaged creatively and imaginatively.

The Awakening functions interestingly as a literary autobiography, which, in tragic prognostication, predicted Chopin's literary (at least) suicide. Viciously attacking the novel's 'obscenities', Chopin's earlier admirers saw her efforts to break with artistic conventions – her new forms of expression – as ugly, immoral and offensive. Another metaphor suggested by the ambivalent ending in the novel (is Edna's drowning a liberation from a perverse society or a tragic defeat?) involves Chopin's belief that to remain within literary conventions and accepted forms is tantamount to drowning one's individuality and creativity in a sea of banalities. By ironizing the conventions of realism (its style and language, its dramatic plot conception, its emphasis on the individual/society conflict, its alleged objectivity of detailed description, its pretended narrative neutrality leading to true representation), Chopin turned realism against itself, ironizing its presuppositions and limitations while using its liberating capacities (from idealization and nostalgia) for her own effects. Chopin undercut realism's most central concept of language as a transparent medium of truth about external reality, by means of lavish, self-conscious use of imagery, metaphor, symbol, and other figures of speech and rhetorical and narrative strategies, to show that description is never just description, never objective or neutral, but always interpretation from some privileged point of view. The Awakening establishes the right of women as individuals to their point of view, both in society and in art. Chopin forged a new style which ironized realism and showed it as inherently decadent, because the greatest illusion of all. For it denies fantasy, the irrational and illusion as a central part of reality which must be grappled with, not repressed.

The Awakening is a relatively short novel, divided into thirty-nine sections of varying lengths, with three major portions identifiable. The first portion occurs on Grand Isle, during the summer, and comprises sixteen sections. Next, the action shifts to the city, where the action of the following twenty-two fragments occurs, and, finally, Edna returns to Grand Isle for the final brief episode. Understatement, surprise and chance characterize the whole, and while a kind of realist objectivity of time and narrative unfolding of events is respected within the fragments, a gap, at times an abyss, can separate the end of one fragment from the beginning of another, thereby alternating between stately, causal, realist narrative progression and fragmentary, episodic, unrelated and subjective modernist narrative gestures. Narrative time is, then, both objectively and subjectively handled; both unity and fragmentation characterize the structure, while the aesthetic effect is one of gently parodying realist notions of order and objectivity as arbitrary and illusory.

Kate Chopin's text suggests throughout that Edna Pontellier's illusions are more complex than Edna realizes. For a time, even the reader is led to believe that the illusion is the notion that (even a loving) marriage and children can be women's main source of fulfilment. Sexual awakening is at first glance the means of liberation from this illusion, albeit not lustful, unloving sex, but sexual love. Later it becomes evident that the numerous awakenings Edna experiences chart the way towards freedom from the illusion that even sexual love and 'possession of the beloved' are a woman's central source of satisfaction. The Awakening portrays rather the idea that individual self-development as human beings is the precondition for fulfilment from other spheres – self-development of the kind portrayed in Greek tragedies such as *Antigone, Oedipus Rex* or *Electra*. Far from suggesting that our awakening is chiefly into free love or even genuine companionship, Chopin's novel suggests an awakening only through existential acts which create a unique individuality for each human being. Like Katherine Mansfield, who argued explicitly for the necessity for women to free themselves from the 'insipid doctrine that love is the only thing in the world' (if the opportunity for happiness and freedom is ever to come), Chopin's *Awakening* rejects, equally forcefully, this doctrine. It does so in an aesthetically impressive gesture of fine congruence between theme and structure.

On the surface level of narration, where the thematics concern Edna's and Robert's relationship and her rearrangement of her domestic life, the liberation appears to be into loving, sexual freedom through Robert. However, the text reveals, on closer scrutiny, a powerful subtext involving Edna and Mlle Reisz which ironizes the surface level in order to shatter its adequacy. This alternative thematic, or ironic subtext, with Mlle Reisz as a central character, establishes the quite different meaning of awakening as not sexual liberation, but existential self-development. Chopin can be said to have woven two separate yet aesthetically complementary plots into the novel which emblematize the two conflicting themes of awakening, the one romantic, the other existential. The subtext ironizes romantic awakening as yet another kind of entrancement – a sleep, a dream – albeit an advance on unloving, contractual marriages or merely lustful sex. It is Mlle Reisz, not Robert, who in the subtext presents Edna with the path to liberation, but it is a liberation through independence, with Mlle Reisz as the model rather than the means. Relationship with her involves self-development; relationship with Robert meant self-immolation and stagnation in a fantasy of sexual love as the central aim in life. The autonomy of Mlle Reisz, at which Edna grasps only blindly and ineffectually, is equated in the novel with the status of an 'artist', but not only artists (in the narrow sense of the word) can achieve it. Chopin showed that the concept 'artist' can be applied existentially and metaphorically to anyone who has

succeeded in creating herself into a genuine individual. Jean Rhys, for example, showed prostitutes achieving autonomy, and such individualities are living, human works of art.

Hence, the notion held by some critics, that the thrust of *The Awakening* embodies the theme that only women who become artists can be independent, is a case of taking literally the metaphor of the artist-figure. The point is, rather, that self-development with existential self-construction is an art of the highest, most demanding kind that a human being can pursue. Indeed, as many artists have argued, art itself is one (albeit paradigmatic) means of self-development; Katherine Mansfield insisted that art *is* self-development. Willa Cather developed the idea in saying that style is the artist's 'very self'. Chopin's use of artists (Mlle Reisz) and artists in the making (Edna) signifies both that life can be lived artistically, whatever one's *metier*, and – most importantly – that if we are to be independent (as opposed to stereotyped products of socialization, playing unoriginal roles in the drama of life), then we must construct ourselves; we must, regarding ourselves at least, be artists. *The Awakening* can be read as, in part, a portrayal of the forces in society and in the psychology of the individual which promote and which hinder such artistry as self-construction, both for women and for men. One of Chopin's clearest insights in the novel, as in the short stories, is her uncompromising exposure of the male delusion that men are free. At least, it seems, some women are aware of the inhibitions to their self-development, whereas men are trapped in the fantasy that emotional immaturity, mothering relationships with wives, and only extrinsically rewarding work are liberation. For Chopin, as for many of the writers discussed here, the struggle women are engaged in is not to exchange one form of dehumanization for another, but to find more fulfilling ways of living than either sex has yet achieved, with rare exceptions.

Mary E. Wilkins Freeman 1852–1930

Mary Wilkins Freeman was born in Randolph, Massachusetts, in 1852, and lived there for much of her life (except for a period in Vermont beginning in her adolescence). She married briefly in 1902, after several years of indecisive engagement; a few months later, she separated from her husband when she moved to New Jersey. After her parents died, leaving her in poverty, she lived for some twenty years with a childhood friend, Mary Wales. Once she achieved literary success after 1881, she began to travel around the eastern United States, and she went to Paris. Her literary career spanned some fifty years, and she won the Howells Medal for Fiction in 1925, as well as being elected one of the first women to the National Institute for Arts and Letters, with Edith Wharton, in the next year. Wilkins Freeman wrote literature for children as well as a whole range of adult fiction, totalling some twenty-six volumes. Her best-known fictions are probably the short stories in the volumes entitled *A Humble Romance* (New York and London, 1887) and *A New England Nun* (New York, 1891), but significant novels are *Pembroke* (New York, 1894, reprinted Chicago, 1978) and *The Shoulders of Atlas* (New York and London, 1908). Other novels include *Jane Field* (London, 1892); a historical novel entitled *The Heart's Highway* (New York, 1900); *The Portion of Labour* (New York and London, 1901), a social novel; and *By the Light of the Soul* (New York and London, 1907), a novel of religious mysticism. Wilkins Freeman also wrote a powerful play, *Giles Corey, Yeoman* (New York, 1893), which involved the Salem witchcraft trials later handled by Arthur Miller in *The Crucible* (1953). She experimented with supernatural tales, which were a long tradition in American fiction, from Irving, Poe and Hawthorne to James and Howells, collected in *The Wind in The Rosebush* (New York, 1903, republished Chicago, 1986). *Edgewater People* (New York and London, 1918) was a later collection of short stories which embody the same artistic achievement as her earlier short fictions. She also wrote a detective story, 'The Long Arm', which explores lesbianism, and she contributed to *The Whole Family: A Novel by Twelve Authors* (New York and London, 1908), along with Henry James and William Dean Howells, her own chapter not diminished by close contact with these more famous contemporaries. Some of her letters appear in *The Infant Sphinx: Collected Letters of Mary E. Wilkins Freeman*, ed. B.L. Kendrick (Metuchen, N.J., and London, 1985).

Wilkins Freeman is usually described as a New England local colourist or regional writer of realist fiction, whose writings explored the harsh rural life of New England after the Civil War and explicitly criticized the equally harsh Puritanical character of her compatriots. Indeed, many of her stories are described as character studies which are less effective through plot or drama than through mood and tones; hence the general preference for her shorter fictions over her novels. Her accurate representation of dialect is seen as a realist gesture which contributes to a persuasive and insightful representation of local character, through studies of Puritanically repressed individuals in the impoverished social system of New England village life. Wilkins Freeman's stories emphasize the isolation and loneliness of this grim landscape, exacerbated by both a material and a corresponding spiritual destitution. Her stories reveal a psychological penetration into the origins of obsession and emotional repression, as characters struggle to endure with dignity the harshness of their lives.

While Wilkins Freeman explored New England family experience, showing its distorted and painful relationships, her stories and novels are more universal than 'regionalism' and 'local colour' imply. For her writings explore general problems involving failures of love and communication amongst people in families and communities. The tragedies of her own youth, the death of siblings and, later, parents, her father's unsuccessful struggle to provide for his family, and the ensuing poverty, provided her with firsthand experience which later inspired her fiction. One of her central themes is the importance of affection and overtly expressed love of children; numerous stories explore the tragic effects of unexpressive, Puritanical parents who oppress their children with duty and obedience without fulfilling the child's need for love in its early, formative years. In 'The Bound Girl' and its sequel 'The Adopted Daughter', a difficult and deeply unhappy child is transformed by affection, as the author took up the familiar idea that moral development is only achievable through love. In 'Patchwork School', a boy is saved from isolation and alienation through sympathy and understanding from an older man.

Many other stories explore the destructive effects on adult men and women of the meanness of spirit, lack of generosity, and harsh pride characteristic of much New England society, and resulting from loveless childhoods. Wilkins Freeman's portrayal, in such stories as 'Luella Miller', of the stagnation and depression caused by stifling emotional needs anticipated Susan Glaspell's depiction of life forces versus death forces in plays like *Trifles*; childhood 'starvation' of emotion leads to powerfully destructive behaviour and adult depression. She also explored the difficulties facing women in particular, and she often did so through strong women who try to maintain their independence in the domestic sphere or by avoiding marriage. She explored the experiences of spinsters, housewives, mothers and daughters, and questioned the traditional roles women are forced to play, leading to frustration, loneliness and waste. She portrayed the ideal of the submissive, domesticated woman as an example of the death force which, through dependence, drains men and women of their constructive energies.

Wilkins Freeman's apparently realist style is complemented, then, by powerful psychological insights which carry her fiction beyond the surface of realism into the depth and mystery of human life. That is, her realism is used suggestively and symbolically as a mere surface, whose carefully constructed detail is designed to convey to the reader the life behind appearances, the unusual behind the ordinary person. Her overt simplicity and restraint are not so much realist as an expansion into a deeper realism suggested to the alert mind by fact and ordinariness. She probed behind the conscious, the overt, the fact, the surface, and found a repressed world of desire, hate, evil, and powerful needs. She exposed the inadequacy of simply denying and repressing these aspects of life and human nature, and her stories show the futility of refusing to face up to frightening elements in human nature if they are to be controlled. Each individual human being is shown to hide depths of desire, evil and creativity as well, behind a facade of realist ordinariness.

Wilkins Freeman also sought to express the mystery of human nature and human life through exploring the relation of humans to nature, and of nature as a symbol of a deeper life reachable through intelligence and sympathy. *Six Trees* (New York and London, 1903), another collection of short stories, most explicitly develops this idea of nature as symbolic of a deeper human nature, but it is evident in the details of many of her fictions, as she depicted the fragility of life, the ease with which our sense of 'at-home-ness' in the world is destroyed, and the fear at the heart of each of us which too often leads to selfishness instead of communal cooperation. The importance of having a home, and the imagination required to create a genuine home, are portrayed in 'A Mistaken Charity' and in 'Gentian' amongst many others, while some stories reveal the ghostly presences which haunt our homes and our souls, if the hidden life is not brought into the open. Wilkins Freeman, then, experimented with a number of types of fiction, from social and historical novels to mystical, religious and symbolic forms. Her supernatural tales are the extension of her interest in our haunted lives, as she sought to develop this popular genre into a psychologically complex form. Her writings for children, her play, her poems and her essays, along with her shorter fictions, stories and novels, anticipate the psychological realism of Dorothy Richardson, Henry James and other writers immediately after her, and also suggest the direction of the movement from realism to the 'novel *démeublé*' and finally to modernism.

Olive Schreiner 1855–1920

The ninth child of missionaries living in the eastern part of the Cape Colony, Olive Schreiner was born in Wittebergen, Cape of Good Hope; she had little formal education, but read widely in literature, philosophy, history of science, economics and sociology. When she arrived in England in 1881, she had already finished two novels and begun a third, but was hardly ever to bring herself to write in the novel form again, though she was prolific in other genres. With the publication of *The Story of an African Farm* in London in 1883 (under the pseudonym Ralph Iron), she was catapulted into fame and the sophistication of London literary and political circles. For the next eight years she roamed over Britain and Europe, lonely and ill in spite of her success, leading a restless, nomadic existence. Admired by Gladstone and Symons, praised by Wilde and Edward Carpenter, intimate friends with Havelock Ellis until her death, Schreiner returned to South Africa in 1889 (after her novel had been a best-seller for five years) to great acclaim from her compatriots. She married in 1894, and for the next two decades took an influential position in South African social, intellectual and political life. Always torn between the intellectual stimulation of England and the vibrant, rejuvenating force of nature in Africa, Schreiner returned to England in 1913, intending to go to Italy in search of relief from asthma and other illnesses. But with the outbreak of war, she was condemned to remain in London, living in desolate boarding houses, often ill, and desperately isolated, as her fame had died down and life had moved on for London society. She returned home again in 1920 and died in a Cape Town boarding house a short time afterwards, having spent much of her life parted from her husband, S.C. Cronwright-Schreiner. After her death, he organized her papers and transcripts and published many texts that had never appeared previously.

The Story of an African Farm (1883, 1987) was in part a complete reworking and transformation of Schreiner's first, more immature novel, *Undine* (published in London only in 1928). *Undine* was a romanticized, autobiographical fiction of Schreiner's own early adolescence, set, however, in a fairy-tale, exotic England, its subject matter being the unhappy love affair of a young woman. Like the later character, Lyndall, Undine dies tragically at an early age; while the novel is an adolescent production which Schreiner never intended for publication, it displays some of the characteristic features of her later, more accomplished work. Thus, we see the pathos of the suffering of extremely young people hardly emerged from adolescence, yet confronted with a terrifyingly brutal and hypocritical adult world, and the theme of the individual, unusually gifted either with intellect or with a capacity to love, who is thwarted by the mean-spiritedness and prejudices of her peers. *The Story of an African Farm* reworks *Undine* into a compelling story of the young girl Lyndall growing into womanhood, her spiritual friendship with Waldo, and her gradual descent into a pathetic death. Part of the greater power of the second novel over *Undine* is Schreiner's recognition that her artistic powers could best realize

themselves by connecting up with the tremendously invigorating African landscape and setting, which give the novel a creative energy, vitality and beauty quite lacking in her first story. Indeed, one of Schreiner's great strengths as an artist was her originality in the rendering of the African karoo landscape, and its symbolical import for the spiritual lives of the characters. Schreiner once explained that her novels were 'written in blood', and this statement refers not merely to the immense energy and effort she poured into them. It is also expressive of the passionate and intense pathos of her two middle novels, including *From Man to Man; or, Perhaps Only* – (London, 1926, 1982), which remained unfinished but surpasses *The Story of an African Farm* in a number of respects.

None of her novels treats of the relations between black and white; the works restrict themselves to South African whites in the main, though her last piece of fiction does handle race issues – yet it can hardly be called a novel, since it is more a political allegory. Both her middle novels handle the terrible inevitability of suffering in life; they utterly reject the notion of a beneficent Being in the face of such suffering, and the sufferers are usually young and innocent women and men at the hands of unscrupulous lovers or elders, whose unmitigated evil, irresponsibility and selfishness blight these young lives. *The Story*'s effect on the reader is such as to give the novel a haunting appeal, and the distinctly detached, yet not indifferent, narrative voice adds to the moving result, as though the narrator were almost numbed by the tragic quality of these blighted lives. Nevertheless, one of the other strengths of the novel is a comic element and sense of humour in the midst of tragedy, and this contributes to the power of the narrative detachment. While the novel moves not so much by plot as by the force of the characters' suffering and their relation to the vastness of the African continent, Schreiner's narrative proceeds in part by stories told by the characters themselves. Waldo returns from his exploration of the world to narrate to Emily his utter failure; Gregory returns likewise to tell Emily of his experiences with Lyndall and her lingering death. Meanwhile, in the midst of all these human comings and goings, an empty, vast Africa stretches out around them – silent, 'unreadable', unchanged and unchanging – hostile or, rather, indifferent to humans, to their suffering, their stories, to history itself. The little farm and the karoo and the lives on it, in this rather anti-pastoral novel, far from being any kind of traditional Eden, are merely a momentary, unnatural bump in the empty landscape, much like the mysterious, innumerable kopjes, those little hills of piled rocks scattered around the flat plains, whose geological origins remain a puzzle.

From Man to Man was Schreiner's only other substantial novel, and it remained unfinished in her lifetime, though her husband published it posthumously in 1926. Again, an episode in the brief life of two girls on a farm in the middle of the karoo is narrated. Rebekah, like Undine and Lyndall, challenges the morality, values and conventions of her world, though, ironically, it is Bettie, the more Emily-like figure, who ends up a prostitute in London (according to Schreiner's intentions, never fulfilled since the novel was never finished). Like *The Story*, *From Man to Man* is a powerful evocation of the African land as a living being itself, but amoral and indestructible. Schreiner explored more explicitly and fully in this novel many of the social, political and intellectual issues which she only touched upon in *The Story*, using Thomas Mann-like conversations and disputes amongst the characters to make this a 'novel of ideas' rather than of the poetic, symbolic genre of its predecessor. In her final 'novel', *Trooper Peter Halket of Mashonaland* (London, 1897), she turned away from fiction to a political allegory, though this ironic narrative is extremely effective as a ruthless satire of the racist atrocities perpetrated by European pioneers and the politics of her ex-friend Rhodes.

Schreiner was deeply engaged in articulating the social and political situation of her times, and much of her rich talent went into non-fiction, such as her famous *Woman and Labour* (London, 1911), a powerful analysis of sexism, patriarchy, and women's rights, which is relevant today in striking detail. In this remarkable work, Schreiner wove within each section of the text an allegory or a symbolical story, which was meant to 'complete' the logical argument or 'illustrate' it, to make it more effective. Art, she believed, had a greater effect on the reader than logic, because it could arouse the intelligence through imaginative and emotive channels; these could more easily influence the mind and shake its preconceived ideas. She was very active in the women's movement, and in striving for the rights of working-class people, black people and other minority groups. She was a pacifist, opposed the Boer War in unambiguous terms – which lost her many friends – and spoke out for pacifists during World War I. Her pamphlet on South African Federation, *Closer Union* (London, 1909), proved to be one of the most prophetic analyses of South African history ever written, as for example when she wrote: 'Any attempt to base our national life on distinctions of race and colour as such will . . . prove fatal to us.' One of Schreiner's greatest achievements was the book *Thoughts on South Africa* (London, 1923), a remarkable collection of essays written about the various peoples and cultures mingling in South Africa, from the European whites, to the half-castes and African blacks. Her understanding of these varied cultures reveals a profound grasp of her society, and a far-sightedness which has stood the test of time. Her own life is a realization of her commitment to the view (shared with Nadine Gordimer) of the artist's role in society as one of awakening others to the social realities of their era, and influencing them to confront painful truths, while probably condemned to a life of loneliness and misunderstanding.

Schreiner's other major contribution to letters was her 'dream' writing, the three volumes of allegories involving dreams, which were meant to express some spiritual, social or moral situation. These sketches and short stories were published as *Dreams* (London, 1890), *Dream Life and Real Life* (London, 1893) and *Stories, Dreams, and Allegories*, ed. S.C. Cronwright-Schreiner (London, 1923); the first two volumes were immensely popular. Her *Letters 1876–1920* were published by her husband (London, 1924), and he wrote a detailed, thorough biography, *The Life of Olive Schreiner* (London, 1924).

Vernon Lee 1856–1935

Violet Paget (Vernon Lee) was born in France, near Boulogne, but she lived much of her childhood in Germany, Switzerland and Italy. Her family was nomadic, frequently changing their household, but Violet's mother, a wealthy, highly accomplished woman, ensured that her daughter received a thorough, indeed remarkable education. For she intended that her daughter should be a writer of the intellectual breadth of a Mme de Staël, and Violet hardly can be said to have disappointed her. (In *The Handling of Words* (London, 1923), Violet described her indebtedness to her mother.) Early childhood letters soon turned into sketches and stories in Violet's adolescence, and one of her earliest sketches, 'Capo Serpente', contains the image of the human in snake form which was to recur in her adult writings. Vernon Lee became fluent in English, French, German and Italian, and by the age of 24 published a book that was to gain her a great reputation and admiration, namely, *Studies in Eighteenth Century Italy* (London, 1880). She also published a collection of stories, *Tuscan Fairy Tales* (London) in the same year, launching herself into the remarkable career in both fiction and criticism which was to make her one of the most brilliant and accomplished women of her time. By 1884 she had continued both strains of her writing career with the publication of several books, including the novel *Miss Brown* (3 vols, London, 1884), and the famous collection of essays, *Euphorion* (London, 1884), containing her well-known discussion of medieval love through literary criticism on Dante, the poetry of Provence and Languedoc, and other Italians. While Henry James had serious reservations about her novel writing, he nevertheless admired her aesthetical work, and described her as 'the most able mind in Europe'. Others, such as Robert Browning and George Bernard Shaw, also expressed praise, especially for her criticism and Italian essays and books. She moved amongst the literary circles of England, Italy and Germany, but became a controversial figure, in part because some of her acquaintances felt her novels indiscreetly satirized her friends.

While Vernon Lee often complained in later life that her writings were ignored by the reading public, this may only reflect the immense reputation she gained so early as for it to be almost unsustainable. Her mature period was marked by aesthetical writings such as *The Spirit of Rome* (London, 1906), *Beauty and Ugliness* (London, 1912), *Music and its Lovers* (London,

1932) and *The Handling of Words and Other Studies in Literary Psychology* (London, 1923). But the collection of essays she published in mid-career, *Genius Loci: Notes on Places* (London, 1899), gained her yet more admiration, and showed her remarkable ability to evoke the sense of place and its powerful effect on the imagination. This empathetic sensibility is one of the strongest elements in her several collections of short stories, for which she is once again becoming known after a half-century of neglect. For throughout her life, Vernon Lee wrote short stories which were published in various collections, such as *Hauntings: Fantastic Stories* (London, 1890), *Vanitas: Polite Stories* (London, 1892), *Pope Jacynth and Other Fantastic Tales* (London, 1904) and *For Maurice* (London, 1927); later these were selected and republished in *Supernatural Tales* (London, 1955). These delightful stories are often compared with Isak Dinesen's Italian tales, as both writers were able to create for their reader a strong sense of reality about the distant historical periods and exotic countries in which they set these probings into love, hate and romance. One of Vernon Lee's stories most comparable to Isak Dinesen's is 'Prince Alberia and the Snake Lady' (1896, reprinted in *Pope Jacynth*), which takes up the image of the human in snake form which she had explored as an adolescent.

These stories and her aesthetical writings show the extraordinary breadth of Vernon Lee's intellect. She was thoroughly familiar with European literature and thought, as her voluminous library testifies; she read from Darwin to Freud in exploring the major contemporary influences, and immersed herself in art and music as well as science and social science. Her writings also suggest her well-known sense of moral responsibility to fellow human beings, and her interest in equality for women. She was strongly feminist in the radical sense, that women should not strive to imitate or be like men. Rather, through personal development and thought, women were to help to challenge present values and evolve new definitions of the good, the true and the beautiful. Through her own intellectual sophistication, her erudition and the almost incredible scope of her writings, from novels and stories to aesthetics, biology, essays and travel writing, Vernon Lee rejected the traditional female roles, and in her *Satan the Waster* (London, 1920), a dramatic trilogy, she, like Virginia Woolf, wrote a pacifist testimony of her belief in the unacceptability of war.

Vernon Lee's *Letters* were published in 1937 (London), ed. I. Cooper Willis, and the same editor made available *A Vernon Lee Anthology* (London, 1929).

Barbara Baynton 1857–1929

Born in Scone, New South Wales, into a working-class background (her father was a carpenter), Baynton spent her childhood in a desolate and lonely part of Hunter River country. The intense physical isolation which she saw women, in particular, enduring in this bush country became one of the themes of her later fiction, and she also described the spiritual or emotional (as well as intellectual) isolation through landscape description. Baynton published her first collection of short stories in 1902 (London) under the title *Bush Studies*, and *Cobbers* in 1917 (London), but she also published a novel, *Human Toll* (London, 1907). Her fiction has been republished in the series Portable Australian Authors as *Barbara Baynton*, eds S. Krimmer and A. Lawson (St Lucia, Queensland, 1980). This small output may in part have led to a neglect of her writing, though further factors may also account for it, such as her refusal to romanticize, idealize or handle sentimentally the people and the life she wrote about. Her stories, with their stark harshness, show the tragedy, but most of all the barbarity, of many bush whites and their often violent and uncivilized ways. Her unsentimental view of this life, along with her use of dialect to portray the crass vulgarity and inhumanity of many characters, no doubt offended readers, as did her tendency to ascribe what civility and humaneness she could find to women.

Her stories have been described as 'nightmarish', and her novel condescendingly dismissed by some critics as a shapeless sequence of scenes, albeit vivid and intense, but totally lacking in that essential element, plot. These descriptions say more about the ignorance of her critics than about her experiments in fiction and her efforts, of an almost modernist kind, to move away from realist conventions (like plot, which artificially

imposed order on life). Her stories reveal a remarkable ability to use the trifling incidents of ordinary life to reveal the depths of human nature, both its depravity and its imaginativeness. In her exploration of such minor details she anticipates such writers as Katherine Mansfield and other modernists, not to mention Susan Glaspell. Other critics have acknowledged Baynton as one of the most powerful pre-World War I Australian writers of short stories, and her classic story 'Billy Skywonkie' is included in the anthology edited by J. Waten and S. Murray-Smith (Melbourne, 1974).

Baynton's portrayal in this story of the hard brutality, uncivilized behaviour, sexism and racism of many bush people, including women, who are often portrayed as slatternly and unkind to each other, is in sharp contrast to much of the contemporary Australian fiction, which took a more romantic line. 'Billy Skywonkie' is a fine example of her poised style and careful use of detail and trifles to point to further resonances and significances. The story reveals a strong viewpoint of detached irony, as the woman protagonist does almost nothing except to observe, with quiet horror, the behaviour of the men (and later women) around her. Wanton cruelty to animals is used as an ironic metaphor for the dehumanization of people in the face of the hard life they lead:

> The listening woman passenger in a carriage between the driver and the bagman heard a thud soon after in the cattle-truck and added another to the list of the fallen. Before dawn that day the train had stopped at a siding to truck them, and she had watched with painful interest these drought-starved brutes being driven into the crowded vans. The tireless, greedy sun had swiftly followed the grey dawn, and in the light that even now seemed old and worn, the desolation of the barren shelterless plains that the night had hidden appalled her . . . The train dragged its weary length again, and she closed her eyes from the monotony of the dead plain. Suddenly the engine cleared its throat in shrill welcome to two iron tanks, hoisted twenty feet and blazing like evil eyes from a vanished face.

The sophistication of this passage both stylistically and in terms of its suggestive power of imagery, personification and metaphor is characteristic of Baynton's fiction.

Her most famous story, 'Squeaker's Mate', first published in *Bush Stories* (republished in *The Penguin Anthology of Australian Women Writers*, ed. D. Spender (Harmondsworth, 1988), is a much more dramatic tale with a powerful theme of breach of faith, involving emotion of Greek tragic proportions as it explores love, hate, revenge, and the power of the human will to overcome adversity. Often Baynton had explored the resourcefulness of women trying to survive in the demanding conditions of the bush, but in this story she does not explore how nature, or drought, or external circumstance is the main enemy; she shows people pitted against each other, and the depths of violence and rage within the individual psyche.

George Egerton 1859–1945

George Egerton was the pen name of Mary Chavelita Dunne, born in Melbourne of Welsh and Irish parents. Her childhood was spent travelling all over the world, while in her twenties she went to Norway for several years, where she was influenced by Ibsen, Knut Hansen and others. She eventually moved to Ireland, and finally to Crawley, having written several novels and plays, the latter being less successful. Egerton was a spiritual predecessor of D.H. Lawrence; though her fiction is not by any means as weighty as his, she went further than contemporaries such as Sarah Grand, for she sought in her writing to explore female sexuality and make it not only a social reality but an appropriate literary theme. She impressed such contemporaries as Havelock Ellis and George Bernard Shaw, not to mention W.B. Yeats, with her efforts to portray emotion and experience from a woman's point of view and her exploration of repression and victimization. Egerton portrayed the process of self-discovery through techniques more characteristic of twentieth-century modernism than of the realism of her time, though it was a transitional period, with many writers exploring impressionistic techniques and 'psychological realism'. At times Egerton's writing moves towards an anticipation of later stream of consciousness techniques, and its rejection of both conventional

morality and conventional literary techniques makes Egerton not only an intrinsically rewarding writer, but a significant figure in the development of fiction from realism to full modernist ellipsis, tremendous trifles symbolically represented, and emphasis upon internal consciousness, as well as other characteristic rejections of realist conventions. Her books include the two collections of stories in *Keynotes* (London, 1893) and *Discords* (London, 1894), *Symphonies* (London, 1897), *Rosa Amerosa* (London, 1901) and *Flies in Amber* (London, 1905). The first two have been republished in one volume as *Keynotes and Discords* (London, 1983).

As with many women writers of the 1890s and early 1900s, Egerton began openly to express disdain for marriage, with crushing descriptions of the cruelty of many relationships, no doubt influenced by her own personal experience. She explained her own intention to explore the '*terra incognita*' of women from the knowledge women have of themselves, instead of the imaginations of male writers. In her representations of this area, she used the natural world symbolically in contrast to society and its constraints, much as Edith Wharton was later to use Italy, as a realm in which women could move more freely to realize their potentialities sexually, emotionally and intellectually. She used interludes of fantasy to explore possible realities for women which would probably have been unacceptable to her audience except as fantasies. Indeed, her explorations into fictional forms which left realism behind were in part due to the need to find formal representations for issues too radical for her readership to accept in conventional realist modes.

Charlotte Perkins Gilman 1860–1935

Charlotte Perkins Gilman was born in Hartford, Connecticut, in 1860, and died in 1935, killing herself with chloroform because she believed her life of useful action was over. She studied art in Rhode Island, later supporting herself as teacher, editor, essayist and writer. Her first, unsuccessful marriage in 1884 left her with a daughter and with severe post-natal depression; the (notorious) treatment led to near insanity, but also to the highly acclaimed novella, 'The Yellow Wallpaper' (Boston, 1892). Gilman wrote poetry and fiction as well as editorial comments, which were published in her monthly magazine *Forerunner* (1909–16). She also wrote some astonishingly foresightful social analyses, such as *Women and Economics* (Boston, 1898), *Concerning Children* (Boston, 1900), *The Home* (New York, 1903), *The Man-Made World* (New York, 1911) and *His Religion and Hers* (New York and London, 1923). Her utopian novel *Herland* was published in 1915 in serial form in *Forerunner* (in book form, New York, 1978). Gilman argued for a rejection of the 'masculinist' society of violence, assertiveness, competition, exploitation and sub-servience, proposing a society of cooperative endeavour, equality and nurturing by all, regardless of gender.

'The Yellow Wallpaper' is Gilman's most acclaimed literary achievement (though stories published in the *Forerunner* and the novel *Herland* deserve republication). The surface thematics of 'Yellow Wallpaper' involve a woman undergoing a rest-cure (as Gilman herself did at the age of 25, to treat post-natal depression). According to her own account in her autobiography *The Living of Charlotte Perkins Gilman* (New York and London, 1935), Gilman was nearly driven mad by this 'cure', which involved preventing her from doing any intellectual work and treating her like a baby. Underneath the surface thematics of patriarchal medical treatment inducing insanity, Gilman developed several metaphorical extensions of this thesis which are apparent from the outset of the story. One involved a social allegory: the rest-cure is a simile for the domestic life that Victorian women of the upper middle classes lived, which often made them ill or drove them mad, as in the case of William and Henry James's sister Alice James, the intrepid and famous travel writer Isabella Bird and many others. Moreover, Gilman's social allegory insinuates that ordinary domestic life turns many women into creeping, crawling creatures, who think they are free while they exist in near-abject submission to male dominance of power, money and status, and to male fantasies of superiority. Marriage and children have often been recommended as the cure for rebellious, independent women entertaining 'inappropriate' desires for fulfilment in male domains of work and public life. Another central

interpretation woven into the fabric of the text involved Gilman's self-consciousness as a writer in a predominantly male tradition. These three strands are carefully interrelated to create a richly complex and extremely dense artifact, further enhanced by skilful use of images reverberating with these multiple thematic significances. The density of metaphorical and symbolical figures is embedded (contrastingly) in a deceptive plain-spokenness, which lends the text a level of detached, ironic, narrative consciousness.

Like Chopin and others, Gilman made clear, both in 'The Yellow Wallpaper' and throughout her writings, the importance of work and of economic independence, without which, she argued, women's intellectual and emotional being could not develop. Her texts do not neglect the portrayal of the consequences of conventional social arrangements, however. Emotional immaturity and selfishness result in destructive love (which pretends to kindness) and can lead to poverty, war and hatred on a large social scale. Gilman never failed to draw out the interrelation between private and public forces, as she revealed psychological and sociological interconnections which inescapably intertwine in individual and social development. 'The Yellow Wallpaper' develops its multiple levels of thematics into a complex artifact by a process of figuration – development of extended figures of speech through imagery and metaphor – which recreates the multiple thematics at a formal, aesthetic level. That is, the unnamed narrative 'I', a kind of everywoman, goes for a rest-cure to an English ancestral house in the country. She is sequestered by her physician-husband, John, and a female housekeeper, Jane, in the large ex-nursery in the attic of the house, where she is looked after and forbidden to work, read or write. The attic room is covered by wallpaper of a ghastly pattern, behind which the narrator begins to see what she calls a sub-pattern, namely, a woman creeping around, trying to get out from behind the imprisoning pattern of the paper. The narrator, at first only an observer of this mysterious woman's efforts at liberation, gradually begins to tear the wallpaper away to help liberate the sub-pattern. In the process of trying to help the woman out, the narrator begins to identify with the creeping woman, until, at the end of the story, she is found creeping around the room along the walls, and announces, 'I've got out at last . . . in spite of you and Jane. And I've pulled off most of the paper, so you can't put me back!'

John, Jane and the narrative 'I' are, Gilman insisted, 'mere ordinary people', and their every-man and everywoman status implicates the reader. Moreover, the 'I', before she begins her own creeping on her knees around the attic room at the end of the story, discovers a smooth groove in the wallpaper, which (it is made clear) has been rubbed by a multitude of previously creep-ing bodies pressing against the wall. Clearly, Gilman is determined not to allow the reader to treat this story as some exceptional tale of mad-ness which has little relevance to the 'sane' reader. While no strict allegories can do the story's complexity justice, it is clear that Gilman's text encourages us to question our own accepted, conventional evaluations of sanity and madness, of our own male and female arrangements, and the meaning of a love which can let cruelty and patriarchy masquerade as kindness and curative treatment. That is, by the end of the novel, at all three thematic levels, the woman narrator's situ-ation has become so intolerable that sanity begins to look like madness, and madness like a kind of liberation, first from insane social dependence and domestic submissiveness, second from a mental 'health' of emotional immaturity to the healing 'insanity' of rebellion, and third from a male tradition of writing.

Liberation from the dominant literary con-ventions is one of the most interesting and carefully crafted themes of 'The Yellow Wall-paper', and it makes the story a powerful attack both on realism and on its ideological principles about the transparency of language and about objectivist and descriptive neutrality. 'The Yellow Wallpaper' also challenges male representations of women, of their experience and of their appropriate role in society. It challenges male prerogatives of control over work, money and privilege, both in the home and in the public domain, by showing the appallingly destructive effects, even of alleged kindness, on women. Patriarchy, the story shows, regardless of its good or bad intentions, is destructive of individual independence. 'The Yellow Wallpaper' can be described as a story of a woman gradually going mad as a result of patriarchal kindness, in both

medical and social domains. It is also the story of the gradual identification of the woman in the attic nursery with the woman behind the wall. And it is the story of a woman writer-diarist successfully embodying her experience in a work of art.

'The Yellow Wallpaper' challenges realism and conventional literary orthodoxies in a number of ways. Apart from its overt thematic challenges to the social, medical and personal forms of pa-triarchy, it challenges novel-story conventions and decorum on nearly every front – theme, form, style, genre, narrative point of view, tone, plot, characterization, and so on. For example, the narrative point of view is the first person voice of a woman going mad. One can hardly get more subjective, unreliable and non-neutral. Further, the short story form is that of a fictional diary which challenges genre notions and dis-tinctions between autobiography and fiction. The writing conveys a present tense of such imme-diacy that the reader almost has to imagine the narrator, by the end of the story, telling, writing and experiencing immediate events all in one identical moment. The present tense finally changes (unnoticeably) to the past only in the final few sentences. So much, then, for realist or conventional demands for objectivity or neutral description. Stylistically and in terms of tone, the story is in a conversational, conventionally unliterary, plain-spoken mode which further establishes the 'validity' of the subjective narra-tive point of view. And the fact that the subjec-tive narrator is unnamed helps towards her interpretation as an everywoman figure, thus, paradoxically, establishing objectivity through subjectivity. The meagre plot – the gradual iden-tification with some hypothetical woman in the wall – is an affront both to realism's emphasis upon drama and to conventional novel plots of events and happenings (as is the thematic attack on patriarchy in all its forms as essentially de-structive). The unreality of the trapped woman in the wall, the emphasis upon the mystical power of the wallpaper, and constant symbolic images involving (1) houses as edifices of society and male privilege, (2) walls as social conventions, (3) wallpaper patterns as social patterns which imprison, (4) sub-patterns behind the main de-sign of the wallpaper as metaphors for the un-conscious, (5) paper as a metaphor for literature, and (6) frequent references to form, formlessness, figures, patterns and designs (which refer metaphorically to literary form, figures of speech and so on) all show Gilman's imagination escaping the bounds of realist and conventional decorum and propriety.

The major images listed above are used systematically throughout the story-diary in such a way as to structure and pattern it, thus creating a level of self-referentiality, which invites the reader to participate fully in an identification with the narrative voice at a literary level: the reader is, through a cleverly designed narrative inversion, transported into the mind of the 'madwoman', and from this inside perspective, what looks like madness from without feels like sanity from within. Meanwhile, the behaviour of John and Jane is now what looks insane. Thus, Gilman questioned social/historical uses of the concept of madness for purposes of repression and discrimination against others; the disobedient daughter, wife, sister or mother is conveniently branded mad, while from her point of view she is perfectly sane. In this, Gilman anticipated the more systematic researches of Foucault and Laing, though they rarely attended to the role of madness as a tool within everyday social/domestic life for ensuring female submission. The aesthetically purposive invasion of the reading mind by the suffering woman makes possible, then, a more thoroughgoing re-evaluation or reversal of attitude towards madness than any amount of discursive argument could achieve. Such invasion of emotions from one person to another is also a powerful psychological truth. The narrator's own gradual identification of herself with the woman in the wall is a metaphoric model for the reader, and it raises intriguing questions of interpretation, whose answers are contradictory and irresolvable.

For example, what is the woman in the wall? Is she the hallucination of a madwoman? Is she a projection onto the wall (as a kind of conscious layer or screen) of what the narrator unconsciously feels is her real self, what patriarchy has made her – a creeping, submissive dependant? Or is it, like Kate Chopin's ending to *The Awakening*, too ambiguous to interpret – because interpretable as both disastrous or tragic and liberating? The woman in the wall is described as a 'formless figure that seemed to skulk about

behind that silly and conspicuous front design'. 'Formless', 'figure' and 'design' all reverberate with self-referential literary connotations characteristic of many sentences in the story, which consolidate both the multilayer thematics and the invitation to the reader to see Gilman symbolizing her own (and the reader's?) plight, as both an individual and a writer, who happens also to be a woman, struggling against social constraints to achieve sanity and individuality at the cost of a place in human society.

Stylistic effects border on modernism, in terms of both short, jerky paragraphing and fragmented, disrupted impressions and observations representative of immediate, impressionistic and subjective consciousness (rather than the incoherence of some types of insanity). Moreover, the fictional diary genre is structurally modernist as well; it makes no pretence of connecting up the fragmented entries, of which there are seven of greatly varying lengths. Gaps of time occur, yet nothing really happens, except in the narrator's mind, where the story remains except for occasional references to people checking up on the inmate. As an early example of the psychological stream of consciousness technique, the story stands as a genuine innovation, just as it does with its stylistic uniqueness and its structural fragmentation at the surface level, while symbolic and metaphoric images weave unifying threads throughout the text, like the colours and motifs of impressionistic painting.

For other writing, see *Charlotte Perkins Gilman: A Non-Fiction Reader*, ed. L. Ceplair (New York, 1991).

Edith Wharton 1862–1937

Edith (Newbold Jones) Wharton was born in New York City in 1862 to a wealthy family, well established in New York society, and began to read and write at an early age. Family and social demands after her marriage at 23 seem to have created emotional conflicts with her vocation as a writer which led to serious depression and illness. Like Charlotte Perkins Gilman, she was treated by means of a rest-cure, but it was the wholehearted commitment to writing and the publication of short story collections in 1899, 1901 and 1904 which set her back on the road to health. *The House of Mirth* (New York, 1905) was her first major novel after *The Valley of Decision* (New York, 1902), followed by nearly a book a year, including *Ethan Frome* (New York, 1911), *The Reef* (New York, 1912), *The Custom of the Country* (New York, 1913), *Summer* (New York, 1917), *The Age of Innocence* (New York, 1920), *The Mother's Recompense* (New York, 1925), *The Gods Arrive* (New York, 1932) and 'Roman Fever' (written 1934 and republished in *Roman Fever and Other Stories* (London, 1982), one of her finest short stories). Wharton also wrote an autobiography, *A Backward Glance* (New York, 1934), and *The Writing of Fiction* (New York, 1924). She won the Pulitzer Prize for *The Age of Innocence*, in spite of having abandoned her writing for war work in France during World War I. From then on, having divorced in 1913, she lived part of the year on the Riviera and part near Paris. One of her greatest sources of pride and happiness was her long friendship with Henry James.

Wharton's novels, novellas and short stories have long been recognized as powerful social and moral critiques, and much secondary criticism has been concerned with these subversive aspects. However, an examination of Wharton's writings as, also, works of art not only enriches our appreciation of them and of her achievement; it also clarifies the moral and social dimensions of her texts and shows them in a new light. Wharton, like many women writers of her day, was deeply sensitive to the woman artist's problematic relationship to a predominantly male tradition. Many of her fictions are constructed around this issue as a subtext, fully developed if the reader is aesthetically aware of the literary details of the text. In many of her texts she constructed sophisticated narrative strategies which develop Jamesean emphases on views and perspectives, thereby building levels of ironic, detached observation which undercut or complicate the surface thematics. Using carefully patterned imagery and extended metaphors and symbols, Wharton designed beautifully textured fictions which repay close reading and attention to artistic strategies, the latter having consequences for the moral and social interpretations. More than is generally conceded, Wharton also challenged, with a number of impressive literary strategies, realist notions of objectivity, representation

and transparent language, which still dominated thought about the novel, in spite of Henry James's success in exploding realist dogmas.

It is through close attention to narrative techniques and to language that one comes most easily to a realization of the extent of Wharton's achievements in forging a kind of fiction which eschews realist dogmas. By means of an intense consciousness of narrative strategies, stylizations and perspective – much of which she learned from her study of painting – Wharton also clarified and articulated in detail the various aspects of the issue of a woman writer establishing a viable relation to a predominantly male literary tradition. In *The Writing of Fiction*, Wharton complained of that 'constricting theory' of the realists, whose emphasis on a 'photographic reproduction' of life and society led to such a mass of detail that what Wharton called 'the larger whole' got left out. This concept of 'the larger whole' refers first, aesthetically, to the failure of any real imaginative fusion and unity in many realist writings and, second, to society. That is, in spite of realist claims to situate the individual in her or his social context, Wharton's texts – as well as explicit statements about realism – suggest that, for her, realism failed, precisely through overemphasis of detailed enumeration of externals, to capture the context in its larger forces and bearings on individuals. Willa Cather, Dorothy Richardson, May Sinclair, Virginia Woolf and other women writers similarly rejected realism as faulty both in its principles and in its practices. Many of them saw the value of the stream of consciousness technique of Gilman, James and others for expressing the fluidity of personality borders, showing how individuals are not as discrete and autonomous as we may think. Individuals flow in and out of each other in their social context; their thoughts and feelings invade each other so that they become mixed up in each other's beings and in their surroundings to an extraordinary degree.

Wharton strongly rejected central planks of the realist ideology when, in *The Writing of Fiction*, she insisted that all representation is better understood not as immediate, objective or truthful. Rather, it presupposes what she called 'stylization' and 'transposition'. This vocabulary she drew from her art-historical researches, which had early convinced her that there is no such thing as representation which is a neutral, objective mirror reflecting facts and objective traits in nature or society. Far from being, as the realists argued, a transparent medium of truth, the language of realism was itself a 'stylization', just as is any other language. Wharton's appreciation of painting gave her another technique for attacking realist naïveté, which she made use of systematically throughout her fiction. This technique involved the reversal of art/life or culture/nature priorities, so that for her it was not so much that art was a mirror or representation of life, society or nature as that nature and society are understood by means of art. That is, we see nature and society by means of the light of imagination incorporated into works of art. Thus, Wharton was intensely conscious of the cultural constructs through which she experienced and viewed life, and her fiction became for her a means of articulating more precisely and clearly both the kinds of cultural construct that shape our experience, and the ways in which a human being can become conscious of those constructs and adopt new ones that make for a more imaginative, individualized existence. Like Jean Rhys's novels, Wharton's writings are often a portrayal both of the success and of the failure of individuals to gain control over the forces of socialization which shape their lives and impede or promote individuality. Whether success or failure is depicted, struggle is always portrayed; Wharton's central characters are engaged in heroic battles which, unlike realism, finely balance the power of the human will and the power of social forces to shape our existence. A kind of existential demand to take responsibility for one's character and circumstances is rarely unaccompanied by a complementary consciousness of the role of chance and context in the development of every human being. This constitutes another departure from realism.

This balance is reflected in Wharton's fiction not merely thematically, but in her individual innovations in style, subject and narrative, which are expressions of her will and uniqueness as an artist. These innovations – the 'stylization' – occur, of course, in the context of the literary and artistic tradition. Most discussions of Wharton's novels have overemphasized the conventional elements – that context – thus reading her as a realist or as an imitator of Henry James.

A more balanced attention to the individuality of her writing reveals her artistic innovations, which constitute her individuality as an artist, her triumph over realism, and her success as a woman artist establishing a voice for herself in a male tradition. Statements such as 'as art is, so is life', or 'there is no short cut to an intimacy', are guides to her innovations in fiction. Wharton used sophisticated literary devices and props such as setting, lighting, colouring and frames to 'strip the veil of familiarity' from things, as the Romantics described art and imagination doing. In her own words, she spoke of 'tearing the gauze into shreds' ('Autre Temps . . .', in *Roman Fever and Other Stories*). Her emphasis on point of view through the use of balconies, terraces, windows and frames constituted a frontal attack on realist neutrality and objectivity as a mere fiction and delusive fantasy, as did her insistence that seeing a situation or a scene in different lights changed it into something completely different.

Only by seeing things in different lights or from different perspectives does one arrive at a genuine intimacy with people or things, with life or art. No one (notionally) objective, neutral point of view exists, any more than there is one neutral, factual language. Wharton's frequent metaphors of journeys and travels – an ancient but powerful literary convention – acted to restate the importance of perspective and of cultural constructs, and also stated the related point about language and life as essentially stylized. When Wharton's characters travel (as did she herself so profitably), they discover that people in foreign countries have different styles – different conventions – about the most basic aspects of life, from eating and food to dress, lovemaking, architecture, and moral and aesthetic values. There is no one right way of doing or seeing things, or of living. Moreover, travel also acts as a metaphor for imagination – and imagination and its product, art, become for Wharton the means by which we succeed in life in creating ourselves, in gaining control over other forces which tend to victimize or imprison us if the imagination fails. Hence comes the systematic use of travel, journeys and foreign settings in her novels, those modern *Odysseys*.

Wharton's emphasis on travel and its metaphorical meaning as perspective or stylization in art, and her use of lighting and times of day as a metaphor for the essence of imagination (as the ability to see things from a variety of viewpoints – imaginative perception), act as two central, complex strategies for establishing herself as a woman artist against realist and other conventional literary ideologies. A related strategy was her tendency, overt in the travel writing and implicit in the novels, to give her readers historical accounts of Morocco, Italy and other exotic places as if these accounts were fantastic stories of fabricated legends. She often drew attention to the fragmentary, meagre basis upon which great historical edifices were built, taking sardonic pleasure not only in pointing out the meagreness of the fragments as the basis of much history, but also in noting ironically that many of these fragments were artistic or literary remains, which were frequently the sole support of history. Thus Wharton re-emphasized her commitment to reversing realism and to arguing that 'as is art, so is life.' History as objective, factual and neutral was as much a myth for Wharton as were realist principles of fiction. History is no more free from narrative views, figures of speech or stylization than are art or life from conventions. Reality becomes meaningful only when interpreted, that is, only when seen from a perspective and by means of some stylized medium. Wharton's novels provide readers with the chance to see their own spectacles in the mirror of the text, to become conscious of other spectacles (or ways of seeing and living), and finally – through imaginative effort – to learn to shift flexibly and easily from one point of view to another, thereby arriving at more imaginative and varied ways of being.

May Sinclair 1863–1946

Born in Rock Ferry, Cheshire, this (today almost unknown) novelist, critic, translator, philosopher and essayist was a well-known and influential London intellectual in her own time. Active in the suffragettes' movement, Sinclair worked with the writer and founder of the Women Writers' Suffrage League in 1908, Cicily Hamilton, and the prolific feminist novelist Violet Hunt; she also helped introduce the psychoanalytic ideas of Jung and Freud to her

contemporaries, wrote and educated friends about German idealism (*A Defence of Idealism*, London and New York, 1917, and *The New Idealism*, London and New York, 1922), promoted the modernism and imagism of such writers as T.S. Eliot, H.D. and Ezra Pound, and defended writers like D.H. Lawrence and Dorothy Richardson. She became an acknowledged expert on the Brontë sisters, with her biography (London, 1912) and her introductions to some of their novels; in her own time she was considered one of the foremost intellectuals of the Georgian period, befriended by, amongst others, Robert Frost, Edith Wharton and Ford Madox Ford. She died in 1946, and is today best remembered for her two novels, *Mary Olivier: A Life* (London and New York, 1919) and *The Life and Death of Harriett Frean* (London and New York, 1922), though she published over two dozen volumes of fiction, two volumes of verse and a verse novel.

In part because of Sinclair's evident awareness of Freud's, Jung's and Havelock Ellis's psychological writings (in many of her novels), her writings are often described as 'psychological novels', *Mary Olivier* being seen as a study in sublimation, while *Harriett Frean* is often described as a study, rather, in repression – where sublimation has failed and the victim's failure is thoroughly psychoanalysed. While these two 'case histories' are greatly admired for their astute investigations into the causes of repression, the means of sublimation and the success or failure of self-development and independence, they are also recognized as more general social criticisms, firmly rooted, however, in a sophisticated awareness of the centrality of social attitudes to sexuality and of the destructive role of much religion and socialization in human life and, more specifically, child development. These novels also betray a considerable interest in nineteenth-century determinism, while at the same time embracing imagist and modernist techniques in narrative and style. May Sinclair adopted Dorothy Richardson's and Henry James's 'psychological realism', or 'stream of consciousness' as she called it, learnt to use complex imagery as a structuring device, and shattered notions of time as objective through several techniques, in both *Mary Olivier* and *Harriett Frean*. She also experimented successfully with narrative perspective in both these novels, and gained the praise even of that most demanding critic, T.S. Eliot.

May Sinclair's praise of Dorothy Richardson's *Pilgrimage* is revealing of her own concerns as a novelist. She, like Richardson, brought to the fore the inner world of the mind, de-emphasizing direct, realist representation of the social context in favour of its indirect portrayal through the consciousness of her characters. She dispensed, like Richardson, with conventional conceptions of plot, anticipating later modernist perfectors of the fiction of non-action. Like Chopin and Gilman before her, she perfected the enigmatic non-ending, which later modernists were also to embrace in the process both of reconceptualizing notions of artistic unity and development, and of challenging notions of meaning as didactic, univocal and determinate. She buttressed her rejection of realist ideology both in literature and in thought by interweaving philosophical ideas and psychological insights (often directly through symbol or imagery), which emphasized certain idealist principles about language, art and consciousness as in need of interpretation and never immediately, transparently knowable or representative of an 'outside'. Sinclair's interest in idealism was less in its transcendental possibilities than in its critique of the naïveté of ideologies which posit unbridgeable dualisms, leading to insoluble problems about the relation of language to the world, art to history and reality, consciousness to external objects, and the individual to society. Aspects of idealism gave Sinclair the critical tools she needed to challenge these dualisms as artificial, man-made constructs, creating pseudo-problems resolved only by a determined refusal of the false, hypothesized dualities upon which they were based. Sinclair's understanding of philosophical idealism clarified the central role of language in conscious experience, and the nature of consciousness as active and constitutive of experience rather than merely passively receptive of an external world. It encouraged her to place language and consciousness at the centre of her novels structurally, thematically and stylistically, instead of relegating them, as realist fiction often did, to by-products of a pre-existing reality.

Sinclair, like so many of her male and female modernist contemporaries, challenged the boundary between fiction and history by breaching the genre divisions between the novel and the autobiography. Anticipating late twentieth-century acknowledgements of the crucial centrality of autobiography in not only fiction but also literary criticism and history, Sinclair recognized, much as Jean Rhys did, that to pretend to objectivity and non-personal, non-subjective thematics was merely one mode of fiction, not *the* mode, or even the superior mode. Astute use of subjective material – that is, of experience – was, for Sinclair, at the heart of all writing. To use it overtly instead of covertly did not somehow invalidate it as fiction. Rather, for May Sinclair, this acknowledged the extent of subjective, personal experience in all fiction, however transformed it may be into public events or plotted drama. In this, Sinclair, Rhys, Richardson, Virginia Woolf, E.M. Forster and Lawrence, for example, were at one, and their emphasis upon subjectivity led eventually to some of the later debates and sophisticated theorizing of the second half of the twentieth century. In this way, Sinclair also ridiculed the realist positing of an omniscient, neutral and objective point of view designed to give us truth from one most ideal perspective. She furthered her modernist experiments by using extreme fragmentation of structure, great leaps of time in the narrative, and an impressionistic style which is also fragmented syntactically; she used word associations and developed extended images to create meaning. Like Jane Austen, Sinclair confused authorial commentary with the thoughts of her characters in her 'indirect free narrative', so that it is impossible to distinguish the two. The notion of objective time is also ruthlessly parodied as the novel *Mary Olivier* rushes towards its enigmatic finish, contrasting almost grotesquely with its stately, leisured pace at the beginning.

Thematically, Sinclair's break with the nineteenth-century tradition came in the form of the centrality in her novels of women's experience and, more specifically, the reality of female sexuality (as well as that of the child). This is tied to the further, psychological thematic of the exploration of the psyche as an unknown, unconscious realm desperately in need of being made conscious if we are ever to come to any self-knowledge. Sinclair anticipated Melanie Klein's understanding of child psychology and Klein's controversial portrayal of the desire to have children as, in part, an infantile wish for dolls. Sinclair also depicted the ambivalent relations between parent and child and the perverse forms that love can take, and portrayed the family as the potential scene of tragedy of Greek proportions. As with Katherine Mansfield, her texts suggest that, until women free themselves from that 'idiotic' delusion that love is the only thing in the world, they will never be able to develop themselves. *Mary Olivier* represents Sinclair's effort to map and track the means (and the hindrances) to personal liberation from convention, circumstance and custom, showing, like Kierkegaard, that it is a path of 'fear and trembling' unto death; never is the seeker free from doubt as to whether she or he has succeeded in transcending the ego or fallen into some kind of self-delusion.

Both *The Life and Death of Harriett Frean* and *Mary Olivier: A Life* begin with the heroine's infancy; the former proceeds more economically (in a novella a quarter of the length of the second novel) to the death at 70 of Harriett Frean. While the sparseness of *Harriett Frean* lends the work an aesthetic compression which is impressive, *Mary Olivier* represents a more thoroughly developed artifact; as such, both novels are experiments in different kinds of writing. *Frean* pushes economy to the limits with immense success, while *Olivier* equally successfully explores the possibilities which a genuine novel-length text provides. Because of the theme of destructive sacrifice in *Frean*, the novel has a distinctly different aesthetic effect from *Olivier*. *Mary Olivier* enacts some interesting modernist experiments which are enormously enhanced by the uplifting and inspiring writing in the last tenth of the novel, describing Olivier's transcendence of her ego in almost Buddhist terms of detachment from things and from the mundane self. The coincidence with the final volume of Dorothy Richardson's *Pilgrimage*, not published until some decades later, is notable. Unlike Wharton, Kate Chopin or Charlotte Perkins Gilman, May Sinclair created a woman who rises above circumstances into an existential fulfilment, and who can say 'nobody told you that after forty-five life would have this exquisite clearness and intensity.' (Vita Sackville-West, in *All Passion Spent* (1931), later portrayed a woman

who, after marriage and children, achieved a similar independence from her family in her widowhood, to the dismayed surprise of her children, grandchildren and friends.) Yet the novel *Mary Olivier*, like its heroine, achieves an exquisite clearness and intensity by the end which testify to an unusual congruence of theme and form. In its impressionistic style, its dexterous alternation between first and third person narrative, its structural balance of fragmentation and unity, its subjective portrayal of time, and its idealist theme of self-construction through thought and action, *Mary Olivier* achieves a uniqueness and individuality as a work of art which its heroine is portrayed as achieving in life. This 'double reflection', as Kierkegaard was fond of calling such congruence, makes an unremitting demand on the reader which is intrinsically rewarding, both aesthetically and morally.

Sinclair's other novels include *The Divine Fire* (London, 1904), *The Three Sisters* (London and New York, 1914) – a study of obsessive love, and *The Tree of Heaven* (London and New York, 1917). Some of these have been recently republished by Virago.

Henry Handel Richardson 1870–1946

Ethel Florence Lindesay Richardson (Henry Handel Richardson) was born in Melbourne, but left Australia at the age of 17 to study music in Leipzig. She lived in Germany and England for the rest of her life, visiting Australia only once to refresh her memory for one of her novels. She wrote four major novels and several short stories, as well as the autobiography *Myself When Young* (Melbourne, 1948). Biographical and critical accounts of her life and writing by Nettie Palmer (Sydney and London, 1950) and Dorothy Green (Sydney, 1973, 1986) show her to be one of Australia's most accomplished novelists. Her first novel, *Maurice Guest* (London, 1908), took her almost a dozen years to write, and is firmly based on her first-hand experiences of student life at the Leipzig Conservatory. At the same time, for 'light relief', Richardson was composing *The Getting of Wisdom* (London and New York, 1910), her Australian autobiographical novel of a young girl's experiences in the confined and oppressive world of boarding school. The ironic *Fortunes of Richard Mahony* (London, 1930), first published in three separate volumes in 1917, 1925 and 1929, is said to be based on her father, and is also an overt exploration of a theme characteristic of many Australian-born novelists, namely, the relative values of life in England or Australia. A collection of short stories, *The End of a Childhood and Other Stories* (London and New York, 1934), and the novel *The Young Cosima* (London and New York, 1939), complete her oeuvre. *The Complete Stories*, ed. C. Franklin, appeared in 1992. Two of her novels, then, are set primarily in Australia, while the other two 'music' novels are set in Germany. Richardson was awarded the Australian Literary Society Gold Medal in 1929.

Richardson's writing belongs to the European-Russian tradition of nineteenth-century realist fiction, with its emphasis on philosophical and existential questions about life and its meaning and worth. Richardson had explicitly stated her belief that the novel should be a study of character and of conflicts of characters as the real drama of life, and her novels testify to her commitment to this principle, most especially *Maurice Guest* and *Richard Mahony*, her two most impressive works. *Maurice Guest* shocked contemporary English and Australian audiences, partly because of its 'Europeanness'; it is an intensely passionate study of sexual repression and resulting obsession, while it also explores the source of conflict amongst people as being essentially in irreconcilable differences of temperament rather than in inadequacy or evil. Richardson's first novel also portrays a theme that was to recur centrally throughout the rest of her fiction, namely the unusual individual whose abilities are not equal to her or his aspirations, and the consequent suffering, failure and even tragedy. This theme of inadequacy and failure is handled by Richardson with an extraordinary detachment, as she refused to moralize or instruct her readers, discouraging judgemental responses in favour of an intelligent appreciation of the variety of points of view on life, morality and art which make it impossible to achieve certainty. The relation of art or genius to morality was another theme which Richardson portrayed as complex in the extreme, as she analysed the difficulty of combining a personal life with an

artist's commitment, much as Willa Cather was to do some years later.

Richardson began her literary career by translating novels from the Danish, which influenced her writing from the start, and placed her firmly in the realist tradition of nineteenth-century European fiction. The relentless inevitability of plot which characterizes *Maurice Guest*, and which some readers find unbearably oppressive, is expressive of a scientific determinism which Richardson employed also in her style, with its enumeration of detail, close attention to setting, attention to the individual's relation to her or his environment, and emphasis on observation and experience. But this realism is complemented by early twentieth-century preoccupations with psychology and sexuality, and in all her novels Richardson explored in greater or lesser depth the self-delusion which leads to repression and obsession. Both *Maurice Guest* and *Richard Mahony* focus on individuals who are neither ordinary nor extraordinary enough to survive; rather, both men are shown in flights from reality, the one from his dreary schoolteacher life in England to the glamorous musical world of Leipzig, the other from wherever he is at the present moment. Even in *The Getting of Wisdom*, Laura is shown, like Guest and Mahony though to a lesser degree, to be confronted with the possibility that it is her own self which needs change and development as much as the inadequate, oppressive world around her, if she is to escape from unhappiness and an intolerable existence. Of all Richardson's novels, however, *Maurice Guest* charted most successfully the causes and the process of the individual imprisoned by her or his own inadequacies, but who deludes herself or himself into believing that fate, or the world, has dealt her or him unfair and intolerable blows. These themes of failure and inadequacy focus on the self as the prison, and impressive psychological studies of the destructive forces which impede self-fulfilment are the result.

Richardson was not simply a realist anti-romantic, however. Her themes were essentially romantic, from the infatuations of a schoolgirl, through the obsessive love of a young man, to the tragedy of mature relationships, as she sought to find means of representing human weaknesses which impede character and lead to madness and suicide. In *Maurice Guest*, Richardson charted with ironic prognostications the final tragedy, whose impact on the reader is not through surprise but through its inevitability and psychological truth. In both this and *Richard Mahony*, the hero is driven, by a restless incapacity to live life, from one continent to the other, as he travels from Australia to England to try to find some environment which he can tolerate. Richardson showed the deficiencies in both societies with a scrupulous neutrality, while dramatizing the real difficulty as within the hero himself.

Thus Richardson achieved an intensely effective fusion of realism and romanticism in her novels, with an unmoralizing presentation of characters and this tragedy of irreconcilable conflicts, due to clashes not between good and evil or morality and immorality so much as between fundamental character differences, which neither love nor imagination is able to bridge. In *Maurice Guest* and in *Richard Mahony* particularly, she developed sophisticated organizational devices for unifying the wealth of incident and variety of characters in each novel: she was a genius at the traumatic scene, and she alternated a variety of intense scenes with Thomas Mann-like intellectual debates amongst her characters and repeated, symbolic images to unify her narrative. The careful accumulation of detail is rarely unenlivened by a powerful narrative detachment and ironic distance, while the detail is never just for itself, but always subservient to the portrayal of character and conflict which so fascinated Richardson throughout her life.

Letters to Nettie Palmer were edited by K.J. Rossing (1953).

Willa Cather 1873–1947

Born in Virginia in 1873, Willa Cather moved with her family to a farm in Red Cloud, Nebraska, when she was 10. The pioneer spirit of many of the highly cultivated immigrants of the region became allied in her novels with the artist spirit, both being expressive of that courage and imaginative energy which are contrasted, as a central theme in her novels, with the powerful forces of mediocrity and convention which destroy the spirit. After taking a BA in 1895 from the University of Nebraska, Cather eventually settled in New York to devote herself to writing fiction; one of her earliest influences was the great New England stylist Sarah Orne Jewett, to whom she dedicated her first novel, *Alexander's Bridge* (Boston and New York, 1912). Cather travelled extensively in Europe with Isabella McClung and later Edith Lewis, but the landscape of her own American Southwest, which she first saw in 1912, proved one of the deepest influences on her fiction. Some of her finest novels, such as *The Song of the Lark* (Boston and New York, 1915), and later *Death Comes from the Archbishop* (New York, 1927), portray the sublimely inspiring landscape with its enchanting, ancient and mysterious cliff dwellings. The supernatural beauty of these ruined human cities hanging in the magnificent cliffs in the sky became a powerful symbol to Cather, not only of art as the perfect balance of the natural and the human, or 'nature humanized', as Coleridge defined the imaginative faculty; these dwellings also became a metaphor for artistic unity, with congruence, harmony and proportion invoked in Cather's description of art. Finally, the excavations of the dwellings, as in the Tom Outland story in *The Professor's House* (New York, 1925; that novella within a novel, which turns digression into main content, and the latter into a frame, and raises Edith Wharton-like questions about history as legend and fiction), turn into a delightful allegory for the nature of reading as the excavation of the language and structure of a novel, and as a metaphor for the human mind itself, with its strata and layerings in need of interpretation.

Oppositions become thematic material and structuring devices in Cather's novels, such as tensions between country and city life, between society and family and the need of individuals for solitude, between America and Europe, between genius and convention or mediocrity, and between the creative and the destructive. These oppositions are also reflected in characters' conflicts, and lead to portrayals of almost heroic dimensions, as characters struggle against each other to achieve fulfilment or to thwart it for themselves and for others. The opposition between nature and art or culture was never a conflict for Cather, however; as with the pioneer and artist, these were shown to be spiritual relations. The urgent conflict was between excellence and the pettiness, convention and mediocrity that imprison the elemental creative forces of the human spirit in greed, fear and passivity.

Cather's novels nearly all display intricacies and complexities of narrative, plot, tone and characters which embody and demonstrate artistically her avowed interest in the novel as novel (as a work of art), and not merely as a document or report of ideas, opinions or truths. She used complex narrative frameworks and personas; she emphasized landscape as both a principle of artistic unity and a metaphor for genius; she used elaborate, emblematic imagery, with symbolic overtones; she foregrounded the act of storytelling in several novels; and she developed a unique style. Like Charlotte Perkins Gilman and Wharton, Cather came to reject realism as restricting the imagination to the ordinary details of surface existence, and marked her rejection by turning to what she called 'romance', for her 'the highest form of fiction', though 'romance', as all her novels testify, is not used in the market-place sense but as a technical, literary term. She was seeking to emphasize the great value she, following Melville, Hawthorne, the Brontës and others, had placed upon the creative imagination, as the instrument both of art and of moral good. She anticipated Flannery O'Connor by decades in arguing that at the basis of all symbolic, imaginative and spiritual achievement is the physical, the concrete and the sensuous, or nature itself. Cather's novels are an exploration of how human beings liberate this elemental energy for creative (and for destructive) forces, and why they fail to liberate it. Thus, her novels have literary, social, moral and psychological strata or dimensions which are carefully intertwined into a beautifully designed whole.

In contrast with realist preoccupations with detailed enumeration and 'over-furnishings', Cather argued for the need to simplify and condense: art, she said, 'should simplify. That indeed, is very nearly the whole of the higher artistic process; finding what conventions of form and what detail one can do without and yet preserve the spirit of the whole.' To simplify, an artist compresses subordinate elements into a few major ones, yet the former hover over the pages by means of suggestion and symbol. Hence, the reader can excavate these hidden layers to discover complexes of unities or strata of meanings. Cather spoke of the 'inexplicable presence of the thing not named'; she wrote of 'overtones divined by the ear but not heard'; she spoke of 'verbal mood', 'emotional auras' which the enumeration of detail destroys; and, along with this 'high quality' of suggestiveness, realism, she argued, destroys 'the spirit of the whole'. Unlike in realism, in Cather's conception of romance the end is always kept in view, through processes of understatement, compression and restraint over the individual elements making up the unity. She believed the contrast between mechanical memory and her 'magical memory' (that selective ally of imagination) to be expressive of the difference between realism and romance, which Wharton had expressed in contrasting the 'mechanical sight-seer' with the 'dreamer and dawdler'. Moreover, Cather believed the artist must learn her principles of craft and technique so thoroughly that they are forgotten, as the arbitrary elements drop away in the face of the intuitive but highly trained power of imagination. Such an imagination becomes a second nature, which controls technique and craft and makes it subservient – in mysterious, often unconscious ways – to the intuited 'spirit of the whole'.

Like landscape, which plays such a powerful role in Cather's novels as to become a character, so magical memory becomes one, hovering over the page, acting now as an astute observer, now as a recoverer and preserver of the past. Through narrative complexity of varying layers of perspective, Cather built into her texts ironic levels of interpretation which comment on each other, creating a remarkable dialogue within the text itself between its thematics and of its structure. In addition to these narrative personifications of memory, nature and imagination, Cather employed framework techniques – stories within stories, a *nouvelle* within a *roman* – freely ironized innocent observers, and used plotless structures, in order to escape the literary conventions of the times. Complicated as the strategies may make her novels at a surface level, they compress and simplify at deeper levels by making possible a critical self-consciousness which is the very essence of much art, that is, a self-awareness of the text's artistry and its aesthetic effect on various types of reader.

Cather was deeply drawn to the naked, 'Blakean' energies of nature and the imagination. Her respect for these – whether used for creative or destructive forces – is an eloquent statement of her belief that the most deadly and powerful enemy of fulfilment and creativity is not so much the abuse of energy, destructive as this can be. Far more deadly and pervasive are the mediocrity and obeisance to convention which kill the human spirit. Her long novel, *The Song of the Lark*, for example, portrays (in one variation after another) the obstacles to the development of genius and personal excellence which convention and narrow-mindedness erect. The suffocation of excellence (out of fear that entrenched beliefs and familiar ways of living will be threatened) is depicted in numerous novels as a 'death-in-life'. Actual bodily, as opposed to spiritual, death was a natural diminution of energy for Cather, so that the mediocrity of ordinary life which kills the spirit was the only death to be feared. Dualities between life and death, and art and nature, are challenged in Cather's novels by an imaginative act which overcomes personal ego in spiritual fulfilment (as in May Sinclair's novels) and which sees art and nature as inextricably one, as symbolized by the beautifully proportioned, harmonious cliff dwellings.

Cather described style as 'the artist's very self', and her love of the Southwest provided her with the inspiration for a unique style. The cliff-dwelling settings became, for her, emblematic of a kind of style, and her writing is suggestive of a re-enactment of the harmony between nature and the human, their perfect congruence and balance exemplified in the canyon cities. Her style emulates their austere beauty, their compression and their shapeliness as expressive of a fine unity, clustered as they often were in harmonious ways around central towers and other architectural foci. In the canyon-city perfection of her novels, excavation also becomes a unifying motif for reading and for aesthetic response: like Tom Outland in *The Professor's House*, the reader is drawn into the excavation of a work of art which not only reveals the intricacies of the canyon city-*cum*-text, but which also turns out (for the reader, as for Tom Outland) to be a construction of one's own individuality, through

the spiritual and moral transformation the mind goes through in the process of rich and complex aesthetic experience.

While *The Professor's House* relies on emblematic figures of excavation as spiritual transformation for much of its power, it also makes use of the convention of the *nouvelle* within the *roman*, and the centrepiece of the novel, Tom Outland's story, shines a spotlight firmly on narration itself as a kind of architecture. In *My Ántonia* (Boston and New York, 1918), other conventions abound and are used with great aesthetic effect. For example, story-telling and narration become central thematic issues, as this plotless novel turns out, upon examination, to be innumerable stories within stories within stories, demonstrating a whole variety of ways of story-telling, not to mention such subsidiary issues as the roles of memory and imagination in art, the question of the possibility of truth, and the relation of history and the past to fiction and the present. In *My Ántonia*, Cather created a 'phoney' narrative frame involving the fictional character, Jim Burden, whom many critics have mistaken for Cather, though he is clearly drawn as a parody of male fantasies about women. This novel further demonstrates Cather's interest in the variety of ways in which women can become fully developed individuals, through the various characters of Lena and the other 'hired girls' as well as Ántonia, not to mention Thea Kronberg in *The Song of the Lark*. Failure of self-development is of course also portrayed, in relation both to men and to women, and the reasons for failure are explored in Cather's writings.

These novels reveal, one after another, Cather's profound interest in Henry Jamesean ideas of views and perspectives, in the relativity of fact, truth and history, and in language as not neutral but stylized and essentially rhetorical. Closely related to these issues, which manifest themselves in structure, theme, style and character, is another central commitment in Cather's art, namely, to the belief that basic perception itself is fundamentally creative, just as nature is a work of art. All Cather's novels function aesthetically to liberate readers from the unconscious assumption that perception is basically a passive receptivity of already constituted external objects, and that reading is a passive receptivity of an author's opinions, intentions or knowledge. Cather not only offered models of active, participatory reading and examples of imaginative perception. Her situations often depict, ironically, the failure of participation and the reasons for not succeeding in escaping from dead metaphors, clichés and stereotypes, which inhibit fresh response and active perception, thus leading to the crippling mediocrity of everyday life.

Other writing includes novels such as *O Pioneers!* (London, 1913), *A Lost Lady* (New York, 1923), *My Mortal Enemy* (New York, 1926) and *Sapphira and the Slave Girl* (New York, 1940). Short stories have been published in *Collected Short Fiction 1892–1912*, ed. V. Faulkner (Lincoln, Nebr., 1970), and *Uncollected Fiction: 1915–1929*, ed. B. Slote (Lincoln, Nebr., 1970). See too the new collection introduced by Hermione Lee (London, 1989). Slote has also edited Cather's essays in *The Kingdom of Art* (Lincoln, Nebr., 1970), and see W.M. Curtin's edition of early articles and reviews, *The World and the Parish: Willa Cather's Articles and Reviews, 1893–1902* (Lincoln, Nebr., 1970). L.B. Bohlke edited another selection of non-fiction, entitled *Willa Cather in Person: Interviews, Speeches, and Letters* (Lincoln, Nebr., 1986). Cather was the recipient of the Pulitzer Prize in 1923 and of a Howells Medal in 1930. She also received numerous other prizes, and half a dozen honorary degrees from, for example, Columbia, Yale, Princeton and Berkeley.

Dorothy Richardson 1873–1957

Dorothy Miller Richardson was born in Berkshire in 1873; she earned her own living from an early age, spending time in Germany before moving to London to work as a dental assistant. Eventually she gave up her job to write; encouraged by H.G. Wells, she supported herself by translation and by publishing some two hundred articles, reviews and sketches, and in 1912 she began *Pilgrimage*, her lifelong, thirteen-volume epic, published (London and New York) between 1915 and 1967 (*March Moonlight* was published posthumously; the other twelve volumes had come out by 1938). She also wrote books on Jane Austen and Quakerism, aspects of which recur in *Pilgrimage*, that early modernist,

stream of consciousness autobiographical fiction, which eschewed conventions of genre, plot, transparent language, objectivity of point of view, external social context and other conventions of the novel, with its radical thematics of the authority of women's experience and viewpoint. Richardson rejected such conventions because, she argued, they represented a male bias characterized not only by egotism (men pretend to portray truths about life, when really they reveal truths only about themselves) but by distortion and misrepresentation of women's experience, by an overemphasis upon analytic reasoning and discursive faculties at the expense of imaginative, synthetic, relational faculties, by intolerance in political and religious views, and by a tendency towards dualistic thinking which creates false problems in life, art and philosophy. These dualistic ways of taking the world and art lead to ways of treating narrative time, structure, language and theme which Richardson sought to replace with an emphasis on time as subjective and flowing at different rates, on structure as less arbitrarily and overtly patterned, on the order of her novel as intrinsic and integral rather than conventional – and on language as problematic in the extreme, rather than clear, determinate and univocal in meaning or representative of an external, non-linguistic reality.

Pilgrimage has been described thematically as the efforts of the heroine, Miriam Henderson, to achieve autonomy, first through economic independence. Her journey, indeed, begins there, as she struggles existentially to construct a more genuine individuality, first by throwing off the expectations of others and the stereotyped roles thrust upon her, and second by moulding herself through work, thought, writing and human relationship. *Pilgrimage*, it has been noted, does not really end; it stops of course, but structurally it remains open-ended, avoiding closure and those false patterns, order and unity which Richardson detested. Its open-endedness expresses the existential idea that self-construction is never over, though it must end in death; but while still living, the individual human being can never be 'finished'. Richardson's novel has also been seen as a study in how far an individual can create herself, and how far she is a product of environment, though it could be argued that this is a false dilemma resulting from an unconsciously assumed duality between the individual and society. That is, *Pilgrimage* functions not to portray these dilemmas and conflicts but to reject them, by showing, for example, that individuals and environments exist only as functions of each other: we express our 'free will' only in struggle with the correlative 'forces' in our environment and our psyches. The contrast is not between free will and determinism, or liberation and imprisonment, but between struggle and passivity. Miriam's attitude to passive women, for example, who collude with men in subordinating women instead of struggling, is ruthlessly critical.

Pilgrimage expresses Richardson's and Miriam's distrust not only of the predominantly male literary tradition, or only of the male view of life, experience and women. It also, paradoxically, expresses a distrust of language itself, even while it has to use language in order to criticize it; hence Richardson's uncompromisingly experimental style. Her experiments in style involve, as did Gertrude Stein's, a challenging of many linguistic conventions, involving grammar, punctuation and semantic dimensions. These were interrelated with her more literary experiments in narrative point of view, unconventional structure, plotlessness and thematics. As has been noted by numerous of Richardson's admirers, she toyed with punctuation, changed verb tenses unexpectedly, and turned sentences into long, rolling paragraphs or short, jerky, ungrammatical fragments. She obscured sense or exploited opacity to express her rejection of univocal meaning and rationalist clarity, and also to express Miriam's increasing uncertainty about basic elements of experience, as she relentlessly challenges accepted 'facts', beliefs, and values about the self, the world, society, language, morality and so on. This deliberate linguistic opacity is repeated at the structural level of the novel: Richardson often leaves great gaps between one part of the narrative and the next, hinting sometimes at momentous events which have occurred without clarifying them (such as the death of Miriam's mother, or Miriam's involvement with Hypo).

Richardson's ambivalence towards language is a repeated theme of Miriam's meditations, and of her gradually increasing preoccupation with silence. The gaps in the narrative are a kind of silence, an example of the possibility even for a writer of communicating indirectly, at least, if not actually wordlessly. The interest in Quakerism is also an expression of the importance of cultivating silence, as Miriam becomes increasingly aware of what she calls the 'intensity of being' and the wonder of mere existence as, for her, the only reason for living. Already by *Deadlock* (London, 1979) Miriam was noting, 'silence is reality. Life ought to be lived on the basis of silence, where truth blossoms.' This may seem an impossible position for a writer to take, yet Richardson's refusal to use the novel as a medium for promoting specific ideas, values and beliefs, so much as one for questioning conventions, makes her distrust of language less paradoxical. Miriam's own journey seems to be one from uncertainty about life to even more uncertainty, in some respects, as thought, experience and language fail to clarify in a positive sense, though they do reveal to her more and more in a kind of negative sense. That is, her awareness of what is *not* possible increases, at least given the facts of a patriarchal society.

Richardson's novel, it could be said, creates, through impressionistic language and an attention to the immediacy of some kinds of experience, an atmosphere which lures the reader into that contemplative silence of which Miriam often speaks. *Pilgrimage* itself may be a testimony to what writers like Eudora Welty or Doris Lessing were, decades later, to say about the relation of words to experience and the mystery of experience:

> Knowing was an 'illumination'. During the last weeks of craziness and timelessness I've had these moments of 'knowing' one after the other, yet there is no way of putting this sort of knowledge into words. Yet these moments have been so powerful, like the rapid illuminations of a dream that remain with one waking, that what I have learned will be part of how I experience life until I die. Words. Words. I play with words, hoping that some combination, even a chance combination, will say what I want . . . the real experience can't be described . . . The people who have been there, in the place in themselves where words, patterns, order, dissolve, will know what I mean and the others won't. (*The Golden Notebook*)

Lessing's Anna goes on to conclude that the condition for this illuminating, wordless knowledge existing at all is, paradoxically, precisely the words, patterns and forms to which, however, it cannot be reduced, and which are not it, nor a substitute for it: 'I know you are there, but we have to preserve the forms, don't we? And perhaps the condition of your existing at all is that we preserve the forms, create the patterns –.' The passionate sense of the wonder of existence, which, Miriam alleges, sets aside all personal problems for a time, is closely involved with a developing sense of a self understood as a unique individuality rather than a socialized role-playing self. This unique self is nourished on solitude, contemplation and silence. Indeed, for it, 'contemplation is adventure into discovery; reality.' Yet, ironically, it seems to have come into being by Richardson's working through the forms and patterns of a new kind of language, through, that is, *Pilgrimage* itself.

Throughout *Pilgrimage*, language crops up as a subject matter, along with other issues such as its relations to thought and to experience, its relation to the world, the possibility of finding a new language less biased by male attitudes, the problem of communication (especially between men and women), and so on. The following passages illustrate several of these issues:

> Scraps of conversation reached her from all over the room; eloquent words, fashioned easily, without thought, a perfect flowing of understanding, to and fro, without obstruction. No heaven could be more marvellous. People talked incessantly because in silence they were ghosts. A single word sounded the secret of the universe. There is a dead level of intelligence throughout humanity. She listened in wonder whilst she explained aloud that she had learned most of her French by reading again and again for the sake of the long, even rhythm of its sentences, one book; that this was the only honest way to acquire a language. It was like a sea, each sentence a wave rolling in, rising till the light shone through its glistening crest, dropping to give way to the next oncoming wave, the meaning gathering, accumulating, coming nearer with each rising falling rhythm; each chapter a renewed tide, monotonously repeating throughout the book in every tone of light and shade the same burden, the secret of everything in the world.

> She wanted to explain that she used to read novels but could not get interested in them

after Emerson. They showed only one side of people, the outside; if they showed them alone, it was only to explain what they felt about people.

> Speech did something to things; set them in a mould that was apt to come up again; repeated, it would be dead; but perhaps one need never repeat oneself? To say the same things to different people would give them a sort of fresh life; but there would be death in oneself as one spoke.

> 'But you must at once finish. They are closing. It is now midnight.' It did not matter. Nothing was at an end. Nothing would ever come to an end again.

These self-referential thematics are characteristic of the novel; the sentence beginning 'It was like a sea, each sentence a wave rolling in' is itself made to roll, to rise, to drop like a wave, gathering as it accumulates. This is an example of Richardson's idea of how language can mean in addition to discursive meaning. It is self-enactment of meaning for which she strove throughout the novel. Moreover, Miriam's intoxication is a metaphor for her later enchantment with an intense awareness of the wonder of existence, through contemplation, silence and solitude. But this passage also reveals a satirical element: Miriam, it is indirectly suggested, is too intoxicated to look critically at her immediate thoughts and feelings, many of which are delusions, as in the first paragraph when she imagines 'eloquent words . . . a perfect flowing of understanding . . . No heaven could be more marvellous.' By such subtle means, Dorothy Richardson critically distanced herself from her heroine, yet without ever pretending to an objectivity which, she believed, was a delusion and which, anyway, can only show 'one side of people, the outside'.

Richardson's non-fiction includes *The Quakers Past and Present* (London, 1914) and *Jane Austen and the Inseparables* (London, 1930). She translated numerous books from German and French.

Gertrude Stein 1874–1946

Born of Bavarian immigrant parents in Allegheny, Pennsylvania, Stein spent the first part of her childhood in Vienna and Paris until her family settled in Oakland, California, in 1879. By 1891, she had lost both her parents, and moved with her brother Leo to the Baltimore residence of her aunt. Stein attended Harvard Annex, now Radcliffe College, and Johns Hopkins medical school, spent time in Italy, New York and London, and finally settled in 27 rue de Fleurus, Paris, first with Leo and then with Alice B. Toklas. She died in Paris in 1946.

Taught by William James and George Santayana, painted by Picasso and Tchelitchew, sculpted by Lipchitz and Davidson, photographed by Van Vechten and Cecil Beaton, and known at one time as the 'mama of dada', Gertrude Stein is more widely known about than read. This is partly due to her imposing personality, her literary and artistic genius, her extraordinary collection of impressionist and post-impressionist paintings (including Matisse, Picasso, Braque, Rousseau, Cézanne and Renoir), and her numerous famous friends (from Hemingway, Virgil Thompson, Anderson and Wilder to Mina Loy, Bryher, Sylvia Beach, Jane Heap and Robert McAlmon), and partly due to the extreme difficulty facing the reader of Stein's radical experiments in language and literature. These experiments range across short stories, plays, novels, poems, autobiographies, 'portraits', memoirs, essays, letters and uncategorizable writings. Indeed, until recently Stein's writings have often been referred to as 'the nonsensical gibberish' of a 'supreme egotist', with the exception of such accessible and immensely popular books as *The Autobiography of Alice B. Toklas* (New York and London, 1933) and *Three Lives* (New York, 1909).

Stein had extreme difficulty in getting her work published in the first few decades of her writing life, which began in earnest in Paris in 1903. *Q.E.D., or Things as They Are*, as it was later entitled, was written in 1903 in Paris but not published until 1950 (Pawlet, Vt.), partly due to its extremely explicit accounts of Stein's lesbian experiences in Baltimore. Her life partner, Alice B. Toklas (whom Stein met in Paris in 1907 and lived with from 1910 until Stein died of cancer), created the Plain Edition press to publish Stein's work, and acted as subject matter, typist, inspiration, proof-reader and general helpmate throughout their life together. During the years before Toklas's arrival, Stein

rewrote *Q.E.D.* into a heterosexual triangle account renamed *Melancthus*. This became part of *Three Lives*, composed while Stein was sitting for her portrait by Picasso, along with the early parts of *The Making of Americans* (completed by 1911), that thousand-page epic 'history' not published until 1925 (Paris), sixteen years after *Three Lives* appeared.

In the meantime, *Tender Buttons* was published (New York, 1914), a series of experimental 'prose poems' which use techniques associated more with poetry than prose, such as those of repetition, 'stream of consciousness', 'denuded language', attention to nuances of sound, alliteration, texture, rhythm and diction, the divorcing of word from meaning, rejection of the primacy of content and subject matter in favour of attention to language, and writing which continually mimics itself. Stein thereby destroyed the supposedly inalienable bond between word and its referent, meaning. She redirected her readers' attention away from content, form or substance towards words (as important in themselves and not as mere signs of meanings or referents 'behind' them) and language (as rich with characteristics in need of the closest possible scrutiny). Stein also explored the effects of unusual use of verb tenses, parts of speech and punctuation. In some early works, such as the early experimental portrait 'Ada' and the erotic poem 'Lifting Belly', Stein wrote in an encoded language to veil her descriptions of lesbian sexual experience; this use of a kind of cypher has led some readers to exaggerate the extent of such encoding techniques, assuming that this explains the difficulty of most of Stein's writing, when in fact it applies to only a small number of her works. Her linguistic experiments went far beyond mere coding techniques, to challenge the traditional concept of language as meaningful by virtue of referentiality.

With the Cubists, impressionists and post-impressionists in painting, Stein was interested in exploring the concept of representation. She took over Cubist and other painters' techniques in a deliberate effort to reject language as primarily important for its representational effects. She was interested, like many modernists, in language as language. But while many other writers of the period concentrated on rhetorical effects, the etymological history of words, plays on natural association and connotations in words, and allusions to extra-linguistic traditions of literature, philosophy and religion, Stein stripped her language of these pretensions of intellectual elitism, adopting a repetitively childish effect that completely stymied the traditional habits and expectations of her readership. Her use of the Cubist technique of 'deformation' (or the intensifying and clarifying of visual effects in order to free painting and language from the prison of representation), along with her adoption and adaptation of William James's liberation of psychology from atomism and sensationalism (with his concept of 'stream of consciousness', or what Stein later called 'continuous present' in her narrative adaptation), contributed to her multiple linguistic experiments. These involved a rejection of the conventional authorial pretensions to have mastered language and the word, or the sacred Logos. Stein, on the contrary, both played with language and let language (as Heidegger might say) play with her, in order to make it reveal to her its secrets in this partial submission to its power, while exerting her own active genius to engage with it in mutual interaction.

Cubism and impressionist methods, as well as William James's ideas in psychology, led to Stein's discovery of a language charged with a self-consciousness of its own principles of operation. Her lesbianism contributed to her attack on what she saw as patriarchal laws of grammar and syntax, which enforce certain restricted relations between parts of speech, use of punctuation, relation of sign to signified and of word to referent, and the operations of a naming process that stipulates the indestructible bond between word and thing. Stein further violated the laws of grammar and syntax by rejecting the serious, decorous tone of much male writing to produce comic, 'unauthorized', playful and arbitrary arrangements and juxtapositions of words and phrases. These often appear to be a result of 'free association' when they are also a sustained attempt to render language self-referential and non-representational but always 'meaningful', even if in a sense that is unorthodox. This 'other' sense of meaningfulness can be described by saying that meaning resides entirely within language, in its textures, sounds, rhythms, principles of operations, and relations amongst words.

Meaning, therefore, is not, for Gertrude Stein, determinate or unambiguous, as it is in the conventional notion. Thus, even the concept of 'encoded meaning' (designed to veil lesbian attacks on patriarchy) is inadequate to describe Stein's experiments which anticipate Kristeva.

Stein's literary attack on the patriarchal privileging of meaning as referential, as opposed to meaning as relational within language itself, was mirrored in her own life, as she meandered exploratively outside the accepted codes of dress, sexual identity, social behaviour, gender roles and value judgements, and totally 'disrupted' and dispersed the domestic tranquillity of patriarchal rules for personal life, writing and social behaviour. Mocked by the patriarchy, even by many modernist writers (who rejected her threatening texts as unreadable), Stein nevertheless became known to a large American and English public, both through Virgil Thompson's opera version of her play *Four Saints in Three Acts* (New York, 1934), which led to an American lecture tour, and through a series of lectures in Oxford and Cambridge, written up as *Composition as Explanation* (published by Leonard and Virginia Woolf's Hogarth Press in London, 1926). Stein's writing anticipates by half a century the critical, stylistic and philosophical insights into language and literature of the 1970s and 1980s that have had a powerful impact upon traditional concepts and values. She is being rediscovered and re-evaluated by a decade of readers able to challenge accepted beliefs, practices and assumptions in life, literature and philosophy, beliefs that have always upheld patriarchal authority and without which it is disrupted.

A useful introductory collection is the *Selected Writings of Gertrude Stein*, ed. Carl Van Vechten (New York, 1946). Donald C. Gallup edited *Fernhurst, Q.E.D., and Other Early Writings* (New York, 1971), and a collection of letters, *The Flowers of Friendship* (New York, 1953). Samuel M. Steward edited *Dear Sammy: Letters from Gertrude Stein and Alice B. Toklas* (Boston, 1977). Memoirs include W.G. Rogers, *When This You See Remember Me: Gertrude Stein in Person* (New York, 1948), and Alice B. Toklas, *What is Remembered* (New York, 1963). See also Linda Simon, *The Biography of Alice B. Toklas* (New York, 1977). Gertrude Stein's papers can be found primarily in the Beinecke Library at Yale, and in the Bancroft Library at the Humanities Research Center, Austin, Texas.

Alice Dunbar-Nelson 1875–1930

Alice Ruth Moore (Alice Dunbar-Nelson) was born in New Orleans and lived there until shortly before she married Paul Lawrence Dunbar and moved to New York City. While still teaching school in New Orleans, when 20 years old, she published a volume of juvenilia, including short stories, poems, sketches and reviews, called *Violets and Other Tales* (Boston, 1895). She later divorced and moved to Delaware; she became an active promoter of civil rights for black people, and continued to publish as well as editing volumes of anthologies of black writers' works. She wrote four novels as well as short stories, journalism, essays, poetry and several plays. Towards the end of her life she gave up school-teaching and worked for black involvement in the world peace movement. Many of her writings have been recently collected in *The Works of Alice Dunbar-Nelson*, 3 vols, ed. G.T. Hull (Oxford and New York, 1988), as part of the Schomberg Library of Nineteenth Century Black Women Writers. An *Alice Dunbar-Nelson Reader* is edited by R.O. Williams (Washington, D.C., 1978), and her diary is available as *Give Us Each Day: The Diary of Alice Dunbar-Nelson*, ed. G.T. Hull (New York, 1984).

After Dunbar-Nelson's juvenilia, four years later she published another, more accomplished collection of stories, *The Goodness of St. Rocque and Other Stories* (New York, 1899, 1969), these two volumes being the only works published in her lifetime apart from single poems, essays and stories. In both these collections, Dunbar-Nelson used many Creole characters and materials rather than black people, about whom she was not to write directly and overtly until somewhat later. But the Creole material may have been a facade, like the style of charm and brightness, used to hide the tragedy, death and racism lurking behind the surface of the texts, indeed often constituting a plot and theme at odds with the easy-going atmosphere of the style. This 'inconsistency' is expressive of the difficulties of self-definition facing black women particularly,

as they were confronted with extremely restrictive social roles that oppressed their attempts at self-realization. In later stories, such as 'The Annals of 'Steenth Street', Dunbar-Nelson wrote about poverty and oppression in the Irish ghettos of New York City, but class oppression is clearly a metaphor for race and even gender difference. In her most overtly autobiographical stories, such as 'No Sacrifice' or 'The Decision', Dunbar-Nelson had used white characters as her vehicles, whether to protect her identity or in the hopes of interesting a larger, white readership we do not know. Images of imprisonment occur throughout her writings, such as closed doors and veils, to express patriarchal constraint restricting the independent self-realization of women, white or black, as in 'Sister Joseph' or 'The Locket'.

A Modern Undine, a novella written about 1900, was published in *The Works* in 1988. This short story shows her writing to be psychologically insightful and complex, as she explored the devastating and crippling effects of jealousy. But she also sought to reach down into the social origins of such jealousy, into the sexist assumptions of female dependence on men. The Undine figure is a means of criticizing the male notion of the ideal woman as passive, submissive, and dependent on men for her very soul. Like Kate Chopin's *The Awakening*, *A Modern Undine* is a subtle analysis of such socialization and a psychological investigation of the crippling effects of dependence. Marion's (the Undine-figure's) deformed child is skilfully used both as a metaphor for the deforming effect on male–female relationships of such 'ideal' sexual stereotypes, and an embodiment of the results of such arrangements in warping personal fulfilment. The novel is the only text of Dunbar-Nelson's to suggest her interest in mystical consciousness and in ideas of the existence of levels of human experience beyond the ordinary, visible world, both unconscious and 'supernatural'. Her use of folklore as well as traditional powerful imagery, such as the sea as a seducer and death-image, reveal Dunbar-Nelson at her most impressive.

Other short stories engage with equally compelling experiences. In 'Natalie', Dunbar-Nelson depicted racism, while 'The Stones of the Village' portrays the more complex racism of black people (and white people) towards light-skinned blacks, mulattos and Creoles. It also portrays the desire of those black people who could pass for white, due to mixed parentage, to hide their race, and the fear of 'exposure' which haunted, and could destroy, their lives. Dunbar-Nelson's stories reveal the racism behind such yearnings, and seek to restore confidence in oneself as black in the midst of prejudice and oppression. Other stories, such as 'Ellen Fenton' and 'Elizabeth', show the author trying to analyse the specific crises of both working women and middle-aged mothers who feel they have been duped into the appearance of a fulfilling life while actually sacrificing themselves so that they are left with no resources. On the other hand, in her satiric novel, *The Confessions of a Lazy Woman*, Dunbar-Nelson took the passive, dependent ideal of woman to its logical extreme, revealing the absurdity and inconsistency of the role to which women were supposed to conform.

In addition to these prose works, Dunbar-Nelson wrote plays and poetry; the latter helped keep her reputation alive. In it, she occasionally mentioned her lesbian feelings, as in 'Fay' or 'You! Inez!'. In her plays, she wrote about black characters, unlike in her prose, and dealt with controversial themes. However, it is in her *Diary* (mainly of 1921 and 1926–31) that some of her finest writing occurs, as well as in her essays and journalism (such as 'Une Femme Dit' or 'As in a Looking Glass'), to which Dunbar-Nelson devoted much of her creativity.

Dorothy Canfield (Fisher) 1879–1958

Prolific writer of fiction and non-fiction, astute educationalist, historian, social critic and war worker, Dorothy Canfield (Fisher) was born in Lawrence, Kansas, but grew up in Nebraska, where she met her life-long friend and fellow writer Willa Cather. She attended Ohio State University and took a doctorate in French literature at Columbia, as well as studying at the Sorbonne. Frustrated in her ambitions to become a musician by the onset of deafness, she was offered a university post, but turned it down in order to look after her parents. Adept at languages from French and Italian to German and Norwegian, Canfield was also deeply interested in children and child development. She wrote

books for children and studied the Montessori educational method in Italy, which impressed her enough for her to write several books encouraging its adoption in America, such as *A Montessori Mother* (New York, 1912) and *Mothers and Children* (New York, 1914). A number of her novels explore the importance of adequate child-rearing for personality development, and expose the effects of inadequate parenting on adults in later life. Often Canfield suggested, as had her predecessor Mary Wilkins Freeman, that a profound immaturity and depression in adulthood were the result of poor or misguided parenting, and her novels explore the roots of destructive character traits and failed marital relations in childhood suffering and parental ignorance. After marriage in 1907, she moved with her husband to rural Vermont, and her writing career began in earnest. During World War I, the entire family moved to France, and Canfield devoted herself to war work and to looking after children orphaned by the war. From 1920, she served for twenty-five years on the selection committee of the Book of the Month Club, shaping the reading of millions of Americans for over two decades. After the death of her son in World War II, she was unable to write fiction, but did publish *Vermont Tradition* in 1953 (Boston), shortly before her death from a stroke in 1958. In all, she published ten novels, most of which became best-sellers. She produced eleven volumes of short stories, around a dozen books of non-fiction and many, many articles and essays on a whole range of social and educational issues.

Canfield was deeply committed to the belief that human fulfilment is achieved in the main only through a balance between work and a rich personal life. Her systematic rejection of a sexist society is based firmly on her understanding that both men and women are deprived of one essential aspect of personality by conventional social arrangements. Her most overt treatment of the stupidity of sexist roles occurs in the novel *The Home-Maker* (New York, 1924), where husband and wife reverse roles out of necessity and find their real talents best realized in their new relationship. Unfortunately, their immediate society is so censorious that they must adopt deceptive ploys to maintain their innovations, but the deception takes a great toll on their self-repect. In a much earlier novel, *The Squirrel-Cage* (New York, 1912), Canfield had explored the destructive effects on women of their entrapment in a draining, conventional marriage. These and others of Canfield's novels emphasize the theme that very few adults have actually grown up in anything more than body. Their emotional, moral and intellectual beings are profoundly arrested, and this lack of development is often the source of tragedy and of mediocrity in adult life. Her novels portray many 'adults' as emotional dwarfs, pitifully unfitted to live their own lives, much less to bring children into the world and rear them. Dorothy Canfield agreed with her great predecessor John Dewey that education and educators were the very foundation of democracy as a social institution, and that parenting was something which needed to be taught, and could be taught. Thus arose her frank exposure in, for example, *Her Son's Wife* (New York, 1926; London, 1986) of the decisive and determining effects of upbringing on an adult character – balanced, however, by a firm belief not only that education can change things, but that compassion in later life can mitigate, at least in a small degree, the character defects and inadequacies of childhood.

Canfield's novels do not only explore the family context for human development. She also looked into social attitudes and arrangements which inhibit maturity – which even, indeed, encourage emotional underdevelopment, especially in men. She criticized the overvaluation of work and external business over the personal, emotional life. She ironized men who put on their hats and got off to work at the first sign of emotions in the home. All these various themes gradually focus around the central theme of self-development, individuality and the nature of human identity. Character transformations and development are the overt themes of *The Deepening Stream* (New York, 1930), for example, and of *Her Son's Wife*, while in *The Brimming Cup* (New York, 1921; London, 1987) the subject is a woman trying to come to terms with the demands of family, social roles and her needs as an individual. This novel is complicated further by Canfield's exploration of sexual needs and their relation to emotional fulfilment, as well as her concern that Freudian emphases on sexuality could lead to a damaging imbalance and immaturity. Infatuation was always to be distinguished from companionship and mature love. The conflict between roles and needs is tied up with character development, of course, but Canfield's novels also expose the conflict between roles and real desires as, often, a result of unimaginative behaviour. That is, women are shown transforming themselves through roles, as well as against them, when they approach them imaginatively as potentially liberating. Thus Canfield's feminism involves insisting both on the importance of work outside the family (as well as financial independence) and on the value, indeed the vitally important nature, of parenting, caring and the personal life.

Canfield's psychological portraits of personal development and transformation – and in some cases, the tragic failure of development – portray human identity as a complex concept in need of careful analysis. Her novels often emphasize that identity and individuality are essentially rooted in relationship and in roles, but that, far from being a paradox or a threat, this rootedness in others is the source of opportunity to develop a multifaceted and rich personal identity. The compassion required to bear the differences amongst us arises, the novels suggest, from a hard-won grasp of the extent to which human beings are paralysed and disabled from taking rational courses of action. Far from being rational animals, human beings are shown 'choosing' destructive behaviour, because they often cannot choose otherwise in their emotionally stunted states. These essentially realistic novels are not deterministic or pessimistic, however, in spite of their systematic exposure of damaging social conventions and personal limitations. For throughout them, Canfield infused a basic optimism, stemming from her faith in the possibility of rationality through education and through improved understanding of child-rearing, the ways to foster emotional growth, and the ways to encourage independence in tandem with social responsibility. Indeed, in Canfield's last novel, *Seasoned Timber* (New York, 1939), personal development is shown to be enriched by, and dependent upon, our accepting a share of responsibility for others, while never abdicating responsibility for our own moral development.

A collection of short stories, entitled *Hillsboro' People*, appeared in 1915 (New York), while a later collection, *Basque People*, was published in 1931 (New York). Other works include the novel *Bonfire* (New York, 1933) and the children's book *Understood Betsy* (New York, 1917).

Catherine Carswell 1879–1946

Fired from her position in Glasgow as a journalist for her praise of D.H. Lawrence's *The Rainbow*, Carswell was a staunch supporter and life-long friend of her famous contemporary. Born in Glasgow and educated at Glasgow University, she was encouraged in her writing by Lawrence's interest in her manuscript of *Open the Door!*, published eventually in 1920 (London and New York, republished London, 1986), and winner of the Melrose Prize. Her only other novel, *The Camomile, An Invention* (London and New York, 1922; London, 1987), is in a completely different vein. After this, Carswell devoted herself to writing a biography of Robert Burns (London, 1930). This was received with considerable acclaim and was followed by *The Savage Pilgrimage* (London, 1932), a biography of Lawrence, and, some years later a biography of Boccaccio, inspired in part by her early visits to Italy. Her autobiography, *Lying Awake* (London, 1950), is unfinished, but includes accounts of her friendships with Rose Macaulay, Rebecca West, Vita Sackville-West, Storm Jameson and others. Numerous articles during her time as drama critic and book reviewer for the *Glasgow Herald* show her to be a courageous journalist and astute critic; these articles (along with her sadly unpreserved letters to D.H. Lawrence from 1911 until the end of his life) were interesting literary documents of this period of English literature and of the reception of major new authors. Lawrence's letters to Carswell (of which there are over two hundred, all published) are supportive and generous, though not uncritical, and are at times referred to as some of the most readable of his epistolary output.

While both of Carswell's novels are based demonstrably on autobiographical elements, they represent two completely distinct novel forms. *Open the Door!* is a conventional novel of plot and romance, though it handles astutely a number of recurring images which give it a symbolic dimension and unify it. Images such as the open and shut door, flower imagery, and systematic use of conventions like the journey and the use of place – Italy versus London and Glasgow – function to enrich and tighten the surface texture and surface thematics. *The Camomile*, on the other hand, uses ostensibly the epistolary and journal form, is much more light-hearted, and contains none of the brooding atmosphere characteristic of Carswell's Lawrentian first novel. Passionate sexual overtones and a tortured preoccupation with desire and fulfilment are replaced in this second novel with a much more sanguine, confident heroine who, eventually, ceases to bother writing letters to her friend, Ruby, and starts writing 'just to herself', and just for herself. In the first novel, fulfilment through love and relationships is the theme; in *The Camomile*, Carswell explored fulfilment through work and writing after rejection of marriage by the heroine. Carswell wrote to a friend that in autobiographical fiction it was essential to detach oneself from the story and to create a narrative persona described as 'cool, critical, perhaps even hostile'. At the end of *The Camomile*, Carswell's heroine Ellen concludes that 'one can never write till one stands outside.'

Lawrence, in a letter to Carswell, robustly condemned her style as 'beastly', but praised her manuscript as 'marvellously good' and 'fascinatingly interesting'. Different as both novels are in genre and style and tone, the central theme is integrity, in the sense that both heroines are portrayed by Carswell as searching for some kind of life in which they can be true to themselves. Both are tempted by security and the approval of their peers, but both have too strong a will towards self-realization to sink into a conventional life, whether it is immolation in sexual passion in Italy or takes the form of respectable marriage and children. Moreover, a corollary of this theme of the search for a way of life true to oneself is the belief that it is only by personal, first-hand experiences that one can discover what is the right way to live for any given individual. Carswell explained this aspect of her novels and echoed Lawrence when she wrote in a letter that 'thought, to be real, must be linked up with the stream of the blood.' Her own central characters are never allowed to be satisfied with borrowed opinions or other people's values, experiences or beliefs. By their trials and their sufferings they live fully, and they not only suffer but learn from their experience, and become transformed by it. In both novels, growth and transformation of character are the central themes, and are contrasted with the cowardice and denial of life – the 'cutting off' from life – that Carswell's heroines are tempted by, but to which they do not succumb. Both novels make for compelling reading in the particular ways in which they depict women struggling to resist mediocrity and self-denial, and both show Carswell experimenting with utterly different literary genres, styles and narrative techniques in her own quest for literary integrity.

Miles Franklin 1879–1954

Miles Franklin (Brent of Bin Bin) was born in the 'Australian Alps' in New South Wales, near Tunent, and grew up in Brindabella, her father's cattle station on the western edge of the Australian Capital Territory. Her family were fifth-generation Australians, her ancestors having come in 1788 with the First Fleet. While her family were pioneers of the Australian bush, Franklin received education with her six siblings from a tutor, who taught her music and literature ranging from Aesop's Fables and the Bible to Shakespeare and Dickens, as well as the budding literature of her own time and country. She also grew up to be a great lover of nature and the Australian mountain landscape, and became an excellent horsewoman. She wrote *My Brilliant Career* (Edinburgh, 1901), her infamous first novel, aged only 16, as an expression of her outrage at the secondary, subservient status of women and the 'degradation' of marriage. After absorbing both the hostile and the encouraging responses to her book, she left home and eventually settled in Sydney for a time. She refused to allow republication of her 'novel', which was mistaken by her friends for autobiography; hence it was out of print from 1901 to 1966. The central pivot of the novel, the claim that women had a right to their own conceptions of self-fulfilment, recurs in her later novels, especially *My Career Goes Bung* (written about 1902–3, but not published until 1946, in Melbourne). While often decrying the slavery of the marriage institution, Franklin's novels portray heroines

(and heroes) in need of 'real' love and companionship, not mere romantic infatuation. Characters such as Sybylla Melvyn and Constance Roberts make this dedication to their writing and their independence clear, without denying their sense of deep loss in their tangled efforts to find a husband who will not be domineering or disrespectful of their work. Some novels conclude on a successful note, while in *My Brilliant Career* the heroine is left rejecting a perhaps suitable suitor, but because she is unable to love him enough rather than because of any paternalism or chauvinism on his part.

Miles Franklin's first teenage novel was hailed as 'the very first Australian novel to be published', in the sense that other novels written by Australians could easily have been written by someone of English or other nationality, because they lacked a distinctive Australian character. Her novel was admired for its powerful evocation of locale and place, and for its fine but unromantic description of nature and landscape, as well as being praised for its sincerity, vitality and, above all, spontaneity. Havelock Ellis praised it as vivid and sincere and of great psychological interest, in its portrayal of the anxieties and adolescent conflicts of a young girl in a predominantly male world. Much of the literature of Australia had been preoccupied with male life in the bush and with codes of fellowship, 'maleship' and honour amongst men, showing little interest in women as human beings with their own intelligence and interests apart from roles subservient to men. Moreover, even such writers as Joseph Furphy (1843–1912), whom Franklin admired, or Henry Lawson (1867–1922), her contemporary, tended to idealize the bushmen, and their nostalgic portrayals of country life were avoided by Franklin, as well as, for example, by Barbara Baynton.

While *My Brilliant Career* is certainly a celebration of the possibilities of the pioneer life, and its freedom from the falseness, artificiality and hypocrisy of city life, it contributed to the creation of an Australian national literature, to which Franklin herself was deeply devoted, in a way which sought to avoid both the extremes of romance, nostalgia or idealization on the one hand, and the formality of European realism on the other. Arguably, Franklin was trying a new conception of what the novel might be, albeit in no revolutionary way, when, in her parodic and ambiguous preface to the text, her heroine asked that it should be read only as a 'real yarn', and nothing else. In this same 'Special Notice', 'Sybylla' says she is writing an autobiography; but the notice is by Sybylla Melvyn, not the author, as though Franklin is making a claim for the worth of her novel in its true-to-real-life character. Franklin also makes her protagonist extol real life over art, and then praise the poet in the very next paragraph. The whole notice, clearly ironic, overtly raises interesting issues about the novel as form or genre, the role of plot, romance and so on. Franklin's other novels, which often verge on the documentary saga, are not always regardful of plot, as though she sought some order, form and unity more 'true to life' than the artificiality of a carefully constructed plot.

Franklin was clearly preoccupied, then, with the relation of fiction to fact, history and life, the question of order, unity, plot and structure, and issues of style and thematics, for most of her writing life. She experimented with a range of types of novel, most especially the 'autobiographical' and the historical saga. Later, in *My Career Goes Bung*, she argued in a similarly ironic and ambiguous preface that *My Brilliant Career* had been written as a parody of the popular autobiographical fiction genre, whereas *My Career Goes Bung*, purporting to be the autobiography of Sybylla Penelope Melvyn, is said to be a truer account, thus taking her spoof of readers' expectations even further. Other novels, such as *Old Blastus of Bandicoot* (Melbourne, 1931) and *Bring the Monkey* (Sydney, 1933), illustrate Franklin's range of fiction.

Franklin's most admired novel is probably *All That Swagger* (Sydney, 1936), a saga of Danny Delasy, an Irish immigrant who goes to Sydney with his bride and whose life, family and descendents are chronicled for the hundred years from the 1830s to the 1930s. Typical of much of Franklin's writing, the novel eschews strict plot development in favour of a wealth of characters and incidents shaped according to their relation to Australia's development as a nation, and the need of a national literature. As in many of the other novels, a powerful sense of natural beauty and of locale is evoked in the writing, and Franklin's love of the region is as evident here

as it is in the 'Brent of Bin Bin' novels published between 1928 and 1956. This pseudonym was used for six novels chronicling the history of several families from 1850 to 1930 and their pioneering life in Australia, giving the reader a clear characterization of the quality of rural society in the Australia of the period.

Franklin left Australia to live in America for some ten years, and while there published the novel *Some Everyday Folk and Dawn* (Edinburgh, 1909) and worked as an editor of *Life and Labour*, the National Women's Trade Union League's journal, before going to Europe. She returned to Australia in 1933, where she lived in Carlton, a suburb of Sydney, for the rest of her life. The themes of artistic frustration, exile and homesickness which occur in some of the Bin Bin novels, such as *Cockatoos* (Sydney, 1954, written 1928/9), or *Up the Country* (Edinburgh, 1928), *Ten Creeks Run* (Edinburgh, 1930) and *Gentlemen at Gyang Gyang* (Sydney, 1956), reveal her commitment to Australia's development as one of the mainsprings of her creativity. In addition to some dozen novels, Franklin had written under the pseudonym Mary Anne for the Australian weekly journal the *Bulletin*, which published work by many Australian writers of the 1890s and 1900s, such as Banjo Patterson, Will Ogilvie, Furphy and Lawson. Franklin also wrote an autobiography, *Childhood at Brindabella* (Sydney, 1963), which, being an openly acknowledged, non-fictional autobiography, makes interesting reading in comparison with *My Brilliant Career*.

Radclyffe Hall 1880–1943

Author of some poetry and several novels, including the (at the time) infamous *Well of Loneliness* (London, 1928), Hall received the James Tait Black Memorial Prize and the Prix Femina in 1926 for her novel *Adam's Breed* (London). Born near Bournemouth to a wealthy family (at age 21, she inherited a fortune which left her financially independent for the rest of her life), Hall began her first novel, *The Unlit Lamp* (London, 1924), when she was nearly 40. Both this and *The Forge* (London, 1924) were extremely well received by critics and buyers alike, though it was *Adam's Breed* which won all the prizes and established Hall's reputation as a serious novelist. With the banning of her fifth novel, *The Well*, in 1928 as 'obscene libel', Hall became the spokeswoman for female homosexuality and moved in circles in London and Paris of lesbian writers and of writers sympathetic to lesbianism. She knew Rebecca West, May Sinclair, Edmund Gosse and Violet Hunt, as well as Natalie Barney and other members of the American expatriate lesbian set living in Paris, not to mention artists such as Augustus John, Tallulah Bankhead and Colette. After *The Well of Loneliness*, Hall wrote three more novels, but none of them was able to sustain her earlier reputation.

While it is true to some extent that much of Hall's fiction is autobiographical – she herself was a committed lesbian and had long, intimate relationships with several other women – only *The Well* takes lesbianism as its explicit, main theme. Even it, it has been argued, is not the fictional autobiography which hundreds of readers and critics have taken it to be. More-over, in recent times, lesbian readers have looked upon this novel with more ambivalence than pre-viously; it is felt that Hall delved too deeply into the psychological anguish and guilt which lesbians today reject as an imposition upon homo-sexuals by a guilt-ridden, prejudiced society. *The Well* is an exploration of the growing conscious-ness of its heroine of her sexual preferences, and the novel is still fascinating today, not only as a document about attitudes and beliefs of the 1920s, but also as an effort to understand sexuality and gender as in part social constructs, with indeter-minate genetic or biological elements. For while it is often claimed that Hall presented 'inver-sion' as entirely inherited, a close reading of the novel shows her exploring the family and social pressures (for example, her father treated Stephan, his daughter, like a son) which may affect children, in addition to biological factors.

Havelock Ellis, the most eminent expert of the day on 'sexual inversion', wrote a fulsome appreciation of Hall's novel, remarking on its 'notable psychological and sociological signifi-cance'. He praised it as being the first English novel to present sexual inversion in a 'completely faithful and uncompromising form'. The novel is quite traditionally realist in narrative style and techniques; it was its explicit theme which con-stituted a radical break with the literary tradition.

This deliberate schism between conservatism and decorum in 'manner' and radical conflict in sub-ject matter functions aesthetically to disorient the reader and disarm prejudices – though in fact it did not succeed, and the book was quickly confiscated. The schism also reflected the psy-chological battle many 'inverts' of the time allegedly suffered: their sexual preferences put them into conflict with the very people they wanted to please and with the traditions to which they yearned to conform. Both Krafft-Ebing and Havelock Ellis gave accounts of the character and special torment of inversion which left the nature/nurture debate unresolved. Hall's novel also explored another problem relatively specific to homosexual relationships, namely, the impos-sibility of having the children of the two part-ners which, Hall's novel suggested, leads to instability allegedly greater than that to which heterosexual relationships are subject.

The Well of Loneliness was hardly alone in its treatment of homosexuality. Contemporaries of Hall's such as Stein, Colette, Proust (even Woolf to some extent in *Orlando*), Djuna Barnes and Natalie Barney, as well as precursors such as Wilde and, of course, Sappho and the writers of the Sapphic tradition (kept alive on the Conti-nent more than in England, undoubtedly), had written about homosexuality. Compton Macken-zie had his book *Extraordinary Women* published in 1928, but it was not banned. *The Well* was (unenthusiastically) supported by many writers during its court battle against banning, though these supporters of its right to be published did not support it as being of 'literary merit', to Hall's great pain. Virginia Woolf, Vera Brittain, E.M. Forster, Storm Jameson, Leonard Woolf and others in fact viewed the book as of no great artistic or literary merit, and regretted that the case should depend on such a 'poor' specimen. Nevertheless, the book sold over fifty thousand copies before the wave of controversy subsided, and continues to be read with enthusiasm today, as does *The Unlit Lamp*, one of Hall's most ac-complished works of fiction.

Rose Macaulay 1881–1958

Rose Macaulay spent several years of her child-hood and early adolescence in Italy, though she was born in Rugby and returned to England to attend secondary school and Somerville College, Oxford, where she studied history. This Italian period made a deep impression on her and influenced her writing; place and locale not only became central features of her novels, but also took on complex symbolic richness. While natural landscape has conventionally been used as a metaphor for inner experience, as well as moral landscape and the unconscious, Macaulay imbued this convention with an individuality which gives nature a distinct character in some of her fiction. This 'power of place', along with an elegant wit and balanced, gentle, but rarely condescending irony, gives a poetic, philosophic quality to much of her writing. In spite of fairly frequent and extensive travel throughout her life, the Mediterranean landscape she loved, with its mixture of wildness and civilization, was never superseded in her fiction by any other locale. Macaulay wrote many novels, as well as travel writing, essays and criticism, and also published a book of poetry, in 1914, entitled *The Two Blind Countries* (London). She was a close friend from childhood of Rupert Brooke, who introduced her to literary life in London, where she moved after living with her family in Wales and Cambridge.

Several early novels, including *Abbots Verney* (London, 1906), preceded *The Lee Shore* (London, 1912), which won her the Hodder and Stoughton award, while *Potterism* (London, 1920) became her first best-seller on both sides of the Atlantic. This satirical novel was followed by others in a different vein, including *Told by an Idiot* (London, 1923, 1983), *Crewe Train* (London, 1926) and *They Were Defeated* (London, 1932). With World War II, and the destruction of her home and library, Macaulay's output was interrupted, but in 1950, with the publication of *The World My Wilderness* (London), she displayed talents in a quite new direction. The satire of her earlier work and its preoccupation with the manners and history of English society gave way to a very different, more compassionate, intense tone, verging on a detached tragic irony, as she explored from quite a different point of view the familiar theme of the failure of marriage, its effects and the effect of war on children, and the conflicting values of passion and propriety. In 1956, her last novel, *The Towers of Trebizond* (London), was published, and won the James

Tait Black Memorial Prize. Some years later a two-volume edition of her letters to J.H.C. Johnson, who inspired her return to the Anglican church at the age of 70, were published as *Letters to a Friend* (London, 1961). One of her most interesting books of non-fiction which has a bearing on her novels is *The Pleasure of Ruins* (London, 1953).

Rose Macaulay's interest in history, along with her love of Italy and her elegant wit, informs nearly all her novels as well as her understanding of the meaning of human life, civilization and its relation to the natural world. These large, universal themes are particularly prominent in the ten novels from 1923 onwards, when, with *Told by an Idiot*, she began to temper her satire of human folly with a more sympathetic tone, which gained greater strength after the death of her long-standing lover in 1942. Her pessimism about marriage as an institution, but also about the complex sexual-emotional involvement between adults inside or outside marriage, can be traced in many novels, as she sought to track the sources of this malaise in the stereotypes and gender roles inappropriately forced upon people regardless of their temperaments and talents. It is notable that many of her characters have names which escape gender indications. She used Stanley and Evelyn for both men and women; but she also tapped the rich possibilities of connotation: the marvellous Helen in *The World My Wilderness*, and her daughter Barbary, as well as Rome Garden in *Told by an Idiot* fulfil the connotation of their names in ways that are neither trite nor ineffective. In *The Towers of Trebizond*, moreover, the gender of the central character is, throughout the entire novel, never made definite, yet the story's effect is in no way marred by this indefiniteness, as if Macaulay were making indirect but strong feminist statements about the absurdity of imprisoning people in gender roles.

Indeed, for her, this part of the English society of the twentieth century was more than just an absurdity. Sexism was an 'inexplicable lunacy', and she avoided both marriage and childbearing, for she saw the untold suffering to which gender roles subjected both women and men. Her feminism, evident in her life and in her literature, led her to question, along with Stevie Smith and others, whether there is any such thing as woman. One of her characters, Imogen, is described in babyhood as having 'neither then nor at any later time, any clear idea about what women ought or ought not to be. Anything they liked, she probably thought. If, indeed, there were, specifically, any such creatures as women.' This is a typical example of Macaulay's detached narrative irony as she puts so controversial an issue into understated, matter-of-fact terms, and in the mind of a 1-year-old girl. Such revolutionary attitudes are rarely presented any more stridently than in this passage, but her analysis of sexism and role playing is trenchant and effective.

There is a powerful backdrop to these social issues of gender, sexism, marriage and politics, however, and it is constructed out of the unobtrusive but ever-present sense Rose Macaulay had of the large, universal scope of not only human history, but natural history. Lurking behind much of her later fiction are philosophical and existential questions of the absurdity of human life, its meaninglessness, its repetitiveness – which is in part what robs suffering and tragedy and life of unmitigated significance. Her later novels are coloured by a sense of history as the wrecking of civilizations by the very human beings who strove to build order and decency, and ruins became, along with the wilderness, an image symbolic of the forces of construction and destruction which exist side by side in the human psyche. Indeed, in these novels a psychological dimension is more prominent than in her earlier work, and the unconscious is figured into the text of *The World My Wilderness*, for example, in quite definite landscape descriptions:

So men's will to recovery strove against the drifting wilderness to halt and tame it; but the wilderness might slip from their hands, from their spades and trowels and measuring rods, slip darkly away from them, seeking the primeval chaos and old night which had been before Londinium was, which would be when cities were ghosts haunting the ancestral dreams of memory.

This, at least, is the fear of men like Sir Gulliver, Helen's ex-husband, and his son Richie; but Macaulay's novel as a whole hardly suggests this is the narrator's fear, objective though it may appear at first. For there may be also Helen's way of dealing with the wilderness, which is neither to tame it nor to be overwhelmed by it, but to live in it and of it, as a source of energy and love.

Susan Glaspell 1882–1948

Born in Davenport, Iowa, to a partly Irish family of early settlers to the Midwest who had arrived as early as the 1830s, Glaspell grew up in Iowa and attended university at Des Moines, where she began publishing short stories and novels while working for the Des Moines newspaper. Her novel *The Glory of the Conquered* (New York, 1909), the tragedy of a scientist who dies on the verge of a major breakthrough, was the first of some ten novels, several dozen short stories, some collected in *Lifted Masks* (New York, 1912), and, most notably, a number of plays which constitute Glaspell's best-known work. After her second novel, *The Visioning* (New York, 1911), Glaspell left Iowa to live in Greenwich Village, where she met her fellow townsman and future husband, the director George Cram Crook. She and Crook gradually established a group of actors and playwrights who became known as the Provincetown Players, after the little village in Cape Cod where they performed plays in a small wharf theatre. They also set up in Greenwich Village the Playwright's Theatre, where such dramatists as Eugene O'Neill, Edna St Vincent Millay and Glaspell saw their new productions performed. Glaspell described her life and her marriage during this period in *The Road to the Temple* (London, 1926; New York, 1927), a biography of George Cram Crook: a small community of friends and colleagues essentially replace the family and conventional society of Midwestern life. Already while living briefly in Chicago, Glaspell had become interested in drama in addition to prose fiction, and especially in the idea of a 'poetic drama' as opposed to verse drama. Influenced in this by a tour of the Irish Players from Dublin, Glaspell migrated to New York, which was becoming the new centre for innovative arts and drama, influenced by European modernism and other movements. Greenwich Village was the focus for artists interested in moving out of the accepted conventions both of art and of life, and bohemianism flourished.

Under the guidance of Glaspell, Cram Crook, Floyd Dell, Eugene O'Neill and others, the group of young dramatists and directors produced a kind of manifesto in which they explained their intentions to establish a theatre in Greenwich Village and in Provincetown where new artists could see their work in performance, since the constraints of commercial theatres influenced by the public's expectation could often not accommodate innovation. They went further, however, to describe themselves as committed to the idea of simplicity in drama – simplicity both in production (minimal setting, costuming, etc.) and in dramatic texts. They argued, in the case of simple production, that such resources not only are unnecessary, but also can be destructive of the dramatic qualities of the play. One of Glaspell's most famous plays, *Trifles* (1916, published Boston, 1920), is a remarkable dramatic realization both of poetic drama and of minimalist aims. In collaboration with her husband, Glaspell had already written her first play, *Suppressed Desires* (1914, published in *Plays*, Boston, 1920), an analysis and satire of psychoanalytical and Freudian issues. She also wrote another novel at this time, *Fidelity* (Boston, 1915), the narrative of a young woman who elopes with a married man. During the next decade, Glaspell's writings were confined to drama, both one-act and full-length plays, such as *Close the Book* (1917, published in *Plays*), an analysis of social hypocrisy, *A Woman's Honor* and *Tickless Time* (both 1918, published in *Plays*, and both satires of escapism), *The People* (in *Plays*), a play about the position of the journalist in a democracy, and *The Verge* (Boston, 1922) and *The Outside* (in *Plays*), two remarkable plays about the efforts of women and, in *The Verge*, the woman artist, to forge an independent life.

In these plays and novels, Glaspell explored the theme of the unusual individual at odds with society. Sometimes the character is explicitly an artist struggling against constraining literary conventions which inhibit innovation, and Glaspell studies the mediocrity and fear that thwart new forms. Sometimes the individual is in conflict with political and social values, though the metaphor of the innovative artist is always evident. But Glaspell's portrayals are characterized by an unusual degree of insistence on the belief that artistic, intellectual, moral and political

innovation must involve an increment in humanity if they are genuine. That is, all her characters possess an unusual level of humaneness which is inextricably tied to their intellectual advances, and this suggests an interdependence between the moral and the imaginative which Glaspell developed to the full in both her novels and her plays. Her longer plays, *Berenice* (1919, published in *Plays*) and *Alison's House* (New York, 1930) – which won the Pulitzer Prize – are a subtle exploration of the effect on others of the death of a relative or friend. Using minimalist techniques of characterization and plot, Glaspell creates a central character, already dead, hovering over the other participants. *Alison's House* is said to be a play referring to Emily Dickinson's death and its aftermath. The other major play of this period is *The Inheritors* (Boston, 1921), a much more conventional but nevertheless extremely powerful drama about a young Midwestern college girl confronted by post-war prejudice against foreign students. This play was ranked by James Agate alongside Ibsen's *The Master Builder*. The themes of racism and xenophobia are also explored in Glaspell's novels; she portrayed them as undermining democracy, and as associated with the equally undermining forces of the unmitigated pursuit of money and of prestige. These forces she saw as threatening the freedom of the individual and of the human race as a whole, and she explored the equally inhibiting effects of family love when oppressive and tyrannical.

The threat to individuality and to democracy which preoccupied so much of Glaspell's writing is broadened to link up with more visionary and symbolic aspects of her fiction and drama, which lend it a poetic dimension. In a number of novels and plays, there is an explicit emphasis upon the importance of the evolution of the entire species for each individual's life. That is, Glaspell showed that the whole human species is carried forward only by the innovation and daring of specific individuals; and she showed too the ignorance and mediocrity which lead people to drag excellence down, and thereby inhibit advance and jeopardize the future. But Glaspell made it clear that, while genius involved a terrible responsibility for gifted individuals to realize themselves fully in order to drag the species forward, this interconnection between the individual and the well-being of the whole species could strengthen the artist or innovator in her or his conflict with convention and mediocrity. Many of her novels, stories and plays portray talented women and men on the 'verge' of desperation and madness in the face of incomprehension, criticism and ridicule. Yet the realization that in their hands lies the future of their fellow humans gives them the strength to pursue their convictions and innovations. Glaspell's transformation of the biological evolutionary force into an intellectual one is extremely effective aesthetically, and gives her work great power and originality in the specific realizations and applications of this metaphor.

Glaspell applied this visionary evolutionism to women's need to give their individual lives meaning independent of men and children or other personal human relationships, representing each triumph against failure and death as a triumph for the whole of humanity. *The Verge* is Glaspell's most successfully experimental dramatic realization of this idea; but it is clear from many texts that for Glaspell, each of us owes it (not just to ourselves but) to the further development and evolution of our whole species to realize our individuality and our talents as fully as possible. Glaspell admitted that while this places a tremendous moral burden on all of us, it also can be what makes an otherwise selfish or meaningless existence rich with significance. Like Willa Cather, Glaspell did not fail to depict the hatred of conventional people for exceptional individuals. Fear of change and the essence of imaginativeness as transformation are the primitive elements in the conflict played out in Glaspell's writing in artistic, social, political and intellectual spheres, as well as in the personal sphere of family relations. Even in the conventional dramatic form of *The Inheritors*, Glaspell expressed this theme of growth, change and transformation as the moving force behind the political veneer. One of her characters stumbles his inarticulate way toward it when he says: 'We are what we are because through all that time there'd been them that wanted to be more than life had been.' And he sees the consequences of not moving forward: 'Then if we don't be – the most we can be, if we don't be more than life has been, we go back on all that life behind us' of a million previous years of painfully won advance. We cannot stand still; either we progress or we

regress. Glaspell's character suddenly explains in a moment of further vision: 'But – why, then we aren't *finished* yet!', and this constitutes another central theme of her texts, namely, the idea that the human mind, reason, imagination and spirit are still evolving, just as the body is. Mind is emerging; contrary to the import of most religions, for Glaspell, the human spirit has not been created by God in his image. It is in an apocalyptic state of becoming, and it is through art, science and humaneness that it will transform itself further into a higher-order degree of mentality. Or else it will stagnate and degenerate. Which of these occurs depends upon each individual making a contribution one way or the other.

Such new levels of existence as Glaspell envisaged are to be achieved by the gradual but substantial restructuring of human sensibility through the power of culture. Or, as one of her characters groped to explain it, 'It's not the learning itself – it's the life that grows up from learning. Learning's like soil. Like – like fertilizer. Get richer. See more. Feel more.' Hence, Glaspell also portrayed the distinction between characters who suffer under the communal prohibition on venturing too far out into innovative living or ideas or works of art and science, and those who stick to creating things merely 'as good as possible of their kind', avoiding the utterly new and hence the virtually incomprehensible and frightening. Individuals are shown risking incomprehension and even madness in their drive to carry the whole human race with them by realizing the best that is in them, however frightening and incomprehensible to contemporaries.

Glaspell's fiction and drama also portray this evolutionary movement and the tragic conflicts engendered by fear of the strange and unusual in the forms of almost Nietzschean and Blakean life and death forces. The creative power which can lead to the evolution of human beings into a higher mentality is portrayed as the essence of the life force itself. Life as a force *is*, she argued, evolutionary and transformative. It is not static, and does not just maintain what is already there in its present living form. The life force is characterized not merely as survival, but as developmental, transformative. Her plays and novels show that for Glaspell survival alone is the death force itself; without growth, transformation and change, life is a mere death-in-life. Not to strive to develop oneself and one's talents is not to live, as she showed most simply and eloquently in *Trifles*. What is perhaps most disturbing about Glaspell's work is the suggestion that this creative impulse, this life force which drags the whole of humanity forward into greater realization, is repressed in so many individuals in varying degrees. Indeed, the implication of her texts is that most 'ordinary' human beings are in the main living a death-in-life, where depression and passivity stifle both the individuals who are depressed and passive and those who live with them.

Other novels began to appear towards the end of Glaspell's dramatic productivity, including *Brook Evans* (New York, 1928), the story of a mother–daughter relationship, *Fugitive's Return* (New York, 1929), a perhaps, in part, autobiographical novel, *Ambrose Holt and Family* (New York, 1931), *The Morning is Near Us* (New York, 1939), and *Norma Ashe* (New York, 1942). Glaspell's last novel, *Judd Rankin's Daughter* (New York, 1945), portrays the life of a philosopher, his family relations, and his struggle against the confining forces that inhibit him.

Katharine Susannah Prichard
1883–1969

Author of a dozen novels, four short story collections, over a dozen plays and two collections of verse, Prichard was born in Levuka, Fiji, but her Australian parents returned to Melbourne when she was 3 years old. She spent her childhood in Tasmania and Victoria, became a governess briefly, and then worked as a journalist in Melbourne and London, where she wrote her first published novel, *The Pioneers* (London, 1915). For this first effort, she won the prestigious Hodder and Stoughton prize for Australian fiction, and with the £250 prize money she was able to return to Australia and continue her writing about Australian life. She next published *Windlestraws* (London, 1916) before marrying and moving to western Australia, near Perth, where she settled for a time and began writing *Black Opal* (London, 1921), her novel about the life of the opal gougers in far western New South Wales,

to be followed by *Working Bullocks* (London, 1926), a complicated novel, set in the Karri forests of western Australia, about the people working in the timber industry. While the setting and overt themes of Prichard's novels explore social realist interests in economic exploitation and class struggle, her early novels almost always structure themselves on emotional struggle and involve an uneasy tension between realism and romance. People are bound to each other by sexual and emotional needs, and these needs and desires lead to conflicts which are portrayed by Prichard in an almost, at times, poetic mode. Already in *The Pioneers* (this romance of settler life in the bush), the conflicting interests of personal fulfilment and social-political responsibility are suggested, but they come more overtly to the fore in *Working Bullocks*. There, the utopian vision of a better world is touched upon, but by the end a realistic view emerges, namely, that change will occur only through a commitment to hard work and through personal endurance and acts of will. One of Prichard's many strong female protagonists first appeared in this novel, but so far, romance continued to balance her interest in social realist representations.

Another major novel, *Intimate Strangers* (London, 1937), was based, as were a number of her further novels, on a play she wrote in 1927, *Bid Me to Love* (Sydney, 1974). This novel is her most thorough exploration of marriage and mature male–female sexual relations. In this (perhaps, in part, autobiographical) account of a failed marriage, which ends with the husband committing suicide and thereby releasing his wife for passionate consummation with her lover, Prichard's interest in the unconscious, along with Lawrentian concerns with sexuality and fulfilment, come to the forefront of the thematics. Issues about sexual repression, which are dealt with more fully in the later novel *Coonardoo* (London, 1929, 1975), are again related to the conflicts between political or social and personal needs. Another central concern of Prichard's fiction is also a major element of *Intimate Strangers*, namely, an analysis of the exploitation of women not only in social and economic terms, but also in sexual relationships. She sought too in this novel to explore the devastating effects of war on individuals. *Coonardoo* is probably Prichard's most accomplished and impressive novel of this first half of her career, however, balancing as it does her analysis of social injustice regarding class, race and sex with her probing investigation of Lawrentian depths of sexuality, nature and repression. It won the *Bulletin* award for the best novel of the year, with M. Barnard Eldershaw's (the pseudonym of Marjorie Barnard and Flora Eldershaw) *A House is Built*.

This novel is also founded in themes which recur throughout Prichard's fiction; its subtitle, *The Well in the Shadow*, gives the reader a sense of the metaphorical and symbolic dimensions characteristic of this and other early novels in spite of their social documentary character. *Coonardoo*, based on an earlier play called *Brumby Innes*, is an extensive study of the devastating effects of sexual repression; one of the central characters, Hugh Watts, a white settler, takes an aboriginal woman, Coonardoo, as a wife after a long period of self-denial and a previous, insipid marriage, but then is unable to deal with his emotions and sexuality. The novel depicts the long but inevitable process of the 'rotting of his very soul' by repression, while Coonardoo is trapped in a tragic cycle of destruction at his hands. This novel was one of the first ever to have an Aborigine as the central character, and also to show the value of Aboriginal culture, instead of portraying it as a primitive, dying society which could be exterminated without loss or remorse. Not surprisingly, the novel had an extremely controversial reception, though it was criticized more for its portrayal of miscegenation than for its condemnation of Aboriginal exploitation. In it, other issues central to Prichard's work are evident; themes of spiritual isolation and the soul-destroying effects of privilege, wealth and pretentiousness are combined with the related depiction of city life as a fallen state and a degenerate version of the more fulfilling rural life. Additionally, Lawrentian themes of the vitality of nature as expressive also of the need for fulfilment, and related themes of artistic creativity as dependent upon natural energies, make *Coonardoo* one of Prichard's most sophisticated novels.

In it, Prichard also achieved some of her finest examples of characterization in the Aboriginal woman and her white lover Hugh. The carefully detailed descriptions of daily life and labour are balanced by psychological analysis and intensely vital depictions of the natural environment, which often mirrors psychological events. Prichard had described her aim as the portrayal of the 'dignity, beauty, and mystery of a primitive people in their natural surroundings'. This novel is a dramatic tragedy rather than a social documentary or economic analysis, though the latter two elements are never entirely out of the picture. It also suggests other concerns, such as Prichard's determined questioning of the assumption of the superiority of European culture over Aboriginal life, which was the basis for the remorseless destruction and exploitation of the latter. The search for spiritual fulfilment in nature, in love and finally in work is also evident throughout this tragic and effective novel.

After the suicide of her husband, Prichard threw herself even more determinedly into her work as a Communist and a pacifist. She had been a committed Communist since 1919, and visited Russia in 1933, after which she wrote *The Real Russia* (Sydney, 1934), a non-fiction account of her time there. Much later she wrote *Straight Left* (Sydney, 1984), ed. R. Throssell, another non-fiction political piece, but the next major stage in her fiction was a three-volume chronicle set in the Australian gold fields. This trilogy included the novels *The Roaring Nineties* (London, 1946), *Golden Miles* (London, 1948) and *Winged Seeds* (Sydney, 1950), all republished by Virago in the 1980s. Historical realism, tempered in her earlier novels by metaphoric, symbolic and at times even modernist-influenced gestures of shifting narrative point of view and virtual stream of consciousness technique, now dominates her writing, reflecting perhaps her own life experience of turning to work for her satisfaction and for bonds with other humans rather than to love, romance or emotional-sexual relations. In these novels, the female character Sally Gough is portrayed as a woman who, through individual initiative and strength of character, finds her only real fulfilment in the independence she achieves through determination and hard work. The male gold miners around her exploit her strength as far as she will let them, but she takes little personal joy from her position; indeed, she suffers acutely at first from lack of genuine companionship. The tension between political commitment and commitment to the writing of fiction evident in these novels is expressive of Prichard's own situation, and is the more convincingly communicated for the personal basis. Through Sally Gough, moreover, this tension and the portrayal of Australia as not merely a man's country, but a country also belonging to women, albeit strong women, add to Prichard's innovations. Sometimes this gold-mining trilogy is criticized for being overburdened by political issues and documentation. Yet the character of Sally Gough and the vitality of Prichard's depiction of life in the 1890s' gold-mining districts give these novels a power and intensity which easily carry the weight of her social analysis.

Prichard's short stories have been collected in *Kiss on the Lips and Other Stories* (London, 1932), and the autobiography *Child of the Hurricane* was published in Sydney in 1963.

Anzia Yezierska 1885–1970

Born during the period of brutal pogroms and repression of Jews in Poland in the 1880s, Anzia Yezierska's family left Warsaw for America in the 1890s. Like so many Jews in Russian Poland, they emigrated to Manhattan filled with the hopes of realizing the American dream of a better life for their children. Yezierska left home as a teenager and worked in the sweatshops and factories of New York to earn independence and freedom from the squalid tenements and the imprisoning patriarchy of her elders. She later won a scholarship to Columbia University, and graduated in 1904. There, she met John Dewey, the great American philosopher and educator, to whom she later turned for advice and encouragement in her fiction. She began publishing stories in *Forum* in 1915, and in 1919 her 'The Fat of the Land' won an award for best short story of the year. In 1920, her first collection of stories, *Hungry Hearts and Other Stories* (Boston and New York), catapulted her into fame and fortune, in a concrete realization of the American dream. Samuel Goldwyn paid her $10,000 for the film rights, and she became an admired literary figure. Her next books included the novel *Salome of the Tenements* (New York and London, 1922), also sold for film rights, another story collection called *Children of Loneliness* (New York and London, 1923), and more novels, *Bread Givers* (New York and London, 1925), *Arrogant Beggar* (New York and London, 1927) and *All I Could Ever Be* (New York, 1932). A selection of her work, *The Open Cage* (New York, 1979), ed. A.K. Harris, and a fictionalized autobiography, *Red Ribbon on a White Horse* (New York, 1950), only appeared after two decades of changed circumstances; for with the Depression, her fortune and fame failed, though her own talents can only be said to have increased. Success did not, however, bring her happiness, but it did bring some relief from the grind and discomfort of poverty, an issue central to Tillie Olsen and Meridel Le Sueur's fiction. Many of her themes revolved around the price of success; for example, the loss of connection with one's family, community and origins.

Two of her most famous stories, 'Hunger' and 'The Fat of the Land', describe the tensions between the poor immigrant (dreaming of and aspiring to a higher life, not through chance or luck, but through determination, hard work, and the conquest of circumstances with individual initiative) and the 'successful', established immigrant cut off from love and community. 'Hunger' is the description of a young woman, Shenah (perhaps a fictionalized Yezierska), who throws off the exploitation of her uncle, and who is committed to an almost existential project of self-development, as the central character eloquently describes 'the hunger to make from myself a person that can't be ousted by nothing or nobody – the life higher!' Like many of Yezierska's stories, and in a style similar to Dorothy Parker's, this one proceeds almost entirely through dialogue, and plot is quite incidental, as it seeks to communicate through speech the intense hopes, fears and terrible disappointment of these vital and intelligent characters. In both these stories, the characteristic point of view of women is a feminist gesture on Yezierska's part, as she portrayed woman's need for self-fulfilment and for financial and emotional independence as entirely natural. While 'Hunger' also describes the pain of rupture from all family patterns, past ways and oppressive or even exploitative love, it rejects romance and marriage as the way out for women. Shenah repeatedly explains to the besotted Sam, 'I got to push myself up by myself, by my own strength.' Her own infatuation with an unreachable man is mostly a symbol of her yearning for something beyond the ordinary, a hope, a hunger 'for light, for the life higher'. The effect of Yezierska's astute alternation between dialogue (which conveys individuality, vitality and intense enthusiasm and hope) and an omniscient narrative (which gently ironizes the characters and realistically portends the difficulties they will inevitably encounter) gives the stories a detached humour and a strong pathos which are finely balanced. These characteristics anticipate Grace Paley's later, remarkable short fictions.

In 'The Fat of the Land', the transformation from rags to riches occurs, but it is not portrayed; only a narrative gap in time, an 'empty hole in the story', is presented, while the beginning and ending are depicted in stark contrast. In the first half, the heroine Hannah is reduced by poverty to irritability and harsh cruelty towards her children, and to a self-pity which makes the reader unsympathetic to her plight. In the second half of the story, decades have passed and Hannah is living in luxury, thanks to the hard work and success of her children, who are now ashamed of their crude and uneducated mother. Here, dialogue is subsumed to narration, and all points of view are presented; no moral judgements or condemnations are made; each character's situation is presented with understanding and sympathy, yet the conflicts are shown to be inevitable. The terrible cost of financial success in alienation from the original sources of energy, namely, family, children and community, restores the marriage as a metaphor for the immigrants' relation to America. Not only are love and romance between people used as an expression of the immigrants' love and romance about America and the opportunities its democracy offers them for self-development; marriage is a symbol too for the need to marry the two opposing groups of immigrants with already-established Americans. The establishment is portrayed as needing the vitality and imagination of the new arrivals. Yezierska's fictions also suggest a need to revitalize and regenerate both Jews and Gentiles by intermarriage, and a powerful fusion of the two cultures, it is implied, is what will make America great. Yet, even as early as *Hungry Hearts and Other Stories*, financial success is exposed as, certainly,

relief from the terrible strains of poverty – strains portrayed by Tillie Olsen and Israel Singer, for example – but not the means of fulfilment of the dream, which requires also companionship, love and community.

H.D. 1886–1961

Hilda Doolittle (H.D.), best known for her eleven volumes of poetry (published between 1916 and 1961), also wrote numerous novels and shorter fictions, adaptations of Greek dramas, Greek translation, film criticisms and memoirs. Born in Pennsylvania in 1886, Doolittle was influenced by the spirituality of the Moravian community to which her mother belonged, and which was balanced by her father's more traditional, rationalist temper as a mathematician and astronomer of note. She met Ezra Pound before dropping out of Bryn Mawr and, a few years later, left for Europe with her friend Frances Gregg. She lived there for the rest of her life. In London, with the help of Pound, she met D.H. Lawrence, W.B. Yeats, May Sinclair, Richard Aldington and others. She also began publishing her poetry in Harriet Monroe's periodical *Poetry*; the first collection of her poems appeared in London in 1916 as *Sea Garden*. By 1921, when she published her next collection of poetry, *Hymen* (London), she had married Aldington, had a miscarriage, been through the horrors of World War I, watched the break-up of her marriage, had an affair and a child, Perdita, with Cecil Gray, met Bryher (Winifred Ellerman, her life companion), been promoted in America by Amy Lowell, and made trips to Greece, which fed her imagination and love of Greek and other ancient mythologies and mysticisms. In 1923 she travelled to Egypt, and she published another collection of verse in 1924, *Heliodora and Other Poems* (Boston and London), and a volume of *Collected Poems* in 1925 (New York). During this period she also wrote novels (some of which were not published until decades later), such as *Her* (written around 1923, published New York, 1981), *Palimpsest* (Paris and Boston, 1926) and *Hedylus* (Boston and Oxford, 1928).

Doolittle followed up her long interest in psychology by submitting herself to analysis with Freud (1933–4), which she described in detail in a later book, *Tribute to Freud* (New York, 1956). Although in 1931 she had published another collection of poetry, *Red Roses for Bronze* (London, Boston and New York, 1931), she turned to Freud in part because of a fear that her creativity was failing her. Her 'war' poetry, *Trilogy*, was not published until 1944–6 (London, 1944, 1945, 1946; New York, 1973), and *Helen in Egypt* followed in 1961 (New York). Various prose writings remain unpublished, though *End to Torment* (her account of her relationship with Ezra Pound) was published in New York in 1979, and *The Gift*, another childhood memoir, in New York in 1982. Other published novels include *Kora and Ka* (Dijon, 1934), *The Usual Star* (Dijon, 1934) and *Nights* (Dijon, 1935).

Like many writers of the period, Doolittle made free use of autobiographical material for both her prose and poetry, emphasizing the value of personal experience and subjectivity instead of devaluing it in favour of some notion of rational objectivity, or of some demand for transformation of life if genuine fiction is to occur. The rejection of genre distinctions, of fiction/reality dualisms, of (phoney) objectivity and narrative omniscience is accompanied by a rejection of notions of neutral, realist, ordinary language in favour of a modernist emphasis upon style. She toyed with poetic forms, first by placing the image at the centre of meaning and structure in poetry, and then by exploring its connotations and semantic reverberations through wordplay – which often involved names – and evocations of mythological elements, especially from Greek and Egyptian traditions. She developed a palimpsest or layering of semi-erased, rewritten meanings (her complement to discursive, narrative development) in both her poetry and her prose.

Doolittle also devised (in her writings over several decades) a revision of Greek and Egyptian mythology, which re-evaluated not only male/female roles but also the concept of knowledge. By drawing on female figures such as Isis and Helen, she gradually created a concept of knowledge not as analytic and objective, but as self-development and self-creation. For H.D., genuine knowledge was better understood as illumination, as inward growth of the personal self, and this constituted a collapse of the distinction between personal, emotional fulfilment and intellectual, public creativity as an artist. Her exploration in prose and poetry of a means of expressing and portraying such creative growth led her, moreover, to see the importance to 'knowledge' of a direct confrontation with one's sexuality and sexual identity. To her, sexuality and creativity in an artist were intertwined; indeed, her writings often suggest that war, aggression and destruction are connected with a failure to grapple with sexuality, a fear of the emotional life, and consequent immaturity and non-development of the psyche.

In the early novel *Her* (or *Hermione*), H.D. wrote in a radically modernist style, which defied the demands for clear, discursive prose, univocal meaning and transparency. Her prose does not merely move forward in a discursive, narrative progression. It swirls around images, metaphors and puns; it creates concentric circles of ever-widening meanings by extended wordplay, toying especially with names, and developing long chains of associations and impressionistic afterimages which often relied on mythological elements. Her prose demands a new and different kind of reading, more akin to poetry, particularly imagistic poetry, but she also used Gertrude Stein's techniques of repetition and of immediacy, though in her own individual way. In the novel, *Her* (and in 'Paint it Now', unpublished but written in 1921, before *Her*), Doolittle explored in a modernist fictional form the process of a young woman's becoming conscious simultaneously of her sexuality and her creativity as a writer. The novel's thematics involved material which was to recur throughout her texts, namely the process of developing an individuality as a unique identity. The elements of this process Doolittle showed to be a quest which took one not only into the unconscious (as both collective and individual), but also into a search through past literature and history in order to understand human culture if one is to recognize oneself.

H.D.'s writings structure this quest in a number of ways, most notably through revisionary mythological elements, characters and images. Another major structuring and thematic device is the portrayal of the transcendence of duality in all its many forms. This transcendence involves an 'illuminating perception' which is almost a definition of her reconceptualization of knowledge not as discursive, analytic or a product of reason, but as self-development, synthesis and a result of imaginative intuition. This illuminating perception is also described as the perception or intuition of the inner radiance or being of things and people, their *'gloire'*. Flannery O'Connor developed this idea some decades later, agreeing with Doolittle that this potentiality involved something 'beyond' the material and visible, but perceived and portrayed only through the concrete, visible particular. This kind of perception can be described, in the poet Denise Levertov's words, as an effort not to flood darkness with the light of reason, as knowledge is traditionally conceived. It involves not destroying 'darkness' or obscurity, but entering into it, journeying through it, so that it becomes experienced and known by the antennae of the imagination, instead of the light of reason.

The transcendence of duality (duality being a grounding, structural character of reason and the visible) in its varied forms was often portrayed by Doolittle through conventional metaphors of quests, journeys and exotic lands; but it was also shown in the hard, devastating images of war, death, loss and suffering, as in the novel *Bid Me to Live* (New York, 1960; written 1927). The lyrical, subjective style of this novel (like the style of *Her*, but showing a marked development as well), while at odds with its subject matter, expresses an ability to transcend war and loss as an aspect of the need to transcend the personal self and the individual consciousness, in order to achieve a more collective, universal experience of being, albeit necessarily through individuality. This form of going above or beyond duality (self/other) Doolittle saw as possible through creative writing, seen as having redemptive power: 'She herself is the writing.' Thus, her writings became records of journeys – word journeys – as she used language to travel into the interior of the unconscious and of human culture, the collective unconscious, through her exploration and reinterpretations of ancient mythologies and legends. Her poems and novels also explore language itself, and how words function to order, shape and bring into being the human reality we experience. Doolittle pressed words to function in new, non-dualistic ways, by creating fluid and dynamic images and linguistic categories. Through images and metaphors of integration and inclusions, through dynamic transformations of one opposition into its other, she questioned the dualisms of reason, such as male/female, fiction/reality, prose/poetry, science/art, life/death, self/other and so on.

Doolittle also rejected traditional narrative structures in both fiction and poetry. In the long poem *Helen in Egypt*, and in *Bid Me to Live*, she avoided definitive endings, as had Dorothy Richardson and Sinclair before her. These non-endings express, paradoxically, both the open-ended nature of the journey towards self-knowledge and the devastation of war as so great as to be never-ending: 'the war will never be over.' The avoidance of conventional unities, development or endings in her writings functions moreover to draw attention to her works as layered structures, palimpsests of meaning, rather than linear, discursive arguments, plots or autonomous, meaningful entities. Her novels and memoirs, for example, work and rework autobiographical material, often overlapping and re-using the 'same' matter, and this repetition, along with extensive revisions of novels, memoirs and poems, raises questions about the very notion of a determinate, single work of art, as these works engage in a dialogue with each other and an irreducible multiplicity of perspectives. Likewise, the personal, conscious self as autonomous was questioned, as Doolittle made full use of Freudian insights into the unconscious, into the importance of recovering childhood through memory and creative acts, and into the role of dreams in recovering our creative selves, as Anaïs Nin was to emphasize decades later in her writings. Doolittle also drew upon Havelock Ellis, the sixteenth-century German poet Hans Sachs and, especially, Jungian ideas about the collective unconscious, art, dreams, mythology, and culture in general as both the expression of the communal unconscious and a means of transcending ego and self-hood. Just as she had questioned notions about autonomous works of art, so she questioned the meaning of the autonomous self, and reintegrated the concept of the individual into both a conception of the psyche as multiple, warring selves, and a concept of the communal or social as the context for individuality.

Images in H.D.'s writings are overdetermined in their meanings: they are not merely ambiguous, but richly multiple, weaving various mythologies and literary traditions into a focal point of imagery. Not only does H.D.'s imagery focus various traditional uses of an image into a single imaginative fusion – a metaphor; she also used such central images as 'flowers' to play on the role of figuration in her own poetry and in the literary or mythological tradition. Flowers are always metaphors for figures of speech, for the latter are the flowers of speech, and, in this way, H.D. recognized the central role of metaphor in language. As for romantic poets before her, and for painters after her such as Georgia O'Keeffe, for H.D. the flower is a particularly expressive metaphor, since it is an image based on the idea of radiation, emblematic of the functioning of the imagination in distinction from linear, discursive reason. Light and song imagery are closely associated with the flower image as other examples of radiation imagery. Moreover, the flower image stands almost as a recipe for how to read H.D.'s poetry. Instead of reading it as developing in some linear progression, whether through narrative, or through ideas, or through specific, evolving metaphors, her poetry accumulates meanings, as petals cluster around a central focus. In her novels, she sought to recreate this poetic method in her narrative technique of spiralling sentences and phrases, swirling around in a field of radiating sounds, patterns and meanings. Like Gertrude Stein's, her fiction demands of the reader a different approach to the language of her quintessentially modernist texts.

Katherine Mansfield 1888–1923

During Katherine Mansfield Beauchamp's short life of thirty-four years, she published three successful collections of short stories and a novella: *In a German Pension* (London, 1911), *Bliss and Other Stories* (London, 1920), *The Garden Party and Other Stories* (London, 1922) and *Prelude* (Richmond, 1918). After her death, her husband, Middleton Murry, published a fourth collection, *The Dove's Nest* (London, 1923), another volume of uncollected stories and fragments, *Something Childish* (London, 1924), and *Poems* (London, 1923). He edited and published portions of her journal (London, 1927), selected

letters (1928), and a collection of book reviews in 1930, called *Novels and Novelists* (London). He also published the revised novella, *The Aloe* (London, 1930). A *Scrapbook* (London) appeared in 1939, followed by fuller editions of letters and journals and collected stories.

Born in Wellington, New Zealand, Mansfield travelled to England and Europe before settling in London in 1908. She quickly found herself at the centre of London literary life; she associated, for example, with D.H. and Frieda Lawrence as well as with Leonard and Virginia Woolf, who first published *Prelude* at the Hogarth Press. Debilitated by her illness in the last several years of her life, she travelled in search of health and cures, spending time in Italy and the south of France. Her New Zealand childhood and the scenery of that beautiful country played a significant part in her stories, as did her relationship with her brother, Leslie Beauchamp (her own name was originally Kathleen Mansfield Beauchamp).

Both Lawrence and Leonard Woolf emphasized the centrality of a sharp, penetrating humour in Mansfield's stories – both in tragic and in predominantly comic contexts. The 'astringent wit' and satire were complemented by a compassion for the suffering in life which, in her stories, occurs as an intense pathos. Mansfield had stated in a 1922 journal entry: 'One must keep ever present a sense of humour. It depends entirely on yourself how much you see or hear or understand. But the sense of humour I have found true of every single occasion of my life.' Lawrence related Mansfield's humour to her ability to create 'tremendous trifles', to turn inconsequential details and events into significant moments through wit, exaggeration and satire. (Mansfield was seen by T.S. Eliot, Kay Boyle and others, on the other hand, as wasting her considerable talents on trifling events and encounters.) Later, Eudora Welty described this characteristic of Mansfield's writing as involving an 'impressionistic intensity', with 'one small situation . . . [but] a large, complex one is implied'. Welty refined this further, in Willa Cather-like terms, when she said that each of Mansfield's stories, 'instead of being a simple situation, is an impression of a situation, and tells more for being so'. Indeed, Mansfield's stories seem almost a deliberate embodiment of Cather's credo that artists 'present their scene by suggestion rather than by enumeration . . . Whatever is felt upon the page without being named there . . . that gives high quality to the novel.'

Mansfield is also known for her 'special prose', which she described in a letter as 'trembling on the brink of poetry'. Even in the last few months of her life, when writing was becoming almost impossible, she continued to be committed to experimentation with style, saying, 'I want to write – but differently – far more steadily.' Elsewhere, she had described prose in general as an undiscovered country, which she wished to explore. Mansfield delighted in an impressionistic style of writing which involved carefully placed details, understatement, symbol and compression. Apparent simplicity and innocence are often a mark for ominous, threatening complexities to do with failures of communication, deceit and cruelty. Another characteristic of her prose is an intimacy which Frieda Lawrence spoke of: 'She can come so close.' Complexity and even indeterminacy of meaning are achieved through imagist devices of the kind that Ezra Pound, Eliot and H.D. were using in their poetry: a single image running throughout the story structures and unifies it while remaining indeterminately symbolic. Mansfield's frequent use of indirect free narrative – that shifting between narrator and central character – adds to a modernist indeterminacy as well as creating an ironic, critical consciousness hovering over the page.

Another familiar quality of Mansfield's stories, that strongly felt pathos, expresses what Welty described as the hidden theme of every story, namely the conflict between life and death. Mansfield described something similar when she wrote, 'even while we live again, we face death. But through life: that's the point. We see death in life as we see death in a flower that is fresh unfolded.' Another origin of this pathos was revealed by Cather in her essay on Mansfield, when she discussed the latter's representation of the tragic necessity of human relationships which are shown as never quite satisfactory. And she described Mansfield's stories as depicting the contradictory (and often tragic) need of human beings for solitude and freedom and also for relationship and commitment. Mansfield's stories certainly explore this theme, as well as the social conventions and socialized responses which make

accommodation of these conflicting needs painful and often impossible.

Mansfield's stories are often designed to shift the reader's attention away from an exclusive interest in the content and towards a more sophisticated literary appreciation of the style, structure and self-referential techniques. Like much impressionistic painting of the time, her prose of light deftness draws the reader's attention both to the medium, the materiality of language of the story and to the act of perception itself, whether in reading, in writing or in living. Stories often have as a subtext the portrayal both of imaginative perception and of the failure of perception and communication. Communication as a theme becomes an allegory for reading, as well as a problem for the fictional characters. Mansfield's stories are explorations of the social conventions and hypocrisy which inhibit intimacy and stunt human development: 'Why do people hide and withdraw and suspect – as they do? . . . it is *lack of heart*: a sort of blight on them which will not let them ever come to full flower.' Themes of development and flowering, and of their failure, also allegorize the problems for the artist of coming to 'full flower', of achieving a unique style and individuality which is the essence of creativity.

That is, for Mansfield, 'Art is absolutely self-development.' This existential commitment to the necessity to develop oneself in life, and to art as one major means of self-development, characterizes many of her stories, letters and journal entries. She wrote that one must 'weave the intricate tapestry of one's own life', implying that, conceived in this existential way, self-construction is analogous to the construction of a work of art: the truly individualized self is a work of art, and living can become the creative construction of such individuality. Life for Mansfield becomes meaningful as the art of self-development, and her stories anatomize the obstacles and the aids to such an artful living. In the story 'Je ne parle pas français', for example, she portrayed a highly self-conscious narrative persona who is trying to create an identity for himself as artist. He then parodies this project from the self-critical perspective of yet another observing self, in an implicitly unending series of meta-perspectives. In 'A Married Man's Story', Mansfield also attended implicitly to story-telling, and made her narrator parody realist notions of pure description, objective truth and neutrality, concluding that he wants to 'write simply . . . no fine effects – no bravura. But just the plain truth, as only a liar can tell it.'

In a criticism of Lawrence, Mansfield described another major thematic aspect of her stories, which relates closely to her idea of art as self-development and the related concept of style as the artist's very self:

> Lawrence denies his humanity. He denies the powers of the imagination. He denies life – I mean *human* life. His hero and heroine are non-human. They are animals on the prowl. They do not feel: they scarcely speak. There is not one memorable word. They submit to the physical response and for the rest go veiled – blind – *faceless* – *mindless*. This is the doctrine of mindlessness . . . here is life where one has blasphemed against the spirit of reverence.

The story 'Bliss', one of Mansfield's most highly regarded short fictions, is exemplary of the above quotation. One character, Bertha Young, strives to articulate her very being, in the midst of romantic illusions which hinder her efforts, while she is surrounded by Lawrentian figures who are likened to cats skulking in the background, lusting after each other. This story is a highly plotted, dramatic play within a story, with numerous self-referential gestures designed to draw the reader into the 'play': Bertha's dinner guests 'reminded her of a play by Chekhov'. Bertha is both actress and spectator, as she is shown throughout the story struggling to make meaning from the fabric of her experience, by articulating her feelings. Language disrupts the smooth surface thematics of personal and social relations, breaking forth frequently as overt subject matter: characters such as Bertha muse openly upon the inadequacy of words, the difficulties of communication, and the ambiguity inherent in meaning. Problems of expression, interpretation and reading recur, as definiteness and certainty escape our grasp. Yet Mansfield's stories suggest that while these, like 'truth', may be unattainable, we can still achieve what matters most anyway in the process of art and self-development, namely reflection upon experience.

Not truth, then, or certainty about life, art,

experience or nature, but reflection is the means by which we develop our humanity. The opposite of imaginative articulation or reflection about experience is that mindlessness referred to earlier, which Mansfield accused Lawrence of idealizing. Mansfield's stories both discuss in allegorical thematics and, more importantly, illustrate through style and structure the many ways in which we can enrich experience by reflection. For example, some stories structure and unify experience by means of complex use of imagery: a single image – such as a pear tree – will recur systematically throughout the story as a focus or centre around which an indeterminate penumbra of meanings coalesce. Such images become both symbolically complex and expressive of themes, and they function to structure and unify a story. Experience is shown to be articulated also by means of metaphors and similes, as characters like Bertha Young try to make sense of their experience through figures of speech, which are not mere ornaments of language but the main vehicles for reflecting intelligently on life.

The *Critical Writings* of Mansfield have been edited by C. Hanson (London, 1987), and the *Collected Letters*, three vols, by V. O'Sullivan and M. Scott (Oxford, 1984–93). C.K. Stead edited her journals and selected letters in 1977, with a very helpful introduction.

Rebecca West 1892–1983

Cicily Isabel Andrews, born Cicily Isabel Fairfield, took her pseudonym, Rebecca West, from Ibsen's *Rosmersholm* (1886), and lived up to her radical feminist namesake in her active life and her writings. Having moved to London at 16 for a stage career, she quickly took up writing for the feminist and socialist publications, and began a long relationship with H.G. Wells. She published a study, *Henry James*, in 1916 (London and New York), and wrote many reviews and articles for the *New Statesman*. She was a strong supporter of the writer and feminist anarchist Emma Goldman, and admired the work of Virginia Woolf as well as that of D.H. Lawrence, about whom she published a critical study (London, 1930). Major novels include *The Return of the Soldier* (London and New York,

1918), *The Judge* (London and New York, 1922), *Harriet Hume* (London and Garden City, N.J., 1929), *The Thinking Reed* (London and New York, 1936) and *The Fountain Overflows* (London and New York, 1957). *The Harsh Voice: Four Short Novels* appeared in 1935 (London and Garden City, N.J.). By the age of 30, West was well known to audiences in both Britain and America. Like her friend Anaïs Nin, she was deeply influenced by Freud's writing – many of her novels treat issues that bring psychological conflicts and sexual behaviour to the fore. She also wrote a well-known anti-Nazi book about the Balkans, *Black Lamb and Grey Falcon* (2 vols, New York, 1941). Several of her other early writings have been edited into a single volume, *The Young Rebecca*, ed. Jane Marcus (New York, 1982). Additional published works include *The Meaning of Treason* (New York, 1947), *The Strange Necessity: Essays and Reviews* (London, 1928; London, 1987), which includes a fine analysis of Willa Cather, and her autobiographical work *Family Memories* (London, 1987), ed. F. Evans.

Each of the novels of Rebecca West stands as a unique example of artistic experimentation, covering between them a range of literary conventions. In her first novel, *The Return of the Soldier*, her predominant experimentation was with narrative point of view, influenced undoubtedly by her study of Henry James a few years earlier, though the related matter of style is also explored. In *The Judge*, another of her finest novels, West seemed to attend intensely to plot and story, creating a complex narrative by introducing into the latter part of the text another novel-story, out of the past, which functions in part as a sinister augury of the future. *Harriet Hume*, on the other hand, is an experiment in fantasy, eschewing many novelistic conventions to create an almost Shakespearean midsummer night's dream of a novel. In part it is an attempt at a unique experiment in the psychological novel, but it also attempts to use an atmosphere of magical illusion – the mental cast of Harriet – to explore the harsh realities of a political-public man in contrast to Harriet's personal world of love and private life. In *The Birds Fall Down* (New York, 1966), West experimented once again, this time with genre in the form of a novel of political intrigue. Prominent actors on

the stage of the Russian Revolution meet on a train journey, and the experiment this time involved the author's making these travellers tell their stories to each other and thereby enact events in actual Russian history, while the train, in allegorical fashion, moves inexorably towards a destination which may be disastrous for one of them. Uppermost in the novel is the relation of history to fiction, and of the blurring of the lines between the two. 'Reality' is turned into legend and story before the eyes of a young girl who listens to the conversations between opposing forces of the Russian Revolution still to come. In *The Fountain Overflows*, there is more experimentation with narrative point of view, as West explored, through the eyes of the adolescent Rose Aubrey, the predicament of both the artist in a hostile society and the individual who sees more truth than it is possible to bear. Each of Rebecca West's other novels can be described as a literary experiment in similar terms, so much so that few novelists have ever achieved the sheer variety and range that West's fiction displays. Reading her corpus of fiction becomes an education in the history of the novel and in its scope as a fictional form.

West's novels are also radical challenges to moral and social conventions, as well as to literary forms, as they take up social issues which continue to interest readers decades later. Marriage is scrutinized and revealed to be, all too often, a soulless, passionless prostitution of the human spirit for materialist interests regarding property, inheritance and ownership of children. Attitudes to extra-marital sex are revealed as hypocritical and destructive, while both marriage as an institution and sex are shown to be inextricably bound up with social class hierarchies that create double standards and perpetuate injustice to women, in particular. *The Thinking Reed*, moreover, was a novel about 'rich people: to find out why they seemed to me to be as dangerous as wild boars and pythons'. The plight of unwed mothers is explored and, depressingly, little seems to change from one generation to another as unmarried women with children are brutally ostracized. Rape is a theme as well, while in other novels West portrayed the 'conflict' between personal, emotional life – typically the concern of women – and public, political life – the arena of men – and showed the corruption each is vulnerable to without the other to balance and contain excesses. In terms of thematic scope, then, West's novels range from the contained, isolated domestic scene to the widest public scope of revolution and political intrigue, almost always, however, focusing upon the particularly problematic situation of women, hemmed in by patriarchal prejudices and social and religious conventions.

West's aesthetic treatise, *The Strange Necessity* (originally entitled *A Hypothesis*), concerned as it is with that 'mystery of mysteries' art, and why it matters so much, provides a useful context for considering her fiction. In this treatise West sought to treat theoretical and philosophical issues of the most abstract kind in a personal, concrete, social way. *The Strange Necessity* constitutes, then, another radical experiment in genre, by its concretion of theory into life. Art matters, it implies, because it is an expression of a fundamental human need, a physiological necessity to learn. Art and science are both the systematic social outcome of individuals engaging in a natural, pleasurable exercise of their higher cerebral cortex, that outer layer of the brain responsible for learning. Relatedly, she argued that art (and science) gives humans a valuable kind of pleasure, while at the same time acting both to identify and to preserve the things in experience which are of value. Works of art tell us something valuable about human experience of the world, and the process of creating works of art is a learning experience for the creator. *The Strange Necessity* is not written in such a way as to demonstrate to the reader Rebecca West's conclusions about art. Rather, the reader watches the author going through the processes of thinking itself in an immediate present, as she wrestles with one possibility after another, chases down an idea only to follow up a different one, drawing upon aesthetic theory, psychology, literature and even practical criticism, which is where she began her investigation. Nothing could be further from the traditional abstract, theoretical, aesthetic treatise than this lively, concrete immediacy of thought and experience, where not only the distinction between life and art is demolished, but also that between a philosophical treatise about thought and thinking itself.

The relation between life (or living) and letters is queried throughout her novels as well, as Rebecca West intertwined her analysis of this relation with the issue so central to literary theory today, namely the distinction between history (and reality) and fiction. One of the central themes of most of her novels, this relation is also worked into the very fabric of her fictional texts as a complex structure of past and present narratives, of memory and present observations. The relation of fiction to reality, and the way in which history and the past are made real by narrating accounts from various points of view, are most overtly dealt with in *The Return of the Soldier*. In this novel, a shell-shocked soldier returns home to a reality which existed fifteen years earlier, the present reality being wiped out by his wartime trauma. Apart from the thematic and psychological insights into passionless marriages, the trifling misunderstandings of life which have such tragic, long-lasting consequences, the neurosis of 'ordinary life', and other reversals of sickness versus cure and reality versus illusion, the novel takes up the issue of truth itself, as the narrator is shown to undergo a complete transformation in attitude. What she had previously seen as genuine becomes utterly false, and her prior confidence in social decency utterly shaken.

While nearly all West's novels reveal a sophistication about the relativity of truth and the fact of perspective or point of view creating multiple realities, like Katherine Anne Porter and others she was also interested in the way even relative truth could be distorted by idealization and self-delusion. Most of her novels suggest, if not directly then at least by implication, that moral and aesthetic judgements must be made and acted upon. Yet, West showed, we need not delude ourselves that they are based on certainties and absolutes, or that such judgements and actions are ever not open to debate. To put it another way, these novels reveal the many forms that moral hypocrisy and aesthetic insincerity take. They delineate the stages and elements in the psychological processes of rationalization of the false into the true, so that by understanding these matters more clearly one is better equipped to resist them. Yet most of her novels end in uncertainty of a moral or aesthetic kind, suggesting that even relative sureness about the false does not lead to truth.

One of the profoundest impressions left by such novels as *The Fountain Overflows*, *The Judge* or *The Birds Fall Down*, as by *The Return of the Soldier*, is Rebecca West's commitment to the social aspect of moral and aesthetic experience. That is, life is undergone by humans not merely as individual, existential beings battling against fate. Life is, for humans, a social affair, and morality and art are pre-eminently matters of social communication. Consequently, moral and aesthetic meanings are social meanings, and bound up in life as conventions and relativities. West's novels portray the way in which conventions are mistaken as facts of nature, as absolute, inviolable truths, thereby imprisoning individuals and thwarting imaginative life. Art can restore the perception that moral, historic and aesthetic realities *are* conventions, not inviolable facts or natural givens. Art, she showed, can give us the courage to relinquish familiar conventions for new modes of ordering and structuring our lives, and the insight both to know when the old ways of thinking have had their day, and what form the new should take.

The Judge, *The Fountain Overflows* and *The Return of the Soldier* all explore as overt thematics the suffering and injustice caused when social, moral or aesthetic conventions are mistaken for absolute truths. *The Birds Fall Down* and *Harriet Hume* also explore this theme, one in the public and one in the private realm. In the former, the uncertainty surrounding past historical events is ironized and intensified by the blatant uncertainty veiling present reality, as history in the making: if present motives and even facts are so uncertain, how much more uncertain will they become when made into past, historical records? *Harriet Hume* and *The Thinking Reed*, contrastingly, analyse social conditions and conventions (the 'rules' of politics and wealth) which seem to make moral or aesthetic discrimination impossible, as hypocrisy and deceit appear endemic. Their inevitably corrupting effects may be an old theme (and seem to be an oversimplification), but in West's astute handling, this issue is explored with revealing and sobering insight. In handling literary conventions of the novel in such an overt way, West succeeded in achieving an impressive congruence of thematic content and formal structure, as she both adapted old conventions to new use, and forged new conventions to express new experiences.

Part II

High Modernism, Other Experiments and the Continuing Development of the Socio-Moral Novel, 1918–1945

Chapter 4

Modernism and Stream of Consciousness Fiction

I

In chapter 2, various writers were introduced who, it was said, anticipated and even initiated modernism, with their rejections of earlier fictional forms associated with realism, naturalism and 'ordinary' language, such as familiar conventions of plot, structure, characterization, narrative description, objectivity, subject matter and so on. The influence of specific psychological developments, especially Freud's and William James's contributions, were also mentioned, but before proceeding any further, one should pause to clarify if possible the notion 'modernism'. Since the early 1950s or so, there has been an explosion of critical writings about the concept of modernism, as well as about specific artists, some of whom it is generally agreed were practitioners of modernist techniques. Yet, it is a platitude to say that there seems little agreement even about the time period to which 'modernism' refers, in addition to there being differences about the practices which constituted modernism, or the writers who should be included as modernists.

In chapter 2 and throughout chapter 3, I have referred to a number of practices as 'modernist', such as stream of consciousness (for a fuller discussion, see below), stylistic experimentation with the materiality of language, changes in conceptions of character, and others. On the other hand, 'late realists', such as Kate Chopin, Edith Wharton and Willa Cather, not to mention Charlotte Perkins Gilman, Olive Schreiner,

Barbara Baynton and Catherine Carswell, for example, were shown already divesting themselves of many predominant nineteenth-century conventions. Strong plot, unity of character, objectivity of point of view, narrative description, emphasis upon public events and settings, sequential development and unity of the text were all gradually dispensed with by different writers. They favoured traits such as interiority, subjectivity, plotlessness, materiality of language, narrative complexity (alternative points of view, framework techniques of story within story), new thematics, resistance to overt formal unity in preference for apparent disorder, fragmentation and time disruptions. However, since many of the techniques described here are characteristic of literature today as well as literature of the past, one should examine how modernism can be better distinguished.

Most critics have admitted that 'modernism' is difficult to define and, as mentioned above, even the historical period to which it refers is widely disputed: critics give varying dates, such as 1857–1920, 1885–1935, 1870–1950, 1890–1930, 1907–1925, 1914–1922, 1900–1940 and 1922–1935. Some critics argue that modernism is essentially still with us, and that 'postmodernism' either is a misnomer or reveals within its own construction the essential continuity of modernism into the 1990s. Other critics have suggested that modernism is better understood as a continuation, with of course alterations and even minor interruptions, of the Romantic sensibility, which can be traced from, say, Blake in the 1780s or so, to the present day. The justification for the extension back into the late eighteenth century, or the amalgamation of modernism into a wider-reaching sensibility, involves a familiar description of Western cultural and intellectual history. That is, this history is described as a series of swings between two major alternative modes, namely the classical or neo-classical enlightenment tradition, with its main emphasis upon reason, science and objectivity, and the romantic and intuitivist tradition, with its emphasis upon imagination, art and subjectivity.

Some critics have proposed that modernism might, instead, be viewed as a break with these alternations, and involve a new sensibility which has succeeded in creating an explosively dynamic fusion of the other two. Others suggest that while modernism is better described as a rejection of the realist/naturalist/enlightenment hegemony of the nineteenth century, it is not a return to an older form, such as Romanticism, or merely a fusion of older forms. To describe modernism as a resurgence of Romanticism or Romantic sensibility is, they argue, regressive, and takes too little account of the new and hitherto unseen developments of art in this period. On the other hand, to describe modernism as a new spirit of the twentieth century which still persists today, albeit with new developments, is also objectionable to many writers, who sense some genuine coherence in the literature and art of the period from around 1899 to 1939, say.

While it is clear that modernism is if anything plural and variously experimental, it is a challenge to articulate the character of some 'sense of real coherence' during a period which included impressionism, expressionism, imagism, symbolism, futurism, vorticism, post-impressionism, surrealism, cubism and dadaism, as well as much art and literature which did not fit into any of these categories. It has been proposed that one way of describing the enormously dynamic and energetic period of literary and artistic activity around this time would be to say that all these movements tended to challenge or at least markedly de-emphasize linearity, sequential unity or developmental structure, and progressive, time-oriented, teleological organization. The strong sense of history characteristic of realist fiction, with its carefully ordered beginnings, middles and ends, its causality, logical categories, and

past, present and future relations, was abandoned by modernists. An emphasis upon the here and the now, this fulgent present, with all its depths, symbolic import, emblematic character and three- or even four-dimensionality, may have been influenced by psychological ideas of the timelessness of the unconscious, its fusion of past and future into present, its rejection of causality, and so on. The literature of this modernist period has been described as seeking spatial expression in language to represent time, by means of layerings and topologies of depths rather than surface geometries of linearity. This was often achieved through the intensified use of extended metaphors or images involving not just phrases but structural properties, as well as characters doubled and even tripled to appear as 'sides' or aspects of a single mind. Narrative time was made to move in spirals and circles, language swirled with connotations and words were overcharged with suggestiveness.

Modernism might also be described as a range of responses to rapidly changing social realities which were characterized by an unusual commitment to continuing experimentation and innovation. The search for 'the new' should, it was said, involve each artist striving to achieve an individual style, and then surpassing and innovating from that. The notion that a few leading geniuses should set the style for others to follow and perhaps vary within the limits of the 'movement' was rejected, then, by some, while a lingering belief persisted, nevertheless, that there were leaders, and they should be models. The alleged emphasis upon the importance of individuality in order to 'make it new' can probably not distinguish modernism from Romanticism, realism or other periods, however, since they too were diverse and innovative, and seemed so to their contemporaries and immediate followers. Perhaps modernism was characterized by a marked rejection of enlightenment and humanist faith in reason and progress, and an increasing awareness of the irrationality within the human psyche and society, more than ever before. The increased globalization of commerce, communication and travel may have added to or at least expedited a seeming tendency towards a normlessness in ethics, religion, social practices, cultural values and personal behaviour. For the intimate knowledge of other cultures can lead to an erosion and even destruction of certainty and the stability of belief, when the provincialism of our practices and values is revealed, and other ways of living, thinking and being are shown to be not only possible, but actual. Moreover, the understanding of the nature of reality itself was being shaken by physics, mathematics and genetics, while both Darwin and later Freud transformed our understanding of the reality of human nature. Both thinkers revealed continuities between humans and animals which had been repressed both by religions and by enlightenment philosophies.

Both the Darwinian and Freudian challenges to enlightenment concepts of reality and the human being as essentially rational were further reinforced by the increasing awareness of Nietzsche's earlier revelations or interpretations of human practices as adaptive survival techniques. Language was not so much a distinguishing sign of a soul or spirituality, which animals do not possess, as a social practice which enhanced survival of the species. It was Nietzsche who reminded twentieth-century intellectuals of the decisive role of language in the construction of human experience of 'reality'. With his 'perspectivism' and relativism, truth, whether artistic or scientific, was seen as a social matter and a linguistic product, the displacement of one set of figures of speech by another, with knowledge the interrelations of signifiers (not signified) in a field of experience made up of prior interpretations. Essentialism was further routed by Nietzsche's inversion of ethical values as power tools for survival and exploitation, and of art as a veil over a reality describable only as wanton, godless procreation. This conception of a dynamic world of supercharged energies of unimaginable force, often in violent conflict and ever-changing relations, came to resemble Freud's concept of the id. Human nature, like nature itself, is not, Nietzsche argued, what it appears to be. The apparently rational surface of consciousness hides a mass of tangled and conflicting desires, impulses and needs. The outer person is a mere papering-over of the cracks of a split and warring complex of selves driven by life and death instincts, as Freud was later to admit. Language was not the transparent tool for the objective representation of a stable reality; ethics was not expressive of a discovered system of absolute

values or religion other than a desire for parental protection throughout life. This Nietzschean subversion of prior assumptions of the long-standing liberal humanist model may have led writers to feel that a change of cataclysmic proportions was occurring – in human nature, human relations and human society.

In the efforts of writers of the period to confront this felt crisis, critics identify a tendency to reunify life and art, to restore art and literature to a more central place in the evolution of a new consciousness. It is often said that, in the face of a growing feeling that 'the centre cannot hold' and that uncertainty and chaos were taking over and old foundations collapsing, modernist writers chose to face the collapse not by repressing or denying but by exploiting that very fragmentation, chaos, disruption and uncertainty, rather than trying to shore up an old, failing order. This pluralization of world views since about 1850 resulted probably from new forms of communication and new classes of social order. Artists are thought to have grasped this freedom with eagerness, even in the face of its darker implications. Exile and travel were ways of thematizing this pluralization and internationalism, and led to further developments in non-representational art. Sometimes novelists portrayed characters in a state of tension and anxiety about these cultural confrontations which threatened their reality. Sometimes they embraced the differences, which offered opportunities for passion and experiences outside what was allowed 'at home'. Indeed, sometimes the texts themselves register a tension between the portrayal of characters out of nineteenth-century fiction lost in the wilderness of twentieth-century literary forms. These 'exiled' character portrayals, which exist uncomfortably within modernist landscapes, register the dislocation evident when, during a period of transition, literary conventions of one epoch linger or stray into the experimentation of the next. Aesthetically, the effects can be very interesting for the reader.

Whether the sensation of crisis resulting from all the above sources was more intense than that of previous periods of transformation in Europe and elsewhere is not clear. There were passionate debates in Europe in the 1790s, for example, about innovations in poetry, as well as the earlier debate between the 'ancients' and 'moderns', the arguments in the Renaissance and Reformation, and the upheavals of the Industrial Revolution and urbanization. If self-consciousness, irony, self-referentiality and the related rejections of representational art, embracing of relativism, and emphasis on experimentation do not distinguish modernism from other periods, perhaps its most salient feature, since it shares all the above-named ones with so many earlier writers, is its internationalism. Not only did modernism imbibe new forms from other cultures: it created a multiculturalism which, while always present in art, became greatly intensified. The border crossings and impurities, the transgressions of decorum along with the new hybrid forms which defied literary proprieties and genre classifications, led to the magic realist and post-structuralist forms whose very character seems internationalist.

In its grappling with the failures of social coherence and cultural integrity, in its defiance of authority, tradition, nationalism, purity and so on, modernism was often associated with 'foreign' ideas which were threatening to the traditional insistence on the importance of, say, Englishness, or Germanness. While modernism is properly understood as the avant-garde of the late nineteenth and early twentieth century, avant-garde movements have always existed and are the very processes of renewal and reinvigoration which prevent stasis or cultural decay. Like most avant-gardes, modernism was characterized by its diverse mixings of 'foreign' elements and its refusal to function as the cultural guardian of the national past. In its rejection of this role in the representation of reality or history, modernism may have shown us that what we label representational art, or literature which looks conventional or uses ordinary language, or even what we call realist, is better seen itself as a name for what has become absorbed into the cultural body of a society. That is, what we have finally been able to assimilate, however resistant we were at first, eventually becomes familiar enough to look representational, conventional and realist. Confusion arises in the case of realism because the word was used to designate a specific form of avant-gardism in the mid-nineteenth century, which itself had rejected the Romance, the Gothic and other familiar fictional forms. The apparent nihilism or decadence of any avant-garde art is explained by its challenge to deeply cherished but often worn-out and inhibiting traditions. For example, modernist texts seemed to lack content and familiar form because, in part, of their challenge to space/time categories of mental organization, by means of intense surface disorder and stylistic innovation. Yet, this apparently cold impersonality was fused with an intensely interiorized, warm, subjective consciousness as 'content'. Moreover, it also made use of silence, empty space or elusive non-messages, experimenting with new 'languages of the night', with the dream and with that 'immediate present', all designed to increase intimacy with the reader. The stress on suggestiveness and elusiveness, or the use of the absent to suggest a complex of present possibilities, led to extremes of minimalism on the one hand, and, on the other, to richly embroidered, gothic, mannered styles. In the latter, ornamentation and elaborate codification displaced any pretence of an extra-linguistic message or content. Words mixed the senses in rich synaesthesia, polypsychism and multiple meanings.

The alleged change in attitudes to human nature and 'all human relations' alluded to by Virginia Woolf may express a sense that the status of the human subject had undergone a revolution which affected conceptions of reality, too: 'the whole world is a work of art; . . . we are parts of the work of art . . . we are the words; we are the music; we are the thing itself.' Gertrude Stein's distinction between 'narrative' and 'narration' was another example of the changes modernism was exploring (and anticipates recent distinctions between the 'book' and the 'text'). Narrative presumes an author, she explained; it requires a distinct point of view, it describes things sequentially, progresses discursively, and is primarily a tool for expressing some ideas, some content. Narration, on the other hand, eschews nouns, substantives and content, in an effort to reconstitute immediacy itself. Stein's continuous present was a new realism, in a sense, a phenomenology of language more than of mind. For narration, as opposed to narrative, evades an agent other than language, which speaks itself. Distinctions between author, reader, text and medium dissolve into a continuous present.

To summarize, nearly all descriptions of modernism apply also to literature of other periods, even taking the most generous breadth of time for modernism. We can describe this literature as intensely self-conscious, as intensely experimental, as stylistically and technically innovative, as poetic prose, as a language preoccupied with itself rather than with subject matter, as an art with multiple points of view, as relatively disorderly and indecorous, as emphasizing interiority, as often structured by images and symbols, as avoiding narrative description of externality, and so on. All these characteristics add up only to a 'family resemblance', but this is perhaps enough. (For further reading, see the end of the chapter.)

II

'Stream of consciousness' is one of the most salient features of many texts associated with that elusive concept, modernism. Yet it, too, is difficult to define, in part because of the diversity of forms it has taken. Normally associated with Dorothy Richardson, Woolf and James Joyce's later novels, as well as some of William Faulkner's fiction (to name only some obvious examples), a prior, related or even embryonic form can, arguably, be seen in the late fiction of Henry James, and in Continental writers such as Proust. Hilda Doolittle's fiction, especially *Her* or *Hermione*, is an example in its fully developed form, while May Sinclair and Gertrude Stein developed versions of stream of consciousness, albeit with distinct individualities. Later, Stevie Smith, Djuna Barnes and Ellen Glasgow produced novels, stories and portions of novels in a full, mainstream version of this modernist feature, while more recently Leonora Carrington, Elizabeth Smart and Marguerite Young have remade this form anew. Contemporaries such as Jennifer Johnston, Toni Cade Bambara, Bessie Head and Kathy Acker, for example, have shown how much more stream of consciousness can be individualized than early practitioners could have imagined.

Thus, the phrase functions as an umbrella term for a very wide range of narrative styles, which, however, have in common both an emphasis upon subjectivity, interiority and psychological states, and, usually, the rejection of an objective authority for the narrative point of view.

Often, the phrase 'internal monologue' is used almost synonymously, but it could be more useful as a term to distinguish another type of related narration, as does, for example, the phrase 'indirect free discourse'. There, the narrator's previously distinct consciousness is, at specific and limited moments, mixed with a character so much that no distinction is possible during those periods. Both Jane Austen and Katherine Mansfield used this form freely, while 'internal monologue' might describe a narrative which is firmly fixed in the point of view and consciousness of one character without necessarily being stream of consciousness, as in some of Jean Rhys's novels. At other times, there is an almost objective quality to the stream, when it is not so clearly confined to a character's consciousness, but seems to come out of that of a narrator. This happens sometimes in Richardson and Glasgow, sometimes in Woolf, and elsewhere.

A brief look at the history of the phrase may give some understanding of its literary applications. William James's use is the first recorded occurrence, in *Principles of Psychology* (1890). It was taken up by Sinclair in 1918, in a review of Richardson's *Pilgrimage*. James sought, with this new phrase, both to escape essentialist notions of mind and consciousness, and to offer a more empirical description than prior philosophers and psychologists, such as atomists, had done. The latter, including David Hume, had assumed consciousness to be a mass of fragments and atoms, discrete sensations and perceptions, related to each other through acts of the mind. Such acts were categorized into either those involving space and time or logical ones, including similarity, difference, causality and so on. Moreover, these postulated atomic sensations were thought to be the 'substance' or material of experience, while the relations established amongst them by acts of mind were purely mental. James believed this account to be both counter-empirical and unnecessarily dualistic. That is, our experience is of a continuously flowing connectedness, which becomes fragmented only upon reflection. The resulting assumption of a dualistic material/mental composite was posited as the nature of experience itself, instead of as a product of reflection about it. Consciousness 'breaks up' into substance versus relation only when made the object of analysis. For James, substance and relation are functions of each other, and experience is already imbued with relations from the outset. Relations are not super-added by the reason to some pre-existing atoms of material or of sensation. Indeed, substance in consciousness turns out to be relations, if it can be said to be anything.

James also contributed to the future development of stream of consciousness fiction when he introduced the idea of the 'specious present', which was to influence first Stein and later Marcel Proust, Woolf and others. This phrase was James's way of describing the arbitrary nature of our time delineations, and the fact that each sense of the present is saturated with the past and the future. Presentness separate from the other two is a kind of fiction. Past, present and future are continuous and merge into each other in consciousness. Any moment we choose to focus upon has, James explained, a halo, a fringe, an overtone. There is a penumbra of other times surrounding it. This is not an unapt emblem for the way in which words mean and function in language, especially in stream of consciousness fiction. While philosophers and psychologists, then, were reanalysing those basic (Kantian) categories of intuition, space and time as subjective and relative, fiction writers began to try to adapt these insights. For example, they attended to narrative-time representation, experimenting with new ways of handling it, in both spatial and non-spatial metaphors, which avoided the old assumptions of linearity, atoms, dualisms and forward movement.

In addition to James, Henri Bergson some years later began publishing his philosophy of 'la durée réelle', in such books as *Time and Free Will* (London, 1910) and *Matter and Memory* (7th imprint, London, 1962; first published 1913), as well as *L'évolution créatrice*, trans. H. Bergson as *Creative Evolution* (London, 1911). Bergson, well informed of James's innovations, gave the stream of consciousness novel a new impetus, himself influenced by such earlier novelists as Edouard Dujardin, with his interior monologue, and by Victor Egger, who published a critical treatise, *La parole intérieure*, in 1881. With the appearance of Richardson's *Pilgrimage*, volume I, in 1915, the technique caught the imagination of readers and writers alike.

Thus, stream of consciousness can be seen as an alternative experiment from that of the realist's efforts to paint the external world of nature and, especially, society in words, and as objectively as possible. There, little or no intrusion of subjective reactions to that external world was allowed to pollute the narrative objectivity. Unlike Romanticists, for example, the realist did not seek to embody, express or record the responses of a subject to nature, love or society – techniques which would give the reader a view of objects and people through a specified perspective. On the other hand, most stream of consciousness writers' ideas differed from Romanticists' aims as well. The mind and its processes were presented as immediately as possible, unobjectified through nature or another person. One of the most significant effects of the stream of consciousness, as well as of internal monologue (and subjective, psychological 'realism'), was the innovative presentation of narrative time. Linear progression, sequentiality and normal, plot-type, forward development of a fiction were displaced by extreme time fragmentation, leaps from present to future (via fantasy or reverie, but also via narrative fiat), and to the past via memory or flashbacks. Objective clock-time is almost erased, and a few seconds of reverie, memory or immediate perception could take pages to describe, while the passage of a year or the occurrence of some decisive event might be glossed over or even left as a gap in the narrative. Thus, Mrs Ramsay's death in *To the Lighthouse*, or Miriam's mother's death or Miriam's affair with Hypo in *Pilgrimage*, are hinted at only, or presented to the reader so casually and briefly as at first to be incredible, then more shocking than any graphic, detailed report could have been.

Another effect of stream of consciousness related to the above is a dissolution of clear boundaries between reality and unreality, public and private, inner and outer, self and other. Fantasy or wish or fear might take on the intensity of reality; memory could be corrupted by the desire to transform the past; the present could be selectively perceived according to needs and prejudices; a probable future could be confused with a longed-for outcome. In addition, characters were shown flowing into each other and the surroundings, losing their own distinct boundaries. Feelings could be shown invading someone near to the person in whom they originated, thoughts were attributed to someone else by suggestion, so that identities became confounded by the intense influences between people, especially those with intimate bonds. All this psychological reality was more readily conveyed by a streaming narrative subjectivity. In extreme cases, what was thought or wished was almost indistinguishable from what was said or actually happened. The borders between rationality or sanity and madness were breached more persuasively for the reader, either momentarily or systematically, as in Gilman's 'The Yellow Wallpaper'.

These blurrings and other techniques demanded from the reader in the 1910s and 1920s a new approach to reading and a restructuring of expectations about fiction, if she or he was to be able to respond imaginatively to these narrative forms, so different from earlier realist forms and other, more conventional, familiar fictional techniques. Further difficulties arose as the reader was confronted not only with the shift from external to internal, but with a shift in emphasis upon the function of language itself. Language for the stream of consciousness writer did not merely shift its function from representation of external objects to representation of internal ones (thoughts, feelings, memories, fantasies). It shifted the focus away from representation of any objects, whether external or internal, and language began to function, one could say, more non-referentially for its significance. This shift is not really surprising, once one considers the role language plays in the internal monologue or interior realm of consciousness. For writers who began using fictional conventions and transforming them to serve better the verbal construction of interiority and processes of the mind, it quickly became evident that the distinction between word and thing was more apparently compelling than that between word and thought or feeling. The latter distinction blurred, since the linguistic embodiment of thoughts and feelings is possibly all we know of them. Struck by this near-congruence of the linguistic embodiment of a thought, and of 'thought' in some hypothetical disembodied sense, writers questioned the substantiality of thought without language. Even the reality of the apparently more acceptable distinction between words and things began to

collapse, as internal and external realities blurred under stream of consciousness representation. Writers especially were in a position to notice how inchoate both inner reality and outer reality are until articulated, and they began to focus upon language itself, its nature, structures and other properties, to see what it might tell them about the mind, the world and reality generally.

Attention to orderings through syntax and grammar, to the semantics of words, phrases and sentences through denotation but also through connotation, and to the materiality of words all led writers to treat language as their subject matter, instead of as merely a vehicle for some other, already existing content. This led to Stein's remarkable experiments, for example, following on Henry James's already extensive linguistic and stylistic innovations (influenced probably by William James's psychology). Punctuation was disrupted, logic/syntax/grammar was toyed with, word complexes of puns, synonyms, antonyms, acronyms and other connotative devices were explored, and repetition, incantation and displacement of linear progression were some of Stein's most frequent techniques. In contrast to Stein's naked, simple diction, Joyce created a rich, dense materiality of language which, like Stein's, seemed unreadable to many, but for quite different reasons. Woolf, on the other hand, took neither of these routes, though she borrowed from them at times, developing a poetic language of imagery, connotation, intensity and suggestiveness, as absences became as important as presences. Words, phrases and images reverberate throughout her fiction, creating fine-spun, delicate but enduring strands of interconnections, as webs of meaning emerge, patterns shimmer into view, and fragile relations accrue reality.

Stream of consciousness fiction often had language as its primary subject matter, then, but this subject matter always led to 'more real' content, like life, death, love and hate. For in exploring language, artists learned about the mind's processes of thinking, feeling, remembering, imagining, hoping, loving, hating, fearing. Exploring language could help one to grasp both logic and intuition as well, throwing light not only on basic processes of perception and living, but also on imagination and reasoning. Understanding how we come to order the world and our experience the way we do might lead to new possibilities for reordering. Yet, to continue to use language in the old way might mean ending up being used by it, once it was realized that ideologies were hidden in linguistic behaviour. Clichés and stereotyped words and phrases could literally determine one's character and experience, given the recognition that the articulation of thought and feeling is decisive for what one comes to feel and think. These issues became a central subject matter for novelists, and stream of consciousness techniques facilitated their representation.

The concept of the self was undergoing critical scrutiny alongside language, since the idea of a field of mental processes, conscious and unconscious, began to seem almost to take the place of a self, as understood in earlier terms. Experience *is* the self, Woolf seemed to suggest, and James described the self as a 'huge spider-web of the finest silken threads suspended in the chamber of consciousness'. As authors sought to transport readers into this chamber of silken threads, their own materiality and that of their readers had to be transmogrified into airy insubstantiality, and text, reader and author merged into a continuous stream of consciousness.

Further reading

Bergonzi, Bernard, ed. *Innovations*. London, 1968.
Bradbury, Malcolm and McFarlane, J., eds. *Modernism 1890–1930*. Harmondsworth, 1976.
Butler, Christopher. *Early Modernism*. Oxford, 1994.
Collier, Peter and Davies, Judy, eds. *Modernism and the European Unconscious*. Oxford, 1990.

Edel, Leon. *The Modern Psychological Novel*. Gloucester, Mass., 1972; first published 1955.
Ellmann, R. and Feidelson, C., eds. *The Modern Tradition* (an anthology). New York and London, 1965.
Freedman, Melvin J. *Stream of Consciousness: A Study in Literary Method*. New Haven, Conn., 1955.
Giles, Steve, ed. *Theorizing Modernism: Essays in Critical Theory*. London and New York, 1993.
Hassan, Ihab. *POSTmodernISM: Paracriticisms*. Urbana, Ill., 1975.
Howe, Irving, ed. *Literary Modernism*. Greenwich, Conn., 1967.
Humphrey, Robert. *Stream of Consciousness in the Modern Novel*. Berkeley, Calif., 1955.
James, William. *The Principles of Psychology*. 2 vols, London, 1890.
Josipovici, Gabriel. *The Lessons of Modernism*. London, 1977.
Karl, F.R. *Modern and Modernism*. New York, 1985.
Kermode, Frank. *Modern Essays*. London, 1971.
Kumar, S.K. *Bergson and the Stream of Consciousness Novel*. London, 1962.
Levenson, Michael. *A Genealogy of Modernism*. Cambridge, 1984.
Leverson, Michael. *Modernism and the Fate of Individuality*. Cambridge, 1991.
Mendilow, A.A. *Time and the Novel*. London, 1952.
Meyerhoff, Hans. *Time in Literature*. Berkeley, Calif., 1955.
Reiss, T.J. *The Discourse of Modernism*. Ithaca, N.Y., 1982.
Spender, Stephen. *The Struggle of the Modern*. London, 1963.
White, Allon. *The Uses of Obscurity*. London, 1981.
Williams, Raymond. *The Politics of Modernism: Against the New Conformists*. Ed. Tony Pinkney. London, 1989.
Wilson, Edmund. *Axel's Castle*. London, 1931.

Chapter 5

Introduction to Novelists, 1918–1945

Diversity in literary experimentation continued to be the main character of fiction in the period, following the intellectual revolutions propelled by William James, Freud, Emily Dickinson, Henry James, Cézanne, van Gogh and others. Changing attitudes to women, to sexuality, to morality, to religion and to social and political arrangements were of course accelerated by the development of the automobile, the telephone and other means of communication. Two of the most notable influences on literature, additional to those discussed in part I, were the Great War and the cinema. Writers responded to these events and transformations in remarkably various and distinctive ways, and while this period is usually described as that of 'high modernism', strong impulses of other kinds of experimentation, as well as of realist and traditional fiction, were felt throughout it. Moreover, literature engaging with issues of homosexuality, political and social adjustments, race and marginality of many kinds dominated this generation, putting paid to the myth that experimental writing is somehow apolitical, amoral and removed from the realities of life.

Writers of this second period of the twentieth century, such as Virginia Woolf, Djuna Barnes, Jean Rhys and Stevie Smith, carried into new realms the modernist experimentation which Gertrude Stein, May Sinclair, Dorothy Richardson, Joseph Conrad, D.H. Lawrence and other early modernists had recently embarked upon. Meanwhile, Susan Glaspell was revolutionizing the drama in America with her minimalist techniques. On the other hand, Ellen Glasgow's *The Sheltered Life*, Elizabeth Bowen's novels and stories, Isak Dinesen's elaborate tales, and Katherine Anne Porter's trenchant stories are only the most obvious examples of the overturning of literary conventions which can occur within the context of an apparently traditional style. In these latter, less categorizable, experimental texts – partly realist, partly modernist – stories are embedded within tales, story-telling is foregrounded, and perception, observation, judgement and interpretation are overt subject matter. Creativity or writing is also a constant, hidden theme, and strong analogies in the thematics with the reading and writing of fiction are conveyed in the texts. Most evidently in this second period, for both the radically stylistically experimental writers like Woolf, Rhys, Barnes, Frances Newman and Stevie Smith, and for the more restrained experimenters like Zora Neale Hurston, Bowen, Christina Stead, Glasgow and Kate O'Brien, there could be no dichotomy between art and morality, for both involve preeminently the imaginative faculty. Such a dichotomy, as well as the view that modernism was amoral and apolitical, is sustainable only if one accepts a social realist premise that art can be 'relevant' solely if it is overtly, dogmatically political and moral, immediately accessible to any reader, and makes no demands on its audience to educate themselves about techniques, traditions and innovations.

During this second period of radical as well as moderate stylistic and formal experimentation,

Katharine Susannah Prichard, Radclyffe Hall, Edna Ferber, Pauline Smith, Jessie Fauset, Winifred Holtby, Storm Jameson and others continued to work within a broadly traditional but updated and vigorous, self-conscious realism. The remarkable individuality and variety of some of this writing suggests the limitations of trying to find a single word to describe such diverse forms of fiction. For the traditional forms of the romance, the adventure novel and the socio-moral novel were flourishing alongside high modernism in South Africa, Australia, New Zealand, the United States, Canada and Britain. Glasgow's *Barren Ground* and *Virginia*, for example, used basically conventional forms, such as a Hardyesque employment of the power of place and landscape in the service of character depiction and thematic representation. Realist plotting and other familiar structural features, such as gradually unfolding moral development, are put by Glasgow in the service of a radical thematics: the young heroines of the novels reject 'the romance' genre of life for that of action and self-realization. Hall followed the example of Prichard and Henry Handel Richardson in Australia. Like Glasgow, Hall turned realism into a tool for exposing the patriarchal values of objectivity and verisimilitude upon which it depends. She and Richardson used emotional and sexual passion, instead of power of place, to infuse their fiction with intensity, while the radical lesbian thematics of *The Well of Loneliness* created a fascinating tension with Hall's orthodox narrative practices.

Regionalists like Ferber, Julia Peterkin, Pauline Smith and Holtby tempered their fiction of local colour to varying degrees with universal social-moral concerns, such as racism and political, class conflicts. Ferber's impressive novel *So Big* almost entirely eschews any romantic elements, in the same tradition as Josephine W. Johnson's splendid *Now in November*; both these Americans depicted in compellingly traditional narrative forms the radical and anti-realist thematics of women outperforming men in farming, labouring and other 'male' domains. Jean Devanny and Holtby, in New Zealand and England, marshalled a modified form of the romance, on the other hand, but to the same effect. Strong women are portrayed supporting less effective but macho men; the romance genre, however, is given a

rude twist at the end, with unexpected outcomes which tend to undercut the traditional aesthetic effect of the romance genre itself.

Peterkin and Fauset both created new fictional worlds in extending literature about American black experiences. Peterkin, a Southern white plantation owner herself, took the step of excluding white people from her narratives, writing about the deeply moving, rural lives of black, impoverished farmhands and the methods they devised to protect their humanity in the face of implacable white exploitation. Fauset, by contrast, set her novels in urban America, and explored the emotionally charged theme of light-skinned blacks 'passing' for white, as well as other issues involving racist attitudes. Her contemporary, Nella Larsen, also took 'passing' as her central theme, and caricatured it in her literary, self-referring versions of it. Fauset adopted what can be best described as a highly dramatic, complexly plotted fiction of fateful, impending revelations of Greek tragic proportions. Pauline Smith, like her great South African predecessor Olive Schreiner, never dared presume to touch directly upon the lives of black people. Yet her powerful, regional stories, and her novel about rural Afrikaner life, show white women being treated like child-bearing animals, good for little else than domestic work and the procreation of progeny for the male landowners, who tyrannize over everyone and everything, except nature itself.

Meanwhile, a 'second generation' of new modernists took experimentation into different and quite unexpected directions. Barnes, Rhys, Stevie Smith, Kay Boyle, Anaïs Nin, Newman and Ivy Compton-Burnett, amongst others, stretched, pulled and framed the novel form into new and unrecognizable canvases, influencing and influenced by William Faulkner, Henry Miller, F. Scott Fitzgerald, Ernest Hemingway, Malcolm Lowry and others. Rhys and Stevie Smith utterly debunked both realism and its 'opposite', the romance, the latter ruthlessly parodying the romance genre and its effects upon young women. Stevie Smith's high modernist, stream of consciousness technique is enriched by a witty and scathing rejection of earlier forms, as she ridiculed the Victorian domestic, romantic and adventure novels and all the gender stereotyping they represented. Her heroine is also a hero, in the tradition of Woolf's Orlando and Vita Sackville-West's Pepita; she goes out into the male world of war and politics, exceeds all male accomplishments, and then rejects male, dehumanizing activities just as she had rejected the female, domestic-romantic sphere. Stevie Smith's three novels form a virtual trilogy which, in a subtext, exposes traditional literary forms as analogies of social-gender stereotypes. Her style is as innovative as Woolf's or Faulkner's, in its challenge to notions of logic, surface order and even sanity, the last a patriarchal tool for subjugating women.

Rhys, on the other hand, while no less scathing and devastating in her critique of society and its gender/class/race prejudices, took experimentation in a new direction, more akin to Mansfield's earlier, indirect free style. Rhys's novels are precursors to Jane Bowles's wonderful immersions in the *demi-mondes* from North to South America. Rhys, like Bowles, used grotesqueries and bizarreries in her laconic and dry explorations of the lives of young and middle-aged women, driven – by their need for personal independence – to selling their bodies, instead of prostituting their souls in marriage.

Barnes and Nin are two other major second-generation modernists, who developed individuality to a degree, expressive of the Mansfield idea that 'art is self-development' and style is 'the artist's very self'. Both were influenced by the revaluations of psychoanalysis; both explored sexuality explicitly, whether lesbian or heterosexual. Both Nin and Barnes developed ornate, mannered styles and avoided plot for monologue, interiorities and emphases upon characterization. They used a direct presentation of thoughts and feelings unmediated by narrative description, objective views of other characters or events. Barnes's writing is also extremely varied; she moved from a style of minimal reportage in her early stories across a whole spectrum of works, until she arrived at the mannered satire of a Shakespearean verse drama. Indeed, within her most famous book, *Nightwood*, the reader discovers a welter of styles and practices, from the overwhelmingly evocative speeches of the doctor, to the baroque descriptions of the initial objective narrator, and, finally, to the mad, ghoulish howlings of the bisexual character Robin, fighting off the demands of categorization.

Other notable experiments in fiction which proclaimed the diversity of the period include Compton-Burnett's knife-like explorations of polite, upper middle-class British hypocrisies. With devastatingly understated simplicity, Compton-Burnett's play-like novel/dramas introduce a quite new genre into this infinitely variable form called fiction. Eschewing psychological development or sustained characterization, utterly excluding nature or landscape for the interior of houses, rooms and public schools, Compton-Burnett dismissed both realist enumeration of detailed description and stream of consciousness alike, with an indifferent flourish. She created a unique dialogue-world of exposed deceits and cruelties, which is almost unbearable to behold in its destructive results. The traditional domestic scene and the romance are turned upside down, as Compton-Burnett marshalled them in the service of an analysis of the selfish human immorality hidden behind a thin veneer of polite, socially acceptable gestures.

As if this range of writing were not already various enough for enjoyment, Isak Dinesen (Karen Blixen) began publishing her intricate and wonderful historical romances of intrigue and self-conscious story-telling, in the *Arabian Nights* tradition already tapped decades earlier by the remarkable British art historian and fiction writer, Vernon Lee. In these fabulous, imaginative tales of seventeenth- and eighteenth-century Europe, especially Italy, Dinesen's ironic, mannered flights of imagination into the supernatural and fantastic take the reader into faraway, exotic worlds of endless digressions, crossroads leading to more forking paths, and mistaken identities, masks and transformations. These and other Shakespearean devices of missent or purloined letters, unexpected trysts and tragic-comic recognition scenes plunge the reader into a fiction unlike anything else.

On the other side of the ocean, in quite a different realm, but contemporaneously, Hurston and Larsen were creating a momentum which became the famous Harlem Renaissance. Hurston, Fauset, Larsen, Langston Hughes, Jean Toomer and Countee Cullen were only some of the major figures of this remarkable flourishing of black literature in America in the 1920s. Hurston's novels owed their unique individuality in part to their author's extensive knowledge of dialect, folk tradition and black culture, which she had studied as an anthropologist in her ethnography work as a university student at Cornell. Hurston's central medium for conveying to the reader her thematics, her characterization and her artistic commitments is the constant reference to the power of language itself as the only means of liberation, when seized upon imaginatively. Her characters are shown struggling to realize themselves, to fight for their very existence as human beings, through their efforts to grasp verbal expression and bring into being a more articulate experience and awareness.

Also in America, Porter, Dorothy Parker and Anzia Yezierska perfected, each in her own inimitable way, innovations in the art of the short story, into which Mansfield had breathed new life. These three great short story writers took the genre into new areas of development. While Parker and Yezierska relied to a great extent upon dialogue, wit and comedy to portray suffering in the midst of the follies of life, Porter displayed a highly sophisticated irony, embedded into an apparently late, modified realism. Her stories and novellas explore most systematically the destructive human tendency towards nostalgia and sentimentality, which, Porter showed, involves a rewriting of the past to fit our selfish, present desires. Consequently, characters are portrayed as moving from one self-delusive state to another, and the consequences of this self-delusion are high tragedy. Yet, Porter's seriousness, like that of Parker and Yezierska, is saturated with an ironic sense of the absurdity of life – one means at least of minimizing the effects of the apparently inevitable delusions which none of us escapes. This theme of false memory and the relation of history to fiction informs many of Porter's best stories.

In contrast, Parker's stories rarely exhibit any narrative description of the kind Porter liberally exploits. Only light, brief passages disrupt the dialogues or interior monologues of these witty fictions. Through an almost uncanny genius for authentic speech, imbued by a cynical yet sympathetic narrative tone, Parker's satirical comedies of human relationships, misguided good intentions and failed communications constitute a wonderful, new short story form. These ironic, witty portrayals of ordinary, everyday incidents had embedded in them, however, surprisingly forceful critiques of sexual taboos and other social 'hang-ups', into which the reader is slyly enticed by the extreme intimacy and familiarity of Parker's 'innocent' tone.

Towards the end of the period, with the continuing late experiments of Woolf, Stein and other modernists, and under the influence of the new wave, comprised of Rhys, Barnes and Stevie Smith, fiction continued to be poured into new and unimagined forms of artistic expression, right up to the early 1940s. Some of the most notable advances were made by Sylvia Townsend Warner, Kate O'Brien and the early Stead, but Zelda Fitzgerald, Holtby, Rosamond Lehmann, Marjorie Barnard, Eleanor Dark and Margaret Kennedy made important contributions. With Bowen's remarkable stories and novels, a new scepticism set in about the radical modernist disruptions. Efforts to take account of the influence of psychology, as well as the cinema, photography and other forms of communication, led to a very conscious reassessment of what forms of expression innovations in fiction could properly take.

Warner's fiction is another example of a corpus of writing most notable for its sheer range and variety of forms. Somewhat in the tradition established by Rebecca West in the earlier period, Warner combined great imaginative skill with a forceful intellect, deeply interested as she was in moral and philosophical issues. Warner imbued her imaginative writings, whether in her historical novels, her romances or her fantastic writings, with the concept of the enabling force of ideas to transform life from mediocrity to fulfilment. Her novels portray women struggling with sexual stereotypes and finding ways round the institutionalized denial of access to power through education, money or influence. Her great Irish contemporary, Kate O'Brien, similarly fused imaginative fiction with profoundly intellectual and moral musings. In her impressive historical novel of sixteenth-century Spanish nobility, *That Lady*, O'Brien depicted the appalling and tragic consequences for a woman who refused to sacrifice her independence for the king's favour. And in her novel of quite astounding aesthetic beauty, *Mary Lavelle*, the equal of any novel in the twentieth century for sheer artistic achievement, O'Brien reached an intensity of passion and emotion, combined with an ironic detachment and intellectual force, which takes the novel of familiar conventions to a new level.

Stead's range is no less noteworthy; the diversity of her fiction can be seen from the innovative *Man Who Loved Children* – an infinitely rich mixture of comedy and tragedy, and wonderfully various in incident, character and ideas – to *For Love Alone*. The latter book is in complete contrast to its predecessor, which had rejected realist plotting, characterization and external correlatives in favour of grotesque tragicomic variety of incident, domestic interiority and family madness. *For Love Alone* shows Stead using conventional realist techniques to create an impassioned, lofty character study of the development of a young woman, from naïveté and romantic idealism to full womanhood. Later still, Stead experimented with an entirely different form, a picaresque novel in the tradition of Defoe's *Moll Flanders*, entitled *Letty Fox: Her Luck*. In spite of the wide diversity of styles and genres of Stead's novels, most of them share one powerfully drawn, systematically recurring theme, namely, the effort of women to throw off patriarchal tyranny in every aspect of their lives, whether financial, emotional, sexual or political.

In contrast to the diversity of the above innovators, Lehmann's fiction is less wide-ranging, though in her later years she branched out into new types. She did, however, perfect both the *Bildungsroman* and the romance; in several novels, she followed the growth of her young heroine from adolescence to adulthood, and while her narrative practices were relatively conventional, within the bounds of the form she achieved an aesthetic perfection and emotional expression of great impact and depth. She too, like her contemporaries, took the romance into new areas of significance, as she explored, for example, not only the reasons for the failure of women to achieve emotional fulfilment; her novels portray the entrapment of men in different but equally tragic prisons of inhumanity, such as ambition, greed, brutal lust and colossal egotism.

Bowen's fiction constitutes a major indication of transition in fiction of this period, from the dominance of modernist and other experiments to a new seriousness and a more direct commitment to a socio-moral literature. This may in part be a result of the soberness induced by World War I and its terrible aftermath, or it

may be that experimentation is almost always followed by a period of consolidation and pause for reflection. Bowen took in the insights of psychological writings, reflected upon the implications for literature of the cinema and other new technological developments, noted the experiments of modernists, and then proceeded to create startlingly original stories and several novels of great merit. Her most noteworthy fictions are, arguably, *The House in Paris, To the North* and numerous stories, though these novels have not always been critics' favourites. *The House in Paris* is a novel of breathtakingly beautiful aesthetic construction and impressive congruence of form and content, rarely so perfectly realized. Under the gaze of a young girl in passage through Paris on a one-day visit, a lifetime of passion, obsession and the struggle for rationality are played out in an Aristotelian unity of time/place/manner, with Freudian ideas fused into the text.

The House in Paris was published by Bowen in 1935, yet six years later Woolf's posthumous novel, *Between the Acts*, brought modernist experimentation to a new intensity and a new style of fiction. In this novel, Woolf achieved a literary work intensely intertextual and self-referential, yet in a much more accessible and superficially conventional narrative than her earlier stream of consciousness and other modernist experiments. This novel anticipates many of the central devices of the next fifty years which are now referred to as post-modernism, as though *Between the Acts* were almost a recipe or a prediction of the direction in which fiction would move and the forms it would tend to take. The text hardly lacks a single characteristic 'post-modernist' element, as frame-breaking, metafictional loops, authorial personas and intrusions, portrayal of audiences resembling readers, recursive embedding, radical instability in meaning, mixings and violations of genre, disruptive direct address, and allusions to other literature enrich the text at every turn. Time and history become the main subject matter of a play within a novel about a play; audiences struggle to interpret as the players literally hold up a mirror at the end, as if to sum up what they have been doing all along; and nature and ordinary life intrude into art, with cows bellowing and airplanes humming overhead. Sinister shadowings behind many events suggest Julia Kristeva's 'chora' intruding into the order and rationality of the surface.

To sum up, by the 1920s, once novelists had had time to absorb the shock of the radical modernist innovations, both literary and social, of the previous twenty or so years, the modernist experiments of disruption, defamiliarization and stream of consciousness were well launched, and were already undergoing considerable alterations. The early modernist changes had been characterized by Willa Cather and others as an avowed desire to clear out the old, heavy, encumbering furniture of realism. Traditional, formal conventions of the novel, which had come to be seen as inalienable characteristics or the 'facts' of the best novels, included carefully ordered plot, stable point of view, relative objectivity, causality, linear time progression, full character development, balance between description and dialogue, so-called 'ordinary' language, and traditional notions of shape, unity and progressive thematic development. Cather, in 'The novel démeublé', amongst other essays, saw the need to sweep away the old props and sets of realism in favour of what she called 'compression', and her own fiction testifies to the success of her rejection. Likewise Woolf, in 'Mr Bennett and Mrs Brown', argued for the need for a new kind of fiction which would challenge the assumptions underpinning the novelistic formalities of the nineteenth century. Moreover, ideas about the nature of the self as a unified identity with autonomy were undermined by Freud's emphasis upon the unconscious, while the function of language and art in life was reassessed in view of the work of William James and C.S. Peirce.

Under the further influence of discoveries by James Frazer in anthropology and the increasing understanding of Darwinism and other ideas about evolution, as well as the new theories about relativity, and so on, literature itself evolved self-consciously into a more relative and diverse form.

Interestingly enough, however, even the radical modernists preserved many of the most familiar motifs and structuring devices of the novel, indeed of art itself, in the midst of their stylistic, linguistic and structural disruptions and upheavals. They made abundant use of the journey, the passage or the outing, as well as travel to exotic places; they revitalized the conventions of the quest, the encounter, the recognition scene, the conflict, the transformation. They adapted the holiday, the dinner party, the circus, the masquerade, the dance; they designed plays within stories and novels framed by storytellers; they portrayed characters struggling to interpret or 'read' each other as well as the meaning of events and themselves. They used motifs of mistaken identity, romantic love, moral struggle and self-development as the vehicles and themes for their experiments in language, form and theme. And they made use of old techniques of the interruptive letter, the diary and other documents, as well as the dream, flashbacks, fantasy and memory to structure their fiction. They used the mirror or looking-glass, the clock, windows and doors, houses and rooms, lamps and other references to lighting, allusions to life as a drama, and other traditional images and motifs to add richness and density to their prose. Thus, these 'patterns' provided much continuity in the midst of modernist transformations.

Chapter 6

Individual Authors, 1918–1945

Ellen Glasgow 1873–1945

Ellen Glasgow was born in Richmond, Virginia, in 1873, to a well-off Southern family, and began writing short stories and poems while in her teens. A draft of *The Descendant*, her first published novel (New York, 1897), was written when she was 17, and was received with considerable praise. Amongst her nearly twenty novels, the best-known are *The Sheltered Life* (Garden City, N.Y., 1932), which shows profound influences from William Faulkner, *Vein of Iron* (New York, 1935) and *Barren Ground* (Garden City, N.Y., 1925), a remarkable epic of harsh, rural life in Virginia, and of a young woman's painful efforts to carve out an independent existence for herself. *The Woman Within* (published posthumously in New York, in 1954) is Glasgow's autobiographical account of both her own painful encounters with deafness at an early age, and her life in Richmond, where she lived until her death, except for a five-year period in New York City and travels in Europe. An extremely successful novelist in her lifetime, she met Thomas Hardy (whom she greatly admired), Joseph Conrad, John Galsworthy and other fellow writers, and was awarded the Howells Medal in 1941, and the Pulitzer Prize in 1942. Her collected stories were published in 1973 and some letters in 1958, and there was an edition of her works as early as 1938. There are a number of biographies of her, and the growing body of secondary literature, including numerous book-length studies, testifies to the rebirth of her reputation as an American novelist of the stature of such writers as Edith Wharton, Willa Cather and Eudora Welty.

In a 1933 preface to *Barren Ground*, Glasgow criticized all her fiction preceding that novel as being so thin that it appeared two-dimensional, except for *Virginia* (Garden City, N.Y., 1913). She argued that in *Barren Ground* and *The Sheltered Life*, an added dimension, a 'universal rhythm', is conveyed. Like Welty some decades later, Glasgow described this three-dimensionality as involving a 'brooding spirit of place', and more, even beneath that, the 'whole movement of life'. As with Hardy, Cather and Welty, one of her greatest achievements as a novelist is her unique, artistic handling of place and the central role which its spirit plays in her texts. Another unique character of her writing is her particular use of Southern US landscape and social life as a means, a focus, a location for writing about human nature, or, as she put it, for illuminating experience by the imagination. Indeed, this was for her the very definition of the novel: 'experience illumined by imagination'. In Glasgow's much longer, more substantial preface to *The Sheltered Life*, she provided her readers with some very useful terminological tools for enriching our response, many of which, as with Cather, Wharton and Virginia Woolf, are rooted in Coleridgean principles.

For example, she referred (though only in passing) to 'the ironic art of fiction' and to the special delights such fiction reveals. *The Sheltered Life* is arguably her greatest success in this, and as such is most lucidly revelatory of what this ironic art is. The novel is structured by means of two contrasting points of view (within a third person unified narrative), which run throughout its almost three hundred pages, except for an extraordinary interlude of twenty-five pages inserted a third of the way into the story. The artistic effect of this interlude is similar to that of Tom Outland's story in Cather's *The Professor's House*, and the father's reveries in Kate O'Brien's *Mary Lavelle*. That is, it acts utterly to disrupt our reading of the novel, completely refocusing the ninety-five preceding pages and the one hundred and seventy pages which follow. It adds, in a single, incredibly impressive artistic gesture, a new dimension and depth to the rest of the story. In this twenty-five page-reverie of the ancient, 83-year-old General Archbald (who represents one of the two points of view, while Jenny Blair, his adolescent granddaughter, represents the other), the plot and drama of the novel are suspended in time. Contemplation and memory are themselves the implicit subject matter of 'The Deep Past', as the interlude is entitled. For Glasgow, this brooding contemplation was the very origin of works of art and the precondition of imaginative activity.

'The Deep Past' constitutes one of the most explicit, naked embodiments of imagination itself that can be found in fiction. It is also a living example of Glasgow's belief in the importance for artistic creativity both of 'a wild sanctuary, an inaccessible valley of reveries' within the psyche, and of artistic endeavour as the effort 'to touch life on every side; but [to] keep the central vision of the mind, the inmost light, untouched and untouchable'. In the interlude, the old general does precisely that, illustrating it, demonstrating it to the reader in one of the most sustained imaginative passages ever written. This passage has often been compared, justifiably, to Faulkner's second chapter in *The Sound and the Fury* (published 1929, that is, three years before Glasgow's novel). In Faulkner's novel, the South is viewed through several eyes, but chapter 2 is the meditative, impressionistic view of Benjy Compson, the 33-year-old 'idiot', in a version of the stream of consciousness technique which shares with the Glasgow interlude a sombre, metaphysical lyricism and technical brilliance. 'The Deep Past' is a *tour de force* of Glasgow's definition of the novel as 'experience illumined by imagination'.

This embodiment of the imagination in part adds the third dimension to Glasgow's novel which she explicitly sought, but it also helps us to an understanding of her phrase; 'the ironic art of fiction'. Throughout the rest of the novel, the two-fold, alternating narrative perspectives of Jenny Blair and General Archbald already constitute an example of what William Blake called two-fold vision, or vision which reaches beyond the discursive reasoning powers into relational apprehension. Youth and age, innocence and experience, view life through different but complementary spectacles, and participate in it accordingly. The interlude seems at first to be merely reminiscence from the General's perspective on his long, painful life, a perspective running also throughout the novel. But gradually it dawns on the reader that we are in the presence of the brooding contemplation of imagination itself; a higher perspective than the General's personal point of view is being depicted, a perspective which is irony itself. While embedded in the General's personal perspective, it is yet something different, which allows the reader to gain a glimpse of a critical consciousness, an artistic self-consciousness perhaps, which is the ironic art. A critical self-watching of the processes of artistic creation, on the one hand, and of meditative rumination, on the other, characterizes irony; a detachment and distance are implied which make space for self-observation and self-criticism, those preconditions for self-construction and self-development. This third dimension is so nakedly portrayed in 'The Deep Past' that, once we recognize it for what it is, we realize that it is built into the whole of the novel and is implicit throughout, even if only explicit in the interlude.

This realization changes the novel. At first, *The Sheltered Life* seems to be primarily a study in obsession, particularly sexual obsession, and its disastrous consequences. This psychological dimension is enriched by a complementary analysis of the social forces which encourage such obsession and its consequent destructiveness. The novel furthers its theme by exploring related forms of suffering, indeed by portraying life itself as too often gratuitous suffering. The title of the novel certainly refers in part to the sheltered, spoiled life of a certain class of people in such a Southern town of the early twentieth century. Glasgow explained in her preface, however, that the title, for her, meant something quite opposite: 'what it implies to me is the effort of one human being to stand between another and life.' This comment occurs in the context of comments about pain, suffering, war and destruction, and she further noted: 'The old man is the real protagonist of the book . . . He represents the tragedy, wherever it appears, of the civilized man in a world that is not civilized.'

These comments, along with some others in the preface, help to take the reader into the deeper strata of the text. For example, Glasgow had earlier described Jenny Blair's point of view in relation to the General's as follows: 'he would remain permanently at the centre of vision, while opposing him on the farther side he would meet the wide, blank, unreflective gaze of inexperience.' 'Unreflective' seems to be one of the key words in this statement: experience not reflected upon, not 'illumined by imagination', is at the root of much pain, suffering and tragedy. 'Inexperience' refers not so much to youth as to lack of reflection, which characterizes people of all ages, though, because reflection comes only with effort and time, youth is particularly vulnerable to it. Eva Birdsong, the local beauty and neighbour of Jenny and the General, was in many ways as inexperienced and certainly as obsessed at 40 as Jenny Blair was at 18. George Birdsong, Eva's husband, was the most unreflective of these three main characters, though Glasgow portrayed him sympathetically, too, in so far as she articulated the social and natural forces which, in part, made him what he is.

The Sheltered Life may be overtly a novel about sexual obsession and the psychological forces and social arrangements which make it happen with such frequency. Yet if we allow the twenty-five pages of 'The Deep Past' to refocus the novel as a whole, as they are designed to do, we find the novel using obsession not as the theme but as a vehicle for the artistic portrayal of a different theme, namely, the importance of imagination, contemplation and reflection in our lives, if we are to gain possession of ourselves as human beings, and not remain at the level of unconscious animal life. The General is the living embodiment of imaginative contemplation, contrasted with obsession and its destruction, which are explicitly portrayed as the nearly inevitable outcome of unimaginative living. For it is imagination alone which can shelter us from the suffering inherent in life. Yet Glasgow raised the stakes, and irony intrudes, when, through the General's reverie, she revealed that imagination cannot shelter us from anything but the lower, animal forms of suffering. The fully ironic consciousness involves the awareness that the greatest suffering and genuine tragedy may occur at the point of greatest imaginative reflection, that 'tragedy of the civilized man in a world that is not civilized'. Imagination, far from sheltering us, brings with it precisely an awareness of the inherent tragedy of human life: tragic in part because of the conflicting needs within us; in part because of the need for intimate human relations which are never entirely satisfactory; in part because of a portion of our unconscious life embedded deeply within human nature which is bent on self-destruction. Yet, experience illumined by imagination not only brings what Glasgow described as a 'release of mind' and a 'subdued rapture'. It is also one of our deepest needs as human beings, as strong as sexual needs and basic hunger and thirst. It is a description of the human mind itself, in a sense, a description of what it is to be a self-conscious, sentient human. Such reflective experience may bring a high consciousness of tragedy, but Glasgow's novel suggests that if life is essentially tragic (at least as humans have so far known it), then to be conscious of this reality is less destructive and more humane than to be unconsciously blundering around in it, increasing the suffering and destruction.

The Sheltered Life is Glasgow's most aesthetically perfected novel because of the fine congruence between form and content. That is, her two overt narrative perspectives express the nature of human consciousness and human experience as not inherently dualistic. The double perspective is integrated, and is also a statement about the necessity both to experience life and to reflect on experience. But the third dimension is reached not as a reconciliation of opposites, but as a further articulation of the necessity to reflect on experience imaginatively, and not only analytically or discursively. At this third level, imagination (embodied in the General as a high level of self-consciousness) is revealed to be the instrument not only of artistic creation, but also of moral good, as it is in O'Brien's *Mary Lavelle*. And this unification of moral good and artistic beauty is at the heart of Glasgow's novel's form and thematics. That is, only through imaginative perception are the compassion and pity at the basis of moral good possible, as the General's reverie confirms. Art and morality become possible in the context of a self-consciousness which is rarefied and deepened by that brooding contemplation leading to moral detachment and to the 'ironic art of fiction', where it is understood not only that 'the wonder in every age was not that most men were savage, but that a few men were civilized.' Irony shows us, tragically, that 'these few were the clowns in the parade'.

Julia M. Peterkin 1880–1961

Pulitzer Prize winner in 1929 for *Scarlet Sister Mary* (Indianapolis, Ind., 1928), Julia Peterkin was born in South Carolina and began a teaching career after gaining degrees at a local college, a career which she gave up upon her marriage in 1903 in order to become mistress of a large plantation, Lang Syne. She took her position very seriously, and entered into the lives of her black employees to such an extent that they became her main subject matter when she began writing some years later, after encouragement from her piano teacher, who was impressed by the stories she told him. After nearly two decades on the plantation, Peterkin began publishing sketches and stories in various journals in the early 1920s. Encouraged by H.L. Mencken, the established critic and literary editor of the *Smart Set* (1908–24), who was delighted to see that his complaints of a literary vacuum in the South were being disproven by Peterkin and other women, such as Frances Newman, Peterkin devoted herself to her authentic and powerfully innovative depiction of black experience and culture on the plantation. Her records of the beliefs, legends, superstitions, values and terrible struggle of black people in the face of an implacable fate not only constitute an immensely valuable historical record; they are also compelling novels whose strengths lie in the authenticity of the characters and the powerful portrayals of incident and plot which give the works a tightly woven unity.

Green Thursday (New York, 1924) is Peterkin's first published book; it is a collection of the sketches and tales published in the *Smart Set* and other journals. Her first novel, *Black April* (Indianapolis, Ind.), appeared three years later; it charts the tragedy of the central character, April, whose elemental force carries him to country-wide success until he is finally defeated through his pride. In this first novel, Peterkin established herself as a specialist in the distinctive life, culture and dialect of the Gullah Negroes, who populated the South Carolina coast and areas further south. She also began the work of portraying with intelligence and understanding the folk culture, values and religious beliefs of the Gullahs to a white audience. *Black April* is most widely acclaimed, however, for being probably the first novel in English by a white author to characterize a black protagonist as a fully realized human being in all his psychological complexity, conflict and depth. *Scarlet Sister Mary*, published only a year later, gained Peterkin even greater admiration, and was dramatized successfully two years later by David Reed after being awarded the Pulitzer Prize. The vibrant strength of its black heroine and Peterkin's deft handling of her passionate sexuality made this character one of the most impressive in American literature of the period, according to many critics and reviewers. Peterkin was praised further for a depiction of black characters of such authenticity and compassion as could normally be expected only from a black person who had actually experienced life from this perspective. Her final major novel, *Bright Skin* (Indianapolis, Ind., 1932), concerns itself with the issue Alice Dunbar-Nelson had broached, namely, the potentially awkward situation of a mulatto heroine in a black world, a subject which Jessie Fauset explored in *The Chinaberry Tree* (1931). Black–white relations were almost never a subject of Peterkin's novels or stories, because she never included white people in her narratives except in a distant world which only occasionally impinged personally on black interrelationships, while all the time it exerted an oppressive and limiting force on possibilities for fulfilment and freedom of movement.

With her realistic and sympathetic representation of the tragedy and harshness of life for black people, as well as its strength and vibrancy in the struggle against a formidable fate, Peterkin genuinely broadened the range of early twentieth-century fiction. She also published *Roll, Jordan Roll* (New York, 1933), a book of photographs with a descriptive commentary which is a visual chronicle of life on her plantation. Her final book, *A Plantation Christmas* (Boston and New York, 1934), is in a lighter vein. Her stories were collected and edited by Frank Durham in 1970 (Columbia, S.C.).

Jessie Redmon Fauset 1882–1961

'The portrayal of black people calls increasingly for black writers', Fauset argued in *Crisis*, the NAACP (National Association for the Advancement of Colored People) journal she edited for a period. Not only did Fauset become a writer of stature herself, she helped and encouraged a number of young black writers whose activities culminated in the Harlem Renaissance of the 1920s and 1930s. She was born in New Jersey of an upper middle-class black family (her father was a minister), and grew up in Philadelphia, later attending Cornell University and graduating Phi Beta Kappa in 1905. She returned to Philadelphia to take a master's degree in 1906 from the University of Pennsylvania, after which, like so many talented young women, she embarked on high-school teaching in the Baltimore–Washington area, specializing in French and Latin. Fauset soon turned to a more literary career, however, when she became editor of *Crisis*, and contributed stories, essays and sketches as well as giving help and advice to other aspiring black writers. In 1924, after having been sent by *Crisis* to Europe, she spent a year in Paris studying at the Sorbonne and experiencing the (at that time) less racist environment of urban France. In the same year her first book, *There is Confusion* (New York), was published. The novel depicts the moral struggle of black women and men trying to achieve a professional life in the context of a racist society. The black heroine strives to become an opera singer while helping a young black man to realize his dream of being a medical doctor. Issues of feminist import as well as racism are central to the text, as they are to her next novel, *Plum Bun* (New York, 1929). In this second work, Fauset took up a theme of interest to many other black writers, namely, the almost existential, moral struggle involved for some very light-skinned black people in accepting and indeed embracing one's race. The novel depicts two black sisters, one of whom finds strength in her heritage, while the other tries to pass for white and is exposed to the brutality and sexism of a white lover.

In probably her best-known novel, *The Chinaberry Tree* (New York, 1931, 1969), Fauset again took these themes of black women struggling with the moral and emotional dilemmas created by their racist environment, and how they find ways of coming to terms with, and even defeating, the destructive elements which are designed to frustrate their self-realization. Issues of existential import relating specifically to black experience are handled with shrewdness and insight. Her characters are often shown in these novels of social mores and constraints as burdened by a legacy from the past which they must escape or turn to advantage, as in her final novel, *Comedy American Style* (New York, 1933). This treats of the anguish and frustration of another black woman struggling with the oppressive, racist, but especially sexist forces constraining her.

Fauset is sometimes said to have been less radical than other black writers because she sought to show, as she argued explicitly in the introduction to *The Chinaberry Tree*, that black people are essentially no different from white people and have the same feelings, needs, and aspirations. But the emphasis of her comments is upon our shared, fundamental humanity, and upon the need to let this shared humanity help to bridge the often harmful differences between people. Fauset was not even implicitly taking the liberal white or black position that black people should aspire to white values or to be like white people. Her literary representation of black characters in her four novels confirms her understanding of the differences that are strengths, and that need to be respected if human societies are to realize the variety at the heart of all creativity.

Fauset mostly used fairly traditional narrative conventions in her novels, but she made skilful use of complex plot in *The Chinaberry Tree*, for example. There, a double plot is finely woven together to express artistically the tensions and conflicts, at the specific thematic level, between the main characters, Melissa and Laurentine. Carefully developed plot and dialogue reinforce Fauset's most energetic technical accomplishment, namely, a fateful, dramatic quality, which hovers over the work and lends a Greek-tragic determinism to the novel. This tone draws all the other elements of complex plot, thematic conflict and dialogue into an impending dramatic revelation about the blood relationship between Melissa and the man she loves, but cannot marry. Fauset explained herself that 'to be a Negro in America posits a dramatic situation . . . the mere juxtaposition of the races brings into existence this fateful quality.' She strove successfully to portray this situation in fictional form.

Pauline Smith 1882–1959

Although Pauline Smith left South Africa at the age of 12 to live most of the rest of her life in Britain, the environment of her childhood made a profound and unforgettable impression upon her, and it was the district in South Africa where she grew up that was the setting for her small but eloquent body of fiction. Born in Oudtshoorn in the southwest part of the Cape Province, in a plateau called the Little Karoo, Smith suffered intermittent ill-health throughout her early life which badly interrupted her education, a matter about which she was painfully sensitive. Her Scottish father was the physician for the entire district, and she accompanied him in his long visits to patients through the often drought-stricken, desolate and flat landscape about which she was to write with great eloquence and feeling decades later. As in the case of Sarah Orne Jewett, these trips with her father gave her an invaluable opportunity, which she did not fail to grasp, to observe the austere and difficult life of the veld farmers. A sensitive and musical ear made it possible for her to reproduce effectively, if not exactly correctly, the dialect and speech patterns of the Afrikaner villagers and farmers whom she observed. Later, these childhood experiences and her father's influence were to provide her with the means of becoming one of the most admired translators of Afrikaans culture and consciousness into the English language and literary tradition. Her stylistic representations of the rhythms and speech patterns of rural

Afrikaans were one of her characteristic literary effects and devices for entering into this Boer world and the daily life of its inhabitants, with such intelligence, authenticity and sensitivity as one could only have expected had she been one of them herself. She conveyed the particular complexity of emotions of these insulated, rural Afrikaners against the backdrop of a severe and at times overpoweringly desolate landscape. These often featureless surroundings function aesthetically to foreground the particularity and distinctiveness of the emotions of these intense but constrained people.

Smith wrote one novel, *The Beadle* (London, 1926), and just under a dozen short stories collected in the famous volume *The Little Karoo* (London, 1925; enlarged London, 1930); all were about Afrikaner life, and were based on her childhood and a few brief visits made later in life, including her return in 1905 and again in 1913. After her father's death in 1898, she began a rather nomadic life with her mother and sister, moving from England and Scotland, where she had been sent to continue her schooling, to the Continent and back again. During this earlier period she had written a number of verses and sketches for children, eventually published in a collection entitled *Platkops Children* (London, 1935); some of her early stories had appeared decades earlier, often under the pseudonym Janet Tamson. In 1908, while staying near Vevey, she met Arnold Bennett, who helped her to overcome her reticence about her writing and the lack of confidence with which her poor education had burdened her. With his encouragement and help, she had a story, 'The Pain', published in Middleton Murry's journal, the *Adelphi*. (Her published account of her relationship with Bennett is called, simply, *A. B.* (London, 1933).) This story is an understated, beautifully austere account of the enduring love of two elderly people who cannot bear to be separated due to the wife's illness. Austerity and simplicity of style were also to characterize Smith's later stories and her novel, and function as one of her central aesthetic formalities, alongside her use of desolate landscape.

The Beadle is Smith's novel of Afrikaner life on the farm Harmonie, which is the centre of the large surrounding district of a sparsely populated valley of farmers and rural labourers.

Like Olive Schreiner, she never touched, except by (powerful) innuendo, the matter of the black labourers or the relationships between white and black people. And, like Schreiner, she adopted another Jane Austen convention: she rarely made reference to life outside the valley, or to the momentous events going on in South Africa during the time Smith wrote her fiction. Her location and dialect are deliberately regional, but her themes are universal, as she wove the lives of various characters around Andrina, the 'orphan' (unacknowledged illegitimate daughter), and her awakening from passivity to sexual and emotional experience. On one level, *The Beadle* constitutes a feminist rewriting of the Biblical Garden of Eden myth, with the innocent woman seduced and deserted by the Englishman Henry Nind. But Smith's interest in both the rewriting of myth and religion and sexuality was too sophisticated not to call into question the Puritanical attitude which equates sexual knowledge with a fall. In her account, Andrina's experience is portrayed as a spiritual and moral transformation, a coming into fuller consciousness of her individual life as a woman, a lover and eventually a mother. That she comes into a fuller existence out of her semi-servanthood through her love of a man unworthy of her (after having been treated as a virtual servant by her own unacknowledged father) is not essentially more than a depiction of normal life by Smith. But it may mark a literary departure from D.H. Lawrence's portrayal of sexual relations as ideally between a master and a servant. For Smith showed Andrina coming to a full spiritual awakening through her equation of sexual love with a divine gift, a ministering to the needs of her own body–soul as well as to that of the loved one. In this novel and in numerous stories, such as 'The Fathers', 'Desolation' or 'The Sisters', the reality of women's lives under patriarchy, whether benign or despotic, is portrayed by Smith through a variety of formal conventions, with a detachment that is more damning than an overt complaint would have been. Women are shown to be seen often as little more than beasts to bear children, so that men can multiply their wealth, while a drought-stricken natural world is itself also described in terms of a suffering, living animal on some occasions, and as a destructive enemy to humans on others. But this humanizing of nature occurs always with an understatement and simplicity which avoid overt moralizing.

Virginia Woolf 1882–1941

Born at Hyde Park Gate to Leslie Stephen and Julia Duckworth, Virginia Woolf settled in London with her sister Vanessa and her brothers in 1904, where they and their circle of friends formed the Bloomsbury Group. In 1912, Woolf married Leonard, having already established herself as a regular contributor to the *Times Literary Supplement*. She published her first novel, *The Voyage Out* (London), in 1915, to considerable acclaim, and she and Leonard founded the Hogarth Press in 1917. While in *Night and Day* (London, 1919) Woolf consolidated her skill with more traditional narrative elements, by *Jacob's Room* (Richmond, 1922) she demonstrated that the modernist elements already evident in *The Voyage Out* would be her central, future means of developing her individuality as a novelist. More radical experimentation with plot, characterization, narrative point of view, style, narrative time, description and event is evident in *Mrs Dalloway* (London, 1925), *To the Lighthouse* (London, 1927) and *The Waves* (London, 1931). By this time, Woolf had complete fluency with such narrative practices as stream of consciousness, shifting narrative point of view, de-emphasized plot and fluid, impressionistic style. All these techniques radicalized notions of artistic unity, the nature of the self, the relation of internal world to externality, and the importance of art – not so much as a representation of external reality, or the novel – as a repository of ideas. Art and the novel are seen as imaginative embodiments of the nature of the human heart and of the intelligible universe within which it lives. Later, Woolf completed *The Years* (London, 1937), and one of her most self-conscious, experimental and successful novels, *Between the Acts* (London), was published posthumously in 1941, after her suicide.

Virginia Woolf not only expanded our conception of the novel; she was also a remarkable critic, essayist, and biographer. *Orlando* (London, 1928) is an imaginative, fictional biography of a male–female character spanning four centuries, while *Flush* (London, 1933) recounts, ironically, the life of the Brownings' dog! *A Room of One's Own* (London, 1929) and *Three Guineas* (London, 1938), are long essays on social issues relating to male/female arrangements, while *The Common Reader* (London, 1925; London, 1932) is a fine collection of Woolf's critical writing. Further collections include *The Death of the Moth* (London, 1942) and *Granite and Rainbow* (London, 1958); see *The Essays of Virginia Woolf*, ed. Andrew McNeillie, 4 vols (London, 1986–94). Letters, diaries and short stories have also been published.

Woolf described the death of her father in 1904 as the opening out of her own life into writing, books and social and intellectual companionship. Her circle included Lytton Strachey, John Maynard Keynes, Duncan Grant, Katherine Mansfield, E.M. Forster, T.S. Eliot, Vita Sackville-West and many, many others. Yet, she described herself as a member of the 'Society of Outsiders', referring not only to the exclusive patriarchy of upper-class educated males, about which Katherine Mansfield had also complained, but to an intellectual and moral freedom, achieved only through an independence of mind which is not compatible with traditional institutions. One of the recurring themes of her novels is the experiences of characters of such an independent spirit and the various modes of coping with insiders and more conventional situations. Also conveyed in her novels is the clash amongst the different mentalities, whether portrayed as within the psyche of a single character or as a conflict between different characters. Indeed, Woolf's novels constantly question the notion of identity and individuality, portraying characters as complex social entities whose boundaries are much less fixed than we usually think. Characters and situations are dynamic and multiple.

Woolf's fiction thus challenges current (humanist and patriarchal) concepts of identity, relationship, society, culture and morality, as she chose to write from the margins, to some extent, and to question prevailing conceptions and dualisms as mere opinion and not fact. For example, she rarely wrote directly of political and large, historical events in her novels. Yet, in such a novel as *Between the Acts*, politics invades at every nuance of action, description and event. It also invades in a more intellectual and pervasive

sense: the politics is in the narrative practices, which break down the political assumptions, prejudices and beliefs which rule our everyday lives and determine our power and social relations, both with each other and within ourselves.

In one of her most famous essays, 'Character in Fiction' (1924, a very close version of the famous essay, 'Mr Bennett and Mrs Brown', and published in a pamphlet by Hogarth Press), Woolf argued for the well-known idea of the centrality of character in novels. She then proceeded, however, to distinguish and qualify her notion of 'character' from that of the Victorians, the realists and other novelists. She argued in this essay, and in many others, against the notion that character portrayal in novels is best achieved by detailed facts, descriptive enumeration of houses, cities and surroundings, or elaborate plots, complex events, and other 'peripheral' matters as the means of creating character. In an essay on Forster around the same time, she extolled the importance for genuine character construction in fiction of a concern with consciousness and the inner life, thoughts, sensations and feelings which crowd our minds and preoccupy us consciously and unconsciously: 'it is the private life that holds out the mirror to infinity.' In essays on Jane Austen, amongst others, Woolf elaborated this idea of the absolute centrality for fiction of conveying inner human nature and consciousness, and, she said, thereby life itself, in all its specificity, oddity and significance. Moreover, this could be achieved, indeed must be achieved, with a few deft strokes, by means of the merest trifles – not through enumeration of hundreds of tangential facts to do with houses and furnishings, dress and external appearance. In 'Character in Fiction', moreover, Woolf explained that a character is real for her if it makes her see and think and feel all sorts of things, but *through its eyes and mind*. We see many things, have many ideas, cherish many values and beliefs, but in character portrayal we must see through the eyes of some character with a particular, specific personality and consciousness not our own. This mastery of a mind's perspective in a few deft strokes is almost Eudora Welty's definition of the imagination and of the art of fiction, as it was P.B. Shelley's.

Another central argument of Woolf's throughout her essays, which ties up with character creation, is her commitment to overcoming the pretentious division between writer and reader. First, she argued that interest in and the reading of character are an essential part of all our daily lives; our relations with people, our happiness and success, depend upon reading character. Second, she suggested that there must be 'a close and equal alliance between us [writer and reader]' if books are to be healthy and strong, for they are a direct result of that alliance. Finally, she concluded by suggesting that a character created in fiction is actually the very 'spirit we live by, life itself'. Truth, reality, life itself are in that character which springs from the lively and fertile fusion of writer and audience.

Woolf's fiction helps us to interpret these comments more fully as we observe her techniques and results in her novels. What comes through in her fictional characters is the essential relatedness and social nature of individuality itself, as well as of language, art and fiction. Individuality is not best understood as some autonomous, independent existence, but as existence embedded in the lives of other people, society and culture. Neither language, nor art, nor fiction is anything if separated from its characteristic being as acts of social communication amongst individuals (those social beings, not those autonomous souls or spirits or independent consciousnesses, for whom relation is an extra, added aspect). Against such ideologies, whether stemming from religious impulses or from philosophical misconceptions about the nature of human consciousness, Woolf's fiction showed that the social dimension of character is its very spirit, and the 'essence' of consciousness is relationship. Consequently, Woolf's fiction portrays reality and truth as never independent of human social interaction and communication: absolute, objective, transcendent, eternal truth or reality is a hypostasization of relations into independent substances. In 'Moments of Being', but also in many other essays, she explicitly defined truth and reality as living only in the daily trifles and common events of our ordinary interactions, not in abstractions, transcendental religions, philosophies or 'objective' sciences. It is not mathematics, science or religion which are our reality; character, human nature and consciousness are our truth, our reality.

Woolf had a profoundly Socratic world view, then. Her attitude to truth, reality and individuality as essentially social has the character of Socratic wisdom. Living neither in some independent individual consciousness nor in a transcendent realm, truth exists in the social, the conventional and the transient. Reality and truth come alive, indeed, in the very clash, the collision, of different consciousnesses – whether two, or three, or a multitude of different points of view within a novel – or in the collision of the novel with a reader's different view. There are no impersonal, objective truths to be winnowed out of these artifacts. Consequently, Woolf's novels end 'without any point to [them]': we modern novelists, Woolf explained, look at human nature, at psychology – not at issues, at societies, at externalities. We see all these things only through the eyes of some character. For her, as for Carson McCullers, for example, each one of us is a 'we', not just an 'I', and reality/truth comes into being only in the collision of varying points of view and consciousness.

There is, then, a celebration of colliding, varying points of view in Woolf's novels, as the fullest possible expression of human life which is our truth, our reality. However, Woolf never presented some resolution of conflicting consciousnesses or of incompatible points of view. Reality – truth – does not lie in the triumph of one character's view over another's. A single point of view, moreover, rarely hovers over the novel as the 'author's' detached consciousness, as it does in much fiction. Points of view are submerged in the characters' cacophony. Meanwhile, the author (as unobtrusively yet as interruptedly as Miss LaTrobe or Mrs Ramsay), tries to direct or observe the goings on of her characters in a way that is limited by the powers that escape the author-observer. Yet these limited powers give such texts their greatest truth, namely diversity of consciousnesses.

Characters in Woolf's fiction are often portrayed as unfinished, as still developing, just as the novels' endings are not conclusive conclusions. Part of their immense vitality comes from this sense that they are not static, but growing, struggling to develop, to understand. Whether we look at Mrs Ramsay or Isa, Lily or Rachel, Miss LaTrobe or the characters in *The Waves*, such as Bernard, or *The Years*, or Mrs Dalloway and Septimus, we see struggle for growth and self-development through greater understanding. Even in death, these characters seem unfinished; particularly in death, for they are so clearly tragic because they cannot develop any more, cut off in mid-growth, as with Susan Glaspell.

In the lively and often terribly painful, even violent counterpoint and opposition of conflicting consciousnesses, the music of life which is our truth and our reality is composed and played. And the music changes as characters are shown to exceed what they had been, developing into something new, because of experiences which broaden and transform their consciousness of their own and other people's being into new and unforeseen melodies. Woolf's texts are a dynamic representation of the continuing, constant tension between variety or multifariousness and coherence or form, which tension is of course nature and life. In her novels, most obviously perhaps in *Between the Acts*, there is no division between spectator and performers, reader and writer, character and society, text and world. As in the Socratic dialogue, the performers are the spectators, and the spectators are the performers. In the play-pageant of *Between the Acts*, the performers constantly watch the audience, as does the 'author', Miss LaTrobe.

Woolf's novels celebrate diversity, and they joy in change as well as in the collision of old with new; they resist absolutism, stasis and so-called objectivity. The collision of 'voices' is a great dialogue of truth, choral truth. Yet this diversity and polyphony are hardly a recipe for chaos, for 'anything goes', for moral turpitude or artistic anarchy. Ordinary human social life gives Woolf the image for a rejection of both absolutism and anarchy:

It is a mistake, this extreme precision, this orderly, military progress; a convenience, a lie. There is always, deep below, even when we arrive punctually, ... with our waistcoats and polite formalities, a rushing stream of broken dreams, nursery rhymes, street cries, half-finished sentences and sighs ... [and] women's writing.

If we compare this (almost a Kristevan description of chora and the semiotic) with another, apparently conflicting remark of Woolf's, we see her view better: 'tumult is vile; confusion is hateful; everything in a work of art should be mastered and ordered.' Both these views aim towards truth.

Between the Acts is probably Woolf's most explicit, self-conscious representation of the preceding remarks. Virtually plotless, the novel weaves the lives of colliding characters into the preparation and then acting out of a play by Miss LaTrobe, which is a pageant of literary history. Both the play within the novel and the novel itself collapse the distance between 'life' and 'art', so that it is impossible to tell what is the play and what is not, what it means, and what its message is. Even the author of the play is presented as a Socratic midwife who helps in the birth of this 'event', which includes equally performers and spectators on one fine Sunday afternoon parish carnival. The ironic title of the novel catches the essential suspension of distance between audience and spectacle, while the constant interruptions of nature and ordinary life (cows lowing, planes flying, the storm, etc.) and of the audience (their systematically reported whispers to each other, the long intervals, the idiot boy's arrival on stage – planned or accidental, no one knows) all make the 'play' into life. As boundaries between work of art and spectator are dismantled, and the participants, both 'performers' and 'audience', watch each other, the play ends as indefinitely as it began. The players hold up a mirror to the spectators, and all breaks up in disarray: 'Is this the end?', 'What does it mean?', 'What did Miss LaTrobe intend?'

The novel itself has two endings, one from Miss LaTrobe's point of view, the other from Giles and Isa's. Neither of them ends except on a note of the 'unfinalizability' of art, life, truth or characters in fiction and in life. For Miss LaTrobe, the ending reads, 'She set down her glass. She heard the first words.' Those 'first words' of her next play may or may not be Giles and Isa's argument, which ends the novel from their point of view of hate and love, tenderness and violence: 'Then the curtain rose. They spoke.' Diverse and often conflicting points of view, which are our reality and our truth, cannot even come into being unless we speak. With speech comes consciousness, point of view, collision, and life and art. For Woolf, there was no other truth, no other reality.

Frances Newman 1883–1928

Frances Newman, whose works were praised by H.L. Mencken and J.B. Cabell, was born in Georgia and worked as a librarian at both the Carnegie Library, Atlanta, and the library of the Georgia Institute of Technology. During her period as a librarian, she became known for her trenchant reviews of the contemporary literature scene, published in New York papers and journals as well as Southern ones. She was encouraged during her thirties by Mencken to finish her first novel, *The Hard-Boiled Virgin* (New York, 1926; London, 1927); Mencken had already published her short story 'Rachel and her Children' in his *American Mercury* magazine. His judgement was borne out by the award of the O. Henry Memorial Prize for the short story. Newman had also already published an anthology in 1924, entitled *The Short Story's Mutations: From Petronius to Paul Morand* (New York). In her introduction to the book, her commitment to the avant-garde and to experimental fiction, evident in her reviews and articles, was consolidated. This commitment was realised in artistic form in the two novels she published in her short lifetime. Influenced by modernism and the modernist's sophistication in style, theme and form, Newman studied such writers as Virginia Woolf and George Meredith before her, and, like Woolf, championed the new fiction, which sought to break with both realism and the less realist but nevertheless fairly traditional fictions of the 1910s and early 1920s.

Newman, then, took to heart Woolf's insistence in such essays as 'Mr Bennett and Mrs Brown' (1924) that innovations in all novelistic aspects were needed if fiction was to be revitalized and made expressive of the new experiences and conceptions developing in the twentieth century. In both her first and her second novel – *Dead Lovers are Faithful Lovers* (New York and London, 1928) – Newman attacked numerous conventions at the levels of thematics, unity and style. Her first novel was then thought offensive enough (though not by today's standards) to be banned in New England, which enormously increased public interest in this avant-garde experiment. Challenging traditional attitudes both to (Southern) women and to 'appropriate' literary representations of women, Newman created a character, Katherine Faraday, and dared to endow her with the capacity to think as well as feel, and to think explicitly about literature, money, sex, relationships and female roles in ways quite unacceptable to traditionalists. In this novel, Newman avoided any use whatsoever of dialogue, using narrative description and a style of writing displaying quite complicated syntactical and logical arrangements, perhaps to emphasize Faraday's ability to think in ways normally reserved for men. The style is also richly and intensely allusive, and the novel proceeds by means of extremely short, pithy chapters. Newman's second novel exhibited the earlier modernist, experimental bent of her first, and the author again turned her attention to women characters. Like Katherine Mansfield, she made use of apparent 'trifles' in ordinary daily life to carry the import of larger issues, and she set up an effective counterpoint and tension between two women characters, one who seeks to make herself attractive to a man through her body and through sex, while the other appeals to his intellect. This overtly feminist thematic material becomes the vehicle for Newman's articulation of the artistic conflicts of her day, and of her efforts to find new forms of expression and models of the new consciousness.

Ivy Compton-Burnett 1884–1969

Dame Commander of the Order of the British Empire, Companion of Literature and Fellow of the Royal Society, winner of the James Tait Black Memorial Prize for *Mother and Son* (London, 1955), and recipient of numerous other honours and accolades, Compton-Burnett was born in Middlesex and died in London aged 85. She is the author of twenty novels written over a sixty-year period, though she rejected the first, *Dolores* (Edinburgh, 1911), as mere juvenilia, arguing that only with her second novel, *Pastors and Masters* (London, 1925) did she get into her mature stride. Compton-Burnett took a degree in classics in 1970 from the Royal Holloway College, and returned home to take up tutoring. She lived for some thirty years with her friend Margaret Jourdain, a historian, who encouraged her writing, until the latter's death. Her novels include *Men and Wives* (London and New York,

1931), *Daughters and Sons* (London and New York, 1937), *Manservant and Maidservant* (London, 1947), *A Father and his Fate* (London, 1957), *A God and his Gifts* (London, 1963) and *The Last and the First* (London, 1971). Radio adaptations made the novelist better known, since her characters' extremely mannered formality of speech, the novels' emphasis upon dialogue (to the virtual exclusion of explanatory narrative), and their restriction to the detached, closed world of the family unrelated to outside events were stumbling blocks to a very wide readership. Though her writing is sometimes compared to the novels of Jane Austen, Barbara Pym and even Henry Green, the general critical consensus is that 'there is nobody in all this writing world even remotely like her.' Or, according to Kay Dick, she has made 'possibly the most consistently original literary contribution of the last half century'.

Compton-Burnett's emphasis upon dialogue in most of the novels virtually creates a new genre of novel, the novel-play, closely related to Shakespearean drama and to Greek tragedy in a number of respects. (She herself described her books as 'something between a novel and a play'.) Power, its abuse, the immense effectiveness of verbal violence in domination, the concentration on the family and many other techniques, such as the use of sub-plots and twists and the intensely central role of multilayered, ironic and witty spoken language, relate Compton-Burnett's novels to the traditions of drama and tragedy. While the characters and their speech are sometimes criticized as too exaggerated and verbally brutal to be real, they will not seem unreal to any observant person acquainted with a cross-section of upper middle-class or upper-class British family life. For one of the effects of the novels is to bring into sharp focus – to make clearly visible – the astonishing cruelty only thinly disguised behind a facade of socially acceptable behaviour. As in some Shakespeare plays, justice does not always prevail and immorality is rarely punished. Or, as Ivy explained, 'I think it [punishment of the guilty] is a literary convention. I think the evidence tends to show that crime on the whole pays.' Compton-Burnett's characters are shown making the most of the upper-class emphasis upon formality and manner

as more important than fundamental decency and morality. Bravado can carry off any cruelty, and with impunity. Any verbal brutality can be uttered without criticism as long as the speaker remains cool, calm and superficially courteous. Form is everything; with the least sign of genuine emotion, one's power is lost. These novels strip the veil of familiarity from the ways in which people manipulate and control each other, and it is only this naked exposure of the real – created by framing what is not usually framed – that makes it appear exaggerated and unreal.

Compton-Burnett's novels have had a varied critical reception; on the one hand, they have been found unreal, pessimistic, difficult, and too unlike anything else in literature to have influence. Moreover, they have been criticized for failing to provide the social/historical setting and context so much in favour amongst realist novelists. On the other hand, this novelist has been said to be '*the* woman novelist of our century . . . with a knowledge of people which would have been held to be impossible' (W.M. Spackman). Most critics have recognized the radically subversive dimensions of these novel-plays, and see Compton-Burnett's starkly ironic exposure of the vacuous pretensions and verbal violence hidden in the ordinary language of educated, apparently cultivated people as her main means of destabilizing their traditional authority as guardians of morality, religion and culture (not to mention wealth). Yet the novel-plays are also enriched in two other obvious respects. First, they build further levels of irony into their structures, by carefully detailed (if occasional and transient) satiric references to both the literary tradition and tradition generally. For example, through names of unusual kinds, Compton-Burnett called up intertextual references to Shakespeare, Greek tragedy, the Metaphysical poets, Chaucer, the Romantics and the Victorians, and then mocked them by inversions and surprising misappropriation. Or she made characters spout platitudes and sentential phrases or sayings which are utterly inappropriate to their own behaviour or intentions. Second, through a systematic interrelationship between her novels (repetitions of familiar situations, satiric naming, and narrative devices), Compton-Burnett's novels became integral pieces of a jigsaw puzzle, which accrue more meaning when related to each other and to a gradually emerging world of fiction-reality. Though criticized, then, for its anti-realist neglect of social environment, Compton-Burnett's oeuvre seems nevertheless to have succeeded in creating a sharply focused world of the family, in which psychological and emotional forms of human behaviour are portrayed as not specific to Victorian life, but characteristic of family and tribal behaviour over a longer period.

Indeed, one could argue that while the overt thematic material of these novel-plays is the tortures, tragedies and sufferings embedded and hidden or repressed in much ordinary family life, the main theme is that of pervasive verbal abuse, which is the weapon of torture delineated by Compton-Burnett in all its various modes. Hidden intentions, disguised insinuations, slips of the tongue, cruel ambiguities, the hypocritical smile sweetening hostile words, the invisible (yet deeply felt) verbal thrusts – all these, used with skill and intensity, reveal the complexities and horrors of much family life which pretends to normality. Deception, insincerity and obfuscation are the means by which quite ordinary people disguise, yet satisfy, their greed, egotism and incapacity for compassion. In his 1985 book on Compton-Burnett, Robert Liddell summed up what he thought to be her most distinctive traits (some of which were mentioned above). He identified her lack of background or narrative exposition and the complete exclusion of her personality from her work, her exhaustive and detailed 'stage directions', her emphasis on dialogue, her ironic use of aphorisms, her fondness for 'stichomythia' (rapid, short speech exchanges) and a slightly ironic employment of the 'great tragic speech'. Given these elements, and given that the happenings of Greek and Shakespearean tragedy are adapted for her novels, Compton-Burnett's writings are more fully appreciated and better understood when read as play-novels which expand the possibilities for both genres in quite new and rewarding directions. Compton-Burnett's writings challenge the conventions of both realism and modernism, of genre and of criticism; her irony, moreover, turns towards her readers and their expectations, and shocks us into either appreciation or rejection.

Isak Dinesen 1885–1962

Born in Denmark to a wealthy family, Karen Dinesen Blixen (Isak Dinesen) studied in Switzerland and Copenhagen (at the Royal Academy of Fine Arts) before marrying Bror Blixen, with whom she departed for Kenya in 1913 to run a vast coffee plantation in the Ngong Hills. Her career as a writer began relatively late; her first collection of short stories, *Seven Gothic Tales* (New York and London), appeared in 1934 (republished London, 1988) with an introduction by one of Dinesen's first admirers, the novelist Dorothy Canfield (Fisher), who had helped her get the book published. A few earlier stories and poems had appeared singly, however, since 1904, in Danish journals. These have now been collected in *Osceola*, ed. C. Svendsen (Copenhagen, 1962). An immediate success, *Seven* was followed by Dinesen's autobiographical account of her years in Kenya, *Out of Africa* (London, 1937, 1984), and then five years later by *Winter's Tales* (New York). Her next publication, a thriller, was entitled *The Angelic Avengers* (London, 1946; Chicago and London, 1978); this has sometimes been seen as a political allegory about the German occupation of Denmark. Set in the nineteenth century, this romantic novel weaves a fantastic plot of the exposure of a crime and its retribution by two young women. It was the only novel Dinesen ever wrote, and was published under the pseudonym Pierre Andrézel. It was followed a decade later by *Last Tales* (Chicago, New York and London, 1957; Harmondsworth, 1986), *Anecdotes of Destiny* (Chicago, New York and London, 1958) and *Shadows on the Grass* (Chicago, New York and London, 1961; Harmondsworth, 1984). Dinesen's *Letters from Africa, 1914–1931* was published in 1982 (London, trans. A. Born, ed. F. Lasson). *Daguerreotypes and Other Essays*, a collection of Dinesen's non-fiction, originally written in Danish, appeared in 1979 (London). Posthumous works include *Ehrengard* (New York and London, 1963) and *Carnival: Entertainments and Posthumous Tales* (London, 1977).

In a letter from Africa, Dinesen had written that 'what I am looking for in imaginative writing is an illumination of . . . the magic of life.' This statement, along with Dinesen's romantic,

Boccaccio-like atmosphere and formal portrayal of the telling of tales as a central part of her narrative thematics, emphasizes her rejection of nineteenth-century realist ideology. For Dinesen ironically used elaborate artifice as a symbol for what is most real – what her stories seem to demand is more elaborate, fantastic and artificial than human life and nature itself. Like Christina Stead, her great Australian contemporary, Dinesen's stories celebrate the story-telling passion in ordinary human beings, and suggest that artistic creativity is not merely the special province of a few gifted geniuses, but the character of human experience itself; magic is to be found in ordinary life, if only the story could be told, however much a repetition of previous stories it will turn out to be. Yet, far from being romantic, fantastic flights away from 'reality', Dinesen's stories are always crucially concerned, as she put it herself, with the life of ordinary people: 'How is one to live?' and 'How are we to create a life for ourselves?' are the constant refrain of her writings, whether we read the letters, *Out of Africa* or her fabulous, ironic stories. She was deeply concerned with human psychology, with gaining a view of the complex inner forces which human beings must come to grips with if they are not to founder. One of our greatest resources, her stories imply, is to look on all this tragic scene with 'gay, glittering eyes'.

Dinesen's writings were admired by such diverse writers as Carson McCullers and Ernest Hemingway; McCullers loved her tales for their portrayal of the magic, absurdity and grotesqueness at the heart of life, Hemingway for their beautiful handling of sexuality and naked nature. Her description in *Out of Africa* of the Masai warriors is almost autobiographical in its application to her own writing. The Masai have, she said, 'that particular form of intelligence which we call *chic*; – daring and wildly fantastical as they seem, they are still unswervingly true to their own nature, and to an immanent ideal. Their style is not an assumed manner, nor an imitation of a foreign perfection; it has grown from the inside.' This virtual 'self-description' can be complemented by Canfield's remarks on Dinesen in her introduction to *Seven Gothic Tales*, where Canfield recognized Dinesen's new, original and strange style in her stories of 'bizarre power' as belonging to a romantic,

grotesque literary tradition. Dinesen certainly remained true to a romantic vision in sharp contrast to the realist, historical or psychological genres, indeed in contrast to the novel genre itself. For her self-consciously literary stories function in a typically romantic opposition to the novel form, and especially to the nineteenth- and early twentieth-century forms. In this sense, at least, Dinesen might be said to be a modernist of sorts, but her commitment to a romantic tradition and its psychological insight, its vision of human life, sets her apart from modernists as well. Her mannered style, her emphasis on complex narratives involving constant self-referentiality, and the parodic self-consciousness of the characters all function as a direct refutation of realism's commitment to objectivity, transparency and 'ordinariness'. Dinesen's romantic vision involves, that is, an unswerving commitment to imagination; as for Flannery O'Connor, reality for Dinesen lies not in the surfaces, which realism sets itself faithfully to reproduce, but in the depths, in the mystery and magic of human life which can only be glimpsed by imaginative power.

In her own complex tales, those versions of the *Arabian Nights*, Dinesen's Romantic kind of ironical awareness of her art – her plays within stories and stories within stories, the foregrounding of story-telling and questioning of authority as well as identity, along with questions of truth versus fiction – all these conventions function to reveal Dinesen's romantic vision of life as art. Consistently anti-rationalist in a vein similar to O'Connor's, Dinesen showed that reason must always be enlivened by the imagination if it is not to dissolve the mystery and magic of life into dead fragments of a dismembered nature. Many of Dinesen's stories also portray, in Blakean gestures of ironic reversal of good and evil, conventional morality as a failure of imagination. Both the good and the true are achieved, Dinesen's tales suggest, by means of artistic, imaginative acts, not through deductive or analytic reasonings. For in the latter, a particular point of view – a theory turned dogma – is allowed to dictate an interpretation of events, a set of explanations. This failure of imagination, this privileging of a single viewpoint or theory over others, represents the opposite of a romantic vision of truth, where partial understandings and a respect for silence and mystery are pre-ferred in deference to a Keatsian 'negative capa-bility': 'it is not a bad thing in a tale that you understand only half of it', said the narrator of one tale in Dinesen's first collection.

Dinesen's strong anti-rationalist vein is ex-pressed in her portrayal of all description as in-terpretation: objective description is a realist illusion; we do not even perceive, much less describe or interpret, objectively. We see through cultural lenses and styles, and this Nietzschean view – of truth as metaphor, of reality as a tissue of fictions (to use Plato's metaphor) – is also an anti-realist, anti-naturalist gesture. Dinesen never passed her stories off as mirrors of reality – as any kind of representation or imitation of real-ity. Her use of artifice as a symbol for the most natural, her use of the fabulous, the absurdly complex and the grotesque in the context of a romance tradition, is a denial that 'objective reality' is an intelligible notion, that personal identity is not a mystery, or that life can be grasped by reason alone. Her stories challenge conventional notions of plot, characterization, narrative time and thematics, as well as style, as they progress by means of apparent digressions – those stories within stories within stories – which turn out to be crucial to the 'main' story, and each of which is a work of art itself. Their opaqueness (in contrast to the transparency of realism) is, moreover, an expression of Dinesen's self-referential emphasis upon the 'life as art' analogy: life, too, is essentially the struggle to interpret human experience, to make sense of events, to give what happens meaning, not by explaining away events according to some pre-ferred notion or theory, not by that irritable reaching after facts and truths. In life we learn to respect the opaqueness of experience, to re-spect the inexplicable, to 'understand only half' of what happens.

Dinesen herself claimed to prefer the stories in *Winter's Tales*; her readers seem to favour *Seven Gothic Tales*, which she found too com-plex, too elaborate and too personal. Repetition, which is a central theme of all her stories, char-acterizes the body of her art as well – we do not find any development from *Seven Gothic Tales* to *Ehrengard*, so much as an Arabian experience of the kind Edith Wharton described in her travel book, *In Morocco* (London, 1920). Reality and history, personal identity and culture are por-trayed in recurring patterns.

Katherine Anne Porter 1890–1980

Author of the well-known novel *Ship of Fools* (Boston, 1962), and of twenty-seven short sto-ries and novellas, for which she won the Pulitzer Prize in 1966, Katherine Anne Porter was born and grew up in Texas before moving to Chicago to work as a journalist for some years. She also lived briefly in New York City, travelled to Mexico where she spent some years, and, after a European trip, settled in Baton Rouge to con-solidate her reputation as a successful writer. Various collections of her stories appeared, named after one of the stories in the group, such as *Flowering Judas* (New York, 1930, augmented New York, 1935), *Pale Horse, Pale Rider* (New York, 1939) and *The Leaning Tower and Other Stories* (New York, 1944). Her only novel, *Ship of Fools*, was made into a film. Some of Porter's non-fiction has been collected in a volume en-titled *Collected Essays and Occasional Writings of Katherine Anne Porter* (New York, 1970), and *Collected Stories* appeared in 1965 (New York).

Porter is a highly regarded stylist; her style has been described as radiant, magical, and ad-mirable for its clarity and precision. Her stories are also notable for what she described as 'co-herent form' created out of a central idea, which, she argued, should not be confused with 'plot', which an author does not really need, 'except in emergencies, when you are trying to manufacture a quick trick and make some easy money'. Porter further explained that her own particular aim in her art of fiction was to understand human motives and feelings, and 'to make a distillation of what human relations and experiences my mind has been able to absorb'. She also described the artist as 'a hostile critic of society', and her particular critical slant she described as a with-ering rejection of 'one of the most disturbing habits of the human mind [which] is its willful and destructive forgetting of whatever in its past does not flatter or conform to its present point of view'. Hence the prominent role of memory in her fiction, and her analysis of the way human beings idealize the unbearable parts of the past into an unrecognizable fiction. This 'betrayal' of the past is a central theme of many of Porter's stories, and is allied to an analysis of the damaging effects of such betrayal in nostalgia, hypocrisy and immaturity.

Porter's stories, as well as *Ship of Fools*, relentlessly expose the many forms which betrayal takes, from self-delusion to characters who live in the future instead of the present. Porter described people who, for example, bow and 'kowtow' to convention, cliché and stereotype, thereby betraying their own experience. The character Miranda, who recurs in several stories, gradually sees through the false pictures of life that her family and acquaintances try to pass off as genuine. Porter's Miranda rejects the pseudo-love of her family which Willa Cather, in *The Song of the Lark*, had depicted as being one of the most formidable enemies to Thea the artist's self-development. Miranda, as well as other characters, learns to distrust and avoid clichéd, stereotyped response which passes itself off as the genuine by invoking convention and propriety. Release from self-delusion, convention and the false is often depicted as happening to a character only in situations of defeat or death, in disease or hallucination. Indeed, confrontation with death is a symbolic encounter with time itself, as characters realize their betrayal of life only when it is too late.

Like Flannery O'Connor, Porter made use of the freak, the fool, the deformed person, the idiot and the drunk to express the spiritual deformity we all suffer from as a result of our self-delusion, our nostalgia, and our deferral of life into some non-existent tomorrow. Porter's novel *Ship of Fools*, like many of her stories, also employs the literary convention of the journey as a metaphor for life and time, while it exposes the delusions and hypocrisies which lead to racism, war, violence, and hatred in personal relations, for example. Many stories make use of familiar literary conventions which Porter revitalized in her own unique style, such as the party, circus or holiday, the cracked looking-glass, the house, the encounter, the witness and so on. She also used framework techniques and self-referential gestures which draw attention to the act of story-telling itself, as merely a version of the narratives we make up about our lives – those fictions which are taken for reality. Porter also portrayed the destructive consequences of

certain types of narrative, and in the character Miranda she represented the partial effort to challenge nostalgia and falsification (through idealization) as the only means of facing the past.

Like Ellen Glasgow, Porter is centrally preoccupied with the need for human beings to reflect upon their past, their experience and their lives, and with the frequency with which this need is denied out of fear of facing unpleasantness and disappointment squarely. The story 'The Jilting of Granny Weatherall' is exemplary of the tendency to distort the past and betray our feelings through denying failure, disappointment and pain. Porter showed that this betrayal is destructive because it means, first, that we deny our feelings and, second, that, since we are always on the run from the past, we look to a future which never comes. We live in tomorrow because yesterday is denied and today is, consequently, unsatisfactory. Characters are portrayed as always waiting for something to happen, never living in the present. Finally, death comes, before we have ever really lived. Time becomes a central character stalking the other characters of each story as they try to escape and deny the past, miss out on the present, and never reach that elusive future, where everything will, supposedly, be different.

Porter's stories are unique in part in their emphasis upon a gaze turned inward into her characters' inner life, thoughts, delusions and fantasies, a gaze which concentrates upon memory, past experience and present lies. Because her stories are actually often located in the inner consciousness of a character, her use of concrete, sensuous imagery and the external world is minimal, and this is sometimes disturbing to readers unused to such an intensely inner location. With the exception of 'Noon Wine', which is firmly set in the objective physical world, Porter's stories are less overtly dramatic than psychologically intense, drawing the reader into a direct intimacy also characteristic of Katherine Mansfield's fiction. Eudora Welty explained that Porter showed us how to see in a new way through her moral convictions, her inner, inward gaze: she 'shows us that we do not have to see a story happen to know what is taking place . . . her vision is reflective . . . Her imagery is as likely as not to belong to a time other than the story's present; . . . it is *memory* imagery . . . a distilled, re-formed imagery.'

'Old Mortality' is a short novel which explores the processes of fictionalizing the past by several different adults, and Miranda's gradual realization of how each has distorted the past to avoid her own particular pain. Yet Porter's narrative point of view does not leave Miranda unimplicated, as the story concludes: 'Let them tell their stories to each other. Let them go on explaining how things happened. I don't care. At least I can know the truth about what happens to me, she assured herself silently, making a promise to herself, in her hopefulness, her ignorance.' (The ironic narrative commentary 'in her hopefulness, in her ignorance' should lay to rest the notion that 'Miranda' is Katherine Anne Porter's voice.) While such a 'conclusion' to a story may explode the myth that we can ever know the truth about what happens, much less what happens to ourselves, Porter's stories – through their detailed, acute representation of processes of self-delusion and of making legends out of the past – at least do make us more acutely conscious of *how* we distort and betray our own experience. By the end of 'Old Mortality', Miranda is shown penetrating the falsity of others' accounts of their past, but she falls into the romantic illusion that she will avoid such idealizing, at the very moment that she promises herself: 'I won't have false hopes, I won't be romantic about myself.'

'Old Mortality', with its explicit exposure of several contradictory accounts of the past, and its acute psychological insight into the ways certain types of character rationalize away the evidence before their eyes, indirectly implicates history on the larger scale as a fiction, and questions the possibility of truth 'even about the smallest, the least important of all the things I must find out'. In the story 'Holiday', Porter's ironic, detached narrative tone, separate from the unnamed, first person narrator (again, not to be confused with Porter's own point of view, as it is so often), ironizes the following remark of the narrator: 'I . . . began making up my first letter to Louise. First I was going to tell her that unless she was to be a novelist, there was no excuse for her having so much imagination. In daily life, I was going to tell her, there are also such useful things as the plain facts that should

be stuck to, through thick and thin. Anything else led to confusions like this.' Porter did not carelessly choose words like 'making up', or miss the chance for self-referential gestures about novel writing, fiction, truth, facts or memory. In 'Holiday', the unnamed 'I' is shown going through a series of complete transformations about what the 'plain facts' are, about her physical surroundings, the relations of her acquaintances, and the inner life of a disfigured woman Ottilie. By the end, there are no 'plain facts', as we watch the central character experiencing both an encounter with death and 'the terror of dying', as well as a moral realization as she bridges the distance between herself and Ottilie in an imaginative encounter (allegorized in the coming of spring) achieved only after an 'ironical mistake'.

In a substantial essay, '"Noon Wine": The Sources', Porter explored the relation of fiction to 'real life', and ended up asking more questions than she answered. In the process of this long 'meditation' (which, she admitted, does not succeed in explaining anything at all, and certainly nothing about the sources for 'Noon Wine'), Porter gradually revealed to herself and to the reader, in discursive form, some of her conceptions about such words as 'real', 'fact', 'truth' and so on, which shed light on many of her stories. The following remark constitutes perhaps the only 'truth' which Porter gives us:

> Is it not almost the sole end of civilized education of all sorts to teach us to be more and more highly, sensitively conscious of the reality of the existence, the essential being, of others, those around us so very like us and yet so bafflingly, so mysteriously different? . . . with some final, undeniable human claims on respect and not to be laughed at, except in passing, for all [their] simple vanity.

In her stories, Porter often portrayed Miranda or one of the other characters having such a revelation 'of the essential being', of the 'reality' of the existence of another human being, and of the need 'to look at another human being with that attention and wonder and speculation which ordinarily, and very naturally, I think, a child lavishes only on himself'. Her stories are often carefully designed accounts of what happens to a person when 'a spiritual enlightenment, some tenderness, some first awakening of charity' occurs, before it is lost again in the midst of self-centredness and self-delusion. Such experiences, which alternate with the more pervasive experience of egotism, are the springs of a more humane, compassionate way of living, without which hatred, violence and greed prevail, as Glasgow had sought to portray in *The Sheltered Life*.

Porter is also the author of a number of non-fiction writings, including *My Chinese Marriage* (New York, 1921), *Outline of Mexican Popular Arts and Crafts* (Los Angeles, 1922) and *A Defense of Circe* (New York, 1955), and she translated two books from French.

Jean Rhys 1890–1979

Praised as one of the 'purest writers of our time', Jean Rhys (née Williams) was born in Dominica, West Indies, in 1890 (it is thought), and came to England in about 1907, where she went to school in Cambridge and later to the London Academy of Dramatic Art. Her novels later drew upon experience derived from the odd jobs which she took (after her father's death) in order to support herself, such as mannequin, chorus girl and model. In the 1920s, Rhys spent time in Paris after having lived with her first husband in Holland and Vienna, where she met Ford Madox Ford around 1923. Ford encouraged her writing, and helped get her first story published in the *transatlantic review* in 1924, as well as writing an introduction to the Jonathan Cape collection of stories, *The Left Bank*, which appeared in London in 1927. Breaking with Ford, Rhys returned to England in 1927 to try to get *Postures* (or *Quartet*) published, a novel allegedly based on her experiences with Ford and Stella Bowen. While Cape refused to publish it for fear of libel, Chatto and Windus (London) took it on in 1928. Only two years later Rhys returned to Cape to publish *After Leaving Mr Mackenzie* (London and New York, 1931). *Postures* and *After Leaving* then went out of print for nearly forty years, though Rhys published two more novels, *Voyage in the Dark* (London and New York, 1934) and *Good Morning, Midnight* (London and New York, 1939), before lapsing into silence for twenty-seven years. After

1966, with the publication of her great feminist revision of *Jane Eyre*, *Wide Sargasso Sea* (London and New York), all her other books were reissued by André Deutsch, two new collections of short stories appeared (*Tigers are Better-Looking* (London and New York, 1968) and *Sleep it Off, Lady* (London and New York, 1976)), apparently written in the 1940s and 1950s, and a sketchy autobiography, *Smile Please* (London, 1979), was published. In 1984, a selection of letters from 1931–66 was edited by Francis Wyndham (who helped rescue her work from oblivion) and Diana Melly (London). *Wide Sargasso Sea* received both the Royal Society of Literature Award and the W.H. Smith Award.

Rhys's comments in a 1934 letter to Evelyn Scott, the acclaimed American novelist, about *Voyage in the Dark*, are relevant to her other novels as well:

> It's written almost entirely in words of one syllable. Like a kitten mewing perhaps. The big idea – well I'm blowed if I can be sure what it is. Something to do with time being an illusion I think. I mean that the past exists – side by side with the present, not behind it; that what was – is.
>
> I tried to do it by making the past (the West Indies) very vivid – the present dreamlike (downward career of a girl) – starting of course piano and ending fortissimo.
>
> Perhaps I was simply trying to describe a girl going potty.

In a previous letter to Scott (1931) and in a slightly later letter (June 1934), Rhys had expressed dismay at the description of her novels as 'sordid and depressing' or 'disgusting' and 'very grey'. While some early reviews had been kind, especially about Rhys's fine style, there was much objection to her themes and characters; her early novels were described in the *Times Literary Supplement* of 1931 as 'sordid little stories' about prostitutes, which were a waste of the author's talents. By the 1940s, it was almost universally accepted by critics that Rhys's novels were essentially about prostitutes who came to self-destruction by the end, whether through drink or drugs, abortion and resulting death, or suicide. The first well-known dissent came in 1950 from Wyndham Lewis, who argued that terms or categories such as 'prostitutes' or 'fallen women' were inappropriate, since Rhys was challenging such evaluations. Yet, the notion Ford Madox Ford initiated in 1927, of Rhys's fiction being about 'underdogs', persists even to the present day, as critics have ignored Rhys's Nietzschean reversal of values.

What almost no critic failed to agree upon, however, was the consummate craft these novels displayed in both style and narrative strategy. Adjectives for Rhys's style such as 'pure', 'original' and 'poised' recur time and again, and her balance and economy, as well as clarity and simplicity, are stressed. Her prose was compared to poetry, with an integrity and intensity of effect arising from its austerity and, yet, density. Very few critics noted or developed, however, Ford's great contribution to insight into Jean Rhys in 1927, namely, her 'singular instinct for form'. In the introduction to *Smile, Please*, Rhys stressed this aspect of her writing when she noted, 'a novel has to have shape, and life doesn't have any; I like shape very much.' This essentially 'modernist' attitude, that life does not have any shape in itself while the central character of artifacts is their shaping ability, was further expressed by Rhys in a letter rejecting the notion that autobiographical material had no place in fiction: 'I know that "parler de soi," is not supposed to be the proper thing to do . . . [but] I feel so fiercely about that. No one knows anything but him or herself and that badly.' Fiction, she explained, involves precisely giving form, shape and body – unity – to that material which is only badly known. However, unlike realism, Rhys's textual forms are not imposed from without, according to arbitrary notions of order, decorum or convention. Like many modernists, Rhys preferred a congruence between form, style and material which could only arise if the first were not imposed upon the other two.

Before looking more closely at the shape of Rhys's novels, a glance at some perspicuous observations about the themes is suggestive of a better understanding of Rhys's novelistic experiments. Already in 1935, one critic described Rhys as a satirist of the hypocrisies of society, *After Leaving Mr Mackenzie* being a book of 'spare, suggestive method . . . profoundly destructive of hypocrisies – social and aesthetic subterfuges'. Rhys had written in a letter in relation to *Voyage in the Dark* that she 'didn't want to use any

stunts and ha[d]n't'. While a number of early critics saw her as a realist, or a follower of Flaubert, this is because of her preoccupation with the *demi-monde*, which was suggestive of realist and naturalist themes and characters. Yet her forms, narrative strategies and style are clearly attacks on and rejections of realist notions of order, objectivity, representations and transparency of language. The 'destruction of hypocrisies – social and aesthetic subterfuges' is a phrase which overtly alerts us to Rhys's concern with liberating the novel from false, realist, aesthetic conventions regarding theme, form and style. All her novels are experiments with these three aspects of fiction in order to try to forge something less false, pretentious and hypocritical in both literature and life.

The convergence of life and literature occurs in Rhys's novels on all the levels suggested above: autobiographical material is shaped into art; both social and literary conventions and hypocrisies are criticized; but most of all, perhaps, in writing her novels, Rhys fashioned herself into a unique individual. Hence, her novels reflect this self-creation, this existential project achieved through writing, as they focus upon not so much underdogs or failures or inadequate human beings as upon women who have lives that are 'of their own making', as one critic put it, however apparently disorderly and shapeless they seem to conventional people. Rhys's novels suggest that people who live lives of their own making cannot belong in society – there is no place for unique individuals, because they do not fit into the categories, moulds or stereotypes which society requires: hence she portrays these uniquely individual women – clearly intelligent, capable of love and compassion to an unusual degree, as well as of suffering – who do not find it possible to 'be conventional'. The focus and theme of Rhys's novels is not so much the underdog or failure, as critics for sixty years have been suggesting. The focus is on the intolerance of a rigid, hypocritical society, which refuses a valued place to people who will not play the games. For as Rhys complained in a letter to her daughter Maryvonne, in 1951, respectable society demands that 'everyone must be exactly alike'. Moreover: 'Christ was quite right about publicans (and about sinners too in my opinion). They are nicer than other people – and I sincerely hope they will walk first into Heaven leaving the holy righteous and respectable outside looking very puzzled.' She put it another way in 1953, in a letter to Morchard Bishop: 'I very much doubt whether any story seriously glorifying the prostitute and showing up not one but several British housewives to say nothing of two nuns! – their meanness and cant and spite – would be accepted.' So much for Rhys's novels being about 'underdogs' or 'failures' or 'neurotic' women. These 'labels' are blatant examples of the prejudice of the critic who has failed to see her 'serious glorification' of the prostitute, because he cannot get out of his social hypocrisies and conventions. Elsewhere, Rhys complained about respectable society as 'the soul destroying middle': 'oh dear the middle way respectable ones – they *can* be the devil – I do think gossip can be such a cruel thing and they gossip so much.'

Rhys's novels are not so much portraits of the same women – much less the same failure or underdog – at different stages of her life as they are studies of the cruelty of normal, ordinary people, hypocritically going about harming others in conventional, socially acceptable ways. These are unacceptable to her women characters, and her novels reveal what happens to people who cannot be like other people, who will not fit into the cruel conventions and destructive hypocrisies of polite society. For example, she remonstrated with Evelyn Scott in 1936:

> I do not agree that there's nothing to defend myself against – I do not agree that my way of looking at life and human beings is distorted. I think that the desire to be cruel and to hurt (with words because any other way might be dangerous to ourself) is part of human nature. Parties are battles (most parties), a conversation is a duel (often). Everybody's trying to hurt first, to get in the dig that will make him or her feel superior, feel triumph.

Another chilling example Rhys gave of cruelty occurred in a throwaway remark in a letter which explains much of her lack of presentation of any typically feminist views in her novels: 'I did think about the Suffragettes. Result of all their sacrifices? The woman doctor!!! Really human effort is futile.' Hence come the portrayals of vicious landladies, destructive aunts, jealous female 'friends', competitive sisters and hypocritical wives, the last being the real prostitutes, who have sold themselves body and soul into the slavery of marriage for their slot in respectable society. It is hardly any wonder that Rhys has been read so superficially, for, as with Jane Austen, her deeply ironic criticisms of marriage, respectability and financial success are too stiff for most of her middle-class, respectable readers, who tend to minimize the extent of her social censures. And as Rhys knew only too well, criticism is not tolerated in respectable English society: 'I know Peggy that you don't care for Americans but they have one great virtue, they don't stifle criticism . . . But not here! The English clamp down on unpleasant facts and some of the facts they clamp down on are unpleasant indeed, believe me.' Rhys's novels lift the veil from the everyday, familiar and normal, revealing it to be cruel, hypocritical and destructive. But her novels are almost as critical of literary conventions as they are of social mores, and each novel is a testimony to her experimentation with new structures, forms, styles and individual women.

For the women in Jean Rhys's novels are not in any meaningful sense the same, except to the eye blinded by convention, which sees a 'prostitute' of varying ages where genuinely individual, unique characters are portrayed who refuse to be like everybody else: like the British housewife, or the professional woman (doctor?). These women are no more the 'same' woman at different stages of life than are Rhys's novels the 'same' novel at different stages of her life. Indeed, the uniqueness of the women characters is inextricably tied up with the uniqueness of each novel – its particular style, unity and subject matter are expressed precisely through the individuality of an Anna, a Sasha, or a Julia, an Antoinette, a Marya. That is, each of Rhys's new women characters becomes a metaphor for the novel's new experiments in style, form, conception and their fine congruence. Like her uncategorizable women, Jean Rhys was creating an uncategorizable novel with a voice, a style of her own. So far as she was concerned, one's very reality is at stake: 'I do find that so many people here are not phoney but *unreal*', as she wrote in a letter; stereotyped behaviour may often involve phoniness and hypocrisy, but for Rhys it involved more importantly the destruction of the only meaningful character of reality, namely, individuality.

Voyage in the Dark and *Wide Sargasso Sea* are both experiments in style, narrative, time and characterization. In both, 'the past exists – side by side with the present, not behind it', so that 'what was – is'. In both, the West Indies (the past) is made more vivid than England, the dream-like present. The reference to the literary tradition is more overt in *Sargasso Sea* than in *Voyage*, yet it is clear that *Voyage* is as much a reference to Zola's *Nana* as is *Sargasso Sea* a reference to *Jane Eyre*: 'I was lying on the sofa, reading *Nana*. . . . I bet you a man writing a book about a tart tells a lot of lies one way and another', she writes in *Voyage*. '*Nana*' is of course an anagram of '*Anna*', the character in *Voyage*. Both *Voyage* and *Sargasso Sea* may be novels 'describing a girl going potty', and both have a carefully constructed, unified shape. Yet they are utterly different, unique novels, and represent remarkable achievements in Rhys's striving for originality. Central themes such as the recuperation of the past (both personal and literary) for the imaginative understanding of the present, and the relation of madness to sanity, are handled in aesthetically unique and different ways. The conventions of the madwoman in the attic and the social outcast are not so much representations of victims, handled compassionately by Rhys, as efforts to explode the valuation of conventional notions of sanity and propriety, revealing them to be not superior but merely stereotyped conventionality – a death-in-life. Thus Rochester is revealed to be insane through his inhuman cruelty – yet he succeeds and prospers and appears sane and proper, while Antoinette 'fails', retiring into herself. Anna either dies of an abortion or lives another death-in-life, depending on whether you read the original ending or the 'mutilated', aborted one. But at least she retained her humanity: she existed, she was not unreal, like the sisters, landladies, phoney friends, aunts and so on.

Rhys drew on an armoury of literary devices and conventions in her marvellously varied experimentation, from journeys to mirrors to windows and curtains and clocks and ships and roads, encounters, quests. Yet these uncategorizable, non-realist, non-romantic, non-modernist, unconventional novels set these literary conventions working in new ways, to help readers see beyond conventional categories, labels and types, into a world of unique human beings and unique artifacts.

Zora Neale Hurston 1891?–1960

Novelist, folkorist and anthropologist, Hurston was born and brought up in an entirely black community, Eastonville, Florida. Educated at Howard University in Washington, D.C., Barnard College and Columbia, Hurston studied cultural anthropology and, specifically, black folklore of the South, as well as of the Caribbean. Her collection of songs, voodoo practices, legends and tales, in *Mules and Men* (Philadelphia, 1935), the first popular book on Afro-American folklore by a black scholar, has been described as the 'most engaging, genuine, and skilfully written book in the field of folklore'. Hurston travelled back to the South as well as to Haiti, Bermuda and Jamaica to record the rich, imaginative folklife of these communities in her characteristically humorous and colourful writing. Alice Walker described Hurston's anthropological writings as 'vigorous work [which] expresses the essence of black folklife'. Another volume of folklore was also published, three years later, entitled *Tell My Horse* (New York and London, 1990), and Hurston is the author of four novels, an autobiographical work, *Dust Tracks on a Road* (Philadelphia, 1942; London, 1986), and some fifty stories and essays. Her most admired novels, *Their Eyes were Watching God* (Philadelphia, 1937; London, 1987) and *Jonah's Gourd Vine* (Philadelphia, 1934; London, 1987), gained her a considerable reputation in her own time, though poverty was never far away, and she died in illness and debt in Port Pierce, Florida, and was buried in an unmarked grave. Her other two novels were *Moses, Man of the Mountain* (Philadelphia, 1939) and *Seraph on the Suwanee* (New York, 1948); the latter is seen as revealing waning powers and a conservatism and loss of courage of which her early life showed no signs, for she was known as a courageous, witty, independent woman who always 'wrote and spoke for herself'. Indeed, this independence of thought gained her much criticism from black people and white people, men and women, alike; the heroine of *Their Eyes*, Janie Crawford, is probably a not inaccurate picture of Hurston herself: Janie is portrayed as transcending exploitation and oppression by gaining power through language, enabling her to analyse her situation and imagine beyond the conventions, stereotypes and expectations of the society around her. Hurston was married briefly twice.

Hurston never underestimated the power of the ordinary talk and stories which surrounded her in childhood; her novels draw on the richness of the African-American dialect, with its vivid, idiosyncratic imagery and syntax, and its energetic figures of speech and turns of phrase. As in Langston Hughes's poems of the Harlem Renaissance, these musical rhythms of speech, incorporated into blues and jazz, also give her writing lyricism, as they did for Gayl Jones and other later successors. Adding to this the thematic elements gained from her extensive knowledge of folk culture – legends, medical and voodoo practices, art, song and religion – which Jean Toomer (novelist and friend of the painter Georgia O'Keeffe) also tapped for his remarkable writings, Hurston achieved remarkable works of art, especially her first two novels. Her analyses of the religious, social and class conflicts firmly focused within a well-researched folk background, along with her refusal to romanticize or falsify Southern black life (as the New York intellectuals often did), contributed to the rich thematics of her fiction, as did her commitment to independence, justice and equality for women. Additionally, her experience of growing up in an entirely black incorporated town, where black people made and kept their own laws, organized their schools, social services, financial and medical institutions, and were relatively free from the daily indignity of white racism, may have given her the strong sense of pride in being black and the deep respect for black people which her novels and folklore studies reveal. Indeed, this is a quality particularly characteristic of Hurston's work; few black writers manage to achieve for their characters the confidence and utter lack of any sense of inferiority or diminishment which Alice Walker, amongst others, has attributed to Hurston's fiction.

Both Hurston's first two novels, *Jonah's Gourd Vine* and *Their Eyes were Watching God*, rely heavily on dialogue – indeed, African-American dialect – and on the genre of the romance, with one or two major characters for their development. And while drawing from autobiographical experiences, these novels convey a strong and vivid sense of the rich culture of the black communities in which the events occur. Also, in both novels, Hurston made use of symbolism from both folk and religious traditions to convey her artistic meaning: both John Pearson in the first novel and Janie Crawford in the second function symbolically (in addition to their import as individuals) to convey the issues of an entire people confronted with a range of moral, social, economic and emotional dilemmas which must be dealt with if black people are to defeat not only racism, but also sexism. In each novel, Hurston's central medium and her central message were the power of language, which, if seized imaginatively and used independently, can liberate individuals to 'speak and write and think for themselves'. *Their Eyes were Watching God* verges on an existentialist portrayal of a young to middle-aged woman who creates herself, shrugging off the powerful social principles which seek to subjugate her, by learning how to use language. This congruence between thematics and form gives these novels still greater artistic integrity, as Hurston kept her 'vehicle' constantly before the reader's eyes: we are watching the language itself, we are inevitably more conscious than usual of it, since she never allowed the overt thematics of personal events to divert our attention from how things are said.

Hurston's imaginative genius is exemplified in her unfailing ability to turn apparently thematic incidents into moral and aesthetic issues of great force and complexity. The terrific storm at the end of *Their Eyes* functions as a powerful metaphor for the external forces (of racism, poverty, etc.) which demand almost unbelievable physical and emotional strength from her characters. Tea Cake's illness, resulting from exposure and exhaustion – a kind of feverish delirium which leads him to try to kill Janie – is a symbol of the destructive effects which racism and poverty inevitably bring in their wake. The truly existential act of the novel, namely, Janie's split-second decision to reach for a rifle and kill him before he can kill her – this unnatural, outrageous act of self-preservation instead of self-sacrifice – inflames her community and leads to a trial for murder. But she is exonerated and freed, even forgiven, in the end, in this powerfully feminist work of great stylistic beauty and formal balance.

Djuna Barnes 1892–1982

Djuna Barnes is one of the foremost examples of a modernist whose work exhibits formal experimentation and an extreme challenge to traditional novel, short story and drama conventions by violating both literary and social codes. Like Gertrude Stein, she experimented with dress, gender and social behaviour – as well as literature – in her search for a more individualistic and liberated way of working, living and thinking. Her prose exhibits radical innovation in style and in plot; she learned from the imagists how images could be developed at the expense of traditional plot and suspense, as well as becoming the means of 'drawing' character, structuring dialogue and establishing a rich materiality of style. Her novels, plays and stories, as well as her uncategorizable writings, explore love, death, desire, obsession, suffering and pain from an unequivocally individualistic female point of view, and an uncompromisingly frank attitude that life is simply not worth the trouble. Barnes lived to be 90 years old; the last forty years of her life she lived as an almost total recluse in Greenwich Village.

Djuna Barnes was born and grew up in New York state amongst a family of writers and artists living an unconventional life. She became a journalist after studying art, meanwhile writing poems and short stories as well as plays, and later illustrating her writings with highly original drawings. She left for Europe shortly before she was 30, and immediately found herself in the literary world of James Joyce, T.S. Eliot, Mina Loy, Ezra Pound, Natalie Barney, Peggy Guggenheim, Bryher and many others. She became one of Joyce's closest friends through his admiration for her work, while Eliot praised *Nightwood* (London, 1936) and thereby helped to secure its reputation. Long before *Nightwood* (Barnes's most famous work, at least today), she had published numerous other works which had attracted the attention of her Parisian peers. The

short story collection *A Night Amongst the Horses* (New York, 1929, published as *A Book*, New York, 1923) was followed by *Ladies Almanack* (Paris, 1928) and *Ryder* (New York, 1928), a satiric novel about a 'female Tom Jones', as Barnes described it. Her blank verse tragedy *The Antiphon* (New York, 1958), a reply to Eliot's *Family Reunion*, was performed in 1961. Editions of her earliest short stories as well as interviews and a volume of illustrated journalism have been published, and an edition of her selected works appeared in 1962. Other works include the collection of 'stories' and drawings, *A Book of Repulsive Women* (Yonkers, N.Y., 1915), an early volume of poems and drawings, several other plays (such as *The Dove*, 1926, and three one-act plays written in the 1910s and 1920s). In addition, Barnes published *Spillway* (New York, 1962, 1972), another version of her short stories, and two further stories, in *Vagaries Malicieux* (New York, 1974); *Selected Works* appeared in 1962 (New York), as did *New York*, a collection of journalism, ed. and intro. D. Messerli (Los Angeles, 1989).

Barnes's texts are experimental in terms of themes, genres, style and language, and in revisions of the conventions of plot, characterization, dialogue and structure. One of the most characteristic aspects of her originality is, paradoxically, her imaginative allusion to the literary tradition. Barnes parodied other texts, plagiarized from them, alluded to them, and derived words, phrases, themes, structures and forms from them to such an extent that she became recognized as one of the most (successfully) consciously literary writers of her generation, admired by Joyce, Eliot and other 'plagiarizers'. Barnes went further and pilloried, appropriated and derived elements from not only literature but life, to both the delight and embarrassment of her contemporaries. Her fusion of her art and her life added to the remarkable individuality of her writing, as she developed her unique personality exactly in relation to her literary and artistic work.

Barnes deployed anti-conventions of stories within stories to ironize narrative; she eschewed plot and mocked endings with her ambivalent, indeterminate conclusions; she used characters to express stylistic experiments, alternated points of view to ridicule objectivity, showed characters openly fictionalizing their past, their present and their future, and challenged the distinction between human beings as rational and animals as irrational by her ruthless portrayal of human desire, obsession, love, hate, sexuality and violence. At the end of her novel *Nightwood*, one of the central (if elusive) characters, Robin, turns into a howling dog. Barnes adopted conventions of the circus, the theatre and the masquerade to arouse the reader to a self-consciousness about the mirror that the text provided for seeing into the misery of one's own soul, face to face with the alienating, enigmatic reality of human existence. She also located sexuality and sexual identity at the heart of human misery, exploring thematically (and reflecting these themes in her experiments in structure and forms) the destructive, irrational forces which are fed by misguided notions of sexual morality, sexual categorizing and sexual roles.

Barnes's novels, stories, plays and parodies confront the incomprehensible pain of living in such a way as to offer little solace to the reader. Her refusal to make concessions to readability and communication mirror one of her central interests, namely, her belief in the hopelessness of finding meanings or rational explanations for life, death, suffering and the inadequacy of human relationships. Her texts explore the exploitation of women, both contemporary and past traditions of degradation, and show the radical subversiveness of lesbianism in a patriarchal society. Barnes, however, is under no illusion that love between women is unproblematic. One of the central themes of *Nightwood*, as well as of other works, is the obsessional, possessive and destructive nature of sexual love and desire, whether heterosexual or lesbian. In that novel, the five characters exist not as individuals but as knots in a network of bondage, driven by uncontrollable needs, whether sexual, emotional or voyeuristic. Many of Barnes's texts seem to imply that the inevitable frustration of meaningful love relationships can act as a central spur towards artistic creativity, as characters such as Dr O'Connor seek to find forms – articulate forms – for their thwarted lives. The distortions, contortions and entanglements which are the forms frustrated living takes are transformed into patterns, articulate styles and structures in art. Yet these artistic 'successes', which contrast so markedly with the convoluted failures of life, are not shown by Barnes to be, somehow, redemptive: to make life meaningful and bearable, as Nietzsche argued. On the contrary, her texts seem to show these adverse constructs as songs of sorrow, almost as laments for life, rather than as celebrations of imagination triumphing over the chaos and formlessness of human frustration.

The traditional, idealistic view of art as redemptive of human suffering, as a substitute for personal fulfilment, as closed off from the misery of existence as if an 'other' in a frame protected from outside life, is shattered by Barnes. She exposed this illusion by revealing that life itself is art – and, consequently, art is as meaningless, indecipherable and irrational as is life, even if the arbitrary order imposed upon it fosters an illusion of definitive meaning uncharacteristic of life. For this 'definitive meaning' achieved by means of arbitrary imposition is shown to be empty, delusory and fabricated. Disruption of the arbitrary categories and dualisms which impose pseudo-form and false meaning on art and life becomes a metaphor in her texts for the need to reorganize human feelings and desires in new forms that differ from the present ones of obsession, possession and mastery. Like Hilda Doolittle's, Barnes's writings exhibit images and metaphors expressive not of dualism and separation, but of integration and dynamic interdependences.

Barnes's writings psychoanalyse the tendency in human beings to turn outwards for artificial sources of security and meaning, to religion, to possessive love, to obsessive work, to idealized art. This turning outwards is analysed as a perpetual quest for an anchor in life to overcome the insecurity within. Strongly hinted at is the suggestion that this childish search for a substitute parental authority can never achieve its goal. An existential project of constructing security and independence within the self, as a precondition for integral interaction with others, is one of Barnes's hidden subtexts, while the overt theme is the portrayal and analysis of the extreme difficulty, perhaps impossibility, of such internal security. In rewriting the 'body' of human literature into new forms, Barnes rewrote human sexuality and desire, by rewriting the relationship of internal/external as not a dichotomy but a dynamic function. The 'human predicament' can be seen, she suggested, as a result of reading experience in terms of dualities, hierarchies, insides and outsides, frames and contents. Her texts explore the details of that arbitrary, dualistic account of human life as utterly, hopelessly destructive and meaningless, and as the source of suffering and frustration. A non-dualistic story, where self and other are not separated, where integration is the pattern which replaces possession, is implicit in Barnes's texts; but the irresolvable ambiguity and resulting hopelessness remain, as the texts give us no reason to believe that integration is achievable as a new form of human existence replacing hierarchy, duality and fragmentation. That is, the analysis or dissection of human misery into its component parts, so that we can comprehend it more profoundly, is no guarantee whatsoever that understanding will bring the power to change ourselves, others or our society, much less the social and literary patterns which perpetuate division and fragmentation.

Other publications of Barnes's include *Smoke and Other Early Stories*, ed. D. Messerli (College Park, Md., 1983; London, 1985) and a collection of interviews, *I Could Never Be Lonely Without a Husband*, ed. A. Barry (College Park, Md., 1985; London, 1987). *New York* is a collection of her journalism, ed. D. Messerli (College Park, Md., 1992).

Dorothy Parker 1893–1967

Close friend to playwright Lillian Hellman, Dorothy Parker was an influential figure in the literary and political life of New York. She was born in New Jersey, named Dorothy Rothschild, and grew up in Manhattan, the daughter of a Scottish mother and businessman father; she became famous initially for her witty verse collection, *Enough Rope* (New York, 1926), which she further consolidated with *Sunset Gun* (New York, 1928) and *Death and Taxes* (New York, 1931), all collected later in *Not So Deep as a Well* (New York, 1936), ironic verse satires on the conventions, whether moral or literary, of her times. One of her most famous set of such satires she entitled 'A Pig's-Eye View of Literature'. She moved further still into the public eye with her sketches, stories, reviews and dialogues,

which were published throughout the 1930s, 1940s and 1950s in the *New Yorker*, after her drama criticism in *Vanity Fair* and her picture captions in *Vogue*. Parker's prose writings were also admired for her focused conciseness, combined with a cynical humour, often in the form of uncannily authentic dialogue involving understatement and innuendo. Her satirical commentaries on all aspects of New York life fascinated and unnerved her friends and acquaintances, as she expressed her disillusionment with society through trenchant analyses and cynical judgements which made her famous. Her short stories appeared in the collections *Laments for the Living* (New York, 1930) and *After Such Pleasures* (New York, 1933), collected together in *Here Lies* (New York, 1939). *A Portable Dorothy Parker* appeared in 1973 (New York), an enlarged and revised version of the (New York) 1944 edition. This includes a selection of her popular book reviews originally published in the *New Yorker* and some of her *Esquire* pieces, including a review of Katherine Anne Porter and the Pulitzer Prize-winning novelist Edna Ferber. She also collaborated with Elmer Rice and Arnaud d'Usseau on the plays 'Close Harmony' and 'Ladies of the Corridor', the latter a sad drama of the lonely lives of two New York City widows. She had two Broadway plays written about her, and a third play included a character modelled on her. *The Penguin Dorothy Parker* was published in 1977, and a *Constant Reader* (1970) contains critical essays.

Somerset Maugham described Dorothy Parker's peculiar tang as her gift for being able to laugh even in the midst of the bitterest tragedies. Her stories, he argued, display this comic element as hidden beneath our woes if only we can see things from an imaginative point of view. She achieved this in part by combining in her stories and verse a sense of the inevitable with the unexpected, and this fusion of two apparent oppositions creates a unity of effect which, Maugham suggested, is the essence of Parker's stories. Like many other critics, both contemporary and later writers praised Parker further for the technical perfection of her style, which maintains an air of utter spontaneity while yet being beautifully polished. Unlike Maugham, however, most readers today seem to take Parker more seriously as a short story writer and as an essayist, rather than finding 'the quintessence of her style in the verse'. Her urbane, multifaceted humour and her flamboyant mode of expression are used in the service both of a trenchant satire of social and literary conventions and as an ironic perspective on her own authorial status, as she cynically parodied both the observed and the observer. Parker had an almost uncanny knack for capturing the idiosyncrasies of ordinary dialogue and contemporary speech patterns, and with a few deft strokes of dialogue she could create a whole character, one, moreover, so familiar and recognizable as to shock the reader into a painful yet comical sense of self-consciousness.

Edmund Wilson, another great admirer of Parker, described her accomplishment in unambiguous terms, when he wrote 'She is not Emily Brontë or Jane Austen but . . . she has put into what she has written a voice, a state of mind, an era, a few moments of human experience that nobody else has conveyed.' This achievement was not easily come by, as Parker herself admitted, in spite of the apparent ease and lightness of her style and mood. Not only did she admit to her writing being anything but effortless and immediate (for every dozen words written, she said she crossed out more than half), but her own life was tumultuous and unstable. She was often suicidal; indeed, she is said to have attempted suicide after an abortion in 1923. She was first married for ten years to Edwin Parker; her second attempt at marriage was even more fraught than her first, it seems, as she divorced Alan Cambell, remarried him, separated, and reunited until his death a few years before her own. She was also active against fascism and worked for the Spanish Civil War effort, only, like so many of her friends (such as Hellman), to be harassed and even black-listed in Hollywood for her political sympathies. Yet in spite of all this turmoil, she retained her sense of humour and succeeded in outliving most of her friends, to her embarrassment. The 'disciplined eye and wild mind', which, she argued, were the prerequisites for a humourist, were hers to an unusual degree, whether in her writing or while wryly commentating on her contemporaries – who were as often disconcerted as they were amused. As Wilson put it, her wit was clean and economic but as flatly brutal as that of Pope, and while it was the wit of her own particular time

and place, it was still a trenchant criticism of life.

Part of Parker's skill can be described as a fine balance of sarcasm and understatement: her dissatisfactions with the world around her, with the pretensions and aims of her contemporaries, are often conveyed in a single, crystallizing word or phrase slipped unobtrusively into an innocent sentence. She was famous both for interior monologue of the indirect free narrative kind (which created an until then almost unheard of intimacy and familiarity with her reader) and for her dialogues. In these two characteristic forms, Parker not only captured the free and extravagant atmosphere of her literary-social circle in the 1920s, but also embedded feminist critiques in her ironic portrayals of ordinary everyday incidents. She was an inveterate critic of sexual taboos and conventional morality, making a mockery of 'innocence' in such stories as 'Here We Are'. Indeed, this story is exemplary of so many of Parker's particular literary strengths as to be an excellent introduction to her fiction as a whole. In the story, the newlyweds are travelling by train to New York for their honeymoon, and the repressed subject matter of their conversation, sex, keeps erupting in spite of all their efforts to talk of anything but that. Neither of them ever mentions sex, and neither of them can think of anything else. The entire, plotless story consists of the tangles the two get into through trying to avoid mentioning what is at the forefront of their minds. This dialogue-story is a hilarious – even embarrassing – study of repression and Freudian slips, while the one immediately contrasting with it, 'A Telephone Call', is an example of Parker's famous monologues. This wry and pathetic sketch of a young woman desperately waiting at the end of the phone for her young man to ring is not only a humorously astute, psychological study of the pains of love. It reveals Parker at her best in creating character without any recourse whatsoever to a descriptive, external point of reference, and yet building into the story an ironic level of observation which unifies her fictions and lends them that marvellous tightness of form, achieved without the usual conventions of plot, action or narrative description. The Porter-like interiority of her texts constitutes their powerful immediacy of effect, while an inferred poised ironist hovers just beyond the reader's view to cast a unity of perspective over the whole which transforms pathos into comedy.

Sylvia Townsend Warner 1893–1978

Most noted for the sheer range and versatility of her writing, Warner was born in Harrow, England, and educated at home, intending to become a musician. One of the editors of *Tudor Church Music* (1916–26), she turned eventually to fiction, poetry, essays, biography and translation. By the end of her life, she had published some eight collections of short stories, seven novels, several volumes of poetry, a study of Jane Austen (London, 1951), a biography of T.H. White, highly regarded translations of Proust and others, and numerous essays. She contributed short stories to the *New Yorker* over forty years, witnessed the Spanish Civil War in 1937, worked actively in politics against fascism, and lived much of her life in Dorset with her companion Mary Valentine Ackland. Her early novels, *Lolly Willowes* (London, 1926) – about a woman who rejects her oppressive upper-class family to become a witch – and *Mr Fortune's Maggot* (London, 1927) – the story of a missionary 'coming of age' in his South Sea island community – gained her a literary reputation in England and across America. *The True Heart* (London, 1929), a mock version of the Cupid and Psyche story, confirmed Warner's remarkable range of theme, setting and style. With *Summer Will Show* (London, 1936), one of her most interesting novels, she extended her virtuosity into yet another genre, the political/historical novel. Yet running throughout these wonderfully varied works of fiction is the theme of personal liberation – especially of women – from the dehumanizing conventions and misguided values of an upper-class, materialist, patriarchal culture.

Warner's fiction is characterized most distinctly by two qualities which can be described as, first, an imaginative power of insight into the minds of people, cultures and periods quite different from her own, with an ability to communicate this insight to readers. The second major feature is the force of ideas in her novels; her main characters, often women, are depicted as coming to terms with their existence through the power of thought, through the enabling force of ideas to which they become committed in the course of experiences which shatter their handed-down, preconceived values and beliefs. Most of Warner's social and political criticism – she was actively political during the rise of fascism in the 1930s – is structured through the personal development of her individual characters, who find a variety of ways of escaping (since they can rarely destroy) the constraints of class-ridden, sexist, materialist Britain. Her faith in the power of thought, of ideas and of the individual will is reinforced by her portrayals of women in past historical periods and different cultures, as well as present times, finding modes of living which allow them more individual freedom than the usual stereotypes of wife and mother. The new modes almost never involve relationships with men, except in *The True Heart* (and there the man is an idiot!).

Summer Will Show epitomizes Warner's versatility and her commitment to the power of the intellect and ideas to liberate women from social stereotypes. The novel opens in rural Dorset, and with exhilarating rapidity proceeds, through the death of Sophia's two children from smallpox, to Paris and February of 1848. In making this momentous passage from conservative England to revolutionary France, Warner detours through a compelling first person narrative by Minna (the Jewess lover of Sophia's husband Frederick) of a pogrom in Lithuania which she only barely survived as a child, while witnessing the death of her parents and neighbours. The next few months up to the counter-revolution are interwoven into Sophia's and Minna's gradually developing relationship, which eventually excludes Frederick. Minna's probable death and Sophia's survival of the July rebellion end this complex novel, with Sophia sitting down to submit herself to the study of revolution and to a life of political commitment. Sophia's determination to leave wifehood and motherhood behind as stereotyped roles of limited usefulness, her probably lesbian relationship with Minna, and her political radicalism explain why her novels had not been reprinted until women's presses in the late 1970s and 1980s began changing our view of fiction.

Lolly Willowes and *The Corner That Held Them* (London, 1948) are equally challenging to the patriarchal oppression characteristic of British life to the present day. In the former, Warner wittily turns Christianity against itself in a searing ironic reversal; at the end of the novel, Lolly commits herself to the devil, recognizing that the other witches in the village have not taken their beliefs to their logical conclusions. In *The Corner*, the novel ends with Sibilla, one of the nuns in the convent which is the setting for the novel, setting off on a secret pilgrimage to Jerusalem. Each of the three endings for Sophia, Lolly and Sibilla is a variation on the central motif of liberation through genuine commitment to one's ideals, however far beyond accepted conventions they may carry one, whether to God, Communism or the devil.

While Warner's novels may at first appear to be conventional historical novels, only a few pages into the texts the reader realizes that this fiction is a remarkable fusion of the historical genre and the novel of ideas, tinged with a *Bildungsroman* dimension. Each novel is startlingly different from the others, and each has a fresh vitality and vividness of detail and context which make it 'present' to the reader, whatever its historical setting and however distant in time it may be. Warner also published several collections of short stories, such as *The Salutation* (London, 1932) and *Winter in the Air* (London, 1956).

Jean Crook Devanny 1894–1962

Born near Nelson, New Zealand, Devanny wrote some seven novels before moving with her husband and children to Australia in 1929. A powerful speaker and political activist for the rights of the poor, women and others, Devanny divided her time between social-political struggle and the writing of fiction. She wrote another nine novels while in Australia, in addition to some short stories, essays, travel writing and non-fiction about the aborigines. Her first published novel, *The Butcher Shop* (London, 1926), was banned for its 'offensive' and explicit feminism, Communism and graphic descriptions of brutal farming practices. This began a long period of deeply wounding struggle with the sexism of left politics – freedom for the *male* workers being the latter's limited goal. Devanny's socialism is a socialism for all people, not merely for the

male half of the human race, as is evident from such novels as *Lenore Divine* (London, 1926), *Dawn Beloved* (London, 1928) and *Devil Made Saint* (London, 1930). Strong, intelligent women characters are depicted in a search for sexual and intellectual fulfilment against the often crushing and tragic obstacles of sexist attitudes.

The novels of Devanny's Australian period emphasize even more explicitly the economic basis of racial, sexual and class exploitation. *Sugar Heaven* (Sydney, 1936), set in the North Queensland sugar plantations, portrays a strike from the point of view of women who see the union boss as as much an enemy as the land owners. This novel also explores the ways in which women see sex, power and money as a complex of oppressive forces orchestrated for economic exploitation. Like Eleanor Dark's, then, Devanny's fiction analyses the relationship between personal aspects of human experience and social-political-economic dimensions, refusing to accept any dichotomy. Her last and one of her most successful novels, *Cindie* (London, 1949), focuses her earlier theoretic concerns and narrative techniques into a compelling story which combines history, romance and realism.

More instructive than many historical accounts of the period (1895–1910) of the development of North Queensland, *Cindie* weaves together a scathing exposure of Australian racism (with its apartheid, White Australia legislation), the brutal exploitation of black island races and Chinese, and the virtual extermination of the aborigines with an insightful exploration of characters, from the creative and energetic Cindie, to the intelligent but impractical Randolph, to the depressed and leech-like Blanche. In an inspiring, vigorous tale, Devanny painted a rich canvas of a fantastically luxuriant nature harnessed by the determination and strength (but also the cruelty and greed) of men and women literally hacking civilization out of the jungle. In addition to her fascinating accounts of the social and political issues which raged at the turn of the century, from the deportation of the long-exploited Kanakas to the arguments about federation for Australia, Devanny constructed a riveting story of the young maidservant Cindie's rise to equality. Thus, this chronicle of the history of the building of Australia revolves around the individual success of a character in building a life for herself, out of servitude and into fulfilment and autonomy, through intelligence and labour. A stark contrast is drawn between Cindie's methods – of cooperation, sharing, and fair reward to the people she works with – and the methods of the white land owners, whose exploitation varies from benign to obscene, but is still exploitation.

The interplay between social-historical context and personal life is evident in all Devanny's novels, but reaches a fine culmination in *Cindie* and in *Sugar Heaven*. Successful in her depiction of Blanche, Randolph and Cindie, Devanny explored, in her last novel, the psychology of three distinct character types, types which are of universal significance. Like Susan Glaspell before her, Devanny used characterization to express powerful natural forces of creativity and destruction, embodied in individual people. This and the depiction of nature are her two main literary techniques, rather than plot, point of view or style. These latter are subjected to the overriding concern of using language and literature to reveal basic patterns in human individuals, and thereby give readers a clearer insight into typical human relationships and experiences. Devanny's efforts to analyse the contemporary social reality of early twentieth-century Australia, then, were always depicted by means of a strong connection between the personal and the political. This faith brought her into further conflict with the radical left, as did her commitment to an art and literature freed from the dictates of social realism. Her championing of women and black people was anathema to the sexist, racist politicians of the Labour movement during that period (and into the present day). Her literary skill in constructing black and women characters of markedly greater humanity, intelligence and maturity than most of the greedy, egotistical white males furthered her social-political philosophy.

Given the diversity and scope of Devanny's fiction and her deft handling of individual characters, complex plot and the natural world as a powerful setting and atmosphere for her novels, there is a need to see more of her novels republished; for they are compelling works of fiction and are also of considerable social-historical interest. Moreover, a sequel to *Cindie*, entitled 'You Can't Have Everything', has never been published, in part because of the increasingly hostile reaction of Devanny's political 'friends'

to her work. Her autobiography, *Point of Departure* (St Lucia, Queensland, 1986), ed. C. Ferrier, was finally published after much delay. *Travels in North Queensland* appeared in 1951 (London).

Marjorie Barnard 1897–1987

Collaborator with Flora Eldershaw (under the pseudonym M. Barnard Eldershaw), Marjorie Barnard was born in Sydney in 1897, where she attended the university and graduated with the university medal for history in 1918. She became a full-time writer in 1935, after working as a librarian for some years (she turned down a scholarship to Oxford). She wrote a biography of Miles Franklin (New York, 1967; reissued 1988), and her novels include, with Eldershaw, *A House is Built* (London, 1929), which, with Katharine Susannah Prichard's *Coonardoo*, won the *Bulletin* prize for best novel of the year. *A House* was then serialized in the *Bulletin*; it charts the rise and fall of a business family in New South Wales, providing an astute account of social and economic conditions in the mid-nineteenth century. Already in this first novel, Barnard and Eldershaw can be seen seeking to expose social injustice. Their later novels continued this strong sense of the novelist's social responsibility, and of the complex relation of fiction to history. That is, fiction does not merely record or document history for Barnard and Eldershaw. Fiction, it is made clear, *is* history; it influences attitudes, values and, eventually, events. Yet literature also constitutes history, both as cultural social event and as pre-eminent record. For Barnard, whose interests in history are concretized in her non-fictional works – her histories, biographies and criticism – the major source for historical accounts is precisely the records and documentation of literature itself. Like Prichard, Barnard and Eldershaw sought a fusion of literature and history in their avoidance of the more symbolic and poetic fictional style of Christina Stead, for example.

Other novels with Eldershaw include *Green Memory* (London, 1931), *The Glasshouse* (London, 1936) and *Plaque of Laurel* (London, 1937), and their literary criticism appeared in the collection *Essays in Australian Fiction* (Melbourne, 1938). In 1943, Barnard published her own short stories, *The Persimmon Tree and Other Stories* (Sydney, reprinted London, 1985). *Tomorrow and Tomorrow* (Melbourne), an extensively censored novel of pacifism, appeared in 1947, with Barnard as the main author, though Eldershaw contributed. Their collaboration is somewhat ambiguously described by Barnard:

> We'd go for long walks together and talk and talk about the book we were going to write until it was worked out thoroughly. After that it didn't really matter who wrote it. Flora had a better brain than I had but I was probably the better writer. I'd write a chapter and she would criticise it and then I'd rewrite.

Restored to its full length, the book was published in 1983 as *Tomorrow and Tomorrow and Tomorrow*, and won the Patrick White Award. In 1984, Barnard received the New South Wales Premier Award, previously awarded also to Christina Stead. This once-controversial novel was given a 'high place in Australian literature', and its subtle handling of complex issues was praised as highly original. It is set some several hundred years in the future, with a historical novelist trying to understand and interpret the earlier events of the 1930s and 1940s, after a third world war. The somewhat utopian framework of the novel seems more a literary device to explore the meaning of the mid-twentieth-century events than an effort to describe an ideal future; for the novel is most powerful in its effective and evocative descriptions of Barnard's own time, as contrasted with the underdeveloped picture of the future. The scenes set in the Sydney of the 1930s and 1940s vividly portray the conflicting claims of war and peace, society and individual liberty, art and politics.

Even a cursory glance at Barnard's short stories, such as 'The Persimmon Tree', should, however, dispel the notion that she was a late social realist novelist. (The stories were reissued in 1989, *But Not For Love*.) As in Prichard's work, the overt, thematic concern with social justice sometimes obscured the fine craft of the novels and the careful structure, and even symbolism, of the writings. This latter quality came across most directly in Barnard's short fiction, where social and political themes are only

suggested by impressionistic, imagistic and symbolic language. The indirect approach to women's relationships with each other and with men, whether in a story like 'The Persimmon Tree' or in 'Habit', suggests that she was anything but insensitive to modernist experiments. Indeed, a close familiarity with these stories makes it possible to read her novels with greater appreciation of the subtler figurations and ironic touches which are often missed.

Kate O'Brien 1897–1974

Playwright and novelist, critic and travel writer, Kate O'Brien saw two of her novels banned for immorality in her home country, Ireland. These were *Mary Lavelle* (London and Garden City, N.Y., 1936, 1984) and *The Land of Spices* (London and Garden City, N.Y., 1941, 1988). Great Irish predecessor of Edna O'Brien, she explored with (apparently offensive) frankness and eloquence the means women adopt to escape the sexual and emotional exploitation of traditional social roles. Influenced by such contemporaries as Edith Wharton, and by their older contemporary Henry James, O'Brien focused her artist's eye upon the insufficiency of accepted social forms of behaviour for the expression of great passion and imagination, anticipating Freud's own similar social criticism from a more overtly psychoanalytical point of view. Her most accomplished novels, *Mary Lavelle* and *That Lady* (London and New York, 1946, 1985), are finely tuned psychological studies, the one of youthful struggle with 'illicit' passion, the other of moral and spiritual struggle, in middle age, against male tyranny.

Born in Limerick, O'Brien attended University College, Dublin, and took a BA before travelling to America and then to Spain as a governess in the early 1920s. There she started to write, perhaps stimulated by a great love of that land, which is the setting for some of her finest writing. Upon her return, she lived in England for some years, working for the *Manchester Guardian* and writing plays, some of which were performed to great acclaim. Her first novel, *Without My Cloak* (London and Garden City, N.Y., 1931, 1986), also met with enormous success, winning two prizes, the James Tait Black

Memorial and the Hawthornden. *The Anteroom* (London and Garden City, N.Y., 1934) followed, a novel which intertwines love and death into a single theme as her next novel, *Mary Lavelle*, was also to do. Other novels include *The Land of Spices* and *As Music and Splendour* (London and New York, 1958). Most of O'Brien's nine novels emphasize characters (often women characters) struggling with conventions, whether moral, social, religious or artistic. Many deal with the specific difficulties for women of gaining independence through education, travel, financial autonomy and self-development. O'Brien was daringly critical in many novels of Catholic orthodoxies, seeking to distinguish the spiritual greatness of that religion from the church's and priestly overlay of unjustifiable dogma.

O'Brien wrote a number of non-fictional books, including *Farewell, Spain* (London and Garden City, N.Y., 1932) and *My Ireland* (London and New York, 1962), as well as *English Diaries and Journals* (London, 1943) and *Presentation Parlour* (London, 1963), a rare autobiographical sketch. In these works, specific reference is made to a theme evident in much contemporary Irish writing, namely the alienation many gifted and imaginative people felt toward the dogmatism and prejudice of Catholic Ireland, which inhibited their personal lives, their artistic efforts and their spiritual fulfilment.

As the works of one of Ireland's outstanding twentieth-century novelists, O'Brien's novels have usually been discussed in terms of their historical and social dimensions and their overt thematics. Like Wharton's writings, however, they are genuine artifacts, which gain their force and inspiration in part from the fine literary representations of the psychological dramas of their characters. Along with the carefully structured thematics, these elements propel the reader forward with the intensity of a Greek tragedy. This concentration of action alternates, however, with more leisured meditations on aesthetic, emotional and moral conflicts, as well as powerfully descriptive evocations of place and setting, beautifully threaded into a novelistic unity of unusual balance in *Mary Lavelle*. On the other hand, *That Lady* experiments more emphatically with meditative narrative handling of moral struggles, so that dramatic action plays a less central role than in the former text. Yet in both

novels, Spain – understood as both splendour of landscape and people – seems to have been the essential inspiration which raised O'Brien to her highest imaginative powers.

Mary Lavelle is arguably her most impressive achievement, if not thematically (*That Lady* holds thematic first place) then in terms of its imaginative intensity, derived from the profundities and intensities of Spain itself, with its harshly beautiful landscape, its brilliant colour, its incomparable paintings, literature and architecture, its long, tortured history, and its dignified and courageous people. As with Thomas Hardy, landscape becomes a central artistic power in this novel, awakening its heroine both to realities and to shadows which, until her arrival in Spain, had lain only on the periphery of her consciousness. The novel begins with various literary devices, such as a series of letters, after a Nathaniel Hawthorne-like, startlingly ironic prologue; the letters give a good deal of background material about Mary, but have been criticized as clumsy. Yet they recur on several occasions in the novel, and function well aesthetically, both to relieve the omniscient narrative perspective and to draw the reader more intimately into Mary's psychology and character. The prologue's irony, on the other hand, is a sharp warning to the reader that this novel is no simple romance. It is a complex work of art, as O'Brien sought to avoid the worn-out literary conventions of the traditional romance genre. She set her exploration of sexual passion, moral dilemma and emotional fulfilment in new artistic structures, but in the context of the tensions between life and death, youth and age, secular and sacred, and sensual and spiritual. Hence, the haunting relationship between Mary and Juanito is restricted in the narrative to a quite small portion of the story, as though O'Brien were following Willa Cather's principle of condensation and suggestion. Yet, small as the amount of narrative given to this relationship is, it is portrayed with such effective power that it is able to function as the backbone upon which the rest of the novel is fleshed out. And, while there is considerable flesh, the portrayal of the dramatic passion of the two central characters carries this weighty intellectual material with stunning ease.

This novel is a triumph aesthetically; O'Brien

117

drew imaginatively upon one aesthetic formal property, motif or convention after another to build up an astonishingly harmonious and well-proportioned unity. Chapter after chapter unfolds with prognostications of the tragedy to come, from the majestic introduction of Don Pablo (Juanito's father and Mary's beloved employer), to the sickeningly beautiful 'Corrida' (the bullfight and an emblem of art itself), to Mary's 'destined' meeting with Juanito, then the trip to Madrid, the 'side-trip' to Toledo, the eventual consummation of love in the Basque country, and, finally, Don Pablo's death scene. Each of these sections functions with fine economy to build up a beautifully complex, unified work of art. Meanwhile, the various scenes in town with the other Irish governesses function, in part, as a sobering yet light relief from the Spanish intensities of the main chapters, and in part both to paint a social portrait of the bourgeois female mentality and to introduce the theme of lesbianism. O'Brien wasted no opportunity of instilling the discrete parts of her novels with symbolic reverberations of the whole. This constant sense that every element of the novel, no matter how small or apparently insignificant, is playing its assigned role in the creation of a total, complex unity of effect wins the novel a tremendous beauty.

Appreciation of *Mary Lavelle* is also enhanced greatly by careful scrutiny of the central aesthetic role of Don Pablo. Like Ellen Glasgow four years earlier in *The Sheltered Life*, Kate O'Brien wonderfully personified imagination itself, here in Juanito's father, and narrated this emblematic force by means of philosophic meditations, memories and evocations of the past. The contrasts between present and past, innocence and experience, youth and age, and sensuality and spirituality which structure the novel are also constructed artistically as inextricable relationship, rather than duality or opposition. Meanwhile, the overwhelming force of Don Pablo's philosophic, detached observation, first of Mary, then of Juanito, and eventually of their tragic love, hovers awesomely over the novel, like Glasgow's own hovering portrayal of naked imagination in the person of the splendid old general. This alternative perspective to the events creates a third dimension to the story, which is like the ironic backward glance so characteristic of the Pindaric ode – it pulls the previous elements together into a staggeringly compelling whole, which leaves the reader stunned into admiration and drained by the sheer force of the narrative beauty. Thus, O'Brien's achievement is truly artistic; she wrote not merely convincing historical novels, not merely sophisticated novels of ideas, but novels of fine artistic integrity, especially *Mary Lavelle*, but also *That Lady* and others. The present emphasis upon structure and artistic unity should not, however, be allowed to diminish her achievement as a stylist or her intellectual power. As can be seen especially in the sections on Don Pablo, or those on Mary and Juanito together, O'Brien's prose achieves great musicality, while her versatility is attested to by the humorous and often tragic sections on the Irish governesses. The sections, however, which stand out for particular stylistic effect are the bullfight, the final love scene and the early portrayal of Don Pablo, where O'Brien's prose reaches a stunning imaginative power, since these sections are emblematic of imaginative creation itself. This power is in part achieved by her thematic fusion of love and death, the explanation for which is given by her most clearly in the bullfight chapter, where art, love and death are united in one force of beauty. The bullfight becomes the symbol both for art and for natural life forces which are constantly thwarted by convention, church and mediocrity: 'it stands for something that you can't defend, but that, in a way, doesn't need defending.' Beauty, whether in love or art or life or death, was, for O'Brien, truth; it was the surest touchstone for spiritual guidance and development.

Winifred Holtby 1898–1935

Described by her biographer and close friend of sixteen years Vera Brittain (in *Testament of Friendship* (London, 1940, 1980) as 'too vital and radiant a creature for death to touch', Holtby died at the age of 37 of kidney disease. Yet, in her short life she produced a quantity and quality of work which few of us achieve. Born in Yorkshire, she met Brittain at Oxford, where she attended and graduated from Somerville College. The two women moved to London and shared a flat, indeed continued to share a home after Brittain's marriage and the arrival of children which Holtby helped to raise. (She herself became engaged only shortly before her death.) Director of *Time and Tide* from 1926 and prolific contributor to other journals and newspapers (such as the *Manchester Guardian* and *News Chronicle*), Holtby soon became known for her intelligent and lively journalism, her progressive, humane politics, her advocacy of peace, her lifelong battle against racism, and her practical (if not theoretical) feminism. While she never gave the time and labour to her journalism which she gave to her imaginative fiction, she became known in the mid-1930s as one of the 'most brilliant' of London journalists. And, though she deplored the necessity for feminism, she pursued that necessity to its social sources in her book *Women and a Changing Civilization* (London, 1934). There, she showed that the origins of sexism lay in a deep-rooted prejudice against a woman's equal right to paid work. She wrote of this issue in her essays, books and articles, guided by her vision of 'a society in which men and women work together for the good of all mankind, a society in which there is no respect of persons, either male or female, but a supreme regard for the importance of the human being'. Her other non-fiction book is a critical study, *Virginia Woolf* (London, 1932); she also published poetry and a satirical work, *The Astonishing Island* (London and New York, 1933).

Holtby's first novel, *Anderby Wold* (London, 1923), traces the demise both of the traditional Robsons and of the fiery, red-haired socialist youth David Rossitur. It received considerable notice and was followed shortly by *The Crowded Street* (London, 1924), less successful than her first, even by her own estimation. *The Land of Green Ginger* (London and New York, 1927) took up more successfully its theme of the yearning for the magical and the exotic behind the veil of everyday life. This novel, like *Mandoa! Mandoa!* (London and New York, 1933), was in part the result of a trip to South Africa in 1926 – South Africa being the land of green ginger, that magical realm which haunts yet eludes the ordinary in life. Though set in a Yorkshire farm, this third novel takes up issues about death, marriage and sexual freedom in the life of the young Joanna, whose death of the spirit is traced in moving detail. *Poor Caroline* (London and New

York, 1931), published to much acclaim four years later, represents a different view – the satiric, ironic treatment of the elderly and of women's organizations generally, though, as usual, Holtby's critical wit is tempered by an appreciation of the basic humanity and even inspiring ardour of Caroline's missions. *Mandoa! Mandoa!* followed shortly, returning to issues of racism as expressed through the character Arthur Rollitt, who pits himself against the brutal, money-greedy proponents of slavery and racism. This novel was a great success, and gave Holtby more financial independence that she had ever enjoyed before. Two collections of short stories appeared in 1934 and, posthumously, in 1937, the year in which Holtby's acknowledged crown of achievement, *South Riding* (London and New York, 1936) won the James Tait Black Memorial Prize, but only after her tragic death.

South Riding, Holtby's most substantial and accomplished novel, was written almost entirely during the last two years of her life when she was critically, disablingly ill. The appreciation of *South Riding* and Holtby's other novels is considerably enhanced by a reading of her short study of Virginia Woolf. There, many of her artistic concerns and related human preoccupations are formulated and expressed more directly and overtly than is appropriate in works of fiction, since they function through indirection, suggestion and metaphor. The study of Woolf emphasizes, above all, Holtby's belief in those 'moments of being' so central to Woolf's fiction and experience: 'There are moments of revelation which compensate for the chaos, the discomfort, the toil of living. The crown of life is neither happiness nor annihilation; it is understanding. The artist's intuitive vision ... these are the moments in which all the disorder of life assumes a pattern.' Related to this faith and understanding is Holtby's conviction that none of us is only or primarily an individual; we are each part of one another. This fine balance and rejection of experience as dualistic, as of self versus other or individual versus society, constitute the heart of Holtby's imaginative vision. Subsidiary issues also arise, especially in *South Riding* – her fullest artistic and formal development of these themes – about the nature of love as capable of transcending differences in opinions, politics, attitudes and ideals: 'In the end – it's not politics nor opinions – it's those fundamental things that count – the things of the spirit.' This remark of the politically committed Mrs Beddows should not be taken too literally. She was arguing that people may be misguided or even wrong in their avowed politics or stated ideals – wedded to old-fashioned, traditional or paternalistic notions. Yet they may still have a spiritual passion, a commitment to the well-being of others, and an ability to be loving – which many people with more progressive views, but less heart, passion or spirit, lack.

South Riding may develop further these themes occurring in the earlier novels, but in formal structure and artistic complexity it surpasses all her earlier writings. Its complexity of plot is beautifully woven together, so that each sub-plot is not only of significant interest itself; these various aspects reflect and draw out specific significances of the more major, more central elements of the novel, such as Sarah's moral development, her growing love for the impossibly conservative Carne, and the crucial importance of local political actions for the social welfare of the individual and the community: 'Maybe all that we do here isn't very splendid. As I see it, when you come to the bottom, all this local government, it's just working together – us ordinary people, against the troubles that afflict all of us – poverty, ignorance, sickness, isolation – madness.' The emphasis here is on both 'together' and 'working', for Holtby knew that until women and men could be ensured meaningful work, no society can call itself civilized.

Elizabeth Bowen 1899–1973

Prolific novelist, short story writer and reviewer, Bowen was born in Dublin to an Anglo-Irish family and grew up in their ancestral home, Bowen Court, in County Cork. Educated in England for the most part, she married in 1923 and soon moved to Oxfordshire, where she socialized with academics and writers, including Rose Macaulay. Macaulay encouraged her and her writing and gave her practical help in getting volumes of stories published in these early years. After inheriting Bowen Court in 1930, Bowen moved with her husband to Regent's Park in London. Her first few novels and short story collections, from *Encounters* (London, 1923) to *The Hotel* (London, 1927), *The Last September* (London and New York, 1929), *Friends and Relations* (London and New York, 1931) and *To the North* (London, 1932), gained her much notice, and she began to frequent Bloomsbury and to associate with Virginia Woolf. Her novels were treated with great respect by reviewers, and she was often compared to E.M. Forster, Henry James, Woolf and others for her technical skill, her fluency in depicting moral-social complexity in a combined analysis of society and personal relations, and her specific interest in moral corruption as a result of a too-great emphasis upon formalities at the expense of fundamental decencies. Indeed, Bowen's near-contemporary Edith Wharton, along with James, may have been a more considerable influence on the development and particular character of her fiction than those she is usually compared with: Ivy Compton-Burnett, Woolf or Evelyn Waugh. Less obviously experimental than Woolf's, yet more richly textured and dense than Compton-Burnett's, Bowen's fiction is in an uneasy relation with either realism or modernism. Much aware of James and the moral uncertainties of experience, much like Wharton in her particular interest in portraying women, innocence, corruption and betrayal in its social milieu and physical-political setting, Bowen made sophisticated (albeit subtle) use of varying points of view and layerings of narrative consciousness to express the difficulty in finding a firm moral footing, even if indecency can be firmly identified.

After this first clutch of novels appeared, Bowen followed it up with *The House in Paris* (London, 1935), *The Death of the Heart* (London, 1938) and numerous works of non-fiction, before *The Heat of the Day* (London) appeared in 1949. Like *The Last September* and *To the North*, *The Death of the Heart* and *The House in Paris* confirmed Bowen's reputation as an accomplished novelist, essayist and prose writer. Memoirs such as *Bowen's Court* (London and New York, 1942) and *Seven Writers* (Dublin, 1942) appeared, as did critical works, such as *English Novelists* (London, 1942) and the play *Anthony Trollope: A New Judgement* (London and New York, 1946). More novels include *A World of Love* (London and New York, 1955) and the enigmatic final novel *Eva Trout* (New

York, 1968), an ironic, masterly study of the counterplay between human will and indomitable life's contingency. This last novel, which nonplussed and irritated most of Bowen's admirers when it first appeared, is the final gesture of a successful writer. With it, Bowen launched at her complacent readership a violent rupture with her past fiction, an almost post-modernist anti-novel. Its disruptive plot, its themes of dislocation and alienation, its gratuitous violence at the 'end', its patchy, sketchy thematics and characterization suggest an effort at an overt rejection of conventions she had previously accepted. Functioning at an almost structuralist level of types and motifs of fairy-tale schematics, the novel can be read as Bowen's gesture towards moving the novel forward into a different landscape, where the real and the fantastic, the probable and the improbable, become almost indistinguishable.

Such sophisticated awareness of the novel as a set of varying conventions, reading as a set of expected responses, and writing as a set of accepted gestures is not absent in earlier novels, from *The Last September* and *To the North* to *The Death of the Heart* and *The Heat of the Day*, for example. In *To the North*, Bowen used – not without considerable irony – the literary convention of the journey, contrasted with the house or home, as the single most powerful structuring device and thematic motif. Journeys are so central a part of the novel as to become its thematics – albeit implying or symbolizing complex moral issues. Described with quite unusual violence, exuberance and vitality, these journeys are the occasion for nearly every significant event in the novel. Similarly, though perhaps less systematically, *The Death of the Heart* is structured around a series of journeys contrasted with the power of the house. No choice or preference for home versus journey is implied, however. Yet Bowen's almost obtrusive foregrounding of travel in these novels alerts the reader to a sophistication in her use of plot, characterization, romance and other conventions to draw attention to the importance of integrating formalities into fundamental decencies. Indeed, one could argue that Bowen, like Wharton and James, used every one of her narrative fictions to explore the idea that most moral corruption (and our destruction of innocence and decency in each other) arises from a divorce between formalities and fundamental decencies. The distinction between what is 'right' (according to rules of courtesy, social manners and custom) and what is 'good' (according to some deeper moral impulse of fellow love, empathy and compassion) comes up repeatedly in Bowen's fiction, and it has its aesthetic counterpoint in the question of what is a correct novel (what an audience expects) and what is a good novel (which may defy the expectations, the decorum, the conventions of contemporary writing).

The schism opened up in society by people opting for the formalities – the trappings of courtesy, the right accent, the proper behaviour, the correct manners, the titles, the proprieties, the dress, the possessions, the appearance of cultivation: all the forms of civility without the heart of it – is the constant preoccupation of Bowen, as it was of Wharton and James. What comes from the heart will be crushed and mocked if the heart has not been schooled in the proper, accepted manners. Here, Bowen's fiction shows its readers, is where corruption flourishes, in the world of mediocrity, where passion, emotion, anger and love are sacrificed to some upper middle-class adherence to notions of superiority. To be superior to the lesser orders is to be imperturbable, emotionless, perfectly controlled at all times, but incapacitated to cope with the unpleasant, the intense, the real. Bowen's acute vision searches out the utter sham at the basis of these pretensions, and condemns a huge proportion of the middle and upper classes for moral depravity, for all their fine manners. Few readers will not be a target of her searchlight.

The House in Paris brings together Bowen's writerly practices into an exquisite unity of aesthetic design. Out of the novel's artistically effective ambivalence between a two- and three-part structure, between the settings of journey and house, time past and time present, passion and decorum, and child versus adult narrative perspectives, Bowen created one of the most accomplished novels of this period. She drew upon the recent psychological discoveries of Freud and others, and upon Woolf's recent innovations, as well as upon traditional techniques. She fused these into an intensely passionate yet profoundly intellectual exploration of human experience, completed by the detached, ironic, watching consciousness of one of the characters.

The duality initially set up in the novel's structure (part I, 'The Present', 50 pages; part II, 'The Past', 125 pages; part III, 'The Present', again 50 pages) is split into three by dividing the present events into a two-part 'frame' for the past, which is the longest section and presented as the unified 'heart' or centre of the novel. Distinctions between frame and centre constantly threaten to elude the reader, however, as both the narrative of the past and its 'other', the present, frame each other as equally central and equally marginal. Thus, while 'The Past' may relate the details of the illicit passion of the adult characters as though subsidiary to and explanatory of 'The Present', that section of the novel itself becomes the very basis of 'The Present'.

The various themes of the novel revolve explicitly and systematically around knowledge – overtly, children's struggles to gain knowledge about parents, but also about sex, passion, origins and adulthood. An incessant questioning by the characters of the meanings of things virtually constitutes the plot of this Jamesean novel. Meaning and interpretation as thematics become the vehicles for Bowen's interrogation of reality, truth and what we mean by concepts such as the self, consciousness, love, good and evil, and so on. Bowen brought in narrative and thematic elements which would dispel in any careful reader's mind the notion that post-structuralism and post-modernism are 'new', moreover. Reading becomes the overt subject matter of a text awash with, for example, letters which arrive but get into the 'wrong' hands, letters missing from empty envelopes, messages deciphered from impressions left on the next sheet of a writing pad (Freud's magic writing pad or *Wunderblock*: see chapter 1). Telegrams which shatter long-awaited meetings arrive altogether too successfully, and characters literally 'read' each other's unconscious motives and feelings on that page called the human visage. Bowen further enriched her text with other familiar narrative conventions such as, again, the journey, highlighting arrivals and departures. She used a doubling of characters who function as alternative points of view, and she placed extreme emphasis upon what is not said, what does not happen, what is absent, missing or lacking. The missing letter

from the mother, Karen, her son Leopold's *Godot*-like waiting for a mother who fails to appear: these non-elements are the very essence of the novel, its plot, its thematics. The portrayal of the expected fulfilment of Leopold's yawning, abysmal desire for his unknown mother, whom he has never yet seen or met, of his gaping lack and longing to be taken away by her forever from his adoptive parents, leads to nerve-wracking deferral. An at first totally inadequate stepfather appears in her stead, legislating, ordering and demanding obedience to his new laws.

All this is observed by the chillingly uninvolved 11-year-old Henrietta, accidentally passing through Paris this momentous day. Henrietta remains an enigma to the reader, until finally one realizes her pivotal aesthetic, self-referential role as embedded reader: observer of events, gradually drawn emotionally into them for a time, and then released completely out of the lives of the players, as the day (the book, the story) ends.

Like many of Bowen's other novels, such as *Eva Trout, The House in Paris* seems almost to constitute a literary enactment of the kinds of psychological insight which were so explosive in the early decades of this century. Metaphors about conscious/unconscious dynamics abound, as repression and denial are explored through constant reference to the unsaid and unsayable, the obfuscated and absent. Bowen's texts confirm that the surest way to invest something with intense meaning is to deny it, forget it, ignore it. Through constant reference to the instability between dualities of self/other, reality/illusion, truth/lie, past/present and so on, Bowen set up a model for the meaningfulness of oppositions as in a perpetual transformation of one into the other. Instability and displacement, through metaphors of travel, exile and alienation, are just as full of meaning as at-homeness and stability. The known and familiar is made uncanny – indeed, this is one of her most characteristic practices. Efforts by the characters to read, understand, know and interpret are portrayed as leading from one letter, event or person to another, all only partly readable and in need of further reading. Gradually, one is filled with the sense that not only is the unconscious unreadable: so is the conscious. Not only are the truths of the subtext unreadable: even the surface is so. Finally, the self is as unknowable as are other persons.

The aesthetically puzzling frequency of journeyings in Bowen's fiction takes on fuller significance from the realization that shuttling from one destination to another becomes a central emblem for knowledge, meaning and the reality of human life. To gain knowledge is to move from one perspective, metaphor or language to another. The act of understanding or of deciphering meaning involves not arrival at definiteness, stability and certainty, but displacement into a different position, relation or 'state'. To 'know' oneself, the texts suggest, or to arrive at knowledge of sex, another person or truth is not to uncover definite meanings. Rather, knowledge is movement, change, the ability to translate and interrelate. Meaning, like characters, travels and circulates, displacing the present meaning for another, displacing the present itself for another interpretation of it.

Surface text and subtext distinctions are also elided, as is unconscious/conscious, or past/present. 'The wish to know / What else is there?' Bowen remarked, thematizing it in this novel to a level of self-referentiality not elsewhere achieved. Leopold's *béance* (see chapter 1), his desire for his mother, becomes the emblem for all desire, including the reader's desire for meaning. In *The House in Paris*, we read of our own reading as desire for knowledge, but Bowen shows that what *is* known is, simply, nothing.

Hermione Lee has edited a selection of Bowen's non-fiction, *The Mulberry Tree*, with a helpful commentary (London, 1986).

Zelda Fitzgerald 1900–1948

Born Zelda Sayre in Montgomery, Alabama, Zelda married F. Scott Fitzgerald in 1920, the year his first novel was published. They soon began their own legendary drama of a fabulous life in the 1920s in America and France, before Scott succumbed to alcoholism (dying in 1940), and Zelda to mental breakdowns. In the meantime, Scott published *The Great Gatsby* (New York, 1925) and Zelda *Save Me the Waltz* (New York, 1932), which she composed allegedly in six weeks of feverish writing in a hospital in

Montgomery and Baltimore after a breakdown. Zelda also published ten stories, later collected in *Bits of Paradise* (London, 1973; New York, 1974), and she wrote a play in 1932, *Scandalabra* (Columbia, S.C., 1980), staged in Baltimore in July in 1933, and published in 1980 in a limited edition. She wrote as well a number of essays and articles for magazines, such as *McCall's*, *College Humor* and the *Saturday Evening Post*, though these have only just been collected again and republished in *The Collected Writings of Zelda Fitzgerald*, ed. M.J. Bruccoli (New York, 1991), with a very helpful introduction by Mary Gordon. This volume does not, unfortunately, include a partially written novel of about seven chapters, entitled 'Caesar's Things', the manuscript of which is in the Princeton University Library with others of Zelda's papers. (The Beinecke Library at Yale University also has papers of hers in its Collection of American Literature.)

It has proven difficult to determine how much F. Scott rifled Zelda's diaries and letters for what he called 'material' for his novels, or how much of her own writing they published under his name, or how much she helped him and collaborated in his work. He certainly 'raised a terrible row when she published her novel' (according to a granddaughter, Scottie Fitzgerald Smith), it encroaching, as he saw it, on his own *Tender is the Night* (1934), which caused him agonies of effort. Elsewhere, Zelda remarked of *The Beautiful and the Damned* (1922) by F. Scott: 'I recognized a portion of an old diary of mine . . . and also scraps of letters . . . Mr Fitzgerald . . . seems to believe plagiarism begins at home.'

Zelda was not only the author of a small but noteworthy body of writings. She had also studied successfully as a ballerina, though it is said that she probably began too late to be first class. Nevertheless, she received great praise from her teachers, and began a career before ill-health defeated it. An admirer of the great American painter Georgia O'Keeffe, she herself twice exhibited her paintings and drawings in 1934, after the physical collapse which made dancing too difficult. In addition to these gifts, she was an impressive personality. Edmund Wilson praised both her writing and her 'delightful, fresh expression', explaining: 'She had no ready-made phrases on the one hand and no straining for effect on the other . . . she talked with so spontaneous a color and wit – almost exactly in the way she wrote.'

Both Zelda and F. Scott drew extensively in their fiction on their own personal lives as well as on the social context of their time, Scott struggling for nearly a decade to finish *Tender is the Night*, his last, most autobiographical novel. Six years later he died of a heart attack; Zelda perished in a fire in a sanatorium in 1948. His final novel is often thought to be a response to Zelda's fictionalization of her life with him in *Save Me the Waltz*, though this, one of his masterpieces, gains much of its passion and commitment from its character as an apologia and defence. Read side by side, the two books offer fascinating alternative views of a marriage, and alternative conceptions of writing, by two relatively modernist novelists; as well, two distinct accounts are offered of the glamorous and often tragic social scene of these remarkable years.

Save Me the Waltz was not particularly well received when first published in New York, but some twenty years later another edition in London received considerable praise, both for its strikingly forceful style and for its formal vitality. It has now been republished several times, both by Jonathan Cape and most recently by Penguin. Like Scott, Zelda was mistress of that transformation of life, shapeless as it is, into art. And like Leonora Carrington, she used her visual, painter's eye for observation of form and colour in verbal compositions of genuine originality and power. Perhaps the most predominant success of *Save Me the Waltz* is its author's evident talent for dialogue as the central narrative device for creating plot, action, character and scene. Zelda Fitzgerald also clearly borrowed modernist disruptive techniques regarding overt progression and unity; a camera lens zooms in and out, jumps from one perspective to another, leaps forward, then compresses momentous occasions into moments of narrative insignificance. The hard-won career of Alabama, the protagonist, as a ballet dancer is snuffed out with the lightest touch, and the juxtaposition of it with the death of her father reverberates with thematic connotations. Narrative understatement is also carried to a fine art, as Alabama's husband David is rarely criticized overtly, and her daughter Bonnie provides an idealized, romantic, mirror-

distortion of events. An ironic narrative detachment creates a stage-like space in which the events of the novel's scenes take on a theatrical resonance; the last sentence of the book is finely expressive of both this and the evocative effects of Zelda Fitzgerald's writing: 'They sat in the pleasant gloom of the late afternoon, staring at each other through the remains of the party; the silver glasses, the silver tray, the traces of many perfumes; they sat together watching the twilight flow through the calm living-room that they were leaving like the clear cold current of a trout stream.'

The vitality and spontaneity of Zelda's writing, its sensual detail and vividness, have often been noted and attributed to her willingness to use techniques of free association and to tolerate, on the surface of her fiction, an apparent disorderliness and fragmentation typical of modernist writing and of life itself. Some writers and critics have compared this to the techniques of surrealists and those influenced by surrealism. But Zelda's writing does not convey at all the surrealistic strangeness of, say, Anna Kavan, Carrington, or even Anaïs Nin's more modified version. Nor is it particularly fragmented or disorderly, as it is usually said to be, even by appreciative friends and admirers. There is nothing particularly 'loose' or 'associative' about *Save Me the Waltz*, or many of the stories. These notions and prejudices could be quickly dispelled by a fresh reading of her fiction, her play or her essays. *Save Me the Waltz* is, in fact, a well-constructed, carefully thought-out unity. It is also a stylistically impressive and sustained piece of fiction; it is an imaginative transformation of Zelda's autobiographical material into a very compelling novel. This finely portrays a young woman's desperately tragic efforts to sustain her self-development, in the face of cruel and largely unconscious personal and social pressures for self-sacrifice, for the sake of her 'more talented' husband.

Zelda's conception of art is expressed in a number of letters to F. Scott, and these reveal an intelligent, theoretically astute mind reflecting on central issues about art, writing and how to live life creatively. A letter dated June 1934 is exemplary of her spontaneous yet reflective bent: 'The artist's business is to take a willing mind and guide it to hope or despair, contributing not his interpretations but a glimpse of his honestly earned scars of battle ... To open some new facet of the stark emotions or to preserve some old one in the grace of a phrase seem nearer to the artistic end.'

Eleanor Dark 1901–1985

Eleanor Dark is one of the most experimental of the Australian writers of her time, anticipating both in theme and technique later developments in literature and in society. She was born in Sydney, but after marriage in 1922 lived in Katoomba, New South Wales, in the Blue Mountains. She began writing poetry as a teenager under a pseudonym but later turned to novels and short stories. Her experimentation concerned primarily narrative time, rather than the stylistic-linguistic experiments of modernists, but in her use of flashbacks, memories, hallucinations, time compressions, dreams and other devices, she explored both the relation of past to present and that of the unconscious to the conscious. Her novels can be said to explore the meaning of fiction itself as a social, cultural and political act, as well as the possibilities for fiction as a form. Dark also explored the significance of the writing of fiction as a personal act of self-development, especially in *The Little Company* (Sydney, 1945), where the apparent conflict between the personal and the public and political is explored fully. Psychology and psychoanalysis also informed her texts both thematically, structurally and in her choice of narrative techniques; innuendo, symbol and hidden meanings become expressions of the power of repression, the unconscious and the past to control our lives, until we search them out through intelligent and imaginative reflection on the meaning of things. Indeed, it could be said that a principal characteristic of Dark's novels is their emphasis upon reflection and imaginativeness as necessary forces for combating prejudice and dogmatism, whether in literature or in life. She embodied this commitment to intelligent reflection in her novels by creating several different narrative points of view or by narrating conflicts amongst characters which emphasize the value of difference, as well as the

problems it generates when people are intolerant and unimaginative about it.

Her first novel, *Slow Dawning* (London, 1932), was followed soon by *Prelude to Christopher* (Sydney, 1934) and *Return to Coolami* (London, 1936), both of which won the Australian Literature Society Gold Medal. During this time, Dark and her physician husband became increasingly radicalized by the poverty and suffering of the Great Depression and by the rise of Hitler and fascism. Indeed, after World War II they were forced to leave Katoomba by the hostility of the community to their radical views. Dark continued to write successful novels, publishing *Sun Across the Sky* (London, 1937) and *Waterway* (London, 1938), and in 1941 the first part of a historical trilogy appeared, entitled *The Timeless Land* (Sydney), probably her most famous novel. This last sets out overtly what had been a theme of earlier novels, namely, time itself, history, and the meaning of both of these for the present. In *The Timeless Land*, the emphasis is on colonialism and its effects on not only the aborigines but also the land itself. Dark's great love for the land – for nature – and her intense respect for it give intensity and vitality to her language and her themes, as she explored the possibilities of natural images as symbols for human experiences, such as the weed in *Lantana Lane* (London, 1959) as a symbol of the unconscious. Both *Prelude to Christopher* and *Return to Coolami* had also been explorations into the meaning of time and history, but in a less directly overt way.

The next two volumes of this classic Australian historical trilogy of the continent and its people are *Storm of Time* (Sydney, 1948) and *No Barrier* (Sydney, 1953), but these only appeared after being interrupted by *The Little Company* (Sydney, 1945), a quite different novel, set in the 1930s and 1940s in Sydney. This is Dark's most self-conscious, self-referential work, a novel of ideas in which she thematized the role of the writer in a community. The central character, himself a writer with a block created by social and political crises, explores how to engage in dissent without being destructive of the elements of society that must be maintained if chaos is not to ensue. Central to this constructive dissent is an emphasis upon humaneness, which is another word for imaginativeness or intelligent reflection. Dark's novel suggests that the growth of consciousness from more private, selfish concerns to more public ones, until the private and the public are intertwined, is essential to defeating prejudice and ignorance, whether it takes the form of nationalism, racism or sexism. In her earlier novels, sexism was portrayed as the fundamental form of oppression in society and treated more overtly than in *The Little Company*. She was, in those novels, sharply critical of women who give in to patriarchy, whereas in this later work her handling of sexism is more indirect. She engaged here in an exposure of the sort of society which traps women into subservient, self-betraying postures, rather than criticizing women as wilfully slavish. *The Little Company* also questions the value and meaning of fiction and its relevance to war, poverty and suffering, as well as its influence on society. It explores too the effects of these crises and cruelties on individuals.

Her final novel, *Lantana Lane*, is in marked contrast to her earlier writing. It is a light-hearted, humorous novel, which shows Dark having sublimated her earlier interests into a symbolic tale about life in a Queensland farm, where she herself lived for some years before returning to the Blue Mountains. Life in this closely knit farming community is not idealized, yet it becomes a symbol for the kind of cooperative, democratic society which Dark strove for. And the lantana weed, against which the farmers have to battle heroically in order to survive at all, becomes a delightful metaphor for all the things human beings have to strive against in order to live decently, whether the forces of the unconsciousness, social evils, or the natural world. The gentle wit and irony of this novel shows Dark at her most mature and detached; the republication of a number of her novels is regaining her a place as one of Australia's most distinguished authors.

Rosamond Lehmann 1901–1990

Born to a literary family in Buckinghamshire, Lehmann read modern languages at Girton College, Cambridge, and later worked with her brother John on *New Writing*, his literary magazine. Her sister Beatrix was a well-known actress, while her father was editor of and a contributor to *Punch*. Lehmann was married twice, with two children, and had a long friendship with C. Day Lewis. Her first novel, *Dusty Answer* (London and New York, 1927), was soon followed by several others, as *A Note in Music* (London and New York, 1930), *Invitation to the Waltz* (London and New York, 1932) and its sequel, *The Weather in the Streets* (London and New York, 1936). These novels established Lehmann as a very accomplished prose writer, and developed her sustained interest in themes of sexual love, obsession and disillusionment or disappointment, which time, maturity and age often bring. These novels depict, then, not only passion, but also the processes of maturation and moral development which often result from the demands which passion makes, upon women particularly. Indeed, Lehmann's reputation as a novelist has probably suffered from her tendency to portray many of her male characters as less capable of maturation and emotional/moral responsibility, beyond the most conventional, socially approved kinds. For while her prose style has almost always been appreciated, her thematics and subject matter have been criticized as too narrow or too lacking in an explicit moral stance, or her characters as too introspective. These comments say more about the critic than they tell us about Lehmann's fiction.

These four novels were followed by *The Ballad and the Source* (London, 1944), one of Lehmann's most substantial novels and of considerable narrative accomplishment; here the mystical elements which were to dominate her later work are introduced by means of powerful imagery. *The Gipsy's Baby and Other Stories* (London, 1946) preceded *The Echoing Grove* (London and New York, 1953), her last novel before the twenty-year gap which led to *A Sea-Grape Tree* (London, 1976), and interrupted only by an autobiographical memoir, *The Swan in the Evening* (London and New York, 1967).

While Lehmann's prose style has been lavishly praised for its intelligent, exquisite artistry and its emotional resonance, her structural and narrative techniques, as well as her thematics, have been undervalued. Like those of Dorothy Richardson, May Sinclair and other female near-contemporaries, Lehmann's courage and determination to write fiction about the authority of women's experience was offensive to many critics, and indeed still is. Lehmann was a skilled innovator in both narrative technique and structure, and while her use of point of view and emphasis upon subjectivity as the starting point for knowledge was similar to that of Richardson and Sinclair, she developed a voice quite distinct from their own markedly individual writings. Her daring, in her thematics, to show the relative immaturity and superficiality of her heroines' lovers and husbands has caused many critics, male and female, to find excuses for undervaluing her novels.

In the mid-career novel *The Weather in the Streets*, Lehmann developed the heroine of her earlier text, Olivia Curtis; now 27 and separated from her husband of a brief few years, Olivia is shown to have changed little in the intervening decade. Still romantic, still attracted to men who are incapable of mature love, Olivia's gradual acceptance of the superficiality of her lover – his sexual passion without emotional depth – is finely portrayed through innovative narrative techniques and a number of familiar modernist devices. Lehmann used fragmentation, gaps in time, indirect free narrative (which subverts any pretence at neutral, omniscient point of view), descriptions by memory, fantasy and interiority, and a Katherine Mansfield-like attention to 'the tremendous trifles' – which have immense allusive power and symbolic force – to create her remarkable, sustained emotional intensity. The ambiguous ending is only one of many indications that Lehmann's refusal of that 'explicit moral stance', for which she has been criticized, was a deliberate moral attitude itself. Insinuations of lesbianism and homosexuality, along with abortion and motherhood, also add a dimension to Lehmann's exploration of the variety of human love, lust and relationships which suggests a far from 'narrow vision'. Like those of Jean Rhys, her contemporary, Lehmann's novels also examine the complex of money, power and prestige from which women are excluded if they refuse marriage or seek to escape an unsatisfactory one. The double standard is constantly under scrutiny, as Lehmann portrayed the freedom of men to commit the very acts for which they ostracize women.

The Weather in the Streets constitutes a genuine literary achievement comparable to those of Rhys, Richardson, Sinclair and Mansfield, then, especially with its daring innovations in theme (its deeply committed presentation of the 'other' woman), including its assertion of the validity of women's sexual desire (and fulfilment outside marriage) or lesbianism and homosexuality as legitimate forms of sexual expression, and of the rights to abortion and an independent life away from the family. To call this vision narrow stretches the credulity of any open-minded reader who does not unconsciously assume that presentation of life experience through the eyes of various different women at different stages of life is an unacceptably narrow project. The finely constructed plot, the astute use of incident and detail to further larger aims, the excellent portrayal of dialogue, and the powerful characterization combine with Lehmann's acknowledged prose style to create works of fiction which reward careful reading and study.

Stevie Smith 1902–1971

Florence Margaret Smith (Stevie Smith), brought up in Palmers Green, London, worked as a secretary to a magazine publisher while writing and illustrating her poetry and novels. *Novel on Yellow Paper* (London, 1936) was quickly succeeded by poems collected in *A Good Time was Had by All* (London, 1937). Two more novels, *Over the Frontier* (London, 1938) and *The Holiday* (London, 1949), and many collections of poetry, often including her remarkable illustrations, followed. In 1981, stories, essays, poems, a radio play (*A Turn Outside*) and a few letters were published in *Me Again* (London). *Stevie*, a play about Smith by Hugh Whitmore (made into a film), has extended Smith's reputation. A remark by Philip Larkin in 1962 about Smith's poetry applies as well to her novels: 'they are completely original, and now and again they are moving. These qualities set them above 95 per cent of present-day output.' Interviews with Stevie Smith are published in *Ivy and Stevie* (London, 1971) and *The Poet Speaks* (London, 1966); *The Collected Poems* of Stevie Smith appeared in 1975 (Harmondsworth). Smith, who never married, lived with her aunt until she died of a brain tumour in 1971.

Stevie Smith is best known for her poetry, which, like William Blake's illuminations, is enjoyed by children as well as adults. Like Blake's,

Smith's poems are often accompanied by illustrations providing ironic and subtle commentary on the poems. Contrary to some curious critical assessments of Smith as pre-eminently a poet rather than a novelist, Smith herself argued that 'there is no very strong division between what is poetry and what is prose.' She went on to illustrate this in the poetic prose of such a novel as *Over the Frontier*, whose density of imagery, figures of speech and materiality of language anticipates such writers as Marguerite Young. Similarly, her poetry often veers towards prose in its direct parody of poetic conventions, as in the long poem 'Souvenir de Monsieur Poop'. More indirectly, Smith parodied poetic (and social) conventions as in the short, pithy poem, 'This Englishwoman':

> This English woman is so refined
> She has no bosom and no behind.

Stevie Smith gained her initial literary recognition from the publication of both her first novel and, a year later, her first collection of poems. Her novels, however, fell into oblivion, while the poetry has thrived. This may in part be because the novels use a stream of consciousness technique, unrelieved by any dramatic plot. The poems, contrastingly, are very accessible at an initial level, though they are complex and demanding at deeper levels. For they are designed, in part, to mirror the strata of the human psyche as well as the rich, disseminative layers in language itself. Indeed, one of the central themes of the novels is an examination of logic, analysis and reason; sanity and madness are also subthemes, albeit covert, while death, violence and love feed thematically into these several strands. Smith's novels and poems function to challenge conventional notions about war, marriage, love, childhood and suicide, for example, not to mention to question literature, and the novel or poem as a distinct genre. Her poetic prose and her prose-like poetry stand as a potent embodiment of her own rejection of some genre distinctions which are often arbitrary and imprisoning. Yet, most systematic was her determination to explore language, in part to reveal the repressed and unconscious material of 'everywoman's' psyche; in part to understand better how language functions.

Many of the poems, and sections of the novels, are examples of disruptive tactics, which fissure the smooth, repressive surface of consciousness. Through such fissures, Smith argued, we can gain a glimpse of the world of the unconscious, which, unbridled, can lead to disastrous violence both in public and in the home. The description at the surface level of the novels involves the rejection of familiar conventions of the novel – of dramatic plot, appropriate style, familiar shape and so on – while in the poetry disruption takes the form of satirizing clichés, punning, inventing new words and referring to previous poems, such as Blake's. Both her poetry and prose are designed to challenge the notion that logic and reason, those tools of analysis, are natural, inviolable and capable of encompassing human experience. Smith's writings deny the dualistic categories of such rationalities, and insist not only that much 'worthwhile' experience (such as that of aesthetics or love) is not adequately structured by logic or reason, but that both of them are themselves conventions, and are completely intertwined with the illogical, the non-rational and the imaginative. The way order arises out of inchoate experience is explored by Smith, and her writings testify to her commitment to finding new forms and styles in order to create and express new kinds of order, new values, new beliefs. Smith's texts destabilize conventional notions of structure, order and style so as to embody experience in words in new and original ways, and thereby make possible still more new experience.

The questioning of logic and reason – what they are and what role they would best play in human life and culture – takes the form of a witty satire in both the novels and the poems. Construing madness and sanity historically and sociologically, for example, Smith related this conventional dichotomy to many others, such as repression and violence, childhood and adulthood. Her poems and novels suggest that beneath the veneer of social propriety lies a 'sick tiger' in every adult, while children are portrayed as anything but innocent. Logic and reason function to order experience, but their particular strategies are far from 'natural'; indeed, for Smith, they are conventions which can be valuable in certain contexts, but which should not be mistaken for absolute universals having a distinct access to truth. Smith's writings constantly breach the dangerous frontier between the logical and the illogical, conscious and unconscious, madness and sanity, as a means of 'connecting up' the psyche. Disruptive techniques on the stylistic and structural level abound, as Smith broke through logic, decorum and poetic convention by means of wit, satire, irony, pun and imagery, in order to reveal the inadequacy of conventional logic and reason to structure experiences. Her texts give the reader glimpses of the powerful forces which exist in each person's unconscious mind, and how such forces can destroy by being ignored and repressed. She did not reject logic and reason, but she did reject rationalists' efforts to set logic and reason up as the ultimate judge of reality, truth and values, excluding the very power of synthesis and intuition which gives logic and reason its connections.

In *Over the Frontier*, the themes described above are worked carefully into the fabric of the novel. In its structure of surface disorder, fragmentation, non-transparency of language and 'unreadability', the novel uses familiar literary conventions of the journey, the parting and crossing the frontier to express and structure its thematics. Crossing the frontier becomes, in this text, a powerful symbol because of its complex, rich associations. It is a familiar literary convention, and Smith taps into this tradition in an original way. In *Over the Frontier*, readers are made painfully aware of the need to cross back and forth from the realm of the conscious to the unconscious (and back again), if we are to gain any self-knowledge and any control over ourselves. Meanwhile, the border crossing involves gender changes, as Pompey dresses up like a soldier and plays at war games. Smith's text illustrates as an artifact a further metaphor, namely, the frightening necessity to cross borders from conventional to new (and at first unacceptable) forms, themes, characters, style and structure. Indirect promptings suggest, moreover, that the frontier is also that between childishness and genuine adulthood and that between madness and sanity. Throughout the novel, Smith strengthened these various themes by showing their powerful interrelations to each other and their direct importance for the reader, who is invited to cross the frontier from outside

to inside the work of art so as to have enlightening experiences.

Yet, there is no overt moralizing, nor is there idealization of the frontier or of the realm on the 'other side'. When Pompey arrives at the frontier, it turns out to be a ditch; her horse panics, and throws her head over heels into that ditch as unceremoniously as can be imagined. The rest of the novel seems primarily to be a long meditation on the dangers of idealization, whether in war and life or in art and reading. In this case, 'the road to excess leads to the palace of wisdom', as Pompey kills a man and only then grasps fully the moral degeneracy of war. What was previously seen as sane is now seen to be insane (war, killing), thanks to first-hand experience of its legitimized form. Pompey's idealization of the war is shown to lead her to a destructive act which confronts her with her own humanity. Other forms of dehumanization are also explored, as, for example, the socialization of children. Rites of passage are exposed as gratuitous cruelty, perpetrated by 'adults' upon children, and Smith's texts, especially her poems, draw out the damage done to children at an early age, damage which leads to war, violence and selfishness.

Smith's texts also explore the illogicality of language, and the violence done to language when we are repressed, thereby losing control of our innermost existence. She explored the inherent nonsense in all sense, and, through wit, playfulness with words, irony and satire, exposed how hackneyed and clichéd all our speech, thinking and feeling are. Her novels are illustrative of new ways of using language, of creating original works of art, and of experiencing values which had been mistaken for facts. They suggest ways in which women, in particular, can break out of imprisoning stereotypes and gender roles which are designed to keep them in domestic service. Thus, the illogicality, indeed insanity, of social codes and conventions is ruthlessly revealed.

The frontier between the text and the reader is another metaphor Smith exploited for challenging dualistic notions of art versus reality or text versus history. Boundaries of this kind are made to collapse repeatedly, sometimes through meta-fictional discourse or direct references to the reader. Sometimes the collapse occurs as a result of visionary designs in which the reader catches herself or himself in the act of passively submitting to the author's view – or actively rejecting it as incomprehensible or merely another feminist tract. Pompey herself draws the female reader into an empathetic relationship, and boundaries collapse again when the reader is confronted by the confusion between dream and reality, which initiates a crack in the golden bowl of the text. For which part is reality and which dream? Does she wake or sleep? And the reader is confronted by Pompey herself, an ordinary woman who is free to go 'out in the world', as Jane Bowles described life. Pompey is single and childless – that monstrous duality which is exacerbated further by her complete lack of guilt at being a New Woman. That New Woman is portrayed as having no maternal instincts, as being as free and brave and adventurous as the social myth paints men to be. Consequently other women characters are not fond of her, for they find her monstrous. But the world of men is not for Pompey either; hence, she retreats into solitude, seeking to carve out for herself some place in the community where she can be an individual, not just a stereotyped role player. As yet, sixty years later, there is still no place for these monstrous aberrations who deny their 'maternal instincts' except in the realm of the imagination, and even then it is very restricted.

Over the Frontier depicts warfare as a metaphor for the insanity and violence of ordinary, accepted social practices. In *The Holiday*, marriage is the Blakean battlefield of the conflict between the sexes. In this, Stevie Smith is indebted to Jane Austen's novels, those powerfully understated revelations of the pressures to conform to insane arrangements, since the (proper) place for women was severely restricted. Austen's irony is pervasive in that it creates a systematic subtext, which is at odds with the surface pretence that courtship and marriage are the meaning of life for women. Smith had no hesitation in abandoning any surface text, as she pushed, pulled, reshaped and restructured both language and social codings, in order to reveal them as conventions in need of change, and in no way natural or gender traits. Smith's heroines are portrayed as different from traditional (maternal) women, and as breaking through into the world of men, only to find that it is no less objectionable than domestic enslavement.

Christina Stead 1902–1983

One of Australia's finest novelists (if controversial), Christina Stead was born in Sydney, where she grew up and attended university. In 1928, she left Australia to live in England and Paris for seven years, before embarking on a nomadic existence which took her first to New York and Hollywood during World War II. After the war, she returned to Europe, and finally, in 1969, went back to Canberra, where she taught courses in creative writing until 1980. She died in 1983, having written some fifteen books, including novels, novellas and short stories. Her first book, a collection of short stories called *The Salzburg Tales* (London, 1934), has much in common with the works of that great contemporary Isak Dinesen, with its Boccaccio-like tales within tales told by a myriad of story-tellers. Unwilling to subscribe to the creed of the artist as a genius set apart from ordinary mortals, Stead made ordinary people her narrators and story-tellers, insisting that every individual is a 'fountain of passion' in some aspect of her or his life. She firmly rejected the hard distinction between art and life, between the artist and the non-genius, in showing that stories permeate every aspect of our lives as we seek to make sense of what is happening to us, and to interpret events. Yet she also emphasized the way in which different points of view led to markedly different experiences and interpretations of reality. These differences are portrayed throughout her numerous novels, as the pressure of reality, as conflicting needs and views, drives characters apart.

Stead's most productive period of writing occurred between 1934 and 1952, when nine books appeared. After over a decade, a new novel appeared, *Cotters' England* (Sydney, 1974; earlier as *Dark Places of the Heart*, New York, 1966; London, 1967). About the same year, Stead published the collection of novellas entitled *The Puzzleheaded Girl* (New York, 1967). But her most famous books are the novels of the earlier years, such as *House of All Nations* (London, 1938), *The Man Who Loved Children* (New York, 1940) and *For Love Alone* (New York, 1944). Other novels from this period include *Letty Fox: Her Luck* (New York, 1946) and *The People with the Dogs* (Boston, 1952). Novels of her late period were *The Little Hotel* (London, 1973) and

Miss Herbert (New York, 1976). She was awarded the Patrick White Prize in 1974. Rebecca West was one of her staunchest admirers, emphasizing Stead's great originality, though she was also praised by fellow writers such as Lillian Hellmann, Saul Bellow, Elizabeth Hardwick, Randall Jarrell and Susan Sontag. The impression persists, however that her reputation remained unstable even after the posthumous publication of *I'm Dying Laughing* (London, 1987) and *Ocean of Story* (Melbourne, 1985), the latter a collection of short fictions.

Like West's, Christina Stead's novels represent an impressive diversity of styles and themes, so much so, indeed, that Stead acquires the kind of protean quality that only a few novelists have ever achieved. While it is true that her way of seeing and representing the world is plainly different from that of other novelists (as Jarrell has noted), her originality goes further; her way of seeing and representing the world is plainly different from one book to the next, as Hardwick implied when she wrote of Stead's 'prodigious talent' and her 'storytelling abundance'. The marvellous story-teller forms of *The Salzburg Tales* quickly gave way to the novelty of *House of All Nations*, set in Paris after World War I and exploring the world of international finance. This fourth novel bears little relation in style or theme to the Australian novel of working-class men and women which was her first, *Seven Poor Men of Sydney* (London, 1934; Melbourne and Sydney, 1965). With the appearance of *The Man Who Loved Children*, set in America yet reputedly an autobiographical novel about Stead's own family, especially her father and herself, she moved into a distinctly new and original mode of writing – of raw excesses, naked violence, intrusive immediacy and overabundance.

Yet, with the publication four years later of *For Love Alone*, Stead moved into an utterly different style again: a narrative, brooding consciousness hovers over the novel, whose passion, verging on the tragic, is in marked contrast to the exuberance, fecund rawness and dense novelty of *The Man Who Loved Children*. For, tragic as the latter may be in theme, it is far from tragic in mood in the broodingly passionate mode of *For Love Alone*. This novel also draws on autobiographical adolescent experiences, but sets them to a quite different purpose from that of

its predecessor. The stream of details of the former involves horror and hilarity alternating as event is piled upon event, until the two are united in Henny's death and Louie's final departure for a 'walk around the world'. In its virtual sequel, *For Love Alone*, Teresa is portrayed almost from the beginning with her quest for life already under way. After breaking out of the confinement of her intolerable family, Teresa's journey into life, love and independence from parents is described by Stead by means of the structuring, plotting device of journeys and passages in geographical space charting emotional journeys. But this 'sequel' to *The Man* is, appropriately, in a tone stripped of the hilarity and the fantastic of the earlier novel. There, plot is utterly subjugated to the need to pile up an abundance of outrage and horror until Louie's credulity is exhausted, and she discharges herself from the prison of her father's chauvinism into a wider world. In *For Love Alone*, the power of plot is central, as details work in the service of charting Teresa's growing awareness of the emotional complexity and neurosis of human beings, and she is portrayed journeying from the exploitative relationship with her father to an equally obscene exploitation by her first lover. Stead is unrepentant in taking the reader through the sufferings Teresa (a very different character from Louie) experiences, to show that her great strength is her ability to learn from experience and thus move out of this prison of neurotic exploitation into a more mature, loving relationship. The richness of detail creates an immediacy in Stead's writing which drags the reader into a more direct relationship with the text: Christina's suffering cannot be kept at a distance. This quality of immediacy is evident in many of Stead's novels: in *The Man Who Loved Children*, we can hear the dishes crashing. Indeed, one feels almost deafened by the riotous hubbub and excess of happenings.

Letty Fox: Her Luck is yet again a testimony to Stead's versatility. Utterly different from *For Love Alone* and its predecessor, it is a picaresque modern-day version of a *Moll Flanders* novel, verging on a formless rapidity and casualness of plot which also distinguish it from *For Love Alone*. Letty's adventures, both sexual, emotional and social, are portrayed as she pursues a (by convention well-hidden but in her case scandalously overt) agenda to find a husband. One of the few novels of Stead's in the first person, this fictional sexual 'autobiography' is a panorama both of male–female relations and of life in New York during the war. Political, social and economic issues inform Letty's personal narrative with a covert richness only possible for an author of Stead's intellectual and political sophistication. Like Jean Rhys and Jane Austen, Stead explored, behind the facade of a young girl struggling for a place in the marriage market, the powerful complex of money, sex and society. *I'm Dying Laughing*, the posthumously published novel written during this period, is in tone and style almost a sequel to *Letty Fox*. Emily's casual leftist political associations, combined with her extravagant fascination with money, prestige and living in style, suggest an adult Letty Fox, corrupted by the contradictions inherent in much liberal thinking: 'they wanted to be on the side of the angels, good Communists, good people, and also to be very rich – well, of course, . . . they came to a bad end.'

Later novels, such as *The People with the Dogs*, show Stead's determination to find an individuality for each of her novels. Once again she explored sexual relations – but also brother–sister relations – with a more gentle, mellow tone than usual. After this 1952 publication, Stead did not publish a work of fiction until *Cotter's England* appeared. Nellie Cotter is the central figure in the novel, and while social issues of poverty, embattled and homeless women, and sexual exploitations are dealt with, the overriding interest is Nellie's manipulation of her brother Tom and its destructive effects on his lover Caroline, as Nellie sets herself up to be a possessive 'mother'. This novel, and Stead's last novel, *Miss Herbert (The Suburban Wife)*, explore the theme recurring in earlier novels of the failure of relationships in its many forms and its multitude of causes. Unlike Teresa Hawkins in *For Love Alone*, Eleanor Herbert cannot mature emotionally; she repeats her earlier failures and is unable to confront her erotic needs and her sexual potency. This novel, not published until 1976, was also written in the late 1940s. It portrays the power of self-deception, and Eleanor is ironized in a passage shortly after the collapse of her marriage: 'Did I marry the wrong man? . . . It's as if there's something I don't understand,

but I do understand, I face all my problems squarely . . . What if we go down? [to Nazi Germany] . . . Can I live where the British Empire does not live?' Like Jean Rhys in her 'implicit exposé' of suburban housewives, Stead exposed, explicitly, their mindless commitment to the glaring inconsistencies and barrenness of propriety and social respectability. This exploration of British female hypocrisy is in (Henry Jamesean) marked contrast, however to the American girl Letty Fox, as though Stead sought to portray the Blakean worm of sexual hypocrisy as a more emotionally destructive and morally contemptible posture.

Clearly, the picaresque narrative mode characteristic of some of Stead's novels – with their brief events and episodic, forward lurches – is in contrast to that of some of her others, where the power of plot propels the action forward in a dramatically calculated formal unity. Even in the latter novels, the detail of incident endows the plot with a richness of thematic material which is only sustained by the passionate power of the action. The brooding authorial presence in *For Love Alone*, for example, prohibits the intimate immediacy and spontaneity in *Letty Fox* or *The Man Who Loved Children*, the sheer noisiness of these rumbustious novels being replaced by a silent intensity.

Like Rhys, Stead refused to be drawn into the feminist movement, and probably for similar reasons. Her characters' battles are fought out in the arena of the family or of sexual relationship. While Stead's portrayals of these battles indicate a profound grasp of the social complex of sex, money and power which intrudes, so that there is no dichotomy between the personal and the political, she never imagined that joining a movement or attending organizational meetings could substitute for fulfilment in sexual, emotional and intellectual life. Exploitation and social hypocrisy cannot be overcome, she observed, by talking about them or writing about them. However much that may help, the battle must be fought in the nitty-gritty of everyday life, from morning to noon to night, and every day.

Kay Boyle 1903–1992

Expatriate American writer Kay Boyle lived in Europe off and on from the early 1920s until the early 1960s, not including the time she spent there with her parents as a young child. Deeply committed to human and civil rights, Boyle, like Lillian Hellman, was an outspoken critic of the hypocrisies of politicians and their voters alike, believing that each one of us must bear a part of the responsibility for the kind of world we inhabit. Born in Minnesota, Boyle attended the Cincinnati Conservatory of Music and then studied architecture, before marrying a Frenchman and beginning her long, twenty-year sojourn abroad. She began writing short stories, a collection of which was published in 1930 as *Wedding Day and Other Stories* (New York), quickly followed by her first, accomplished novel, *Plagued by the Nightingale* (New York, 1931). A succession of novels and short stories followed, including perhaps her finest novel, *Year Before Last* (New York, 1932), as well as *My Next Bride* (New York, 1934) and *Avalanche* (London and New York, 1944). Story collections include *The White Horses of Vienna and Other Stories* (New York, 1936), *Thirty Stories* (New York, 1936) and *The Smoking Mountain: Stories of Post War Germany* (New York, 1951). She had already won the O. Henry Award for 'Wedding Day', repeated in 1941 with 'Defeat'. She has continued writing novels, short stories, essays, poetry and journalism, and was foreign correspondent for the *New Yorker* 1946–53. She was awarded Guggenheim fellowships in 1934 and 1961, and has been visiting fellow at numerous academic institutions since she returned to live in America in the 1960s. An autobiographical account of her time in France, co-authored with her friend Robert McAlmon, *Being Geniuses Together: 1920–1930* (London, 1970), gives a fascinating account of the period when Boyle knew such figures as Djuna Barnes, Gertrude Stein, Sylvia Beach, James Joyce, William Carlos Williams and many others. Non-fiction collections of essays include *Words that Must Somehow Be Said* (London, 1985), and *The Long Walk at San Francisco* (New York, 1970).

The contexts for much of Boyle's fiction include war and European suffering in the aftermath, politics, conflict and violence, espionage and the lives of expatriates; these historical contexts provide the more universal thematics of moral-ethical issues which recur throughout the fiction and non-fiction. Romantic love also

functions as such a context – it is rarely a theme, since it is the background against which situations requiring responsibility and great courage are portrayed, as in her first and second novels. Like many writers, Boyle rejected the ideology of realism, with its illusory fiction of objectivity of point of view, its notion of pure, unstylized language, its overemphasis on dramatic plot, external social setting, careful structuring of events into a rational order, and so on. Her narratives eschew omniscience; she avoided artificial drama and overemphases on plot; and she explored the potentialities of language in her own, unique way. While *Plagued by the Nightingale* is a momentous achievement as the first novel of a relatively young writer, *Year Before Last* is arguably her most accomplished piece of fiction, at least in terms of prose writing, and bears closer scrutiny, even if some of her other novels are more notable for their fineness of structure or congruence of theme and art. Like Kate O'Brien with *Mary Lavelle* (1936), or E.M. Forster with *Passage to India* (1924), Boyle rose, arguably, to one of her highest aesthetic achievements in her novel of the tragic last years together in life, love, art and death of Martin Sheehan and his lover Hannah.

As *Being Geniuses Together* makes clear, this novel drew much of its inspiration from Boyle's romance with the fatally tubercular Ernest Walsh in the mid-1920s. And inspired it is too, infused with a language of passion and imagination which is its very substance, and before which plot, drama, characterization and setting pale into insignificance, as they did later in Elizabeth Smart's *By Grand Central Station* (1945). This must be a part of the novel's uniqueness, that its language so utterly subsumes everything else through some three hundred pages. These pages chart Martin and Hannah's exile from one place to another, as each proprietor's fear of Martin's illness drives them from hotel to hotel, through spring, summer, autumn and winter, from the sea-level Mediterranean blue of Nice and Cannes to mountain snows and cascading streams in Barcelonnette. Words pour over the reader in shimmering blues and cascading whites, and create a thirst for what Hannah or Martin will think or say next, almost banishing the conventional suspense aroused by what will happen next, as in the following example:

When Hannah came in the door, there Martin's hunger gaped on the pillow in his deep motionless gaze, there Martin's silent love waited. His hands fell on the open books and the words written on them as if they were beautiful stuffs, texture to feel between thumb and finger, the silk and satin of other men's mouths to fumble and touch.

Read me some more, said Martin's voice . . .

Read me some more, like a man starving . . . read me some more, he whispered, his fingers twitching over the pages, another man's banquet served to his liking . . .

All day they read, and half the night.

Thematic issues are woven into the poetic texture of the prose with fine congruence, as the novel's portrayal of Hannah's, Martin's and Eve's (the jealous aunt) dilemmas remind us of the central role of language in our lives. How we discern the aesthetic and moral qualities of experience is shown by Boyle as largely dependent on our use or abuse of language. How we cope with illness and death, hate and love, wealth and poverty, depends in part at least upon how finely tuned an instrument of thought and feeling our own language is. Kierkegaardian issues of conflict and choice between moral commitment and aesthetic commitment, conflicts between love and art, life and word, recur throughout the novel. Yet *Year Before Last* suggests that any choice between these pairs will be a kind of death, whichever you choose. Somehow the conflict has to be resolved not by choosing, but by creating a situation in which both are possible, not only because human beings need both, but also because the distinctions between the pairs are not divisions in experience, but only points of view. That is, Boyle's novel shows the inextricability of moral and aesthetic experience, of art and love bound up in each other, of life and art interdependent and inseparable. Conflicts which create the necessity for choice tend to arise because of failures of imagination, characterized sometimes as selfishness, greed, stupidity and fear. Like Katherine Anne Porter's, Boyle's fiction suggests that we must often take decisions to act even though 'failure' is inescapable, since sometimes an existential gesture is more important than the outcome. Both Martin and Hannah show such courage, as do many of

Boyle's numerous characters, but Boyle rarely achieved the richness of moral and aesthetic experience which her language brought to life in *Year Before Last*.

Anaïs Nin 1903-1977

Born in Neuilly, near Paris, to a Spanish pianist and composer father and a Danish-born mother, Anaïs Nin lived much of her childhood in Europe and her adolescence in New York, before returning to France and establishing her home at Louveciennes in 1929. This house became a centre for artists and friends whom Nin was to write about in her diaries, published only some fifty years after they were first begun at the age of 11 on a ship from Spain to New York. In the meantime, various novels and short stories were published, including the short story collection *Under a Glass Bell* (New York, 1944), the novel *A Spy in the House of Love* (New York, 1954) and the five novels comprising *Cities of the Interior* (Denver, 1959), including *House of Incest* (Paris, 1936), *Winter of Artifice* (Paris, 1939) and *Ladders to Fire* (Paris, 1946). Other books include *Seduction of the Minotaur* (Denver, 1961), *Delta of Venus* (New York, 1977; London, 1978), *Collages* (Denver, 1964) and a critical study of D.H. Lawrence (Paris, 1932), Nin's first book. She also wrote *The Novel of the Future* (New York, 1968), and essays, interviews and lectures have been published in *A Woman Speaks*, ed. E.J. Hinz (Chicago, 1975). Seven large volumes of her diaries have now been published in Quartet Books (1966–80), ed. Gunther Stuhlmann, and they represent a selection of the vast diary manuscripts covering the period from 1931 into the 1970s.

Anaïs Nin made it clear that while she understood and appreciated the power of our surroundings to influence our lives, she was an existentialist by temperament. That is, she had tremendous faith in the ability of human beings to shape that surrounding power by means of will and imagination. Or, in her own words, 'it was the faith that we must turn to ourselves as a creative piece of work – not only in the arts but in the creation of our lives.' All her writings are a testimony to this philosophy of life, this personal vision that our identity as human beings is constructed by each one of us, ourselves, and that if we can develop our imaginations we can become artists of that most important work of art, our own beings. Indeed, there is a suggestion throughout her works that one of the most significant aspects of labour is its contribution to the construction of a self distinct from a socialized cardboard cut-out, or Herbert Marcuse's 'one-dimensional man'. Like Jean Rhys, then, Nin saw the writing of her novels, diaries and art criticism as contributing decisively to the human being that she was striving to become. For her, the central value of education was to develop the power of will and imagination so that people could make informed decisions about what to be, how to live, how to die. Clearly, Nin was drawing upon central existentialist strains from Greek tragedy and European literature, which were contemporaneously informing developments in the psychoanalysis of Freud, Jung, Rank (with whom she worked), and many others.

In addition to the importance of her writings as a record of the efforts of a woman and an artist in the twentieth century to resist the pressures of convention to become a non-person, a mere stereotyped, role-playing, non-individual, Nin's writings are a remarkable contribution both to modernists' experiments in fiction, and to the literary and intellectual history of the twentieth century. Her appreciation of the import of psychoanalysis at a time when it was violently disparaged, and her recognition of the value of new trends in literature, reveal her as one of the more insightful critics of her time, playing a crucial role in nourishing and furthering new ideas, new art and new ways of living. She was an astute critic, too, of the ideologies and unconscious assumptions which inhibit self-development and fulfilment. Noting the almost irresistible pressures upon women for self-sacrifice to children and husbands, she commented:

> The will to create, or creative will, which pursues the artist, and haunts the artist, I find to be as applicable to our individual life, to our personal life, as it is to a work of art. That is, we do have a will, a possibility, and a potential to change ourselves, and doing that is not an egocentric or turned-in activity. It is an activity that ultimately affects, influences, and transforms an entire community.

This essentially Coleridgean or Shelley-like vision, that our most important contribution to our community is genuine self-development (which was branded as egotism by unimaginative commentators), was developed by Nin both as she built her own imaginatively constructed personal identity and as she revealed the forces, within the psyche and without, which either inhibited or facilitated the gradual strengthening of the imagination – that faculty of creative will. Her novels and diaries depict life as a Kierkegaardian project of thought, thought being conceived of as congruent with (not distinct from) action. The word is the act, and language is understood by Nin as a more or less sharply refined tool for reflecting upon life and art in intelligent ways which lead to growth, transformation and renewal. Thus, her texts both explore thematically and depict stylistically how to sharpen our language and our thinking, so that we can live more intelligently and become more unique and individual. Nin's diaries in particular are a powerful 'defence of poetry', as she showed that art is our most powerful ally in resisting conformity and superficiality. Art is not only the primary record for a society of the striving for spiritual individuality; it is the primary vehicle by means of which individuals and societies achieve a life which goes beyond material comforts and nourishes the whole human being.

Nin's writings make explicit and overt the concerns of many other writers, such as Kate Chopin, Ellen Glasgow, Djuna Barnes, Marguerite Young and so on, which are often badly misunderstood. That is, readers have often failed to see that the artist is used in many novels as a metaphor or prototype for any individual, since we must all be artists of our self-construction, our very identity and individuality. For if we do not construct ourselves, social and psychological forces will turn us into puppets who do the bidding of others, when we think we are being most ourselves. Nin realized the valuable role which psychoanalysis could play in recapturing the unconscious for conscious life, by delivering us out of the hands of powerful external, social pressures, as well as internal, subconscious powers. She emphasized both the dream and art as the means of gaining entrance into a larger experience of human life, which tends to be shut off from exploration by the demands of the group.

This commitment to art and to the unconscious was at the basis of her determined rejection of ideologies such as realism and rationalism, which overemphasize the surface of experience at the expense of its depths. Like Flannery O'Connor and Eudora Welty, amongst others, Nin explicitly argued that mystery, fantasy and imagination *are* reality, while so-called reality is often a stultifying illusion which deadens us to the rich possibilities of human experience.

Consequently, Nin wrote revealingly about the literature of her times, viewing criticism not as a means of judging literature so much as one for helping readers to perceive more fully. Her writings on Anna Kavan, Young, Maude Hutchins, Barnes, Isak Dinesan, Zelda Fitzgerald, Georgia O'Keeffe, Rebecca West and many others invariably reveal ways of appreciating these artists, ways which involve cleansing the doors of perception of the prejudices, whether realist, sexist or others, which inhibit response. Nin exposed the prejudice behind much criticism of women writers, analysing the reasons why so many fine women artists were denigrated. She penetrated the false ideologies of the objective, whether in art or in criticism, insisting upon the value of the subjective, the personal and the domestic. She argued that criticism was never objective, but was the better for being a personal vision, especially if it was freed from unconscious prejudices. Only through personal vision, through the subjective, can we arrive, Nin argued, at the sources of our human life and our humanity. Nin also preferred to use criticism as a means of showing how different writers can nourish us at different times; what at times seems bad may at other times feed us. And she explained that, as writers, women need to reveal the ways in which they have been beguiled into colluding with and contributing to the mystification of the feminine.

As a novelist, Nin was deeply committed to experimentation and innovation; her diaries are a record of her efforts to support the experiments of contemporary artists to develop new ways of writing, living and being. Since she saw sexual repression as the cornerstone of convention, she was particularly interested in writing which challenged the orthodoxies of respectability, sexuality and conventions regarding gender. She was also, like Kavan and Leonora Carrington,

attracted to surrealism, with its emphasis upon psychological reality and individuality, and its claim that 'one can only find reality by discarding realism.' In her own writing, she sought to find the different levels of conscious–unconscious psychological life by means of recurring symbols and images which would make the passage from one level to another easier. Her fictional writings also suggest that only by exploring the depths of our personal lives can we reach into a life beyond the personal. In her fiction, she used dreams, fantasies and illusions not merely as a decorative element but (as did Jean Rhys and later Young) as essential components of art and life, arguing that our conventional notion of reality as reason is the biggest delusion of all, like the related notion that we arrive at truth by means of logical, univocal, discursive statements. For Nin, we must learn the language of symbolism, since without it we remain in a one-dimensional, passive state. Moreover, Nin explained the necessity to overcome silence and shyness when she wrote: 'I connect articulation with growth, and I say that women . . . need the expression. Because expression is tied to our awareness. We cannot be aware of something in a non-language state. Our awareness somehow is connected with language. . . . Women . . . must learn to articulate, to become focused.' In her fiction, as in her diaries and other non-fiction, Anaïs Nin explored the ways in which unexamined language could oppress us, and how we need to invent new languages if we are to find better ways of living.

Molly Keane 1904–

Successful playwright as well as a prolific novelist, Molly Keane was born in County Kildare to an Anglo-Irish family who were prominent members of a sporting, hunting and horse-riding community, and was educated only by governesses. Her writing career included over a dozen novels and several plays, some of which were remarkably well received by critics such as James Agate and Hugh Walpole. Many of her early novels, before her husband's death when she was in her mid-thirties, were written under the pseudonym of M.J. Farrell. These include

Taking Chances (London, 1929), *The Rising Tide* (London, 1937, an account of the small but intensely emotional, manipulative world of upper middle-class rural family life), *Two Days in Aragon* (London, 1941), *Loving Without Tears* (London, 1951) and *Treasure Hunt* (London, 1950). After some decades of virtual silence, Keane renewed her career as a novelist, under her own name, with the publication in 1981 (London) of *Good Behaviour* (shortlisted for the Booker Prize), followed two years later by *Time After Time* (London), and finally by *Loving and Giving* (London, 1988). While some of her earlier novels explored the powerful sexuality driving the violence of the hunt and horseback-riding, later novels explore a quite new territory, often portraying characters – outsiders – intruding into the claustrophobic, closed world of Anglo-Irish country life and creating considerable, indeed catastrophic, disturbances. Keane's final three novels form a corpus of literary achievement which exceeds her earlier work in technical grace, stylistic felicity, imaginativeness and humour. Compared often to Elizabeth Bowen or Jean Rhys, Keane established herself in the last decade of her life as an artist of the comic novel. (See also chapter 8 for further discussion.)

Good Behaviour is the first person, light-hearted narrative of a painfully oversized young woman, the daughter of a wealthy land owner, who experiences rejection by her mother and her brother's friends, condescension from the servants and pity from the neighbours, until her father's death. Thereupon, thanks to her father's will, which leaves her virtually everything, the novel ends with the reversal of power and the restoration of the woman's self-esteem. Keane's techniques throughout are fairly conventional, until one realizes her quite unusual gift for humour, for comic situation, and for turning pain and tragedy into bearable absurdity. Her gifts as a playwright are brought to the fore, as the novel proceeds by dramatic scenes and dialogue rather than description or plot development. Indeed, in this novel there is virtually no plot, only dialogues amongst characters, until the final ironic

reversal of roles more characteristic of the drama than of fiction. Thus, what at first appears to be a rather conventional if immensely amusing novel shows itself to be unusually original in the narrative techniques of comedy or humour and dialogue.

Time After Time represents an even greater accomplishment than its predecessor *Good Behaviour*. In the second of Keane's late novels, more powerful and varied techniques and themes are evident, as she portrays the life of three ageing sisters and a brother on an estate in southern Ireland. At Durraghglass, the arrival of a quite unexpected, alien element from the depths of the past, Cousin Leda of Vienna, shatters the fragile peace and arouses passionate loves and hates amongst these ageing gentry. Unlike *Good Behaviour*, *Time After Time* is a carefully plotted novel, though it does draw extensively on Keane's earlier talents of comedy, dialogue, scene creation and sharp wit. The third person narrative creates a quite different effect from the intensely subjective, small-world atmosphere of *Good Behaviour*. Here, one has the sense that the novel is constantly being made to refer to larger psychological and historical diversions in its portrayal of the upheavals at Durraghglass. Leda's arrival and subsequent impact take on mythological or at least symbolical dimensions, which Keane had rarely attempted before, though elements of this exist in her D.H. Lawrence-like representation of sexuality in *The Rising Tide* through the violence of the hunt and other sports. To make a rather unlikely analogy, Leda disrupts the inbred world of Durraghglass as a psychological force of repressed desire, much as Geraldine does in Coleridge's poem 'Christabel'. Additionally, as a figure from the siblings' past, she functions to unify that past (youth) with the present (age), raising questions about time itself, as well as shattering prejudices against age. Keane's novel suggests both the persistence of the past in the present and the tendency of history or of personal history to repeat itself, and she implies that the 'safety' of repression is a most unreliable refuge.

Part III

Neo-Realism, the Post-War Novel and Early Post-Modernist Innovations, 1944–1975

Chapter 7

The New International Literatures in English

Change in the period 1899–1941 involved a gradual destabilizing of elements which had become so predominant in the nineteenth century, and even authoritative, as to inhibit fresh response. Conventions such as certain conceptions of causal plot, overt unity, stylistic decorum, and emphasis upon the message to the apparent neglect of formal medium were once themselves innovations. But by 1899, they had become so dominant as to pass for essential facts of the novel instead of alterable conventions. Marked disruptions and alterations, from minor challenges to major assaults, occurred. It is not surprising that after forty years of certain types of relentless renewal, something of a change from these 'changes', these modes of experiment, were needed. The experiments of the period had constituted a subversion of the assumption that the socio-moral form of the novel, characterized by realism, was the appropriate or 'natural' form of the novel. A number of writers, by the end of the 1930s, were rejecting some aspects of modernist experiments as themselves now dominant and oppressive. Yet, it would be a mistake to characterize this next period as a reactionary, conservative one, lacking in innovation and seeking to reinstate the socio-moral form of the novel, or the novel of ideas. Some authors may have sought to do this, but, in the main, the self-consciousness of the period continued, maintaining the transformation of the novel, albeit in at first apparently familiar garb. The novels of Malcolm Lowry, Graham Greene and William Golding, or Christina Stead, Flannery O'Connor,

Carson McCullers and Jane Bowles, for example, are remarkably experimental, and in no way constitute a return to realism.

While the literature of the 1930s, 1940s and 1950s, then, displays continuing innovations and experiments in form, style and thematics, as the individual author entries confirm, the criticism and reading of this period often blinded itself to these innovations, and argued that the novel was returning to the socio-moral form most proper to it. The absurdities, excesses and overt disruptions of modernism, critics claimed, had been defeated and shown to be transient aberrations. The novel of ideas, of realism, of documentary, was back. Some critics and readers welcomed this alleged return, while others saw it as the regressions of a 'literature of exhaustion'. The novel, apparently, was worn out, dead; for it had come full circle, and a new form would supersede it, some thought. These views can now be seen to be notions which arose out of inhibiting preferences, either for realist forms or for modernist ones. Had critics and readers been more open to the diversity of appropriate novel forms and experiments, they would have been able to see this next period from 1935 to 1965 as varied, innovative and progressive, indeed, as anticipating the astonishing fecundity of recent decades.

One of the most outstanding transformations of English literature in the last half-century or so has been the rapid growth and consolidation of fiction writing by women and men all over the world in the English language. These international English writings may have begun in past

141

centuries in some geographical areas, but in recent decades writers have begun to create a body of literatures, including both primary and secondary material, of considerable note. This systematic emergence of both self- and communal expression in a highly sophisticated cultural form has had numerous consequences. People previously colonized politically, or presently colonized linguistically, culturally or economically, have gained for themselves the many advantages of literary expression, from a more incisive historical grasp of their situation, to a greater sense of identity as both individuals and communities, to a development of imaginative and linguistic capacities which free them from colonization and other forms of exploitation in specific ways. For women especially, this increased access to the control of communication, as well as to its formation, confers meaning and authority on the experiences of those who earlier were less able to express them, or less able to communicate their expressions and thereby validate and confirm them. This greatly enhanced meaning leads to empowerment, as women particularly have increased courage to act on shared, collective experiences.

A highly developed imaginative capacity is part of what makes it possible to shift from one way of looking at things to another, from one person's experience to another's. This shuttling back and forth is the vehicle for revealing that all aspects of society, nature and culture are subject to challenge, and are changeable, because constructed and not natural, absolute or god-given. Once this 'natural attitude' – that perceived, present reality just is what it is – is exposed as only one very limited reality, then the possibility for change becomes an actuality. Literatures, both primary and secondary, are powerful mechanisms which women can adapt for changing sexist, patriarchal, colonizing cultures which seek to portray themselves as natural. Moreover, literary writing is a social occasion, primarily, however solitary the moment of writing or reading may seem. Writings are a communal exercise of imaginative perspectivism, and as such, they develop in women the faculty of being able to see that things can be constructed otherwise than what seems at the moment natural. International literatures can be a particularly revealing critique of political, social, moral and aesthetic arrangements, and

often a more powerful one than non-fiction, being indirect and able to evade the conscious censors which block direct approaches. Techniques of irony, metaphor and multiple perspective create a relativity of perception which makes scepticism possible about the status quo, and which subtly introduces alternatives under the guise of innocence.

Imaginative writing in English from all over the world, with its access to a variety of long views rather than to short-term, immediate ones, can not only awaken readers to value multiple, 'foreign' worlds and 'alien' ways of seeing, knowing, judging and believing. It can also exercise the writers' and the readers' minds in empathetic identification with people of different nationalities, experiences and values. Literatures in the 'new Englishes' are a powerful means of broadening the otherwise narrow viewpoints which blinker our literary appreciation. The increase in these literatures in the second half of the twentieth century enables us, through imaginative writing, to enter into the experiences, attitudes, values and beliefs of cultures and peoples quite different from our own. In reading, we can break out of acquired preferences. These can be strengths when used as instruments for further extension of appreciation beyond those initial acquirements; yet they too often become weaknesses, because they are used not for extensive but for exclusive purposes. The cultural imprints of a specific group, moreover, do not preclude us, as outsiders, from entering into the enjoyment and available range of meanings of artifacts of 'other' cultures, any more than the individuality of an artist prevents communication with others within or without her or his cultural group. It is precisely by means of literature (and the other arts) that people do communicate.

International literatures in Englishes allow us, through a relatively common language, to cross bridges and borders which would, without that language, remain much more alien and inaccessible. In such border trafficking, we learn more not only about others but about ourselves. For the art of other cultures in a familiar language gives us views of ourselves and our own cultural values which we would never be able to have without that distance or that specific point of view. These exchanges and increments in understanding occur not pre-eminently by the collection of historical facts and information, or by reasoning and the accumulation of ethnological, contextual detail, though these may help (or hinder). Enhancement of understanding occurs more by means of the imaginative installation of ourselves in social, sexual and aesthetic forms which are at first incomprehensible, alien and even at times objectionable.

It is probably inevitable that what these new literatures in Englishes can mean to an 'outsider' will be different in substantial ways to what they mean to those within the given group. Yet, this in no way deauthenticizes one's responses. (Distortion and offensive appropriation of another culture's literature for one's own blinded purposes of exploitation are always possible, but never necessary.) That one should reproduce exactly the viewpoint of others is never the aim of art or appreciation, anyway. The nature of artistic achievement is always to facilitate the movement of perspectives for appreciative audiences from other origins. Distortion or failure of such communication across barriers, whether cultural or personal and temperamental, will not be prevented by false claims of 'priority of authenticity' of response for those within the cultural group from which the artifact initially arises.

The new literatures in Englishes by women, through the imaginative variations they embody, provide people with the insights they need to penetrate that complex of prejudices we have named the 'natural attitude'. These literatures expose the details of a given, privileged reality and its suppression of other realities, which involves marginalization and denial of others' experiences. The new international literatures challenge dominant notions of genuine literature, purity of English, individual worth, and sexist, racist or nationalist assumptions of status. There are many competing ideas about how these challenges should be made. Some writers, for example, argue that post-colonized peoples must first of all avoid 'recolonization', whether by language, economics, cultural hegemony or other pressures. This may require, it is said, the rejection of Englishes and a return to native languages, native literary forms and native aesthetic values, if such repetition of dominance is to be avoided. Other writers argue, on the contrary, that Eurocentric and American hegemony can best be repelled by using English, and thereby communicating better and confronting more directly these oppressive attitudes. Even in using English, disruptions of grammar, syntax, diction, spelling, idiom – practically everything – can be made to work against ideologies. Additionally, literary conventions and genres can also be altered successfully, so that the new English literatures capture the power offered in these forms while expressing their own uniqueness and specificity, yet in a language accessible to hundreds of millions of readers.

Other theorists of the new literatures in Englishes suggest that multiculturalism and internationalism are the way forward through many forms of exploitation and marginalization, whether within a culture or between cultures. While one needs to avoid the syncretism or 'melting pot' effect, which destroys valuable distinctions and even cultural identities, nationalism is not without dangers of reactionary exclusiveness. Yet, the divisive tendencies of nationalism can be balanced by a more positive form, which can provide the means of preserving cultural identities without necessarily leading to oppressive attitudes. Thus Caribbean and Canadian writers may often protect themselves from undue 'Americanization' by invoking certain national or regional qualities, while Africans, those from the Indian subcontinent and Australasians may need to reject many aspects of Englishness or Britishness to preserve a distinct identity.

Many writers in this field agree at least on one thing, namely the need to avoid essentialist concepts, whether about literature and literariness, identity, ethnicity, sexuality or authenticity. Both post-structuralist and feminist theories have contributed to an emphasis on this recognition of the political and constructed nature of such concepts. In some parts of the world, women writers of the new literatures in Englishes have been practising this awareness for decades, if not even longer. Thus, these new literatures have probably been as much a stimulant to these theories as stimulated by them. The flood of new writings in Englishes since World War II may well have intensified a sense of multiculturalism and relativism which had already been deepened by modernist attitudes. Women writers of Englishes have been dismantling and disabling structures of belief imposed upon their cultures in many ways, transforming English into Englishes, and

English literature into new literatures, by every possible disruption and transformation. They have used mimicry, parody and irony to disestablish hegemonies of all kinds, disrupted punctuation, diction and syntax, and created new genres by incorporating oral techniques and women's experiences and preferences. The reading practices of dominant groups, whether within their culture or outside, have been challenged and then changed to suit the needs of marginalized, previously silent people.

Discussions about the dangers of 'cultural esperanto', on the one hand, and an overemphasis on national, ethnic and race or sexual identity, on the other, along with concerns about cultural appropriation and recolonization, abound in the critical literature about these new Englishes. Many writers have noted the contributions to the analyses of Euro-, American- and ethnocentrism generally, of 'Orientalism' and the tyranny of Western critical theory as well as literary and aesthetic values, by such writers as Edward Said, H.K. Bhabha, Gayatri Spivak, Wilson Harris, Barbara Christian, Frantz Fanon, Helen Tiffin and many others. A striking characteristic of some of these contemporary discussions, including many fine introductory writings which give astute surveys of the major issues about empire, race, post-colonialism, ethnicity and so on in the new literatures in Englishes, is their studied neglect of women writers. In some of these books, nine out of ten literary examples are from men writers. Whether prejudice or ignorance of the wealth of women's writing is the reason, there can no longer be any excuse for such contradictory 'imperial' behaviour in books allegedly devoted to disestablishmentarianism. Sadly, this preoccupation with male writers is a characteristic of anthologies and histories as well as critical works. Such sexist attitudes go a long way towards undermining the integrity of these literary critical writings, which claim to be de-centring and demarginalizing empire hegemony.

Some critics have avoided the continuation of this long tradition of the male empire (now no longer only white male empire, but still male), but even in the work of these writers, there is not always a strong enough emphasis upon the need to look more closely at the familiar theorizing about the new literatures in Englishes. For these theoretical writings usually contain some underlying assumptions which disable or confuse their insights. The most obvious one is in the analyses of self–Other, colonized–imperium. Many surveys and histories do not stress enough that the imperial power is itself a flawed and cracked construction, and not unified, pure and harmonious within itself as they assume. The conflict between the imperial power and the colonized people is, that is, an exact replication of the 'colonization' going on at home, within one's own country, in the factories, in the homes, on the land. The imperial power has always marginalized and colonized both within and without. Otherness, colony, margin and exploited exist within the centre of power itself. The undivided, unified centre is a myth, the belief in which contributes considerably to the perpetration of its influence and power at home and abroad. Not only, then, did Europe create a conceptual apparatus about the Orient, for example, which took little if any account of the experiences of Oriental peoples; Europe created a conceptual apparatus about its own monolithic nature by ignoring the 'Orient' within itself. Its own Oriental Other was its women, its working classes, its gypsies, its homosexuals, and so on. This apparatus was harmful to European colonialized people within, just as it was to those abroad. The reification, by theorists of post-colonial literatures, of the empire-power into a smooth surface of homogeneous identity goes a long way towards explaining the exclusion of women authors from the literary corpus of texts in the new literatures in Englishes.

One of the surest means of 'recolonization' succeeding is the fostering of the myth that the colonial power, old or new, economic or political, is unified instead of split, torn and self-enslaved. If we make unnecessary enemies of each other, instead of recognizing fellow marginalized peoples, then we do the work of the centre for it, as indeed we have almost always done. Moreover, this hypothetical 'centre' is not so much any group of people as a set of attitudes and beliefs, prejudices and preconceptions, which must be replaced by new values. As a character in Bessie Head's *When Rain Clouds Gather*, Ma-Millipede, explained to Makhaya, he must not hate even his 'oppressor':

'It is because of the great burden of life', she said quietly . . . 'You must never, never put anyone away from you as not being your brother. Because of this great burden, no one can be put away from you.'

'Who is my brother, Mama?' he asked.

'It is each person alive on the earth', she said.

This philosophy of life may be the most powerful means women have of rebalancing power from patriarchal structures. For it debunks the myth that the 'powerful' are themselves not weak, vulnerable and burdened portions of humanity in the face of that great leveller, life and death. We invest others with power to oppress us when we mistake for reality their self-assessments as privileged beings. Bessie Head's Ma-Millipede suggests that the psyche of every individual, whatever their race, sex, nationality or class, is riven with the Otherness she or he represses – emotions, needs, desires unfulfilled, humanity itself. Surely it is a strange and wonderful idea that the ultimate satisfaction in life is to become a dehumanized robot, with insatiable needs for status, wealth and power over others. If the new literatures in Englishes by women have been subversive, creative and revitalizing of our lives and our literatures, it has been in part because they have so vigorously exposed the meaninglessness at the heart of patriarchal ideals. We may never agree on the alternative ways of living, but diversity flourishing is perhaps the best protection against exploitation.

The new literatures in Englishes have not only expanded the canon, they have displaced it to the margins. Dialogues amongst constantly changing authors and readers with new texts as the subject matter *are* the centre. We can now marginalize the notion that an identifiable body of literature should exist about which any educated person will know. At the new centre will be the metaphor of maps (not bodies) and travel, movement across borders, shuttling from one centre/margin to another margin/centre. Moreover, all concepts of, for example, ethnicity and identity, race, nationality, gender and so on, are already split and problematic at their origins.

Purity is already hybridity, homogeneity is always heterogeneous. Self, group, tribe and culture are always mixtures from the start. The balance between maintaining diverse cultures and ethnicities while avoiding hierarchy and privilege which marginalize others is an inherent difficulty, not a result of external forces. For diversity is the nature of identity and 'purity', the latter being only a mythic construction for certain ends and purposes.

Further reading

Achebe, Chinua. *Morning Yet on Creation Day*. New York, 1973.

Ahmad, Aziz. *In Theory: Classes, Nations, Literatures*. London, 1992.

Ashcroft, B., Griffiths, G. and Tiffin, H. *The Empire Writes Back. Theory and Practice in Post Colonial Literatures*. London and New York, 1989.

Bhabha, H.K. *Nation and Narration*. London, 1995.

Brydon, Diana. 'The Myths that Write Us: Decolonizing the Mind'. *Commonwealth* 10 (1987), 1–14.

Christian, Barbara. 'The Race for Theory'. *Cultural Critique* 6 (1987), 51–64.

Fanon, Frantz. *Black Skins White Masks*. London, 1986.

Gates, H.L., ed. *'Race', Writing, and Difference*. Chicago and London, 1986.

Harris, Wilson. *The Womb of Space: The Cross-Cultural Imagination*. Westport, Conn., 1983.

Johnson, Barbara. *A World of Difference*. Baltimore, 1987.

Ngugi, N. wa. *Decolonizing the Mind: The Politics of Language in African Literatures*. London, 1986.

Parry, Benita. 'Problems in Current Theories of Colonial Discourse'. *Oxford Literary Review* 9 (1988), 27–58.

Said, Edward. *Orientalism*. New York, 1978.

Slemon, S. and Tiffin, H., eds. *After Europe: Critical Theory and Post-Colonial Writing*. Sydney, 1989.

Spivak, G.C. *The Post-Colonial Critic*. London, 1990.

Spivak, G.C. *In Other Worlds: Essays in Cultural Politics*. New York and London, 1987.

Chapter 8

Introduction to Novelists, 1944–1975

The post-World War II period avoids, in the main, the pyrotechnics of modernist experimentation, whilst still searching for innovative modes of expression that will keep the writing of fiction vigorous, compelling and fresh. While this period was sometimes regarded as one of retrenchment to old, familiar forms, novelists did re-examine the usefulness of traditional conventions regarding plot, narrative time, characterization, description, explicit logical development, overt unity and ordinary language. This hesitancy to accept modernists' rejections unquestioningly is often interpreted as an admission of the failure of modernist innovations. More probably, it expresses a quite natural wish to find new ways of handling fictional conventions, ways which modernists had not discovered. The assumption that the fiction of this period represented essentially a return to the novel of ideas or the socio-moral novel is further disputed by the actual texts produced. Even the less overtly experimental novels are usually more than merely neo-realist. A remark by Elizabeth Bowen aptly describes the clear differences from realism of this new, mid-century writing, and suggests some notable similarities with modernist aims: 'The new literature, whether written or visual, is an affair of reflexes, of immediate susceptibility, of associations not examined by reason: it does not attempt a synthesis. Narrative of any length involves continuity, sometimes a forced continuity: it is here that the novel too often becomes invalid.' Bowen's remark suggests that fiction was not regressing naïvely to realist familiarities; if

anything, fiction writers had learnt from modernists, post-impressionists, imagists, symbolists and other experimentalists; they were now searching for new ways of reinventing and reinvigorating fictional forms, which had grown stale in late modernism.

Flannery O'Connor was another writer whose remarks on realism indicate how different and innovative mid-twentieth-century fiction was from its earlier relative, in its adaptations of previous conventions and traditional elements. Her use of the grotesque, combined exotically with a powerful regionalism, led to an impressive if small body of fiction which expanded realism to include the mystery and depth behind the surface of human life. O'Connor explicitly argued for a 'realism of depths', having criticized nineteenth-century realism as one of surface facts and enumeration of descriptive details which did not necessarily reach down into life. Carson McCullers's fiction used overtly carnivalesque effects, as in *The Ballad of the Sad Café*, her most outstanding work. There, realist traditions are hilariously mocked while yet being exploited to the full, especially in the all-out, knock-down fist fight between the characters Miss Amelia and Marvin Macy. Representing, as caricatures, the genres of romance and realism, they are outdone by a flying dwarf, a misfit, an uncategorizable being, itself representative of the new fiction. McCullers's and O'Connor's fiction are fine examples of this 'misfit' who barges in and takes over from the old, familiar traditions. Their texts are exemplary of a continuing experimentation in the post-war period which led to genuinely innovative short stories, novellas and longer works. If the literature of the late 1930s to the early 1960s, say, looks different from earlier writings, this is as much to do with the need for continuing, progressive innovation as with some retrenchment from experimentation. Malcolm Lowry, Henry Green, Henry Miller, Anaïs Nin, Kay Boyle, Elizabeth Smart, Jane Bowles and Leonora Carrington, for example, are further instances of an earlier generation of writers who lived through modernism, participated in it, and then sought new and diverse ways of transforming aspects of the novel.

While the bizarreries and grotesqueries of Bowles, Green, O'Connor and McCullers (discussed further below) function within the realm of the ordinary world, surrealists such as Nin, Carrington and Anna Kavan took fiction into the realm of Kafkaesque exoticisms. These writers can be said to have borrowed much from painting of the period, but also from the early writings of Kafka in the second decade of the twentieth century, with their remarkably innovative attacks on realism. Kafka both parodied realism by using dream characteristics in reality and making reality a 'nightmare', and used the impossible or even supernatural in the midst of deadpan, realist narrative conventions. 'Metamorphosis' ('Die Verwandlung') is only the most obvious example of his additional jokings, such as with enumeration of details about settings, other naturalist descriptive gestures, and strict reference to clock-time, as his cockroach roams about the walls and ceilings of his room in this virtually plotless novel of interiority: the mind of a cockroach.

Carrington, Nin and Kavan were all influenced by Kafka, and their surrealism uses these techniques, some of which clearly owe much to psychological writings of the 1910s and 1920s. Carrington's *The Stone Door* and *The Hearing Trumpet*, the latter written decades later, use quite different techniques from each other, however. *The Stone Door* is almost a glimpse into the illogical, disorderly world of the unconscious as Carrington conceived it, while *The Hearing Trumpet* establishes itself in a more Bowles-like world of bizarre, grotesque, witty incidents. Nin, on the other hand, tapped fully the resources of the dream, the unconscious and Freud's and Jung's

theories, seeking to grope her way into the depths of the psyche where sexuality and desire rule. Kavan's surrealism, however, testifies to the uniqueness of each of these three writers' transformations into fiction of Freudian and surrealist ideas. More influenced by Kafka than either of the other two, she built realms of ice and frozen stasis which were metaphorical constructs for the landscape of portions of the mind rarely explored by less intrepid souls.

An alternative tradition used forms of narration more closely associated with familiar conventions, yet even these novels are vigorously individual in style. In this broad tradition, Jessamyn West and the early Molly Keane, along with Jean Stafford, Martha Gellhorn and Ann Petry, continued the exploration of the sociomoral novel. Jessamyn West's novels are typical examples of a kind of fiction which seems to proceed with fairly traditional narrative practices, at least until one looks more closely. Through the sophisticated use of flashbacks and other digressions from the main development, West's fiction establishes a convincing interrogation of concepts of fact, history and reality versus fiction, the novel and illusion. A constant concern of many of her novels is how the human mind constructs the reality which it mistakes as given, and what the social and personal contributions are to the sustaining of such a construct. Her questioning of the role of desire and of storytelling, metaphor making and other means of ordering and patterning our experience is at its most overt in *The Massacre at Fall Creek*, but other novels, including the self-referential *A Matter of Time*, explore aesthetic issues regarding both narrative time and thematic content. Hence, the content of the latter turns out to be not only life time, but narrative time, as West surprised her readers with constant examples of congruency of form and self-conscious content.

Molly Keane's early novels are also fairly conventional fictions in terms of narrative practices, style and theme, yet they are not without interest for their insights into the hypocrisies of upper-class Anglo-Irish society. Her later fiction, however, breaks entirely with this decades-earlier form, and moves into realms of stunning originality, comic absurdities and inventive, bizarre characters and incidents. Written in her 70s and 80s, these novels have a Bakhtin-like, carnivalesque character in their mixing of high and low, comic and tragic, and a circus-like world of unreality. Plot and sequence are at a minimum, unlike in Keane's earlier Irish novels of manners, while characterization is to the fore, but in a mode quite unheard of in socio-moral novels. For character presentation itself is parodied in these wildly improbable, often ageing, virtually lunatic, idiosyncratic originals. In the context of such characters, the traditional, realist use of the Irish country house for the shenanigans of these eccentrics also takes on a parodic aura. Thus, Keane seems to have subjected the literary techniques of her youthful novels to a hilarious satire both of herself when young and of realist fictional practices generally.

In complete contrast to these contemporaries, Gellhorn, Stafford and Petry drew upon an extremely rigorous form of social realist traditions in fiction. Gellhorn lent her considerable talents to documentary fiction about the poverty and consequent spiritual degradation in both urban and rural America, North and South, in the Depression and in later decades. Occasionally she set her fictions in other countries, such as Africa, and then wrote more about the pretensions and repressions of well-off expatriates, but her most moving works detail the appalling human cost of poor social organization. Petry's narrative techniques in her most famous novel, *The Street*, are suprisingly non-realist, given the social documentary nature of the thematics. Petry's novel is also a fine character study, however, in addition to being a compelling representation of a street in Harlem, and the lives of the black people struggling to contain the outrage and violence engendered by white racism. This moving novel of the individual will of a young woman, Lutie, pitted against apparently indomitable forces of sexism, racism and poverty, is unified further by reference to the existential faith in acts of the will whose value is not negated even by failure. For the novel suggests that whether Lutie succeeds in her goals or not is less significant morally than whether she succeeds in trying, in activating her will, and in facing these odds, even if they do turn out to defeat her.

Stafford began her writing career with some very traditional forms which led to *Boston Adventure* and numerous short stories. With a later novella,

Mountain Lion, however, Stafford achieved her finest novel in structural and stylistic terms; as it happens, it was also her least realist fiction. Plot in this text is completely rejected as Stafford tapped into the resources of symbolic incident, into the pretended innocence of the child's point of view, and into powerful undercurrents of irony which implicated both the lives and attitudes of her characters, and her art. That is, realist presumptions about objectivity, morality and truth are placed under the cold eye of a detached narrator, and the reader's assumptions are included in this harsh scrutiny of values.

Ironically, socio-realist working-class writers like Meridel Le Sueur, Tillie Olsen and Jessie Kesson, also concerned with themes of poverty, sexism and rural farm life or labouring life, were often much less documentary in style than Gellhorn, Petry or Stafford, amongst their contemporaries. They each wrote of the socio-political arrangements which deform whole classes of individuals, and the elements of the human spirit in each one of us which try to resist such deformation, which try to continue to create beauty and humanity in the midst of crushing poverty and waste. Each was markedly innovative and developed new forms of plot and a nonobjectivist point of view. Most of all, they were innovative in their styles. Each of these writers wrote of working-class people in an inspiring, lyrical prose of quite astonishing beauty and passion which, while incongruous with their subject matter at a superficial level, expressed deeply held beliefs about human life.

Olsen had tried to explain the appropriateness of this seeming incongruity when she wrote of the imagination as the most basic nature of humane life, and its expression in literature as a need shared by all peoples, whatever their schooleducation or book-learning. Her fiction is an irrefutable proof of this democratic instinct, in contrast to the classism of such writers as T.S. Eliot, who espoused a deadening elitism about education, literature and the life of the mind. Through concepts of 'transport, meaning, and community', Olsen's writing achieved an elevated style which she herself believed to be the very heart of genuine democracy. The fresh, lively and poetic prose styles of these three writers, so distinct from traditional 'ordinary-language' stylists, is a pressing reminder of the life of the imagination in people of all classes, levels of education, sex, colour and creed. Moreover, there is nothing inaccessible about its legendary beauty and lyricism, so similar to the later Bessie Head's writing. The notion of social realists that only 'ordinary language' is truly accessible to all people is revealed by Olsen's, Le Sueur's and Kesson's magical prose as nonsensical ideology. Through the elevated style of other writers such as Jennifer Johnson, also fusing a lyrical prose with brutal, harsh, rural life, this fine diction demonstrated that beauty in everyday life is the rightful property of all human beings.

The contrast between the magical fusions by Kesson, Johnson, Le Sueur and Olsen of their naturalist themes with elevated, lyrical prose, on the one hand, and the documentary styles of other socio-realists (in addition to Gellhorn, Petry and Stafford) such as the early regionalists Harriette Arnow and Marjorie Kinnan Rawlings, and the early fiction of Doris Lessing, on the other hand, is a reminder of the amazing fecundity of the novel form. All these 'new realists' were too sophisticated to imagine, however, that their realism could be objective or neutral, any more than photography could be. They were all clearly aware, as their texts indicate, that both linguistic and photographic representation are stylized, no matter what mode one uses. Lessing was to embody this recognition most skilfully in *The Golden Notebook*, where she completely debunked the idea that realism could be appropriate any more in its nineteenth-century form. In that text, Lessing fragmented a central conventional, realist novel, *Free Women*, into several pieces, interrupted, indeed completely disrupted, by 'marginal', non-objective forms of writing, such as diaries, notebooks, memoirs and drafts of novels. Even the newspaper cuttings with which the central character begins to wallpaper her house, in a last grasp at sanity conceived as objectivity, are shown to be biased, utterly unreliable and even lies. The very concepts of truth and reality are questioned along with realism itself, and disruption, fragmentation and breakdown are seen as new realities which may, if faced up to, lead us to hope, if not to truth.

In a similarly sophisticated questioning of realist fictional forms and assumptions, Iris Murdoch began publishing her fantastic parodies of neo-realism, funnier than even she expected,

perhaps, for the parody was missed by critics for years. A.S. Byatt, an accomplished novelist herself, was one of the first critics to appreciate the sophistication of Murdoch's interrogations of fictional form and traditions. It was Byatt who saw Murdoch, contemporaneously with Lessing, engaging in a systematic exploration of how to create a literature which could explore moral and intellectual issues characteristic of realist fiction, without imagining one could go back to such an earlier form. For one would have to ignore the existence of modernism, psychology, technology and all other social and cultural changes, and write in a style no longer expressive of a new era.

Another notable event was the failure of critics, readers and publishers in the 1960s to appreciate Barbara Pym, for example. After an immensely successful set of six novels from 1950 to 1961, Pym's fiction became unfashionable, probably because misread as neo-realist, conservative and 'irrelevant', it was said, to the new times. In the late 1970s, however, Pym was reinstated and republished as one of the most sophisticated and original writers of the period – not soon enough to undo the damage of years of neglect. (She died soon after being taken up again by her fickle public.) It seems that her wonderfully playful and self-conscious, innovative fictions had been read as provincial, old-fashioned romances. This instance of critical folly should be a painful reminder to all readers of how easy it is to blind ourselves to the value of fiction, and how easily we fail to spot innovation. This is partly because we 'see' what we have learned to expect. It is also because we often fail to appreciate subtleties that do not fit into our narrow tastes and prejudices, which we imagine to be infallible measures of value. Moreover, it is often we readers, reviewers and critics who are *projecting* conservatism into texts which do not happen to fit our idea of experimentation. If we see the only real kinds of experimentation as the modernist or postmodernist, then we are destined to overlook much that is new and valuable in fiction of any period.

Such limited notions lead to the 'depressing and outdated folklore', as Malcolm Bradbury eloquently described it, that the post-war period, especially in England but also elsewhere in the English-speaking world, signified the imminent 'death of the novel'. The critics who made such predictions must be a distinct shade of pink today, for the novel has flourished in the last thirty years as never before. When Susan Sontag's *Against Interpretation* appeared in 1966, it too drew attention to one of the main reasons why the literature of the two previous decades had seemed to some readers less progressive. The novel, Sontag argued, is too readily treated by critics as a repository of ideas when it is not brashly experimental. Unless, Sontag explained, the novelist forces us to attend to formalities and to artistry and craft, usually through shocking, unreadable breaches of the familiar, we readers tend to allow our attention to drift towards overt subject matter, and become mesmerized by it. Because we ignore the forms through which such subject matter is expressed, we not only fail to perceive the artistry, literary qualities and innovative character of much fiction; we even miss, she argued, the significance of its subject matter, misinterpreting it because we separate it from its artistic embodiment. In pleading for the congruence of forms of expression with thematics, Sontag also avoided in her criticism the alleged excesses of the 'new criticism' of the late 1940s and early 1950s, with its tendency, it is sometimes said, to overemphasize form.

Elizabeth Hardwick's novels are examples of this interest in congruence of form and content. Like Harper Lee in *To Kill A Mockingbird*, Hardwick interrogated truth itself, and how language can express or embody such an elusive entity. Both she and Lee created meta-fictional situations via apparently simple content, namely a trial for murder to establish the 'simple truth', with the attention on the observation and interpretation of events rather than the events themselves. In both cases, the reader is herself or himself mirrored in the text, misinterpreting the simple truth. Contrastingly, Elizabeth Smart's *By Grand Central Station I Sat Down and Wept* uses late modernist stream of consciousness techniques and meditates on love as a linguistic effect, which, she showed, is no less devastating for being so. Janet Frame's fiction was equally experimental, but not in being late modernist. Frame began with traditional narrative conventions, but gradually developed techniques which are so post-modernist as to place her firmly in that school of experimentation, while her contemporary, Ann Quin, was even more ahead of her time. Writing radically experimental novels in

the 1960s and 1970s, before her early death in 1973, Quin anticipated strategies that have only recently begun to come to the fore again in such writers as Kathy Acker and Christine Brooke-Rose. Quin's *Berg*, *Passages* and other novels should undoubtedly be recovered as major experiments in new forms of fiction. That this writer has been unknown for two decades is quite inexplicable, as any reader should immediately see.

By the end of this wonderfully varied period, which had found new forms of expression for the new experiences of the post-war period no less innovative for being different from modernism, Bowles, Eudora Welty, Muriel Spark, Margaret Laurence, Frame and Elizabeth Spencer had published fiction from all corners of the earth. The novel could have hardly been less dead, as Welty brought forth her elegant and mysterious fictions, from *A Curtain of Green* to the fairy-tale revision *The Robber Bridegroom*; Bowles astonished the literary world with *Two Serious Ladies*; and Laurence in Canada, Frame in New Zealand, and Spencer in Italy were weaving spells over readers enchanted by this old-new writing. While one of the central characteristic forms of the post-war period was said to be the use of the grotesque or carnivalesque to shock the reader out of complacency and out of preoccupation with subject matter to the exclusion of form, other typical modes used were the comic, experiments with voice and narrative personas, and the power of place and setting.

Bowles's *Two Serious Ladies* is one of the earliest and certainly the most significant example of this interest in bizarre, eccentric, grotesque styles. Part of a tradition which led to O'Connor's originals and McCullers's 'cases', Bowles was greatly admired by her contemporaries and is surely one of the original stylists of the mid-twentieth century. Her hilarious and witty stories and novel, and her tragic drama *In the Summerhouse*, are of too much literary merit to be ignored for long. Bowles's novel shares the religious and moral concerns of Flannery O'Connor, and succeeds equally with O'Connor in subordinating those concerns to the demands of her art. Limits are constantly tested and breached by weird and wonderful characters, from lesbians, to prostitutes, to bums, to thugs and inhabitants of a *demi-monde* which gets mixed up with the world of ladies and gentlemen. Bowles's inventiveness seems inexhaustible, as her fiction and drama transgress the borders of the acceptable, the proper and the 'good' in life, literature and reading. In a not entirely different vein, her contemporary Muriel Spark achieved great fame for a time, yet only recently have her novels been seen as early examples of post-modern literature. Her constant thematizing of reading, of audiences and of interpretation is embedded in a thematics explorative of power relations, authorities and obediences. As with Pym, Murdoch and Lessing, it has taken some years for critics and reviewers to realize that Spark was figuring them into the tapestry of her fiction!

Other contemporaries of the post-war period include the Canadian Margaret Laurence, whose characteristic practice was to experiment with narrative voices. Laurence achieved a truly remarkable diversity of narrative personas through whose personalities we see the world, as in *The Stone Angel* or *A Jest of God*. A later novel, *The Diviners*, thematizes a writer's efforts to distinguish autobiography from fiction, fiction from fact and history, and to reconcile the impossibility of objectivity and neutrality with the need for truth and the need to live life. Welty was similarly fascinated with these issues, but she was especially interested in the artist's ability to present narrative points of view and take the reader with her or him into the minds of the most improbable people. For her, this ability to leap across the boundaries of the self into the soul of a fellow human was the essence of imagination and of art generally. Such leaps were facilitated by the ability of the author to create for the reader a strong sense of place, of atmosphere and of natural setting. That is, the establishment of an imaginative landscape is a step in the difficult business of arousing the reader to imaginative response. Welty's fiction is also notable for its wide diversity of styles and genres, from stories and novels verging on regionalism, and relying upon dialect and locale for their impact, to fiction of universal, timeless character.

Other important contributions to the fuller development of fiction in the mid-twentieth century include the work of the incomparable Marguerite Young. This writer represents a radically experimental stream of fiction which was developing in the 1960s and 1970s, and which will be

further discussed in chapter 11, because it constitutes one of the earlier radical examples of postmodernism. Hortense Calisher's fiction must, however, be mentioned as another early postmodernist form. In one novel, for example, Calisher rewrote *Gulliver's Travels* from a woman space-traveller's point of view, challenging both male and earthling centrism, while in *The Railway Police*, her heroine gives up all the previous disguises, wigs, masks and costumes of her earlier life, and goes forth into the world completely bald!

Other writers of the post-war period, some of whose work reaches right into the 1990s, include Nadine Gordimer, whose fiction is a fusion of the political realities of life in South Africa with the literary techniques of an artist of great integrity. Using a detached irony as her primary mode of communication, Gordimer interrogates every barrier between human beings, from the most obvious, apartheid, to the less evident forms involving temperament, class, sex and age. She has experimented with realist practices, a form of stream of consciousness in *July's People*, and a rich materiality of language in *Burger's Daughter*. Ruth Prawer Jhabvala, Kamala Markandaya, Mavis Gallant and Elizabeth Spencer have also experimented during this period with narrative practices, albeit within basically accessible conventions. Yet each one of them has achieved an individuality of style within this tradition – a continuing testimony to the inexhaustibility of the novel form.

In 1965, with the explosion on the literary scene of Young's *Miss MacIntosh, My Darling*, shortly to be followed by Jean Rhys's *Wide Sargasso Sea* (1966), Richard Brautigan's *Trout Fishing in America* (1967), Thomas Pynchon's *The Crying of Lot 49* (1966), Christine Brooke-Rose's *Such* (1966), Kurt Vonnegut's *Slaughterhouse-Five* (1969), Gore Vidal's *Myra Beckenridge* (1968), Philip Roth's *Portnoy's Complaint* (1969), Frame's *State of Siege* (1966), Calisher's *Extreme Magic* (1964) and Quin's *Berg* (1964), the era we call post-modernism was ushered in. This era was certainly influenced by the *nouveau roman*, and by the writings of Vladimir Nabokov, William Burroughs and John Barth, for example. It also constituted a vigorous, new direction for the fiction of the post-war period, so much so, indeed, that the notion of the death of the novel was laughable. After the mid-1960s, when the novel was supposed to have died or at least been exhausted, a period of literary richness and diversity set in which was more international, more diverse and more lively than ever before. Consequently, the canon is gradually collapsing under the weight of an international cornucopia of styles, forms and practices. We surely cannot continue to cope with such diversity by relying on outdated and inappropriate notions of canon.

The old mappings and charts are no longer viable. The new reader has standards, but lots of them, not just a small, elite set based on ignorance of the tradition. The old hierarchies identified a few dozen books per decade (usually by male, white writers) as the literature worth notice: the new reader reads and enjoys for herself or himself the particularities of a whole range of texts from all over the world, in all kinds of style, form and practice.

Chapter 9

Individual Authors, 1944–1975

Anna Kavan 1901–1968

Born in Cannes as Helen Woods, Kavan began publishing under her first married name, Helen Ferguson. After a second marriage broke up, and after two periods in an asylum, she changed her appearance, and her name to Anna Kavan. This name may have been taken as a result of the influence of Franz Kafka's writings, which is evident in the second period of her career. As Helen Ferguson, Kavan published several early novels, including *A Charmed Circle* (London, 1929), *Let Me Alone* (London, 1930), *A Stranger Still* (London, 1935) and *Goose Cross* (London, 1936). In her second period, as a symbolist-surrealist writer, Kavan published a whole range of novellas and collections of short stories, thanks to the support and encouragement of, especially, Peter Owen, but also her friends Rhys Davies, Raymond Marriott, Dr Bluth and Brian Aldiss. These works include *Asylum Piece and Other Stories* (London, 1940), *I Am Lazarus: Short Stories* (London, 1941), *Sleep Has His House* (London, 1948: a novella), *A Scarcity of Love* (Southport, 1956), *Eagle's Nest* (a Kafkaesque fiction: London, 1957), *A Bright Green Field* (a short story collection: London, 1958), *Who Are You?* (Lowestoft, 1963: a novella), *Ice* (London, 1967: a surrealist, almost science fiction novella, which surely influenced Doris Lessing's *The Making of a Representative from Planet X*), *Julia and the Bazooka and Other Stories*, ed. Rhys Davies (London, 1970) and *My Soul in China: A Novella and Stories*, ed. Rhys Davies (London,

1975). Kavan was also an accomplished painter throughout her life, and earned a considerable amount of money from restoring and redecorating houses.

Greatly admired by a number of her contemporaries, including, for example, Jean Rhys, Kavan was probably first written about and praised extensively by her spiritual friend Anaïs Nin in her book, *The Novel of the Future* (1968). Kavan was, like Nin, enthusiastic about the French *nouveau roman*, though she is said to have had a predilection for male writers, due perhaps to her poorly hidden jealousy of other women novelists.

While Kavan's second period is much more experimental and unconventional than her first several novels, these early works are by no means without interest, and they certainly contain elements which became intensely emphasized and exaggerated later. For example, while situated in the familiar, everyday world of ordinary reality, *Goose Cross* (particularly) enters into a realm of the psychological and of mental experience suggestive of Ann Quin's earliest work. Preoccupations with loneliness, alienation, and emotional coldness – patterned through the central character, Julia's, intense feelings, images and events – presage Kavan's later concerns. Relationship with others and the question of identity – 'Who are you?', 'Who am I?' – saturate her fictions' thematics. After breakdowns in the late 1930s, and her change of name and identity in 1939–40, Kavan began her experimental period, which she was to continue until the end of her life; she

153

died from an overdose of heroin (she had been a registered addict for some thirty years).

Kavan described her writing to Rhys Davies and to others as an effort to move away from 'realistic' or 'straight' fiction into realms she sometimes referred to as fantasy, dream or even madness. One of her central symbolic, surrealist or imagist techniques was to portray the interior world of thoughts and feelings by means of descriptions normally applied to external, natural landscapes and scenery. *Ice* is the most systematic and extreme example of this externalization of the interior life, this 'naturalization' of human feelings and thoughts, which functions to defamiliarize utterly, by avoiding the usual language of psychological, mental experience. The nightmarish, surreal technique of *Who Are You?*, on the other hand, a kind of surreal rewriting of the earlier *Let Me Alone*, has more in common with Leonora Carrington's mode of 'making the unconscious conscious' through bestial images and rather weird juxtapositions and other images. Kavan explained her experimental writing in a letter to Peter Owen: 'I wanted to abandon realistic writing insofar as it describes exclusively events in the physical environment, and to make the reader aware of the existence of the different, though just as real, "reality" which lies just beyond the surface of ordinary daily life . . . I am convinced that a vast, exciting new territory is waiting to be explored by the writer in that direction.'

In the same letter, Kavan further remarked that it would not be possible for a writer to explore and describe this 'new territory' by conventional means of plot, characterization, description, thematics and so on. She needed to experiment with ways of writing that were differently structured and radically adapted to capture a 'three-dimensional effect – an effect in depth'. Like Marguerite Young, Ann Quin and, later, Christine Brooke-Rose and Kathy Acker, Kavan sought to create in her language a sense of multiple, contemporaneous realities in every moment, for every event, without merely resorting to alternating narrative perspectives expressed in a linear narrative. Though she did at times make use of this technique, she sought to reinforce it, or even surpass it, by means of an intensely imaginative, symbolic language, a language expressive of the richness of the world of the unconscious saturating every conscious thought or feeling we experience. Like Djuna Barnes's *Nightwood* (which Kavan admired), her writings seek out a language of the dream, the nightmare – a 'nocturnal' language which can communicate and connect us to other realities than the familiar one, which tyrannizes over our imagination and blocks fresh perceptions and new experiences. The most obvious example of this 'language of the night' is *Sleep Has His House*, which contains 'summaries' in ordinary, realist language of each of the chapters, a set of stylistic alternations designed to show the inadequacy of 'realistic' or 'straight' writing.

With *The Eagle's Nest*, Kavan devised a still different mode of symbolic-surrealist language, much influenced by Kafka's writings. There, haphazard, arbitrary and nightmarish events have indecipherable meanings: 'Signs wrongly read, wrongly combined or chosen, can result only in false conclusions, and judgements that are unreliable.' This may be the first of Kavan's novels in which it becomes pellucid that her fiction is not merely autobiographical, or self-referring to the writing of fiction. In *The Eagle's Nest*, as in *Ice* and other later writings, the so-called post-modernist preoccupation with the reader and the reading situation is starkly, undeniably delineated. Extreme self-referentiality invades these works, as Kavan not only wrote about the plights of her characters, but made these plights symbolic of the plight of an author, a text and a reader. Like Young, Quin, Carrington, Brooke-Rose and Acker, she rejected without hesitation the 'laws' that govern the novel and alleged literary success, though, curiously, *The Eagle's Nest* is in some respects ironically conventional and accessible, unlike many of her other works. In *Who Are You?*, for example, the reader is confronted with alternative endings: a nightmarish one occurs at page 94, and the other, more realist, happens twenty-four pages later; but both are inconclusive and 'indecipherable'.

Like Kafka, then, Kavan – along with many other contemporary writers, such as the imagists and modernists – rejected realism, in her case adopting surreal, fantastic, grotesque and absurdist techniques. Her writings reveal the strong influence of the new psychoanalysis of Freud, Jung and Havelock Ellis, amongst others, on writers. Her fiction explores the nature of realities different from the familiar one, and she, like Kafka, portrayed these realities as in part illegible, unknowable by the rational, logical processes, and yet not at all meaningless. These new and different territories and experiences waiting to be explored by the writer are realms which elude the confines of the reason, which involve paradoxes and inconsistencies, which are constantly shifting and changing, so that certainty and definiteness are lacking. Sometimes Kavan's writing describes reality as basically an enigma, and she emphasizes this by portraying characters confronted constantly with life as an impasse. Ambiguity is the essence of meaning, as Kavan showed the conscious mind saturated by various levels of the unconscious: every gesture, every utterance is layered with (often contradictory) meanings. The process of fiction is shown, in part, to be that of facilitating the passageways between the various strata of the human mind, and expressing these multiples through fusing them in images, metaphors and symbols, or by surrealist juxtapositions. Indeed, not only are the various layers and meanings within the psyche fused by symbols, etc.; the psychological, interior complex is fused by the writer with the physical, natural, exterior complex world. Familiarity with the inner landscapes of our lives eventually can illuminate the mysterious realms of the human mind which, otherwise, remain unreachable.

Jessamyn West 1902–1984

Born to committed Quaker parents in Indiana in 1902, West is the author of the well-known linked stories *Friendly Persuasion* (New York, 1945), made into a remarkable film in 1955. This, her first book publication, has sold several hundred thousand copies as a result. It is a beautifully written, moving account of Jess and Eliza Birdwell and their lives as Quakers in the second half of the nineteenth century. West wrote several other collections of linked stories, including *Cress Delahanty* (New York, 1953), *Love, Death, and the Ladies' Drill Team* (New York, 1955) and *Except for Me and Thee* (New York, 1967), the last of which fleshes out the lives of the Birdwells of *Friendly Persuasion*. Novels include *The Witch Diggers* (New York, 1957), a tragic account of the failure of love in the face of shame regarding

sexual passion, and *South of the Angels* (New York, 1960), a saga of California families trying to settle the desert near Los Angeles (this novel covers a single year, in which the need for water is chronicled through the use of a powerful seasonal metaphor of birth, sexual love, death and revival). Other novels include *A Matter of Time* (New York, 1966), *Leafy Rivers* (New York, 1967) and *The Massacre at Fall Creek* (New York and London, 1975), as well as *The Life I Really Lived* (New York and London, 1979). In several of these, West drew on personal experiences but also on historical facts, in an exploration of the relation of art to life and fiction to fact. How history shapes reality, rather than merely reflecting it, is a central theme of many of her texts. West also wrote a number of non-fictional works: *Hide and Seek: A Continuing Journey* (New York and London, 1973) is an account of several months spent alone in the wilds on a bank of the Colorado River. It is an overt expression of West's admiration for Henry Thoreau and his commitment to the idea that a life lived in independence is the basis of all healthy community. Powerful themes of the 'value of life' as inherently entangled with 'courage in the face of death' emerge in the autobiography *The Woman Said Yes* (New York and London, 1976), a book in part about euthanasia, and in part about West's mother, who is portrayed as a force of love, creativity and life-enhancing power with which she sought to endow her children.

'Reality' is a concept under continual scrutiny in West's fiction as well as her autobiographical works. In *The Life I Really Lived*, one of West's finest novels, the book's epigraph reads, 'One's real life is the life one does not lead.' This oxymoron is a way of stating West's constant interest in how reality emerges as story, or how the mind organizes and perceives events through patterns, metaphors and unities which express not so much an external, unitary reality as the kind of perspective that any particular mind takes. For example, *A Matter of Time* is organized almost entirely by flashbacks, as the older of two sisters reconstructs their lives through memories, while they 'wait' for the moment of impending death by euthanasia. The present illness, age and death provide a frame within which their lives are valued for being unique – lived 'in their own way' – and the novel expresses the importance of intellectual independence, and the Thoreau-like determination to resist convention and die in one's own way, in one's own time. Most of all, West's fiction expresses this independence through the need to tell one's story in one's own way. Yet, how to negotiate one's way through the pitfalls of illusion, evasion and falsification is one of her central sub-themes, as in *The Massacre at Fall Creek*.

This novel is her most experimental in terms of narrative strategies and, like Mari Sandoz, in her interest in 'reality', 'history' and fiction. She explained in her non-fiction 'Valedictory' at the end of the novel that 'My intention was not to reveal historic facts in a fictional setting, but to open questions of more abiding truths. And that is quite a different matter.' Based on an 1824 Indiana murder trial of white men accused of killing American Indians (perhaps the first time in US history that white men were executed legally for the murder of American Indians), official records of which had been destroyed in a courthouse fire, this 'historical novel' is constructed through a variety of methods, from extensive extracts of letters to newspaper reports to traditional authorial commentary. A romantic sub-plot enriches the main plot of the trial proceedings. It functions further as a kind of allegory reflecting the issues involved in the trial, as well as the larger issues of reality versus illusion, what truth is, what a lie is, and how human beings order their lives in the midst of uncertainty and relativity. West was attracted to this particular event because of its relevance to her Quaker values of non-violence. She was certainly also struck by Sandoz's idea (in *Battle of the Little Big Horn* (1978)), that in Canada the westward expansion of European civilization had not been accompanied by the wholesale slaughter of Native Americans on the way. This had been avoided by efforts to relocate and compensate them, however unsatisfactorily. West's novel includes two Indians (one amongst the murdered) who adhered to a nineteenth-century religious philosophy, like Gandhi's, of non-violence (which today still has a following of several thousand Iroquois).

In the course of constructing this dual narrative of trial and romance, the novel proceeds partly via comments by the focusing consciousness of Charles Fort, the young lawyer who writes letters to his newspaper editor father to provide a basis for the latter's journalistic reports of the event. Gradually, digressions and asides (about the subjectivity of any 'account' due to the distortion arising from selection of material, condensation, limitation of point of view, and so on) begin to swamp the narrative. Charles notes the effects of certain kinds of language and rhetoric, along with the inevitability of stylization. He concludes that narrative shapes events and makes them meaningful, rather than merely reporting already-shaped, significant events. Charles's reports and the authorial comments about the problem of reportage and narrative, audience response, point of view, prose versus poetry and personal versus publishable all become the covert subject matter: language is also on trial, especially our abuse of language through unconscious, careless assumptions about it. West showed how problematic the relation of words to experience is, and how this relation complicates our notions of truth, reality and justice, but also love. In the midst of all these relativities and uncertainties, there are, the novel suggests – especially in the romance, but also in the trial – guidelines, even if there are no absolutes, and non-violence is one of them. Another is love, understood as recognizing other human beings as people like ourselves. Another again is the need to be able to discriminate, even if only relatively and not absolutely, between values and needs that are humane, and the cravings for money, power and prestige which dehumanize us. *The Massacre at Fall Creek* makes no concessions to the lack of absolutes in life, but it also shows – and this is the central aesthetic role of the romantic sub-plot – that discrimination and judgement are essential, even if provisional and subject to change. That is, we must act, even if we can only act on uncertain bases; for to act pretending that it is based on certainty is surely a deception, and the source of intolerance and selfishness.

Martha Gellhorn 1908–

War correspondent in Spain (1957–8), Finland (1937), France and Germany (1943–5), Vietnam (1966) and Israel (1967), not to mention China (1940–1), England and Italy, Gellhorn is the author of over half a dozen novels and several collections of novellas and short stories. Married to Ernest Hemingway (and allegedly the original of the girl in Hemingway's play *The Fifth Column*), she received the O. Henry Award in 1958. Born in St Louis, Missouri, she attended Bryn Mawr College before beginning a distinguished career as a journalist and a parallel one as a fiction writer. Gellhorn has not been an overtly experimental or innovative writer in terms of narrative or stylistic techniques, yet she has produced a number of finely crafted and moving, insightful texts, all of which are a testimony not only to her own genuine sense of compassion and strong conscience, but also to the power of the novel as an art form to break down the destructive prejudices of colour, class, sex and religion which blind us all to our common humanity. Gellhorn is the author of several non-fictional works as well, including *The Face of War* (New York and London, 1959), *Travels with Myself and Another* (London, 1978; an autobiographical account of a trip through the Caribbean) and *The View from the Ground* (London, 1989). Her novels include *A Stricken Field* (New York, 1940), *Liana* (New York and London, 1944), *The Wine of Astonishment* (New York, 1948), *His Own Man* (New York, 1961) and *The Lowest Trees Have Tops* (London, 1967).

Some of Gellhorn's novellas written about the Great Depression, and published in a 1936 collection entitled *The Trouble I've Seen* (New York and London), are successful social realist documentaries – but also powerful emotional fictional narratives – about the struggle (or failure to struggle) of various types of individual, against the crushing effects of deeply rooted poverty, whether in the Southern United States, the Midwest or the East. Elements of *The Trouble I've Seen* originated in a report Gellhorn was commissioned to write for the US Federal Emergency Relief Agency. 'Mrs Maddison' is a well-designed example of Gellhorn's ability to adapt familiar realist conventions in vigorous and individual ways, thereby capturing the reader's interest on behalf of people probably far removed from our own situation. This story also exemplifies Gellhorn's aesthetic principle of a refusal to simplify complex social and psychological issues. She portrayed Mrs Maddison as not only up against a difficult social situation, but ultimately defeated by the fecklessness of her children.

These immature young adults are portrayed almost as failed artists: as unable to rise to the extreme demands placed upon the moral fabric of individuals during the Depression. In the novellas 'Joe and Pete' and 'Ruby', Gellhorn explored, on the one hand, through a starkly naturalist style the courage of factory workers striking in vain against a powerful management, and, through a more lyrical language on the other, the way poverty drives a child of 12 into prostitution – a child who is so innocent as not to comprehend what is happening to her.

After experimenting with a number of other styles, forms, topics and themes throughout the 1940s, 1950s and 1960s, in 1980 Gellhorn published another collection of novellas set in Africa, entitled *The Weather in Africa* (New York). This book included 'On the Mountain', 'By the Sea' and 'In the Highlands', and in all three tales Gellhorn revealed a passion for the beautiful landscape of Africa and a fine descriptive talent for nature. This is especially true of the final novella in the collection: 'In the Highlands' reminds readers that while Gellhorn often wrote in a documentary, realist style, she was capable of great lyricism and poetic prose. While many of her novellas are ostensibly concerned, at the thematic level, with social and economic issues, they always function at another, aesthetic level. In this case, we have a story of the morally creative effect of African people and magnificent landscape upon certain types of human nature, and the healing power of a life lived close to nature.

In one of her most successful novels, *Liana*, Gellhorn drew on her experiences of a trip on a small potato boat in the Caribbean, when she was becalmed for some days on a small island, totally isolated by German submarines and the hurricane season. Using the setting of this Eden-like island, Gellhorn turned to dramatic conventions and constructed the compelling tragedy of a young black islander taken up by a white land owner, then a young Frenchman, and finally abandoned by both, emotionally if not financially. *Liana* describes the selfishness of both men's exploitation of Liana, as two quite different forms of 'love' which lead to despair and suicide. This novel is one of Gellhorn's most original and expressive works. In the afterword to her novel, the author explained that 'there is only one iron rule for fiction: it must not bore.' Readers are encouraged to understand a story in their own way; indeed, Gellhorn argued that no readers react to the same book in the same way. She also explained that often writers have no other intention in fiction 'beyond a private wilful wish' to tell their stories. Gellhorn's stories rarely bore, and their compelling narratives are formally, aesthetically rich enough to stimulate a variety of different responses, even from the same reader, at different times. That is, they can withstand numerous re-readings, which suggests that Gellhorn not only succeeded with her story-line; she also managed to interest her readers in the way she wrote her tales, in part through the strength of her own candour combined with a passionate interest in how she could portray other people in fictional forms. For her novels emphasize, above all, the fictional achievement of characterization; Gellhorn's great strength as a writer is, in part, her ability to fuse strong characters into a well-designed plot, with both communicated by means of a clear, candid prose.

Ann Petry 1908–

Described as 'one of the best novels ever written about Harlem', *The Street* (Boston, 1946) was published to immense response; it sold over one and a half million copies, and has been reprinted in 1985 and 1986. Petry's first novel, creating a new wave of literature after the Depression had depleted the powerful creative period of the Harlem Renaissance in the 1920s and early 1930s, constitutes a shift towards an emphasis upon a more naturalistic social and economic critique than was typical of that earlier wave of black creativity. A year later, *Country Place* (Boston, 1947), a second novel, was published; Petry also published four children's novels and some poetry, a third adult novel, *The Narrows* (Boston, 1953), and a collection of short stories, *Miss Muriel* (Boston, 1971). She has been a visiting lecturer at the Universities of Yale, Berkeley, Hawaii and Suffolk, and still lives in Old Saybrook, Connecticut, where she was born. She took a BA in pharmacy from the University of Connecticut before marrying and moving to New York City, where she had a daughter and worked as a journalist for several years. A Houghton-Mifflin Fellowship in 1945 helped her to complete her

first novel, which established her as a major literary success. This occurred in spite of the extreme chauvinism among male black American writers, which has persisted into the 1990s (considerably weakened by Ntozake Shange's and Toni Cade Bambara's publications in the 1970s).

The Street, recognized early as a work of 'transcendent and enduring literary artistry', is not only a social documentary; it is not only a profoundly compelling protest novel and indictment of racist society; it is not only a moving analysis of the inhumanity of a capitalist economic system based on exploitation of women, black people and the working classes. It is a fine achievement of narrative subtlety, complex and effective plot, unpretentious style and insightful characterization. Petry focused her novel on the central character, Lutie Johnson, a young mother in her early 20s separated from her husband. This thematic and narrative centre is balanced in an aesthetically sophisticated way by the large, looming figure of Mrs Hedges, who observes almost everything from her street-front window. In addition to this added eccentric observer, Petry devised a further complexity: while using a third person narrative throughout, the point of view is almost never omniscient. It shifts with the weight of each major character, creating several interior monologues. Indeed, Petry's narrative is a naturalistic stream of consciousness so intimately bound up and identified with the predominant character at any given time that the reader is ushered in and out of the consciousnesses of Lutie, Bud and Super in a painful proximity which intensifies the tragedy of all their lives.

Another major unifying and stylistic technique of the novel is Petry's ability to bring to life and sustain her personification of the street itself. The street is used first as an emblem of society and environment. Once this symbol is established, Petry proceeded by imagery and stylistic techniques to turn the street into the other main protagonist in conflict with Lutie Johnson. Of course, Lutie's struggles involve poverty, racism, sexism and the destructive jealousy of other women. Each one of these conflicts is portrayed through specific characters. But all the characters against whom Lutie has to battle are portrayed almost as mere tools of the all-powerful street. It is the street, the environment, the society which will defeat her, not some individual, or even several individuals. Her individual will (or theirs), strong as it is, is shown to be a mere toy in the face of the implacable determination of society to keep certain people 'in their place'. As a consequence of this technique of personification, Petry's novel depicts a society at war with itself and exposes the psychological mechanisms of how individuals are manipulated, divided, and taught self-destruction and destruction of their own peers. Further, the text sets up an illuminating tension between individual will and social, environmental forces: there is no dichotomy, Petry showed, no genuine conflict, for individual will is only meaningful in the context of an environment which recognizes individuality. A racist environment precisely denies the individuality of its targets. Hence, it is a non-environment, that is, not a meaningful environment. Petry subverts the grounds of the distinction, and shows the hollowness of the debate – a white man's debate only.

Yet her analysis goes even deeper. In the one brief scene including white people, Petry depicted the utter poverty of their spiritual lives, and showed money and consumerism to be at the roots of their loveless, empty existences. The overvaluing of money and property is at the basis of sexism, racism and other forms of prejudice, as Paule Marshall and others would argue. The gradual shift in the 1970s and 1980s from protest fiction and tragedy and towards hope may suggest that the strength of the illness is being diminished by the creativity and speech of black women working together.

Eudora Welty 1909–

Recipient of the Pulitzer Prize in 1973 for *The Optimist's Daughter* (New York, 1972), Eudora Welty was born and has lived most of her life in Jackson, Mississippi. *A Curtain of Green and Other Stories* (New York, 1941), her first collection of short stories to be published, was introduced by Katherine Anne Porter, whose fiction Welty had long admired. Other stories were collected into volumes in 1943, 1955 and finally in 1980, as *The Collected Stories* (New York and London). Welty's novels include her notable *Robber Bridegroom* (New York, 1942), which takes

a folklore, fairy-tale setting, and, like Margaret Atwood decades later, rewrites the legend in provocative prose. *Delta Wedding* appeared in New York in 1946. For *The Ponder Heart* (New York, 1954) Welty received the Howell Medal. A later novel, *Losing Battles* (New York, 1970), is a Homeric, epic account of an extended family reunion. Finally, *The Optimist's Daughter* is again a novel with Greek tragedy elements, infused nevertheless into an essentially humorous tone, as a middle-aged woman is confronted with her immaturity in the face of her father's death.

In 1984, *One Writer's Beginnings* (Cambridge, Mass., and London) appeared, an autobiographical account of Welty's childhood and family. Earlier, in 1971, Welty published *One Time, One Place* (New York), a remarkable collection of photographs from the 1930s, when she worked for the Works Progress Administration in the Mississippi Countryside; the photos record the lives of black and white sharecroppers and other workers in that poverty-stricken era. Many of her short stories can be read as verbal documentaries of the lives of these Mississippi farmers and labourers struggling with the effects of the Great Depression and its aftermath. In 1978, *The Eye of the Story* (New York) was published, a selection of Welty's essays and reviews, including pieces on Willa Cather, Isak Dinesen, Porter, Katherine Mansfield, Jane Austen, Virginia Woolf, Elizabeth Bowen and others.

A number of essays in *The Eye of the Story* give insight into Welty's conceptions of fiction and story-telling. In a 1965 essay, 'Words into Fiction', she explored, in an imaginative prose comparable to Ellen Glasgow's preface to *The Sheltered Life*, the mystery, as she called it, 'in the use of language to express human life'. Fiction is not, she explained, the effort to solve this mystery so much as to rediscover it, take advantage of it. Welty makes it clear in this essay that language and art do not somehow follow or supplement already felt experience; rather, without the artist and her or his interpretation or understanding of human life, 'experience is the worst kind of emptiness; it is obliterated, black or prismatic, as meaningless as was indeed that loveless cave [of her childhood]. Before there is meaning, there has to occur some personal act of vision.' Then she described a finished work of fiction as a letter mailed to a reader, who must enliven it

159

beyond the author's meaning, which is distanced once the text is finished: 'fiction finished has to bear the responsibility of its own meaning, it is its own memory.' Imagination she described as above all 'the power to reveal, with nothing barred'. Imagination can reveal the mystery of life itself, as well as that of putting experience into language, but not in the sense of dissolving that mystery. Like Flannery O'Connor (though without specifically religious overtones), Welty argued that reality is best accepted and understood as mystery, while realism as a form of writing can portray and reveal mystery.

The purpose of revealing mystery and respecting it, rather than trying to resolve it into universal meaning and rational discourse, is made clear in Welty's stories and novels, as characters are shown struggling both to reveal themselves (yet fearing such exposure) and to gain a vision of the essential reality of 'the other' as a human being like themselves. The result of such visions or revelations by means of imaginative seeing is not to solve the mystery, but to arouse a sense of the complexity and wonder of things which leads to compassion, tolerance and loving understanding of others, even while we lack a rational understanding. That is, Welty's stories and novels both portray and demonstrate (through her own hovering presence) the value she places on loving without necessarily being able to understand, in genuine tolerance of another person's different character and values, which may be incomprehensible to us. This requires a great leap of imagination, for it involves going beyond empathy – that power of identifying with another – to respect without being able to identify. This, one might say, is compassion, and loving compassion is one of the most intense qualities of Welty's writing.

She described this imaginative compassion in the preface to *Collected Stories* (1980) as 'the act of a writer's imagination that I set most high', namely, the ability to 'enter into the mind, heart, and skin of a human being who is not myself'. She called this, and the writing portraying it, a leap into the dark which requires great daring, for it involves jumping off into some new way of seeing and feeling. Welty emphasized that fiction of any value always involves experimentation with forms and styles, and each text represents something new which a writer has learned in the

process of shaping that fiction. Criticism, she argued, too often tries to dissolve mystery and reduce the complexity of fiction and imagination to something two-dimensional. Instead of reading to resolve mystery, she suggested (in words O'Connor might have used) that we can read another way: we can yield to what has been suggested by the writer – with all her or his available means – and in this yielding to suggestion we gain a vision which allows us to 'see for ourselves a certain distance beyond what is possible for [the writer] simply to *say*'. She concluded, with O'Connor, that in this sense all fiction can be seen as a symbol.

In Welty's essays on Cather, D.H. Lawrence, William Faulkner, Mansfield, Porter and others, the symbolic nature of fiction is thoroughly explored, as she discusses how, for example, a single tree is 'a whole wilderness falling to civilization' or 'the whole history of a land and people crowds into one chapter'. She writes also of the fact that, in Faulkner's 'The Bear', for example, reality 'not only *is*, but *looms*, as Faulkner alternately diluted reality to the reach of abstraction and brought it home with a footprint'. Her comments about Faulkner are clearly descriptive of her own concerns, as she noted the prevalence of such literary conventions in his writings as the hunt, quest, search and encounter, the journey, the passage, the arrival. She then explained that the plot of nearly every story ever written is the conflict between life and death, the struggle to survive, the quest for continuing life as more meaningful, communicative existence. Many short stories, she explained, show another story over and beyond the overt world portrayed, and in this sense fiction is also a symbol; hidden, secret lives are suggested beyond the surface, and they are endlessly explorable.

Welty's stories and novels give her readers another way of seeing human life, of seeing beyond the surface into the interior of her characters, into their inner conflicts and struggles. This interior portrayal is characterized in her fiction almost always by being situated in some distinctive place, locale or setting. Feelings, she argued, are bound up in place, and fiction depends for its very life on place: 'location is the crossroads of circumstance, the proving ground of "What happened? Who's here? Who's coming?"' Welty's fiction is characterized by a strong sense of place;

for her it is the base of reference, she explained; it *is* her point of view. Place does not merely provide some needed background for actions or characterization in fiction; it actually contributes to the reality of fiction, to the central mystery it seeks to reveal. For Welty, as for O'Connor, symbol and reality can occur only in the concrete particular, but that concrete particularity is what makes universality possible. Every story or novel, she argued, would be a different one if it occurred in a different place, because the feelings in all fiction pertain profoundly to concrete locale. And intensity of feeling is a measure of the reality and concreteness of fiction for her. Put another way, place in Welty's novels and stories is the frame through which the reader glimpses the reality expressed in her fiction.

Welty's first ever published short story, 'Death of a Travelling Salesman', embodies many of the qualities which were to become characteristic of much of her later writing from *Delta Wedding* to *The Optimist's Daughter*. The Greek tragic drama of her novels, which revolve like the plays of her Athenian precursors around the family as the scene of moral and emotional conflict, are – unlike Faulkner's – set in a context and tone of comedy and humour which give her writing part of its distinctive character. Her first novel, *The Robber Bridegroom* (a fairy-tale revision, and a mode to which Welty never returned, interestingly as she handled it), is a departure from her concretely 'placed', regional fiction, but 'Death of a Travelling Salesman' constitutes almost a prognostication of the later fiction. Making use of traditional literary conventions of journey, encounter, misapprehension and then recognition, the story's plot is literally about the conflict of life and death. But it also, as one who knows Welty's writing might guess, involves a sudden revelation to one of the story's characters of the emotional paucity and selfishness of his own life, just as death overtakes him. Influences from Porter are more evident in this story than in Welty's later fiction, where her own originality of shape, style and plot is more marked. Nevertheless, these more overt influences are not so much inhibiting as revealing of Welty's own concerns, as already her distinctive voice is evident. Time, as in Porter's works, stalks the entire story from start to finish, and nostalgia transformed into a moral revelation is one of the

central themes, while the story itself is a monument to Welty's ability to take the most commonplace literary conventions and make them show something new.

In one of her finest novels, and her most recent, *The Optimist's Daughter*, Welty tapped into the powerful feeling of Greek tragedy again, much as Eugene O'Neill did. She took an Electra theme and set it in the Greek chorus of a small Southern town. There she explored the process of Laurel McKelva's psychological maturation as she struggles to overcome the irresistible forces of jealousy and hate engendered by her father's remarriage to a woman so much younger than herself as almost to become her daughter, and then her father's sudden blindness and death. In both her first story and this latest novel, fiction as symbol and reality as mystery are intensely realized; the powerful feelings evoked by place and locale are also part of the story and the novel, and we see the way place establishes a frame for the fiction's reality as mystery. Moreover, in both this first story and this final novel to date – so utterly different from each other on the surface – another shared quality of Welty's writing is displayed, namely that belief in the importance of the ability to get into the mind and heart of a character different from oneself. While *The Optimist's Daughter* may in some senses be the most autobiographical of Welty's fiction, it still represents a notable example of her powerful imaginative vision into the life of other people, and represents her astonishing success in that mysterious process not only of putting experience into words, but also of communicating to her reader the irresolvable mystery of reality, even when revealed to the reader's imagination by the writer's imagination. Welty also wrote numerous works of non-fiction, including 'Place in Fiction' (1957; reprinted in *The Eye of the Story*), *Short Stories* (New York, 1949), and *Three Papers on Fiction* (Northampton, Mass., 1962).

Marguerite Young 1909–

Probably the most underrated novelist of the post-war period, Young was born in Indiana and by 1936 had an MA from the University of Chicago. She taught the novelist John Gardner while at Iowa between 1955 and 1957, and he was later to describe her Joycean, titanic epic, *Miss MacIntosh, My Darling* (New York, 1965; London, 1966) as 'extraordinary for breadth of mind and verbal genius'. William Goyen and Bernard Bergonzi wrote about this massive fable similarly in book reviews of 1965 (*New York Times Book Review* and *New York Review of Books*). Recipient of the prestigious Guggenheim Fellowship (1948), as well as a Rockefeller Fellowship (1954) and various other awards and grants, Young taught at several universities (Iowa, Columbia, Indiana, the New School for Social Research and Fairleigh Dickinson) while writing her 1,198-page, three-and-a-quarter-pound picaresque fantasy, over some eighteen years. She also published two volumes of verse, *Prismatic Ground* (New York, 1937) and *Moderate Fable* (New York, 1944), and a genre-busting historical reconstruction describing the nineteenth-century utopian New Harmony community, entitled *Angel in the Forest: A Fairy Tale of Two Utopias* (New York, 1945, 1967). Despite further appreciations of her massive novel by such writers and critics as Anaïs Nin (1969), A.S. Byatt (1966) and R. Durand (1975), and interviews in *Book Forum* 3 (1975) and in C. Ruas's influential *Conversations with American Writers* (1985) some thirty years after publication, Young has only just begun to be noticed again. Recently, her remarkable avant-garde *tour de force* has been re-read and again lavishly praised, with one critic explaining the silence surrounding it as due to our not knowing how to read a book this original, experimental, and opaque, dense and rich in language. Described by Goyen (1972) as a 'picaresque journey, a Faustian quest and a work of stunning magnitude and beauty', in *Contemporary Novelists*, the novel explores every aspect of language – its musicality, its ambiguities, its punning power, its symbolic and metaphorical properties, its connotations, assonances, alliterations and dissonances; in short, its incredibly fertile and procreative capacities, if only one allows oneself to break the rules of syntax, spelling, denotation, punctuation and order. While Young's language and thematics cannot be easily appreciated if readers impose realist or traditional expectations, the novel exemplifies immensely enjoyable, radiant prose if one is willing to subject oneself to its unique and peculiar music. Young not only experimented radically with language,

she also explored new ways of handling narrative time, thematic organization, characterization and points of view. And she experimented innovatively with literary conventions of the quest, the journey, the encounter and the dream; she parodied beginnings, endings, middles, plots, conventions of order, structure and unity, as well as using images of pregnant women who never give birth as emblems of art. She wove stories within stories and treated fantasies with as much attention as real events, dissolving the absoluteness of the boundary between external and internal experience.

Nin was one of Young's first fellow writers to appreciate the resonant, witty and oceanic incantations of her characters – Miss MacIntosh, Vera and Catherine Cartwheel, Mr Spitzer, and the ever-pregnant waitress Esther Longtree. Later, Nin was to write an introduction to the new Harcourt edition (1979), but already in *The Future of the Novel* (1968) she repeatedly and systematically discussed Young's Joycean and Faulknerian linguistic, syntactic and stylistic experiments, as well as the extraordinarily original formal and structural features. The novel's effective narrative progress – not through plot or time or causality, but through accumulative, massive, resounding organic growth – involved efforts to explore time as Proust had done, and to create a formless form as Doris Lessing was contemporaneously doing in *The Golden Notebook* (1962). Young's novel represents the triumph of synthesis over analysis, in its efforts at an all-encompassing, organic unity, a shape or form with no stable external boundaries. This oxymoronic statement may be a paradox for the reason, but is an apt figure for imaginative products and activity: centre and circumference keep changing as our point of view alters. For Young, the reader's point of view alters the further she or he reads into the novel; this Hegelian alteration causes the novel's shape to expand continuously outwards, so that the novel never really ends or begins; after 1,198 pages, there is only a 'sign' for Esther the waitress to hang on the door, saying 'owt to luntsch. Bee bak in a whale.' Indeed, Esther's 'everlasting' pregnancy is an emblem of the book itself; this voluptuous waitress, procreative and fertile, serving up endless meals to her customers, never actually gives birth. She explains that it is the endless waiting for birth which endows her with the patience to play life as a game of deferrals, which is of course also a description of the novel itself and the reader's experience.

Miss MacIntosh, My Darling begins with Vera Cartwheel's quest across the Midwest for a Miss MacIntosh of her childhood, who can probably never be found, since she is thought to have drowned in the Atlantic, though her body was never recovered. Traces – a black umbrella, a red wig, an old raincoat, a corset or false bosom – were all that was left behind. Vera's quest, her journey, is, however, immediately swamped by the 1,000 pages of oceanic memories, fantasies, dreams and hopes of her own, Esther's, her mother's and others'. After these pages of a labyrinthine complexity, an apparent disorder and a serpentine motion, Vera's voyage resurfaces out of this phantasmagoric plurality of multiple times, multiple characters and multiple worlds. This radical plurality is an expression of the nature of modern reality: the acceptance of chaos, the avoidance of familiar categories, the expression of the desire for flux and fecundity, and, above all, the acceptance that reality itself is essentially a fantasy. That is, for Young, reality is a product of imagination, and not something other than the imaginative. Thus, Mr Spitzer becomes an umbrella stand, a chair is transformed from a basket of grapes: everything is potentially something else; everything is metaphor. Or, the denial of the reality of fantasy and desire in our everyday lives is the most prevalent and delusive fantasy of all. We are all permanently, endlessly pregnant with unfulfilled and unrealizable desires and fantasies. That such desires and fantasies can rarely be brought to birth, or realized, does not diminish their real power over our lives.

Transgressing the boundaries between external action and interior life, Young avoided the demarcation of dialogue in favour of various characters' monologues, which mix and mesh and interpenetrate each other; characters flow into each other; 'real' external events are fleshed out with fantasies, memories, dreams and hopes; labyrinth upon labyrinth is built into the thematics by means of the language and form. Endless deferrals, innumerable detours, excessive repetitions and multiplications constitute the very nature of immanent, immediate experience: its chaos and flux are a source of joy and fecundity. In avoiding origins, ends, overt orders, climax, ordinary logic and hierarchical organization, Young substituted for phallic and genital dominance pleonastic excess, nurturing and fecundity. Male and female distinctions collapse, as men become pregnant with fantasies – 'a real, pregnant man who suffered from a dream'. The language and images of the phallus, of reason, of hierarchies and categories, or origins and ends, is not supplemented so much as decentred by the resituating of an 'other' language to share the centre. Opposition and dichotomy, hierarchy and distinction are pushed aside to make equal room for synthesis and cooperation, nurturing and fecundity.

The characters in the 'long, tidal rhythm' of *Miss MacIntosh, My Darling* are often described by Young as drowning: they submerge themselves into the life of dream, fantasy and subterranean realms which are the hidden depths of our conscious, surface lives. As Nin explained, it is the surface which is the illusion, the fantasy. Ordinary people's lives, lived in a small American town – their nostalgia for the past and their homesickness – are transformed by symbolization and myth making into a fabulous, symphonic work of dense materiality and phantasmagoric universality. Nin described Young's novel as a 'poetic prose without the complexities and multilanguages of Joyce'. She continued:

> Her work is completely subterranean, an epic dedicated to the theme of reality and illusion. She took figures from American folk life, stock characters – the prize fighter, the country doctor, the old maid, the lawyer, the banker, the nurse, the suffragette, the bone-breaker – and plunged them into the revivifying waters of the unconscious, and they emerged as mythic figures, in an ocean of waking dreams, visions, reveries, monologues, so that we could *see into the depths* of the full richness of the mind. The book has an oceanic form, parallel to its contents . . . the tragicomic elements are native, natural, and far-reaching. She has roots in the simplest reality, in the earth, but a power of levitation accorded to very few poets. She uses everything and transforms it into a symbolic drama, investing it with meaning.

The theme that reality is embedded in fantasy, not opposed to it but utterly dependent upon it – that reality has to be imagined and that what is most real is the most fantastic – recurs in the form, structure, style and language of the novel. These several elements are congruent with each other, as dichotomies collapse, and the reader is drowned in tidal monologues of images proliferating other images; or, as Goyen described it:

> Vera Cartwheel begins a search for her drowned reality which was, in ironic effect, illusion. This is the theme and ground of this sweeping, swelling and inexhaustibly breeding fiction, which pulls behind it, on and on, page after page, loads and burdens of images proliferating images; precise cataloguing, inventories and enumerations of facts, plants, hats, heraldries, geographers, birds, rivers, cities ancient and modern, kings and dynasties and archeologies. It breaks into conceits, images, metaphors, preciosities, bizarreries. Concrete character detail elaborates into huge metaphors, into musicalizations, rhapsodies, repetitively rolling and resounding and doubling back upon themselves in an oceanic tumult.

Goyen's review further notes wryly that the book is readable but only through hypnosis and enchantment; in a full-throated outbreak of song, the novel, by 'soaring into the universal, has rooted itself in the American reality'. Illusion and reality cannot, ultimately, be distinguished; or, as Vera complained, 'What shall we do when fleeing from illusion we are confronted by illusion? When falling from illusion, we fall into illusion?'

Miss MacIntosh is to Vera the incarnation of reality, completely different from her mother, Catherine. Catherine 'presumed that things were not what they seemed . . . that her life was this play of illusion, that there should be nothing certain but uncertainty . . . all her days were her nights, and all her nights were her days, and there was eternal twilight.' Vera goes on her quest for truth, for reality – for Miss MacIntosh, only to learn that her head of beautiful red hair is a wig. She used spectacles to see by, and she disappeared, mysteriously, into the ocean of being. The reader voyages with Vera and experiences her gradual realization that her mother, Cousin Hannah, Mr Spitzer and all the other characters in her life are no less real than Miss MacIntosh,

and that all are equally illusory, including Vera's own image of herself.

Hortense Calisher 1911–

Recipient of numerous awards and grants to support her writing, Calisher was born and brought up in New York City, graduating from Barnard College and teaching literature and writing at various universities while she was publishing her remarkable and often experimental fiction between 1951 and 1977. Her books include the collections of short stories *In the Absence of Angels* (Boston, 1951), *Tale for the Mirror* (Boston, 1962) and *Extreme Magic* (Boston and London, 1964), and *The Collected Stories* appeared in 1975 (New York). Amongst her novels are *False Entry* (Boston, 1961), *The New Yorkers* (Boston, 1969), *Queenie* (New York, 1971), *Standard Dreaming* (New York, 1972) and *Eagle Eye* (New York, 1973). Two novellas, *The Railway Police*, and *The Last Trolley Ride*, were published to acclaim in 1966 (Boston). Calisher's latest novel, *On Keeping Women*, appeared in 1977 (New York), and a memoir, *Herself*, was published in 1972 (New York).

By the time Calisher came to write her memoir, her fiction had undergone considerable development, and her sophistication as a practitioner of the art of narrative is evident in the ironically titled *Herself*. For this autobiography tells its reader very little about Calisher the person, and much about Calisher the artist. In her memoir, Calisher explained her views and theories about art, from the most abstract ideas about narrative practice to more thematic issues of sexuality in literature and the overturning of stereotyped gender roles as they function in fiction. For these affect the writer, the representation of characters, and the reader, and may also affect practices traditionally available to female, as opposed to male, novelists. That is, readers' expectations about what is appropriate for female authors can intrude into their estimation and appreciation of a text. Equally, writers' expectations about what is 'decorous' for women to write about and what practices are appropriate for women writers constitute palpable psychological pressure upon the artist, both from within her own psyche and from without.

Calisher's writing challenges these unwritten rules, prejudices and expectations in a range of ways, from extremely complex plot to elliptical style, penetrating insight into character, and faintly scandalous situations. One thinks immediately of the scene in which the women at a formal dinner party take off their blouses and sit bare-breasted for the rest of the meal. *Queenie* is probably Calisher's most overtly sexual novel, an intertextual dialogue with the sexually explicit male novels of her time, such as Roth's depiction of the randy Portnoy in 1969. In addition to this dimension of Calisher's fiction, there is also the powerful thematic material in, for example, *False Entry*, the novel of 'Pierre Goodman's' testimonies against the Alabama racists, in a trial of the murder of a black man by the Ku-Klux-Klan. The novel was published at the height of Southern activism against segregation in 1961, and its protagonist, 'Goodman', is known only by his pseudonym. This is not only a gesture acknowledging the real danger in his anti-racist activities, but also a literary device to problematize the notion of character depiction in fiction or in history.

Calisher's fiction underwent considerable development in the course of her twenty-five-year publishing life. Her earliest novels are more accessible and use more traditional conventions regarding plot, style and theme, as in *False Entry* and *Textures of Life* (Boston and London, 1963). They are not to be disregarded for their familiar practices, however, for they represent genuinely impressive fiction of great intelligence and imaginative empathy. Calisher was richly endowed, from the first, with that genius which Eudora Welty believed to be the central and greatest gift of a writer, namely, empathetic identification with human beings utterly different from oneself. And, as with Welty, Calisher's penetrating insights into the human psyche are always tinged with a detached, but never condescending, humour. Moreover, the stories of this period were already anticipating the elliptical and magical quality of her later fiction. In 1965, Calisher published her challenge to literary genre, *Journal from Ellipsia* (Boston), her delightful rewriting of *Gulliver's Travels*, as her heroine Gulliver zooms around the solar system, and we glimpse her world from different narrative perspectives.

In the year following this imaginative and inventive dialogue with the literary tradition, Calisher published one of her most remarkable novels, *The Railway Police*. Like Nathaniel Hawthorne's cleric in 'The Minister's Black Veil', the novel's protagonist confronts her acquaintances with their own unacknowledged masks and disguises of ordinary, everyday life. Unlike the minister, who puts on a veil, she takes her disguise off. That is, Calisher's central woman character, who had acquired an extensive array of wigs of all kinds, in order to be able to face the world in a variety of different identities, suddenly casts all of them off, and goes 'out in the world' naked and exposed with her bald pate. This novel centrally thematizes what is at the margins of nearly all Calisher's writing, as with many novelists, namely, the question of who we are, what identity is, whether we are unified or split within ourselves, how we disguise ourselves to ourselves and to others, and so on. But Calisher always managed to turn her thematic material to corresponding questions about fiction, art and artifice itself, and its relation to reality. The wigs, the masks, the pseudonyms, the clothes, the rituals, the roles, which she used as motifs and metaphors, are also meta-fictional vehicles which carry the reader into meditations about what is involved in the reading and writing of such narratives.

Kylie Tennant 1912–1988

Journalist, playwright, novelist, and children's author, Kylie Tennant was born in Manly, New South Wales. Her first novel, *Tiburon* (Sydney, 1935), was published in the *Bulletin*; it was a vibrant drama of the Depression, but full of wit and satire, the two recurring characteristics of all her fiction. Her novels are often described as picaresque, and this certainly applies to her next two, *Foveaux* (London, 1939) and *The Battlers* (London, 1941). While *Tiburon* was set in a small country town, her second novel depicted the urban working class, and her third portrayed rural life for a band of wandering unemployed. All of the novels dealt humorously with the absurdity of human life, while Tennant's comic handling also portrays a hopefulness about the possibilities for change. In *Ride On Stranger* (Sydney, 1943) and *Time Enough Later* (New York, 1943), Tennant contrasted the values of country and city life, and especially the tendency towards decadence in the latter, but these and other serious social issues are always handled with a buoyant wit and comic tone. Other novels include *Lost Haven* (New York, 1946), *Tell Morning This* (Sydney, 1967; this is the complete version of *The Joyful Condemned*, London, 1953), *The Honey Flow* (London, 1956), and a collection of stories, *Ma Jones and the Little White Cannibals* (London, 1967). *Speak You So Gently* (London, 1959) is a tough but witty travel description of the exploitation of aborigines, full of the wealth of incident and dialogue characteristic of her fictional work. Tennant also wrote several plays, biography, criticism and other works.

Some decades later, *Tantavallon* (Melbourne, 1983) continued in the picaresque mode; that is in dramatic, farcical scenes with little plot, and with good-humoured satire and witty handling of both scene and characterization, Tennant explored the absurdity of human life. *The Missing Heir* (Melbourne, 1986) is Tennant's fascinating autobiography, which crowns over twenty-five published books.

The following extract from one of her finest short stories, 'The Antagonists', is exemplary of her style and characteristic verve, and it and the story as a whole suggest the intellectual power behind her novels:

It was a morning breathless, as it leaned over the mirror of the lake, with the sight of its own beauty. Like the painter, it could not turn away from its reflection. The bush was rapt, withdrawn. A slight trembling might send down all the priceless silver of the leaf-hoarded, last-night rain. Even the big old black barn, where the carcasses used to hang, had taken on a luminous quality from the shield of light behind it, the blaze of water. The forty-acre paddock breasted the still mere as though it would slowly float out as an island, all its plumage of bladey grass and bracken spread like a swan's wings.

Like most of Tennant's fiction, this story treats of a serious subject, but with the light hand of a detached wit. The antagonists are a hermit-like painter, who seems to be on the verge of madness, and a hoary old rancher who lets him live on one of his paddocks and do a little work, while basically getting on with his painting. The complete failure of understanding between the simple old rancher and the 'educated bloke' leads to a destructive obsession on both sides, but the real interest of the story is neither in the theme nor in the plot, but in Tennant's skilful handling of the two chasmically separated points of view with characteristic comic irony. Her own description of the best short story as 'like a beam of light through a crack, illuminating something significant' is applicable to this story.

Tennant is also the author of *Australia: Her Story* (London, 1953, revised 1964, 1971), an account of Australia which expresses her ability to fuse history and documentary with stylistic verve and descriptive acumen. Like Martha Gellhorn's, Tennant's concern for the 'poor and struggling' is evident throughout her prose, fiction or non-fiction. Yet, her political and social ideals are almost always subordinated to the demands of her art. While most of her central characters are working-class, she occasionally turns an eye to others, and, as in 'The Antagonists', satirizes pretensions and hypocrisies on the one hand, and prejudice, ignorance and boorishness on the other. Irony – but especially wit and humour – permeate the picaresque adventures which make up her anti-realist, plotless novels, in the tradition of Daniel Defoe and Lawrence Sterne, and demonstrate Tennant's ironic self-awareness about her own art and her role as writer of imaginative fictions.

Tillie Olsen 1913–

Political activist, jailed in the 1930s for attempts to help organize factory workers, harassed by the FBI during the 1950s, Olsen is the recipient of the O. Henry Award, 1961, for 'Tell Me A Riddle', later made into an emotionally moving film. She has received a Guggenheim Fellowship, a Ford Foundation and National Endowment for the Arts awards, and the Award for a Distinguished Contribution to American Literature. She has received honorary degrees, been on the faculties of Amherst College, the University of Massachusetts, the Radcliffe Institute and Stanford University, and published several books of fiction and non-fiction. Her most famous fiction is the collection of stories and a novella *Tell Me a Riddle* (Philadelphia, 1961; London,

1964), containing four remarkable stories of working-class life, and *Yonnondio: From the Thirties* (New York and London, 1974), a novel written in the 1930s but not published for forty years (part of the first chapter appeared in 1934 in *Partisan Review*). Olsen has also published a famous collection of essays, *Silences* (New York and London, 1978), which includes her eloquent essay on the nineteenth-century writer Rebecca Harding Davis (an essay first published in a 1972 edition of Davis's fiction, *Life in the Iron Mills*, Old Westbury, N.Y.). Olsen has been at work on the second half of her novella, *Requa I* (part published *Iowa Review* I (1970), 54–74), and has published *Mother to Daughter, Daughter to Mother: A Day Book and Reader* (Old Westbury, N.Y., and London, 1984) and *Dream-Vision* (London, 1984). Born in Nebraska, married, with children, Olsen now lives in California.

Described as 'epitomizing the best of its time', Olsen's fiction constitutes a small but invaluable corpus of fine technical strategy, stylistic excellence and thematic passion, all rarely unified into a prose art of indescribable power and beauty. The individuality and uniqueness of Olsen's genius is evident on nearly every page of *Yonnondio* especially, but also in 'Tell Me a Riddle' and the other stories. While Olsen's thematic concerns are well-known ones (analysis of the social/psychological exploitation of women and the working class, which makes writing or other professions extremely difficult), she nevertheless explored these with originality, insight and compassion. She deplored not only the tragic waste of human talent 'which society cannot afford'; she deplored too (as did Margaret Walker) the socially engineered conflict between child-rearing and intellectual fulfilment, the social institutions which deform whole classes of people, and the political structures which mean that 'any person who is lucky enough to achieve recognition does so at the expense of those who do not get a chance.' Like Doris Lessing, Olsen has a profound sense of the responsibility we all share for the brutality of our social-political arrangements. Olsen explored the moral-aesthetic concepts of 'transport, meaning, community' which are denied most people, especially women (but also working-class men), since they must live *for* people instead of *with* people. Her stories explore the details of the institutionalized forces which

deform, maim and stunt human development, and they show the specific characteristics of the obscenity and insanity of an economics which condemns and wastes the talents of huge sections of humanity.

Olsen was deeply committed to the centrality of art and culture in human life, because she had seen the truth early in her life that every human being is endowed with some kind of creativity. Or, as Christians have expressed it, in every individual there is a portion of Christ. Olsen's fiction explores the idea that the development of this humanity–divinity in each and every person is essential for a sane and healthy society: each one of us is diminished when a fellow human is wasted. She called imaginative writing 'the incomparable medium' for nurturing the coming into being of individuality and fulfilment, and for thwarting the destructive effects of our defective social machinery in order to realize the 'human ecstasy of achievement'. Olsen's life and her writings are an insistence upon art, culture and writing as not some mystical property of highly privileged, gifted (male) geniuses. They belong, as the great American philosopher John Dewey had insistently repeated, to all people, regardless of their class, sex or colour. If we choose to keep great portions of humanity ignorant and uneducated, we simply waste vast human resources of energy, vitality and imagination, and emasculate the white/male/upper-class spirit by the moral decadence resulting inevitably from exploitation. Olsen's texts constitute, further, one of the most impassioned and tragic expositions in all literature of the conflict between creativity and procreation; the latter she described astutely as the very 'core' of the oppression of women. Yet she also analysed the entangling web of love for men which makes sexism possible, men who with rare exceptions are themselves no more than children – indeed, often more demanding of time, energy, self-sacrifice and support than any child. As one reads her fiction, one is constantly confronted with the questions, 'Why have children? Why love men?' And while Olsen's fiction suggests that these parts of women's experience provide some of that 'transport, meaning, community', that 'ecstasy necessary to make life liveable', the questions still linger as though this answer were not enough to justify the price paid for exploitation and self-sacrifice.

The stylistic, narrative and structural techniques Olsen deployed for the artistic embodiment of her themes cannot be overestimated. Using aesthetically effective multiple points of view and changing narratives, using extremely fragmented structures while rejecting conventions of plot, narrative time or sequence, Olsen wrote a staggeringly beautiful prose which constitutes the most powerful demonstration of her central thematic insistence on the inherent beauty and creativity in every single human life, as in the following passage from *Yonnondio*:

> The Farm. Oh Jim's great voice rolling over the land. Oh Anna, moving lightly from house to barn so that the happiness with which she brims will not jar and spill over. Oh Mazie, hurting herself with beauty ... But land is here. Days falling freely into large rhythms of weather. Feet sinking into plowed earth, the plow making a bright furrow ... Drama of things growing.

Like Bessie Head's, Olsen's prose draws upon elemental forces of creativity in the land, the sky, growing things and the sun to create a biblical, legendary power in her writing which awakens the reader to Olsen's spiritual faith in beauty. This faith creates a fine aesthetic congruence between her central thematic concerns and her style and formal structures. That is, her democratic belief in the fundamental role of art, culture and beauty in human experience is a condemnation of elitist notions. Her most significant aesthetic achievement is precisely the revelation to the reader of the profound beauty in everyday life and its appreciation by ordinary people. A contemporary of John Dewey, she expressed his insistence that art springs from ordinary social intercourse, as the history of human society testifies. Only in recent centuries has art become both divorced from life and, allegedly, the preserve of an elite. Olsen's writing finds literature in the stories of people; she finds art in their weaving, cooking, dress, gardens, basketwork – in their utensils of life, not in some privileged realm.

Barbara Pym 1913–1980

Legendary now not only for her novels, but for being one of the 'most underrated' writers of the century in a *Times Literary Supplement* survey in 1977, Pym was rescued from fourteen years of obscurity only by Philip Larkin and David Cecil. Born in Shropshire and educated at Oxford, Pym worked for twenty-eight years at the International African Institute, where she met her biographer to be, Hazel Holt. During this period she published six successful novels with Jonathan Cape, only to have her seventh, and then further novels, summarily rejected as no longer publishable and out of date, though 'well-written'. When the *TLS* survey was published, Macmillan began to publish all her previously 'obsolete' novels, and Cape reissued the earlier ones. For example, *The Sweet Dove Died* (written 1963–9, published London, 1978), described in the late 1960s as 'impossible to publish', made the 1978 best-seller list in *The Times*. While Pym's novels went unpublished from 1963 to 1977, she continued to write, producing in addition *An Unsuitable Attachment* (London, 1982), *An Academic Question* (London, 1986), *Quartet in Autumn* (London, 1977) and *A Few Green Leaves* (London and New York, 1980), in that order. It was the publication of *Quartet in Autumn* by Macmillan (after the 1977 survey) and being short listed for the Booker Prize which broke the log jam that Pym had suffered for fourteen years. This new novel was received with tremendous popular and critical acclaim throughout Britain and America. Pym's novels have become, increasingly, the subject of numerous book-length studies as well as articles, and her letters and journals were edited and published in *A Very Private Eye* (London, 1984).

Pym began her career as a novelist with the publication in 1950 of *Some Tame Gazelle* (London), and this was quickly followed by *Excellent Women* (London, 1952), *Jane and Prudence* (London, 1953), *Less than Angels* (London, 1955), *A Glass of Blessings* (London, 1958) and *No Fond Return of Love* (London, 1961). (These novels have all now been reissued.) Only three years before her death was she to see one of her rejected books finally published; one more appeared before she died, but that original stumbling block, *An Unsuitable Attachment*, was only published posthumously, along with several other novels, some written as early as 1936. According to Philip Larkin, Pym's first novel 'is as practised as the last', and no obvious development of her oeuvre is discernible. Larkin had long been an admirer of Pym, and they corresponded for some fourteen years, finally meeting in Oxford in 1975. Larkin admired, above all, he explained, Pym's quiet, unobtrusive irony: 'It is so strange to find the level good-humoured tender irony of your style unchanged by dealing with the awful end of life: I admired you enormously for tackling it, and for bringing it off so well.' David Cecil wrote of Pym in similar terms:

> No other living novelist writes books that amuse one as yours do; they enlarge my imagination too, by introducing me to new worlds ... All is vitalized by your particular vein of humour and keen observation. I was also impressed by the way you did for once introduce death ... and yet kept the Comedy atmosphere and this without giving in to that, to me, displeasing phenomenon called 'black humour.'

Cecil's comment, that Pym introduces us to new worlds and new perceptions, was taken up many years later by her fellow novelist and admirer, Shirley Hazzard, who puzzled as to how we had managed 'pre-Pym': 'What did one do, pre-Pym, with those observations and imaginings to which she has given form?' Other admirers, such as Pamela Hansford Johnson, Francis King, Francis Wyndham (who had helped rescue Jean Rhys from oblivion) and many other writers and critics contributed to Pym's resurgence as a major figure, and in 1978 she was made a Fellow of the Royal Society of Literature. A few months later she was diagnosed as suffering from terminal cancer, and she died only a year after, in January 1980, by which time her reputation as a novelist of considerable achievement was well established.

Pym's novels and other comments in letters and journals indicate how high a value she placed on humour and on irony. In a letter referring to her work of reading novels for the Romantic Novelists Association awards, she remembered that of the ten read so far, 'they are extremely varied ... the one thing they lack is humour or irony – and of course one does miss that. But in a way they do seem to reflect some aspects of life that may be valid for the fortunate ones! As much as Doris Lessing or Edna O'Brien, or even B. Pym.' It may be this 'level good-humoured tender irony', amounting to a powerful, Katherine Mansfield-like understatement, which

obscured from Pym's readers the sophistication of her narratives, their astute use of literary conventions, and her 'torpedo-like' penetration of pretensions and hypocrisies. Like Jane Austen or Mansfield, Pym explored the domestic world around her, and its manners and morals, in thematic terms which involved no events outside prosaic, ordinary life. Like Rhys, her central female characters often exhibit a courage and will which offend conventions – but they do it quietly, unobtrusively, so that the careless reader may overlook the turmoil beneath the surface. And, like Alison Lurie's, Pym's novels are designed to decentre the reader's focus, so that several views of the same event, person or place are presented. While in many novels it is London which is the multivalent text to be deciphered – the central character which contextualizes all the other characters – in *An Unsuitable Attachment*, for example, it is Italy which becomes the focus of interpretation, and the scene of Pym's most systematically self-referential gestures. With her typical irony, Pym made repeated allusions or intertextual gestures toward precursors like Henry James and Edith Wharton; for her – unlike for them – a trip to Italy is, however, not the occasion for the eruption of repressed passions or the consummation of previously deferred feelings. In Pym's Italy, all potentially passionate encounters hilariously flop, while Pym uses the Italy trip as an opportunity for humorously self-referential remarks to the reader about the multiplicity of interpretations, views, attitudes and responses possible to any such 'text' as Italy, or her novel.

While a darker tone is evident in her later novels, *Quartet in Autumn* and *The Sweet Dove Died* – which portray more overtly the harshness and isolation of, for example, old age – Pym's characteristic irony, humour and, above all, that sharp, self-conscious observation are evident throughout. Perhaps Anne Tyler summed up Pym's continuing appeal when she noted, 'Whom do people turn to when they've finished Barbara Pym? The answer is easy: they turn back to Barbara Pym.'

Elizabeth Smart 1913–1986

Born in Ottawa, Canada, Smart published several volumes of poetry, wrote journalism, and was the literary and associate editor of *Queen* magazine after World War II. She is probably most famous, however, for her impassioned, 'novel' of dazzling poetic prose, *By Grand Central Station I Sat Down and Wept* (London, 1945), and for its sequel, *The Assumption of the Rogues and the Rascals* (London, 1978). The former piece is said to have been, in part, a chronicle in fiction of her love affair with the poet George Barker, with whom she had four children. These two books were republished in 1991, after Smart's early journal, *Necessary Secrets* (London, 1986), edited by Alice Van Wart, appeared. A second volume of later journals has also recently been published (1994). In the midst of extensive travels both to many parts of Europe (twenty-two trips in the 1930s alone!) and to Mexico, New York, California and around the world, Smart wrote some of the poems published recently in *Collected Poems*, introduced by David Gascoyne (London, 1992); the thirty-nine poems in the volume *A Bonus* were published in 1977 (London); other poems followed, all published in *Collected Poems*, including *Eleven Poems* (Bracknell, 1982). *In the Meantime: A Collection of Poetry and Prose* was published in 1984, ed. A. Van Wart (Ottawa), and contains the early novella 'Let Us Dig a Grave and Bury Our Mother', which helps, when we are reading *By Grand Central Station*, to focus our attention away from Smart's love-affair with Barker and towards her intense love of language and poetry.

Smart had been writing poetry, plays, stories and essays from an early age (see the *Juvenilia*, ed. A. Van Wart (Toronto, 1987). Her journals also began early, and they provide fascinating documentation as both records of her life, loves, thinking and travels, and also as repositories and sources for her published poetry and prose writings. Smart first went to England at 19 to study piano at King's College, London, but soon realized her apprenticeship to language and poetic forms was her predominant passion. She began studying Virginia Woolf and Katherine Mansfield, amongst others, and, in the midst of extensive travelling, began writing 'My Lover John', her first known attempt at a novel-length piece of prose, where she experimented with narrative point of view, style and other formal literary conventions. During this period Smart travelled frequently between Canada and Europe as well

as within Europe, establishing an active social life in London, and later worked in New York, Los Angeles and Ottawa. She became involved with Barker in the summer of 1940, and gave birth to their first child in August 1941, two weeks after she finished her novel *By Grand Central Station*. A year later, she left for London, pregnant with their second child, and remained based in England until her death some forty-four years later in Suffolk.

Brigid Brophy, who wrote a brief and insightful introduction to the 1966 edition of Smart's first 'novel', described it as one of 'half a dozen masterpieces of poetic prose in the world'. Further described as 'a genuine novel, as well as a rhapsody and a lament', *By Grand Central Station* is said by Brophy to be a 'masterpiece of metaphor', which succeeds in yoking together the intense and the banal, the high and low, by a kind of metamorphosis of life into art and language, of pain into beauty. Lorna Sage also explained that Smart's 'story' in the novel is not so much her personal love-affair as her affair 'with the high style (poetry and tragedy) which came to a sticky end in the low-mimetic mode'. Its sequel over thirty years later, *The Assumption of the Rogues and the Rascals*, charts, she explained, Smart's effort to articulate the very struggle to articulate, to write, to make forms and metaphors, to create poetry out of the ordinariness and banality of life: '*The Assumption* . . . becomes the story of its own difficult conception. She must be her own Muse, fertilize her own imagination, against the rules of nature, and only precariously supported by the tradition of art.'

Smart's first novel (which was banned in Canada in 1945) is in a radically experimental poetic prose which, in its rejection of realist narrative, creates a stream of consciousness, a subjective and almost plotless text. The novel internalizes the externalities of nature, other people and events, and further articulates them by means of the formality of rich allusion to other literature, from the Song of Songs through Shakespeare, Milton and the metaphysical poets, to Emily Brontë, Emily Dickinson and twentieth-century literature. A constant ironic awareness, both of the absurdity of love, hate, pain, suffering and joy, and of the effort to structure these experiences verbally, is intensified by Smart's continual yoking together of human reproduction, desire and sexuality with literary-linguistic creation and beauty. Smart's literary constructions are an eloquent testimony to the power of verbal articulations to 'create' or at least intensify the feelings and thoughts to which they give a name. Plunged into the narrative, which ends as abruptly (and uncompromisingly sparely of explanatory details) as it began, the reader is allowed no reprieve from unexplained narrative gaps in time, or only elusively presented encounters, such as those with the police and other authorities (literary protocol?), and other external events. The narrative is divided into ten distinct fragments, which end in both loss and gain, as the lover departs but pregnancy remains, and the novel ends on a mixture of ironic self-criticism and unrepentant longing. Smart's novels, moreover, bring up again and again earlier journal and letter statements about her experience of being a woman artist; especially, by the time of her second novel's publication, this theme had become more overt. It also expresses the self-conscious themes and techniques of so much of her poetry, as, for example, in *A Bonus*. The effort to keep alive the energy to create forms of words out of life, and a life thereby incalculably enriched by the created words, the terrible exhaustion of work, child-bearing, child-rearing and love, all are charted through formal literary structures in the 'sequel' to Smart's first novel, as she rejected any dichotomy between life and work or art. She also avoided clear thematic distinctions between autobiography and fiction in both her novels and in her poetry. Her experience of her years with George Barker is contrasted with his own autobiographical novel, *The Dead Seagull* (New York, 1950, 1965), which expresses a deep-rooted misogyny still characteristic of much of the literary 'male world'.

Jean Stafford 1915–1979

Winner of the Pulitzer Prize in 1970 for her *Collected Stories* (New York, 1969), Stafford is the recipient of numerous awards and grants which confirm her reputation as a distinguished American writer of mid-century fiction. She won the O. Henry Award in 1955, the National Press Club Award in 1948 and *Mademoiselle's* Merit Award in 1944, and received a Guggenheim fellowship, a National Institute of Arts and Letters grant, and several other grants. She taught at Columbia, Wesleyan University, and elsewhere. Born in Covina, California, Stafford took a BA and MA from Colorado before spending a year in Heidelberg. She was married for several years to Robert Lowell and then to A.J. Liebling, and her father, John Richard Stafford, was the author of Western novels. She published her first novel, *Boston Adventure* (New York, 1944), to considerable acclaim, and two other novels followed, first *The Mountain Lion* (New York, 1947) and then *The Catherine Wheel* (New York and London, 1952). After this, collections of novellas and short stories appeared, such as *Children are Bored on Sunday* (New York, 1953) and *Bad Characters* (New York, 1964). She has published fiction for children and the remarkable non-fiction book *A Mother in History* (New York and London, 1966), a series of interviews with the mother of Lee Harvey Oswald, who assassinated John Kennedy.

Stafford's fiction is best known for its insightful depiction of adolescent consciousness, but her ruthless exposure of the snobbism and hypocrisy of adults sets up a powerful opposition in the fiction. This opposition, like, for example, Harper Lee's, illuminates all stages of life, in using adolescent narrative perspective as a critical lens through which to view the absurdities of adults. *Boston Adventure* is ostensibly a study, by means of such tension, of the destructive falsity of 'society', with all its pretensions and empty, inhumane values. Yet Stafford enriched this social critique with a finely developed study of human emotional and moral maturation; adolescent Sonia achieves adulthood by living out the childish fantasies that money, power and prestige are worthwhile achievements. Stafford's moral dimension is progressively revealed: pretensions and snobbism represent emotional immaturity, as well as moral decadence. All Stafford's novels and many of her stories emphasize this psychological insight, too rarely remembered, namely, that emotional immaturity and a failure to develop into genuine adulthood are at the root of our false values. Hence Stafford's systematic use of the narrative point of view of children and adolescents, who are struggling against the pressures of family and society which stunt their growth and individuality. This explains, in part

171

at least, why so many of Stafford's adult characters are portrayed as childish: that is, Stafford's fiction reveals how few adults can actually be said to have lived through their childish fantasies and fought their way into a more adult set of values. Like Harper Lee, Stafford drew not only on contraries, but on symbol and religious imagery to convey her analysis of the reasons for the endemic immaturity of her fellow humans. By means of a carefully crafted irony, Stafford implicated herself and her readers as well, thus avoiding condescension or preachiness.

While *Boston Adventure* is built around a structural opposition in two major parts, reflecting its complex thematic oppositions (which include reflections on madness and sanity as well as social and moral discriminations), *The Mountain Lion* is arguably Stafford's most technically accomplished and aesthetically effective novel. Much shorter and more spare than *Boston Adventure* (which Ellen Glasgow implied would have been improved by ruthless cutting), it is beautifully constructed out of a complexity of symbolic relations and of tensions so multiple as to stimulate a whole range of reflections about its effect. What the mountain lion symbolizes, its relation to Molly, the aesthetic significance of Ralph's shooting (accidentally) of his sister Molly, the thematic centrality of Ralph's adolescent sexual awakening and Molly's resistance (she is two years younger), Uncle Claude's and Grandpa Kenyon's opposition to Mrs Fawcett, the role of place (Colorado and the mountains versus East and West coast), male/female differences – all these and others contribute to a carefully constructed novel with its Willa Cather-like symbolic evocations of nature and landscape. It is no accident that the final chapter of the novel is set (more emphatically and symbolically than any other section) well up in the mountains near where Molly had made a summer refuge for herself and her writing.

In *The Mountain Lion*, Stafford achieved a stylistic perfection not as evident in her other two novels, and which is only comparable to that of several of her short stories. Combined with the novel's spare structure and fine use of place and landscape, and with its clear thematic focus and astute use of symbol, this stylistic achievement, in a novel which subordinates plot to character, gives *The Mountain Lion* a real

significance in American fiction. Stafford focused her material and style by dispensing with plot more effectively in this novel than in almost any of her other writings; this work becomes a study in the use of symbolic incident to replace plot. It is also a study in sophistication of narrative point of view: indirectly alternating between Molly and Ralph's consciousnesses, Stafford's third person narrative is imbued with the irony and suggestive undercurrents liberated by her indirect free style. This novel's stylistic achievement reveals powerful influences from Cather, with its lucidity, its suggestiveness, its sparseness and its subtlety. The following lines are, typically, emblematic of the moral and emotional issues Stafford portrayed through literary forms:

> Garland Peak . . . was one of the lowest . . . In the summer she went up the face of it, but since this involved scaling three chimneys, she had to change her route when the storms came and was obliged to approach it indirectly, first climbing half way up a higher peak and then cutting across a wash, down a gulch, and up the opposite bank to the northern base. The ascent was not an easy one at any time of the year, but it was worth all the fatigue. From the summit she commanded a view of the entire valley, of the range as far as the eye could see, and of Cuthbert Pass, beyond which, disappearing finally in a gauzy blue, were the highest mountains of all, the Arrowheads, which seemed as far away as the end of the world. In the summer the mesa below was like a sheet of rusted metal with densely growing Indian paintbrush . . . She had been here in the fall when the aspens show like honey among the conifers on all the foothills and the high fields were dark green with the first shoots of winter wheat.

For the alert reader, the simplicity and clarity of such writing, combined with the condensation Cather, after Coleridge, recommended, give Stafford's novel a powerful, meditative aura, which derives much of its aesthetic impact from that ability to 'humanize nature'.

Margaret Walker 1915–

Author of the monumental *Jubilee* (Boston and New York, 1966), as well as other novels, poetry, a biography and an autobiography, Walker was born in Birmingham, Alabama, and took BA, MA and PhD degrees from Northwestern and Iowa. She won the Yale Younger Poet award for the collection *For My People* (New Haven, 1942), when she was 26. Already at 19, Walker had begun the thirty-year period of research and writing which was to go into *Jubilee*, the titanic historical folk novel about slavery. During this time she taught a brutal schedule at Jackson State College, Mississippi, from 1949, in order to support herself, her sick husband and several children. She described, in her autobiography *How I Wrote Jubilee* (Detroit, 1971), the gruelling programme of teaching, writing and domestic obligations which fell upon her (not to mention her own ill-health), though her only rancour was for her harrowing exploitation by the Jackson State College administrators. Other poetry includes her most recent, 'This is My Century' (in *Confirmation: An Anthology*, eds Amini and Amiri Baraka, New York, 1983), preceded by *Ballad of the Free* (Detroit, 1966), *Prophets for a New Day* (Detroit, 1966) and *October Journey* (Detroit, 1973). She wrote the biography *The Daemonic Genius of Richard Wright* (New York, 1985), and she has worked recently on other novels, including the manuscripts 'Mother Broyer' and 'Minna and Jim', the latter a sequel to *Jubilee*.

In *Jubilee*, Walker set out to write a 'new historical version of slavery' as well as the story of her great-grandmother. This is a project which Toni Morrison continued in *Beloved*, and which other black women are interested in expanding. The book took so long to write in part because Walker was determined to educate herself fully about slavery, about its social, political, historical, moral and economic dimensions, and about the psychological aspects of the phenomenon of racism. Walker explained in her autobiography that she not only wanted to write a book which would give a different perspective on slavery, since the three versions she knew of (white Southerner's, white Northerner's and black male's) were based on stereotypes or false myths, or failed to describe meaningfully the actual human experiences – male and female – which slavery engendered. She also wanted to show how essential an understanding of this past is to a grasp of the twentieth century. Segregation and prejudice are still so much a part of American

life today that Walker sought to give her readers a historical grounding in their present experience by writing a historical novel that was also a folk novel about real human beings. The story of Vyry, the mulatto mother heroine – who has to choose to leave her children behind if she is to escape slavery – is told within the context of a rich and varied African-American cultural realm, which sustained individual slaves suffering untellable outrages. Walker wove the events of Vyry's life into a colourful tapestry of song, oral stories, ritual and folklore, so that *Jubilee* itself constitutes a collection of folklore of the kind that writers such as Zora Neale Hurston had earlier sought in their own villages and towns. Through religious hymns, spirituals, folk songs and popular songs, Walker developed her story of the tragedy of slavery for black people (but also for its perpetrators, in a moral sense). The music which constitutes a leitmotif in the novel is the central strand around which an entire tradition of folk wisdom evolves, including medical lore, moral instruction through tales and through socialization in the black community, religious training through hymns and spirituals, literary training through the art of story-telling and myth, and historical instruction through stories about origin and future hopes – of freedom, of course.

Walker's *Jubilee* is a testimony to the history of slavery and to black folk heritage, but in addition to these two great themes it is also a testimony to the humanity of individual black people. Walker made it clear that not only racism but sexism was an issue in the novel; not only black people but specifically black women are often construed as dehumanized: 'equated with animals and having subhuman status: wild, savage, and uncivilized. This, in the face of great African civilizations and cultures.' Walker wanted to challenge the stereotypes not only of white writers, but of black male writers. The latter, she explained, were often more inclined to stereotype black women as subhuman than as people. Freedom, as in the case of many calls for it, is reserved for men only. Nevertheless, Vyry in *Jubilee* finds the strength she needs to survive the ravages of slavery – but not in herself alone (though great personal strength and courage *are* required). She is depicted by Walker as also drawing energy and sustenance from her identity with her community, with its art, music, poetry and literature;

its morality, religion, history, and economics of sharing and cooperation. Walker has herself played a pivotal role in creating and sustaining a new community of black women, who are reconstructing new images of themselves, rewriting history to include women, challenging the fictions and prejudices of earlier historians which distorted facts, and constructing a new folk heritage of their own. No longer silenced, stereotyped or dehumanized, they express themselves in their own image, their own words.

Elizabeth Hardwick 1916–

One of the founders of the *New York Review of Books* in 1963, Hardwick has had a long career not only as a writer of fiction but also as a 'brilliant literary and social critic'. Better known for her essays and articles in *Partisan Review*, *Harper's*, the *New Republic* and the *New York Review of Books*, she has been praised repeatedly and lavishly for her fine prose style and literary discrimination. Her novels are *The Ghostly Lover* (New York, 1945), *The Simple Truth* (New York and London, 1955) and *Sleepless Nights* (New York and London, 1979), and her short stories, not yet collected, appeared in *Sewanee Review* (1946), *Partisan Review* (1950, 1951), *Kenyon Review* (1953) and the *New Yorker* (two in 1956 and one each in 1957, 1959, 1979). She collected some of her finest essays on women (such as Plath, Woolf, the Brontë sisters, Dorothy Wordsworth and Zelda Fitzgerald) in *Seduction and Betrayal* (New York and London, 1974), while others appeared in the collection *A View of My Own: Essays on Literature and Society* (New York and London, 1962). She has also edited *Selected Letters of William James* (New York, 1961) with an introduction. Hardwick was married to Robert Lowell from 1949 to 1972, and had a daughter with him in 1957. She was born in Lexington, Kentucky, and took a BA and an MA from the university there, after which she attended Columbia University from 1939 to 1941. She lived in Europe between 1950 and 1953, and later settled for some years in Boston. She received a Guggenheim Fellowship in 1947, which she spent writing short stories. In 1969, she was awarded the George Jean Nathan Award for outstanding drama criticism, and her final novel was greeted with unanimous acclaim.

Hardwick's first two novels were published to only mixed critical response and much misunderstanding, however. Both *The Ghostly Lover* and *The Simple Truth* were criticized for lack of plot and failure of characterization – the protagonists were described as woefully flat and lifeless. In spite of these 'flaws', her prose style was praised, lavishly at times, and she was described in one book review (1945) as 'a new writer of great talent and promise'. Both the novels explore the loneliness of human life and the fragility of communication – the difficulty indeed of knowing 'the simple truth' about anyone, including ourselves. In addition to her 'burnished' prose style, Hardwick's other great accomplishment in her fiction was precisely what her early critics took to be the two central flaws of poor plot and characterization. That is, Hardwick strove to avoid imposing those 'false patterns' and that arbitrary order on human life which so many novelists of the modernist period, especially, had also sought to avoid. And, as Virginia Woolf lamented in 'Mr Bennett and Mrs Brown', readers kept expecting fiction to fit the old realist conventions and prejudices, instead of opening themselves up to new kinds. Hardwick dispensed with plot as far as she could, especially in *The Ghostly Lover*. Even in *The Simple Truth*, where there is an apparent plot (the progress of the murder trial), it is not the representation of the trial and its progress which matters to Hardwick. Rather, she focused on observing the observation of the trial. This meta-perceptual level was complex: not only are the two central observers watching the jury, but the narrator is 'watching' the two journalists. At times, indeed, the author seems to be 'watching' the narrator, as though constantly preoccupied with the difficulty of communication, perception and articulation.

Similarly, *The Ghostly Lover* is not a novel with thematic or narrative aspects which require strong plot or vivid characterization. Its object is to explore the mysterious ties between people, in this case between a daughter and her mother most especially, though others are also involved. Hardwick seems to have set out to explore the strange ghostliness of many of our relationships; the tenuousness of our communication with each other, of our knowledge of each other, is again the substance. Hence, she constructed her characters, such as Marion or her mother Lucy, in such a way that we know them only through a mist – just as they know each other only vaguely, just as they know themselves only vaguely. That Hardwick's avoidance of strong plot and characterization, given her clear aims, should have been criticized is presumably yet another in the long line of critical blindnesses arising from misplaced expectations and unconscious prejudices. Her fine prose also explores the fantasies which inhabit the psyche, fantasies about love, protection and security, which condemn most of us to the shelter of 'safe' lives and relationships. Marion Coleman quietly but steadily, even unconsciously, explores these 'securities' of parents and husband and family which she has clung to, and then lets them go, just as quietly walking out into 'an icy ray of light'.

Part of the power of Hardwick's prose comes from a strong sense of interiority, a meditative quality, as though, paradoxically, the reader were inescapably separated from Marion and yet had a strangely intimate view of her thoughts and feelings. This 'strange intimacy' of style also characterizes Hardwick's individuality as a writer, and is congruent with her novels' thematic preoccupations with the tenuousness and difficulty of communication. Her novels constantly remind us, then, of the extremely problematic nature of fiction; the assumption that it can communicate truth or reality, about either people or events, is quietly but ruthlessly rejected. In *The Ghostly Lover*, Hardwick described the relation of two of her characters in a way which has application to her technique: 'Hattie and Mrs Gorman knew of each other's existence in the way one knows historical personages. To each the other was a series of manageable and separated traits, unencumbered with the contradictions and possibilities of a living human being.' By the end of the novel, Marion rejects this simplicity, just as the alleged simplicity of the Iowa townspeople is rejected in *The Simple Truth*.

Sleepless Nights is a fictional, autobiographical memoir which Hardwick referred to as a novel, in which she explored more explicitly memory, knowledge, communication and articulation. Plot and characterization are so clearly inappropriate for this diverse, fragmented memoir-novel that it has had much greater success than Hardwick's first two works of fiction. Yet *Sleepless Nights* makes a reappraisal of *The Ghostly Lover* and

The Simple Truth unavoidable, since it makes clearer her exploration in those novels as well – if less overtly – of the elusiveness of truth, the way fact 'is to me a hindrance to memory.'

Jane Bowles 1917–1973

Jane Bowles was born in New York in 1917. When she was only 25 she wrote *Two Serious Ladies* (published New York, 1943), a novel celebrated by writers in her own time, and exemplary of modernist fiction. Having lived for a time with her husband, Paul Bowles, in a Brooklyn Heights, New York, boarding house (where Benjamin Britten, Carson McCullers, W.H. Auden and Gypsy Rose Lee also boarded), she and her husband began their nomadic existence, living in central America, then Mexico, Europe and Ceylon, before settling eventually in Tangiers in 1947. The play *In the Summerhouse* (New York, 1954) and a number of verses and some short stories, collected in the volume *Plain Pleasures* (London, 1966), were completed before Jane Bowles suffered a cerebral haemorrhage in 1957 which made writing extremely difficult. She died in a convent hospital in Malaga in 1973.

While much of Bowles's writing concentrates on the experiences of unusual women, her analysis of the social constraints that inhibit individuality, autonomy, creativity and happiness should interest both men and women. A constant theme in all her writings is human apartness; but a related one is the way in which men and women constrain and inhibit each other from achieving individuality. People enforce on themselves and others stereotyped social relationships, roles and forms of behaviour that suffocate originality in behaviour, dress, sexual conduct and thought. Bowles's novels and play exude a surrealism that arises in part from the suspension of any normal logic of behaviour between people. Categories of relationship are blurred and social conventions are constantly overstepped. Her characters speak and act in ways just off-centre enough so that the reader is made aware that nearly everything we say and do is a cliché or a form of game playing. Rules are unconsciously followed when we think we are being spontaneous, original and most ourselves. Those who fail to follow the rules are looked upon as interesting eccentrics at best,

175

and more often as troublemakers, degenerates and outcasts with whom it is dangerous (for one's social acceptability) to become involved in any way. Bowles's fantastic blend of realism and the grotesque, of tragedy and compassionate comedy, of the bizarre and the familiar, is austere in its total freedom from any moralizing.

All these thematic characteristics are reflected in Bowles's eccentric and original style. There is no exaggeration in Tennessee William's description of her as 'the most important writer of prose fiction in modern American letters'. John Ashbery called her 'one of the finest modern writers of fiction in any language', while Truman Capote, in his introduction to *The Collected Works of Jane Bowles* (reissued New York, 1984), wrote of her as 'a modern legend' and 'one of the really original pure stylists'. Ashbery identified *surprise* as the factor that gives Bowles's style its power, 'the surprise that is the one essential ingredient of great art'. 'Surprise' involves precision, conciseness, unpredictability and a refreshingly bitter wit, all of which are major characteristics of Bowles's biting, original literary voice. Capote called her stories 'sloppy, marvelous stews [built] atop an electric burner'. He further described her style as richly varied, uniting the extremes of Moorish colourings and natural light, as it meanders through the tortured paths and labyrinthine alleyways of human eccentricity in life (and in artifacts).

Bowles's prose is one of the most sustained attempts ever made to render transparent the literary and linguistic conventions that normally remain obscured by subject matter. Here, subject matter is an almost constant metaphoric dramatization of the literary conventions of storytelling, characterization, plot, creation of setting, establishment of narrative point of view, and so on. Metaphors involving dress, food and social behaviour are endlessly varied and repeated as Bowles illuminates the inner workings of art, language and society. Garments and clothing are used both as a metaphor for language and art, and as an example of the way in which behaviour is encoded and values communicated. Social rituals involving food and drink become metaphors for artistic technique and linguistic devices. Diction, linguistic mannerisms, and conventions of ordinary speech and literary language become

Bowles's subject matter, in part, as she reveals the way in which hackneyed and clichéd language leads to stereotyped, one-dimensional behaviour. Put another way, fashions or 'styles' in food, dress, behaviour and art are closely peered at, observed and then slightly altered. These alterations are signposts to the reader to attend not merely to the overt subject matter but also to the language in which it is garbed.

In *Two Serious Ladies*, the protagonist Christina's games as a child and an adult involve repeated occasions of taking off her dress and doing dances of worship to the sun. Bowles's prose takes off the dress of conventional literary language, or 'style', and, in its own dancing, mixes up categories of diction, style and subject matter – from children's books and fairy tale to serious adult literature. This creates a brilliantly original tone that is more than a mere surrealist pastiche or *mélange* of forms not ordinarily mixed together. Impropriety and promiscuity of language and decorum become the road to sainthood and to genius. For Bowles, literary style is merely a 'hostess gown adapted from a central European peasant costume'. Moreover, like people's growth, fashions and 'styles' (whether of literary languages or of dress) change, and though Bowles's 'unfashionable', 'unstylish' prose may, like Christina, seem 'at this time [to be] very heavy and her [its] legs quite fat', it 'may be impossible to foresee that she [it] would turn out to be a tall and elegant lady'.

Two Serious Ladies is a novel involving two almost distinct novels, lightly, even casually intertwined at the beginning and the end. No particular effort is made to integrate the bipartite text, itself broken up into fragments. The novel contains three distinct sections of rather varying length (30, 87 and 90 pages). Two main characters are drawn whose actions constitute all three parts of the novel, though the two women rarely meet, for they are only acquaintances. Both are portrayed by Bowles as escaping from the mundane boredom of everyday life, 'out into the world'. Each, a perfect 'lady' at the outset, gets involved with an electrifying *demi-monde* of characters like Jean Rhys's, from prostitutes and drug addicts to drunkards and crooks. Bowles, like Rhys, sought to portray such marginalized people as individuals, instead of dehumanized categories merely to do the bidding of white males. Both the two main characters, Mrs Copperfield and Miss Goering, are portrayed as breaking out of stifling conventional relationships, struggling for independence and gaining, perhaps, some self-knowledge through imaginative identification with other oppressed groups. Sexuality, gender, lesbianism, friendship and love are explored, as the two women become utterly enthralled by their 'downward path to wisdom'.

Like Gertrude Stein before her, Bowles sought to live out her art in her life; thus, her novel tends to portray innovations in dress, eating rituals and social behaviour as parallel to her artistic innovations. Along, then, with the overt thematics mentioned above is a stratum of implications for the reading and writing of the text. Stylistic and other artistic issues are rooted in personal living, as Bowles, like many other women writers, rejected any dichotomy between art and life, insisting that each is a supplement to the other. She experimented passionately with life, as she did with writing. The striking originality of style, tone and structure is a testimony to her unique voice and to her individuality. The overt thematics of two women 'degenerating' into freedom is paralleled at the covert level of thematics by a rejection of familiar stereotypes and literature; Bowles's style shocks the reader into a more imaginative appreciation of the novel as an artifact, and not as merely an exciting repository, of a writer's ideas, values and opinions. Thus, Mrs Copperfield and Miss Goering's degeneration into the *demi-monde* is a metaphor for Bowles's experimentations ('degeneration') with the grotesque, the improper and the criminal, as she broke some of the laws of literature and created a style of her own and an original structure.

As for Rhys, categorizations for Bowles are a central means of the dehumanization which leads to stereotyped behaviour, clichéd speech and second-hand opinions. Her characters, in going out into the world, cease to fit into any categories yet established for classifying human beings. This escape from traditional roles occurs as Miss Goering and Mrs Copperfield confound any efforts to judge them or label them. The travel metaphor, or journey convention, is once again used as symbolic of inner transformation as well as outward 'freedom', as the women travel geographically and spiritually away from patriarchal constraints. No nostalgic or sentimental illusions are encouraged, however, for it is not paradise which they reach, but the gutter, a goal Nietzsche would have heartily applauded! Travelling suggests further the thematic point that there is no place for a woman in a patriarchal society, apart from mothering. To escape these constraints (for however rewarding mothering is, it is, like anything else, not the whole of experience), not only are the two women portrayed as exploring a social *demi-monde* of experience; the journey is also a metaphor for delving into the unconscious. Bowles's stories and novels, as well as her remarkable play *In the Summerhouse*, thematize the unconscious as the ruling force of the psyche, tantamount to an all-powerful male being. No freedom is envisaged by her until the realm of sexuality, love and need is known to the conscious mind. Or, as one of the characters puts it: '"The idea," said Miss Goering, "is to change first of our own volition and according to our own inner promptings before they impose completely arbitrary changes on us."'

The spiritual/grotesque quest these two women embark on is presented to the reader as one of the most effective means of breaking out of the repressive constraints of patriarchy. Images of transformation recur as a symbol of existential self-development. Unlike many of her contemporaries or predecessors, Bowles did not chose to make the woman artist a metaphor for imaginative living (as Kate Chopin did, or Doris Lessing, or May Sinclair, to name only a few). Perhaps she rejected this image as misleading, if taken literally to mean that only artists can 'escape'. She avoided this misunderstanding by seeking spiritual regeneration for ordinary women through morally 'degenerate' companions. The latter gave the two heroines a completely new perspective on the world, just as a long look into the unconscious can achieve this. Bowles's style of writing struck many readers as bizarre, and this bizarreness, along with surprise, opens the reader up to her or his own imaginative quest.

Bowles's unpublished MS 'Out in the World' is in the Humanities Research Center, University of Texas at Austin, as are some of her other papers. *Selected Letters 1935–70* was edited by Millicent Dillon (Santa Barbara, Calif., 1985), and Dillon's biography of Bowles appeared in 1981.

Leonora Carrington 1917–

Surrealist painter and companion to Max Ernst in the mid-1930s, Carrington (not to be confused with the Bloomsbury group's Dora Carrington, b. 1893) grew up in Lancashire before leaving home to study painting in London, in the year of an influential surrealist exhibition which completely captured her imagination. Departing from London with Ernst for Paris and the south of France, she continued painting and writing intensively, until Ernst was imprisoned as an enemy alien. Rescued from a breakdown in a Madrid asylum, Carrington married and left Europe for the safety of New York and, eventually, Mexico City, where she lived for some forty years, was widowed, married again, and had two children. While she often wrote her stories in French, she also wrote, in English, two novels, *The Stone Door* (London, 1977) and *The Hearing Trumpet* (London, 1976), both of which also appeared in French translations in 1976 and 1974. Her stories have been collected in *The House of Fear: Notes from Down Below* (New York, 1988) and *The Seventh Horse and other Stories* (New York, 1988). Many of them were translated into French and then first published in that language, or translated from French. Some of the stories were written in the late 1930s in a Provençal farmhouse where Carrington lived and painted with Max Ernst, who was inspired by her person, her writings and her art. She was a close associate of such other surrealists and artists as André Breton, Paul Eluard, Peggy Guggenheim, Leonor Fini, Roland Penrose, Remedios Varo (one of Carrington's closest friends in Mexico City), Robert Capa and Imre Weisz – whom Carrington later married.

While *The Hearing Trumpet* is Carrington's most substantial piece of fiction, her novella *The Stone Door* – written in the 1940s – is a fascinating tale of a quest across legendary lands for love. Other stories of considerable interest include 'The Debutante', 'The Neutral Man' and 'A Mexican Fairy Tale', while 'Down Below' is an account of Carrington's breakdown; encouraged by Breton, she tried to put into writing her voyage into madness, and the result was published

in English and French in the 1940s. *Little Francis*, a novella written in 1938 (and first published in *The House of Fear*), can be read as a *roman-à-clef* about the period in 1937 when Ernst and Carrington set up house amid conflicts with Ernst's wife. The novel also explores mystical and magical ideas about androgyny, the quest for enlightenment and wholeness, and journeys of maturation and discovery of the 'nahual', or animal soul within every human soul. Surrealistic to the extreme – like all Carrington's writings – *Little Francis* makes use of both natural and imaginary bestiaries; Carrington argued that within every individual's psyche is an inner bestiary, suggestive of the wildness, the marvellous, the fantastic and the blasphemous which surrealism revered. Animal imagery functions to express the surrealist belief in the need to recapture the feral, unconscious, sexual-animal nature of the human mind if it is to realize its fullest imaginativeness. Using dreams, fantasies, memories and desires, with the macabre, grotesque, oxymoronic and fantastic, Carrington wove tales which defy reason, logic and meaning, and which appeal to the unconscious and the imagination.

While *The Stone Door* makes overt use of familiar mystical and legendary writings and imagery, its construction is a complex puzzle which defies logic, ordinary time progression and the distinction between reality and dream. The story draws the reader into layer upon layer of dreams, narratives and dream narratives, along with a confusion of place, time, ontological levels and character identities, so that ordinary logic is suspended in favour of a dream-like receptivity to powerful, recurring imagery and patterns of symbols. It cannot be read sustainedly as a precise allegory or *roman-à-clef*, for the power of the tale's images sweeps away any coherent narrative meaning couched in ordinary logic. Instead, we are offered a view of the rich tapestry of the unconscious, freed from rational constraints.

The Hearing Trumpet departs less radically from comprehensible narrative plot and time logic than *The Stone Door*, but is equally fantastic in its comic and absurd portrayal of 92-year-old Marian's quest for the Holy Grail. Using webs of symbols from alchemy, magic, astrology and other ancient wisdom – from books from China and Tibet to Mexican Indian lore – Carrington made use of the surrealist ideas of chance as a principle of art, and of life as more marvellous than art. Interweaving ordinary daily activities of cooking, eating and sleeping with mystical rituals of alchemy, dream and quest, Carrington transmuted the familiar into gold by her imaginative witchcraft. These artifacts she presented to her readers as a perfectly ordinary repast; but like her famous contemporary Jane Bowles's great, sloppy stews, these magic, golden broths, when consumed by the reader, nourish and fortify us to the end of the quest, namely, self-knowledge.

Carson McCullers 1917–1967

Lula Carson Smith (Carson McCullers) grew up in Columbus, Georgia, where, at the age of 15, she took up writing as a substitute for a career as a concert pianist, which ill-health made impossible. By 17, she had made her way to New York City, where she studied writing at Columbia University, publishing the successful story, 'Wunderkind'; by the age of 23, she had already published her highly acclaimed first novel, *The Heart is a Lonely Hunter* (Boston, 1940). This novel led to friendship with Tennessee Williams, W.H. Auden and Jane Bowles, and she also gained numerous awards, grants and fellowships to continue her writing. Other novels quickly followed, such as *Reflections in a Golden Eye* (Boston, 1941), *The Member of the Wedding* (Boston, 1946, made into a successful Broadway play), *The Ballad of the Sad Café* (Boston, 1951) and *Clock Without Hands* (Boston, 1961), and a play, *The Square Root of Wonderful* (Boston, 1958). A posthumous collection of essays, stories and poems was published in 1971, *The Mortgaged Heart* (Boston), ed. M.G. Smith. Two of McCullers's novels have been made into films, and two biographies appeared as early as 1975. A reminiscence of her by Williams, 'Praise to Assenting Angels', is paraphrased in the introduction to *The Mortgaged Heart*. Illness and strained relations with her twice-divorced husband characterized McCullers's adult life, side by side with a remarkably successful literary career.

Like Flannery O'Connor and Djuna Barnes, McCullers used grotesque and violent means to portray spiritual limitations as well as moral transformations and revelations. Racial issues in some of her fiction, along with Southern locale, identified her with other Southern writers, such as Williams, William Faulkner, Ellen Glasgow and Eudora Welty. However, her themes and literary techniques were not seen as regional, but as universal, as she explored in ways uniquely her own the issues of spiritual and moral deprivation, which had fascinated O'Connor, too. Nearly all critics have focused on the 'quest for identity' depicted in much of McCullers's writing, and the opposite yet complementary quest to belong to a group or community through love and communication. McCullers explored the interactions of these two at times opposing, at times cooperative moral motives. In *The Member of the Wedding*, for example, she portrayed the need of the young heroine to be more than an I-person, to be a we-person. McCullers explained that her characters are almost without exception in search of the 'we of me', thereby uniting the two quests for identity and community into one moral vocation. Moral isolation is shown to be not only intolerable for the individual, but also the source of much fear, leading to racial hatred, class elitism and violence. This leads to McCullers's second recurring theme, namely the nature of love and of communication between individuals.

McCullers explored love as the central means in human experience for finding the 'we of me', but she also depicted the perverse forms of love that loneliness and immaturity can lead to. Maturity and processes of maturation are portrayed as the process of mastering loneliness (the identity problem), and maturity is, then, the record and history of the relations between the individual and society. In *The Ballad of the Sad Café* and *Reflections in a Golden Eye*, perverse, obsessive forms of love (as essentially immature) are sharply focused, and related to their origins in an imperfectly realized moral identity which leads, in the one case, to emotional obsession and violence and, in the other, to sexual obsession and promiscuity, as Glasgow had portrayed in *The Sheltered Life* (1932). McCullers described her portrayal of love as involving the moral judgement that the passionate love for an individual is inferior to the love of our fellows, or brotherly or sisterly love – what she described sometimes as love of God. This, she explained in the essay 'The Flowering Dreams: Notes on Writing', was the unifying idea of *The Ballad of the Sad Café*.

The strange and inexplicable – even perverse – love of Miss Amelia for the little hunchback, Cousin Lyman, is portrayed via grotesque figures – people, McCullers explained, whose physical incapacity is a symbol of their spiritual incapacity to love and of their moral isolation. Sometimes the conflicts portrayed, as between the three characters in *The Ballad*, can also be seen as Lawrentian, Blakean conflicts within the individual human psyche. Struggles between conscious and unconscious become the scene for the development of a maturity and identity which are shown to be the preconditions both of satisfying relationships and of original works of art.

For McCullers, the struggle to become an artist was a part of the effort to gain moral maturity, because art essentially involves communication, just as this is the essence of love. Like O'Connor, she believed that the romantic notion of the lonely, isolated artist was a destructive fiction. Artists, she argued, need above all to communicate with their contemporaries. Artistic creation is not mere self-expression: it needs to be communicated, shared and understood, or else the artist must fear retreating to a solitary, alienated moral and spiritual death. She explained, however, that innovation – the very soul of art – is liable to conflict with the possibility of understanding between writer and reader, because artistic innovations often look awkward, ugly and offensive at first. Breaching conventions leads to much misunderstanding, and only time can heal the failure of communication which results. McCullers's novels testify, however, to the inextricable interrelation between self-expression and the need for communication: neither can occur without the other, just as the quest for personal identity is achieved only in the quest for communal belonging.

McCullers's novels also make it clear that communication between writer and reader is not a matter of the reader passively accepting a writer's opinions, judgements or values. She argued, indeed, that much misunderstanding in literature occurs precisely because the reader adopts a passive posture, expecting the writer to take the moral responsibility to categorize and classify experience. As a writer, McCullers posed certain basic questions which arise out of human emotional experiences and values, but she refused to answer them. She explained that an artist must be able to depict clearly the confusion of values and conflicts of belief which may be occurring, but that the author should not take on the 'spiritual responsibility', which must be left to the reader, if art is not to degenerate into maxims and ideologies and individual preferences. She insisted that her responsibility as a writer involved clarity of vision and the artistic intuition for representing that vision in appropriate forms. But she rejected the responsibility of interpreting either her vision or her embodiment of it: all her novels portray the necessity, both in art and in life, of tolerating and accepting spiritual inconsistencies and the impossibility of resolving them. This refusal of sentimentality and emotional pandering to the reader gives her novels a modernist flavour, as indeterminacy of meaning and moral significance are her central theme.

Like O'Connor, McCullers was impressed with the insoluble, symbolic inexplicability of art and of life, but she too insisted that in the embodiment of this intuition, concreteness was vital to symbolic art. Concreteness is not to be understood as moral determinacy, however. McCullers argued that we live in a world of mystery and irresolvable disorder and disharmony, which lead to an irresolvable, uncertain system of values. This uncertainty leads in turn to the only knowledge we can have, namely, that of the meaningless absurdity of life. Her novels pose over and over again the question of whether life is 'precious enough to justify the struggle'. Southern writers of her time found that the grotesque was a powerful way of expressing this inherent instability of moral meaning in an absurd world. McCullers described this grotesque technique as the 'bold and callous juxtapositions of the tragic with the humorous', the fusion of anguish and farce, which is often shocking to the reader. As she went on to say: 'Farce and tragedy have always been used as foils for each other. But it is rare, except in the works of the Russians and the Southerners, that they are superimposed one upon the other so that their effects are experienced simultaneously.'

McCullers argued that Southern American fiction of the early to mid-twentieth century could be better understood if its relation to Russian realism of the nineteenth to twentieth century were appreciated. While it might not be possible to compare them in terms of artistic achievement, she believed that the two different streams of fiction showed a similarity in the approach to their material. That is, while both Southern American writers and Russian realists were interested in raising the great moral and metaphysical questions about existence, they never made the mistake of trying to supply authoritative solutions to problems of human life and human suffering. She agreed that Russian realists sought to transpose 'the painful substance of life around them as accurately as possible', without dissolving the spiritual contradictions found there. Southern writers likewise assumed the philosophical responsibility of analysing the nature of such existence and suffering, without imposing inadequate rationalizations and logical structures upon it. The following passage from *The Ballad of the Sad Café* is a typical example of McCullers's insistence on the active moral and aesthetic participation of the reader in the aesthetic struggle evident in all genuinely original art:

> During a struggle like this, when the enemies are as quick and strong as those two, it is worth while to turn from the confusion of the fight itself and observe the spectators. The people had flattened back as close as possible against the walls. Stumpy MacPhail was in a corner, crouched over and with his fists tight in sympathy, making strange noises. Poor Merlie Byan had his mouth so wide open that a fly buzzed into it, and was swallowed before Merlie realized what had happened. And Cousin Lyman – he was worth watching. The hunchback still stood on the counter, so that he was raised up above everyone else in the café. He had his hands on his hips, his big head thrust forward, and his little legs bent so that the knees jutted outwards. The excitement had made him break out in a rash, and his pale mouth shivered.

While this instance is one of the most explicit in McCullers's fiction of a mirroring of the audience–reader situation, it is not at all uncharacteristic of her texts. Indeed, in both *The Member of the Wedding* and *Reflections in a Golden Eye*, for example, she built into her novels a consciousness of observation and interpretation which mirrors the reader's role. She reflected both lazy, passive, voyeuristic readers and more active ones, and showed how the former are destructive of communication and moral transformation, while revealing the impediments to, as well as the means of facilitating, the latter. In *The Member*, Frances is shown to be trapped in a childish stage of voyeurism of her brother and his fiancée's relationship. The struggle for 'participation' of a selfish kind is contrasted with maturation and genuine participation of a more imaginative kind. In *Reflections*, characters interact from self-centred id-worlds of sexual and emotional obsession, watching each other as a substitute for genuinely communicating. Passive beholding eventually leads to a murder and to an outbreak of violence in other respects.

The Ballad of the Sad Café not only depicts the reader's struggle for communication with the author and characters, and with herself or himself. The fight at the end is an archetypal struggle of the artist wrestling with conflicting materials and conflicting purposes. The symbolic value of the struggle is increased as we realize that, all along, the three central characters have resonated with psychological symbolism and are aspects of a single psyche fighting for control of each other. The novel focuses its interest on balancing between opposition and conflicts rather than reconciling them or resolving them one way or the other, when McCullers shifts the moral balance again:

> At last she had him down and straddled; her strong big hands were on his throat.
> But at that instant, just as the fight was won, a cry sounded in the café that caused a shrill bright shiver to run down the spine. And what took place has been a mystery ever since. The whole town was there to testify what happened, but there were those who doubted their own eyesight. For the counter on which Cousin Lymon stood was at least twelve feet from the fighters in the center of the café. Yet at the instant Miss Amelia grasped the throat of Marvin Macy, the hunchback sprang forward and sailed through the air as though he had grown wings. He landed on the broad back of Miss Amelia and clutched at her neck with his clawed little fingers ... Miss Amelia was beaten.

The end of the novella involves the portrayal of Miss Amelia imprisoned in her obsession, while a chain gang of prisoners is singing with a 'music that causes the heart to broaden and the listener to grow old with ecstasy and fright'.

Muriel Spark 1918–

Recipient of numerous literary awards, author of studies of Mary Shelley (Hadleigh, 1951, 1974) and Emily Brontë (London and New York, 1953) amongst others, and much written about by academic critics, including Frank Kermode, Malcolm Bradbury, Patricia Stubbs, David Lodge, Karl Malkoff and others, Spark, born in Edinburgh, is the author of over a dozen novels and some stories, plays and poems. Having worked as the editor of *Poetry Review* in the 1940s, she took other writing jobs while beginning to write her 'African' short stories, based on experiences on that continent in the late 1930s. Her first novel, *The Comforters* (London and New York, 1957), charts autobiographically the (self-conscious) process of a young woman becoming a writer of fiction instead of a literary critic of fiction. From this first novel right through to her most recent book, self-conscious, meta-fictional elements saturate her short, economical, but intensely dense, satiric and well-formed fictions. *Memento Mori* (London and Philadelphia, 1959), her third novel, introduces another frequent technique, namely, the irruption of 'natural' supernatural elements into the characters' realities, which set up an analogue between the divine creation of the world and the creation by a writer of a novel. Other issues, of free will or determinacy, for example, add post-modernist connotations to the overt plots of these novels; many of the novels, indeed, seem to attend almost at surface-level thematics to the nature of plotting itself, as well as to the creation of characters. Other novels followed, including *The Bachelors* (London and New York, 1960), and focus on another central element of most of Spark's novels, namely, an almost obsessive interest in the ways in which characters can gain power over others, and the moral uses or abuses of such psychological authority. Like Elizabeth Bowen before her, Spark often thematized the complications and disasters which occur when innocent or decent characters are psychologically overpowered and manipulated by selfish or morally corrupt acquaintances. In spite of self-conscious, intricate plottings and character relations, however, Spark's novels – with only a few exceptions – verge on the length of the novella, with Spark indicating a deliberate aesthetic preference for a spare, tightly controlled structure.

Her most famous novel is probably *The Prime of Miss Jean Brodie* (London, 1961). Her sixth, it was made into a film as well as a television series, and has received much critical acclaim. Later novels have proven to be still more admired, by critics at least, such as *The Public Image* (London and New York, 1968), *The Driver's Seat* (London and New York, 1970) and *Not to Disturb* (London and New York, 1971). More recent works include *The Takeover* (London and New York, 1976), *Territorial Rights* (London and New York, 1979) and *Loitering with Intent* (London and New York, 1981), amongst others. Spark has also published *Collected Stories I* (London, 1967) and *Collected Poems I* (London, 1967), and a biography, *John Masefield* (London, 1953).

Given Spark's recurring (if not constant) interest in power relations amongst characters (and the moral and psychological dimensions involved), it is hardly surprising that she has shown a corresponding interest in the relations of an author to her or his characters, plot, style, structure and themes, as well as the analogous relations of author to readers and of novel to readers. These levels of thematics are rarely covert in her novels, and are emphasized even more sharply by Spark's characterization of one of the main differences between story-telling – relating the experiences one has had or a character has had – and experience without that concurrent narration of it. That is, in a memory, story or narrative, as one writer has put it, everything is told from the focus which the outcome of the event or experience gives. Contrasted to this, in 'living' experiences, we do not usually know what the outcome is, so that the filter or point of view is utterly different. Kermode, one of Spark's most enthusiastic readers, called this the 'sense of an ending'; indeed, *Memento Mori* uses the literal ending of life as a way of exploring this issue, which has aesthetic dimensions for the author and for the reader, and moral dimensions involving power relations.

For all her novels' satire, irony, wit and sharpness, Spark's fiction develops its aesthetic concerns in tandem with moral explorations. In often almost existentialist strains (and existentialism has some strongly shared principles with Catholicism, to which she converted in 1954, at the practical level of living life), Spark's characters struggle to interpret complexity, to gain the courage to act – even in uncertainty – and come face to face with the fact of mystery and the lack of absolute certainties by which they can judge themselves, each other, or the events they experience. Endings, then, are not definites, not truths – their significance is a matter of point of view.

Doris Lessing 1919–

In 1949, Doris Tayler Lessing arrived in England from Rhodesia with the manuscript of her first, then unpublished, lyrical novel, *The Grass is Singing*, immediately recognized as a notable achievement in twentieth-century fiction. Soon after its publication in 1950 (London and New York), the first volumes of the Martha Quest series appeared, beginning in 1952 and ending in 1969, when the final volume was published, entitled symbolically *The Four-Gated City* (London and New York). Meanwhile, Lessing had published her best-known novel, *The Golden Notebook*, in 1962 (London and New York), as well as numerous short stories which have been collected into various groupings, including, most notably, *African Stories* (London, 1964). Lessing's two novels *Briefing for a Descent into Hell* (London and New York, 1971) and *Memoirs of a Survivor* (London, 1974) follow up themes in other novels, such as breakdown and survival, but in new ways, while *The Summer before the Dark* (London and New York, 1973) explores symbol and image more fully than usual. In the 1980s, Lessing began experimenting with novels involving large-scale interplanetary life, such as *The Making of a Representative for Planet X* (London and New York, 1982) and *The Marriages Between Zones Three, Four, and Five* (London and New York, 1980). Given how prescient her earlier novels have been about social and civil breakdown, these novels may give us a glimpse into a future closer to our own coming reality than anything we have a right to expect. *A Small Personal Voice* (New York, 1974), *Going Home* (London, 1957) and *African Laughter* (New York and

London, 1992) are autobiographical essays, memoirs and travel writings. Her first volume of an autobiography, *Under My Skin* (New York and London), was published in 1994.

Lessing's writings, from her first novel in 1950 to her most recent autobiography of 1994, represent impressive experiments with literary conventions of form, genre, style and thematics. While *The Golden Notebook* is perhaps the most sustained and multifaceted of these experiments, Lessing's innovative art is evident from *The Grass is Singing*. Already in that earliest novel (arguably one of her finest), she was not writing as a realist so much as scrutinizing realism. The novel begins with a short, factual newspaper clipping about a murder of a white woman by a black employee, and becomes a lyrical meditation on the questionable possibility of realism, on the inadequacy of documentary writing to do justice to the richness, complexity and indeterminacy of human experience, and on the way in which language functions, contradictorily, both to dehumanize or reduce and, on the other hand, to constitute the very possibility of humane existence. Characters are carefully 'placed' to establish irony, to create variety of point of view, and to raise questions about what we mean by 'truth'. Social and psychological pressures are shown in their dynamic and complex interaction. Indeed, Lessing was already exploring the idea that 'personal, psychological problems' are never just personal and psychological, but always the results of sociological and interpsychical energies and trends. If we ignore the sociological dimension, we will never get a purchase on 'psychological' matters. The context for personal (as well as racial) conflict is staged, then, as an expression of communal, shared experience. Already, form and language are, moreover, central thematic issues threaded amongst issues of racism, marriage, bush life and other matters, as the conventions of the 'conventional novel' itself are put under examination.

Over a decade later, Lessing was to publish her most direct, systematic interrogation both of the novel as a genre and form and of language, in *The Golden Notebook*. In the 1950s, she had experimented with a conventional realism in the early Martha Quest novels, a style and genre which she returned to only occasionally throughout the next forty years. Realism, she saw, could never encompass her fiction, however. For already in *The Grass is Singing* it is evident that the orthodoxy of realism itself was to her a kind of delusion, a fantasy of objectivity, of rationality as the real, and so on. Lessing explored this orthodoxy relentlessly in *The Golden Notebook*, and ruthlessly revealed its inconsistencies and assumptions. That novel explicitly rejected language as a transparent medium or representation of some rational reality; it rejected the dualisms inherent in realist assumptions, such as language–world, art–reality, fiction–history, fiction–truth and so on. It rejected the notion of a 'reality', of 'an objective point of view', of 'a neutral observer'. In the final section of *The Four-Gated City*, Lessing had already introduced ideas about communication and existence relating to aspects of Sufism which overtly threatened realist and materialist assumptions. Then, in *Memoirs of a Survivor*, she explored modes of representation contrary to realist ideology, developed even further in *The Marriages Between Zones Three, Four, and Five*. Other novels further emphasized her life-long dialogue with the realist and modernist traditions, as she sought tirelessly for a form and style which could do justice to the specific character of much twentieth-century experience. She courageously explored nearly every genre available to her, from the fantastic, utopian, mystical and supernatural to science fiction, the documentary of a madman, allegories and 'straight' forms.

Remarkable as is *The Grass is Singing*, impressive as many later writings are, *The Golden Notebook* is, arguably, Lessing's single greatest achievement. In terms of form, structure and unity, it is a staggeringly innovative text. In sheer scope of thematics, characterization and stylistic experimentation, it is overwhelming. To describe it as 'a documentary autobiography', as some critics have done, is rather superficial and misleading, and ignores the fact that that phrase describes one of the main characteristics of many novels which *The Golden Notebook* ruthlessly ironizes. Put somewhat crudely, *The Golden Notebook* is an all-encompassing but unconventional unity, including a short, conventional novel entitled *Free Women* which is broken up into five bits. Then there are four separate 'notebooks', the red, yellow, blue and black, also broken up into four parts each. Finally, there is 'The Golden Notebook', a penultimate section of the whole *Golden Notebook*. The various coloured notebooks include an effort at a diary, the partial, fragmented, disrupted manuscript of a novel, a 'historical', 'factual' record of events involving the Communist Party in London in the 1950s, and the manuscript of some biographical material telling of the main character Anna's life in Rhodesia, a kind of 'history'. Systematically and repeatedly throughout all the notebook fragments and the conventional novel fragments of *Free Women*, issues involving truth, fact, point of view, objectivity, neutrality and the capability of language or fiction to say anything at all are at the forefront of Anna's experience. This creates a level both of self-referentiality and of irony, as both Lessing's project as a writer and the reader's project of reading are problematized. Indeed, intelligible experience, reason or sanity, and the possibility of going on living in the face of such extreme uncertainty as is inherent in modern life become the central subject matter, still further undercut by Lessing's relentless refusal to accept conventional categories even about these central, basic matters. That is, the novel interrogates, for example, basic issues of sanity and madness, and shows how they mean different things, both in different contexts (historical, personal, cultural) and from different points of view. Sometimes sanity can be seen as insane; sometimes madness is the only means of protest against so-called sanity; and so on. Lessing also scrutinized what we mean by normal, everyday living, and revealed it to be not only violent and destructive at times, but also a death-in-life. As with Flannery O'Connor, the 'normal' is shown to be distortion and disfigurement when seen from another viewpoint.

The Golden Notebook is a radical experiment in form, broken up into twenty-two fragments of vastly varying lengths and organized in various 'hierarchies'. The conventional novel *Free Women* is literally in fragments, a superficial, fragmented layer of consciousness underwritten by the layers of the fragmented and various notebooks. This form is almost a parody of psychoanalytic accounts of the mind, as the marginal, secondary and supplemental notebook writings represent the unconscious, and act also as a commentary on the 'conscious ego' of *Free Women*.

That work is exemplary of the novel-reportage which Anna heartily detests as utterly false to experience, imposing false order, false unities, false meanings and false security on human experience. The diaries and notebooks, the unfinished fictional manuscripts and the unfinished factual one, fragmented, disordered and incomplete as they are, are less false than the phoney unity and superficial order of *Free Women* – that primary, smoothly polished, finished 'novel'. Indeed, they – these secondary, supplemental writings – are all that give any depth or any meaning to *Free Women*.

In terms of style, *The Golden Notebook* is also radically innovative, but in a quite unexpected way. Instead of using opacity, materiality, punning or etymological jokes, or other familiar 'innovations' in style, Lessing took hold of 'familiar', 'ordinary' language, and turned it inside out more systematically than almost any previous writer. That is, she revealed the inability of so-called ordinary language to do what realists and ordinary-language adherents claim it does, namely, to represent reality or human experience accurately, neutrally and literally. Lessing's *Golden Notebook* presses familiar, accessible language (unlike modernism's inaccessible language) to its purest, extremest forms, thereby revealing its inherent impurity: its prejudice, its blatant ideology, its irrationality, its figurativeness, its inability to say anything at all, much less to tell the 'truth'. This thoroughgoing exposure of realist, ordinary language as itself rigidly stylized and ideological is mirrored in Lessing's exposure of the conventional form, structure and unity of the novel-report, *Free Women*. Its language is shown to be as stylized as – if not more so than – any of the other types of writing explored in *The Golden Notebook*. The stylistic technique of *The Golden Notebook* is innovative, then; without resorting to typical, earlier innovations in style (which became conventions), Lessing managed to explore a whole range of styles of writing. And in every case, she arrived at what, for example, modernism (as well as other experiments – surrealism, absurdism, etc.) could reveal only by more overt acrobatics and pyrotechnics, namely, that dualisms and other false orderings of language are inadequate, that every concept – from 'sanity' to 'reality' to 'language' – is in desperate need of constant reflection, and that facts and truths are values which must be revised and replaced in the light of new experience. She showed that the simplest statements are not univocal, that a radical indeterminacy saturates our experience and language, and that history and reality are always contextual and from some limited perspective.

The central theme of *The Golden Notebook* is breakdown, and thematically the novel is perfectly congruent with its fragmented form. Yet it is precisely fragmentation of conventional forms (of novels, of human beings) which leads to a kind of end of fragmentation, namely (oxymoronically) formlessness. Structurally and thematically the novel expresses this idea that health, sanity and unity are achieved partially, and only, at the expense (the breakdown) of imprisoning orders. 'Formlessness' is a word which expresses unconventional form, original and particular. There is nothing shaped or formed or unified like *The Golden Notebook*; hence, no familiar form can describe it. It has achieved individuality at the expense of categorization. Lessing, however, embraced earlier, familiar techniques or conventions of 'disunity' and formlessness more overtly than ever when, at the end of *The Golden Notebook*, she makes the novel swallow itself up in a möbius-strip effect, as the first sentence of *The Golden Notebook* is written into a golden notebook by one of the characters in 'The Golden Notebook'. Fiction becomes reality as Saul dictates to Anna her first sentence, 'The two women were alone in the London flat'; character distinctions collapse as Molly and Anna are seen as two aspects of a warring personality in breakdown. Authorial distinctions are blurred as Molly, Anna, Saul and Doris merge into each other, so that familiar categories of self–other collapse into a fiction. As *The Golden Notebook* circles round on itself and devours its own beginning, it devours the authority of categories, concepts, distinctions, characters and dualities which order us and our lives. It challenges our notions of what constitutes sane behaviour and mental health, as well as our beliefs about history, reality, the self and the function of language. In its extreme congruence of form, theme and style, it is one of the most impressive literary 'documents' of the twentieth century.

Iris Murdoch 1919–

Prolific writer of some twenty or so published novels, two plays as well as adaptations of her novels, poems, and books on philosophy (Sartre and Plato), Murdoch was born in Dublin of Anglo-Irish parents and spent her childhood in London. After taking a BA in classics at Oxford and working for the civil service and the UN, she began an academic career as a philosophy lecturer at Oxford (after a short time in Cambridge) which continued until 1963, whereupon she took up writing full-time. She married the scholar and critic John Bayley in 1956. She was created a Dame Commander of the Order of the British Empire in 1987; she has been presented with numerous honours; three of her novels have been awarded major literary prizes. Relatively early novels such as *The Unicorn* (London and New York, 1963) express her consciousness of the literary tradition as a problematic context, involving issues of influence and rejection and the role of experiment and convention in contemporary fiction. Ten years later, *The Black Prince* (London and New York, 1973) was exemplifying the epistemological problems of contemporary fiction through an ironic 'portrait of the artist'. Frequent allusion in the text to other works – from Shakespeare to Nabokov – along with exploration of the moral consequences of art (the relation of the true, the good and the beautiful) indicates the issues of originality and tradition in the articulation of human experience, including novel writing. In this and in other novels we find the overt thematics alluding to a level of self-conscious narration – a novel which narrates the story of its own composition, to use a familiar phrase. Other novels, such as the monumental *The Sea, the Sea* (London and New York, 1978), which won the Booker Prize, seem more traditionally realist and less ironically self-conscious, as they explore Blakean alternations between love as selfish or obsessive and as imaginative and unpossessive. Indeed, Murdoch's novels suggest a fascination with the central moral principle that the good in human relations is essentially the ability to perceive others as beings like ourselves, rather than as objects for exploitation, and that art can develop this imaginative faculty. In an essay on the sublime in 1959, Murdoch stated that 'freedom is

knowing and understanding things quite other than ourselves.'

These moral, aesthetic and philosophic concerns in part account for Murdoch's commitment in her later novels to developing characters who are separate, distinct individuals capable of acts of will and self-determination. Before immersing herself in these more familiar, realist concerns, however, Murdoch, for example in her first novel *Under the Net* (London and New York, 1954), had already written what A.S. Byatt has described as 'a fable about realism' or a 'conceptual game', in which Murdoch sought to establish the need for new literary, narrative, thematic and stylistic conventions leading to a new kind of realism. Byatt, like Malcolm Bradbury, has written convincingly of Murdoch as a writer who has made the dichotomy between realism and modernism or experimental writing almost redundant. For Murdoch, like other precursors and contemporaries, has 'experimented' with 'realism'; like, for example, Margaret Drabble most recently (to a lesser degree, however), Murdoch has subjected realism to systematic scrutiny, parody and self-consciousness. This creates a new fiction, a 'strong, agile realism' more accessible than modernism, post-modernism or other overtly radical experiments. Yet, it no longer accepts the (often dogmatic) assumptions in nineteenth-century realism of objectivity, transparency of language, art as an accurate representation of an unproblematic reality, and so on.

Murdoch's techniques for going beyond either traditional realism or explicitly experimental writing involve what Bradbury has described as 'rococo plots', 'surrealist comic fantasies', and systematic speculations about language, knowledge, perception, art, form and so on. That is, from as early as the 1950s' fiction, Murdoch was writing self-consciously about the impossibility of taking language and communication for granted, since she was acutely aware of the need to interrogate the concept 'reality' and the notion of art as 'referring'. Like Flannery O'Connor and other near-contemporaries, Murdoch came to see reality as, ambiguously, a kind of mystery, and her attention turned away from what we perceive to how we perceive. The tension between reality and metaphor arose as she developed her fictional language to express this ambiguity of reality as mystery, even as fantasy, and as essentially a metaphorical construct. Marguerite Young developed a quite different form of writing to express this very insight, following in the modernist mode of linguistic and literary virtuosity, but Murdoch, like Doris Lessing and Alison Lurie, for example, seemed determined to find a more accessible style. That is, she strove for a kind of experimental writing which is as self-conscious as modernism and postmodernism, but which proclaims and comments upon its own artifice in such a way that this level of philosophic self-consciousness is not intruded upon the reader. Disguised parodies of Shakespearean plots, rich, dense but subtle allusion creating an intertextual network, unobtrusive but self-conscious games with the reader, and many other modernist techniques – learned from Samuel Beckett, Elias Canetti and others whom she admired – continued to appear in Murdoch's later novels, even while moral/aesthetic concerns were increasingly dominating the texts.

Murdoch's fiction has divided critics – a not unusual occurrence – in a more clear-cut way than is usually the case. Not only is there little agreement as to whether her novels and her style are 'good'; there is even less agreement as to how to classify her, as realist, ironist, experimentalist, romantic or moralist. Byatt, Bradbury and Frank Kermode have tended to avoid such judgements and classifications, concentrating on improving our understanding of the details of Murdoch's strategies and artistries. Other, more censorious critics have evaluated her work and found it wanting. Her meticulous attention to (traditional) realist conventions of setting or environment (usually London, but also Ireland and elsewhere), the problematic relation of individual characters to the powerful social forces in that setting, and moral themes, as well as the apparent accessibility of her style, have led to accusations of conservatism in politics, morality and art (in spite of her long-standing left-wing attitudes). Ironically (and perhaps revealingly), it is often the more overtly conservative critics who have rejected Murdoch. This may suggest that she has found a way of writing – neither realist nor experimental in the traditional senses of those words – which is remarkably accessible, yet also rather subversive. Indeed, it is the tendency of many critics to maintain realist myths and reject not only overt experimentalism, but most especially the experimentalism which absorbs realism (Lessing, Murdoch, Muriel Spark, etc.), that may account for the critical disagreements about Murdoch.

In addition to the novels mentioned above, other fiction includes *The Nice and the Good* (London and New York, 1968), *The Sacred and the Profane Love Machine* (London and New York, 1974), *The Philosopher's Pupil* (London and New York, 1983) and *The Book and the Brotherhood* (London and New York, 1987).

Elizabeth Spencer 1921–

Author of several novels, novellas and some forty short stories, Spencer was born in Carrollton, Mississippi, and attended Belhaven College in Jackson, Mississippi, where she first met Eudora Welty, with whom she formed a long friendship as a fellow Southern writer. She took an MA at Vanderbilt University in 1943, where she was influenced by Donald Davidson, the well-known Tennessee poet and friend of Allen Tate, and published the first of her three Mississippi novels, *Fire in the Morning*, in 1948 (New York). This novel depicts four generations of rural Southerners by means of a complicated intricate plot, including a minor character, Amos Dudley, on whom she focused in her second novel, *This Crooked Way* (New York and London, 1952). Here, complex plot is replaced by attention to psychology and to the use of religion for egotistical gains; Spencer experimented with multiple narrators and the use of the journey convention, as well as with allusive images with symbolic import, as the obsessed Amos moves West and uproots his family. *The Voice at the Back Door* (New York, 1956), which Spencer wrote in part while holding a Guggenheim Fellowship in 1953, is the last of these 'regional' novels, and explores black–white relations in a fiction of more overt social and political criticism, not unlike Harper Lee's *To Kill a Mockingbird*. Meanwhile, Spencer began publishing numerous stories in the *Virginia Quarterly*, the *New Yorker* and *McCall's*, and in 1960 won the first McGraw-Hill Fiction Award for her European novel, *The Light in the Piazza* (New York, 1960; made into a film), a novella of Jamesean moral complexity and subtle narrative ironies. Her years in Italy before her marriage to her English husband brought about the change in setting from the US South to the European south. Like Edith Wharton, Spencer made use of the perceived sensuality of Italy to explore the 'underworld' of the human psyche.

By this time, Spencer was well established as a precise, technically highly accomplished stylist. She received O. Henry Awards, the Rosenthal Award, and the Award of Merit Medal (of the American Academy of Arts and Letters) for the short story, as well as the Pushcart Prize, and she consolidated her work with the publication in 1965 of one of her most admired novellas, *Knights and Dragons* (New York). Ten stories were collected in the volume *Ship Island* (New York, 1968), dedicated to Welty. Later, in *No Place for an Angel* (New York, 1967) and *The Snare* (New York, 1972), set in the underworld of drugs and crime in New Orleans, Spencer explored more explicitly, in complicated plots and vivid characters, the interior moral-psychological world of her characters and their unconscious motives and drives. In 1981, the *Stories of Elizabeth Spencer* (Garden City, N.Y.), with an introduction by Welty, appeared, containing the ten *Ship Island* stories and twenty-three others, including *Knights and Dragons*, the so-called Marilee stories (three stories published separately in 1981 and narrated by Marilee Summerall), and many other previously uncollected ones. Spencer lived for some years in Montreal before settling in North Carolina with her husband.

From the first, Spencer was admired for the clarity and lucidity of her style; even after she began to write much more morally complex, Jamesean fiction, her attention to moral ambiguities and psychological complexities was said by the critics to be hidden behind a clear and accessible prose. Moreover, her range and thematic versatility have by now become evident, as has her impressive development as a writer, from the early Mississippi fiction to her Italian and, eventually, New Orleans writing. Welty, in her foreword to the 1981 *Stories*, praised Spencer most for her ability to handle what Welty had argued elsewhere (*The Eye of the Story*) was one of the most important elements of much fiction, namely place, locale or setting: 'What is *unerring* about her writing . . . [is] the sense of place.' Welty also wrote of Spencer's 'capacity for cool detachment' as part of the source of her power

as a writer of fiction, along with 'finely-shaded perception', which Welty argued was comparable to Katherine Mansfield's. These comments fit with Spencer's own remarks; she spoke of one of her central concerns in literature as being the depiction of 'how you take up residence in the world'. This involves moral and spiritual residence as well, however; indeed, a central preoccupation of Spencer's Italian novella, *Knights and Dragons*, is Martha Ingram's growing sense that her life in Italy is affecting her moral discriminations and values. That is, Spencer explored the effect of place upon one's very moral dwelling. Similarly, in the earlier Italian novella *Light in the Piazza*, Margaret Johnson finds herself inhabiting a quite different world of values from those in her American residence.

Clearly, then, in many of Spencer's writings, place and locale function powerfully as symbolic of moral realms. Wharton and Henry James had found, similarly, that setting could function in this way, enormously increasing the aesthetic effect of the narrative. No doubt Welty placed so much value on 'the power of place' for the same reasons, namely, that moral values are as much conventions as are time and place, and can be represented as 'locations'. In exploring how moral beliefs vary from place to place, and how easy it is to become 'infected' (as one of the characters liked to describe it) by alternative values, Spencer revealed the moral ambiguities of all our lives, with which James and Wharton were so preoccupied. As moral absolutes crumble, as familiar, local attitudes and regional certainties fragment in 'foreign', often exotic surroundings, Spencer's characters experience the irresolvable dilemmas which result from an awareness that moral actions can never be based on anything but questionable motives and relative conventions. Yet, Spencer's fiction also depicts the emotional attraction of 'evil' – its exotic, sexual allure: characters are often portrayed as wanting to escape from the mundane, 'virtuous' world of mediocrity and familiarity, risking security and convention for the 'underworld'. This attraction is explicitly portrayed in *The Snare*; as in Jane Bowles's novel *Two Serious Ladies*, the protagonist, Julia Garrett, seems to feel that she must explore the extremes before she can accept ordinariness. Elsewhere, as in *Knights and Dragons*, the world portrayed is one of sexuality, infidelity and desire, where moral judgement is blurred beyond any normal limit for Martha Ingram, usually because of conflicting or morally questionable desires.

Spencer, then, combined a number of modernist techniques with familiar conventions of the traditional novel in her fiction. Plot and characterization are handled with vitality and subtlety, while dislocation in narrative time (whether through memory and flashback or through hallucinatory memories), multiple narrative perspectives, symbolic, allusive imagery, and extreme thematic elusiveness and moral ambiguity are skilfully deployed.

Spencer has also written a few non-fiction articles in *Delta Review* (1964), *Notes on Mississippi Writers* 3 (1970), and *Weekend Magazine* (12 August 1978). Her papers and manuscripts reside in the University of Kentucky Library at Lexington.

Mavis Gallant 1922–

Born Mavis de Trafford Young in Montreal, Gallant wrote feature articles for the *Montreal Standard* before leaving Canada in 1950 for Paris, which she made her permanent residence. A long connection with the *New Yorker*, which published her first story in 1951, and many subsequent stories, gained her a reputation in the United States which exceeded that in her home country for some decades. Over one hundred stories have now been published, as well as a novella, *Green Water, Green Sky* (Cambridge, Mass., 1959) – which reads like a cycle of interrelated short stories – and a novel, *A Fairly Good Time* (New York, 1970). There is a collection of essays and articles, *Paris Notebooks* (Toronto, 1986), and a play, *What is to Be Done?* (Dunvegan, Ontario, 1983). Gallant's stories have appeared in a variety of collections such as *The Other Paris* (Cambridge, Mass., 1956), *The Pegnitz Junction* (New York, 1973), *From the Fifteenth District* (Toronto, 1979), *Home Truths* (Toronto, 1981), *Overhead in a Balloon* (Toronto, 1985) and *Across the Bridge* (Toronto, 1993). She won the prestigious Governor General's Award of Canada in 1982, and was writer in residence at the University of Toronto, 1983–4. She was made an Officer of the Order of Canada in 1981, and is now recognized as one of the first stylists of the

English language writing today. Her prose displays a rare elegance and subtlety; its polish and intellectuality compare with precursors such as Jorge Luis Borges. Yet her constant preoccupation with history, politics, war and questions of national identity and exile give her fiction an overt thematic dimension. Like that of another great precursor, Katherine Mansfield, Gallant's fiction effects considerable aesthetic response by means of bitter irony, complemented by sharp wit which characterizes her detached narrative voice.

In *Green Water, Green Sky*, Gallant explored mother–daughter relations to portray the destructive moral effects upon a young girl of an overprotective, manipulative mother, while in the later *A Fairly Good Time* she explored in a bitterly comic vein the failure of the marriage of a young, unbelievably inexperienced girl. In the Linnet Muir sequence in *Home Truths*, one finds more overtly feminist themes and autobiographical elements; a young woman writer struggles to free herself from the encumbrances of family attachments, in order to devote herself to her profession. As in Mansfield's stories a half-century earlier, some women are portrayed as colluding with patriarchal structures in order to keep their female competitors from escaping the oppressive confines of the world of women and children – 'the kitchen is a slum', as Gallant liked to describe it. While portraying marriage as ruthless and victimizing, she also showed the vulnerability of children to the moral irresponsibility and caprices of parents. Throughout these explorations, the narrative voice, whether first or third person, is characterized by a detached, acerbic irony and wit, as incisive observations of human psychology and the pressures of history and politics upon individual human beings are explored. While the detachment of the narrative verges at times on the callous, this sharpness is usually mitigated to a compassionate pessimism by the end of a story.

While Gallant's stories suggest that we are all victims of larger historical, economic and political forces, she often focused particularly upon World War II and its after-effects. In sometimes markedly complex stories, with archaeological layerings of meaning and systematic historical and anti-fascist allusions, we find an effective interplay of narrative points of view. These function aesthetically to reveal the cruel and destructive pretensions which pepper our everyday dealings with our fellow humans, and which render our lives petty and empty. Themes of the exile, the alien and the stranger function symbolically and are expressive of the main quality in our relations with each other. Sometimes, characters may actually manage to communicate with each other or be generous, thereby overcoming their strangeness in a moment of shared experience. Yet these successful encounters are the exception; often people are shown leading spiteful and empty lives, though the astute narrative voice reveals such lives as governed by fears and vulnerabilities which lead to harmful defences. The sheer skill and polish of Gallant's verbal texture is combined, then, with three-dimensional thematic complexity involving anti-fascist politics and the embedding of human experience in its social and historical surroundings; indeed, these external surroundings are often the means by which she conveys her characters' internal psychology.

While Gallant wrote about both post-war and contemporary life, about both Canadian and European characters and setting, her stories all demonstrate a Jamesean interest in point of view, a modified, compassionate irony, and an interest in North American–European relations. Gallant also marshalled ambiguity and indefiniteness of meanings and endings in post-modernist gestures which recall the absurdist methods of the 1940s and 1950s. These are contrasted with overt, accessible themes about racism, genocide, destruction and dislocation, which are almost always, however, presented through memory. Like Katherine Anne Porter, Gallant analysed the way memory can manipulate, select, and expunge: 'Some things are better left as legends.' Deemphasizing plot in favour of style and ambience, she achieved a sophisticated, elegant prose and a unique voice which make her one of North America's most distinguished stylists.

Nadine Gordimer 1923–

Author of numerous novels, essays and short stories (over half a dozen collections) as well as criticism (*The Black Interpreters*: *Notes on African Writing*, Johannesburg, 1973) and recipient of the Nobel Prize for literature, Nadine Gordimer was born in the Transvaal and lives in South Africa. Because of the saturation of everyday life by intense political conflict, Gordimer's fiction was initially appreciated for its condemnation of the evils of apartheid; only later did attention focus upon her writing as literature, indeed, literature which challenged the usefulness of notions of any art as apolitical. In such highly acclaimed novels as *Burger's Daughter* (London, 1979), *July's People* (London, 1981) and *A Sport of Nature* (London, 1987), and in short story collections from *Some Monday For Sure* (London, 1976) to the most recent *Selected Stories* (London, 1975), which reprints stories from numerous earlier collections, Gordimer's narrative strategies, stylistic innovations, use of irony and point of view, and shaping, unifying skills have been evident, functioning congruently with her overt thematic material. Other novels include *The Lying Days* (London, 1953), *The Late Bourgeois World* (London, 1966), *A Guest of Honor* (New York, 1970) and *The Conservationist* (London, 1974). While Gordimer's novels and stories often focus upon the tensions inherent in apartheid, her fiction investigates human relationships and experience in many other domains; she explored sexual relationships, family conflicts, and the nature of friendship and of violent enmity, and she became highly skilled at the portrayal of moral transformation and of the forces which encourage or inhibit such growth. Moreover, her fiction engages in a subtle dialogue with both realism and modernism, as she developed techniques from each tradition in order to find the most coherent and sharply focused modes for her specific material.

Gordimer's fiction, at its best, confronts the reader with the passivity and paternalism inherent in the very act of reading (as well as in life, generally). Her motto in the novel *Burger's Daughter*, 'I am the place in which something has occurred', confronts the reader with the potential, full force of art when imaginative participation allows her or him to experience moral transformation, instead of watching characters experience it (or fail to achieve it). Relatedly, communication and the hindrances to it are explored as a central issue in the fiction, along with the violence and sterility resulting from the paternalism at the basis both of apartheid and of the refusal to communicate with others as another self. Like Katherine Anne Porter some decades earlier, Gordimer designed carefully crafted situations in which characters (and the reader) are led to the revelation that other people have a reality as essential as one's own. Whatever their age, their sex, their skin colour, their language, their status, Gordimer shows us human beings 'in the real', coming alive to each other, as the scales of egotism and the skin-thickening effects of greed drop away at moments of crisis, leading to 'views' into the essential humanity of another individual.

Gordimer's fiction portrays paternalism as a central attitude inhibiting imaginative communication and relationship amongst people. Indeed, paternalism, her novels and stories show, leads – almost inevitably – to violence and injustice, both in personal relations and in the larger social-political sphere. Paternalism is anatomized as the attitude that other people are not full human beings; somehow they are incomplete, lacking in some way which means they cannot be allowed to make their own choices. They are either children or like children, and therefore do not have the moral, intellectual and emotional maturity to direct their lives. Gordimer examined paternalism and the people who behave paternalistically, and revealed the sources of much paternalism in greed and economic exploitation. She also portrayed the results of paternalism, as she sought to demonstrate the imperviousness of deeply rooted paternalistic attitudes to reason, compromise and negotiation; hence violence is the only means of resisting such arrogance. Gordimer's fiction also portrays the infinite masks and disguises which paternalism adopts in order to pass itself off as acceptable and even rational.

Paternalism in the literary tradition was engaged with in a number of ways, as well. Gordimer challenged accepted conventions involving theme, character, unifying techniques and style, often frustrating readers' expectations of novels as realist representation passively observed by a spectating mind. The spectating mind often gets confronted by the limitations of its own inner country instead of that of a character; or it is frustrated in its efforts to arrive at determinate sense and motivation. In *July's People*, for example, Gordimer developed an almost modernist narrative technique of elusive meaning at the surface level, in order to express the total indeterminacy and unpredictability of the nature of the relations between black and white when the familiar order collapses. In *Burger's Daughter*, a psychological realism of a plotless kind reflects the theme of the story, namely, Rosa Burger's gradual moral transformation and personal maturation – and the many events and ties which fail to deflect the gradual unfolding of her character. Congruence of theme, form and style is the predominant character of these two novels in particular, which make for interesting contrast, as *Burger's Daughter* formulates Rosa's construction of herself, while *July's People* appears, on the surface, to chart the breakdown of a society, a marriage and, perhaps, Maureen Smoles. Yet, behind the breakdown is, inevitably, the suggestion of the construction of something new and different – and possibly better, but only after much destruction and death. While *July's People*, in style, narrative and content, portrays fragmentation and breakdown, *Burger's Daughter* adopts an almost Greek tragic tone of narrative distance and inevitability, of impersonality and detached observation, as the will of a modern Antigone is developed into full maturity. A paradoxical balance of determinism and individual freedom is the result, as the origins of such a heroine are explored and analysed. *A Sport of Nature* further demonstrates Gordimer's splendid variety, as a completely different narrative technique and style are created to map the development of a woman from chaos and mediocrity into dignity and a role in state affairs.

In some of her non-fiction, Gordimer remarked that 'my approach in these stories, as in many others, is that of irony. In fact, I would say that in general, in my stories, my approach as a short story writer is the ironical one, and that it represents the writer's unconscious selection of the approach best suited to the material.' This statement occurred in the context of a discussion of point of view, when Gordimer explained that her fiction rarely presents the author's point of view. Rather, it seeks to portray what she called the 'consciousness of the era', for the writer is a medium through which a society's values and beliefs are brought into consciousness, and a society's values and beliefs are, she insisted, rarely shared with the artist. 'Irony' in this context, then, is suggested to be a complex narrative point of view: a questioning (through exposure by the light of imagination) of a society's accepted values is unobtrusively built into fiction through the indirect mode of ironic consciousness. Irony in Gordimer's texts is achieved in many ways; some of them are familiar literary conventions. To construct an ironic consciousness, Gordimer uses ambiguity, indeterminate endings, strata of meanings, extended metaphoric situations, complex tone in the narrative, and other strategies which act to question accepted values without paternalistically prescribing answers or univocal solutions. Gordimer never explicitly defined what she meant exactly by 'irony', but the term is closely associated with issues of paternalism, communication, illumination and violence.

Traditionally, irony involves self-knowledge; associated with Socrates and Sophocles most specifically, it is not merely satire or prognostication, but a word designating a 'flip of perspective': an observer thinks she or he is watching something happen to someone else, but suddenly realizes it is happening to her or him. In Gordimer's novels and short stories, this traditional artistic convention is adapted by Gordimer for her own specific purposes to create unique works of art which yet demonstrate many familiar literary conventions. Irony often occurs in Gordimer's text as a mirror for racism, whether in characters or readers, liberals or reactionaries, but it is also a mirror for other familiar forms of paternalism. Moreover, through ironic structures using tone, metaphor, self-referring gestures and other mirroring techniques, Gordimer's fiction analyses the ways in which the various forms of paternalism are related, both to each other and to the social, economic, psychological and political assumptions which support these attitudes. Sometimes an individual's psychology is at the forefront of analysis; sometimes the society dwarfs the individual characters. Yet, whichever is emphasized, the context in the one case and the agent in the other are never wholly excluded. In 'Is There Nowhere Else Where We Can Meet?' or 'The Train From Rhodesia', characters, as is usual in short, short stories, are subordinated to action; in a few deft strokes, Gordimer sketched the sharp outlines of the salient features of life under apartheid, the kinds of conflict that seem inevitable, and the human consequences for everyone.

In the novels, characterization is still often subordinate to action; even in *Burger's Daughter*, Rosa is subordinated to her heroic role. This is not a flaw; on the contrary, it is an example of irony – 'the writer's unconscious selection of the approach best suited to the material'. For the novel portrays precisely the dilemma of individual fulfilment achievable only through social-political action – only through apparent abnegation – in certain historical situations. Paradoxically, Rosa seems to achieve her fullest humanity and individuality only by rejecting the form such fulfilment would take in a European as opposed to a South African setting, thereby accepting her heroic destiny. And yet the ambiguity and uncertainty remain built into the texture of the novel, as to what, if anything, she can achieve in that way. Perhaps, the novel seems to suggest, it is the willingness to risk everything, rather than the outcome, which defines heroism, but the sort of society which still needs heroism is closely scrutinized. If the reader, however, allows overt political thematics to obscure literary craft, she or he will miss Gordimer's fine artistic control, her impressive congruence of form and subject matter, her impressionistic use of landscape and setting, the exquisite imagery and the particularity of her style, all of which contribute to beautifully designed illuminations in moral, social and aesthetic experience in which the reader can participate.

Gordimer's most recent fiction includes *My Son's Story* (London, 1990) and two collections of stories, *Crimes of Conscience* (London, 1991) and *Jump and Other Stories* (London, 1991). Nonfiction publications of recent date are *The Essential Gesture: Writing, Politics and Places*, with S. Clingman (London, 1988), *Lifetimes Under Apartheid*, with D. Goldblatt (London, 1986), and *What Happened to Burger's Daughter: or How South African Censorship Works*, with others (Johannesburg, 1980).

Janet Frame 1924 –

Author of numerous novels, short story collections, poetry, three volumes of prize-winning autobiography, and a fairy tale, Janet Frame was born in Dunedin, New Zealand. Her early fiction was published as *The Lagoon: Stories*

(Christchurch, 1951; Auckland, 1990), and six years later her first novel (and one of her best-loved) appeared, *Owls Do Cry* (Christchurch, 1957). Numerous books followed over the next thirty years, including some ten novels, such as *Faces in the Water* (Christchurch, 1961), *The Edge of the Alphabet* (Christchurch, 1962), *Scented Gardens for the Blind* (Christchurch, 1963), *A State of Siege* (New York, 1966), *The Rainbirds* (London, 1968), *Intensive Care* (New York, 1970), *Daughter Buffalo* (New York, 1972) and *Living in the Maniototo* (New York, 1979), which won the New Zealand Book Award for fiction. Frame meanwhile published a number of short story volumes, many of which were later republished in *You are Now Entering the Human Heart* (Wellington, 1983), which includes stories selected by Frame from *The Lagoon*, *The Reservoir* (New York, 1963), and *Snowman, Snowman* (New York, 1963). Some of her poetry is collected in the volume entitled *The Pocket Mirror* (New York, 1967), while her three volumes of autobiography are *To the Island* (New York, 1982), *An Angel at My Table* (New York and London, 1984), and *The Envoy from Mirror City* (New York and London, 1985).

In Frame's writing, the boundary between life and art is more thoroughly dissolved than in that of most other writers, however much others have investigated this 'interface'. Moreover, her fiction is an exploration of that house of being, language, and the ways in which life is burdened or liberated in this its dwelling. Much of the intensity and aesthetic effect of the fiction originate in Frame's ability to 'bear too much reality' and in her adeptness in constructing, out of these views of 'reality', communicable records of her experience. These records – her writings – are disturbing to many readers, though nevertheless compelling, because she makes no concessions about the nature of human existence as a painful journey of suffering through the relentless rounds of birth, time and death. In this context, Frame's art undertakes to discover and reveal how, through language, we can construct a self, a world, sanity, relationships and a life: this artistic process of discovery is her life, which her writing has constructed. Her fiction reveals that there need be no dichotomy between writing and living; nor can either be secondary to the other, contrary to general opinion. Indeed,

as a record of one individual's success in creating a unique individuality, her works are unsurpassed, while they can be threatening to conventional orthodoxies about what constitutes successful living or happiness.

One of the central techniques of Frame's fiction is the contrast between the normal, the conventional or the orthodox, and 'other' ways of being and living. Throughout her work, characters are shown living under the pressure to 'fit' into a role, a mould and a niche in order to survive. Many of her 'heroines' fail to make a place for themselves in the grammar of social behaviour; yet these marginal figures' inner lives are revealed to the reader and made familiar. Frame revealed the centrality of our language games in social behaviour and in individual psychology as a means of fitting in and adopting roles and stereotypes. She revealed our normal forms of behaviour, interaction and relationship to be a language of dead metaphors, stale clichés and worn-out banalities. Normality, it is suggested, condemns people to forms of behaviour and relationship which are as essentially meaningless as are the clichés that dominate our thought. Such normal, everyday language as we all use, like our normal, everyday behaviour, is empty of spirituality, vitality and individuality. Through such social role-playing, wrought by our normal language games, any uniqueness of character, any imaginativeness, is stifled. Some of Frame's 'anti-heroines' register the shock and horror that an 'abnormal' psyche experiences when, gradually, through adolescence and early adulthood, these unique minds are confronted head on by the pressures to fit in, and the unwillingness of others to tolerate their eccentricity, their ungrammaticality in the dead language of social interaction.

Frame's exposure of normality as a total corruption of the human imaginative life is usually presented through both indirect narrative techniques and indirect thematics. We see the ordinary world through the eyes of a range of marginalized people, and this view, in part, exposes us to the sadism and deadness of normal, 'successful' people – often people in caring professions, ironically. Because of the 'centrality' in the fiction of such 'marginal' characters, we, as readers, experience their almost incredible vitality, their unique individuality and the variety of their mental lives. By contrast, the supposedly successful people who are often 'looking after' these mindless 'lunatics', these idiots, seem like automatons, going through the stereotyped motions demanded by their roles as nurses, doctors, husbands, wives, parents, friends and so on. The normal is seen as dull, unimaginative, and often sadistic; like their speech and language, the thoughts and feelings of ordinary people are seen by the heroines as repetitive, predictable and unoriginal, for the most part. This analogy between life and language – that social behaviour and personal 'inner' experience consist of acts which are like sentences, and are governed by rules of grammar, syntax and semantics – is developed throughout Frame's fiction and reaches its climax in *Living in the Maniototo*. There the heroine, a writer, is waiting, like the characters in *Godot*, for life to recede so that she can write her novel, only to discover that the 'life' events were the sentences in her 'fiction' she thought she had not been 'writing'.

Frame, then, courageously confronted the boredom and fear characteristic of normal life, but denied by nearly everyone, because they cannot face too much reality. She also described the damage done to unusual minds and the shocked horror they experience when pressed to deny their vision of this terrifying reality which is life, time and death. Yet in nearly all her novels, especially the later ones, there are evidences of her painstakingly discovering limited ways of existing in time, which are neither devoid of imagination on the one hand, nor madness on the other. Often, these two ways of being, namely, dehumanization or madness, seem the only possibilities, although a third is the silent withdrawal from life into autism, usually involving a rejection of the dead language of ordinary speech and a refusal of the equally dead language of relationship. This third way is explored in *Scented Gardens for the Blind* and *Intensive Care*, while *A State of Siege* explores the theme recurring through most of Frame's novels, namely, that life is a battle, a conflict not merely with other people but with forces greater than the individual will, forces both within the psyche and outside it. In *Intensive Care* and *A State of Siege*, this conflict results in death for the central character, while *Scented Gardens for the Blind* depicts the battle of life as leading one character to silent

withdrawal and the other to blindness and sensory deprivation: a living death.

Central to Frame's novels, then, is a narrative point of view which reverses fundamental values and interpretations in life. This involves not so much the familiar reversal of sanity and madness; rather, Frame showed us that human beings who are usually treated as though they have no inner life, no real humanity, are often more mentally alive and humane than 'normal' people, who have dehumanized themselves in order to fit into the familiar grammar of social life. A literary counterpart to the reversal of values is also uppermost in all of Frame's novels, namely, her exposure of realist fiction – that 'normal', 'ordinary' language and order in fiction – as a virtual stripping away from *art* of imaginativeness. Many of her novels are so saturated with either symbolic, surreal, fantastic, inexplicable or mysterious elements that they constitute a direct challenge to realist notions. Moreover, her challenges to realist, ordinary fiction also take the forms of a rejection of straightforward authorship, as she alleges, for example, that the manuscript about to be read 'was found among the papers of Thora Pattern after her death, and submitted to the publishers by Peter Heron, Hire-Purchase Salesman' (*The Edge of the Alphabet*). The 'author' of *Living in the Maniototo* discusses multiple authorship throughout the novel, and relates it to the fundamental question of identity: 'What, who am I?', 'What is it to be an I? a self-conscious creature?' In *Scented Gardens for the Blind* and *Daughter Buffalo* (as overtly in *Living in the Maniototo*), fantasy and reality are so utterly blended that the reader's grasp of the novel's reality is proved mistaken at the end: the autistic world and the 'real' world keep turning into each other. Throughout some novels, Frame drew on the old literary convention that death is the reality, while life is the dream. This paradox is useful for raising questions of a metaphysical and existential nature, but it has the further use of being a metaphor for the theme of normal life as a death-in-life, while abnormal mental and physical states of insanity, autism, retardation and so on are more alive and imaginative than 'fitting in' is.

In *Scented Gardens for the Blind*, not only are fantasy and reality indistinguishable; the individuality of the characters is undermined, as they take on each other's characteristics. By the end of the novel the reader is encouraged to suspect that the whole story is a world of imaginary fictions going on in the mind of a single character: all the people and all the events have been imagined by her, but presented as 'real' to the reader. Even this interpretation is undermined, however, first by the fact that the final chapter has no more status in reality than the rest of the book. Second, one of the doctors in this 'frame' to the rest of the novel is starting to take on schizophrenic characteristics exactly like Erlene-Vera Glace's. Clearly, one of the central themes of this and other novels is the figurative nature of our self-conceptions; we are similes of each other: 'there seemed to be a secret likeness between all people, as if some borrowed the characteristics of others, for a day or two, or kept them for life and for death . . . in an attempt to efface all individual identity, to escape from the responsibility of owning a unique essence and a *name*.' Likewise, *Daughter Buffalo*'s two central characters, Edelman and Turnbury, are both reality and fiction: one is a fiction of the other's imagination, but we cannot see which is which. In *A State of Siege*, the central experience and largest portion of the novel involves the terrifying experience a woman lives through alone during a violent storm at night with repeated knockings on her door. At the end, she is found dead, perhaps of a heart attack. Realistic frames at the beginning and end of the novel are connected with suggestions throughout the text that the experience of terror is 'simply' the result of a fevered mind due to heart illness. Yet for Malfred, the heroine, the experiences involve spiritual revelations about herself, her psyche, the human mind: the haunting, intrusive presence of an unacknowledged past locked away in a secret 'room' of her psyche is being charted as it intrudes into her consciousness, so powerfully that it overcomes her present conscious existence, which dies. This 'reality' coexists with the world that designated it 'mere' fantasy.

Faces in the Water, Frame's fictional documentary, is another ironic gesture at realist assumptions. Written in the first person, it is the narrative of Istina Mavet, a seriously deranged woman who, strangely, narrates her story in a perfectly sane, orderly way. What is notable about her narrative is its unique, intensively imaginative

language, its vitality in expressing her experiences in startling and innovative, unclichéd words: 'I did not know my own identity. I was burgled of body and hung in the sky like a woman of straw. The day seemed palpable about me yet receded when I moved to touch it, for fear that I might contaminate it.' Istina's grasp of the depths of reality seems far greater than the flat surface on which her carers live. In *Intensive Care*, the confrontation with the inadequacy of realism and normality takes a different form. The novel is in a panoramic, social realist, 'historical' genre – but set in a ghastly post-World War III 'future'. Much like Atwood's *Handmaid's Tale*, this 'document' records society's survival of the war only by total dehumanization, as all 'misfits' are condemned to death by a computer. One of them, Milly, killed because she is a useless autistic, keeps a diary. Far from being a retarded, simple-minded idiot with no inner human life of her own, Milly reveals herself in her diary to be a remarkably imaginative, creative being whose grasp of language is a testimony to her personal uniqueness: she has her own language, which much resembles the Joycean language of Frame's poetry, in its playing with words, spellings and connotations, so as to reveal amazingly multivalent resources in all language.

Throughout her writing, Janet Frame seemed to implicate language as a powerful means by which we are socialized, not civilized, and subjugated, not liberated. Yet, while this indictment of the way language is used in our society to deaden our imaginations and destroy our individuality recurs as a systematic theme, Frame's target is, evidently, the abuse of language, not language itself. As she was acutely, personally aware, it was the ability to release the power of language to work in the service of imaginativeness, to create uniqueness, individuality and novelty, that made her life what it is. Yet, as for Kate Chopin and others, the writer is a figure of speech, not to be taken literally, for her novels are a constant evocation of the potentiality in every human being to be a Shakespeare in the dream that is life.

Kamala Markandaya 1924–

Novelist and journalist, Markandaya (Kamala Purnaiya Taylor) was born in India and educated at Madras University; she has worked in both India and Britain, reporting on a variety of social issues, such as the rural poor and the problems of urban, industrial India. Many of her novels portray directly or indirectly the familiar conflict between Western attitudes, technology and modernization and Indian concerns with detachment, contemplation and the ultimate spirituality of life stripped of materialist cravings. This large cultural conflict is interwoven and complicated by Markandaya's concern with the underclasses in Indian society, the caste systems and the second-class status of women. Her novels include, *Nectar in a Sieve* (London and New York, 1954), *Some Inner Fury* (London and New York, 1955), *A Silence of Desire* (New York, 1960), *Possession* (London, 1962), *A Handful of Rice* (New York, 1966), *The Coffer Dams* (Delhi and New York, 1969), *Two Virgins* (New York, 1973) and *The Golden Honeycomb* (London, 1977). These display a range of genre within the form and styles of narration which is impressive, and which makes Markandaya one of the most notable post-R.K. Narayan or post-Raja Rao writers. Two of her most interesting novels, *A Silence of Desire* and *The Golden Honeycomb*, are examples of two 'opposite' kinds of novel, the former an exploration of personal relationship and developing spirituality in a wife, while the latter is in a more conventional historical genre. It ranges over three generations of contemporary British rule, and balances this larger social world with a portrayal of the intimate life of an Indian prince as well as his struggle with the British and Indian democracy for emerging power.

A Silence of Desire is a powerful novel which weaves into a single, unified artistic effect several strands of conflict, which is the main structure of the novel: there are conflicts between male and female, Eastern and Western, and the need for solitude as well as relationship. A characteristic simplicity and clarity of language mask a sophisticated treatment of the impossibility of any easy resolution amongst these claims. Moreover, Markandaya constructs a highly dramatic plot, which moves forwards with an intensity considerably indebted to her sense of irony, an irony fully revealed only at the end of the novel. For the protagonist, Sarojini, in her search for physical health, finds herself on the path of spiritual development through the help of a swami.

Caught up into 'the way', through detachment from not only material goods but personal attachments or relationships, she begins to neglect her household, her teenage daughters, her young son and her husband. Eventually, her distraught husband, Dandekar, pressures the swami to go away to some other distant village, so that his wife will be forced to return to her mundane, temporal existence. She does return, but greatly ennobled and spiritually developed, in part due to her months of attendance to the swami's teachings, and in part due to the ability to break her attachment of all attachments, namely, that to the swami himself. Even her husband perceives the irony in her giving up far more than he ever attempted (and failed) to detach himself from. Markandaya also ironically draws the portrait of the husband much more fully than that of the wife, but his greater development as a character is a structural expression of the thematic fact that he is more attached to life, and therefore has more personal characteristics. The wife, in marked contrast, is underdeveloped, almost nothing but a sketch of a woman in the stages of spiritualization, depersonalization and growing detachment. Moreover, the narrative alternations between descriptions of the disturbances and uproars of ordinary life – usually involving Dandekar – and the serenity pervading the scenes with the swami and Sarojini, express the thematic concerns of spirituality in contrast to ordinary, material life. In a fine gesture of balance and of acknowledgement of the power and reality of ordinary life over spiritual transcendence, Markandaya gives Dandekar the last word; but this postscript seems an ironic concession rather than a sincere effort to rebalance the impossible imbalance between the demands of the spirit and those of the body and mind.

Flannery O'Connor 1925–1964

Flannery O'Connor, born in Savannah, Georgia, wrote two novels, two short story collections, and a collection of essays and lectures in her short life of thirty-nine years. She lived most of her life in Georgia on a farm, except for a brief period at university in Iowa (MFA, 1947) and Connecticut. Her novels are *Wise Blood* (New York, 1952) and *The Violent Bear it Away* (New

York, 1960), and her short story collections are entitled *A Good Man is Hard to Find and Other Stories* (New York, 1955) and *Everything That Rises Must Converge* (New York, 1965). Her prose is collected in the remarkable volume *Mystery and Manners: Occasional Prose*, eds S. and R. Fitzgerald (New York, 1969). In an essay on O'Connor, Alice Walker wrote that many of O'Connor's readers assume from her fiction that she was an atheist, until they read in *Mystery and Manners* about her surprising commitment to Catholicism. Walker argued that her Catholicism did not in any way limit her art (O'Connor herself argued that it deepened it), and concluded that O'Connor was incapable of writing dogmatic fiction. Walker described the 'essential' O'Connor as the portrayal of spiritual growth, or those moments when an individual comes face to face with her or his own limitations, and comprehends 'the true frontiers of her own inner country'. Or, in O'Connor's terms, to know what we are is above all to know what we lack, so that the first result of self-knowledge is humility. Walker explained that these moments of revelation tend to occur at times of extreme loss or crisis (as in Katherine Anne Porter's stories). Moreover, these revelations in O'Connor's stories show that, for her, art is not so much an idealistic view of what we ought to be as a revelation of what people actually are, in all their inner, hidden deformity and limitations. Hence, O'Connor wrote stories about characters, about people who are 'poor, afflicted in mind and body', and who have little (or at best a distorted) sense of spiritual purpose, since to her that is the norm.

Walker also pointed out that O'Connor's stories are a record of the spiritual growth of the author, as she struggled with what Walker called 'the moral imperative of the serious writer'. O'Connor had herself made it clear in several essays in *Mystery and Manners* that the reader's participation (of a moral and spiritual kind) was also at stake. This participation is not at first evident, for O'Connor's characters are often overtly grotesque and abnormal individuals. That is, unlike most of us, they wear their deformity on the outside, instead of hiding it behind a veneer of normality and social acceptability. She portrayed idiots, misfits, murderers, demented and illiterate characters, people who are afflicted in both body and mind, who, as we said earlier,

have little more than a distorted sense of spiritual purpose. Eventually, it becomes evident to the reader that O'Connor's 'originals' are, after all, just the observed in society: the things which appear natural to us are exposed as the distortions that they actually are. O'Connor argued in her essays that she was showing an often hostile audience what we all are at any particular time and under given circumstances; the audience is hostile because self-knowledge is the thing we resist most intensely, since it inevitably involves smashing our fantasies and seeing ourselves in all our limitations. Hostility and resistance from the audience makes necessary the grotesque, violent means to which she often resorted in her stories. In the process, O'Connor destroyed what Walker described as the last vestiges of sentimentality in Southern writing.

In her essay 'Some Aspects of the Grotesque in Southern Fiction', O'Connor discussed the concept of realism, and argued that there are deeper kinds of realism than those associated with sociology, psychology, economics and history, much less literary realism. The 'realism of fact' (of the nineteenth-century European realists, in particular, but also twentieth-century 'fact' realists) can limit rather than broaden a novelist's approach, so that realism and naturalism, taken literally, can be badly abused. Art, O'Connor argued, is essentially selective, and what is natural to life is not natural to art. O'Connor then explained that in her own fiction, realistic, concrete details are designed to accumulate meaning and become symbolic. Symbols are understood as concrete details which have their essential place in the surface level of fiction, but which also function at a deeper level, so that both writer and reader need a kind of vision which can perceive different levels of reality in a single image, concrete detail or specific situation. As O'Connor put it, she sought to make the gaze extend beyond the surface until it touches the realms of prophets and poets.

Fiction, O'Connor emphasized, is at a fundamental level concrete; its nature is determined by the nature of human perceptions, namely, the five senses. Since human knowledge begins in concrete, particular sense experience, fiction must also begin there, avoiding abstractions, generalizations and universals on its surface, though these are clearly pointed to via symbols.

Through concrete, surface observation alone can the writer reach into the depths of things, and it is there that we reach meaning and reality, she argued. These depths lie beyond the sociological, psychological, economic or rational determinants in what O'Connor called mystery; that is, fiction moves away from typical social patterns and stereotypes towards the unexpected, the unique, the mysterious. This mystery and unexpectedness she described as the true realism, because life and human experience are essentially mysterious. Realist fiction, then, pushes out towards mystery which, for O'Connor as for Eudora Welty, is best understood as the nature of reality itself; as a writer O'Connor felt the need to guarantee a respect for mystery. Moreover, the mysterious process of spiritual growth depicted in the thematics and characterization of the stories and novels is reduplicated for the reader in her struggle to face the truth that the grotesque is merely the observed in society, while it 'takes considerable courage not to turn away from the storyteller'.

In trying to reach into the depth of reality to the experience of mystery, O'Connor showed, like H.D., that we do not experience mystery by dissolving it with the light of reason or the structures of familiar logic. As a writer, O'Connor was interested in what we do not understand, not in what we do understand. She argued that meaning, then, only begins where science, sociology or psychology, for example, or other types of determinism, have been exhausted. Like Jane Bowles, she emphasized the importance of the unexpected in fiction to express mystery. The grotesque is one form which the unexpected can take in literature. Hence, her characters 'lean away from typical social patterns', but this abnormality of surface expresses in part the mystery of individuality and uniqueness. Indeed, authors who use the grotesque regarding characterization may not, O'Connor argued, consider their characters as anything other than ordinary, fallen human beings. Hence, the task of the author will be, in part, to bridge this gap between what is visible to the eyes of the author's imagination and what is visible to an audience unaccustomed to such 'prophetic vision', as she called it. Like Carson McCullers, then, O'Connor saw the freak, the misfit, the fanatic and so on as a symbolic figure representative of the essential displacement of all human beings. For her, the ordinary businessmen in their pin-striped suits are much more grotesque than the freaks she was writing about.

O'Connor described fiction as an *incarnational* art, in order to emphasize the importance of concreteness in the spiritual. For her, there was no question of heading straight for the spiritual without the mediation of matter; hence, the importance for her of concreteness of detail, of fleshing out ideas and emotions, and of drama and plot in her stories. Symbol exists only through concrete particulars of actions, place and character, and meaning arises out of symbols, defined as details which have their essential place in the literal level of the story, but which then operate in depth, expanding the meaning of the story in every direction. But, with Willa Cather before her, she emphasized also the importance of understatement; too much surface detail will obscure the depth which is the reality behind appearance. Moreover, O'Connor insisted that art is a way of having an experience (for both writer and reader) which is valuable in itself. This experience involves seeing different levels of reality in one image or one situation. Such 'prophetic vision' is needed by both writer and reader, and O'Connor's stories often depict a character experiencing such a moment of vision. In such epiphanic instants, moral judgement is shown to be part of the very act of seeing. Fact and value are not allowed to exist as if separable in human experience. Hence, facts change, reality changes, as our values are changed by transformations in our experiences of moral growth.

O'Connor placed great value on plot, on action, on drama in the short story. For her, narrative art was essentially a dramatic art; in fiction, especially in short stories, something has to happen, or else the art itself is missing, and you have another genre of writing – an essay, perhaps, a memoir, an impression, but not a story. Fiction for her was essentially dramatic, because what is involved in art is the having of experience, as the astute American philosopher John Dewey put it. That is, fiction is a plunge into reality for both writer and reader, shocking to the system, and hence essentially dramatic. Writing fiction and reading it are, O'Connor insisted, not an escape from reality, then, but a deepening of the sense of what reality is behind the visible veneer of appearance. Reading and writing involve a dramatic confrontation with the discrepancies between the visible world of the familiar and acceptable, and the invisible world of the uncanny and unfamiliar – the real. The writer, she believed, must be a 'realist of distances'. The look of such fiction, she explained, is going to be wild, violent, comic and grotesque, precisely because of the discrepancy it seeks to combine between the ordinary and the real but hidden.

Fiction, then, is essentially an experience, for both writer and reader. Each of them experiences a sharpening or increment in the organ of 'sight'. But this organ is understood by O'Connor to be both of the senses and of the intellectual and moral sphere. There is no possibility of separating these from each other. To see concrete particulars more clearly, to see facts, is to sharpen the moral judgement, to enhance the perception of values. This Blakean/Nietzschean process of enhancing the organs of perception as the sole means of developing the imaginative and spiritual realms of our being is depicted in each of O'Connor's fictions, but in a different way. Each of her stories is a unique individuality which requires fresh attention from the reader if an aesthetic/moral experience is to be achieved. By cleansing the doors of perception, O'Connor shocks her readers into a view of the grotesqueness of normal, everyday lives and transforms our experience. As Elizabeth Bishop wryly remarked: 'Critics who accuse her of exaggeration are quite wrong . . . I lived in Florida for several years . . . Nothing Flannery O'Connor ever wrote could seem at all exaggerated to me.' Whether we live in Florida or London, O'Connor's stories are no more grotesque than the life around us, if only we take a long look.

Margaret Laurence 1926–1987

Born and reared in Neepawa, Manitoba, Laurence did most of her writing when she was not living in her native Canada. Her famous Manawaki series of five volumes was written after she settled with her daughter and son in England in 1962. Not yet an established writer, Laurence published *The Tomorrow-Tamer* (Toronto and London, 1963), a collection of short stories set in west Africa (published as *New Wind in a Dry Land*, New York, 1964). She drew from her own experience of living in Somaliland, 1950–2, and in Ghana, 1952–7. During that period, she collected Somali poetry and tales, which she translated and published as *A Tree for Poverty* (Nairobi, 1954), and she wrote *The Prophet's Camel Bell* (Toronto and London, 1963), an account of her life and travels in east Africa. Her first novel, *This Side Jordan* (Toronto, London and New York, 1960), was written during a brief period between Ghana and England while she was in Canada, and she also published collections of essays and four children's books. She was a fellow of the Royal Society of Canada, and started to live fairly permanently in Ontario by 1972, where she resided until her early death at 61. In 1971 she was made a Companion of the Order of Canada.

The Manawaki series was published between 1964 and 1974, and comprises four novels and one collection of linked stories. The volumes are *The Stone Angel* (Toronto, London and New York, 1964); *A Jest of God* (Toronto, London and New York, 1966), made into the film *Rachel, Rachel*; *The Fire-Dwellers* (Toronto, London and New York, 1969); *A Bird in the House*, the stories (Toronto, London and New York, 1970); and *The Diviners* (Toronto, New York and London, 1974). For the second and final books she was awarded the Governor General's Award. These five volumes represent a remarkable range of characters, narrative techniques and subject matter, beginning with a 90-year-old woman surveying her past while living her last few weeks of the present. Told in the first person, the novel reveals to the reader not a middle-class, educated young woman's travails in love and at work; Laurence steps out of traditional mid-twentieth-century social realist subject matter, style and narrative time, into a world of small-town women and men struggling to gain some control over the pressures of the parochialism and conventionality which threaten the educated and uneducated, the middle-class and lower-class alike. By extensive adaptation of modernist techniques (and resistance to the prevailing neo-realism of the 1960s), Laurence fleshes out a world picture which could rival any realist panorama, but by means of harnessing both the force of the subjective, limited, first person narrative point of view of 90-year-old, crotchety Hagar Shipley, and the power of systematic flashbacks which constitute much of the novel. The constant interruption of the present narrative time with past memories, fantasies and reveries forges a 'literary time' which has a powerful aesthetic effect upon the readers.

Like Vita Sackville-West's *All Passion Spent* (1931), Molly Keane's *Time After Time* (1983) or Cynthia Ozick's *The Shawl* (1989), *The Stone Angel* shocks the reader into a rare sympathy with elderly people, into an intimacy with their humanity which is often forgotten in our too-frequent penchant for dismissing them as unfeeling, inhuman. In addition to this social-moral effect of compassion and imaginative identification, Laurence also created a technically fine narrative style, overcoming the chasm between present and past, young and old, as she revealed indirectly to the reader the mythologizing and sentimentalizing of the past. Indeed, Laurence's preoccupation with how one is ever to reconstruct one's past without distorting it beyond any meaningful truth or accuracy is the central theme of all of her five Manawaki volumes, with the possible exception of *A Jest of God*. Even there, Rachel Cameron changes her present life only because a shockingly painful experience has given her a new view of her past fifteen years of waiting futilely for something to happen. Her past, brilliantly personified in her intolerable mother, ceases to tyrannize over her only when she reaches out for illicit passion, and, for the first time in fifteen years, actually lives in the present. Notably, this passion she embraces, which awakens her from her stupor, involves a complete disobedience, rupture, and rejection of everything she has been taught to respect and adhere to in order to be happy. Once again in the first person, Laurence's *Jest of God* also constitutes a rejection of the dominant literary conventions, as she revealed the stunning power of subjectivity, limited point of view and female experience to portray human life with truth and authority.

While *A Jest of God* touches upon lesbianism and religion, it also explores, in almost Herman Melville-like symbolism, Rachel's flirtation with death, suicide and birth. A touchingly funny encounter with the undertaker at midnight helps Rachel on her journey out of past sentimentality and into a new present. After all, it was her undertaker father's death which forced her to return to Manawaki after her escape at 18 to Winnipeg University. Nor is it accidental that Rachel and her mother are made to live above the funeral parlour. Death, symbolically, is directly beneath them, and will dominate their lives until Rachel, like her sister, drags her depressive mother away to (of course) California. Laurence's novel also raises interesting issues about the 'cancer' or illness of women who place too much emphasis upon children and child-bearing for their fulfilment. Indeed, this novel is her most explicit challenge to the sexist myth that whatever else women may achieve, they are first and foremost mothers. Rachel's pregnancy is not only literally an illness, after all; it is also a symbol for the destructiveness of equating womanhood with motherhood. *The Diviners* takes this theme even further, and shows Morag Gunn struggling with herself to make her life meaningful in ways that do not depend upon her daughter or her own maternity. Gunn is constantly worried that it is impossible to justify giving birth, bringing children into a harsh and difficult world, creating a centre of suffering that might have been spared. Through this Buddhistic conception of life as predominantly, at least, a wheel of suffering, Laurence introduces a social, personal and psychological conflict which few women or men writers have been prepared to explore fully. She no longer allows her protagonist to agonize merely over how to let her daughter lead her own independent life. Laurence shows Gunn facing up to the insoluble question of how to justify having children.

The Diviners is Laurence's most self-conscious novel, both in terms of personal issues discussed above, and in artistic terms. It is the final volume of the Manawaki series, and is also her last major (published) work of fiction. This novel is her most autobiographical, but autobiographical in the sense of exploring her developing consciousness as a writer of fiction, who has concerned herself throughout her career with exploring the way apparent limitations of language and memory can be transformed into strengths. Laurence, like Doris Lessing, reveals in her fiction almost Nietzschean reversals of truth and lie, reality and fiction, past and present, memory and imagination. And like Katherine Anne Porter, Laurence sought to expose the processes of nostalgia and sentimentalization which degrade language, memory and truth. Her fiction shows that the problem of the truth of the past is really the same as that of truth of the present – both are problematic because truth itself is so. For all our experiences occur from specific points of view, and the process of clarifying and focusing experience by language is narration, metaphor, 'arbitrary' order and so on. Laurence gradually discovered that these apparent limitations are only limitations when the concept of truth is misconstrued as objective, neutral and omnipotent. Once we understand that it is always only intersubjective, then weaknesses can be reassessed as strengths which reveal how language functions as our most powerful tool for social intercourse of all kinds, rather than as a means of inadequately representing some rational reality.

Harper Lee 1926–

Recipient of the Pulitzer Prize in 1961 (and various other awards) for her novel *To Kill a Mockingbird* (Philadelphia and London, 1960), Harper Lee became instantly famous as the (until then unknown) author of a book which captured the imagination of Americans, and sold over ten million copies in the next few years. Made into a film in 1962, it was never followed by that 'second novel' which Lee was said to have started shortly after this first major publication. Her publications include, consequently, only a couple of brief essays of a personal nature, in *McCalls* 89 (December 1961) and *Vogue* 137 (1961), and some reviews and editorials published in University of Alabama student publications, where Lee studied law between 1945 and 1950. She left for New York City to learn her writing trade shortly before she was due to finish her degree, having taken a year to attend Oxford University as an American exchange student. Lee supported herself in New York by working for an airline while she wrote stories and essays, which she eventually showed to a literary agent. Encouraged to expand one of the stories into a novel, Lee wrote the first version of *To Kill a Mockingbird*, and submitted it to Lippincott in 1954. She was advised to strengthen the structure, plot and unity of the novel, which she did, and it was then published in 1960 to considerable critical acclaim and to a popular reception.

Harper Lee was born in Monroeville, Alabama, a neighbour of Truman Capote, with whom she was friends until he left for the North at the age of 10. Each author has appeared as a character in the other's novels. Lee's novel is an apparently simple narrative (told from the point of view of a precocious 6–9-year-old girl) which introduces, however, complex social and moral issues in a skilful, technically accomplished way. While the overt thematics involve racism, prejudice, and the false allegation against a black man of rape of a white woman, these themes are also developed by Lee through sophisticated literary formalities to explore the significance of courage and its centrality for a meaningful life. While Lee was initially criticized by some overly literal-minded reviewers for trying to tell a morally and socially sophisticated story from the point of view of a young child – they called her project 'impossible' – it was her general reading public who proved how entirely possible and how aesthetically successful her plan was. The novel spans a period of three years in the life of a small-town Alabama society, yet it conveys universal human experiences, in part by means of a complex model of related oppositions and in part through symbols and symbolic characters, such as the mockingbird, the snowman and the village recluse. Moreover, Lee's central thematic pivot – the alleged rape of a white woman by a black man – uses symbol too, for it is a symbolic event which represents deep fears, hatreds and insecurities which are at the foundation of racism, sexism and other forms of prejudice. Still more interesting is the way she subordinated this thematic pivot to attend to processes of perception, judgement, observation and interpretation. As with Elizabeth Hardwick's *The Simple Truth* (1955), neither the rape nor even the trial of the rape is the subject matter of this remarkable novel. Rather, the subject matter is more properly understood as the efforts of the lawyer's children (and the reader) to grasp the events and formulate them to fit into a rational world view. This project is shown by Lee to be doomed to failure, and the children are initiated into the adult world, as the reader is initiated into a sophisticated novel if she or he realizes its covert subject matter.

The novel is a substantial technical achievement, at the level of both style and structure. While the publisher's readers had criticized the first, 1954 version as more like a series of linked stories than a novel, Lee was able to make use of her story-telling abilities – her talent for plot, situation, event and dialogue – to enrich the final version in ways best explained, perhaps, by Willa Cather some decades earlier, when she remarked that every good novel must contain within it a dozen or more stories. Nearly every incident in *To Kill a Mockingbird*, however apparently trivial, functions to further Lee's central theme, namely, courage – and its necessity if life is to be lived meaningfully. At one point in the novel, Lee makes Atticus Finch, the lawyer father of the narrator, Scout, explain what courage is in relation to a reformed woman drug addict who has recently died: 'It's when you know you're licked before you begin but you begin anyway and you see it through no matter what.' Atticus contrasts this with the conventional definition of courage, which often involves such notions as a man with a gun, and rejects this violence which parades as a virtue. This theme is at the heart of the novel, and it also describes the concept of 'tragedy,' especially Greek tragedy in literature. But the novel is not itself a tragedy, though it contains within it the tragedy of Tom Robinson, killed, violently, while trying to escape after a verdict of guilty reached by the racist jury in the face of clear proof of his innocence, as well as the tragedy of a society committed to forms of violence and racism. It is a novel which explores explicitly the means by which children can be brought up to reject such violence and prejudice. And the means, which are implied throughout, are essentially a knowledge of other people as fundamentally like ourselves, so that trivial differences of appearance, whether skin colour or facial type or whatever, are not allowed to create a mystique of differentness which is then used to justify cruelty and ill-treatment.

This theme of our common humanity, along with that of the courage required to realize it, recurs throughout the novel, which is built up out of a series of events expressing related sub-themes. These circulate around the central story of the allegation of rape, the trial, the verdict and the dramatic aftermath, when Scout and Jem are nearly killed, saved only by the village recluse, who had been a figure of fun and mockery. Lee draws on her considerable knowledge of judicial procedure and law, but the literal trial

is made by her to function as a symbol of life itself, as well as one of the process of maturation and moral development. Life is shown, in the novel, to be full of trials which demand both moral courage and practical intelligence, and these conscious, symbolic gestures of the author enrich the novel's narrative and formal levels. Lee's narrative point of view is also a central thematic meaning in the novel. For while many novelists have attacked deeply rooted prejudices against the elderly, Lee's fiction not only forces us to a greater respect for the mentality and moral sophistication of children; she also reveals how such respect for children from their earliest years is a crucial element in their later capacity for full moral development. The implication is quite clearly that children who are treated with condescension and who are subjected to authoritarian decisions at an early age will internalize this behaviour as their misguided ideal, and become that way themselves.

Ruth Prawer Jhabvala 1927–

Winner of the Booker Prize in 1975 for *Heat and Dust* (London), Jhabvala was born in Cologne, Germany, but fled to England in 1939 with her Polish parents. She attended school and London University before marrying an Indian and moving to Delhi in 1951, where she brought up a family while writing several novels and short stories. Since 1975, she has spent part of the year in New York, and has written numerous film scripts and screenplays as well as further novels. Her most recent novel, *Poet and Dancer* (London, 1993), is set in Manhattan, unlike most of her earlier novels and stories, which tend to have India not only as their setting but as their very subject matter. Her other novels include *Three Continents* (London, 1987), *In Search of Love and Beauty* (London, 1983), *The Nature of Passion* (London, 1956), *The House-Holder* (London and New York, 1960) and *A Backward Place* (New York, 1965), and several collections of short stories have appeared, such as *How I Became a Holy Mother and Other Stories* (London and New York, 1976), which combines two previous collections and an autobiographical introduction. In that introduction, Jhabvala discussed both the particular problem for Europeans of living in India and the more general problems of expatriates living 'abroad'. Like E.M. Forster and Henry James, Jhabvala was predisposed to explore the very problem of living at all, but located in the expatriate situation, which focuses human difficulties in a certain way. Her introduction also describes another theme of her novels, namely that of Indians themselves trying to find a way of living in India, especially middle-class, educated or 'Westernized' Indians in the midst of poverty and of material and social backwardness.

Yet, while the confrontation between East and West is usually the context, many of Jhabvala's novels and stories use this to focus upon a central problem in life of making the passage between childhood and adulthood, and the analogous passage from egotism and materialism to universality and spirituality. Indeed, sometimes the process of adjusting to a new country is presented as a powerful metaphor for these passages and for the adjustment necessary to cope with life as an adult, on one's own and without parents there to sort out emotional or financial difficulties as they always did when one was a child. Yet even this is only a metaphor for the passage from ordinary life to spiritual fulfilment. There is a suggestion in some of Jhabvala's fiction that living in a foreign country offers opportunities both for heightened self-consciousness and development and also for greater folly and failure than might be likely had one remained within the 'familiar' world.

Heat and Dust is arguably Jhabvala's most successful novel, and has been described as a 'minor masterpiece' by some critics. It is certainly her most sophisticated piece of fiction in terms of narrative structure, and it may have influenced A.S. Byatt's most impressive novel, *Possession* (1990). Like *Possession*, *Heat and Dust* is a development of the narrative convention of telling two apparently unrelated stories separated in time by fifty to a hundred years; at least one of the modern characters is related to one of the more distant figures; as the stories unfold, they begin to have an uncanny similarity, suggesting that the present is only ever a variation on the past.

Jhabvala's novel raises a host of fascinating issues, as a Pandora's box of irresolvable puzzles is opened by the double narration. 'What is individuality?' is an insistent query. More insistent still is the way in *Heat and Dust* Jhabvala

foregrounded the difficulty of reconstructing the past as analogous both to the problem of interpreting present happenings and to that of writing both history and fiction. And, of course, in the novel she explored the relations of history to reality, of fiction to history, and of fiction to reality. The novel proceeds with a first person narrative by one of the characters who has come to India, ostensibly to trace the story of her paternal grandfather's first wife, Olivia, 'who had eloped with an Indian prince'. The story is told by means of the 'I's' journal over a period of several months, alternating with quotations and paraphrases from letters Olivia allegedly wrote to her sister in 1923 over several months – in large part reconstructions of Olivia's feelings and experiences with the characters Douglass, Harry and others, which rarely refer to the letters as source and go beyond anything letters ordinarily convey. The uncanny sense of the present repeating the past, though in variation, is heightened both by the fact that Olivia and her modern counterpart become pregnant (presumably, but not definitely, by Indian men), and by the fact that the 'I' has 'returned to the (precise) scene' of Olivia's Indian life to reconstruct for herself Olivia's past, her 'story': 'this is not my story, it is Olivia's as far as I can follow it.' The unexpressed (and perhaps inexpressible) relation between 'my story' and 'Olivia's story', fiction or history and reality, history and fiction, haunts the novel as with an uncanny presence. The fact that the 'I' is unnamed and also has such direct access to Olivia's mind blurs the distinction between the two, and the distinction between the 'I', Olivia and the reader. Eventually, sub-themes running through the novel – at first involving the characters Chid, Maji and others – converge at the novel's end, as romantic love, spiritual passion for a higher life, and pregnancy are fused into a vision of 'staying on': not turning back, not going back to 'England', but going higher into such a full experiencing of life that there will be no going down again, no going back into the shelter of innocence, childhood, England or the familiar. In the journey into the exotic world of India – that metaphor for vision and imagination – cosy conventions and protective familiarities are left behind as Jhabvala portrayed a character – an everywoman – who is yet unfeminine, an androgynous being; who 'stayed on' for the sake of 'the view – or vision – that filled her eyes all those years and suffused her soul'.

Edna O'Brien 1932–

Greatly loved Irish writer of novels, stories, poetry and non-fiction prose, O'Brien was born in the west of Ireland. Recipient of the Yorkshire Post Award in 1971 for her fiction, she has also received much praise from fellow novelists and critics, including her Irish American contemporary Mary Gordon, John Berger, Philip Roth, John Updike and Clair Tomalin, amongst others. O'Brien immediately gained appreciation with *The Country Girls* (London and New York, 1960), one of her earliest publications, and followed shortly by *Girl with Green Eyes* (London, 1964) and *Girls in Their Married Bliss* (London, 1964), both sequels to the first novel about Baba and Kate. *August is a Wicked Month* (London and New York, 1965) and *Casualties of Peace* (London, 1966) portrayed unrelievedly the darker side of sexual involvements, while *A Pagan Place* (London and New York, 1971) moved, through impressionistic and imagistic first person narrative, into the mind of a young adolescent struggling with the shattering revelations of maturation. *Zee and Co.* (London, 1971) followed, a study of the eternal triangle; then came the remarkable *Night* (London, 1972), which John Updike so admired. Mary's stream of consciousness swirls the reader into a torrent of memories and emotions, of past events and people, of passion and pain in a captivating novel of compelling writing.

Throughout this period, various collections of short stories had been appearing, such as *The Love Object* (London, 1968), *A Scandalous Woman* (London and New York, 1974), *A Rose in the Heart* (Garden City, N.Y., 1979, earlier published as *Mrs Reinhardt* (London, 1978) and *Returning* (London, 1982). From these collections of stories, *A Fanatic Heart: Selected Stories of Edna O'Brien* was compiled (Harmondsworth, 1984). Other novels include *Johnny I Hardly Knew You* (London, 1977), a near-stream of consciousness depiction of a woman's mind as she is about to face trial for the murder of her young lover. More recent books are *Some Irish Loving* (London and New York, 1979), which is a collection of non-fiction essays, fragments and poems on love by numerous Irish writers, as well as *The Dazzle* (London, 1981) and *A Christmas Treat* (London, 1982).

While O'Brien is usually known for her novels and stories of overt romance, obsessive love and the pain of mother–daughter relationships, her power as a writer who can chisel intense emotion into the bed-rock of ordinary language is underestimated. Her fiction represents a much wider range than the popular or academic image of her as the author only of the *Girl with Green Eyes* or *The Country Girls* would suggest. For it includes explorations of language and narrative conventions which constitute a painful protest against imprisoning, prejudiced images of women writers, young women in love, and also mothers as busy with the 'trivial' matters of marriage, child-bearing, romance and human relations generally. The vigour, clarity and sparseness of her writing, combined with a probing analysis of the human psyche, make her a novelist worthy of detailed study. Nearly every one of her novels from the 1960s onwards is an experiment in the conventions of fiction. Many of them, like Jean Rhys's or Stevie Smith's earlier texts, are meditations on the genre of the popular romance, which exceed that genre in numerous interesting ways. For not only is O'Brien a craftswoman of lucid, sparse language for intense emotions and a visionary of the human psyche; she has also explored numerous narrative devices, such as extensive variation in point of view, stream of consciousness, use of memory and flashback, and the power of place as an emblem of the psychological terrain being explored. Sometimes, she has emphasized typically realist devices of detailed description of setting, landscape and exterior events or plot. At other times, O'Brien has shown herself to be most fluent with later, typically modernist devices, which emphasize interiority, materiality of language, split psyches and plotlessness. Clearly influenced by her great predecessors Kate O'Brien, Rhys, Elizabeth Bowen, Molly Keane and Virginia Woolf, O'Brien has learned from them all, and recognition of her achievements is only delayed by the prejudices which have blinded and continue to blind readers to the artistry, self-consciousness and sophistication of many women writers.

Already in the early novels of the 'country'

girls, O'Brien was interested in the external forces which act on human feelings, especially women's, to encourage emotional maturation, moral growth and personal independence, or to inhibit them. Contrasts between the country and the city, Ireland and England, Catholicism and Protestantism, and innocence and experience are deftly intertwined to reveal the falsity of such oppositions and such analogies. In 1965, with *August is a Wicked Month*, O'Brien was extending the grasp of narrative point of view and thematic complexity. With *A Pagan Place*, she moved into new, Proustian territory, reconstructing a young girl's past as part of her existential struggles to achieve a future self-construction. *Night* pushes further into memory reconstruction; dispensing even more with plot than in the previous text, which has little enough, this time O'Brien treated not innocence but experience. Narrative conventions of journeys and travel to foreign territory are invoked in invigorating ways to give fresh power to these ancient metaphors.

These two novels lay the groundwork for *Johnny I Hardly Knew You*, one of O'Brien's finest achievements – a skilfully shaped novel, which circles round upon itself to demand a new reading, using the images of imprisonment and trial as emblematic of woman's estate, but also of language and literature themselves. Structures of signification both ensnare and liberate the character who is trying to understand her tragic action, while the reader sees herself or himself equally grasping at meaning. Meaning, however, flits away tantalizingly, while the text remains more full of colour and energy in flight than if pinned down, as it ends self-referentially: 'Dawn, day, dark, frost, cloud, sprinkling, icicle, a fall of snow, bare places covered over, sparrows and red wings, daisy, hollyhock, wall marigolds . . . Ah ye world that I hold dear, soon now you will be slipping away.'

Susan Sontag 1933–

One of America's most admired and famous non-fiction prose writers, Sontag is the renowned author of several major works of non-fiction, as well as novels, short stories and plays. Born in New York City, she grew up in Arizona and California, but took degrees from Chicago and Harvard before

spending time at Oxford in 1957. She has taught philosophy at various American universities, directed films, and received Rockefeller, Guggenheim, MacArthur Foundation and American Association of University Women fellowships, and numerous other awards and grants. Her fiction includes *The Benefactor* (New York, 1963), *Death Kit* (New York, 1967), *I, Etcetera* (New York, 1978; a collection of stories), *The Way We Live Now* (New York, 1991) and *The Volcano Lover: A Romance* (New York, 1992). Her non-fiction includes *On Photography* (New York, 1977), which won the National Book Critics Circle Award; the earlier collection of essays, *Against Interpretation* (New York, 1966), which first established her as a major figure; *Trip to Hanoi* (New York, 1968); and *Styles of Radical Will* (New York, 1969), another collection of essays. These were followed by *Illness as Metaphor* (New York, 1978); then her third major collection of essays, *Under the Sign of Saturn* (New York, 1980), including a remarkable piece on Walter Benjamin; and *Aids and its Metaphors* (New York, 1988). *A Susan Sontag Reader*, intro. Elizabeth Hardwick (New York, 1982), contains, amongst other things, Sontag's famous essay on Roland Barthes.

Sontag's fiction and non-fiction are in constant dialogue with each other. While this is true of many writers who have written both, it is more marked with Sontag's work, so that the reader steeped in both streams gains a richer appreciation of both her intelligence and her achievements. In her (in)famous essay in 1964, 'Against Interpretation', Sontag daringly ended with, 'In place of hermeneutics we need an erotics of art.' Already in this early essay, revealing aesthetic and philosophical commitments expounded by, most especially, Barthes in the decades to come, Sontag made clear her impatience with the mode of criticism of art prevalent throughout most of the twentieth century. This mode, she argued, sought to tell us what art means; it sought to analyse and 'intellectualize' what is pre-eminently aesthetic. It used analytical categories of biography, politics, history, economics, morality or religion, sociology, psychoanalysis and so on, instead of appreciating art as a distinctly aesthetic experience. She argued that, even with the New Criticism, which sought to restore distinctively aesthetic appreciation to art, a tendency towards analysis and abstraction prevailed, as the unique, particular and sensuous delight of works of art was subordinated to analytical models and structures for 'explaining art'.

In both her fiction and her prose non-fiction, then, Sontag has sought above all to restore pleasure and delight to aesthetic experience. Criticism and interpretation, she has explained, *do* have a function, but that function is not to tell us what texts mean or how they should be rated. Rather, interpretation can function to help us to learn how to respond to art with pleasure, by improving our 'vision', our appreciation, our insight (not into what texts mean but) into how art 'is what it is', even 'that it is what it is'. Criticism, that is, eroticizes our response to art by helping us to reawaken our dulled senses: 'What is important now is to recover our senses. We must learn to *see* more, to *hear* more, to *feel* more.' Sontag (like John Dewey some forty years earlier) has sought to liberate art from criticism/interpretation which reduced its meaning to categories other than the aesthetic. Criticism, then, ignored art's most salient, characteristic being, namely, that which initiates an aesthetic experience – an experience of pleasure arising from a gradual culmination of feeling, which is essentially erotic in the broad, Freudian sense of the word.

Sontag's fiction embodies these aesthetic and philosophical insights, first, by challenging realist assumptions about the nature of art as representational of 'reality', and therefore as a coded commentary on reality in metaphorical, verbal and other forms which the critic must decipher to reveal the message. She has argued that criticism should not view art as something to be replaced essentially by something else (commentary, meaning, message or story). This attitude debases both criticism and art: both are 'depleted' and 'impoverished'. Her fiction and non-fiction explore how criticism can function differently to reveal not meanings (through paraphrase, or 'in other words', as Eudora Welty complained). Criticism can function in a new way to reveal artifacts as what they are and how they are – their sensuousness, their luminosity, their erotic, pleasurable character as fundamental to aesthetic experience. In this insistence upon restoring pleasure to the text or artifact, Sontag anticipated the direction of criticism, theory and art

too for the rest of the twentieth century. She may have been unaware that she was extending the shared and continuous tradition of Dewey, William James and the Romantics, who had also sought to preserve the essential sensuousness of aesthetic experience against over-intellectuality. Their method was slightly different from Sontag's. They knew that while thought can become divorced from feeling and the senses through empty abstraction and intellectualizing, it is nevertheless rooted in them for its very existence. Sontag knew her Nietzsche, but she knew less well Dewey (and his embracing of much of Nietzsche on art), Coleridge and Blake, perhaps – or chose not to recognize them.

Her fiction of the 1960s and 1970s challenges our notions of reality, like so much fiction of the period – as, for example, that of Marguerite Young, Leonora Carrington, Ann Quin and Christine Brooke-Rose. Later, Kathy Acker carried on Sontag's eroticism of art, extending the tradition of Anaïs Nin, Henry Miller and others, though their more explicit, overt sexuality is evident. Sontag, like Young and Quin, adapted modernist rejections of plot, causality, traditional narrative time as sequence, language as transparent, and so on, in order to try to prevent the reader or observer from maintaining a separateness from the artifact which obstructed aesthetic response (as opposed to other kinds of response). Like Brecht, for example, she was aware that a too-unselfconscious immersion in the subject matter, plot, story or thematics and ideas of a work of art actually inhibits aesthetic/erotic appreciation. By frustrating clear thematics or unambiguous story-lines in her novels and short fictions, she has sought to direct the reader to an immersion (not into what happens to somebody else, but) into 'the very processes of seeing and knowing'. This attention has sometimes been described as meta-fictional or even meta-aesthetic, but Sontag has shown that this is the aesthetic *par excellence*. Art, then, itself directs the reader's attention towards not merely content or form, but towards the way any particular work of art is unique in achieving a congruence of form and content. Thus, art and criticism are close relations, and inhere in each other, since criticism must be 'artful' in helping us to cleanse our doors of perception if it is to be criticism worthy of the name, and not some poor substitute.

In *The Benefactor*, Sontag created a radical ambiguity about 'reality', as she did later in *Death Kit*. The distinction between inner and outer is not sustained, as what the characters 'actually' do, as opposed to what they imagine, dream or think they do, is irresolvable. Related issues about the reality of the self – 'Which self is real?', 'What is a self?', 'Is it one or many?' – arise, as does the problem of freedom and free will. But these thematic elements are not allowed to distract the reader from the processes of perception, thought and feelings themselves. The results of those processes are always presented as ambiguous in meaning, and in need of constant reconnection with those which construct them. Her most recent novel, *The Volcano Lover*, is an inventive post-modernist reconstruction of the historical romance which lays bare the conventions of such a novel and its thematic resource in order to 'pleasure' the reader by illuminating its nature as a work of art – why it is, how it is, what it is.

Ann Quin 1936–1973

Radically experimental novelist of the 1960s and early 1970s, Quin published four novels in her short life, and a portion of a fifth appeared after her death. Her first novel, *Berg* (London, 1964), was well received and won her the D.H. Lawrence Award in 1964 and a Harkness Fellowship in 1964–7, which made it possible for her to complete her second novel, *Three* (London and New York, 1966). *Passages* appeared in 1969 (London), and her final published novel, *Tripticks*, in 1972 (London). After her death, a portion of an unfinished fifth novel, 'The Unmapped Country', was published in *Beyond the Words*, ed. Giles Gordon (London, 1975), a collection of experimental writing. Quin also wrote several short stories and two early unpublished novels; her papers can be found in the Lilly Library, University of Indiana, Bloomington. Born in Brighton, Quin left school early to pursue theatre and writing interests; she apparently suffered from several breakdowns, and her death by drowning is thought by some to have been suicide.

Like her immediate contemporary Marguerite Young, Quin rejected realist writing as the greatest fantasy of all, and questioned some of the most basic assumptions which inform both the writing of fiction and our grasp of the world. That is, her fiction dispenses with notions of the centrality of certain kinds of order in our mental lives, and challenges the centrality of logical, rational meaning. Familiar order and logic, her novels suggest, are far less basic and 'native' to our experience than is normally admitted, either in philosophy or in fiction. The realist imposition of order through its various conventions is quite arbitrary and unrepresentative of our experience. As one reads Quin's fiction, from *Berg* through to *Tripticks*, progressive experimentation with new means of depicting consciousness and experience is evident. All her novels raise, in slightly different ways, questions about personal identity and individuality – the multiplicity of the self and its relations to other 'selves' – questions about the relation of fantasy to reality, or, more accurately, the fantasy which reality is, and about language and literature and how they function in our lives. Quin's fiction represents a search for literary and linguistic techniques for depicting and expressing inner consciousness which avoid the conventional assumptions of order and wholeness that cut us off from other possible experiences and perceptions.

For example, in *Passages*, the narrative proceeds by means of a radical alternation between chapters composed of first/third person mixed authorship, short passages, and pieces from a diary with marginal notes. Each chapter is predominantly authored by a woman and a man, presumably lovers, who are constantly travelling 'because' the woman is in search of her dead brother. Nearly all Quin's novels involve thematically a quest, the commitment to which by the character is usually ambivalent, and the object of which is never achieved. Both *Passages* and *Tripticks* take the ancient, worn-out literary convention of the journey, and infuse it with new life and new significance, as Quin played upon the word 'passages' to mean paragraphs, journeys and life itself as time. Moreover, *Passages* is littered with 'plagiarism' and unacknowledged borrowings from other literature, as she wove, for example, notebook entries from Coleridge on dreams, first and second consciousness, and single and double touch into her narrative of passages.

Eschewing not only realist conventions of

order, such as plot and description, Quin also 'unravelled' distinct character identities. For example, in her second novel, *Three*, the three characters lose their distinctness, as the characters in *Passages* do. In *Tripticks*, the single character's consciousness seems to merge into the almost surreal world of her perceptions, so that characters merge both into each other and into the world. This had already occurred in *Berg*, where fantasy and reality, memory and perception, present and past are jumbled together. Yet *Tripticks*, with its marvellously effective use of pop art scattered throughout the novel (sometimes in the margins, sometimes at the centre, sometimes over the whole page) and its anticipations of Kathy Acker's pop art tone, is a genuine advance on *Berg*. All Quin's novels share a refusal to present experience by means of familiar dichotomous categories, distinctions, hierarchies and orderings. Unconscious fantasies of sex and violence intensify and eroticize the conscious perceptions of the characters. In all the novels, the distinction between outer and inner is non-existent: consciousness *is* reality. Reality is not characterized by wholeness or order so much as by fragmentation, jumble and multivalent layers of immediate perception, thought, fantasy, dialogue and memory mixed into a discontinuous, ongoing passage of language.

Quin's novels use their thematics explicitly to explore how language can construct experience, and how language can function to reveal experience in fresh ways. Her novels are a reminder of how stereotyped our experiences can become if we forget that our modes of organization are mere conventions. And they remind us that there is no absolute separation between life and art: to be concerned as a novelist about language, the novel as a form and modes of articulation is not to ignore life. Our most central conceptions about life, from personal identity to relationship with others, from the value of work or love or money to how we cope with illness and loss – all those 'life' issues are dependent for understanding upon our grasp of how language, logic and other forms of order shape our experience. Quin's overt experiments with logic, order and language, and her efforts to find new ways of ordering the chaos of our experience – in order to reveal new values and new facets of it – go to the heart of how we cope with life and make life meaningful. Her novels can be said perhaps to express William Blake's conviction that either we create our own system or else we are enslaved by another's. *Tripticks'* final sentences are these: 'I opened my mouth, but no words. Only the words of others I saw, like ads, texts, psalms, from those who had attempted to persuade me into their systems. A power I did not want to possess. The Inquisition.' This is followed by six drawings of portions of a building, the final one of which is a staircase disappearing upwards into a wall.

Part IV

Further Internationalism, Diversification and Experimentation, 1970–1995

Chapter 10

Post-Structuralist Theory and Fiction

Post-structuralist theory, like post-modernist literature and magic realism, has been much influenced by early twentieth-century psychological writings, by modernism, and by the development of the 'new literatures in Englishes'. It has done much to expose and encourage the dismantling of authoritarian, patriarchal structures in literature and in life. Through its analysis of dualism and phallocentrism in language, it has influenced fiction writers and poets, and encouraged astute articulation of feminist theory, theory about post-colonial literatures, and gender and gay theory. Its political implications have been greater than the more overtly politicized formulations such as Marxist literary theory and the new historicism, contrary to much opinion. For post-structuralism challenged the hidden ideologies – those 'natural attitudes' which are the basis of restrictive ideologies. By comparison, the politics of Marxism and historicism are limited, the one by a profoundly sexist refusal to include women in class liberation, the other by a return to historical dualisms (history/text, reality/art) which repeat Marxist basis/superstructure dualisms and reinstate old hierarchies and categories as 'natural' realities.

Strong influences from Nietzsche with his existentialist, pragmatist orientation, along with the later philosophies of language of Martin Heidegger and Ludwig Wittgenstein, and the deconstruction of Western metaphysics by John Dewey and William James, have operated on theorists since the 1930s particularly, from Jacques Lacan to Mikhail Bakhtin, Roland Barthes, Jacques Derrida, Julia Kristeva and Michel Foucault, for example. These influences refocused intellectual literary debate, in both fiction and non-fiction, explicitly and systematically around language and discourse, for the first time in nearly a hundred years, since German and English Romantic philosophers and poets had taken up and re-examined Berkeley, Hume and other eighteenth-century language theorists and their relation to Plato, Aristotle and the Neo-Platonists. Borrowing much from the English and German Romantics, Nietzsche, Dewey and James elaborated for philosophy what the French theorists were to bring later to literary theory and criticism. Nietzsche's influence was probably first mediated through Freud, while Dewey and James were – as part of a revival of Americana after World War II – studied extensively at the Sorbonne and elsewhere. It is unlikely that any student or teacher in the late 1940s and 1950s would not have learned Dewey and James, as well as their great precursor Charles Sanders Peirce, thoroughly. Peirce is an acknowledged source of early structuralist ideas about language as a system of arbitrary signs or symbols, while James, almost contemporaneously, began the deconstruction of metaphysics with *Pragmatism* (Cambridge, Mass., 1907) and *The Meaning of Truth* (Cambridge, Mass., 1909).

It was Dewey, in *Experience and Nature* (Chicago, 1925), who began the systematic twentieth-century revolution in philosophy which has continued into the present day, through Willard van Orman Quine, Nelson Goodman and other philosophers of language, to influence literary writers, critics and theorists such as Derrida. In attending to the role of discourse, Dewey subjected language to close scrutiny to clarify its impact upon human experience, and both Heidegger and Wittgenstein followed this direction later. Communication through some form of language – some kind of system of artificial, arbitrary signs – was said by Dewey to be the very condition of consciousness. That is, paradoxical as it may sound at first, mind emerges, and events and objects become perceptible and identifiable, only through 'concretion in discourse'. (Or, as Coleridge had put it a hundred years before, to think is to 'thingify'.) By thinking with language, we thingify or make objective and perceptible – bring into conscious existence or awareness – things and events, whether mental or physical. Brute, meaningless, undifferentiated chaos turns into objects and subjects, into things with meanings, through articulation in language. Things pass from the plane of external pushing and pulling to that of revealing themselves to humans because language concretizes them, and enables us to live in a world of things which have *meaningful* existence. However, unlike the Platonist theorist, who mistook the structure of discourse for the structure of nature or things in themselves, Dewey, like James and Nietzsche, recognized these structures as social constructions – the forms which things and events assume under the influence of social cooperation amongst human beings. He rejected, then, the essentialist, absolutist mistake of taking a work of human social art for a nature independent (and argued that Platonists, not Plato, had made this error). This 'outness prejudice', as we might call it, is at the root of all dualisms and essentialisms, and its exposure has laid the foundations for many of the insights of post-structuralist theories. Of all things, communication and language are, Dewey reminded us, the most wonderful and the most in need of study. For they affect our lives in all areas of experience.

Mind, also, is a social product, not a natural one, except in so far as social life is itself natural, of course, in the practical sense of the word. Mind emerges, as does meaning, through the shared social practices of communication and exchange. While words, things and meanings

certainly correspond to each other, they cannot properly be said to correspond prior to discourse, Dewey pointed out. Further, the world of inner experience is also dependent upon the extension of language: thinking and conscious awareness are a result of social communication and not prior to it. Or as Derrida later phrased it, both speech and inner speech (the thinking once called a private language) cannot be prior to the social institution of language, represented by, say, writing. Language and the distinctive thought made possible by it are not spiritual, non-material, supernatural events, however. They are the natural functionings of human beings in association and interaction. Moreover, language leads to the increased significance of objects and natural events, for through language, bare physical events are enriched and accrue character. They become more than mere occurrences without significance because they take on, via language, perceivable consequences, implications and results. The reasoning and inference which are made possible by language, and which then influence the further development of language into greater sophistication, involve 'reading the message of things, which things utter because they are involved in human association'.

The age-old dualism of the rational and the sensible, which has had an effect upon literature and the arts and their perceived value relative to science in revealing truths, can be shown to be one merely of application, not of essence. That is, rational categories describe the relatively extensive operations of things in relation to each other, on the one hand, while the sensible describes local, restricted interactions of things, on the other. No person or thing is merely individual and solitary; everything, in so far as it is known and knowable, is in interaction with other things. This associative element in all existence Dewey called 'participation', following that early 'sceptic', Socrates; Dewey suggested that participation rather than referentiality is at the heart of linguistic practices. Meaning is the direct result of this participatory, cooperative sharing in human discourse. Words, for example, accrue meaning when use of a sound establishes a genuine community of action, and words have numerous meanings which vary with new conditions and new intentions or experiences. Essences are the result of taking one meaning and then hypostasizing that partiality into a primary and constitutive form of existence.

Hence, words are not arbitrary in meaning, exactly. As results of communal modes of social interaction, they are objective in being intersubjective, but not in the sense of being absolute and unchangeable. Like words, our values and beliefs are also only objective in that sense: they are not merely subjective, either, because they are not the products of an exclusively individual mental state. The same comments apply to works of art, which are never the products of an exclusively individual mental state, for no such state exists: individuality and consciousness only exist because of social, communal interaction. To create a work of art is to participate intensely, actively in a communal practice. Thus, artifacts are variously meaningful and variously valuable and like all linguistic utterances, spill out beyond intentions or responses in quite unlegislatable ways.

The foregoing review of the roots of post-structuralist theory in early twentieth-century thought shows how fundamental is the analysis of language as the condition of human consciousness. Nature and mind both emerge from concretion in discourse; language is shown to be a social, communal and quite natural, not a spiritual, supernatural practice, and meaning is the result of usage and practice, not the discovery of essences or ideal structures. These insights cleared the path of twentieth-century theorists and led to specific analyses of prejudices in literature and in society. Post-structuralism, with its feet firmly planted in this thoroughly political-social analysis of language, led further by drawing on insights from Ferdinand de Saussure, Nietzsche and Freud, and by recognizing the import of this re-emphasis upon language for literary criticism and literature, not to mention the extension to other disciplines. The profoundly democratic, anti-authoritarian, anti-patriarchal spirit of these earlier insights informs post-structuralism at all levels, and makes it a powerful tool for feminist critics and theorists of the new literatures in Englishes.

Challenges arising out of the deconstruction of metaphysics through the better understanding of language have involved related queries as to what constitutes a literary text and how one decides this. What kind of special language is literary language, and how does literature differ from philosophy, criticism, history or autobiography, for example? Who legislates, and according to what rules? Moreover, how is the meaning of a text determined, how much is the author's intention a limiting factor, and what is the role of the critic? What is the relation of literature to the world, to history, to reality? Do authors act as individuals, or more as tools of powerful, external forces of economic, biological or social nature? Correlatively, what is a reader's role; indeed, what do we do when we read? How much do we project, and how much do we discover? Is interpretation objective or subjective? Indeed, what is a text? Is it a repository of discoverable meanings, or a site for appropriation, conquest or play by the reader/critic?

Most readers will be familiar with post-structuralist challenges to the unconscious assumptions of some literary practices and criticism. In the systematic insistence that the questions above need reflection, post-structuralists examined nearly every assumption of traditional, literary practice. They came to emphasize multiplicity of interpretation, perspectivism or limitedness of any one point of view, and the difficulty of evaluating, once familiar conceits and hidden assumptions behind familiar practices were exposed. These orthodox, generally accepted practices were shown to be saturated with hidden ideologies, prejudices and partialities, while pretending to objectivity and professionalism. Evaluative abilities went wildly wrong, as texts such as Kate O'Brien's *Mary Lavelle*, Ellen Glasgow's *The Sheltered Life*, Susan Glaspell's *Trifles*, May Sinclair's *Mary Olivier*, Jean Rhys's *Voyage in the Dark* and Rebecca West's *The Judge* (to name the merest few) were consigned by male professionals to the dustbin of obscurity. Immature and sometimes even emotionally vapid texts by men were raised to canonical status, and all this on objective, literary merits, it was alleged. Post-structuralist audacity has turned into that quiet voice of reason which Freud hoped would be able to penetrate the depths of unreason and rob it of its energy.

Some of the most interesting results, for interpretative reading practices as well as for creative writing, have been an investigation of desire, the erotic and the sexual nature of all literary activity. Relatedly, individual readers or writers are revealed as projecting themselves into the thematics of the text when they are least aware of such autobiographical activity. The effort to keep erotics out of decorous (or indecorous!) literature and criticism, and to keep the self out too, has been shown to be a naïve illusion. The gradual increase in theorizing about autobiography in both literature and criticism, whether in reading or writing, revolves around the idea of desire as inherent in language. Language, which is said to be the structure of the unconscious, is permeated with sexuality and portents of desire which can be repressed but not eradicated. The traces can be found scattered liberally throughout the text, in the puns, metaphors, images, thematics; in the gaps, flaws and alleged infelicities or weaknesses of the text.

Such reflections have led to an increased sensitivity to ideas about the multiplicities and indeterminacies of self, text, language and reality. Ideas of the unity of the text are displaced by notions of split and fractured layers of the text with inconsistent meanings; language itself, from the word to the whole text, is shown to be a 'heteroglossia', with centrifugal and centripetal forces acting to preserve the old while transforming it by the new. Theorists such as Bakhtin, then later Barthes and Derrida, for example, have shown language to be inherently ambiguous, sexually, sinisterly insinuating and self-referring, whatever the 'intentions' of the author or reader. Like the word or sentence of language, the text exceeds the control of author, reader or critic; its meaning cannot be successfully legislated, any more than the unconscious can be fully interpreted or known. 'Interminable analysis' applies to the text as to the psyche, and ideas of play are gradually replacing those of criticism as legislation and prescription. Contextual/historical/biographical material is seen as just as likely to mislead as to inform; however interesting it may be intrinsically, it can no more legislate the limits of acceptable interpretation than can author, critic or reader. This loss of the legislation of meaning and value has come as a relief to those who have been impressed by the bigotry and sexism of earlier legalities.

Such rampant relativity and unlimited perspectivism have been anathema to many critics; but others have grasped the opportunity to deconstruct old hierarchies and ideologies, and replace them with more pluralistic, democratic, less canonically oriented approaches to writing, reading and criticism. Much of this perspectivism can be traced to Nietzsche most recently, and expressed more clearly through his ideas about the revaluation of all values, which are pertinent to all the recent revaluations by marginalized people. Related to Foucault's later excavations into language, Nietzsche's ideas revolve around the central theme of the 'will to power', which results in the fabrication of the world, the self, society and all morality and religion along the lines of artistic fabrication and making processes. This power agenda involves what Nietzsche called 'appropriation', or the making like of things, and has clear implications for theorists of post-colonial literature, feminists and gay theorists. As in eating, where we take into our bodies an unlike substance and transform it into our body, so, in mental processes, consciousness involves making unlike things like, through, for example, metaphor. Overcoming differences, we create a world of experience through appropriative, metaphoric processes which are merely a mirror of bodily ones. These latter must be repressed and forgotten if consciousness is to emerge; otherwise we would be swamped by them. Beauty, truth and the good are merely aesthetic anthropomorphisms, not traits of some notional reality. The process of knowledge and revelation of meaning is not the gradual disclosure of truth about reality. It is, Nietzsche argued, merely the incessant appropriation, through figuration and interpretation, of prior interpretations, appropriations and figures of speech. There is nothing original or originary, and the mind is just as much a function of metaphor-making and appropriation as is the world. Mind, self, the subject, nature, world and reality are figures of speech, effects of language. Finally, appropriation can function either to exploit others or to empower ourselves and others, as Foucault was later to argue in his reinterpretation of Nietzsche.

These Nietzschean insights run as central strands through post-structuralist theorizing. Geoffrey Hartman's question opens the debate:

'What complexity have we overlooked in forgetting reading, reducing it to the status of mere passivity?' Moreover, he asked, what is it even to 'open a reading' and to make reading more active play? This challenge to traditional critical assumptions involved the necessity for an increasingly self-conscious reading. The subversion of the concept of the 'book', this closed, univocally meaningful representation of reality, was occasioned by the concept of the 'text', that organic tissue of ever-changing relations, which reached out into the world and textualized reality itself by refusing the dichotomy between frame and content, representation and represented. Barthes added to the fray by talking of reading as a 'form of life', as Wittgenstein had written of language behaviours. Barthes erased the dichotomy between writers and readers, and spoke of 'writerly readers' and 'readerly writers', readerly texts and textualized readers. In his rejection of the law-abiding search for author's intent or best interpretation, Barthes reintroduced the notion of desire and eroticism, of autobiography in all writing and criticism. Readers rewrite the text according to their desire, while writers re-read earlier written texts according to their own desires, in a constant process of plagiarism and influence, conscious and unconscious.

Other critics such as Hillis Miller and Barbara Johnson elaborated on these ideas, with notions of reading and criticism as a 'lateral dance' of meanings and movements, leading to a proliferation and dissemination of meaning as opposed to univocity, in Miller. Johnson wrote about 'engendering textuality' and the subversion of textual identity for 'difference within'. This involves both insoluble ambiguity of meaning and a rejection of new historicist dualities between text and reality. The 'difference' between text and reality inhabits each, so to speak: reality is textual because it is a construction out of language, and already interpreted. Moreover, a central character of our real lives is our constant narration of what happens, our textualizing of experiences to make them intelligible, meaningful and even real.

In addition to Miller and Johnson, Harold Bloom and Paul de Man have contributed to the interpretation and elaboration of post-structuralist theorizing, with ideas of reading as basically 'misreading' and misprision, and of influence from previous writers being so great as to lead to intertextuality as the substance of all texts. All readings, that is, are partial and inevitably incomplete, even erroneous. For de Man, reading, moreover, is not a hermeneutics, or decoding of a message to reveal truth, but a disseminative activity. Reading is not the determination of truth but the proliferation of possibilities for response and effects which a text offers. Moreover, all texts are inhabited by the allegory of ways of reading them, through rhetorical, figurative language. Indeed, for some critics, texts contain not only allegories of reading, but ironic portrayals of criticism as well as self-critical gestures. Criticism for these critics is not a search for meaning or truth, since language is essentially, not ornamentally metaphoric, equivocal and indeterminate. Truth is an 'army of metaphors . . . truths are illusions whose illusory nature has been forgotten', to quote Nietzsche. Truth, univocal meaning and knowledge are relinquished for 'écriture/writing', valuable for its performative play rather than constative meaning. Criticism is reconceived, too, as free play, not the cracking of codes containing decisive messages. The goal is not to resolve responses into determinate meanings or intents, but to multiply the responses and the effects a text has on a reader.

Additionally, there is no meta-language of criticism; the language of criticism, as of philosophy (that criticism of criticisms), is revealed to be rhetorical, figurative, metaphorical. The literal, the meta-, is a dead metaphor. Criticism becomes the effort to narrate reading experiences, Miller explained. Derrida's Freudian interminable analysis is a free play without truths or origins. For de Man, what he calls rhetorically conscious readings are vital if criticism is to be useful. Consequently, all language must be seen for its inherent metaphoricity, whether science, fiction, history or criticism. Barthes had much earlier argued that critical language is 'textual' too, that is, polyphonic. This polyphony leads to the dissolution of boundaries between literature, criticism and other discourses. Objectivity and referentiality are displaced by the subversive movements of rhetoricity.

De Man suggested that criticism could shift its attention from the thematics of texts (treated as repositories of ideas and beliefs) to the aesthetic effects, phonic dimensions and linguistic/ rhetorical structures. Once attention is shifted to how a text works, figurative themes reveal inconsistencies in interpretation which display the rhetorical deceit of referentiality and truth, the falsity of questions of author's or text's intent. Relatedly, Johnson suggested that texts are 'less about something than about "being about"'. Texts, she oxymoronically remarked, are thus 'framed' by their contents. She saw the effort at analytical mastery of the meaning of a text as a futile attempt to tame and delimit the uncontrollable language of texts. Johnson adopted Barthes' and Derrida's erasure of the distinction between literary language and meta-, critical, or ordinary, non-figurative language. (Some deconstructive critics do not give up this distinction so readily.) Literary language is simply 'écriture', not some privileged form of writing. Literal, or ordinary, language is just as 'infected' with ambiguity, irony and undecidability (figuration) as is rhetorical language. Stanley Fish has suggested the metaphor that literary language is ordinary language 'framed' – regarded with a particular self-consciousness, a resource which all language has always possessed. Nietzsche had anticipated these debates when he stated, 'No such thing as an unrhetorical, natural language exists that could be used as a point of reference.' (In this he followed German and English Romantic theories.) Tropes, then, are the truest nature of language, and the question of referentiality is 'bracketed' – put to the side as misconceived, badly posed. For language is not meaningful so much because it refers to something extra-linguistic (nature, society, consciousness, experience); figuration defies referentiality as the essence of language and meaning, for the world to which reference is allegedly made is a construction of metaphors and linguistic effects, a text: as Derrida says, 'there is nothing outside the text.' Textuality is the character of our experience, and this 'writing', this écriture, is not engraved on stone and univocal in meaning. It can not only be interpreted differently, it can be rewritten. Feminism, gay theory and post-colonial theory are a rewriting of patriarchal texts which can proceed in several ways. They can reveal the anti-patriarchal elements within those very texts which

are, then, self-subverting, and they can introduce new emphases and perspectives, which change the story, alter the plot, and create a new style, genre and language.

Throughout this period of the last thirty years or so, influences from South America, such as Gabriel García Márquez, Jorge Luis Borges and others, were reinforcing structuralist and post-structuralist adaptations of German and English Romantic concepts and American pragmatist transformations. Magic realism and postmodernism both inspired and were inspired by critical theorists and other thinkers such as Bakhtin, Foucault, Pierre Macherey, Jean-Paul Sartre, Louis Althusser and others. One of the major thematic interests which can be identified as expressive of these abstract theorizings involves the idea of displacement, which has almost become a redefinition of truth. It rejects the hermeneutical notion of the revelations of meanings or the decodings of pre-existent, hidden messages. Displacement, for truth, expresses the idea that all truth involves movement (not static or stable essences): movement from one metaphor or figure of speech or discourse to another, from one set of terminological expressions to another, from one fiction to another, from one way of talking to another. In short, truth is relational, not substantive, and it is movement, not body – process, not product. We learn to talk and think about things in terms of other things and other thoughts; when we extend our knowledge or increase understanding, we expand the verbal web of relationships amongst things. We expand our field of known expressions into new areas, through relating words which create new metaphors or revitalize old ones.

Both criticism and fiction have been radically affected by this field/web/map metaphor, since this figure precludes stasis and hierarchy in its emphasis upon the value of constantly expanding relations, shifting the place of the centre to connect elements in new ways. The power of the theme of travel, and all its related themes of exile, foreignness and alienation, is drawn in part from its expression of this human experience: that gaining knowledge is like travel. Another powerful theme of literature is the simile of life as a drama or story, with characters trying to read each other's meanings and those of events.

If fiction is now often perceived as always a form of deceitful autobiography, then life too is portrayed as story, and reality is dependent on story making. There is no escape outside fiction into some reality, since reality and truth are the result of stories, evolving by the displacement of one fiction or metaphor or story for another. Hence, the implicit subject matter of all art is the making of art itself – the analogy for the existential project of self-fashioning. Thus, paradoxically, at first, when literature is most self-referential, it is most life-like. For the character of life is the making of stories. This simile of life as story leads to the infinite regress whereby life becomes a fantastic mosaic of others' texts, others' lives; 'pure' originality is non-existent, as we plagiarize from each other to make sense of our lives, to fashion ourselves, and to achieve meaning by shifting, shuttling back and forth from one account to another, from one metaphor to another. Memory and imagination vie for the agency of writing our intertextual lives, which become unique only because of the way we read them. Displacement and travel can also express the endless deferral of any arrival, the constant breaching of borders and transgressing of boundaries. Transgression is thematized in literature as itself the law; narrative time becomes the only content of all our stories, our lives, our metaphors. With unreadable lives, indecipherable stories, we stand on the threshold of the law of life as meaningful, and we wait for meaning, or create it, depending on our temperaments.

Further reading

Collier, Peter and Geyer-Ryan, Helga, eds. *Literary Theory Today*. Cambridge, 1990.

Fish, Stanley. *Is There a Text in this Class?*. Cambridge, Mass., 1980.

Hartman, Geoffrey. *Saving the Text: Literature/Derrida/Philosophy*. Baltimore, 1981.

Johnson, Barbara. *The Critical Difference*. Baltimore, 1981.

Johnson, Barbara. *A World of Difference*. Baltimore, 1989.

Johnson, Christopher. *System and Writing in the Philosophy of Jacques Derrida*. Cambridge, 1994.

Llewelyn, John. *Derrida on the Margins of Philosophy*. New York and London, 1986.

Man, Paul de. *Allegories of Reading*. New Haven, 1979.

Norris, Christopher. *The Contest of Faculties*. London, 1985.

Rorty, Richard. *Consequences of Pragmatism*. Brighton, 1982.

Spivak, G.C. *In Other Worlds*. New York, 1988.

Veeser, A. *The New Historicism*. London, 1989.

Wheeler, Kathleen. *Romanticism, Pragmatism, and Deconstruction*. Oxford, 1993.

White, Hayden. *Tropics of Discourse*. Baltimore, 1978.

Chapter 11

Introduction to Novelists, 1970–1995

Marguerite Young's Joycean epic *Miss MacIntosh, My Darling* (1965) now seems prophetic of a period of exuberance and almost wanton variety and profusion in fiction. If critics in the earlier decade thought the novel was dying, it must have been because they were not reading Young, Christina Stead, Jane Bowles, Flannery O'Connor, Eudora Welty and many other women writers. Experimentation may seem to have waned somewhat in the writers they were reading, such as Barbara Pym, Muriel Spark, Iris Murdoch, Doris Lessing and Nadine Gordimer, because innovations were not understood or perceived as such. In the last thirty-odd years, since recognizable, overt experimentation has set in again with an avant-garde, post-modernist and magic realist vengeance, we have witnessed the renewal of a genre of literature which has shown itself to be both resilient and responsive to the needs of almost any race, sex, class, creed or nationality. From South and black Africa to Anglo-Saxon and ethnic minority England, from Asian America to the East Coast, from the Caribbean to Canada, and from New Zealand and Australia to the Indian subcontinent, new, international fiction has blossomed in a glorious and breathtaking profusion. Such global fiction demands new responses, new attitudes, and most of all an acceptance that 'canon' is probably becoming an outmoded and less useful concept. No such security, convenience or exclusiveness is needed any more for the reader who reads with a 'passionate desire for intimacy' with diverse texts (to use Edith Wharton's terms). Without an acquaintance with the vast diversity of modern international fiction, whether overtly experimental or not, the reader who persists in believing that white Europeans or Americans of the male sex probably write the 'best' novels, with a few exceptions which prove the rule, is not only ignorant of contemporary literature; she or he is also out of touch with reality. She or He is hardly even in a position to respond imaginatively to what those favoured, canonical writers are doing.

Another major stream of literary experimentation and innovation in this last part of the twentieth century is, once again, the writings of the radical experimentalists. This easily identified stream is often called post-modernism, since it shares much with modernists' overt experimentation while innovating in other important ways as well. Young is the most obvious early example of this stream, with her 1,200-page Odyssey of Vera Cartwheel in search of her (probably already dead) childhood nanny, Miss MacIntosh. Making labyrinthine, proliferating journeys within journeys and interiorities within maze-like further interiorities, questioning origins for events and meanings, questioning the meaning of meaning, fantasizing reality and realizing fantasy, Young's novel breaks narrative frames and makes the real story inaccessible. Rich allusiveness and complexities create a seemingly, endless 1,000-page deferral, so that the novel is a story about what never happens. Reality recedes and the story-teller becomes a fiction, engendering another self which evades authority for this non-fiction fiction; all these disruptive elements, which can in fact be found throughout the history of Western literature, are 'made new' by Young through her inimitable imaginative genius.

Ann Quin (discussed in part III) followed immediately Young's 'late modernist', early post-modernist novel with several radically experimental texts, which uncannily predicted the direction fiction was to take. Thomas Pynchon's *The Crying of Lot 49* (1966) spelled out many of these predicted characteristics of the new post-modernism, which was to permeate the work of dozens of writers to come. Cynthia Ozick's most post-modernist novel, *The Messiah of Stockholm*, not published until 1987, took typical devices such as recursive embedding, meta-fictional loops and *mise-en-abîmes* or abysses of endless interpretation to new extremes, engaging the reader in a 'game' of a search for a text, a father and an identity. Other novelists in this broadly post-modernist form of experimentation include such radical post-modernists as Christine Brooke-Rose, Angela Carter (who also uses magic realism) and Kathy Acker, in addition to Quin, Young and Ozick. Yet these are the practitioners of post-modernism at its most extreme; many other writers have used aspects of it, such as Grace Paley, Elizabeth Jolley, Emma Tennant, Margaret Atwood, Janet Turner Hospital, Maggie Gee, Janet Frame and Rachell Ingalls, for example.

Twentieth-century fiction has systematically examined and theorized about the age-old pastiche character, where the artifact is built up not only out of the author's individuality and innovations, but out of other artifacts preceding it. Post-modernist fiction has, in particular, engaged in an intensely vigorous dialogue with other literature and other art, both contemporaneous and antecedent, and in a whole range of fascinating modes of allusion. Such 'intertextuality', as we have come to call it, has been apparent this century from Henry James through Virginia Woolf and Isak Dinesen, for example, to Young, Elizabeth Smart, Frame and Lessing, culminating in the extreme overtness of Brooke-Rose's, Quin's and Acker's dialogues and toyings with other texts. While intertextuality is a character of all literature, twentieth-century authors have both revived old forms and invented new ones, such as extensive pastiche, allusion, plagiarisms and so on. The very act of writing intelligible literature at all is, of course, an act of participation in some tradition, which leaves its marks and traces everywhere in the 'new' text, whether deliberately or not. The more perceptive and informed a writer is, the more these dialogic elements will be conscious. And, depending on the aims of the writer, they can be obscured from the reader's eye for some aesthetic purpose, or called to our attention for another type of response.

Brooke-Rose, in *Textermination*, and Acker, in numerous novels, are only the most extreme examples of authors using two very visible types of intertextuality. Jean Rhys, in *Wide Sargasso Sea*, rewrote an aspect of *Jane Eyre*, the 'Bertha story', bringing to light the subversive, repressed 'Other' in that earlier novel. Aritha van Herk, in *Places far from Ellsmere*, did not so much rewrite as re-read *Anna Karenina*, while Emma Tennant, Hortense Calisher and Jane Gardam also used 'classic', canonical texts as the starting points for their fictions, such as *Gulliver's Travels* and *Robinson Crusoe*. Other overtly intertextual fictions have come from A.S. Byatt, in *Possession*, while Michèle Roberts has rewritten Christian texts, Maxine Hong Kingston has incorporated the famous Chinese legend of the 'Journey to the West of the Monkey' into a *Portrait of the Artist as a Young Man*, and Atwood, Welty and Carter have rewritten fairy tales, folk legends and mythology, and have drawn overtly and systematically from fiction from medieval times to the present.

These intertextual devices are one of the central characteristics of post-modern literature, though they are found in literature from Greek and Sanskrit times, through Shakespeare and Cervantes, to the present day. Perhaps what is new today is the systematic use of intertextuality, or its overtness and deliberateness; the author tries to call the reader's attention to the allusions, instead of meshing them into the texture of the fiction. (Borges liked to joke that texts are 'unique because of the way we read them'.)

Thus, such writers as Young, Quin, Acker, Carter and Brooke-Rose use extreme disruption in style, form or thematics, as did the modernists, but with a distinctly post-war character which distinguishes it from modernism. They also often privilege a subjectivist interiority or inner consciousness, in which the boundary between internal and external is dissolved. Characters split into numerous selves, flowing into each other and the world, while narrative point of view is alternating, confused and even indeterminate, as in Brooke-Rose's *Verbivore* or Quin's *Berg* and other novels, for example. While it is true that these techniques draw on aspects of the stream of consciousness technique characteristic of modernism, with rare exceptions there are also marked differences which cannot be overlooked. Additionally, plot is endlessly deferred, parodied or ridiculed openly, while content is openly flaunted; language itself, as well as the writing and reading of fiction, becomes the subject matter, and fictionality is queried along with reality.

An emphasis upon fantasy is another characteristic of such experiments; its relation to reality is inverted: reality is said to be the biggest fantasy or illusion of all, as modern physics is constantly reminding us. Elaborate speculations about fictionality are also couched in labyrinthine plots with meta-fictional loops. The boundary between fact and fiction collapses, as narrative frames are broken into by authors and readers intruding into the story. The artistic illusion is mocked, and fictional facts are threatened. Moreover, there intrude into the text narrative personae who are those of the author or reader of this very book you are reading right now, especially in Acker, but also in other writers. Plagiarism can be overt and acknowledged, as in Acker or the later Brooke-Rose, or borrowings can be strewn throughout to surprise and delight the reader who recognizes them. Brooke-Rose's *Textermination* is an oxymoronic example of total pastiche and plagiarism and total originality, showing the two extremes to be, themselves, fictions. That is, all writing is marked with the traces of other writing; nothing is wholly original or free from borrowings. Unique as these texts may seem, none of their devices is unrelated to earlier modernist practices.

Another feature of post-modernism which invites comparison with modernism is the insertion of erotic, sexual thematics into the texts. Sexual desire becomes another central theme, especially in Young, Acker, Carter and Quin. Reading is eroticized, as is writing, and the pleasure of the text is sexualized. Acker, for example, sets out to shock her readers, as had Anaïs Nin and Henry Miller decades earlier, out of their complacencies, by fusing virtually pornographic writing (*Kathy Goes to Haiti* or almost any of her other novels) with literary sophistication. Concepts of pornography and propriety are put under erasure, as Acker explored the political dimensions of sexual repressions and inhibitions, as did Carter. Sexuality was a central theme of nearly every Carter novel, as she explored the issues of repression, propriety, gender, homosexuality and the body as itself textuality. Carter's fiction, some of the most original writing of this period, is almost a fusion of post-modernist devices and magic realism (discussed below). She employed ideas and techniques described best by the theorist Bakhtin as carnivalesque, mimicry, parody and heteroglossia, for example. Nearly every novel she wrote was different from her others, and this wide diversity was achieved in part by her use of literary devices and thematics from fairy tale and folk legend, medieval romances and ballads, Shakespearean tricks, and writers from all over Europe, America and the rest of the world. Her erudition informed her vigorous imaginative energies to push at the frontiers of fiction.

In addition to this eroticizing of literature, self-conscious meta-fictionality is taken to another degree, as reading (not just writing) is made an almost constant subtext in these writers. The nature of reading is no longer taken for granted, but is raised to the level of a philosophical question. None of these writers accepts the notion that reading is a passive (or only somewhat active) receptivity of someone else's ideas. Part of the difficulty in reading their texts results from their determination to involve the reader in an active, participatory way. Their texts also challenge the notion that the novel has some content independent of its form and style, which it is the work of the reader to identify and take away. Both the novel of ideas and the socio-moral novel encouraged this view, and almost all experimentalists reject it. Radical experimentation makes it almost impossible for the reader to read passively, or to extract meaning from the formal artistry of a text. Textual meanings, content and even plot are made indeterminate and destabilized by such authors. Endless deferrals and maze-like proliferations prevent any univocal, single story, plot or meaning from emerging.

Other techniques include the mixing of apparently non-fictional elements into the text.

Journals and diaries, letters, newspaper clippings, historical or sociological reports, anthropological documents and so on are strewn throughout the fictional prose. Autobiography, biography, history, travel and science are incorporated into the text, in order to show how fictional non-fiction is, with its metaphors and other figures of speech, its conventions and its formalities, not to mention its often unconscious assumption of a narrative persona and a reader. Another technique of post-modernism is to introduce the idea that reading is a game, a joke, an activity which is essentially playful. Reading and writing, like games and jokes, conform to rules only partially. Part of the game is to breach the rules, to see what might happen. Writers devise plots in which the reader is ensnared in a game of transgressions; the laws of literature are noted, then breached. Wit and humour play central roles in such disruptions, as the seriousness and academic pedantry of much criticism is mocked.

Many of these techniques have a long history, but their systematic eruption in the late nineteenth and early twentieth century perhaps marked a new intensity, as their use became more widespread. As modernism waned, writers such as Borges took up and developed further its ideas. Borges probably influenced, and was influenced by, the *nouveau roman* and *el realismo mágico* in the 1950s and 1960s. These Spanish American and French practices were also felt in the United States in the post-war period, and somewhat later in England and elsewhere. Borges's emphasis upon metaphors and figures of speech as the essential character of language, his interest in language and how it means, how we construct our experience/world out of it, how and what we communicate, focused again issues which Gertrude Stein and Henry James had made their thematics. Borges added to this concern a central interest in how the familiar world can be made marvellous. His stories 'about' reading and writing, with their themes of deception, deceit, duplicity, plagiarism and lying, expressed the realization that art involves pretences, falsities and deceits at its very inception. That is, false notions abound in literature, such as that reality provides an origin to which fictions refer for meaning, that fiction is original, that authors are objective, sincere or detached, that fiction is about a familiar, ordinary world which already exists

independently of it. These issues rise again to the forefront in post-modernism and magic realism, where that ordinary world is shown to be a fantastic, magical realm of unbelievable beauty and novelty, if only we choose to see it that way. Characteristic motifs, both for the estrangement of the familiar and for the attention to language and art as thematic focus, include complex courtyards, mazes, mirror reflections, split selves, mysteries and quests, endless journeys and passages, exotic beings, magnificent scenery and extraordinary occurrences.

'Magic realism' is another major stream of recent fiction, distinct from realism, the socio-moral novel and post-modernism, while using many narrative practices familiar both in experimental, alternative forms of fiction and in the more conventional types. Initially associated with the fiction of South American writers such as García Márquez, Alejo Carpentier and others, magic realism was historically understood as a reaction against or deviation from European forms of avant-garde fiction and experimental writings of the late 1920s and 1930s. Originating, in these early stages, in the writings of such authors as André Breton and Franz Roh, *lo real maravilloso* of the 1930s and 1940s, as it was sometimes named, had strong links with surrealist and other atraditional forms of art. Surrealism in literature was associated later with Anna Kavan and Leonora Carrington, for example, and earlier with David Gascoyne and the young Herbert Read. It was an alternative form of experimentation to that of modernist innovations, and was greatly influenced by psychoanalysis and psychology generally. Early writers such as Franz Kafka had anticipated many of these later forms in their fictional dialogues with the literary traditional and their efforts to find ways out of the limits imposed by realist traditions. With the constant intercourse between South American writers such as Borges and European artists and writers, especially in France, Spain and Italy, *lo real maravilloso* and all its associated forms travelled from Europe to South America in the late 1940s and began influencing art and literature in startling ways.

Borges himself, not usually thought of as a magic realist so much as an anti-realist, intellectualist and post-modernist, was nevertheless a major influence in the shift from authoritarian social realism and socio-moral forms of fiction to avant-garde experimentation of all kinds. Having spent several years in Europe and especially in France in his adolescence, Borges was influenced by these early European innovations, and became one of the major literary influences in South America. His own stories, poems and essays from the 1930s to the 1970s make use both of postmodernism and *lo real maravilloso*, but were quite distinct, from the beginning, from European avant-garde and surrealist techniques. The encouragement, both by example and in person, to other young South Americans to break with the authoritarianism of social realist forms of fiction helped to establish a flourishing South American, Spanish literature into the 1960s and later.

Borges's and other Spanish American writings were translated into English in the 1960s and 1970s, and created an imaginative shock which is still reverberating today in the writings of, for example, Kingston, Leslie Marmon Silko, Toni Morrison, Gloria Naylor and many others, and which could be said to have begun with the 'pure' *realismo mágico* of the ironic and parodic Carlos Castaneda books, from 1969 for the next decade. (Borges had been translated into French much earlier, and his writings may well have influenced the development of the *nouveau roman*.) Excoriated in his own country and throughout South America for his (alleged) apolitical, uncommitted, intellectualist and 'decadent' writings, Borges's *ficciones* and essays became one of the greatest sources of inspiration for a new kind of Spanish American writing. It, in turn, has unleashed *el realismo mágico* into the North American continent, where it has flourished as one of the major forms of fiction of the late twentieth century. European surrealism, the avant-garde and the *nouveau roman*, on the other hand, have never flourished in the Americas in the same vibrant and intense way.

According to Carpentier, this is because one of the central strengths of *el realismo mágico* fiction is its characteristic clash of cultures, such as that of European with Native American, which releases imaginative energies and resources unavailable to the purely European forms of innovation. These latter he saw as sterile and barren, in contrast to the fertility and vitality released by fusing cultures, as happened historically in the Americas, especially in South America. Carpentier saw *el realismo mágico* as a hybrid, border-crossing fiction which was vital enough to produce imaginative innovations that could change our sense of what reality is, was, or can be. This alteration in our perceptions of reality is at the heart of all types of magic realism; it involves fiction which, through various techniques, shocks, frightens and awakens us to a view of familiar reality as merely one possible description of the magical, marvellous and incomprehensible natural world which we inhabit. Our ways of perceiving nature are shown to be merely learned attitudes and beliefs, which drastically reduce imaginative responses and inhibit us from being able to gain access to the powers and enriching natural forces, both within and without, which can enhance our daily lives.

Neither Carpentier, García Márquez nor Borges, however, was under the illusion that this infusing of ordinary reality with the magical and the marvellous was something new in fiction, some indication of an evolution of fiction into new realms. 'Stripping the veil of familiarity from the familiar' in order to reveal the incomprehensible, stupendous universe in which we mysteriously find ourselves was a character of literature and human culture since its beginnings. Moreover, Borges had argued that he learnt his own (post-modernist, magic realist) innovative strategies and devices from none other than Cervantes, Ariosto, Dante, Shakespeare, Chaucer, Goethe and the dozens of other writers from Spain to Russia and Scandinavia which he read so voraciously in his youth. Everywhere, he found writers throughout the centuries of European (and other) culture trying to make the familiar strange in order to awaken readers from their custom-induced stupor and 'see' with new eyes the almost incredible fact of there being anything at all, much less this world of nature and human consciousness.

The fiction of magic realism itself can be seen to have quite distinct strands, such as that of novels which focus upon landscape and nature and emphasize the stupendous powers of the natural world, often using the supernatural to heighten the effect of strangeness, magic and exoticism. An example of this would be Silko's

Ceremony. Another stream emphasizes the human side of this equation, sometimes by embedding magic into the historical in order either to construct a speculative history or to rewrite the history of the Americas from another, previously marginalized point of view. García Márquez's *One Hundred Years of Solitude* (London, 1970, trans. Márquez himself) is an example of speculative history, while Toni Morrison's *Beloved* exemplifies the latter. In other novels, such as Kingston's *Tripmaster Monkey. His Fake Book*, a slightly different stream of magic realism is evident. Here, the emphasis is upon an individual's self-construction and history, and upon her or his self-creation through imaginative acts of the will, which often involve a whole community. Moreover, Kingston makes use of extensive postmodernist devices as well, as does Rachel Ingalls. The latter's *Binstead's Safari*, with its self-referring account of the origins of legends, combines the natural and the human in a powerful African setting, while Gloria Naylor's *Mama Day* tends toward a type of *realismo mágico* which fuses historical and individual reconstruction in an imaginary landscape.

In most forms of *el realismo mágico*, whether emphasizing nature or the human psyche, history or the life of an individual, we find constant exhortations to question our perceptions of reality, to see reality as merely one of many possible descriptions. Our perceptions of reality can, then, change; reality itself can be changed, that is, by imaginative fiction which gives us new viewpoints from which to perceive, new models by which we interpret, and new 'eyes' by which we actually see new things we never saw before. In addition to this central theme of magic realism, we find consistent rejections of cultural assimilation into European-American-white consumerist values. Cultural differences are emphasized in these novels, and indeed, the fiction often becomes a virtual document of cultural songs, legends, rituals, stories, myths and values woven into the fabric of the narrative, and preserving this culture from disintegration and loss. 'Assimilation' as an aim is contrasted with 'transculturation' as the goal, and traditional values of mastery, purity and hierarchy are rejected in favour of cooperation, hybridity, miscegenation and equality. Challenges to white male

constructions of reality, history, fiction and truth are enacted by means of a rhetoric of speculative historiography, fabulous possibilities and the elaboration of divergent realities – or descriptions of realities – which enlarge and enrich the scope of human potentialities. Thus, in Nietzschean reversals of value, migrancy, mixed genealogies, hybridities, impurities, transgressions and border trafficking, as well as border-defying forms of fiction, are sought for and elaborated.

While complex genealogy, or the embedding of *cuentos*, fabulations or talk stories in history, along with imaginative geography, the supernatural, constructions of speculative histories, hybridity of all kinds and transculturation, as well as conflicts and clashes of cultures, may characterize *el realismo mágico*, its own impulse for border-defying gestures takes it to its logical conclusion. That is, this fiction mixes fluently with alternative forms, such as post-modernism, and, of course, with so-called realism. While Silko's *Almanac of the Dead* or Kingston's *Tripmaster Monkey* may be the obvious examples, Morrison's *Song of Solomon* and Naylor's *Linden Hills* are also *mélanges* of these modern streams of writing. Louise Erdrich's novels, from *Love Medicine* or *Tracks* to *The Beet Queen*, offer yet another mode of transculturation, as do Patricia Grace's Maori novels and some of Paule Marshall's more recent fiction, such as *Praisesong for the Widow*. Carter's magic realism, like Jeanette Winterson's, is a distinctive European type, drawing upon medieval traditions, central European legends, Irish myths and Chaucerian ribaldry in a modern form to enrich Carter's fiction with divergent, licentious and elaborate improprieties. Perhaps one of the most successful examples of this almost unclassifiable, hybrid modern form of fiction is Anita Desai's recent *Baumgartner's Bombay*, which, in part because of its stylistic particularity and originality, rises, like Kingston's *Monkey* and Silko's *Ceremony* (amongst other novels mentioned above), beyond any 'type' of fiction, to escape into a magical region of its own.

By means of making the familiar strange, intertextuality and self-referential meta-fictionality, in all their various forms described above, writers achieved an intense self-consciousness about their practices, and communicated this increased awareness to the reader. There is nothing apolitical or amoral about self-consciousness; on the contrary, one could argue that it is a precondition of any viable moral or political position. Such a high level of theoretical awareness, about fiction, art, language, reading and writing, led to a questioning of accepted conventions and beliefs in magic realism and post-modernism. Issues about the relation of language to the world and of fiction to reality were explored; language was shown to be essentially figurative, and our known world a construct of metaphorical relations. Dichotomies collapsed, as opposites were seen to be interdependent for meaning. Hierarchies were reversed, and then abandoned, as distinctions were seen to be conventions and not facts about reality. Not merely the text but the world too was viewed as a metaphorical construct; history and other accounts of reality were reconceptualized as interpretative gestures, not true descriptions. Reality, world, self and text are all 'texts', in need of interpretation and 'reading'. Reading is a kind of appropriation tantamount to a rewriting of the text, while writing is redefined as a reinscription of what was always already there. The reader is kept in a constant state of passage, of transition, of journeying from one metaphor to another, one point of view to another, one frame to another, one loop to another.

This idea of passages (explored by Quin in the novel with that title) is also related to recent theorizing about decolonization and the deconstruction of ethnicity, race, class and gender. Concepts of displacement of centres and margins replace traditional fixities; colonies are decolonized, canons decanonized and centres decentralized. Ethnicity, race, class and sexual identity are deconstructed, as values of 'purity' and identity as homogeneous are replaced by ideals of hybridity, mixings, border crossings. The 'Other' is not only seen as a source of strength instead of as a threat to notional purities, but also recognized as not so much outside, external, or marginal to identity, ethnicity or centres, as within. Centre, identity, sexuality and gender, are all heterogeneous mixes of other and self.

Other writers, including Rose Tremain, Alice Thomas Ellis, Jolley and more recently Erdrich and Winterson display a rich imaginativeness allied with great wit and an emphasis upon fantasy in some cases. In a quite different vein, Margaret Laurence, Jayne Anne Phillips, Buchi Emecheta, Ellen Gilchrist, Joyce Carol Oates and Margaret Drabble draw on different modes of realism and even 'use realism against itself'. Great stylists have also emerged, such as Desai, whose novels also constitute a range of impressive variety. Similarly, Alison Lurie, Anita Brookner, A.S. Byatt and Anne Redmon use post-modernist devices within their search for a clarity of style which alerts the reader to aesthetic issues of artifice and of artistic form and relationship.

A rich variety of practices within other Canadian-American writing is evident in Alice Munro's wonderfully witty and sophisticated linked stories, Anne Tyler's domestic tragi-comedies, Bobbie Ann Mason's and Susan Kenney's studies of family life and Ingalls's often exotic romances. Indian-born writers such as Nayantara Sahgal, Bharati Mukherjee, Suniti Namjoshi, Shashi Deshpande and Kamala Markandaya have explored domestic life in a quite different setting in some cases; Namjoshi has been the most experimental in creating her witty and incisive, Gertrude Stein-like fictions. Ama Ata Aidoo, Miriam Masoli, Grace Nichols, Tsitsi Dangarembga and Ntozake Shange, amongst others, are stretching the English language into new spheres of experience which enrich the novel still further. On another front, Roberts is rewriting Christianity to expand its limited horizons, while Jennifer Johnston educates us about Ireland, the English and the destructive blindnesses on both sides. Mary Gordon and Ellis give us a new view of religious faith in two utterly different forms of fiction, as had Flannery O'Connor thirty years earlier, while Fay Weldon, Joanna Russ, Erica Jong, Alice Walker and many others ridicule patriarchy in undisguised lambasts. Additionally, Ursula Le Guin, Emma Tennant, P.D. James, and Marge Piercy, for example, have broadened the scope of the novel to challenge conventions of 'literariness' and of genre. Hardly a woman novelist mentioned in this *Guide*, moreover, has neglected to challenge accepted fictions about women and images of women or sexuality, in one way or another. The act of writing has itself backed up those words of challenge by the deed. Women have a literature of their own; it is probably up to them, however, to learn to value it at its true worth, rather than continuing to see it (or themselves) through the eyes of that 'other' sex. Women break their silences all the time; other women are needed to listen and to read those disruptions of the law of literature. Someday men may follow that example.

Chapter 12

Individual Authors, 1970–1995

Meridel Le Sueur 1900–

Described as a 'brilliant maverick' and the voice of the people, Le Sueur is the author of two novels, novellas and numerous short stories, as well as essays, articles, history and social documentary. Her first piece of published fiction, 'Persephone', her story 'The Horse' (a dialogue with D.H. Lawrence's 'St Mawr') and her autobiographical essay 'Corn Village' won her awards. But her best-known works of fiction are the novel *The Girl* (Minneapolis, 1979), the collection (a novel and two novellas) *I Hear Men Talking* (Minneapolis, 1984) and the collection of historical and documentary fiction in *American Folklore: North Star Country* (New York, 1945; Minneapolis, 1984). Other collections include *The Harvest and Song for My Time* (Minneapolis, 1977), containing thirteen stories, and two pamphlets, *Women on the Breadlines* (Minneapolis, 1978) and *Worker Writer* (Minneapolis, 1981) (all by the West End Press, Minneapolis, Minnesota) plus *Ripening: Selected Work of Meridel Le Sueur 1927–1980* (Old Westbury, N.Y., 1982).

Born in Iowa, Le Sueur grew up in Kansas and later resided in Minnesota; a Midwesterner through and through, she was devoted to the beauty of the vast and boundless prairies which rolled over hundreds of thousands of square miles and became the breadbasket of America. Brought up by politically active parents, Le Sueur was a deeply committed democrat, who exposed the way human lives are blighted when money, success, power and property become their goals.

Following Agnes Smedley in *Daughter of Earth* (1929), she explored the effects of capitalism on society, showing how it turns creative life forces into mere commodities. Thus, for example, women's sexuality is debased into something for men to consume, while imaginative art is valued for its commercial worth. Le Sueur handled with greater ease than did Smedley, Olive Dargan or Myra Page, for example, the deep-rooted sexism of the left, and its unwillingness to deal with the extremely subversive emphasis upon women's issues. In capitalist systems, Le Sueur argued, a crippling imbalance arises between the individual and the community. Individuals are set up against each other by race, sex, class or religion, to be exploited and manipulated. Early in her life, Le Sueur had been shocked by the chasmic difference between European-American economics and the economic systems of Native American Indians. In the essay 'The Ancient and the Newly Come', she described the latter's (now well-known) symbiotic and holistic relationship with nature and their sharing, cooperative, communal balance with each other.

Throughout Le Sueur's fiction, whether in the lyrical *The Girl* and *I Hear Men Talking* or in *American Folklore: North Star Country*, with its historical, documentary emphasis, themes of rape of the land, genocide (of the American Indian tribes), exploitation of women and of the working class, and sexual repression of women and men are woven into an integrated vision of the potential inherent beauty of everyday life. Le Sueur's fiction fuses the democratic and the symbolic, art and life, as she avoids dogmas in a flexible pragmatism based on compassion and a profound respect for the human spirit within every individual. *North Star Country* is a deeply compelling mosaic of the lyrical and the documentary, of fiction and history, as it proceeds through reports, diaries, letters, ballad and song, tales, legends and histories, to unfold the appalling genocide and rape of nature during the nineteenth-century westward development. Yet Le Sueur's regional history burns also with the commitment to democracy and a faith in working women as well as working men, unlike that of many sexist male socialists. Her writing is alive with the voices of ordinary people, as she drew on oral traditions and expressed her belief that the arts of a people help them not only to understand the world, but to change it:

> For the people compose a story that never ends, a river that winds and falls and rushes to the sea. The people are a story that is a long and continual coming alive from the earth into better wheat, percherons, babies, engines – persistent and inevitable. The people will always know that some of the grain will be good, some of the crop will be saved, some will return and bear the strength of the kernel, that from the bloodiest year some will survive to outfox the frost.

In this characteristic passage, Le Sueur's metaphors interweave to create a nexus of imagery relating humanity, nature and art to each other fundamentally. Images of seeds recur throughout her writing to reinforce the value of growth and transformation over stasis and possession. Le Sueur's Penelope, in *I Hear Men Talking*, for example, gains the emotional strength to fight off reduction to an object of (sexual and physical) consumption when she assists at the birth of a male child, and has a revelation of the pathetic vulnerability of men. Freed from her socialized fantasies of men as strong, protective and fatherly after this illumination, Penelope, symbolically, blinds her self-appointed lover in his second rape attempt. A moment later, he is accidentally killed by the gun of one of his fellow rapists; a cyclone hits immediately after, and Le Sueur ends the novel not with its arrival but with fantastic and lyrical descriptions of it by the townspeople: 'Voices fused together, talking, of what

they had seen and would see, of a tide they knew now carried them and did not separate them doing battle against each other.' Only natural disasters can, apparently, overcome the differences and competitiveness which separate American Indians and Europeans, men and women, black and white; but Le Sueur made clear her own hope that a more balanced, cooperative mentality could be fostered eventually, even if only out of sheer necessity (as had happened to the American Indians):

> I do not care for the bourgeois 'individual' that I am ... I want to be integrated into a new and different way as an individual and this I feel can come only from a communal participation which reverses the feeling of a bourgeois writer. What will happen to him will not be special and precious, but will be the communal happening ... I can no longer breathe in this maggotty individualism of a merchant society ... I hope to 'belong' ... in a living whole.

In the afterword to *I Hear Men Talking*, Le Sueur made clear her conscious struggles with form, style, thematics, characterization and description in her fiction, in her own struggle to make a 'new and different way' as an artist. The above quotation already suggests that part of this new way would involve changing the balance in the writer between individual imaginativeness and communal expression. She also expressed the necessity for transformation, for growth and change, based, she argued, only on action which unites opposition and differences, which creates democratic relationship rather than hierarchy, duality or domination. She also wrote of her efforts to avoid 'the manipulation by the author of the reader who is a consumer, the brazen and often brutal design of our literature to intensify the image of brutality'. Le Sueur sought to create an alliance between herself and her reader by creating new forms, structures and 'images of being together'. These new forms of literature would 'name the enemy' and then 'limn the image of solidarity', so that cruel dichotomies such as male/female, rich/poor, could no longer blind, kill and cripple people. Both her lyrical fictions and her documentary, fictional histories stand as monuments to ordinary people who are a story, a river that never ends.

Grace Paley 1922–

Political and community activist as well as poet and short story writer, Paley was born in New York City to Russian immigrant parents. Her marriage at an early age to Jess Paley ended her education at Hunter College, but her fame from her first collection of short stories, *The Little Disturbances of Man* (New York, 1959), brought her a teaching position in Columbia University and, later, at Sarah Lawrence College. After raising two children, Paley was awarded a Guggenheim Fellowship in 1966 and awards from the American Institute for Arts and Letters in 1970, not to mention an earlier grant from the National Endowment for the Arts (1966). She published two further collections of stories, *Enormous Changes at the Last Minute* (New York, 1974) and *Later the Same Day* (New York, 1985), which won the PEN/Faulkner Fiction Prize. Elected to the Institute of Arts and Letters in 1980, she then began publishing volumes of autobiographical poetry, including *Leaning Forward* (Penebscoot, Maine, 1985), and *365 Reasons Not to Have Another War: Peace Calendar 1989* (New York, 1988). She had also published stories in the *New Yorker* (1978, 1979) which have not been collected, as well as in *Delta* (1982), *American Review* (1977) and *Iowa Review* (1981). She has written several articles for magazines such as *MS* and *Esquire*, and numerous interviews with her have been published.

Like Eudora Welty, Paley has been fascinated by the mystery of the articulation of human experience; she has wanted 'to show how mysterious ordinary life is'. As for Welty, this emphasis upon mystery implied no duality, for without words and story-telling, experience is the 'barest meaninglessness'. Paley has shared with Welty (and Susan Sontag) another central artistic belief in the need to encourage readers to resist trying to paraphrase stories and other art forms into meanings, allegories or ideas. These women authors have encouraged active reading of a different kind, for the former is a passive acquiescence in what one believes to be the authority of the writer, but which is almost always merely a projection of the reader's expectations, prejudices and set attitudes. Paley has wanted to leave the reader 'enough space to move around'; while her object is communication (with an emphasis upon the profoundly communal, social essence of language and stories), what is communicated is not for Paley or Welty or Sontag to authorize. Paley explained that her stories communicate by 'illuminating a dark object, or person, or fact', but they do not tell the reader what to see or how to moralize. Thus, Paley's stories are often made up of stories, or fragments of stories, and are either explicitly about story-telling (as 'A Conversation with My Father') or implicitly involve stories, as 'The Long-Distance Runner' or 'The Immigrant Story'. They toy with narrative time, linear plot, beginnings and endings. Paley has authorized multiple points of view and played with elusive thematics and paradoxical events (avoiding allegory and symbol). In short, she has realized in her stories post-modernist theoretical issues in an astonishingly accessible, concrete form. This may be one way of articulating her fiction's power and appeal: its ordinariness and simplicity, its stunning plainness (to speak oxymoronically) are a concretization of the very theoretical sophistication which many writers have found almost impossible to narrate convincingly. Paley's stories, then, are a rare triumph of theory and practice, of sophistication and accessibility. Unmarred by the overt artificialities and artistries characteristic of so much contemporary fiction, not enervated by the extreme self-referentiality and self-consciousness of some (almost dehumanized) recent fiction, Paley's humane, readable stories should influence a whole generation of writers who are fascinated by post-modernist insights, but have been unable to find convincing modes of artistic expression.

One of Paley's general devices for humanizing the intellectuality of Jorge Luis Borges-type techniques has been to create an interlocking set of stories which gradually evolves into a unified work but is not a novel, yet not merely a collection of stories either. Alice Munro and Jane Gardam have engaged less systematically in this interconnecting of tales, while Louise Erdrich has written a novel (*Tracks*) by means of various 'stories'. Paley's stories achieve a similarly innovative form as they circle around in never-ending spirals, referring forwards, sideways and backwards, creating a multiplicity of voices, perspectives and emphases, so that centre and margin are indistinguishable. Life is too varied, relative and open-ended to be portrayable from a centre or a margin, Paley has argued; we need several centres at once, while centres become margins and margins centres.

'Enormous Changes at the Last Minute' illustrates in a number of ways Paley's congruence of Borges-intellectuality (or self-referential fiction) and the depiction of 'ordinary' life experience. References to mirrors, points of view, recognition scenes, truth as a barrier ('she placed between them a barrier of truthful information'), interruptions of poetry and 'framed' prose into the fiction, references to other literature, irruptions of past reflections into the present narrative, newspaper reports, catalogues of objects, references to reality versus illusion, self-referential comments about art, language and how words relate to ideas, absurd surreal gestures, incredible gaps in narrative time, understatement and a meaningless ending – all these gestures explode any pretence that the story is mimetic of reality or that reality is an origin. Moreover, Paley intruded sarcastic references to psychoanalysis to discourage such 'readings', and she related tragic events in a comic way to discourage allegories. More sarcasm at psychoanalysis is injected into the explicitly self-referential story 'A Conversation with My Father', which mocks notions of 'simple truth' much as Elizabeth Hardwick had done. In this tale, Paley joked about the art–reality, language–world dualities, joked about readers' 'realist' expectations, and rejected plot as too meaningful (imposing pattern and moral dimensions where there are none). Her narrator wants to leave a lot out to 'allow for change, for other possibilities'. In this story, Paley mixed ontological levels, that is, she broke narrative frames: 'fiction' intrudes into 'fact', and literary 'fact' is shown to be interpretation. Her narrator's rationalist doctor father accuses his story-teller daughter of joking around too much, not attending enough to tragedy, truth, plain stories, facts, reality, definites, endings.

In 'The Long Distance Runner', Paley explored the limits of plot absurdity, rejecting motive, reason and explanations for actions, as Faith – a character who recurs throughout her stories – runs off from her family, stays unexpectedly in her old apartment, where a black family now lives, for three weeks, and then returns, her absence unremarked, to her own family. Violations of plot and thematic conventions abound, as characters behave in Jane Bowles-like off-centre ways which stretch the readers' credulity to the breaking point. Moreover, this incredulity is mirrored by the characters, who cannot make sense of each other's words: 'He listened to me for a while. Then he said, I don't know what she's talking about either . . . I repeated the story. They all said, What?' Ending on this note, Paley's story 'breaks the law' of what is literature, and shatters the illusion of fiction as a depiction of a knowable reality accurately represented in words.

Elizabeth Jolley 1923–

Educated at a Quaker school and born into a German-speaking family, Jolley grew up in the Midlands of England, but emigrated with her husband and children in 1959 to Australia. Having tried her hand at a range of jobs, including nursing, she has been a part-time teacher at the Western Australian Institute of Technology. When she was 50-some years old, Jolley published her first book, *Five Acre Virgin and Other Stories* (Fremantle, 1976), followed shortly by *The Travelling Entertainer and Other Stories* (Fremantle, 1979) and *Woman in a Lampshade* (Melbourne, 1983), another collection. Her novels, which sometimes seem to have grown out of a short story, include *Palomino* (Melbourne, 1980), *The Newspaper of Claremont Street* (Fremantle, 1981), *Mr Scobie's Riddle* (Melbourne, 1983), *Miss Peabody's Inheritance* (St Lucia, Queensland, 1983) and *Milk and Honey* (Fremantle, 1984), followed by *Foxybaby* (St Lucia, Queensland, 1985), *The Well* (Melbourne, 1986), *The Sugar Mother* (New York, 1988) and *Cabin Fever* (New York, 1990). *Milk and Honey* was awarded the New South Wales Premier's Literary Award, and Jolley's other novels have been received with enthusiasm by critics, reviewers and her contemporary novelist peers. Angela Carter, for example, described her texts thus: 'Her fiction shines and shines and shines, like a good deed in a naughty world.' Susan Hill, more specifically, emphasized the originality and imaginativeness of her fiction: 'She has tremendous, idiosyncratic talent, she is very wry, very funny, most adept at handling complex narrative forms.' Jolley is a mistress of the art of fantasy, comedy and irony, and is often compared with Muriel Spark.

Like many of her contemporaries, Jolley has exhibited a remarkable fluency with the novel's potentiality for weaving fiction and 'reality' into a tight texture, so elaborately constructed that the reader is subtly but relentlessly drawn self-consciously into the tale. Especially in her more recent novels, Jolley has developed the art of allegorizing life into the *writing* of fiction, so that such novels as *Miss Peabody's Inheritance* and *Foxybaby*, as well as *The Sugar Mother*, suggest a subtextual theme of post-modernist character: the reader reading, and the writer writing, are engaged in adventures analogous to the erotic and sexy shenanigans of the characters. This mirroring technique, characteristic of post-modernism but hardly peculiar to it, is developed by Jolley in her individual, dizzyingly elaborate way; yet the labyrinthine reverberations of self-referentiality are firmly rooted in a humane, subtle craft of social comedy and mordant psychological insight. Like her fellow novelists (and unlike numerous reviewers), Jolley has had a clear view of the crucial import for life of post-modernist emphases upon allegories of reading and writing. Far from being 'purely literary', or artificial, or art for art's sake; far from being somehow decadent and frivolous because not attentive to love, life, death and tragedy; these post-modernist techniques of thematic multidimensionality and structural self-referentiality are shown by Jolley to be a crucial means of urging the reader towards a more sophisticated awareness both of literary forms (as opposed to merely overt themes) and of the need for self-criticism, whether in reading, in writing or in living.

For example, in *The Sugar Mother* the central character, Edwin, is a literature professor embarked on an academic study entitled 'The Study of Man'. He seems to have almost no self-knowledge, however. When he writes his lectures, moreover, he quotes extensively from unknown sources, and peppers his conversations with phrases and sentences of literary allusions whose origins he has usually forgotten. In *Foxybaby* and *Miss Peabody*, fact and fiction are also indistinguishable. Miss Peabody becomes so absorbed in the reality of her author friend's characters that she begins looking for them in the streets of London! Eventually, she goes to Australia to meet her author friend Hopewell; but, arriving only a few days after the friend's death, she is inadvertently absorbed into Hopewell's life, to the extent that she starts not only living in her life but writing her fiction. Reader becomes author, and writing a kind of reading, it seems, especially in *Foxybaby*, where the drama which the playwright Miss Porch is 'sketching out' (for her pupils to 'fill in' the details) suddenly becomes 'life'. Not only does the playwright meet her characters on the lonely beach she is walking along on her final evening, but after this unexpected reversal, the novel ends with a new beginning, a rewriting of an earlier incident. Moreover, Jolley has unflinchingly developed erotic undertones of reading and writing in a Roland Barthes-like realization of the 'pleasure of the text'. Desire is always at the centre of her thematic complexities, sometimes heterosexual, sometimes homosexual, sometimes obsessional, but most often gender-free polymorphous perversity, as her bawdy and her inhibited characters interact in hilariously evocative ways, which do not allow the reader the status of voyeur.

Aroused by the passions of the characters, the reader is ushered into an erotic world where desires are not shameful, where literature is sexy, and where genital, phallic sex is just one aspect, not the goal or centre, of the playful eroticism of imaginative activity. Jolley's fiction expresses a Nietzschean faith in knowledge as 'of the body', allowing no dualistic separation between the intellectual and the physical. It gives the lie to the mistaken interpretations of Freud on sexuality; while embodying Freudian insights into human energies of all kinds as erotic, bodily, playful, Jolley has shown that this is not a 'reduction of everything to sex'. In reuniting the bodily and the imaginative in her fiction, Jolley has created works of exhilarating individuality which reward the reader on every 'rewriting' with unexpected, previously unnoticed details, which delight and arouse.

Alison Lurie 1926–

Winner of the 1985 Pulitzer Prize for *Foreign Affairs* (New York, 1984), Lurie is the author of numerous novels including several for children, two volumes of essays (*The Language of Clothes* (New York, 1981)) and *Don't Tell the Grownups* (London, 1990), and *V.R. Lang: A Memoir* (private printing, 1959). Born in Chicago, she later attended Radcliffe and then moved to Los Angeles and, finally, to Cornell University in 1968, where she taught writing courses. She received an award from the American Academy of Arts and Letters in 1979, and is the editor of *The Oxford Book of Modern Fairy Tales* (Oxford, 1993). *Love and Friendship* (New York, 1962), her first novel, takes its title from Jane Austen and establishes from the outset Lurie's conception of her literary influences and heritage. A biting, if often deadpan satire, Lurie's irony is, like Austen's, focused upon male–female relationships. Also as in Austen, a thoroughgoing ambiguity exists about the extent and result, for social-political issues, of Lurie's irony. That is, she has been read both as socially and politically a conservative and as a radical. Yet this indefiniteness is, as in Austen's texts, an essential part of Lurie's techniques of forcing onto the reader an acceptance of an active role in the construction of meaningful attitudes and experiences, whether of texts, other people, one's feelings, or the natural–cultural world.

Such popular novels as *The War Between the Tates* (New York, 1974), a play of words on the War between the States, increased the frustration of readers and critics who were intent on placing – or categorizing – Lurie. Using war as a unifying image, the novel weaves together the personal and the political in a satiric and subtle treatment of the late 1960s and early 1970s in middle-class America. Yet in this novel, as in earlier ones such as *Imaginary Friends* (New York, 1966) and *Real People* (New York, 1969), or later ones such as *Foreign Affairs*, the satire and subtleties are not confined to the overt thematics. Like many of her contemporaries, Lurie has embedded in her fiction constant and systematic self-referential thematics about reading, writing and interpretation, so well woven into her overt material as to be often overlooked by careless reading. Another self-referential technique, which Lurie has in common with such writers as Jane Gardam and Barbara Pym, is her fondness for surprising her readers with familiar characters from other novels. This disruption of conventional textual frames and boundaries constitutes a challenge to the notion of the book as a unitary, independent product, and has several effects on the reader. First, it connects the reader to previous experiences of reading, and it reminds her or him of the arbitrariness and limitedness of the particular novel-world at hand: things might have been (would have been) quite different if this or that central character were only a marginal figure.

In these mid-to-late-career novels, Lurie's embedded thematics constitute a superbly ironic commentary or level of criticism of a quite sophisticated nature, which has not always been fully appreciated by critics or readers. *Imaginary Friends* is a carefully systematized study of how values, standards and attitudes – regarding morals, politics, religion, art and behaviour – are a reflection more of power and politics than of some truth or beauty or goodness notionally independent of the form. This novel explicitly questions the politicization of madness and sanity, whereas Lurie's next novel, *Real People*, concentrated on the analogy between literature and society, and the hypocrisies and pretensions which undermine the creative impulses in both by a valuing of superficialities over fundamentals. The diary form of the novel (frequently interrupted by dialogues with other characters) works well as a focus upon the writer-heroine's growing realization that her writing is her very self, developing and changing and growing: the analogy between the construction of a work of art and the construction of a 'real' self is finely drawn so that the notion of reality itself is questioned as an imaginary construct.

Foreign Affairs and *The Truth about Lorin Jones* (Boston, 1988) further explore the nature of reality, the self and fiction as discursive constructs; that is, as always multiple and interpreted from different points of view. In the latter novel, interviews with different people are interspersed amongst narrative passages to reveal the amazing variety of perceptions about who Lorin actually is. In *Foreign Affairs*, it is England itself which becomes the text to be read, interpreted and evaluated. Through a series of fantastic fairytale encounters, tasks, quests and recognitions, the characters in *Foreign Affairs* are seen through their own changing and contradictory readings of that Bible of all texts for the English literature

professor, namely, English society itself. There
is no one English society, though; there are,
rather, views, fantasies, illusions and attitudes
about it. Using the power of the journey metaphor to the full, Lurie set her characters in an
intertextual reality, drawing heavily on Henry
James, Edith Wharton and others, to reveal the
destructive effects of unimaginative, unconscious
stereotypes and the possible modes in which
characters can recreate themselves into something more genuinely imaginative. The literary
convention of foreign places as the scene for
imaginativeness and increments in self-knowledge is exploited by Lurie with fine discretion.
Fairy-tale illusions are shattered as the beauty
turns out to be the beast, the frog a prince and
54-year-old Vinnie a Cinderella, and Prince
Charming returns to his wife. 'Readings' of
England, interpretations of what it is really like,
what is the real England and so on abound, and
provide the context and frame for characters'
transformations. *Foreign Affairs* shares this fascination for the liberating effects of foreign places
with its contemporary *An Unsuitable Attachment*
(1982), Pym's splendid satiric exploration of her
character's conflicting readings both of Italy and
of each other. Both Lurie and Pym, then, follow
in the Henry James–Edith Wharton tradition in
their use of conventions, their emphasis upon
views, and their interest in moral ambiguity, self-
deception and self-development or moral maturation. Moreover, the counterpoint in *Foreign
Affairs* – the alternating chapters in which central characters are marginalized and marginalized
ones are centred – keeps the reader off balance
enough to prevent unconscious identification with
one point of view as *the* point of view. And the
balance between England and America is poised:
Americans may be trying to read England and
the English, but the English are also shown observing, reading and misreading their American
observers. While the analogy between reader and
text may not be as explicitly drawn as in *Lorin
Jones*, it still haunts the novel, as it haunts
James's, constantly reminding the reader that
not only is the novel a discursive construct, but
so are the subject, the reader and the author,
and the reality to which the text 'refers'. For
Lurie, the reader inevitably collaborates, whether
knowingly or not.

Christine Brooke-Rose 1928–

Arguably one of Britain's most important novelists of the second half of the twentieth century,
Brooke-Rose's radically experimental fiction can
be compared with that of James Joyce, Marguerite Young, Ann Quin, Kathy Acker and the
plays of Samuel Beckett. Influenced – both before and during her long period of residence and
teaching in Paris, from 1968 onwards (she now
lives in Provence) – by the French *nouveau roman* and such writers as Alain Robbe-Grillet,
Nathalie Sarraute and Claude Simon, she has
pushed still further their challenge to realism
(its claim, for example, of the novel as representative of an extra-linguistic reality, and so
on). Her radically innovative use of language,
especially metaphor, and her emphasis upon the
need to perceive in new ways, formulate new
literary structures and imagine new realities have
taken her beyond the 'conservative' techniques
of her compatriots, who rarely break decisively
with realism of character, plot, style or structure. The characteristic self-consciousness about
one's literary heritage, the frequent use of alleged non-fictional modes within fiction (use of
documentary material: letters, journals, 'found'
manuscripts, essays, etc.), the self-reflective
awareness of writing and reading in the thematics,
and other familiar post-modernist devices everywhere evident in recent British fiction did not,
Brooke-Rose has indicated, go far enough in
challenging the authority of our commonsense
notions of reality, whether about personal identity, psychology, the 'Other', society, science,
literature, history, the arts, the natural world or
whatever. Few recent writers, then, have gone
as far to try to change our perceptions and draw
our attention to new possible perceptual processes
as has Brooke-Rose in her fiction, criticism and
theoretical writings.

Brooke-Rose was born in Geneva of a Swiss
American mother and an English father, and
learnt French before she learnt to speak English.
She took a BA in philology at Somerville College, Oxford, in 1949, and a PhD from University College, London, in 1954. The PhD led,
indirectly at least, to her academic study of the
language of English poetry, *A Grammar of Metaphor* (London, 1958); she had already published

her first novel, *The Languages of Love* (London, 1957), and some poetry. *The Sycamore Tree* (London, 1958), *The Dear Deceit* (London, 1960) and *The Middlemen* (London, 1961) preceded the truly experimental and impressive fiction of Brooke-Rose's middle period, though they are not without interest. Indeed, some of her later, more radical concerns are already evident in these four early texts. By 1964, with the publication of *Out* (London), which won the Travelling Prize of the Society of Authors, Brooke-Rose had suffered a serious illness which, she suggested, contributed to a kind of literary conversion; this involved a recognition that her earlier work had capitulated too easily to the prevailing conventions. With this novel and its sequels – *Such* (London, 1966), which won the James Tait Black Memorial Prize; *Between* (London, 1968); and *Thru* (London, 1975) – Brooke-Rose broke with realist notions of unified plot and character, logical narrative, causal order and time sequence, transparent language, and predominantly literal language or single, unified discourse.

These new non-realist techniques had already been introduced in her early work, but in the middle period Brook-Rose flooded her novels with these devices, utterly sweeping away the realist props which are usually allowed to frame, structure and authorize even relatively post-modernist descriptions and challenges. Gone are unified characters or narrative points of view, gone are distinct thematics or causal plot, gone is use of language predominantly to convey meaning. Instead, language is foregrounded as essentially metaphoric and not the vehicle of meaning, but the means by which we can and must refresh and revitalize our perceptions, our reality and ourselves, if we are not to degenerate into unthinking robots tyrannized by clichés. As Sarah Birch has shown, Brooke-Rose has experimented with all forms of metaphor, and she expanded the meaning of the concept 'metaphor', using puns, misquotations, scientific discourse taken out of context, mixed discourses, slips of the tongue, synonyms and so on, in order to elaborate upon and demonstrate the Nietzschean idea that all knowledge-discourse is based on metaphors and is essentially fictional. Through a process of 'recontextualization', of both words and entire discourses, Brooke-Rose's fiction functions

to challenge the natural and the universal (especially science) – that objective authority alleged by scientific discourses, for example. She has revealed science to be strange, exotic, metaphoric, and just another of the possible discourses for experiencing and perceiving the world.

Recontextualization, then, is one of Brooke-Rose's primary literary strategies for engaging in the radical break with realist unities which most post-modernists have only tampered with. Recontextualization is, essentially, metaphoricity, and it involves the usual conceptual 'displacement' of one thing for (or like) another, or what Nietzsche termed 'appropriation'. 'Displacement' also becomes a frequent thematic element in Brooke-Rose's novels of the middle period, whether in the form of global catastrophes (as in the works of Doris Lessing) or of changes in values, beliefs or other kinds of cognitive decentring. This thematic metaphor functions polysemically to suggest not only how reluctant people are to change their perceptions, but also what it feels like when circumstances – illness or some other necessity – force new views and new, alien attitudes upon us. Psychologically cataclysmic and terrifying, such changes often threaten our sanity, or at least seem incomprehensible, as in new literature, philosophy or art, which is often perceived as chaos until one finds the new words needed to make possible new responses. For to try to force such new perceptions into old forms would deprive us of the opportunity to enlarge, enrich and make new our perceptions, our concepts, our realities and our forms of consciousness.

One of Brooke-Rose's central preoccupations in the search for a new kind of fiction and language has been her concern with social, political and psychological realities. Like those of Jorge Luis Borges, Jacques Derrida, Nietzsche and others, her linguistic and artistic endeavours have been firmly rooted in these 'realities'. Indeed, her fiction has sought to expose the destructiveness of certain conventional notions about personal identity, character, morality, social relations and power. Like Michel Foucault, she has sought to reveal these realities as conventions or even illusions which *can be changed*. Gender relations have also been one of her concerns; indeed she looked at the fact/fiction dichotomy from the focus of gender, and how that focus changes our perception of such dichotomies. Coercion and authority, and notions of purity and competition, are replaced by fraternization, reversibility, exchange, flow and hybridity – or what Keats called 'negative capability' – the ability to hover amongst or between yet within apparently contradictory or exclusive terrains. Through metaphoric reversibility, Brooke-Rose has challenged hierarchies, dualisms and familiar illusions mistaken for inviolable truths, and reconceptualized subjectivity, objectivity, society and art. By making words, sentences and concepts interact in new and unexpected ways, Brooke-Rose has shown us how we can revitalize our language, our feelings and our lives by reimagining and remaking our most basic assumptions, which pass for inalterable realities.

Later novels, such as *Amalgamemnon* (Manchester, 1984), *Xorandor* (Manchester, 1986), *Verbivore* (Manchester, 1990) and *Textermination* (Manchester, 1991), sometimes referred to as the 'Intercom Quartet', constitute a further departure by Brooke-Rose, away from the radically anti-realist techniques of her middle novels, and towards a questioning of the novel in a highly technological era. Other related questions about the novel and about fiction and language itself involve an analysis of the concept of communication, the nature of reading, writing and storytelling. Brooke-Rose's texts explore what is possible in the way of more dynamic, interactive narration, without capitulating to the familiar, ordinary devices of realist fiction. The ontological status of characters, plots, themes, social realities and other elements of novels is explored, as Brooke-Rose has shown us that the process of reading involves not the determination (of a multiplicity) of correct interpretations. Reading inevitably leads to unlimited variety – Derrida's endless free play of interpretation – and Brooke-Rose's fiction presses us to let ourselves think of fiction, art, criticism and appreciation in ways that may at first seem preposterous and impossible. Her novels, while experimental to an *almost* alienating degree, are made 'appropriable' by their humour, geniality and sheer virtuosity: they are readable if we learn to read in a more light-hearted way, as is the case with the works of Quin and Acker.

In her most recent novel, *Textermination*,

Brooke-Rose filled the text with characters from other novels, from Jane Austen's Emma to Emma Bovary, for example. Authors also appear, including, for example, Goethe, Tolstoy and others. Moreover, readers and critics also attend the literary conference where all these characters gather annually in the USA. The novel begins with that ancient literary convention, the journey – in carriages, on horseback, in aeroplanes, by foot – endless descriptions of journeys taken from other novels acting to introduce the 'fictional' beings who will populate the novel. Fiction and non-fiction (of a kind, at least) intermingle irretrievably, as the reader is drawn into the profusion of events at the conference of characters, authors, readers and critics. From violent terrorist attacks by gunmen (only simulated, apparently, since they are 'killed' and then reappear later) to simple romances, jealousies and accounts of conference talks and debates, *Textermination* takes the reader into a fictional world of fiction like nothing ever experienced before in a novel, at least not in this systematic way, though Walter Scott comes close.

In *Xorandor* and *Verbivore*, Brooke-Rose used fiction as the subject matter of her novels in a somewhat less overt and direct way. 'Natural' computers – not human-made, that is – which look like small, shapely stones and which have existed peacefully on earth for thousands of millions of years, begin to intrude into the computer screens of humans. The Xorandors object to the amount of verbiage spewn out by all these personal computers and other machines, which is causing intolerable 'noise' and pollution to the Xorandors of the natural world. Consequently, they interrupt human computers, causing deadly plane crashes and radio and TV failures, and thereby terrify the human race into a more ecologically minded attitude. In telling the story of the 'verbivores', Brooke-Rose used many postmodernist techniques as well as some new devices of her own. Recursive embedding abounds, as do disrupted syntax and obfuscation of narrative point of view, while ontological loops and other meta-fictional devices delight the reader. In *Xorandor*, the novel is entirely 'dialogue' (including 'dialogues' with Xorandor), but reported dialogue, as the two children who discover the verbivores 'dictate' their incredible story into their word processor. They thereby stumble upon all the problems of how to tell a story. In the sequel, *Verbivore*, many narrators tell stories, all interrelated and endlessly, recursively embedded, usually typing into their word processors with interruptions from the verbivores.

Often, in *Verbivore*, it is impossible to 'tell' who is narrating or on which meta-fictional loop we find ourselves: a playwright creates characters who have encounters in the 'real' world, he writes them into plays, they confront him with his false accounts, he becomes a creation of theirs, and so on. Likewise, in *Amalgamemnon*, a character in the twentieth century becomes fused into the texts of Herodotus and mixed up with Cassandra, and all boundaries between fiction and historical fact or reality collapse.

One can also note that earlier experiments in *Out*, *Such*, *Between* and *Thru* similarly mocked conventional dualities, and described the world, experience and consciousness as a text. In *Thru*, Brooke-Rose amalgamated Roland Barthes's, Derrida's and many other writers' writings and ideas about literature and theory into a novel which keeps erasing itself, starting a new text, changing the characters, the events, the accounts. And it mixes self-commentary and analysis with that of a writing teacher commenting on the text, so that the meta-fictional loops exceed anything Brooke-Rose had done before. Romance intermingles with classes on literature, creative writing and dialogues between 'characters' in the (fictional) class, and radical disruptions of format, syntax and spelling abound. It makes no sense to ask what is real and what is fiction, what the author is trying to communicate, and so on. Literary theory and life experience are interwoven into a quite simply hilarious 'self-consuming artifact'.

All this overt experimentation began with the novel *Out*, after Brooke-Rose's illness. There, Brooke-Rose described a character who returns from the dead to be drawn into emotionally strained relationships with his family and friends, who do not know what to make of his return. A constant interweaving of the memory of his 'other-world' encounters (with 'luminous balls of being' or circles of light) with his present encounters (with corresponding people in his worldly life) creates a fascinating narrative of radically innovative images, metaphors and stylistic effects, as 'Lazarus' drifts towards betrayal

and disappointment after his miraculous recovery. To sum up, each one of Brooke-Rose's novels is a different type of radical experimentation and, hence, stands as an example of her remarkably imaginative reinvigoration of fiction, language and life.

Anita Brookner 1928–

Born in London of Polish parents, Brookner established herself as an expert in the art history of eighteenth- and nineteenth-century France. Several books on the subject won her a readership at the Courtauld Institute, where she had earlier taken a PhD, having done a BA at King's College, London. She is also distinguished by being the first woman to hold the Slade Professorship of Fine Art at Cambridge University in 1967–8. In addition to her books on art history, she has written numerous articles and reviews for the *Times Literary Supplement*, the *London Review of Books* and other periodicals, journals and newspapers. In 1981, at the age of 53, she published her first novel, self-consciously entitled *A Start in Life*, also known as *The Debut* (London), then *Providence* (London, 1982) and *Look at Me* (London, 1983). Her fourth novel, *Hotel du Lac* (London, 1984), won the Booker Prize, and other novels followed, such as *Family and Friends* (London, 1985), which moved away from the familiar milieu of her earlier four novels to portray a Jewish family transplanted to London before World War II. With *A Misalliance* (London, 1986), Brookner returned to her treatment of more solitary female characters. By this time, she had moved beyond the overt and systematic intertextual allusions of her first few novels, with their specific references to Balzac (especially *Eugenie Gandet*) and other nineteenth- (as well as eighteenth-) century 'realists'. Such direct intertextuality is replaced by more subtle allusions in the later works, such as *Lewis Piercy* (London, 1989) or *Brief Lives* (London, 1990), which depicts the difficult but rewarding friendship between two women. *A Closed Eye* (London, 1991) portrays the nature of a conventional marriage or family and the results of its stifling of feelings, such as the suffocation with love of a daughter by her frustrated mother. The atmosphere of ruthless determinism in the novel may suggest the almost irresistible power of sexist conventions about marriage and about women servants. In *Fraud* (London, 1992), Brookner developed an extremely ironic tale about a woman, Anna, who disappears from her normal life, and the 'portraits' by her acquaintances and friends which the police enquiry turns up. These 'photographic' images of the woman are, apparently, precisely what Anna has sought to escape by taking off to Paris to recreate herself.

This recent novel, *Fraud*, is an emblem of all Brookner's novels and their central, if variously depicted, preoccupation with how accepted images of women function to coerce them into exploitable postures. Like Angela Carter's, Brookner's fiction constitutes a ruthless and daring exposure of the mechanics of the psychological manipulation, on a large social scale, of girls and women. Through parents, schools, films, literature, painting, politics and so on, women are shown in Brookner's novels to be coerced into preposterous wants, needs, desires, fantasies and, in general, notions about fulfilment or happiness which are doomed to failure and designed to render women dependent and exploitable. The novels expose the anatomy of such manipulation: girls are fed images of themselves and nourished on doomed fantasies, and this image creation is the crucial mechanism for exploitation. Brookner does not whitewash the extremely painful, even terrifying process of delegitimizing images of the 'good girl' and 'virtuous woman'. Her characters encounter almost unbearable depths of loneliness and denigration, at the hands of both men and entrapped, jealous women, when they try to create new images, whether of themselves or of what is desirable or of what constitutes happiness. Through techniques of irony and humour and through self-referential narrative devices, Brookner's fiction explores the literary analysis of such images, and rewrites the canon.

Not surprisingly, Brookner's fiction has generated considerable fury and often an ugly defensiveness, mostly, though not entirely, from male readers and critics. Most of the criticism mistakenly centres on the 'contents', since Brookner's fine style and her structural and narrative achievements are generally acknowledged and even lavishly praised. Her fiction, a sustained assault – through literary formalities concretized in the thematics – on the social, political and literary images of women, men, happiness and relationships, must be very threatening to readers committed to the status quo and its related securities. Perhaps the most devastating aspect of her fiction is not so much its exposure of the images which entrap people and which need to be replaced. Its most shocking implication is not even Brookner's courageous if often comic depiction of the pain and loneliness involved in divesting ourselves of 'safe' stereotypes. Its most outrageous, offensive aspect is its (albeit indirect) suggestion that marriage, love, motherhood, status and money, in their familiar, pervasive forms, are empty platitudes; that lives lived conventionally are a death-in-life; that the mediocrity of ordinary people bowing and kowtowing to approved behaviour turns the heart to dust. Like Jean Rhys's, then, Brookner's fiction contributes to an 'innovative' tradition of literature which is dismissed by the unimaginative reader as stories of 'depressed women', 'underdogs', 'failures'. For that is apparently how unconventional women look to the mediocre eye, women who have the courage and humour to endure the pain and loneliness which are the first stage of smashing the mundane shell of stereotypic images. As Doris Lessing showed in *The Golden Notebook*, challenging conventional roles, images and values looks like insanity to the obedient, and 'breaking out' can look like breakdown, since the pressure to conform is ruthlessly exacting. As in life, so in literature: Brookner's literary and thematic innovations are attacked as, of all things, conservative realist texts.

Brookner's women rarely do break down in order to break out, unlike Lessing's characters; nor do they take the route Rhys's novels describe, of destitution, prostitution and drug addiction. Perhaps Brookner's fiction is more optimistic, and perhaps that optimism is a sign of outward social progress, for her women characters are often represented as finding a viable way of living. That they are frequently portrayed as lonely and as unable to succeed at marriage may be depressing to some readers. It may be merely realistic to others, especially since 'happy' and 'successful' marriage and family relations are bought almost always at the price of one's very self-same happiness. Brookner's thematic forms outrage some readers precisely because they dare to suggest that *that* kind of happiness is not worth the name. Brookner has offered a Kate Chopin-like warning to women that they must begin slowly, 'strengthening their wings' before they fly off from their familiar imprisoning world – or else they may be overwhelmed by madness and suicide. These latter may often be the result of the quest for self-realization and escape from image-prisons, but they may be avoidable if we proceed with patience and care in divesting ourselves of the lies we are nourished on from infancy.

Brookner's women, these new artists of life and self, often divest themselves gradually of their illusions and recreate themselves in new images by becoming aware of the fantasies of 'perfection' in relationships which function to oppress women. Perfect mother, perfect wife, perfect romantic lover and sex provider, perfect house – or else it is *your* fault. Meanwhile, the men romp through the novels in a state of complete, self-centred, irresponsible immaturity with respect to human relations and emotions. By gradually accepting the destructive, enslaving effects of illusions of perfection, Brookner's characters are able to begin, albeit stumblingly and awkwardly, to cobble together some patchwork, bricolage existence, which avoids the phoney happiness and seamless unity of conventional 'family values'. In *Hotel du Lac*, for example, Edith recognizes that the cold marriage of convenience offered her by Phillip is not objectionable because it is an inferior form of marriage; it is objectionable because it is just like most marriages, once the heady illusion of romantic attraction has inevitably expired. Edith preserves her limited but passionate affair, instead of trading it for status or sullying it with infidelity and triviality. By challenging all these basic linguistic structures – these concepts – Brookner's fictions suggest new ways of seeing not only women, but men, marriage and child-bearing.

Perhaps such 'moral' dimensions add to the controversy about Brookner's fiction. Her novels depict the 'terrifying' possibility that women who reject society's images of virtue and decency (wifehood, motherhood, dutiful daughters), in order to construct their own versions of themselves, may be realizing a far greater humanity, goodness and decency than either conventionally obedient or conventionally, flamboyantly re-

bellious women. Accused by some radical feminists of being 'conservative', Brookner's fiction is perhaps provoking them by suggesting that their often exhibitionist rebellions are merely the twin of obedience. While we must work together to decentre conventions, we each must also be allowed to forge her (or his) own unique path. Brookner's novels portray both pain and fulfilment, but they depict women making their own unique way through these pressures in terms helpful to readers on similar journeys. For they suggest that noisy, showy displays are often only superficially unconventional, while a quiet, determined pursuit of independence is a more reliable – if less overtly political or feminist – path. If this commitment to non-exhibitionist self-construction and self-recreation is conservative, then so be it.

Jane Gardam 1928–

Fellow of the Royal Society of Literature since 1976, and author of several collections of linked stories and of novels (as well as children's books), Gardam was born in Yorkshire as Jane Pearson and took a BA in English in 1949 at Bedford College, London. After three further years as a research student, she took editorial jobs with journals such as *Time and Tide*, until child-bearing interrupted her career. She published her first book, *A Few Fair Days* (London), in 1971; it and her next two books, *A Long Way from Verona* (London and New York, 1971) and *The Summer After the Funeral* (London and New York, 1973), are often regarded as books for adolescents, though they are also good reading for adults. *Black Faces, White Faces* (London, 1975), published as *The Pineapple Bay Hotel* (New York, 1976) in America, has been treated as Gardam's first adult fiction, and won the David Higham Prize for a first novel, when it might better be treated as a collection of stories with characters and themes recurring throughout. This book also won the Winifred Holtby Memorial Prize in 1976. *Bilgewater* (London, 1976) is arguably a book for adolescents; it is, however, an intricate, comic novel, verging on the frivolous, about the trials and social tribulations of a teenager on the verge of adulthood. The next novel, *God on the Rocks* (London, 1978), is written at the outset from the point of view of 8-year-old Margaret Marsh, but is clearly an adult fiction. Later, the point of view shifts to the various adult characters and their quirks, caprices and promiscuities. *The Sidmouth Letters* (London and New York, 1980), another collection of stories, followed; its title story alerts the reader to Gardam's use of literary allusion in much of her writing, though in this story it is overt, as the existence of two love-letters of Jane Austen become the focus of an academic controversy. *Bridget and William* (London, 1981) and *Horse* (London, 1982) are children's books, while *The Hollow Land* (London, 1981) is another collection of linked stories with Cumbria as the setting, as is *The Pangs of Love* (London, 1983), which won the Katherine Mansfield award. *Kit* (London, 1983) followed this collection, and Gardam's next novel, *Crusoe's Daughter* (London, 1985), is set on the east coast of England; it begins in the first part of the twentieth century, and traces the whole of the century through the eyes of Polly Flint, 87-year-old translator of *Robinson Crusoe*, who is also working on an analysis of *Crusoe* as a spiritual biography.

In *Crusoe's Daughter*, Gardam experiments most overtly with post-modernist techniques of self-referentiality, through direct use of themes about writing, reading, teaching and the interpretation of literature, though this A.S. Byatt-like mode was also anticipated in *The Sidmouth Letters*. Throughout *Crusoe's Daughter*, but especially near and at the end (when Polly teaches a class on 'the novel', and then when this novel closes with a dramatic scene including Robinson Crusoe himself and Polly), Gardam has created an ironic level of self-referentiality. Fact and fiction are interwoven in an inextricable complicity, as the shadowy presence of Crusoe takes on a substantiality which eclipses that of Polly Flint.

While intertextuality (or systematic literary allusion) and self-referentiality are two features of Gardam's witty, exuberant fiction, another interesting feature of the short stories is the intricacy and surprise of their linkages. The interconnections amongst the stories are not mere ornamentation; they often function to give a startlingly different viewpoint. *The Pangs of Love* is a particularly rich example of expansion of viewpoint; moreover, because the first and last story

turn out to involve the same two characters, the connection shapes the entire book into an unexpected unity. This artistic form raises interesting questions about order and shape, and focuses the reader's attention on the very processes of perception, or the struggle for pattern or relationship. *Black Faces, White Faces* is another collection where the links between stories have a quite startling effect upon the reader's attitudes towards the characters and the action. Even more than in other authors' linked stories, such as Alice Munro's or Louise Erdrich's, Gardam's manage to arouse in the reader a rather rare state of mild shock at the difference which an altered point of view can make upon factual, moral and aesthetic perceptions. Like an impressionist painting, Gardam's stories and her fictions are unusually effective both in drawing the reader's attention to the psychological and perceptual processes of ordering and structuring experience, and in shocking the reader into the sudden, unexpected experience of seeing the 'same' things differently.

Some of Gardam's novels and story collections are also notable for the importance of setting. *Black Faces, White Faces* is set in Jamaica, and themes of racism are predominant in this novel–story collection. *The Pangs of Love*, on the other hand, is a collection of stories set in various places, from India to Hong Kong to the north of England, the Isle of Wight and London. Yet, in each story, setting functions not merely as an accidental background but as a central issue in the thematics of the story. Indeed, it could be argued that one of Gardam's most evident characteristics is an economy achieved in part through the congruence of means and ends, parts and whole, structure and thematics, and in part through a spare and precise style.

Cynthia Ozick 1928–

Recipient of numerous awards and grants, and long-time resident of New York City, where she was born, Ozick has written poetry, criticism, short stories, novels and translations of Yiddish poetry into English. She took a BA from New York University in 1949 and an MA from Ohio State a year later, receiving her first major fiction award in 1971, the B'nai B'rith Jewish Heritage

Award. In 1972, she won both the Edward Lewis Wallant Memorial Award and the Jewish Book Council Award for fiction. Three years later, an O. Henry Short Story Award was conferred on her, and numerous other awards have followed. Grants from such sources as the National Endowment for the Arts and a Guggenheim, amongst others, helped her to continue her writing. Her work has been translated into a number of languages, and she has been called, by *Newsweek*, one of the best American short story writers. She is also a prolific essayist, writing for numerous magazines, newspapers and periodicals.

Ozick's novels include *Trust* (New York, 1966), *The Cannibal Galaxy* (New York, 1983) and *The Messiah of Stockholm* (New York, 1987), while some of her stories are collected in *The Pagan Rabbi and Other Stories* (New York, 1971), *Bloodshed and Three Novellas* (New York, 1976), *Levitation: Five Fictions* (New York, 1982) and *The Shawl: A Story and a Novella* (New York, 1989). Her collection of essays, *Art and Ardour*, appeared in 1983 (New York). Throughout her stories, novellas, fictions and novels, Ozick has increasingly made use of post-modern techniques. They are combined effectively with Jewish elements of, for example, the golem (a man or woman created out of magical art, or sometimes also meaning as yet unformed matter), other religious images, icons and idols, often in the context of feminist writing. This involves preeminently affirmation of the equality of people, rather than a feminism of separatism or difference. For Ozick, as for Virginia Woolf, the human psyche is 'androgynous, epicene, asexual'. The characters in her fictions display this quality; indeed, 'epicene' is an apt word for describing Ozick's commitment, in her writing, to our common humanity. The emphasis, in her case, is on overcoming barriers resulting from both sex and race, as well as religion, as it is in such writers as Maxine Hong Kingston and Nadine Gordimer, for example. This is not to suggest that Ozick has been uninterested in the exclusion of women from many aspects of society and religion, however. On the contrary, she is active in her insistence on the necessity not to exclude half the Jewish people from its culture and intellect, or else another generation of women will be 'born to have no ancestry and . . . no progeny'.

A recent novel, *The Messiah of Stockholm*, illustrates Ozick's evolving fluency and interest in post-modern techniques, though these were already evident in earlier works, such as 'Rosa', 'The Shawl' or *Cannibal Galaxy*, for example. This fluency is enriched by Ozick's interest in what she called 'a new culture-making', involving the creation of a Jewish 'liturgical fiction'. Such fiction involves, for Ozick, the rejuvenation of the Hebrew form of writing known as midrash – the ancient method of exegesis. Ozick also suggested that if we disinherit ourselves from our own culture – in her case, her Jewish culture – the result will be a kind of creative stagnation: 'It is the final shudder of spent thought: out of which no literature, Jewish or otherwise, can hope to spring.' Midrash functions in Ozick's fiction to keep the text alive, both by connecting it with the textual tradition and by making it constantly self-renewing. It is a method which, Ozick realized, could fruitfully employ post-modernist devices to achieve those two aims. Midrash involved interpreting the Bible in a way that allowed of several coexisting accounts, leading to polyvocal commentaries which prevented the Bible from becoming a set, static, unalterable object. The method of midrash also functioned to 'fill in' the written text with oral, social, living traditions, so that the text did not become isolated from its environment or insensitive to historical and social changes. The text is, then, understood to be productive always of new meanings and therefore open, not closed. For Ozick, the text – and culture generally – is preserved by augmenting it with new reading, new writing, and the filling in of elements previously left out, missed or disregarded.

In this case, it is the voice and experience of women – women's writing – which need to fill in the spaces of Jewish culture and literature created by their prior exclusion. While Ozick cautioned her readers in the late 1980s that midrash should not be the sole form of Jewish literary revitalization, her handling of these larger issues in *The Messiah of Stockholm* fuses with post-modernist devices to create an impressive work of art.

The novel adopts primarily the post-modernist techniques of, for example, embedding one text within another, creating a central character whose identity is problematic, violating genre

distinctions, emphasizing plot over characterization, raising questions of authorized versions,
originality and plagiarism, attending to literature as a form of self-referentiality and so on. In
the case of this novel, more specifically, recursive embedding occurs when we realize that the
quest for a missing manuscript – whose existence is even in doubt – involves a novel entitled,
itself, *The Messiah*. Identity is problematized in
a protagonist who is an orphan, who has made
up his name, having lost his own, and who claims
nevertheless to be the son of Bruno Schultz
(Freud?), the author of *The Messiah*. When the
manuscript finally turns up in extremely suspicious circumstances its authenticity is suspected,
but never disproven. After a hair-raising series
of deferrals, the protagonist (Lacan?) manages
to 'read' the manuscript, but the effect of the
reading is only to create more uncertainty:

> What was in *The Messiah*? Lost! Chips of
> dream. It was nearly as if he had stumbled
> into someone else's dream. Whose? . . . He
> could not remember what he had read five
> minutes ago. A perplexity . . . fragments of
> some vague insubstantiality, folklorish rem-
> nants; a passage of oxygen-deprivation per-
> haps. It has receded, whatever it was – he
> retained nothing, . . . only the faintest tremor
> of some strenuous force . . . Lamentation
> remained. Elegy after great pain.

Moreover, the protagonist now has a rival: Adela,
who has allegedly brought – rescued – the manuscript from a cellar in Poland, claims to be the
daughter (Kristeva?) of the author of *The Messiah*
– the authentic messenger of the word, the text,
is a woman. Our anti-hero cannot accept her
authority; he feels it threatens his status as self-
proclaimed son of *The Messiah's* creator, and
loses his faith in himself, in his ancestry and in
the manuscript – which he destroys in a violent
act of setting fire to the text.

Throughout *The Messiah of Stockholm*, the
reader is confronted with insistent references to
the Holocaust; indeed, in such stories as 'The
Shawl' and 'Rosa', this is the overt theme of the
texts. References to a persistent 'smell of something roasting' disturb the reader throughout the
text, as do Ozick's frequent reminders of the
events in Poland which led to the present fictional
situation. This Walter Abish-like mixture of fact

and history with fiction is accomplished in such
a way that the reader becomes confused, even
as to the fictional 'facts'. The references in the
text to the reading of *The Messiah* as like an
intrusion into someone else's dream, along with
unifying themes throughout the novel of plagiarism, the questioning of origins of both characters and the manuscript, and attention to themes
of deceit, lying and duplicity are all typical post-
modernist modes of drawing attention to the
artifice of the text, and of life itself. Art at its
very inception, that is, is duplicitous, as is the
author: pretences of sincerity, objectivity and
authority, pretences of the art being a mimetic
representation of reality, or of having some reality as its origin to which it refers for its meaning
– all these 'duplicities' are exposed. The author
is shown to be an impersonator whose stories
only trace the lines of her or his own face, to use
Jorge Luis Borges's terms. *The Messiah of Stockholm* is the story of an interminable deferral of
certainty and truth, while history and time themselves are implicated as fiction.

Paule Marshall 1929–

Daughter of immigrants from Barbados, Marshall
grew up in New York City and studied at Hunter
and Brooklyn College. Most famous at first for
her early novel, *Brown Girl, Brownstones* (New
York, 1959), Marshall has continued to publish
for nearly forty years. Her fiction includes three
other novels, *The Chosen Place, the Timeless People* (New York, 1969) about Merle Kinbona,
Praisesong for the Widow (New York, 1983) and
Daughters (New York, 1991). Collections of short
stories include *Soul Clap Hands and Sing* (New
York, 1961) and *Merle and Other Stories* (London, 1983, published as *Reena and Other Stories*,
New York, 1983). Alice Walker has described
Marshall as 'unequalled in intelligence, vision,
craft, by anyone of her generation, to put her
contribution to our literature modestly'. Numerous critics have noted Marshall's thematic interests in the relation of mother–daughter, that is,
the way female identity is often developed
through connection with the mother (and then
the eventual need to break away from the
mother's dominion to establish autonomy). The
process of establishing a meaningful, viable

relationship as an adult with the mother is shown to have larger social-political-historical import; the mother–daughter relationship functions as an emblem in Marshall's (and other writers') fiction of the land, the people, the past, the heritage – all of which must be renegotiated to achieve self-identity. The extreme difficulty of getting right the balance between autonomy and relationships, personal identity and community, present and past, is not glossed over, as Marshall's novels explore the dilemmas which arise in people's efforts to balance these often conflicting demands.

All Marshall's novels explore the specific particularities of black people's encounters with these human demands and conflicts as they occur in racist societies. While *Brown Girl, Brownstones*, set in New York City, explores a young female adolescent's process of establishing her autonomy relationship with her mother/land/history/people, *The Chosen Place, the Timeless People* depicts the memorable character Merle Kinbona on the mythical island of Bournehills, set in the Atlantic Ocean, also struggling, in her middle age, to find herself a home for her spirit. Travels to England, marriage there, child birth and a lesbian relationship have only increased her alienation and confusion. Her return to Bournehills initiates the process of reconstruction which leads, through connection with the past, her history, her people and her land, to a greater peace. In *Praisesong for the Widow*, a widow still older than Merle is depicted by Marshall as having also to confront her personal and communal identity if she is to gain relief from the spiritual malaise which is gradually overwhelming her. Here again, place is central, as Avey Johnson travels back to Carriacou, a Caribbean island, where she reappropriates her cultural heritage. In both of these later novels, the emphases upon island settings, upon repossessing 'discredited knowledge' in the form of rituals (communal excursions, dances, healing sessions and celebrations) and other mythic forms structure the narratives in distinctive ways. In her most recent novel, *Daughters*, Marshall used these elements and also looked at the father–daughter relationships introduced in the second and first novels more tangentially.

While each of Marshall's novels can stand alone as a fine artistic achievement, read together they form an even more powerful, eloquent artistic embodiment of the experiences of women of all ages struggling to achieve an identity distinct from the stereotypes and conventional roles normally allowed them. Like Gloria Naylor, Marshall has drawn on 'the power of place' as 'the gathering spot' of feeling, to give her novels themselves a distinctive and unique 'identity', just as the characters are struggling for such identity. *Praisesong for the Widow*, while not as panoramic and substantial as its predecessor *The Chosen Place*, fuses all the most effective elements of Marshall's novels into a powerful unity. Avey Johnson, on a cruise in the Caribbean, has a dream vision of her great aunt calling her to come home; the awareness of the spiritual malaise triggered by the dream grows to unbearable intensity, until Avey abandons the cruise. Before she can escape her destiny on a plane back to New York, she meets the ancient, ageless sage Lebert Joseph, who senses her spiritual illness and encourages her to join the yearly excursion to Carriacou to celebrate community, the past and one's connection with one's people and land. On this 'second' journey (within a journey), Avey becomes violently ill and is purged by her sickness, then partially healed by the ministrations and personal power of Lebert's daughter, who lives on the island. That evening, at the fête, Avey's past is restored to her through a ritual dance, and her spirit is freed from its debilitation. This novel is structured around a variety of finely arranged conventions – including journeys, fêtes, dances, healing encounters and transformative rites, as well as natural 'supernatural' (but never explicitly so) elements: dreams, visions and ancient sages as well as curing, magical rituals. Such 'discredited knowledge' is repossessed by an insistence in the novel upon its natural power, its imaginative force, as a completion of the rational forces of Western science and medicine (represented in *The Chosen Place*, for example, by the socialist anthropologist and his wife). While *Praisesong* covers only a two-day period, through memories, fantasies and dreams, Avey's life is unfolded before the reader to show the demands and conflicts which have made her ill in spirit.

One of these central conflicts involves her family's efforts to overcome the poverty and social injustice in a racist society designed to exploit and impoverish black people. As she counts up the terrible price she and her husband have paid for respectability, she realizes that her husband lost his identity and became a stranger to her before he died. Then she realizes she has lost her own, from wanting 'too much' material goods, too much money, because she identified with the single-minded white majority's pursuit of money as an end in itself, instead of as a means only. They could have had both freedom from poverty and spiritual riches, if only they had been more 'vigilant': 'the means needed to rescue them from Halsey Street and to see the children through, while preserving, safeguarding, treasuring those things that had come down to them over the generations, which had defined them in a particular way. The most vivid, the most valuable part of themselves!' Marshall's novels, from 1959 to 1991, embody this most valuable part of human life in compelling fiction which speaks to all readers, of whatever race, creed or sex, and reminds us that the value of money is to release us from poverty, so that we can then pursue emotional and intellectual fulfilment. Marshall's fiction portrays people without such fulfilment as empty of all meaning, however wealthy they are. When money becomes an aim, rather than an instrument for the achievement of humane values, then human life is no longer human.

Ursula Le Guin 1929–

Daughter of Afred and Theodore Kroeber, Le Guin was born in California and took degrees from Radcliffe and Columbia, before embarking on a career as a writer and a teacher of writing at universities throughout the USA and Europe. Many of her books are overtly for children, but the distinction between adolescent and adult fiction is not easily maintained, as her powerful fantasy writings capture the imagination of adult readers. The latter often see her work functioning as a critique of contemporary and conventional language, life and attitudes, revealing the hidden political agendas and assumptions which inhibit freedom. Le Guin has won numerous awards and prizes for various of her fifteen novels and short stories, and she has also written non-fiction essays, collected in the two volumes

The Language of the Night (New York, 1979) and *Dancing at the Edge of the World* (New York and London, 1989). Le Guin's command of language, her psychological insight and her passionate convictions have given readers a new respect for the entire genre of fantasy and science fiction; indeed, she has breached the boundaries not only of adolescent/adult fiction but also of canonical/non-canonical literature. This 'genre busting' is an example of Le Guin's interest in examining the categories and distinctions which govern our lives, structure our experience and constitute our world. The categories and patterns by which we organize and order our world, our experiences, our thoughts and feelings are analysed by Le Guin through naming and renaming. That is, she has examined the power of words as acts, as political acts indeed. How we categorize our experience – by means of names – is an expression of our values and attitudes, and we can question, adapt and transform our values only by using words and language in a more self-conscious, politically aware way. For Le Guin, because life is evolutionary, because it is constantly changing, we need to adapt and evolve new values and ways of living which are more appropriate to new developments and social and personal experience. We cannot do this if we go on clinging to all the old categories and names and ways of thinking, feeling and experiencing. For Le Guin, it is not the reason but fantasy and imagination that are the sources of new names, new categories; reason can only analyse what is already known. Fantasy literature and science fiction get much of their power from releasing into the conscious mind, for the use of the reason, unconscious, 'irrational' or non-rational elements, by means of new words, names and categories.

Archaic, legendary and heroic characters, situations, images and words are used in Le Guin's fiction to defamiliarize ordinary, everyday language, as well as to draw upon the power of these mythic, primitive and universal elements. Quests, encounters and journeys, along with animal allies and helpers, dragons and witches, and other effects such as shadowy selves (animus, anima, emanations, etc.), issues of power and balance between nature and the human, and imagery of light and darkness make up Le Guin's worlds of fiction. Some of her most accomplished novels are the 'Earthsea' trilogy, *A Wizard of Earthsea* (Berkeley, Calif., 1968), *The Tombs of Atuan* (New York, 1971) and *The Farthest Shore* (New York, 1972). *Tehanu* (New York and London, 1990) is a fourth part, published eighteen years later. *The Left Hand of Darkness* (New York and London, 1969) describes a race of beings who are ambisexual; it raises interesting questions about gender demarcations and how we might more creatively view ourselves and our sexuality. In *The Lathe of Heaven* (New York, 1971), the central character's dreams actually remake a world desecrated and spoiled by pollution and abuse. Other novels include *The Word for World is Forest* (New York, 1976), *The Beginning Place* (New York, 1980) and *Always Coming Home* (New York, 1985). Many short stories have been published in numerous magazines such as the *New Yorker*, and essays in *Science-Fiction Studies* and other journals.

Jennifer Johnston 1930–

Born in Dublin, daughter of actress-director Shelah Richards and playwright Denis Johnston, Jennifer Johnston left Trinity College before taking a degree. Having written plays since her adolescence, she turned to novel writing after raising a family. She found at first no publisher for her novel *The Gates* (London, 1973), which was accepted only after her second novel, *The Captains and the Kings* (London, 1972), won several prizes including the Yorkshire Post Fiction and Robert Pitman Literary prizes. *How Many Miles to Babylon?* (London, 1974) charts the tragic friendship of two young soldiers, while *Shadows on our Skin* (London, 1977) – nominated for the Booker Prize – explores adolescent love and jealousy and its dire consequences. *The Old Jest* (London, 1979), probably a dialogue with Bowen's *The Last September* (1929), describes the maturing effects of the violent death of an older man on a young female admirer. Death again is a central theme in her next novel, *The Christmas Tree* (London, 1981), while in *The Railway Station Man* (London, 1984) Johnston gave us her most complex novel of human relationship, art and violence. *Fool's Sanctuary* (London, 1987) represents perhaps the quintessence of her art, finely described by Anthony Burgess:

'This is a unique and perfect art, born of a time and place and temperament, not contrived against their grain. It represents no movement, and one can learn nothing from it except the ancient virtues of human concern and verbal economy.'

To all her novels, Johnston's dramatic skills have contributed a classical verbal and structural economy, with her adept dialogue, terse, accurate diction and austerity of plot. In these short, intense novels, the author usually adopts a pseudo-objective autobiographical point of view: one of the characters is the focus of the (often) past, recollected events, but their immediacy for the reader is overwhelming. Usually set in Ireland, usually encompassing violence, love and death, often exploring relationships across boundaries of age, sex, class or religion, Johnston's novels avoid political and moralistic or religious dogma, yet use, as vehicles for her art, political, moral and religious themes. Like Winifred Holtby in *South Riding* (1936), Johnston has explored the deeper human currents which draw people of quite different, conflicting 'surface' opinions together. While Holtby was preoccupied primarily with class divides, Johnston explored nearly all the dualisms of our social arrangements, and her fiction traces the powerful attractions between people of different beliefs brought about by empathy in temperament, character and values. Part of the tragic effect of her novels lies in E.M. Forster's idea that accidents of age, nationality, religion and class inevitably divide passionate, loyal and generous natures from their 'natural' fellow spirits.

In her recent novel *Fool's Sanctuary*, Johnston achieved – even by the measures of her own intense and terse art – a perfection of quiet immediacy and interiority, as she framed and focused the violently dramatic tragedy of Miranda's youth with the apparently rambling yet pointed consciousness of an aged, dying, drugged Miranda. Indeed, the frequent, periodic interruptions of later commentary into the 1919–20 narrative create an alternation in narrative focus which effectively destroys any sentimentality in the reader, as ironic, satiric and self-referential comments about the characters of 'my play . . . having more reality' remind the reader that this may be fiction, but it is also history and reality. One of the most recurring themes throughout the 'present', dying Miranda's fragmentary but

243

systematic narratives is the way emotional intensity can make the past, a dream or a memory far more real than the present. As with most of Johnston's other novels, *Fool's Sanctuary* focuses upon a moral dilemma of conflicting loyalties which are irresolvable, and which lead to the death of an admirable, courageous being. Similarly, irresolvable moral dilemmas in *How Many Miles* and *The Old Jest* portray morally developed or developing humans trying to find their way through the massive tangle of violence and social upheaval which threatens their commitments to decency and love. Thus, while set in Ireland, while exuding the life and breath of Irish existence, Johnston's novels explore the artistic forms most expressive of the very heart of human moral and spiritual dimensions, bridging the terrible gap which divides British and Irish people and prevents them from seeing each other as people, instead of as the enemy.

To sum up, Johnston has achieved in her artistic forms a rare and breathtaking fusion; she has plumbed the depths of human life while setting it in an acutely realized historical locale; she has fused human complexity with a brevity and artistic spareness of quite unusual intensity for the novel form. While it is sometimes said by reviewers that her novels are more like expanded short stories, this quite fails to capture the breadth and depth of her fiction. Her characters are highly developed and have a profound impact on the reader; the structure of the novels is complex and multilayered; landscape, locale and setting are powerfully, if tersely, drawn. The thematics are rich and encompassing vehicles of her formal achievements. If her novels are short, they are still novels; but they may be said to be 'exemplary novels', that is, paradigms of how rare an art brevity is, of how much can be compressed into a few carefully chosen, deft sentences.

Toni Cade Bambara 1931–

Recipient of the American Book Award for her novel *The Salt Eaters* (New York, 1980), Bambara was born in New York City. She took a BA from Queens College and an MA from City College of New York, and taught at various universities before moving to Atlanta, Georgia, where she lives with her daughter. She has also published two collections of short stories, *Gorilla, My Love* (New York, 1972) and *The Sea Birds are Still Alive* (New York, 1977), and has edited two anthologies, *The Black Woman* (New York, 1970) and *Tales and Stories for Black Folks* (Garden City, N.Y., 1971). She is the author of numerous articles, book reviews and film scripts, and is a great enthusiast of the cinema. She has recently published *Those Bones are Not My Child*, a book about the 1980–2 'Atlanta murders'. Her fiction represents the perspectives of a black, woman artist concerned to explore and delineate the 'state of war' of contemporary society – political and moral as well as aesthetic: 'the war is also being fought over the truth: what is the truth about human nature, about the human potential? . . . the truth works, it releases the Spirit and . . . it is a joyous thing.' Like Tillie Olsen, Bambara is sensitive to the forces that prevent creativity or which construe it as the province of white, male, upper- or middle-class people. She has argued in various essays and books that writing can be the major 'tool for self-instruction and self-development'.

Both her novel and her short stories experiment with language, form and narrative technique, and, like Toni Morrison's, her fiction explores the means of survival offered to people through finding their voices, their identities, their history and culture by means of articulating stories: 'Stories are important. They keep us alive . . . The storyteller snatches us back from the edge to hear the next chapter. In which we are the subjects . . . That is what I work to do: to produce stories that save our lives.' Admittedly impatient with linear literary conventions and conventional narrative postures, Bambara rejected the notion that omniscient narrative perspective, linear narrative time or objective realist ordering of events could ever give the truth of human experience. In writing about her efforts to devise a fiction and voice expressive of her insights, Bambara has explained that she had tried to find a different kind of point of view, of shape, of order: 'Both dream and meditation hint at another possibility – the narrator as medium, the camera eye as permeable.' She has credited her great predecessor Zora Neale Hurston with not only writing against the 'stereotypes of the day', but also offering her readers new ways of seeing the world, new images of women, new ways of conceiving literature. Clearly, Hurston's achievements are in part Bambara's aims, too. She has described many of her stories as being provoked by her daily observations of police, parents and others violating moral and legal contracts, but her stories also chart the necessity to disrupt laws and conventions of behaviour which are an insult to morality, creativity and human development: 'We are at war' is an assertion which relates Bambara to Kathy Acker, however different their modes of construing this social state.

The Salt Eaters, her most substantial work of fiction, represents aesthetically accomplished experiments in structure, point of view, style and thematics. Bambara has constructed a remarkable fiction transcending narrative time, with a continuous present which fuses present, past and future. Moreover, the central focus of this 300-page novel, Velma Henry's single hour with the community healer Minnie Ransom, functions as an emblem for the self-destruction and breakdown of an entire civilization into insanity and self-isolation. During the course of the novel the sources of the self-destruction at both micro- and macrocosmic levels are depicted, as are the means of return to health. The novel emphasizes the importance of integration into a community (and the deadly dangers of withdrawing into 'a safe place where no one could follow, probe'), of synthesis, and of a long tradition of communal struggle and resistance. These factors lead to transformation, renewal and salvation. Bambara's fiction also explores the role of language and of narrative in this process of renewal: language will fail us if it is treated merely as a medium or tool of expression, just as art fails when it is used merely as a vehicle of ideas. Both language and art must be reconceived as central acts of participation in a communal life: they are the very means of social participation and human reality. They are not merely tools or ornaments, but the modes through which we build our *human* experience, our experience of meaningfulness – of aesthetic, moral or scientific significance.

The Salt Eaters is a narrative suspended in Velma's drugged semi-consciousness, with excursions via memory and other characters into the world that brought Velma to her debilitated spiritual state. Dichotomies between dream and reality, present and past, self and other, real and

supernatural collapse as the reader is led down the labyrinthine paths of Velma's wandering memories, triggered by words and phrases of Minnie the healer's invocations. Bambara's novel questions other dualities too, such as the personal–political, art–politics ('I really began to realize that this [writing] was a perfectly legitimate way to participate in struggle'), and the false opposition between 'warriors and healers'. She has explained that the novel was an effort 'to investigate possible ways to bring our technicians of the sacred and our guerrillas together'. The novel also seeks to overcome the duality between subjective and objective in its search for an imaginative narrative point of view: 'Omniscient author . . . presumes too much. Finally I found . . . the narrator as medium through whom the people unfold the stories, and the town telling as much of its story as can be told in the space of one book.' 'The narrator as medium' – elsewhere, Bambara has expressed a related idea, that 'the dream is real, my friends. The failure to make it work is the unreality.' Like Anaïs Nin's, Bambara's fiction connects surface with depth, in order to release the human spirit into the joy of living. To be cut off from one's unconsciousness is to be cut off from one's community, one's ancestors and one's history.

Shirley Hazzard 1931–

Author of the book *Defeat of an Ideal: A Study of the Self-Destruction of the United Nations* (London, 1973), Hazzard was born in Sydney. After extensive travel in the Far East and the USA, she became an American citizen, and worked for the United Nations before resigning to become a full-time writer. Hazzard is also the winner of the O. Henry Short Story Award and the National Book Circle Critics Award for best fiction in 1980 for *The Transit of Venus* (London, 1980). She has written three other novels and collections of short stories (such as *Cliffs of Fall*, London, 1963). Her non-fiction study is about the United Nations and the Waldheim case (she worked for the UN for ten years until 1962–3, when she devoted herself to writing and married the writer Francis Steegmuller). One of her early novels, *People in Glass Houses* (Melbourne, 1967), is a satire on the UN and its bureaucratic complacency and waste, while two other short novels, *The Evening of the Holiday* (London, 1966) and *The Bay of Noon* (London, 1970), are studies of romance. Her most substantial achievement in fiction is undoubtedly *The Transit of Venus*; a D.H. Lawrence-like, brooding passion enriches the novel as it progresses through complex patterns of symbols and carefully designed, intricate plots to a final, destined conclusion.

The Transit of Venus makes use of the power of the journey as a literary convention to structure the novel from beginning to end. It begins with an evocative description of Ted Tice's journey to a country house where he meets Caroline Bell; the next 330 pages map out the complicated series of journeys which eventually bring them together again, after twenty years of emotional and moral development for Caroline. The symbolism Hazzard uses to describe Tice's arrival at the house sets the tone for the rest of the novel, as, following Thomas Hardy, she deploys nature as a character of immense proportions prophesying devastation and storm and destiny: 'That noon a man was walking slowly into a landscape under a branch of lightning. A frame of almost human expectancy defined this scene, which he entered from the left-hand corner. Every nerve . . . waited, fatalistic. Only he, kinetic, advanced against circumstances to a single destination.' Hazzard develops this first scene of Tice's walk over the hill and through the vale to the house, Peverel, with its fine Greek detail, as elements in the scene turn out to be prognostications of events to come. Concise descriptions of the house reveal future character, as 'one enlarged high window – an intentional, frivolous defect like the piercing of an ear for an ornament' becomes, we realize later, an insight into Paul Ivory (it is his window), the obscenely destructive character whose humanity is literally 'defective'. Next, the brief, accidental meeting with Caro is described again with careful symbolism, as she looks down on Tice from an arc of stairs, and then turns away because she was expecting someone else. Throughout the twenty years of the novel, she 'expects someone else', until, finally, in a recognition scene of dramatic, tragic significance, she realizes that Tice was her destiny. She had simply been too naïve and morally undeveloped to recognize him.

Other techniques are used by Hazzard to great effect in *The Transit of Venus*. Caro Bell's sister, Grace Bell, is intricately woven into the novel to function as a contrast to Caro, or a light (though lovely) touch whose aesthetic effect is greatly to strengthen Caro's moral and emotional hold upon the reader. And Grace's presence functions further to emphasize Tice's strength of character: though he meets Grace first and appreciates her moral and physical qualities, his passion is utterly unaroused until Caro walks into the dining room. Other techniques which Hazzard deftly handles are flashbacks, establishing the context of a personal past which has required of Grace and Caro great emotional stamina and moral strength to survive. After the death of both parents in a shipwreck (on a journey back to Australia), the sisters were 'brought up' by a half-crazed, severely depressed elder half-sister, Dora. All three eventually arrive in England to begin a new life. The thematic strand of Dora's experiences – after the sisters become independent – weaves in and out amongst the two strands of the sisters' own contrasting lives, adding a depth and complexity to the novel. And Hazzard proves adequate to exploring the psychological aspects of three such utterly different personalities. Yet Caro's character development provides the central, unifying focus around which these other two women's lives are painted in considerable, but supplementary, detail. Meanwhile, the four male characters are also perfectly worked into this tapestry, albeit entirely dependent thematically on their corresponding female characters.

There is, however, no simple paralleling of these seven characters, as Hazzard relates Ted Tice, Adam Vail and Paul Ivory to Caro, Christian to Grace, and only transient ne'er-do-wells to Dora. Caro's 'journey' from Ted to Paul to Adam and finally back to Ted is depicted with great moral subtlety, as Hazzard introduces the shadowy figure of Adam to function as a long (and nearly final) detour for Caro, until he tragically dies, and Caro resumes her moral, emotional journeyings. Running alongside the depiction of Caro's long journey is Grace's appalling marriage and the effects of her husband's moral mediocrity upon her, as well as Dora's endless wanderings, which always end in self-destruction and crisis. Grace's stasis at home is contrasted first with Dora's endless, hapless circlings and second with Caro's purposeful progression – for when she returns to Ted twenty years later they are not returning so much to a (fictional) starting point as meeting, perhaps inconclusively, in a foreign land (Scandinavia). Indeed, Hazzard's decision to conclude the novel inconclusively with a journey – which involves Ted going north and Caro going perhaps to Rome, to meet Ted later and take up a new life with him, but perhaps also to New York, in a denial of the possibility of taking up a new life with him – is a bold aesthetic stroke, which leaves the reader on the threshold of a journey of unknown destination. The ambiguity is made almost aesthetically unbearable if the reader remembers (and who can forget?) the prognostication made about Ted Tice by the narrator early in the novel: 'In fact, Edmond Tice would take his own life before attaining the peak of his achievement. But that would occur in a northern city, and not for many years.' This sentence haunts the reader throughout the novel, and yet no such event ever materializes, as if it were a narrative 'mistake'. It is also balanced by the causal comment toward the end of the novel, 'For the last time, Caroline Vail lay in a bed alone.' The possible ambiguity of the meaning of the novel's conclusion is sustained even in the imagery; the roar of the plane taking off is likened to 'the intake of humanity's breath when a work of ages shrivels in an instant; or the great gasp of hull and ocean as a ship does down', referring to the sinking of the ferry which drowned Caro's parents and initiated her into her wanderings across Europe and America.

Hazzard's *Transit of Venus* can be compared to Henry Handel Richardson's *Maurice Guest* (1908), for it has the same brooding, passionate atmosphere, which gives these novels a rich materiality. Hazzard was also writing within the context of other Australian women novelists, such as Olga Masters, whom she has probably influenced. For although Masters was born in 1919 she began her career very late; her *Loving Daughters* appeared only in 1984. It explores the theme of a lover who conflates two sisters into one ideal woman; her prize-winning book *Home Girls* (1982) also owes something to Hazzard. The latter may have been influenced by such Australian writers as Thea Astley (1925–) and Elizabeth

Jolley (1923–), all of whom were trying to find new forms and themes more relevant to women's experience and more effective for creating new kinds of novels.

Toni Morrison 1931–

Winner of the Nobel Prize for literature in 1993, Toni Morrison (Chloe Anthony Wofford) was born in Ohio and educated at Howard and Cornell. She has taught at several universities, including Yale, Rutgers and Princeton. She won the National Book Critics Circle Award for *Song of Solomon* (New York, 1977), her third novel after *The Bluest Eye* (New York, 1970) and *Sula* (New York, 1973). *Tar Baby* (New York, 1981) was followed by what many readers see as the crowning achievement of her twenty-five-year career, namely, *Beloved* (New York, 1987), which won the Pulitzer Prize in 1988. While senior editor at Random House, she oversaw books by Angela Davis and Muhammad Ali, as well as *The Black Book* (1974), an anthology designed to express the experiences of 'anonymous' black Americans. In 1992, another novel, *Jazz* (New York), was published.

All of Morrison's novels testify to her commitment to experimentation with the forms and conventions of fiction and of language in order to find adequate means of shaping her experience into literature. Influencing and influenced by such contemporaries as the novelist Toni Cade Bambara and the poet Lucille Clifton, not to mention earlier writers such as Virginia Woolf and William Faulkner, Morrison's novels explore a variety of themes, characters and narrative techniques in her panoramic depiction of black experiences in America, until finally, in *Beloved*, she succeeded at last in telling the story that 'was not a story to pass on', the story that had haunted all her other novels, and which haunts America and American literature, as the character Beloved herself haunts the house at 124 that is the setting for much of the novel. Throughout Morrison's earlier novels, experiments in narrative points of view, language, time and other elements are evident as she strove to shape her material into aesthetic form. *Beloved* is most impressive in its complex narrative technique, as it weaves a present out of past events, experiences and the memories of the characters Sethe and Paul D, both through direct narration by characters and through indirect understatement. The confrontation with the past which they experience on a personal level, first through the haunting of the house and second through the incarnation of Beloved, is mirrored in the text by the confrontation with America's slave-holding past, an America which continues to be plagued by prejudice, forgetfulness and denial of that past. Morrison's novel, like her earlier narratives, also reveals the inextricably intertwined themes of sexual inhibitions and racial hate (explicitly charted decades earlier by Lillian Smith in *Killers of the Dream* (1949, revised 1961).

Earlier, in *Song of Solomon*, Morrison made the relation of the present to the past the pivotal point of an individual's search for meaningfulness and identity. Indeed, the very structure of that novel is expressive of the problematic relationship between the two. For there, the present as portrayed by the first two-thirds of the novel is artistically disjointed from the journey to rediscover the past, and it is only in the final third of the novel, called (perhaps ironically) 'Part II', that the exploration of a character's and a family's past pulls the whole novel together. Part I becomes a meaningful narrative rather than simply a rambling tale of a group of family members. Both *Song of Solomon* and *Beloved* suggest thematically and formally, then, that the present is virtually meaningless and often intolerable, until the past is released into consciousness, into the here and now in an overt and explicit way. Formally, Morrison expressed this psychological insight very differently in *Beloved*, however. There, instead of 200 pages of the present, followed by 100 pages of a 'journey into the past' (which is portrayed as a heightened present), she dispensed with journey metaphors or ancestral homes for buried treasures. Instead of literal bags of bones or gold coins with symbolic, erotic significances, instead of the powerful metaphor of flying used throughout *Song of Solomon*, instead of exploring the way folk song, legend and myth can be decoded to yield personal and historical knowledge, in *Beloved*, by contrast, Morrison both wove the past inextricably into the present by means of narrative, and harnessed the supernatural in the figure of Beloved to haunt the here and now. In *Tar Baby*, the confronta-

tion with the past is also the main theme of the novel, as pairs of characters are shown being destroyed by a past they will not confront or cannot cope with. The two central characters, Son and Jadine, watch their relationship break when Jadine is unable to accept Son's identity (she has kept trying to change him) once he connects up with his past and roots himself in it. In all cases, emotional maturity is shown to hinge critically upon successfully dealing with a past made fully conscious to the individuals concerned.

Beloved, the embodiment of the 'dead' past, threatens to drag Sethe back into the darkness of death, the unconscious, the forgotten and the inchoate until Sethe, reliving her past in an almost Freudian recreation, tries this time to murder her 'antagonist' instead of her babies. Through this confrontation, through the retargeting of her rage onto her assailant, and through the determination of her daughter Denver to seek the help of the community instead of remaining a proud and isolated individual, Sethe is able to absolve the 'ghost' of the past. Even then, she needs the help of Paul D and Denver to drag her out of sickness and lethargy into a living present which has future possibilities.

Particularly notable in *Beloved* is the unique way in which Morrison marshalled a narrative technique which fused past and present, while at the same time further fusing past and present through characterization, plot and thematics on both a personal and a social-political level. This quite unusual congruence of all these elements is one way of explaining the powerful aesthetic effect of the novel. Such a unification of past and present is recreated in the reading experience, as strands from earlier pages of the novel get taken up again much later, and repeatedly, so that the reader is engaged in a piecing together, a quilting together, of the fragments of the narrative into patterns which only emerge gradually. The arrival of Paul D from out of an eighteen-year distant past, his efforts to forge a relationship with Sethe and Denver, his temporary failure as Beloved takes over the house, and his eventual return form the beginning, middle and end of the overt plot. Along this forward-moving line of narration, the 'bare bones' of the novel, is fleshed out a past for both him and Sethe which constitutes the body of the writing. Past events, usually introduced to the reader via the memory of Sethe or Paul D, but sometimes by the narrator, intrude into the present plot so much that the intrusions become the substance, and hardly a page is read which is not saturated with past events. The past is further merged into the present by means of character, as first, Paul D arrives, having last seen Sethe at Sweet Home where they had both been slaves, before her escape and the journey over the river into Ohio. His and Sethe's narrated memories and interpretations of the present through the past constitute alternating male/female black experiences of slavery and then freedom, which are woven into a unified chorus of horrendous castigation of the white Americans who perpetrated or condoned these atrocities. As in much Greek tragedy, moreover, the atrocities occur 'off the stage', but by means of Morrison's genius with understatement, they have an even more powerful effect upon the reader than any direct account would achieve.

In addition to Paul D, Beloved descends into Sethe's present life, the incarnation of Sethe's year-old baby murdered some seventeen years ago by her own hand, to save this child from slavery. Along with the plot of Paul D's arrival and efforts to win Sethe away from Beloved is the counterplot of Beloved's efforts to win Sethe away from Paul, Denver and life itself. Beloved is not only the figure of the dead baby, she is the 'incarnation' of Sethe's unresolved, unconfronted past; but she can also be read as the incarnation of America's slave-holding past, as the embodiment of the sufferings of black people and the guilt of white people for what happened, and for what is still happening. Morrison's novel thus functions at psychological, interpersonal, social and political levels of significance. Moreover, the personal struggles of Sethe and Paul D in the Ohio of 1873 are so firmly placed in the context of American racism that they spill over beyond their specific time and place, so that the past, 1873, becomes the reader's present: racism still haunts us all today. This use of the supernatural rooted matter-of-factly into a historical, realist setting is another source of the intensely effective artistry of the novel. Flannery O'Connor had argued in her essays (and illustrated in her novels) that there are deeper kinds of realism than those forms expressed by sociology, history, psychology and economics, and by so-called

realism in the nineteenth-century novel. Realism, she argued paradoxically, resides in the depths of life, not in its surface facts, and while this depth is revealed by means of concretes and definites, it is constituted not by surface, concrete facts, but by mystery. Fiction she described as an incarnational art needing a vision of depth. Beloved functions symbolically not only as a concretion of the unconfronted, unconscious past, of the unacknowledged American past of slavery, but also as a representation of art and the imagination, and of fiction and the novel itself. That is, as a supernatural figure in the novel, her presence creates a dissociation from reality for both the characters and the reader. She can only be grasped imaginatively, not by the reason alone. Moreover, the casual, matter-of-fact juxtaposition of this supernatural figure with the realist context of the novel creates a further dissociation from literary realism. This use of the supernatural, along with Morrison's unique narrative interweaving of present and past by means of extreme understatement and the artistic congruence of the text discussed earlier, constitutes an artistically significant and intensely imaginative challenge to the implied orthodoxy of realism and rationalism in mainstream English literature.

In Song of Solomon the aesthetic effect which the supernatural performs in Beloved is achieved instead through the metaphor of flying, which runs throughout the book from, literally, the first page to the last. Flying, traditionally a metaphor for sexual experience and potency, is also a metaphor for imagination. Morrison related the symbolic imagery of flying to the song, the 'air', the legend, throughout that novel. Yet, the importance of this relation becomes evident only at the end, when Macon's search for identity through acquaintance with his past and his ancestors succeeds by receiving and decoding the Song of Solomon, about his great-grandfather who flew away home to Africa, leaving his American slavery behind him. Throughout the novel, the importance of names – their ability to store the past and make it recoverable, as well as to create and mark identities and individualities – is emphasized. As Macon stumbles on his confused way into his past, he finds the names recorded in towns, on rocks, in caves, which take on personal and historical meaning instead of being meaningless labels only when he learns the song, the legend, of his great-grandfather, his grandparents and his own identity as a member of the family of flying Africans. By decoding the legend-song, he is able not only to reveal to his Aunt Pilate truths which mean more to her than life; he also gains the strength to 'fly out' and meet his adversary, Guitar. Legend becomes reality, once reality is discovered encoded in the legend, the song of Shalimar-Solomon, while Macon's courage and imagination are awakened as song, poetry, literature and art are imaged in 'the air'. If you surrender to the power of song, of art, if you can fly, you can 'ride on' air. To sing is to fly, and both are symbols for imaginative living, the only kind of living worth the trouble, as Macon eventually learns when he realizes the value of Pilate, Ruth and Hagar. In a heroic leap of imagination, he turns his back on his former life of useless selfishness to face, of all names, Guitar – the name of a musical instrument – while Macon Dead becomes a wheeling figure 'as fleet and bright as a lodestar', and the novel concludes: 'it did not matter which one of them would give up the ghost in the killing arms of his brother. For now he knew what Shalimar knew: If you surrendered to the air, you could *ride* it.'

Macon Dead becomes a star, a figure of speech, a simile at the end of the novel, which rejects any resolution of the contest or conflict between Guitar and Macon as irrelevant. Puns, plays on words, and phrases suggestive of Biblical legends incite the reader to decodings, such as of 'Shalimar' from Shalom, the Hebrew root of both Solomon and Jerusalem, meaning peace, and the wisdom of inner peace which can 'ride out' outer conflict. No strict allegories are possible, but the rejection of realist endings for metaphors, plays on words and ambiguities, suggestive of the power of songs, airs, legends – those flights of imagination – and the power of words, names and language, leave the reader, like Coleridge's Wedding Guest, stunned into silence.

Alice Munro 1931–

Admirer of Eudora Welty, Flannery O'Connor and Carson McCullers, and influenced by fellow Canadian Mavis Gallant, Munro was born Alice

Laidlaw in Wingham, Ontario, and went to the University of Western Ontario in 1949, before marrying in 1951 and setting off on a remarkable and celebrated career as one of Canada's finest authors. First published in journals and magazines, her stories were collected in 1968 into *Dance of the Happy Shades* (Toronto), followed in 1971 by the interconnecting stories/novel *Lives of Girls and Women* (Toronto) and then by *Something I've Been Meaning to Tell You* (Toronto, 1974). *Who Do You Think You Are?* (Toronto) was another set of linked stories published in 1978, and was followed by *Moons of Jupiter* (Toronto, 1982); both these collections tended towards tales about women, whereas the earlier books had focused on adolescence and initiation into adulthood. With *The Progress of Love* (Toronto, 1986), Munro introduced her first major male narrator, and continued her exploration of women and men, often in love triangles, which she developed further in *Friend of My Youth* (Toronto, 1990). Munro moved back to the area of her birth, to Clinton in southwestern Ontario, to live with her second husband in the 1970s. This region informs much of Munro's fiction with a powerful sense of place, which Welty had argued could be a central means of embodying the imagination in images of the senses. Munro's central recurring themes of encounters with death, sexual initiation and love are usually focused through the consciousness of young, adolescent girls growing into women in the earlier stories, though the later ones encompass both older women and men as narrative filters, in either the first person or the third.

Munro remarked in an interview that her aim in writing fiction was to recreate 'that intense feeling of light on buildings, and streets, and trees . . . that is the secret of what I'm after.' This desire to illuminate (rather than to interpret, to preach or to teach), whether the external world or the internal psychology of her characters, forces plot into the margins, and leads her to foreground the 'secret' (or mystery, as Welty called it) of 'painting' – of putting the world and experience into words. Munro's interest in this process of language, words and story-telling lurks within all her stories and often becomes explicit, systematically so in the 'Epilogue' to *Lives of Girls and Women*. It is also indirectly expressed in her repeated fascination with incorporating photographs, cameras and paintings into her fictions, as for example in 'Ottowa Valley', 'Winter Wind' or *Lives*, where she emphasized the way even photography fails to be able to record any objective reality. Her extremely complex narrative use of time, with layer upon layer of present–past points of view, commentaries on those points of view, and multiple narratives (especially in the later collections), and her self-referential and meta-fictional drawing of the reader's attention to this complexity, relativity and subjectivity, show Munro to have a sophisticated awareness of issues of realism, modernism, ontological and epistemological disputes of what there is and how we perceive or know it, and issues of the dualities of appearance/reality, surface/depth, fact/fiction, objectivity/subjectivity, word/object and so on. Many of her stories verge on post-modernism in this self-referential awareness and in narratives which combine meta-narratives, ambiguous, open-ended 'conclusions', use of an autobiographical persona, typical fondness for mocking realism with funny lists and catalogues, repeated, explicit discussions of writing and of describing 'reality', and overt emphasis on the way memory and imagination rewrite history and the past.

The growing sophistication of Munro's narrative techniques, as well as her increasing interest in mosaic narratives, 'stereoscopic vision' or complex use of narrative time and multiple voice, mixing of limited and omniscient narrator, and attention to dualities, oppositions and contraries leads the reader of her stories to the realization that Munro is not so much showing how story-telling and language inevitably distort reality. Nor is she suggesting so much that language and words are inadequate, or that silence is a superior truth – that experience cannot be captured by language. Rather, like Welty's, Munro's stories suggest that 'ordinary life' is, precisely, its opposite: marvellous, mysterious, exotic, when that dull, familiar world is illuminated by the light of imagination. Paradox is at the heart of Munro's style, imagery and structures, then, as her stories illustrate the enigma that ordinary life is an incredible mystery when seen imaginatively. This account suggests Munro's determination to challenge the dualistic way of seeing the world: reality versus appearance, fact versus fiction, experience versus words, history versus story, and so on. Munro's techniques, style and thematics urge the reader precisely towards a more imaginative, stereoscopic vision where many realities, many truths and many points of view are perceived, but without privileging one over another as *the* reality, *the* truth, *the* point of view. Her often oxymoronic language – things are both strange and familiar, marvellous and ordinary, and so on – is at the basis of her fiction's commitment to reality as paradox, as fiction, and yet as true – 'not real, but true' is one way she puts this oppositional duality, as opposed to static duality.

Munro's stories do not, in their modernist preoccupation with story-telling, suggest, then, that language, words or stories distort reality inevitably. Her techniques suggest more radically that such dualisms are nonsense. She has challenged in her fiction the very basis of dualistic thinking, showing in her fondness for photographic images, for example, that nothing can record reality accurately because there is no such thing as a reality to be recorded. Language, art, words and story-telling do not distort some pre-existing or coterminous reality, because this notion of such a reality is itself, as Marguerite Young showed, a mere illusion, a fantasy, a fiction. Language, art and story-telling are the very means by which we build up our realities, and reality is always multiple and always a product of an ordinary, perceiving, mind – itself a product of its own activities and not some pre-existing reality. Munro has explored *Bildungsroman* and *Künstlerroman* genres, especially in *Lives of Girls and Women* with its penetrating psychological analyses of the pains and embarrassments of adolescence; she has analysed why women usually feel their very meaning in life to be bound up with relationships with men in *Who Do You Think You Are?* and *Moons of Jupiter*. She has explored the extreme difficulty of crossing the abyss between sex and age in her characters' efforts to communicate. All these domestic and familiar, ordinary themes are, as in Margaret Laurence, infused with Munro's sophisticated consciousness of the problematic nature of fiction as an expression not of some inevitably distorted reality but of the mystery of putting human life into words; life which, until it is so put, is not some pre-existing reality but, rather, the 'barest meaningless', the most complete nothing.

That Munro has at times emphasized the greater appropriateness of silence on certain occasions in no way contradicts this description of her fiction. Rather, it expresses her awareness that there are often other more appropriate 'languages': verbal language – words – are only one form of social interaction or communication, as is brilliantly illustrated in the 'Epilogue' to *Lives of Girls and Women*, when Bobby, the 'mad' neighbour, performs an act which the unimaginative eye might not even have noticed, much less described in the following way. Del Jordan 'sees' it for her reader, illuminating the dull and ordinary with 'intense light':

Bobby Sheriff spoke wistfully to me, relieving me of my fork, napkin, and empty plate. Then he did the only special thing he ever did for me. With those things in his hands, he rose on his toes like a dancer, like a plump ballerina. This action, accompanied by his delicate smile, appeared to be a joke not shared with me so much as displayed for me, and it seemed also to have a concise meaning, a stylized meaning – to be a letter, or a whole word, in an alphabet I did not know . . .
Yes, I said, instead of thank you.

As an emblem of Munro's fiction, this image captures well her sense of the mysterious beauty of life, and the affirmation, 'yes', gives us a sense of her endings, avoiding closure or resolution, as in that of *Something I've Been Meaning to Tell You*, with its post-modern self-consciousness: 'If I had been making a proper story out of this, I would have ended it, I think, with my mother not answering and going ahead of me across the pasture.' Munro has moved amongst modernist and post-modernist techniques with extraordinary ease and familiarity, making those normally obtrusive and alienating, even artificial devices seem entirely ordinary. Her transparent, lucid style expresses, paradoxically, her ability to give herself up to the control of her imagination at the loss of arbitrary will and surface determination, thereby giving a stereoscopic vision which more fully illuminates human life and constitutes that fusion of realism, modernism and post-modernism which only a few contemporary writers have succeeded in creating.

Fay Weldon 1931–

Playwright and novelist, shortlisted for the Booker Prize in 1978 for *Praxis*, Fellow of the Royal Society of Literature, and winner of a number of awards for her radio plays, Weldon was born in Worcestershire but spent her early childhood in New Zealand with her mother and sisters. After returning to London with them at the age of 14, she later took a BA and then an MA in 1954 from St Andrews in psychology and economics. She began writing novels in the 1950s, but her first novel, *The Fat Woman's Joke* (London), was published only in 1967. Numerous novels and plays followed, although she was often working full-time in, for example, advertising, while raising four sons. Weldon's novels explore recurring yet wide-ranging themes and issues about women's relationships, the role of power structures in their lives, and their vulnerability to nature, that is, their bodily processes – always contextualized by a concern for moral well-being. Her narrative techniques constitute an impressive range of experimentation with dialogue and play excerpts within prose, stories within stories, alternating narrative points of view, fluid use of time, stylistic shock, Shandyesque digression and authorial intrusions, and the ironic use of the supernatural, as well as literary allusion. Weldon has 'fractured' her prose by setting off short paragraphs, making it episodic and terse, in the modernist tradition; she has also experimented with punctuation, introduced scientific diction as well as sociological facts into her domestic themes, and has toyed with conventions of diverse genres, from romance and realism to science fiction and the thriller. Her writing is characterized by a sardonic wit and detachment, as she has articulated human experiences in ways that undercut traditional and realist narrative conventions mistaken for facts. Anita Brookner has described Weldon as 'one of the most astute and distinctive women writing fiction today'. David Lodge has added his appreciation for her experiments in fiction and narrative techniques which, through 'surprise, wit, irony and lyricism', have led to a complex and multilayered narrative. Numerous other writers and critics, such as Bernard Levin and John Braine, have prized the originality and virtuosity of her fiction, though she has sometimes been criticized for weak characterization, especially regarding her male figures. This latter criticism may result from a rejection of Weldon's intentionally picaresque use of fairy-tale or legendary types which are designed to give her social satires greater universality.

One of Weldon's most evident strengths is her ability to synthesize effective innovations of earlier as well as contemporary writers into a vital and original fiction. Using dialogue to flesh out her plot and replace narrative description, she has drawn upon Ivy Compton-Burnett's novel-play genre, especially in such works as *Female Friends* (London and New York, 1975) and, more overtly, *Remember Me* (London and New York, 1976). In the latter, Weldon added Compton-Burnett-like analyses of the hostile insinuations hidden within ambiguous, apparently innocent comments. Like her near-contemporary Iris Murdoch, Weldon has sought to find a new form of fiction which was accessible to a wide-ranging reading public, yet free from the ideology of realism. This new form of writing would be experimental, yet, like Murdoch's, within the context of moral, humane dimensions involving personal responsibility and an understanding of the power of social forces to undermine it. Unlike Murdoch, but like Angela Carter, Margaret Atwood and other, earlier writers, Weldon has explored the possibilities of legendary character types, drawing upon fairy tale, myth and folklore as well as earlier literature. Her psychological insights have generic force, though her characters are not always as flat as some critics have complained, and often show interesting peculiarities and quirks which suggest an astuteness of observation about individuality. Drawing on myth and fantasy, Weldon yet retains the gritty ordinariness of everyday life in her fiction, and this 'naturalist' streak is one of her most evident effects.

In more recent novels, such as *Puffball* (London and New York, 1980), *The President's Child* (London, 1982), *The Shrapnel Academy* (London, 1986) and *The Hearts and Lives of Men* (London, 1987), Weldon has expanded her themes and settings as well as her techniques (discussed above) to deal explicitly with the various forms of exploitation (sexual, racial, economic and class), the origins of violence and war in the human psyche and their institutionalization in our social structures, and the role of biology or nature, science and the past in our everyday attempts at free will, to defeat genes, fate and external forces. The relation of the individual to the state, an analysis of urban versus rural myths, and our persuasive myths about sex, romantic love, the 'place' of women, the 'rights' of men and the pursuit of money and possessions are all examined, but by means of continually evolving experiments in narrative, stylistic and structural techniques, which Weldon has fused into vigorous, witty and enormously readable fiction.

Eva Figes 1932–

Author of several experimental novels, as well as the classic *Patriarchal Attitudes* (London and New York, 1970) – a major, very early challenge to sexism with its laser-like dissection of the prejudices underlying male–female ideologies – and other non-fiction books, such as *Sex and Subterfuge: Women Writers to 1850* (London, 1982), Figes was born in Berlin and came to England in 1939 with her family. *Little Eden: A Child at War* (London, 1978) is an autobiographical account describing her childhood difficulties in adjusting to her new environment. Influenced by European writers such as Proust and Kafka (she remained fluent in German), and fascinated by the developments of the *nouveau roman* in France by Alain Robbe-Grillet, Nathalie Saurraute and Claude Simon, Figes belongs to the experimental (sometimes even avant-garde or post-modernist) tradition of the 1960s, 1970s and 1980s. Drawing upon Virginia Woolf, Katherine Mansfield and Samuel Beckett, Figes dispensed with overt plot, characterization, progressive development and dialogue, and sought to capture the 'stream' of experience without allowing for any stable dichotomy between inner and outer. Her second novel, *Winter Journey* (London, 1967), won the *Guardian* fiction award and is probably her most popular novel. Later novels, such as *B* (London, 1972), *Days* (London, 1974) and *Waking* (London, 1981), became more experimental and less accessible to readers not conversant with the conventions of such texts. Even in somewhat more accessible novels such as *Light* (London, 1983), which draws on

253

Mansfield's novella 'At the Bay', or *Nelly's Version* (London, 1977) or *Konek's Landing* (London, 1969), the last of which reveals influences from Kafka, Figes's return to almost modernist experiments is everywhere evident. A stream of consciousness is substituted for plot and characterization, lyricism and poetic prose with intense imagery dominate her style, and small incidents carry large, symbolic import.

Figes's novels are experimental also in trying to capture in words the processes of consciousness – of thought and feeling – which both distinguish individuals from each other and connect them. Like impressionist painters and modernist writers, she has sought to focus upon the act of and nature of perception itself – of how we perceive, rather than what we perceive. In parallel, she has attended to how we think and feel, and to how those perceptions get transformed into verbal experience. Figes's writing reveals how words and phrases are meaningful more by connotation, ambiguity and suggestion than by denotation or reference to things. And it demonstrates that language is always polyvalent: words are surrounded by a penumbra or cluster of meanings. Moreover, the complexity of language reflects, for Figes, the complexity of experience and the psyche as composed of unknown meanings beyond the visible, the rational and the conscious. Thus Figes, like the modernists before her, has repositioned subjectivity and made it the central thematics, while realist truth and objectivity are marginalized as complete fictions.

While *Konek's Landing* uses Kafkaesque, nightmarish events and monologic passages to explore the insanity of the Holocaust, *B* is more self-referential in its questioning of the relation between fact and fiction or reality and illusion. This novel charts the strange tale of the novelist Paul Beard, who writes about a (real or fictional?) novelist friend B. The two 'characters' epitomize the post-modern device of 'breaking the frame' around art or fiction so as to erase the boundary between it and the reality it purports to represent. In *Nelly's Version*, another novel overtly concerned with concepts of identity and the relation of reality to fiction, the heroine Nelly Dear, who is amnesiac, sees an aged old lady in her hotel-room mirror. This unrecognizable 'repetition' of her 'self' sets up a theme of the radical ambiguity of all experience, in which we

are doomed both to indeterminacy of meaning in the story and to endless repetition. *The Seven Ages* (London, 1986) is one of Figes's most successful novels; there she has combined metafiction with compelling thematics concerning women's bodies, pregnancy and child birth. The novel is structured by stories within stories, stories by women which draw on legendary and mythic material, stories told by different narrators, stories in different times and places, yet with a marked continuity achieved by returning to earlier characters and themes. Her most recent novel is *Ghosts* (1988); written in short paragraphs, it continues Figes's exploration of the concept of identity, as well as the relation of a 'self' to others, in lyrical, intense prose.

Eva Figes has contributed articles to the *New Review* (summer 1978) and to several critical works, such as *Woman on Woman*, ed. M. Laing (London, 1971), and has translated numerous books, including Martin Walser's *The Gadarene Club* (London, 1960) and Renate Rasp's *A Family Failure* (New York and London, 1970).

Alice Thomas Ellis 1932–

Born in Liverpool, mother of seven children and married to the late Colin Haycraft, who was a publisher at Duckworth, Ellis (Anna Haycraft) worked as fiction editor at Duckworth while writing numerous novels. (She was fiction editor for Beryl Bainbridge's books, for example.) She has written two cookery books and, for the *Spectator*, numerous articles on the family, entitled 'Home Life'; and she has collaborated with Tom Pitt-Aikens to write books on juvenile delinquency. Her first two novels, *The Sin Eater* (London, 1977) and *The Birds of the Air* (London, 1980), received awards from the Welsh Arts Council. *The 27th Kingdom* (London, 1982) was nominated for the Booker Prize, and was followed by *The Other Side of the Fire* (London, 1983) and *Unexplained Laughter* (London, 1985), which won the Yorkshire Post fiction award. In 1987, 1988 and 1989, Ellis published three related novels; the same plot is developed using a different narrative point of view. These novels, *The Clothes in the Wardrobe* (London), *The Skeleton in the Cupboard* (London), and *The Fly in the Ointment* (London), were republished in 1991 as *The Summerhouse Trilogy* (Harmondsworth). *The Inn at the Edge of the Wood* (London, 1990), a supernatural black comedy, was followed by Ellis's autobiography, *A Welsh Childhood* (London, 1990).

Most of Ellis's short novels (they never exceed 50,000 words) rely on Catholic symbolism, imagery and theology, while, like Iris Murdoch and Anita Brookner, Ellis has used literary allusions freely to enrich her multilayered style. This style is characterized by a rich, punning and connotative vocabulary, and its density and complexity of meaning make unnecessary the expansive, explanatory prose characteristic of many novelists. Ellis has also experimented with narrative techniques and point of view. In such novels as *Unexplained Laughter* and *The 27th Kingdom*, not to mention *The Summerhouse Trilogy*, point of view is foregrounded and also varied. In *Unexplained Laughter*, a mute, disabled child is made the narrator of short, well-spaced portions which have the quality of legendary, supernatural and even Biblical wisdom, and which function as a strange and revelatory commentary upon the events narrated by a more conventional voice. In *The 27th Kingdom*, a similar, fragmentary narrative is used to convey the progress of a comic but supernatural event at a convent: the apple picked by a young nun before her departure out into the world to test her vocation fails to decay until it is time for the nun to return. Indeed, in this novel, narrative point of view is further confused as the novel begins and ends with direct self-reference to the 'storyteller': 'The story I shall tell begins like this.' and 'As for me, the story-teller, I was in the pub.' The reader is confronted with the weird possibility that the story-teller/pub inhabitant is no other than the drunken Major of the novel. Further mystifications abound in the plot and thematics of the novel. An unknown, mystery man lurking near the characters' residence, Dancing Master House, is chased into the river, from where the saintly nun, Valentine, rescues him and breathes life back into the drowned man's lungs. The man turns out to be an amalgam of several other characters who have occurred in the novel, both in the present and in the distant past. Debt-collector to Aunt Irene and Mrs Mason, bereaved victim of her sister's folly to Valentine as well as to Mrs O'Connor, threaten-

ing, silent telephone caller perhaps to the reader, the miraculously revived man ends the novel, pulling together several disparate strands, but leaving many others untied; the other characters all take their departure on the final page to their widely ranging destinations.

The 27th Kingdom could be said to be Ellis's most overtly successful attempt in her fiction to create a kind of writing which begins in familiar facts and daily life, only to take off into the nether realms of symbolism, Flannery O'Connor-like 'reality beyond appearance', and the supernatural embedded in ordinary life. Or, one could argue, Ellis's fiction expands the ordinary into the extraordinary by revealing its partially hidden miraculousness. No duality exists between the two; it is simply a matter of perception, or point of view. To the imaginative, awakened eye, there is nothing ordinary about everyday life; it *is* the miraculous. Hence, thematics and plot function essentially in the service of revealing this genuinely miraculous ordinariness, as apparently trivial or disconnected events and incidences interconnect, not at the surface of the thematics, but only at the level of religious symbolism and literary metaphor. This 'behind-the-scenes' reality of networks and interconnections gives the surface of Ellis's novels a quality of radical discontinuity and illogicality, a kind of fantastic whimsicality and comedy, which whirls the reader along a kooky series of events with varying degrees of plottedness or lack of plot. The 'substance' is in these methods, and in the connotations and symbols which, ironically, flesh out the meanings and significances of the surface events, and catapult the reader – whether believer, atheist or agnostic – into a realm of the spirit where we can explore the great issues of art, life, death, love and time. Ellis's achievement in her fiction is all the more remarkable because these thematic issues are not made to intrude upon the reader in any dogmatic or sectarian way. Rather, committed as she has allegedly been to the fundamentals of Catholicism, Ellis, like O'Connor, has expressed spirituality and morality in universally graspable, artistic terms. Through the fantastic, the symbolic, the supernatural and the comic, Ellis has scrutinized the most profound aspects of human existence in finely structured fictions of admirable inventiveness.

Miriam Masoli (Tlali) 1933–

The writings of Tlali, who was born in Johannesburg, first began appearing in the 1970s in the Raven Press series of writings by South African writers, which was an extension of their journal, *Staffrider*; Tlali contributed a column, 'Soweto Speaking'. Her first novel, *Muriel at Metropolitan*, was published in 1975 (Johannesburg), and then included in the Longman Drumbeat series (1979). It is alleged to be the first novel by a black woman to have been published in South Africa. Her second novel, *Amandla* (Johannesburg, 1980), was also published by the Raven Press. Along with her first, it was banned by the South African censors. In 1989, a collection of short stories, *Footprints in the Quag* (Johannesburg), appeared, published abroad as *Soweto Stories*. Like Bessie Head, Tlali made the theme of power one of the unifying forces of her book; indeed, 'Amandla' means power, and the novel is a response to the 16 June 1976 uprising in Soweto. Miriam Masoli took her pen-name from some ancestors who ran a printing press in Lesotho, called Tlale and Company, which had published a newspaper for some decades. This discovery, and the gradual realization of the existence of preceding and contemporary black writers (who were numerous enough to form a literary tradition of black South African literature), gave her confidence in her own abilities and strengths. Throughout her novels, the raising of black consciousness, the presentation of black characters and their varieties of attitude, experiences and values, and the empowerment of black people became some of the main thematic concerns, for which she found authentic literary structures, forms, and styles.

Like her immediate literary predecessor, Head, Tlali is a story-teller in the ancient African tradition. While her novels concern themselves with racism, sexism, paternalism and other forms of inequality, the ideas are not presented discursively, but worked into the narration in ways that are integral to the action, incident, plot, character and dialogue of her novels. Indeed, dialogue is often the means by which Tlali creates dramatic incidents or narrates somewhat absurd, funny events; but both her novels are carefully unified into focused constructions through unity of place, characterization and point of view. A tone of ironic, slightly humorous and mocking tolerance towards racist and even liberal, well-intentioned white characters is underpinned by a more serious, less tolerant tone, which becomes dominant in her second novel. In her first, more autobiographical novel about a young woman, Muriel, set in an urban locale (which conveys the life of black urban dwellers throughout South Africa), the moral dilemmas of black people confronted by a white-dominated system of authority and financial power, in which they must participate in order to survive, is explored through irony and amused condescension towards the ignorance of prejudiced, racist white people. Often, black characters are shown confronting the paternalism and rudeness of white fellow employees and bosses, but in nonviolent ways. In *Amandla*, written after the Soweto tragedy, Tlali portrays resistance as a more violent and, especially, a more communal experience. Unlike the characters in *Muriel at Metropolitan*, who tend to resist individually (Muriel complains that she cannot 'stage a one-man protest'), those of *Amandla* unite to form a more powerful protest against apartheid. 'Ordinary' people are shown being driven to ruthless violence in their fight against the even more ruthless white oppression. The Soweto events are chronicled, but artistically and subjectively, through the eyes of a family influenced by the uprisings to take to more active protest. The radicalization of young and old black people by the police violence is characterized in the figure of Pholoso, who, after protest, arrest and torture, is forced to choose exile, since there is no safety for him in his own country. Numerous other characters are shown, too, in their responses to this momentous event, but Pholoso is the literary centre around which the reader sees township life revolving, and this theme of the relationship of the individual's identification with her or his community is at the forefront, as the novel concludes: 'Talking about this land is talking about ourselves.'

Other writings include *Mihloti* (Johannesburg, 1984), a volume of concise, fictional pieces of a documentary-autobiographical kind, describing life in an apartheid society. Both Tlali's novels were unbanned in the late 1980s, and she has written plays which have been performed abroad, such as the unpublished *Crimen Injuria*.

A.S. Byatt 1936–

Winner of the Aer Lingus and Booker Prizes (in 1991) for *Possession: A Romance* (London, 1990), A.S. Byatt (sister of Margaret Drabble) was born Antonia Susan Drabble in Sheffield. She attended Cambridge University and then became a lecturer in English at University College, London, until establishing herself as a novelist and literary critic by 1983. She has published books on Coleridge and Wordsworth (1970) as well as on the fiction of Iris Murdoch (1965), and she has written five other novels and collections of short stories including *Sugar and Other Stories* (London, 1987) and *The Matisse Stories* (London, 1993). Her novels range from *Shadow of a Sun* (London, 1964) and *The Game* (London, 1967) to *The Virgin in the Garden* (London, 1978), *Still Life* (London, 1985), the pair of novellas *Angels and Insects* (London, 1992) and *The Djinn in the Nightingale's Eye* (London, 1994). A further book of criticism, *Passions of the Mind*, appeared in 1991 (London). She has written numerous introductions to the Virago editions of novels by Willa Cather and Elizabeth Bowen and of stories by Grace Paley, and she has edited an edition of George Eliot's essays, poems and other writings. She is a Fellow of the Royal Society of Literature and received a CBE in 1990.

Byatt's several novels represent a determined effort to experiment with the novel and its conventions. Open display of her artistry, along with overt intellectualizing of her toyings with plot, narrative point of view, framework techniques, style and imagery, and her interest in the relation of fiction to history, biography and autobiography are evident in most of her longer fiction, especially the later works. While both *The Shadow of a Sun* and *The Game* seem to represent an artistically interesting if painful process of turning autobiographical experience into fiction, according to fairly conventional methods, Byatt's later novels appear to concentrate more upon self-conscious experimentation, beginning with *The Virgin in the Garden*, with its stylistic achievements of complexity, erudition and density of language, allusion to the literary tradition, and alternating narrative perspectives. (Even in *The Game*, however, she had already introduced some density of allusion and symbolism more characteristic of her later novels, as for example in her

use of the Eden myth and her central motif of the game itself.)

Both *The Virgin* and its sequel, *Still Life*, made use of realist (and other nineteenth-century fiction) conventions, such as a Tolstoyan sweep of highly analysed characters, beautifully set in a fully embellished social milieu, with carefully detailed enumeration in the description of object, character and setting. Unlike realist authors, however, Byatt introduced a baroque, almost mannered style, achieved not only by means of allusion but also through density of metaphor, image and symbol, drawing upon conventions from medieval and Renaissance literature. Equally unlike realism, Byatt's later fiction is systematically, overtly self-referential, like so much literature of the period. In *Still Life*, one of the central themes of the novel is the debate between a male academic critic, who is vehemently anti-realist regarding the writing of modern fiction, and a young woman student who meekly points out how like realist fiction her own family was. This parody of the tradition in the 1920s and 1930s of representing the realist as an authoritarian male is simply an acknowledgement of how anti-realist attitudes had become the 'dominant ideology'. Like Doris Lessing before her, Byatt shows a character trying to write a play in ordinary, unfigurative language, and failing to be able to exclude the metaphors and similes which are the very stuff of thought.

Possession: A Romance is acknowledged to be Byatt's most impressive achievement. Like Jhabvala before her and Anita Desai after her, Byatt adopted the novelistic convention of interweaving two distinct stories set in different historical periods, which gradually and uncannily are revealed to be, in certain respects, mirror images or symbolic of each other. The 'inner novel' – a Victorian 'romance' between Ash and LaMotte, two poets – is narrated to the reader through letters, diaries, journals and literary texts (usually long narrative poems) attributed to one or the other of them. The romance is told almost as a detective mystery, since their brief, illicit relationship (the male poet was married) was said to be carefully covered up by elaborate, but ultimately unsuccessful, precautions. Byatt has drawn upon a host of familiar literary techniques; through a most extraordinarily persevering quest, various unknown literary remains are found and read, and a grave is exhumed, to confirm the final suspicion that the woman had a child by her lover. This child, it transpires, is probably the great-great-great-grandmother of the heroine of the 'outer' novel, Maud. She, and her evolving romance with fellow academic Roland, is the focus of a contemporary 1970s world of academic plots and subterfuges, which functions as a superficial analogue to the passionate, brooding intensity of Ash and La Motte's relationship. The entire novel within a novel is, moreover, a spoof on academic criticism, which attends to biography and thematics, rather than to narrative practices and to texts as artifacts.

In her essay 'People in Paper Houses: Attitudes to Experiment in English Post-War Fiction', Byatt has given a very accurate description of her own most recent novels, and her efforts in them to get beyond the notion that there is an antithesis between realism and modernism. This reconciliation between the two dominant traditions of nineteenth- and twentieth-century fiction has so far taken the form primarily either of parodies of realism (Iris Murdoch), or a self-conscious artifice so overt as to be itself a parody of modernism, or an overt fusion of realism and modernism (as in Byatt's case). What one can also find, however, in modern fiction, are examples such as *Tripmaster Monkey* (1989) by Maxine Hong Kingston, or *Ceremony* (1977) by Leslie Marmon Silko, which move beyond both parody (of either tradition) and an often unconvincing effort at fusion. Margaret Atwood's *Surfacing* (1972) and Bessie Head's *Maru* (1971), or Angela Carter's *Nights at the Circus* (1984), to give a few examples, suggest ways forward into a new kind of fiction that moves beyond parody and overt efforts at fusions.

Anita Desai 1937–

One of India's most original and distinguished novelists, Anita Desai grew up in Delhi and attended university there; she has lived for extended periods in Bombay, England and America, and she has been professor of English at Mount Holyoke College as well as an honorary fellow of Girton College, Cambridge. Desai wrote several books for children, such as *The Village by the Sea* (London, 1982); her earliest works included

Cry the Peacock (London, 1963) and *Voices in the City* (London, 1965). A collection of short stories, *Games at Twilight* (London), appeared in 1978, preceded by a remarkable novel, *Fire on the Mountain* (London and Delhi, 1977), which won the Winifred Holtby prize and the National Academy of Letters, India, award. Her next novel, *Clear Light of Day* (London, 1980), shortlisted for the Booker Prize, continued the distinguished writing of *Fire on the Mountain*. With the publication of *In Custody* (London, 1984, also shortlisted for the Booker Prize), Desai's range and intellectual variety became evident, as in *Baumgartner's Bombay* (London, 1988) and *Journey to Ithaca* (London, 1995), her most recent book. Several of Desai's stories and novels have been translated into numerous European and Indian languages.

Like Flannery O'Connor, Desai has argued that 'reality' is a matter of depths, not surfaces; the realist dogma that art should reflect facts, in the discourse of sociology, psychology, economics, politics and so on, leads only to a superficial understanding of life and death. Consequently, her novels reveal efforts aimed at an intuitive grasp of the intelligible universe through concrete particulars, which lead to symbolic and imaginative depths, reverberations and significances. Desai's conviction that art is not an accurate reflection of surface facts and concrete particulars, but uses concrete particulars as the starting point in its gropings into the depths of life, leads to a rich style of writing involving the use of recurring images and motifs. These latter are suggestive of a personal, imaginative vision involving moral and aesthetic values which, however, escape definitive reduction into discursive statements. For these implied values are thoroughly embedded in a fundamental predilection for growth, change, and transformation. Desai's novels are definitive about one thing only, ultimately, and that is faith in the necessity of intelligent, imaginative articulation of human experience, if experience is to be made meaningful. Through an imaginative interrogation of our experience alone can we progress beyond selfishness, prejudice and stupidity.

Since intelligent analysis of the received opinion which constitutes much of our sense of reality can be accomplished only by a finely honed instrument, language and style are central concerns for Desai. Her novels work relentlessly against reduction to repositories of ideas, beliefs or value statements; thematic matter is so elusive as to slip through the winnows of discursive dogmas and criticism. Ambiguity pervades the texts in an almost modernist vein, preventing the reader from projecting her or his own predilections into them. Plot is mercilessly subordinated to craft and style; narrative time is designed not to further the action, but to thwart such superficial progression along surface lines, by delving into the minds of the characters, into their past, their aspirations, their hopes and their fears. Consequently, both style and structure in Desai's novels are characterized by a quality of rich proliferation. Both the language and the structure reverberate with depths and with elusive resonances, whose imaginative vitality resists univocal statement. More 'like' life than any realism of fact could ever be, Desai's stylistic richness is vital and organic in the way that life itself is, with its depths, its ambiguities and its evolutionary essence.

One of Desai's most striking accomplishments is her success in unifying the outer world of social life with the inner realm of her characters, so that the distinction between the two dissolves into the order which reintegrates them. Thus, in her artistic effort to design, out of the meaningless chaos of life, an imaginative composition, Desai has achieved a unity of vision which completely overcomes the dualistic philosophies arising from mere surface facts. This unity involves a congruence of style, structure and thematics characteristic of intensely imaginative fiction, and such congruence is perceived by the reader as aesthetic beauty, a beauty, however, which is alive to change, to growth and to transformation. This character of Desai's novels is first evident to the reader in the fine balance observable in the texts between the teeming, powerfully alive social life, portrayed in rich, colourful language, and the internal lives of the characters caught in the midst of this streaming humanity. Whether in *Baumgartner's Bombay*, *In Custody*, *Clear Light of Day* or *Fire on the Mountain*, each of the main characters functions as a relatively still point in the rush of life, not out of it altogether, of course, but 'not in the mainstream' either, not completely caught up in the hubbub because incapable of not observing, meditating,

contemplating. This contemplative posture is portrayed by Desai in quite different ways, from the deliberate distancing from life of the grandmother in *Fire on the Mountain* to the less voluntary distancing of Baumgartner, Tara and Deven. Yet, however various Desai's portrayals, conflicts between the need for detachment and solitude and the need for relationship are never resolvable.

Thus, the characteristic way in which Desai's central characters tend to appear to be swamped by the clamorous world around them is to be understood not as a flaw, but as functioning aesthetically in the novel, with the explicit aim of questioning the assumption that an active life, conventionally understood, is categorically superior. Related challenges to literary orthodoxies arise, too, as the value of superficially dramatic plot and action is re-evaluated, as are 'strong characterization' assumptions. Readers' expectations are thwarted, and redirected away from certainties and unambiguously stated values, away from strong portrayal of characters and dramatic plots, away from reductive thematics and towards style, language and contemplation. Textual complexities arouse the mind to meditation about the meaning of art, life, love and death. But such meditation as Desai's novels encourage the reader to engage in does not function to resolve and dispel moral complexity or aesthetic ambiguity so much as to inspire appreciation of points of view and ways of being which were previously alien to us. Such appreciation is the mode *par excellence* by which we enrich our moral, aesthetic and spiritual beings, and it is by means of Desai's beautifully crafted style that we expand our grasp of attitudes, beliefs and forms of life different from our own.

The narrative structures of several of Desai's novels are suggestive of an axis formed by the opposition of the individual characters to social forces surrounding them; that is, narrative time plunges into depths of psychological, inner realms by exploring both past, remembered experiences and present feelings and thoughts. Then, suddenly, instead of exploring depths, the narrative moves forward in an orderly, linear way to connect the character with her or his surrounding world, her or his relatives, friends or community. This structural character reflects one of the central themes of many of the novels, namely the conflict between duty, relationships or participation and the individual's need to withdraw or her or his inability to relate. Characterization reinforces this thematic dimension; people are shown in every degree of relationship and apartness. Yet, as the novels succeed in overcoming the duality between past and present, depth and surface, by revealing the latter elements to be constructed out of the former, they also dispel any easy, clear distinction between individuality and relationship. Most obviously, Desai's texts question the adequacy of accepted forms of relationship, and reveal a whole range of possible forms which have their integrity, too.

It is, however, by means of a subtle, carefully construed language that Desai opens her readers to a more expanded grasp of the sheer diversity of human relationship. Through finely drawn distinctions and subtleties, the writing itself arouses us to a more imaginative sympathy. The power of Desai's language to reveal prejudice, to remove the veils of custom which blind and deafen us to others, involves the perfection of perception itself. The very facts and surface particulars are transformed through metaphor, imagery and motifs. We perceive worlds of experience belonging to others of utterly different temperament because of the power of the language of Desai's texts, not because the thematics of the text lead us to certain conclusions. Having created a language and style which enlarge and quicken our experience, she leaves moral and intellectual appraisal to her characters. This is essentially a technique of irony, and it reinforces other devices, such as indirect free narrative and de-emphasizing of plot and content, in the text's construction of meaning, which defies the reader's treating it as an authoritative box of ideas for consumption like chocolates.

Patricia Grace 1937–

Author of the first collection of short stories by a Maori woman writer, *Waiariki* (Auckland, 1975), and mother of seven children, Grace was born in Wellington, New Zealand. *Mutuwhenua: The Moon Sleeps* (Auckland, 1978), her first novel, was followed by another short story collection, *The Dream Sleepers* (Auckland, 1980), and by two children's books, *The Kuia and the Spider*

(Auckland, 1981) and *Watercress Tuna and the Children of Champion Street* (Auckland, 1984). Her second novel, *Potiki*, appeared in 1986 (Auckland; it won the 1987 New Zealand Book Award for fiction). *Electric City and other Stories* (Auckland, 1987) was her third collection of short stories. In 1993, a third novel, *Cousins* (London), consolidated Grace's reputation as an accomplished and compelling novelist, short story writer and author of children's books. Writing Fellow at Victoria University in 1985, Grace has also taught in schools at both primary and secondary levels. She contributed stories to the Maori literature magazine *Te Ao Hou* (founded in 1952) when she first began publishing. Her fiction is set within the familiar context of issues regarding biculturalism – Maori/pakeha (white) relations – both at the personal level of interracial marriage and friendship, and on the larger social/political scale of battles with the pakeha world for equality, return of stolen land, and resistance to the assimilation and death of Maori culture, language and tradition. Her fiction explores with wit, irony and seriousness the pakeha mindset of the 'Mr Dollarmen', that is, white people unable to appreciate values which transcend transient gratifications of money and extreme individualism at the expense of community, spiritual/imaginative values, and culture, heritage or tradition. The importance of land to the Maori, and of both the preservation of what white people have not yet appropriated and the return of stolen land, is a unifying thematic principle, and is of symbolic value too. For natural landscape becomes a metaphor for the 'landscapes of the heart', which are said to make Maori people what they are. Grace's fiction explores the difficulty of responding to change and progress while not being destroyed by it. Maoris must find ways of adopting aspects of progress, but in their own way, making their own decisions about how to reconcile progress and heritage, instead of allowing their culture to be swept away.

Grace, like a number of other Maori writers such as Keri Hulme or Witi Ihimaeva (1944–), has constructed complex narratives involving various points of view, time shifts, supernatural elements, dream, myth, ritual and symbolism. Her overt use of Maori legends, oral poetry and imagery, which frequently occur as stories and poems in their own right within the progress of her fiction, create a fine unity suggestive of how Maoris can preserve their heritage, even in the context of a powerful pakeha literary environment. For example, myths of the Maori legendary figure Maui are related to Christian myths of Christ, as in *Potiki* (much as Keri Hulme did in *The Bone People*, 1983), with the supernaturally gifted child Toko who, born of the simple-minded Mary and Joseph, the transient beachcomber, has a visionary knowledge of past, present and future. Deformed and condemned to an early death, Toko becomes a source of great strength, joy and inspiration to his people, as he transcends individuality in a powerful fusion of the personal and the communal. His extremely subjective, individual perceptions are depicted as a form of objective, communal wisdom; his narrative perspective in the chapters bearing his name are only Grace's most intense rejection of a realist, objective, omniscient narrative. Her chapters avoid such a pakeha myth, as her fiction moves across a range of perspectives of stream of consciousness, free indirect thought, interior monologues, first and third person limited and retrospective views, and so on. Dream, memory, vision and indirect report replace any illusions of faithful depiction of a reality in favour of the importance of experience closely connected to subjective perceptions.

Patricia Grace's first novel, *Mutuwhenua*, is a magical expression of the inner life of Ripeka, who is nearly destroyed by her inability to trust the strength of her pakeha husband's love in the face of supernatural Maori forces, which threaten her life. Less experimental than its successors *Potiki* and *Cousins*, *Mutuwhenua* is a compelling fiction, nevertheless. The two later novels develop its themes in much more complex narrative forms, and extend the content to the larger social/political arena, where individual struggles and relationships are firmly situated within the larger Maori community, history and efforts to preserve their heritage. Both novels expand their scope further by drawing in whole extended families and even communities, where *Mutuwhenua* had emphasized more the personal relationship between Ripeka and Graeme. This extension is handled with admirable skill by Grace, yet in quite separate ways in *Potiki* and *Cousins*.

In *Potiki*, Grace has infused the everyday with

legendary and symbolic dimensions; the whole novel could be read as not only a piece of fiction in the Western literary tradition, but also as a Maori document, designed itself to function as a written repository of oral legends, myths, stories, poems, rituals and history – the writing down of which, in this way, is a central means of preserving Maori life from the destruction of pakeha society. Thus, Grace has adopted a European form (the novel) and then made it serve Maori culture. Its narrative progresses from a 'Prologue', recording the tale of a legendary carver, into the initially subjective, everyday experiences of the Tamihana family. Yet, this ordinariness is, very early, raised to the level of myth and religion, and the incredible birth of the Maui–Christ figure, Toko, is recounted. Indeed, hardly a chapter of the book passes without some legend, myth or ritual structuring the everyday life, until the novel gradually expands into the communal/symbolic, and reaches a crescendo of transcendence in, first, the rebuilding of the burned-down meeting house. The finishing of the final poupou (the carving referred to in the 'Prologue'), the telling of the final few legends from an unknown narrator, and the prophetic 'Potiki', the last chapter, told by the 'dead' Toko, take this book to a level of significance far beyond that of most novels, for it constitutes a vital document of Maori culture which will function to strengthen the survival of this threatened people.

Bessie Head 1937–1986

One of the most remarkable South African writers of the century, Bessie Head was born in Pietermaritzburg of a white mother and a black father. After a traumatic childhood, first with foster parents, then in an orphanage, and finally in a missionary school, Head gained a teaching certificate and lived in Durban, Johannesburg and Cape Town, where she also worked as a journalist. In 1964, she was given a one-way exit permit to the British Protectorate of Bechuanaland, now Botswana, where she began another difficult period of her life, harassed by the local male authorities for her independence and reserve to the point of nervous collapse. She left the village of Serowe to live with her young son in

Francistown for the period 1965–8. Throughout the 1960s she had been publishing essays and stories in such journals as the *New African*. After returning to Serowe, she finished and published her first novel, *When Rain Clouds Gather* (New York and London, 1969), received with great enthusiasm. It is the story of Makhaya, a political refugee in Golema Mmidi, a village in Botswana, and his efforts to become a part of the community as it struggles to survive in the face of a severe drought and in the face of the ignorance, prejudice and traditions which prevent it from benefiting from modern farming techniques. Her next book, *Maru* (London, 1971), was greeted with even greater praise; it is a remarkable novella about a young Masarwa, Margaret. In Head's own words, this is a novel 'on the hideousness of racial prejudice. But I also wanted the novel to be so beautiful and so magical that I, as the writer, would long to read and re-read it.' The novel is certainly magical, and is an example of the 'prophetic' writing which E.M. Forster described as the highest form of fiction: '[the writer's] theme is the universe, or something universal; he proposes to sing, and the strangeness of song arising in the halls of fiction is bound to give us a shock.'

In 1973, Head made yet another enormous stride forward in her craft in publishing *A Question of Power* (London), her most substantial work of fiction. In this third novel, Head charted the mental tortures of the character Elizabeth in an intensely internal narrative mode which was so different from the style and narrative of her earlier fiction as to confound many of her earlier admirers. Narrative progression and clarity are sacrificed to the embodiment of Elizabeth's suffering in a powerful picture-language which overwhelms her and cuts her and the reader off from any objective, external world or reality. In 1977, a 'collection' of stories, *The Collector of Treasures and Other Botswana Village Tales* (London), was published. This Head explained, was a series of linked 'tales' whose order was crucial to the presentation of the unity of the book. Her next book, *Serowe, Village of the Rain Wind* (Cape Town and London, 1981), is a semi-documentary account of the Botswana village where she lived, the largest such south of the Sahara, and its history. The last book to be published in her

lifetime was *A Bewitched Crossroad* (Johannesburg, 1984), a legend of the history of Africa focusing upon the Bamangwato and their chief, Khama III, who lived in Serowe. Posthumous publications include *Tales of Tenderness and Power* (Johannesburg, 1989; London, 1990), a collection of twenty-one shorter writings, three of which had not been published. Others had been published in journals, anthologies and magazines between 1962 and 1981, but were not easily available until collected. Other posthumous collections should appear soon, and an invaluable selection of her letters has recently been published as *A Gesture of Belonging* (London, 1991), ed. Randolph Vigne, to whom the letters were written. Other letters (several thousand) and papers are in the Bessie Head Archive in Serowe, Botswana. Articles and essays, such as 'Some Notes on Novel Writing', published in *New Classic* (5, 1978), give further insight into her imaginative writings. In all, then, Head is the author of six full-length works, some twenty-five shorter fictions, various essays and some journalism, and several thousand letters, which it is hoped will one day be published in a complete edition.

Head's fiction is closely rooted in her own personal experience, but it also draws upon the immediate political and social events around her, as well as the history of Botswana and its people. Her ability to fuse autobiographical elements with social documentary and history into symbolic, imaginative fiction is one of the central characteristics of her work. The particular way in which she achieved this fusion through the shaping powers of her imagination is a mark of her individuality and originality. Because her fiction is intensely prophetic, it can be discussed in terms of philosophic and universal, metaphysical issues as well as immediate social, political, psychological and personal concerns. However mundane the events are that provide the incidents in the stories, then, they always reach straight back into universals. One of the most frequently recurring themes of these novels is that of life itself as a common burden which binds each and every one of us together, however different we may be. The character Ma-Millipede in *When Rain Clouds Gather* explains to Makhaya, the refugee, why he must not hate even his oppressors:

'It is because of the great burden of life,' she said quietly. 'You must learn only one thing. You must never, never put anyone away from you as not being your brother. Because of this great burden, no one can be put away from you.'

'Who is my brother, Mama?' he asked.

'It is each person alive on the earth,' she said.

The novels explore, of course, themes of the racism inherent in most cultures (*Maru* shows the blacks of Serowe to be as racist towards the Masarwas as whites towards blacks) and the brutality of the sexism of black men and its power to destroy a woman's sanity. Yet they also explore the great decency and generosity which can come out of some apparently ordinary people. Head also depicted the profound human need for community and for cooperation if a self-identity was to be realized, thus insisting on the interdependence of individuality and community. She showed how exile and exclusion from the sense of belonging and loving can unbalance people, and she emphasized the importance of the relation of people to their land, their earth, the very soil they till for sustenance. She ended *A Question of Power* with two sentences which unify the themes of the book, in writing of Elizabeth, 'As she fell asleep, she placed one soft hand over her land. It was a gesture of belonging.' The soil or land as a symbol both of roots and of the self-identity which must ground itself in the land, or die for lack of sustenance, recurs throughout the fiction as a unifying image. Other themes involve the stultifying effects of ignorance and the need for education if traditions and customs which promote inhumanity, poverty, sexism and racism are to be overcome. However, the theme which dominates all others, and which unifies all her writings into one body of work, is that of power.

The way Head handled power makes her writing prophetic, particularly *Maru* and *A Question of Power*. In the latter, there is a deft alternation between everyday scenes of reality and dream, nightmares and hallucinations. While spasmodically confused and then realistic, these alternations are only incidental to the spiritual theme of the quest for power and the battle against evil – seen as the abuse of power. Both *Maru* and

Power realize this quest, as does *When Rain Clouds Gather*, in the overt form of a life-and-death struggle, or, in Forster's terms, a contest, but one which is articulated not by theme, arguments, issues, talk or speech. The contest is conveyed essentially through 'its prophetic song, [which] flows athwart the action and the surface morality like an undercurrent. It lies outside words.' Both action and surface morality – whether involving issues of racism or of sexual love – function less to convey any beliefs or attitudes than as a vehicle for the song and its value as music. In a passage in *Maru*, Margaret is described as realizing the importance of art as a means of controlling an otherwise destructive and consuming power within her body and her psyche: 'Something was more powerful than her body could endure. It had to be brought under control, put on a leash and then be allowed to live in a manageable form.' Moreover, it is not so much the characters of the novels who are in conflict with each other; this level of personal conflict is also made purely incidental to the larger contest between power and its abuse. Indeed, the characters lose their distinct identities so much that they begin to look like forces within the individual psyche, much as William Blake's characters in the prophetic books are.

While with *A Question of Power* Head reached into new areas of experimentation with style, narrative and psychological exploration, it could be argued that *Maru* is her most perfect achievement. In this short novel she reached her most intense congruence of form and matter and her most radiant song. The first paragraph of the novel sings the motif:

The rains were so late that year. But throughout that hot, dry summer those black storm clouds clung in thick folds of brooding darkness along the low horizon. There seemed to be a secret in their activity, because each evening they broke the long, sullen silence of the day, and sent soft rumbles of thunder and flickering slicks of lightning across the empty sky. They were not promising rain. They were prisoners, pushed back, in trapped coils of boiling cloud.

and the final paragraph states the refrain:

When people of the Masarwa tribe heard about Maru's marriage to one of their own, a door silently opened on the small, dark airless room in which their souls had been shut for a long time. The wind of freedom, which was blowing throughout the world for all people, turned and flowed into the room. As they breathed in the fresh, clear air their humanity awakened.

The complete inadequacy of describing this novella as a contest between Maru and Moleba for Margaret's love is an indication of the more universal plane on which it moves. A further indication is the lack of suspense as a force in the novel; the first six pages of the tale are set in a time far into the future of the rest of the 120 pages. Moreover, Margaret and Maru are never described as meeting after their first brief encounter, and she is hardly ever described in encounters with Moleba. Rather, the incidents of the story which are related make it impossible to describe the novel as a romance. It is written in a legendary style and tone, as though all the particulars and incidents are meaningful only in so far as they are understood as concrete embodiments of ancient wisdom. Certainly Head should be read as a tale-teller in the ancient African tradition, as is also evident from *A Bewitched Crossroad*. For example, her description of Maru is, throughout, elemental, as in the following lines: 'there was a depth of secret activity in him like that long, low line of black boiling cloud. There was a clear blue sky in his mind that calmly awaited the storm in his heart and when all had been said and done, this earth could be washed clean of all the things he hated.' His vision of a new world is described in equally simple, concrete but elemental terms: 'A little brown, dusty footpath turned away from the roaring busy highways of life – yellow daisies grew alongside the dusty footpath and danced in the sun and wind, and together the footpath and the daisies would make his heart bound with joy.' Elsewhere, Margaret is said to see Maru in words that are implicitly self-referential: 'He was not just anything but some kind of strange, sweet music you could hear over and over again. She was beginning to listen. It was not strange. She had heard it before.'

This description of Margaret's impression of

Maru is of course also one of the effects the novel is meant to have upon the reader. Other central elements in the novel are equally self-referential: Margaret paints a picture which depicts a dream that Maru has had; she also begins to dream his own dreams. These are like the legends of whole cultures, tribes and races, as are the nightmares Elizabeth has in *A Question of Power*. Gradually it becomes evident that power is to be understood not in any worldly sense but in a spiritual one, a personal power that makes the individual a visionary who has the insight to realize her or his deepest dreams and needs. The dreams and nightmares, the hallucinations and fantasies are the means by which the characters enter into their own deeper realities, in order to discover both the monsters that threaten them and the nature of their real needs. In Head's novels, it becomes clear that the quest for power is a visionary, personal one which involves not only the community and the land but all of humanity. Elizabeth explains in *A Question of Power* that 'Africa isn't rising. It's already up. It depends on where one places the stress. I place it on the soul. If it's basically right, there, then other things fall into place. That's my struggle, and that's black power, but it's a power that belongs to all of mankind and in which all mankind can share.'

Head's autobiographical writings have been collected in the volume *A Woman Alone*, ed. Craig MacKenzie (London, 1990).

Joanna Russ 1937–

One of the earliest overt critics of gender stereotypes of the post-war period, Russ was born and brought up in New York City. She attended Cornell and Yale, taking BA and MFA degrees, and has taught at various universities throughout the USA. Her fiction has been recognized as exemplary of some of the most interesting experimental writings of the post-modern period, though it was at first often relegated to second-class status as 'merely' science fiction, utopian or feminist literature. Russ has combined all these elements into a post-modernist literary achievement which challenges such genre classifications; like that of Ursula Le Guin, Emma Tennant and others, her fiction disrupts hierarchies previously established by male critics and writers. She has also revealed the emptiness of the charge against much experimental writing, that it was amoral or apolitical, by showing how politically subversive the disruption of literary conventions, styles, forms and genres essentially is. For literary conventions are shown by Russ to express moral, political and social attitudes, power structures and values. One of Russ's hallmarks is, however, her systematic and insistent interweaving of gender criticism into all her writing, so that gender is revealed to be an issue at the heart of literary, moral and political beliefs. From *Picnic on Paradise* (New York, 1968) to *And Chaos Died* (New York, 1970), the immensely well-known *The Female Man* (New York, 1975), then *The Adventures of Alyx* (New York, 1983), *Extra (Ordinary) People* (New York, 1984; a collection of narratives) and the non-fictional *How to Suppress Women's Writing* (Austin, Tex., 1983), Russ has engaged in a systematic exposure of the role of gender stereotypes in all our thinking, and how it infects our political, social, moral and literary ideals.

The Female Man is typically post-modern, not in its use of meta-fictional devices or metaphysical questioning so much as in its imaginative reversal of prejudices, attitudes and notions, often to do with gender, which pass themselves off as facts of nature or of reality. The four characters in this science fiction, utopian genre-disruptor can be seen as the fragmented multiple self of a single narrative persona. This multiple narrative 'self' breaks down the boundaries not only between the characters, but between characters and narrative persona; more radically, the boundary between narrator/persona of the author and the persona of the author of this book is breached, especially as one of the characters is named Joanna. Thus, Russ's narrative point of view is sophisticated, multiple, varied and indeterminate in post-modernist ways: the world of fact intrudes into the world of fiction as ontological realms and levels are confused. Fictional fact, fictional fiction, factual fiction and factual fact are all mixed in 'frame-busting' tactics which create typical effects of recursive embedding, instability of distinctions and multiple realities. As in her other novels, Russ also adapted the conventions of 'non-literary literature', both to escape male evaluations of what constitutes the

literary, and to see how sexual difference might be reconceptualized in alternative forms not involving the familiar hierarchies and privileges. Russ drew too upon the psychoanalytic analyses of such writers as R.D. Laing to sharpen her perceptions of how traditional prejudices are established and become 'facts', and the detailed methods of how they can be overturned. Her remarkably readable *The Female Man* uses a number of other post-modernist techniques flavoured by science fiction devices. The narrative 'progresses' and 'backtracks' by means of both short, jerky fragments and longer pieces interspersed between the one-, two- and three-sentence sections. The events in these fragments occur sometimes in the present and sometimes in the 'contemporaneous' future, sometimes in New York City and sometimes in Whileaway (earth and non-earth, nine hundred years from 'now', or 'then'). Sometimes the narrator is one or another first person narrator, sometimes there is an unknown, third person narrator. Sometimes the events are fantastic, supernatural, surreal, sometimes they are quite ordinary.

Throughout *The Female Male*, men change into women, women into men, while Joanna, Jeannine, Janet and Jael gradually interweave into each other. Meanwhile, their increasingly multiple yet unitary self is interrupted by hilarious scenes with men trying to reason 'women', especially Janet, into doing their will – usually copulation. Writer, narrator and characters no longer maintain distinct identities, as Russ explored our concept of identity, how women are stripped of any sense of self through self-sacrifice, and what new conception of identity we could evolve to balance individuality with communality. In her collection of novellas, *Extra (Ordinary) People*, she developed further her use of science fiction, utopian and feminist conventions. ('Souls' received the *Science Fiction Chronicle's* highest award, the Hugo prize, in 1983.) Russ's fiction, like much avant-garde and post-modern writing, frustrates readers' attempts to make the text meaningful by imposing already familiar patterns and structures upon them. That is, traditional codes of reading and interpretation do not work, precisely because Russ has tried to get out of the old forms and orders – with all their ideological baggage – and offer us new and unfamiliar codes, concepts and logic. Russ's fiction demonstrates what a number of conventional science fiction and utopian writers have found, such as Mary Staton and June Arnold; namely, the new metaphors, styles, images, structures, themes and techniques available in such a genre outside the mainstream give the writer opportunities for subverting and disrupting prejudices and conventions which otherwise go unchallenged.

Further publications by Russ include *Kittatinny: A Tale of Magic* (New York, 1978), *The Two of Them* (New York, 1978), *On Strike Against God* (New York, 1980), *The Zanzibar Cat* (Sauk City, Wis. 1983) and *The Hidden Side of the Moon* (New York, 1987).

Emma Tennant 1937–

Fantasist, satirist and author of books and plays for children and adults, Tennant was born in London to Scottish parents, though much of her adolescence was spent in the family castle in Scotland. Influenced by mythology, the supernatural and the imaginativeness of science fiction, Tennant began experimenting with a range of approaches to fiction after the publication of her first novel, *The Colour of Rain* (London, 1964), under the pseudonym Catherine Aydy. She was also an avid reader of Henry Green and of South American fantasists, while admiring precursors like Thomas Hardy (she has a cottage in Dorset). Her writing is marked both by allegory and by overt intertextual devices – she often 're-writes' earlier novels, myths or stories in order to present their themes from a feminist perspective. Political or social satire is rarely absent and often overtly systematic, while her fiction also explores the dichotomies between sanity and madness, reality and illusion, and issues of identity, violence and desire.

Tennant's explicit exposure of the ridiculous limitations which social notions about women's roles place on intelligent, creative people takes a number of different forms in *Woman Beware Woman* (London, 1983), playing upon Thomas Middleton and Prosper Mérimée. The protagonist goes quite mad under the pressure of life in frustrating, murderous Ireland. In *Alice Fell* (London, 1980), the Alice–Persephone figure is condemned for a time to the underworld, while Britain crumbles around her in the midst of

political upheavals. In *The Bad Sister* (London, 1978), a rewriting of James Hogg's *Confessions of a Justified Sinner* (1824), Tennant portrayed a young woman, Jane Wild, who becomes psychologically disturbed/demonically possessed and kills her sister and father. A journal of Jane's is 'framed' by an editor's commentary which functions also as an interpretative gesture. In *Queen of Stones* (London, 1982) – a take-off of William Golding's *Lord of the Flies* (1954) – Tennant continued her ruthless exploration of women and violence, depicting a group of adolescent girls who execute one of their members under the leadership of another Jane, who adopts violence as her only mode of rejecting the female roles imposed upon her. Finally, in another intertextual parody, this time of R.L. Stevenson's *Dr Jekyll and Mr Hyde* (1886), Tennant described a woman who degenerates into a split other self, a seductress and murderess of men. This novel, *Two Women of London* (London, 1989), charts the breakdown of a mother whose sanity is dependent on illusions of happiness and simplicity which are not congruent with reality. Violence in Tennant's novels is often presented as virtually synonymous with insanity. Far from simply condemning it, however, the author presents readers with a quite detailed psychological analysis of the path of breakdown into violence and its causes in social injustice. Yet all is presented in a parodic, satiric vein, with culture and the literary tradition (both previous fictional works and also narrative conventions) made some of Tennant's prime targets, and closely related to the moral, social and political dimensions which types of literature perpetuate.

Tennant has been described as one of our 'most original writers' and as a 'rare fantasist'. While critics have often been bemused by her fabulous, supernatural and symbolic devices, most agree on the excellence of her style, describing it as striking, elegant, beautifully measured and graceful. Her imagery and parody have been praised, especially in such novels as *Hotel de Dream* (London, 1976), *The Time of the Crack* (London, 1973) and *The Last of the Country House Murderers* (London, 1974). While the latter two are allegories of British society, *Hotel de Dream* adds an additional psychological dimension, so that public, social life and private, personal life become interwoven: one person's dreams invade the psyche of another person and become reality, in one of Tennant's most imaginative novels.

In addition to over a dozen and a half novels, Tennant has written children's books, was founder-editor of the literature magazine *Bananas* (London), 1975–8, and has published an anthology of contemporary literature, *Saturday Night Reader* (London, 1979).

Shashi Deshpande 1938–

Born in Dharwad, south India, Deshpande was educated in Bombay and at Bangalore University, taking degrees in both law and economics. She began publishing short stories in various periodicals while working as a journalist, and eventually collected her stories in four volumes, *The Legacy* (Calcutta, 1971), *The Miracle* (Calcutta, 1986), *It Was the Nightingale* (Calcutta, 1986) and *It Was Dark* (Calcutta, 1986); she has also written children's books. Her novels include *The Dark Holds No Terrors* (New Delhi, 1980), *If I Die Today* (Sahibabad, 1982), *Come Up and Be Dead* (New Delhi, 1985) and *Roots and Shadows* (Madras, 1983). This fourth novel won an award as the best Indian novel in the English language for 1983. Her next novel, *That Long Silence* (London, 1988), is published by Virago, and concerns the writer, wife and mother Jaya, who retreats from everyday life into a kind of exile, in part due to apparent financial irregularities in her husband's job. This exile is symbolic, however, of Jaya's barrenness as a writer with a block. This novel is intensely and overtly feminist, as she has analysed the physicality of women's lives as it impinges upon and both enriches and hinders their spiritual lives. The novel relentlessly exposes the ritualization of sexual and emotional life to the point of dehumanization and permanent frustrations. Themes of self-fulfilment in conflict with social needs are carefully woven into the implied theme of how 'ordinary' life hinders and yet nourishes the creative life, the life of art, of writing and of imagination. Another novel, *The Binding Vine* (London, 1993) has recently appeared.

That Long Silence is a novel constructed out of oppositions carefully intertwined both thematically and in narrative terms, through plot, characterization, tone, and rhetorical devices such as central, controlling metaphors and images. Oppositions between men and women are overt, as their differences in status and power are criticized. The opposition between the past and the present becomes a controlling metaphor, as the novel explores symbolically the role of memory in imaginative acts of artistic creation. In order to grasp the significance as well as the origins of her present barren situation, Jaya returns to confront a past which had been represented and denied by means of silence. Indeed, she and her husband literally return to a previously occupied flat, during this present period of exile, where Jaya's setting helps her to explore her unconscious life, both past and present, and to learn how to order with language and reason this repressed life, which has led her to the present total impasse of writer's block and dissatisfaction with her family relationships. Sexual repression is also explored, as Jaya analyses the limitations of marriage in the context of Indian attitudes. The novel constitutes a reinstantiation of women's creativity, vitality and worth when they disrupt the silences that destroy their very lives.

Margaret Atwood 1939–

Novelist, short story writer, essayist, poet and restorer of Canadian literary achievements, Atwood in her writing systematically thematizes the personal quest for fulfilment as inextricably involved in a communal quest for cultural identity. Born in Ottawa, Ontario, Atwood attended the University of Toronto and Radcliffe College while establishing herself as a major writer. She published her first volume of poems, *Double Persephone*, in 1961 (Toronto), followed by many more throughout the next three decades, interspersed with novels, including *The Edible Woman* (Toronto, 1969), *Surfacing* (Toronto, 1972), *Lady Oracle* (Toronto, 1976), *Life Before Man* (Toronto, 1979), *Bodily Harm* (Toronto, 1981), *The Handmaid's Tale* (Toronto, 1985) and *The Robber Bride* (Toronto, 1993). Collections of stories include *Bluebeard's Egg* (Toronto, 1983), *Dancing Girls* (Toronto, 1977) and *Good Bones* (Toronto and London, 1992), and her *Selected Poems* (Toronto) first came out in 1976. Atwood has also compiled *The New Oxford Book of Canadian Verse in English* (Toronto, 1982) and *Survival: A*

Thematic Guide to Canadian Literature (Toronto, 1972), which is a 'map' of Canadian literature. Her poems and her fiction are often organized thematically around images of both cultural and individual issues of survival, as she has sought to portray the entrapment of woman in patriarchy, and of men and women in suffocating social-cultural imprisonment. Allegories of writers trying to escape the inhibiting effects of an overly revered literary tradition are implied throughout. More notably than almost any recent writer, except perhaps Angela Carter, Atwood has drawn explicitly upon folk tale and mythology to reveal the constraining effects of these aspects of cultural heritage, as well as their role in socialization and perpetuation of questionable values.

Like Stevie Smith and many other writers, Atwood has made systematic use of the journey metaphor, both as a quest for identity and to characterize that quest as necessarily passing through uncharted territories into unknown lands (the unconscious, the past, sexuality). Recuperation of the past for present uses (to free us from the crippling effects of nostalgia and sentimentality) and repossession of the unconscious for consciousness has involved gaining control of material in order to survive and to develop into a person. Atwood's novels and poems explore the forces which prevent or inhibit such development by preventing exploration of the 'other side', the 'underground', the unknown, the unconscious, or the hidden prejudices which otherwise control us. Images of diving and surfacing (which Adrienne Rich used in *Diving into the Wreck* (1973) – one year after *Surfacing*) strengthen Atwood's challenge to patriarchal aspects of psychoanalysis and to rationalism, as she reveals the depth beneath the surface and argues that language means more what it represses than what it says. Her poetry and fiction subject both language and its various discourses to 'psychoanalysis', in order to reveal the structures which shape it, and to show the ways it can be used to victimize not only women but also men. Yet, throughout her explorations of language and discourse, she suggests that language is available either to entrap us or to liberate us, whether men or women. The biggest myth of all may be that men are not themselves slaves and victims of social constructs which inhibit self-realization.

Like Doris Lessing in *The Golden Notebook* (1962), Atwood has searched to create a language which does not fragment and debase either women or men. She has rejected the univocal statement or any concept of meaning or truth as single and determinate, noting that she 'uses words for evocation rather than for denotation'. She has described writing as 'uncanny', as 'spell-making', and has explained that we must learn that what is not said is often more important than what is said. She has developed further the literary convention of language as surfaces and depths, as a palimpsest which hides what it means, and she has toyed with the deceptive devices of rhetoric and figures of speech, especially metaphors, as essential to language. She has shown that deception is inherent in language, that figures are fundamental to it and are not merely ornaments, and then has insisted that language is available as either a release and a transformative power or as a trap and a force of subjugation. Her poems and novels express these issues, often through powerful images which are literary conventions revitalized to take on further powers and symbolic meanings.

Atwood's writings exhibit a range of familiar techniques for exploring language and demonstrating both its modes of entrapment and of release. Her prose is much more dense than it may at first appear, when the reader examines its rich materiality to discover punning, satirizing and the foregrounding of clichés and stereotyped speech to reveal its presuppositions. Her puns, her neologisms, her repeated use of familiar idioms to expose their assumptions, her extended imagery, her systematic metaphors, her play on words from other languages and discourses, her indirect references to psychoanalysis (and its sexist assumptions) and her mocking of euphemisms, along with many other devices, turn her prose into highly poetic language, conscious of itself as shaping experience into certain moulds. Self-conscious language is, for Atwood, language liberated from its own unconscious presuppositions of, for example, patriarchy or rationalism. Her writing suggests that such awareness is a prerequisite for 'survival', for control over language – otherwise language controlling us will victimize us with its hidden assumptions. Control over language releases it for creative and artistic purposes, for innovation and transformation of experience, literature, history and self. As in Toni Morrison's writings, Atwood's fiction and poetry explore the means of survival – and explore who survives and who does not.

Atwood has explored the various modes of gaining control over our lives, as she has shown that the past must be regained, the unconscious made conscious and language made creative – free from clichés, stereotypes and dead metaphors. Images of transgression of boundaries and breaching limits abound, as characters are shown that they have the power to become 'other' in a number of senses: other than what they were; 'the other' – able to project themselves into another person to emphasize and escape egotistical confines; the other as the unconscious which, without powerful imaginative analysis, controls the conscious; other in the sense of new and never before experienced; and so on. Atwood has suggested that powerlessness and silence go together; by revealing how language imprisons, we can discover how to use it in new ways which liberate.

In 'On Being a Woman Writer' and 'Writing the Male Character', essays in the volume *Second Words* (Toronto, 1983), Atwood dismissed, specifically, the sexist assumptions hidden in language which prevent women from taking hold of words, and from writing themselves into new, powerful identities. She also revealed that text produces gender; gender is not 'natural' but social – gender does not produce texts. In those essays, Atwood also exposed implicitly the sexist prejudices of much psychoanalysis and medical discourse, and, as in novels such as *Surfacing*, examined notions of madness and illness as both escapes from victimization and forms of it. Like Michel Foucault's writings, Atwood's texts show the historical and cultural nature of such 'natural' phenomena and subject them to control by analysing their hidden assumptions. Her novels often look like portrayals of a search for alternative roles of a more viable kind for both men and women seeking to escape the preferred, 'sane', conventional, socially approved roles. Rejection of the victimization of negative roles is explored, as is the difficulty of escape. But these projects are never isolated from the cultural, social and communal contexts in which they occur, as characters are shown to have 'problems' which are rarely merely personal, but always microcosms of larger, communal and social issues. Sociology and psychology are not, then, separable for Atwood: the individual exists within a community, and escape from victimization can occur only when not merely the individual but also the community – and its manifestation in language, art and history – are subjected to relentless, intelligent scrutiny.

Atwood is well known to have made extensive use of mythology and folk-tale in her writings. Greek and Latin mythology, along with fairy-tale and folklore elements, are borrowed by her, whether as images, characters or situations, in explicit, overt ways in order to revise and rewrite these legends by exploring their hidden or overt sexism, and then changing them. She herself has ironically confirmed that '*Grimm's Fairy Tales* was the most influential work I ever read', an ambiguous comment suggestive of the importance for a patriarchal society of socializing its members from as early as possible. Figures of Artemis, Diana, Hecate and Aphrodite or Venus abound, as Atwood uses these familiar archetypes to expose sexist assumptions and rewrite situations which involve either female figures avoiding traditional stereotypes or male figures exposed as tyrannical. Through her explicit and systematic use of familiar images of mirrors, labyrinths, wolves, eggs, forests and so on *ad infinitum*, she has engaged in self-conscious, self-referential gestures. She has consciously written into her texts the tradition which is their context, thereby gaining control over it instead of being 'influenced' passively or unconsciously by it. She has also provided mirror situations for her readers, opportunities for them to gain control of her texts by her efforts to illuminate to her readers the nature of art and fictions as self-reflective, that is, as including parodies of readers and reading which can be both models of imaginative reading and anti-models of victimized readings. By taking hold overtly of the 'art as mirror' convention, Atwood reveals that art is not a mirror or representation of nature, but a reflection of processes of writing, reading and interpretation; fiction images the reader into the texts, into both its language and its situations and characters. The reader who recognizes herself or himself in the language of the text is no longer a victim of that language's hidden assumptions, of that writing's hidden values.

Surfacing is Atwood's most remarkable novelistic achievement, in which she has managed an imaginative fusion of the range of issues discussed above in an artistically innovative language and form, which set the novel apart from the others. The density of imagery and metaphor, the powerful symbolic dimensions, the fusion of psychological with larger cultural-social themes, and the revitalization of effective literary conventions all combine into a spiritual search for some identity other than the conventional roles available. The novel is noticeably economical, as each character, each event and each stage of development contributes to the drama and reverberates with multiple significances. The unnamed narrator's tortuous excavation functions on many levels as a search for self-knowledge which makes no concessions to any short cuts or easy routes towards this goal.

Surfacing is a work of tremendous emotional resonance, successfully humanizing and embodying theoretical insights from Freud and Jacques Lacan to Foucault and Jacques Derrida. The unnamed protagonist is engaged in an archetypal quest for her missing father, which eventually turns into an encounter with her past, her childhood, her unconscious, her dead parents and primitive social origins. These encounters lead to a self-knowledge which liberates her from oppressive patterns of victimization which had previously entrapped her. These patterns include a failed marriage and an abandoned motherhood, as well as a deeply wounding abortion. In a remarkably suggestive conclusion, comparable to the interpretative enigma of Kate Chopin's *Awakening*, *Surfacing* portrays the heroine on the threshold of a present at last infused with a consciousness of the past, but no less uncertain for all that. The last word of the novel is 'nothing'; the 'I' and her partner are waiting for each other; however, 'the journey back' is not portrayed.

Atwood's narrative strategies draw systematically for structured unity upon familiar literary conventions, regenerated by theoretical gestures towards feminism, colonialism, theories of the gaze, the camera, the victim, psychoanalytic metaphors and deconstructionist images of maps, cyphers and hieroglyphs. The entire novel is structured by endless journeys, excursions and outings, as well as journeys within journeys.

Sometimes the journey metaphor is complicated by reference to photographic metaphors of shooting, rape and victimization. At other times the journey involves the traces of deconstructionist images of maps of the locations of American Indian hieroglyphs, which are supposed to be clues that lead, eventually, by means of almost endless detours, to the location of the missing father. This ostensive quest for the father turns into an Oedipal discovery of the self (enacted on the archetypal site of a cabin in the wilderness) only when the 'I' is left to herself, once her friends depart, and only when she destroys all the trappings of socialized life. All rituals are deferred, her clothes destroyed, the inside of the cabin and all its contents smashed (including the scrap books and photo albums of her past). She 'dives into the wreck', in search of a location in her mind where she can recontact her body and gain access to 'natural' powers destroyed by socialization, but whose restoration may give her the strength to resist further victimization.

Atwood's novel constitutes a powerful exploration of the labour involved in such psychic regeneration. Her heroine is depicted struggling to divest herself of the social myths which cripple her personal power. Her quest for her missing father takes on all the power of the quest for certainty, for ultimate meaning in life, for the final solution to the cypher. In the process, she comes to believe that her father went mad, then she discovers that the madness was 'anthropological research'; then she discovers that he was 'making up' the American Indian cypher drawings to send to an academic researcher; then, when she finds his body drowned in the lake, she does not 'recognize' him, but sees instead an image of her aborted foetus. When friends of the family later come to tell her they found her father's body in the lake, drowned by the weight of his enormous camera, she accuses them of fictions. She then 'goes mad' herself, in her ultimate gesture of sanity; Atwood inverts the two to reveal their socially constructed nature, along with the socially constructed 'nature' of woman which the 'I' is successfully escaping.

The protagonist's journey to find the appropriate site for her own psychological and emotional deconstruction (for the sake of reconstruction – movement from stereotyped self to individuality or self-construction) is portrayed as a journey back to the past, to nature and to the unconscious. The novel is structured to reflect for the reader precisely this journeying back. That is, the novel is not legible on the surface, in the present reading. It has been designed to necessitate repeated re-readings and rejourneyings through its pages, just as the 'I' journeys variously around the lake and over her past haunts, following one false lead and then another. When she finally finds her dead father she cannot recognize him consciously, but after this shock she returns to the site of the cabin and, nevertheless, begins her violent desocialization. Via repeated re-readings, we are able to 'decipher' this hieroglyph of a novel, this map of misreadings, and fashion some kind of account. But the account is unrecognizable, like the dead father, as the meaning of the novel. For there occurs the supplementary ending, namely, the process of violent desocialization, which exceeds completely the meaning of the finding of the missing father. The quest for the phallus, the father, God, presence, being or meaning has led to 'nothing'. Moreover, the 'I's' self is nothing essential either; Atwood has depicted the self instead as the location, the scene where the primordial Oedipal conflict drama occurs, and where eventual regeneration can take place. In the process of regeneration, the 'I' smashes all socialized images of herself, rejects all socialized established roles and rituals, and adopts the pre-social, pre-photographic, pre-human state of nature. The latter, however, the 'I' figure does not idealize or make a ground or origin, a substitute phallus, father cypher or privileged point of view. Rather, she used this fictional state of nature as a place-holder; nature and primitiveness are portrayed not as an end or an origin, but as a site, a place, a metaphor for power and self-'construction'. The 'I' knows that this is how many American Indians tapped into natural power, not by mistaking nature as a God or origin or ideal. They and she see nature as a metaphor for empowerment: nature can be read as a self-constructed place where the conflict of life and death unfolds. But if taken literally, nature is an excuse for violence and exploitation: 'it's natural.' Atwood's novel postulates the enigma of a civil nature (a culturally constructed nature) as the highest achievement of nature itself. That is, nature is metaphorically portrayed

by her as imagination, as a power, not an essence, origin or ideal end. As for writers from William Blake to Marguerite Young, for Atwood imagination (nature in *Surfacing*) is the place or site or scene of action; imagination is the Nietzschean will to power through appropriation or metaphor making. *Surfacing* is Atwood's finest example of figuration as both the record of imaginative passages and the means by which we travel in journeys of self-construction, whereby we leave the safety of familiarity, convention and sanity, and in exploring the unknown (the Other, the unconscious) through shifting metaphors, learn new ways of being and living which exceed anything we dared expect. For the reader, then, *Surfacing* functions as a map made out of hieroglyphs about living and reading which may end in 'nothing', but we are not where we were when we started out. For now we have at last begun to ask 'Where is here?', anyway, and 'Who am I?', questions which we did not know we even needed to ask.

Atwood's writing demonstrates the way language and experience interact with metaphor as the mirror of that interaction. In order to survive, we must gain some control, at least, over our experience, and we can do this through language: 'this above all, to refuse to be a victim.' Atwood's novels not only reveal sexist, patriarchal assumptions hidden in language and culture generally. She has also built into her texts a level of analysis which explodes the myth of men as free, and has detailed the victimization of men which a patriarchal social system institutionalizes.

Margaret Drabble 1939–

Committed to a realist narrative style in her fiction, Margaret Drabble has nevertheless shown a sophisticated awareness of the presuppositions and limitations of realism. Seeking to reach a wide audience through what she found to be a more accessible style than most experimental writing, Drabble has expanded traditional realist narrative conventions and, like Doris Lessing and Iris Murdoch (though to a lesser degree), has questioned traditional notions of objectivity, opacity and unity, which earlier realism tended to presuppose. Using various non-realist, non-conventional narrative techniques – overt intertextuality, inconclusive endings, alternating points of view, narrative self-consciousness, systematic patternings of images, and overt emphases upon the subjectivity of her various characters' experience – Drabble has succeeded in her aim not to present some alleged objective reality, but to 'document' (albeit from her own specific point of view) the lives of British women and men during the 1960s–90s. In one sense, at least, her considerable success constitutes an overturning of traditional realist assumptions even more than some radically experimental writing. For her novels 'use realism against itself', to use a cliché. That is, they expose the assumptions of realism – objectivity, unity and stability of text, self, characters, plot or reality – as an illusion, which (so-called) 'ordinary language' fosters only when used naïvely. Drabble's texts, then, portray truth and reality as subjective; they portray the self, the characters, reality, the structures of the text, the endings and the meanings of the themes as elusive, relatively indeterminate, and certainly often dependent upon point of view. Perhaps one could call this the 'new' realism, or post-realism, if we want to distinguish Drabble, Lessing and other such writers from earlier realists.

Drabble was born in Sheffield and is the younger sister of A.S. Byatt; her second husband is the biographer Michael Holroyd. She has a BA in English from Cambridge, and began her career as an actress until she became pregnant, whereupon she took up writing. Her first novel, *A Summer Birdcage* (London, 1963), was widely acclaimed as innovative for its detailed documentation of the domestic, ordinary lives of girls and women. She has written about motherhood, marriage, initiation into the world of sexuality, conflicts between duty and happiness and between career and traditional female roles, and other 'ordinary' issues which confront women and demand great strength from them if they are to survive. Other early novels include *The Garrick Year* (London, 1964) and *The Millstone* (London, 1965). Later novels, such as *The Needle's Eye* (London, 1972), *The Ice Age* (London, 1977) and *The Middle Ground* (London, 1980), represent an increasing narrative complexity and a widening of thematic material away from exclusive focus on personal relationships, and

towards an inclusion of society as the powerful, influential context for those relationships, which are decisively affected by its specific, contemporary characteristics. This broadening out represents an embracing of traditional realist modes of expressing an interest in determinism versus free will, and in representations of the types of environment in which individuals can either prosper or wither. Further novels include *The Radiant Way* (London, 1987) and *A Natural Curiosity* (London, 1989).

Drabble has also edited *The Oxford Companion to English Literature* (London, 1985), is the author of a book on Wordsworth (London, 1966), and has written short stories, screenplays and *Arnold Bennett: A Biography* (London, 1974). *A Writer's Britain: Landscape in Literature* (London, 1979) is a collection of essays.

Angela Carter 1940–1992

Angela Carter, born Angela Stalker, published novels, short stories and essays, as well as a body of as yet uncollected journalism (except for the small book *Nothing Sacred*, London, 1982, and the later *Expletives Deleted*, London, 1992). She lived in Japan for two years, as well as in America and Australia, and finally resettled in London, where she died in 1992. Her first novel, *Shadow Dance* (London, 1965), was followed by *The Magic Toyshop* (London, 1967), for which she won the John Llewellyn Rhys prize. *Several Perceptions* (London, 1968) took the Somerset Maugham Award, and other novels and stories followed quickly, such as *Heroes and Villains* (London, 1969), *Love* (London, 1971) and *The Infernal Desire Machines of Doctor Hoffman* (London, 1972). Collections of short stories, *Fireworks* (London, 1974), *The Bloody Chamber* (London, 1979) and *Black Venus* (London, 1985), appeared side by side with the novels *The Passion of New Eve* (London, 1977) and *Nights at the Circus* (London, 1984). Carter's incisive cultural critique, *The Sadeian Woman: An Exercise in Cultural History* (London), appeared in 1979. In 1986, she published an anthology of short stories by recent women writers called *Wayward Girls and Wicked Women*, and edited *The Virago Book of Fairy Tales* (2 vols; London, 1990; London, 1992). Some poetry appeared in various

British journals, and *The Magic Toyshop* was made into a film, as was 'The Company of Wolves', Carter's rewriting of 'Little Red Riding Hood'. She also wrote two children's books, which adults, too, enjoy reading, *Miss Z. The Dark Young Lady* (London, 1970) and *The Donkey Prince* (New York, 1970). Carter additionally translated the fairy tales of Charles Perrault. Her most recent novel, *Wise Children* (London), appeared the year before her death (1991), and *American Ghosts & Old World Wonders* (London) appeared in 1993.

One of Carter's recurrent metaphors is the idea of the need for a decolonization of language and habits of thought; she used language to free women (and men) from the colonizing of middle-class males (since many men are also marginalized). Her writing represents a transformation of language and fictional forms, as she sought, like Margaret Atwood, to avoid helplessly using the 'language of the oppressor'. Her novels and stories are experiments and explorations of how fiction works, what language can do, and what other ways there are of writing besides realism; hence her extreme experiments with styles, genres, form, imagery and language. Her novels often depict the observation or experience of life and the world from the point of view of marginalized people, of freaks and outsiders, as with Flannery O'Connor or Carson McCullers; so-called normal people are shown 'to be in trouble with their souls', as O'Connor said. Carter's fiction invites the reader to relinquish the point of view of the dominant class and its ideology in order to experience other views and hence other worlds, and she struggled to create a new language and new style in order to do this. She argued, moreover, that the reader needed to share in both the imagining and the writing of the stories.

Carter took up Simone de Beauvoir's axiom, that women are made not born, and explored the way cultural norms inhibit women, in such novels as *The Passion of New Eve, Nights at the Circus, Love* and others. In Nietzschean reversals of value, she deconstructed the traditional, social and literary image of the virtuous woman, and showed her to be a masochistic, passive, self-deluded victim. Gender definitions are exposed as mere cultural prejudices imposed on obedient women and men. Relatedly, Carter

showed in her writings that not only women and gender definitions are 'made not born'; history too is not some irresistible fact; we are, in part at least, its makers and not its slaves, while sexual relations are not immutable natural facts but contrived forms of social interaction. Carter's fiction relentlessly analysed in detail the specific myths and cultural archetypes invoked to entice women into complacency and submission. False universals are mocked and scorned, as she attacked essentialist notions of masculine and feminine, showing the culturally defined nature of all relations between the sexes as historically determined, particularly by economic dependence leading to emotional and intellectual submission. Hence, sexuality and its occurrence in our lives as set forms of behaviour are a major theme. Images of woman as the great, fecund mother nature who receives passively the male seed and plough are exposed, especially in *The Passion of New Eve*, as destructive fantasies which dehumanize and deindividualize both men and women into anonymity. Additionally, these novels reveal the importance of each individual's realization that personal problems are less personal than concrete expressions of social-economic-historical contradictions, symptomatic of systemic social injustices playing themselves out in our everyday lives. Madness, illness and transgression may be indications of a strong character's refusal to submit to oppressive archetypes and destructive myths.

Carter described her surrealist, baroque, fantastic, grotesque and picaresque writing as 'magic realism', that oxymoronic term which suggests the moribund state of the realist/anti-realist debate. Magic realism, that marvellous realm of verbal transformations, involves word play, name play, puns and the shattering of pure, traditional images and tropes with the crude, the obscene and the explicit. Carter argued that these imaginative explosions need to be counterbalanced, even controlled, by preciseness of detail, economic use of symbol and concreteness of landscape and setting. Her imaginative shattering of traditional literary images and conventions, as well as cultural norms, involved using imagery from the unconscious – the realm behind everyday 'appearance' – in order to reinterpret the reality hidden behind the veneer of propriety and pleasantness. She also drew, as a supplement to the unconscious, on medieval romances and fables, on Irish folktales and legends (as in *The Magic Toyshop*), on the tradition of the picaresque (involving outrageous adventures followed by extensive discussion of them by characters, she explained) and on French surrealism. As a result, her style was often deliberately mannered, and narrative devices from eighteenth-century novels added to the mannerisms. Ordinary life, the normal, decorous and proper, is estranged in Carter's fiction; this strangeness functions to shatter the acceptability of normality by revealing its inherent neuroses and insanity, its conventionality, manneredness and *un*naturalness.

One of the central features of Carter's fiction (at the levels of thematics, form and style) which it shares – but in its own unique particularity – with modernism and other experimental forms, is the quality of mosaic or patchwork. Seamless unity, purity of style, coherence of thematics and logical plot development are all systematically disrupted. The assumptions of realism, science and logic are all disrupted in a celebration of designed destabilization of literary, cultural and social pretensions that convention is nature. Even biology, not merely gender, is shown to be a cultural prejudice, since the meaning of biology is culturally and historically constructed. Sentimental notions about literature and art are also exposed in Carter's disturbances, as her overt, deliberate narrative contrivances disrupt the highly prized literary illusion, and the reader is confronted with the constructed, arbitrary fictionality of the text. Her patchwork of medieval romance, surrealism, folk tales and so on creates a pluralization of discourse which defies any single point of view and rejects the notion of artistic products as pure originality, as spontaneous overflow of natural feeling, showing her texts to be a mosaic of texts from previous eras, previous genres and previous cultures. These stylistic, formal and thematic examples of intertextuality are related to her rejection of prevailing ideologies which privilege objectivity, decorum and unity.

Carter's disruptive bricolage techniques also involve parodies of literary conventions and stereotypes which relate to cultural and social forms. Familiar folk tales and stock motifs, for example, are altered and radicalized to invert universalizing myths which inhibit individual-ity. In 'The Company of Wolves' and *The Magic Toyshop*, the dynamics of female desire are brought to the fore as readers' expectations are demolished. Like Atwood's, Carter's reinventions of fairy tales and legends expose cultural formations as sexist, racist and dehumanizing, because they encourage stereotypes at the expense of individuality. Not content simply to invert hierarchies – which merely reinforces stereotypes, but in inverted values – Carter's fiction points towards a world free of patriarchy and matriarchy, a world of cooperation, not parental nurturing, a world where individuality is negotiated, instead of stereotypes being adopted. Identity, for example, is shown, as in Jacques Lacan's works, to transcend gender or biology; indeed, identity is portrayed as multiple or oppositional within the individual. Carter's characters are as much quilted together as are her novels: she displays the 'subject' as in no need of a fixed, stable identity (which leads to stereotype), but rather as capable of shifting and changing subjectivities; hence, metaphors of masquerades, circuses and dressing up for the stage abound. The unitary self, shown to be an illusion, is replaced by a self in constant process and constant transformation. Moreover, this multiplicity of the subject and the emphasis upon process rather than product or finality imply a denial of either objective knowledge, subjective authenticity of experience, or definitive meaning in the the text. Knowledge as unitary is replaced by experience as bricolage, as a quilting together, and as partial.

Both femininity and masculinity are at times ridiculed as mere masquerades in the circus which is our 'real' lives. Control over our multifaceted sexuality and, particularly for women, control over our bodies are portrayed as a central plank in the effort to construct one's own (albeit multiple) identity as an individual instead of a social stereotype. Feminine women are ridiculed as mannequins and robots, as Carter explored the dynamics of female desire not merely for sexual indetermination, but for women's right to their own points of view, as Henry James had done (more decorously) in *The Portrait of a Lady* a century earlier. The carnivalesque, patchwork quality of real life is exposed in Carter's texts pre-eminently by the defamiliarization of the naturalness of sexual relations and behaviour, by exposing the arbitrary constructedness of our images of ourselves and the opposite sex. The fabulous and absurd are presented as normal, while normality is revealed to be perverse, obscene and repulsive. For example, within the house of marriage and the family, incest and lechery predominate in *The Magic Toyshop*, while *Love* describes love as a 'private chamber of horrors'. Ferrers, in *Nights at the Circus*, grows wings which are interpreted as showing 'how nature had equipped her only for the "woman on top" position'; male/female stereotypes collapse at the end of the novel, and women are installed as beings of power in this imaginary world. Carter's novels portray sexual and gender stereotyping as at the centre of social dehumanization of all kinds, as the cornerstone of prejudice; all forms of exploitation are variations on this bedrock of privilege, which is constant throughout all classes, all nationalities, all races, all religions. Like Henry Miller and Anaïs Nin before her, Carter confronted sexuality as a political reality, not a moral dilemma, which has the potentiality to transgress patriarchal laws, demystify the most sanctified images of women as crippling stereotypes, and liberate enormous energies for the realization of individuality.

Rachel Ingalls 1940–

Graduate of Harvard University, Ingalls spent much of her childhood and adolescence in Cambridge, Massachusetts. She was also educated in part in Germany. Five years before her first publication, a novella entitled *Theft* (London, 1970), she moved to London and developed an interest in film and radio, as well as theatre. A collection of stories, *The Man Who Was Left Behind and Other Stories*, was published in 1974 (London), and this was followed by the novel *Mrs. Caliban* (London, 1982). A group of four novellas first published separately appeared as *Four Stories* (London, 1987). Other fiction includes the stories *Three of a Kind* (London, 1985), *The Pearlkillers* (London, 1986) and *The End of Tragedy* (London, 1987). *Black Diamond* (London, 1992) is still another collection of three short stories and the two novellas 'S.S. and Bud' and 'Be My Guest'. Her greatest triumph, according to many readers and critics, is her other novel, *Binstead's Safari* (London, 1983).

Praised by a variety of critics and fellow novelists for, in particular, her mastery of the novella form, Ingalls is also respected for her almost poetic compression of style and the resulting force of effect, whether she aims at terror and suspense or the revelation of psychological insight. Like many writers of the second half of this century, Ingalls has rejected the realist/modernist/romance debate as no longer productive, substituting for such dichotomies a quite original fusion of the natural and realistic with the supernatural, legendary and mythical. The mixture of the mundane and the magical, the ordinary and terrifying, is achieved in part by means of drawing on psychology, ethnology and anthropology.

Binstead's Safari exemplifies Ingalls's techniques and story-telling accomplishments at their most powerful and sophisticated. Neither a romance nor an adventure nor a supernatural tale, it transcends these categories as it obliquely explores the social and sexist presuppositions which destroy genuine love and companionship, and which condemn men to childish bullying. Meanwhile, Ingalls's story progresses overtly by means of the magically handled literary convention of the journey, as Stan and Millie, apparently together on safari in Africa searching for lions and other big game, begin their diverging Odysseys, in Millie's case one of self-exploration. Ingalls's novel takes on the force of a powerful, Bessie Head-type legend, as she employs, literally, the further convention of the death-and-life struggle – as Eudora Welty described the (hidden) theme of every novel – by means of a sophisticated, ancient, literary-dramatic device. That is, Ingalls creates a Greek chorus out of a group of African villagers, who reveal gradually to the reader and to the characters both the actual facts as they evolve and the hidden significances, both of which constitute symbolic and supernatural developments. In a sense, Ingalls shows legend in the making, but more significantly she also shows that reality itself is made out of legend, as the two intermingle, become entangled, and finally are woven together in a single strand. Greek tragic conventions are exploited by Ingalls in this powerful and dramatic novel, as reality becomes entangled with myth through her heroic figures, legendary transformations, ironic prognostications and haunting 'recognition' scenes. She follows Sophoclean conventions of shifting from one viewpoint to another (from one chorus to another or from chorus to hero and heroine and back again) – in this case from African to European – to create an utterly unbelievable story and ending which the reader accepts like the Wedding Guest in Coleridge's 'Ancient Mariner', stunned into silence.

Ingalls's novel is only overtly a romance – one of the lovers dies with a full third of the novel still to take place. The rest of the novel is devoted to a theme repeatedly hinted at from its beginning, namely, an ethnological study of the way primitive legends about heroic or mythic figures arise, and their specific relationship to the society that engenders and faithfully preserves them. By transforming these to fit new circumstances, social groups keep such legends literally alive and in constant evolution and relevance to the immediate present. Stan had come to Africa not primarily to shoot big game, but as a university professor of ethnology planning a book on the transformation of the hero in the hands of story-tellers, who shape a legend's events to fit present realities. Little did he, Millie or the reader realize that they would all three become the central characters in 'Stan's' book, or rather Ingalls's novel-myth, as she became one of those 'generations of storytellers [who] shaped the incidents in their hero's career'. Thus, Ingalls's novel is also Stan's book – an ethnological account, fictionally presented, of the African legend of the lion-human who takes one form and then another. Stan and Millie, at first observers and recorders, are implicated by the legend; Millie, through passion, becomes a central legendary character herself. Legend turns out to be reality, and *Binstead's Safari* a fiction on the legendary nature of life when lived passionately.

Maxine Hong Kingston 1940–

Winner of the National Book Critics Circle Award for non-fiction for her first book, *The Woman Warrior* (New York, 1976), Kingston, who was born in California, soon followed this with the still more remarkable *China Men* (New York, 1980) and then with her first novel, *Tripmaster Monkey. His Fake Book* (New York, 1989). Already with these first two books, her writing refused easy categorization, as fiction and non-fiction intermingled, and legend, myth, fact and history alternated with each other, even fading into each other. It might be just as accurate to describe the first books as linked stories set in specific and recognizable historical contexts, with a first person narrator, as to describe them as autobiographical. Indeed, in an (ironic) essay 'The Coming Book', in *The Writer and Her Work*, ed. Janet Sternburg (London, 1992; first published in 2 vols, New York and London, 1981, 1991), Kingston explained (perhaps tongue in cheek) about her new book: 'Right now I don't know who these people are . . . But it is not me . . . So, with The Book, I will make a break from the "I" stories I have been writing.' This essay is not itself non-fiction in the usual essay way. Like her other 'non-fiction' books, it is written in parables, metaphors and images and with irony and wit, as is the case with many novelists and poets who write about their work. And we can glean all the more from it for its being in this idiosyncratic, visionary strain, but we must beware of its irony. We should also be aware of the tradition and context of Chinese and Chinese American writing in which Kingston worked, including the writings of Jade Snew Wong (1919–), for example, whose *Fifth Chinese Daughter* (1945) and *No Chinese Stranger* (1975) provided precursors for Kingston's experiments in biographical and autobiographical fiction.

For example, Kingston emphasized that her 'coming book' would 'sound like the Twentieth Century . . . The Book will not be a collection of nonsense sounds but English words, a translation of music.' Yet she also discussed the visions which 'come assailing', and closed the essay with a parable about getting lost in the mountains amongst optical illusions. She concluded: 'Apparently you have no choice about what shows itself. What I did learn was: Don't trust the deer trails; they meander and fade. Head downhill, where you'll come to a stream; follow it to town.' Gradually, the force of her characteristic irony comes home to us as we realize, however, that 'The Coming Book' seems to describe, at times, The Book which people want her to write, or expect of her, but which is impossible, a fantasy, a mere comfort. Perhaps the phrase 'The Book' refers to Jacques Derrida's distinction between 'The Book' and the text: 'If I could finish it, I would never have to write again; in it would be the last word. So far we have only written approximations.' From many of the other ambiguous comments made about 'The Book' ('If the Book is an archetype, I needn't be the one to write it'), the reader of this essay begins to recognize Kingston's 'mastery' of the art of irony and indirection even in her other three books. Her essay is, clearly, addressing itself, like her longer texts, with wit and parody to critics' and readers' preoccupations with thematics and other attitudes towards both her earlier writing (non-fiction, memoir, autobiographical, hence 'limited') and towards novels as a whole (after James Joyce, what can ever be left for a novelist to do; the novel is dead; the novel of the late twentieth century must be this or that; and so on). Hence, unless we read her essay and her writings prior to it and aware of the irony, we will be wildly misled about *Tripmaster Monkey. His Fake Book*, Kingston's Chinese American rewriting of Walt Whitman's poetry.

Moreover, not only does the essay follow the mode of *China Men* and *The Woman Warrior*, mocking many conventional notions about autobiographies, novels and books generally; it further raises questions about novelistic conventions. Already having questioned the novel–autobiography (fiction–non-fiction) distinction in her writings, Kingston also joked around with narrative distinctions, such as 'first-person narrator and "I" stories'. It is implied that the 'I' of *China Men* and of *The Woman Warrior* was just as fictional, inevitably, as is the third person narrative in *Tripmaster Monkey. His Fake Book*. As the character Wittman Ah Sing's story unfolds, moreover, life becomes a theatrical spectacle, wherein distinctions between audience and actor collapse, while life and play are inextricable, since the drama was designed to be, in large part, impromptu. As in Virginia Woolf's *Between the Acts* (1941), the unscripted elements intrude more and more into the play, until the play turns into a wedding celebration of Wittman's (perhaps invalid!) marriage to Taña. Meanwhile, the novel has become a celebration of life lived creatively, of originality and of the courage needed in

the face of prejudices and conventions which dehumanize.

Themes of racism, sexism, materialism, war and the daily violence of social stereotyping, which grinds down individuality, are woven into the dramatics of this plotless text. These are little more than the fairly mundane experiences of Wittman: working in a toy store, losing his job, searching for other jobs, meeting friends at parties, getting to know Taña, seeing his parents and so on. Yet Wittman's wit and imagination transform this mundaneness into a rich and colourful picaresque novel of Don Quixote-like tiltings and challenges, so that Wittman's 'ordinary' life is a fabulous canvas of originality and art so powerful that the reader is propelled along a rushing stream of imagination. This stream will have a different character, different depths and layers, as this piece of rich writing has, depending upon the many ways in which readers are able to plunge into it. Yet there is something in this marvellous rush of human life for everybody to enjoy, to identify with and to participate in. For while the central character may be an avowed artist – a playwright and poet – he is portrayed to a large extent as an artist of life. That is, he is an artist in the way that we can all be artists; he is a figure – a metaphor – for the human being who lives life artistically, that is, by challenging conventions, stereotypes and mindless obeisance to clichés of thought, feeling, expression and behaviour. Wittman also has the gift of showing others how to participate in such a life, of creating opportunities for them to develop more fully their own individuality. Kingston, like Woolf, draws her audience/readers into the book, and, for a space, they can actively participate in a Whitmanesque-American 'triumph of life', as they read this 'fake book'. It is, after all, only an approximation, a text, not The Book; no archetype perhaps, but an examination of 'some other sightings, like the town I saw when I got lost in the woods'. Or is it the other town, the one downstream? Illusion, reality, last word or only approximation, epic symphony or rock song – this fake book includes them all, includes us, in a common humanity.

Tripmaster Monkey. His Fake Book can also be appreciated for its reference to that most popular book in East Asia, *Journey to the West*, otherwise known as *Monkey*, the Chinese folk legend written down by Cheng'en Wu (*c*.1505–80). Monkey and Hsuan-Tsang, his Buddhist monk companion, set off on a journey to recover Buddhist scriptures from India to take back to China. One hundred chapters of allegorical encounters with demons, spirits, and all manner of obstacles confront them (and the reader) on their path. These obstacles, however, are only 'illusions', it is implied. Yet they are powerful enough and no less real for it, especially as life itself is *maya* – illusion – for Buddhists. Kingston's own 'fake book' is a contribution to this story in a Western disguise, and is enormously enriched when set into the background of spiritual and intellectual allegory provided by *Monkey*. By engaging with this legend, the author releases its tremendous energy into her own new version, without sacrificing her particular purposes and originality. *Tripmaster Monkey* becomes a delightful *mélange* of East and West, as it mixes the literature of China and America into a new and fabulous fusion.

Bobbie Ann Mason 1940–

Recipient of the Hemingway Foundation Award in 1983 for *Shiloh and Other Stories* (New York, 1982), Mason was born in Mayfield, Kentucky, and attended the University of Kentucky, where she took a BA. Eventually, after taking courses at the State University of New York, she took a PhD at the University of Connecticut in 1972. A journalist in New York City for a time, she wrote and published two academic studies, on Nabokov (*Nabokov's Garden*, Ann Arbor, 1974) and on heroines in children's books, (*The Girl Sleuth*, Old Westbury, N.Y., 1975), before she began writing fiction. The sixteen short stories collected in *Shiloh* generally take place in rural Kentucky, and depict the lives of those ordinary, working-class people who so fascinate A.L. Kennedy, Mason's Scottish literary near-contemporary. Mason has also published two novels, *In Country* (New York, 1985) and *Spence + Lila* (New York, 1988), and another collection of short stories, *Love Life* (New York, 1989). Many of her stories and her two novels adapt familiar literary techniques of ambiguity and indeterminacy to express thematic conflicts between past and present, educated, urban, wealthy

and uneducated, poor, rural life. Her fiction also engages with social and political issues, as she examines the effects of the Vietnam war on a shell-shocked character in *In Country*, as well as the struggles of a young woman to establish herself independently of her family. Mason's fiction is characterized by an immediacy and flow, as if she had taken Gertrude Stein's invocation of the 'continuous present' to heart and recreated it in a 1980s version. This effect is achieved in part by the use of the present tense in the narration, especially in *Spence + Lila* and some of the short stories, and in part by a sense of the arbitrariness of the beginnings and endings of the novel, the chapters and even the elements within the chapter.

Made into a film in 1989, *In Country* is Mason's most substantial piece of fiction. As its epithet indicates, it is to some extent a 'road novel': 'I'm ten years burning down the road / Nowhere to run ain't got nowhere to go', with all the metaphorical dimensions of the journey convention. While its centre tends to be around Sam Hughes, a young teenage woman, the novel also weaves into Sam's 'journey' that of her Uncle Emmett, who has returned some years earlier from Vietnam, badly damaged, but still alive. His brother David, Sam's father, was killed there while she was still in the womb; her journey involves, in part, an effort to gain access to her father's reality, and an effort to root herself more solidly in the present. Emmett's journey also involves past concerns and present instabilities, due to his war-damaged mind and body, and his grief at the loss of friends and relations in the horrors and questionable motives of the Vietnam war. (See Jayne Anne Phillips's similar use of the war to explore American consciousness in the 1960s and 1970s.) These two psychological journeys are woven into the literal journey by car of Emmett, Sam and her grandmother, Mamaw, from Kentucky to Washington, D.C., to see the Vietnam Memorial and the names of Sam's father (and Mamaw's son) and Emmett's comrades engraved on the great, black marble. The visit not only releases more grief; unexpectedly, Sam sees her own name amongst the many Hughes's, listed near her father's: 'She touches her own name. How odd it feels, as though all the names in America have been used to decorate this wall.' The novel does not quite end on this ironic note, however, for when Uncle Emmett discovers that the name of a comrade – whose fate he has not known for fourteen years – is not on the wall, 'his face bursts into a smile like flames.'

Mason's handling of her complex point of view, which includes the literary convention of both the youthful, inexperienced Sam's perspective and Emmett's ravaged, cynical knowledge, is especially notable when we realize the full narrative sophistication of this novel's structure. The two alternative but complementary perspectives of innocence and experience are created through the unifying technique of a journey forward, which is disrupted by the long narrations of events preceding the trip to Washington. This is not an uncommon technique (see A.L. Kennedy's *Looking for the Possible Dance* (1993) for the most contemporary example), but Mason has infused it with a meaning as she has chosen her everyday events carefully and positioned them along the line of the journey, which 'frames' the novel and is in the present tense, unlike the 'body' of the text, which is narrated in the past. Her finest effect is the unpretentious simplicity of her prose, and of her characters and scenes, best described in a quotation from *Spence + Lila*:

> The way doctors throw their forty-dollar words around like weapons is infuriating. Spence knows big words, plenty of them. He prefers not to use his vocabulary in conversations, though, for fear of sounding pretentious. At times there is no way on earth he can say what he feels ... Real love requires something else, something deeper. And sometimes a feeling just goes without saying.

Mason experimented in her second novel with a quite different narrative technique, though the themes of tragedy and coming to terms with illness and death – handled with her light, ironic deftness – are everywhere evident in *Spence + Lila*. Here, her narrative voice is even more sophisticated and varied than in *In Country* or the *Shiloh* stories, for now she has moved with even greater ease and fluency amongst her characters' viewpoints. Never pretending to any narrative omniscience, Mason has nevertheless eschewed direct subjectivity, as though she has wanted to avoid any pretence at a first-hand knowledge of

her characters at which she knew she could only guess. Her narrative veers primarily between Lila's and Spence's experiences, and her often short, choppy snatches of chapters, of less than a page at times, flick like a television drama from one view and scene to another, shifting from the present reality of Lila's hospitalization and surgery to memories from the past of both Lila and Spence. These memories, which function as formal, structuring devices, interrupt the narrative of Lila's weeks in hospital and fill out the present tragedy with the reality of Spence and Lila's whole life together. As with *In Country*, plot is at a minimum, as characters' relationships predominate, and as Mason's novel explores the formal capacities of language for expressing that 'something deeper'.

Susan Kenney 1941–

Recipient of numerous awards for her fiction, Susan Kenney is also the author of the novels *Sailing* (New York, 1988), *Garden of Malice* (South Yarmouth, Maine, 1983) and *Graves in Academe* (South Yarmouth, Maine, 1985), as well as the acclaimed work *In Another Country* (South Yarmouth, Maine, New York and London, 1984), which won the 1985 New Voices Literary Prize. A portion of this latter novel, 'Facing Front', also won the O. Henry Award for best short story of the year in 1982, and the book as a whole was praised by such contemporaries as Anne Tyler. *In Another Country* might better be described as a series of linked stories; yet because the six sections are so intimately tied together, the whole text seems designed to bridge the gap between story and novel. Kenney's later novel, *Sailing*, adopts many of the fragmentation devices of its predecessor, but thematic and narrative unity pushes this more substantial work into the clear category of a novel.

Kenney is clearly a writer interested in exploring all kinds of narrative conventions, including genre; her experiments help her both to develop an originality and to create unique works of art which expand our conceptions of narrative possibilities and fictional forms. *Sailing* is a further development of the last three fragments of *In Another Country*; thematically it fleshes out the story of the characters' Phil and Sara's battle against his cancer. Narratively, it is more determinedly experimental than *In Another Country*, though it uses many of the techniques of that novel, too. In both, Kenney has juxtaposed segments of a present against various experiences, and complicated this segmentation with narrative accounts of dreams, fantasies and explicit memories. In *Sailing*, she has also mixed narrative points of view, while *In Another Country*, though more thematically fragmented, is unified by Sara's narrative consciousness. Apart from themes of illness and death – or rather, the struggles against illness and death, which almost seem to define life itself for the narrator – Kenney's texts are further unified or structured by an unusually effective use of central, organizing metaphors which dominate her writings. These metaphors enrich her overt thematic concerns by setting off a series of semantic echoes which create networks of relations. They are also suggestive of a sophisticated self-consciousness about art and about the act of writing and reading, and function to encourage reflection about the role of art in life.

These relations and reverberations are successfully charted in all Kenney's novels, and have been particularly well developed in *Sailing*; there, distinct episodes of sailing alternate with episodes at the hospital and more normal life at home, when Phil is well enough. Throughout the novel, sailing is used as a powerful metaphor as, for example, in the following lines:

> Sailing is not so much a science as an art, and thus demands complete attention . . . there are so many variables, wind strength and direction, tide changes, rocks and shoals, so much to watch for. And then there are matters of discretion, whether to sail closer to the wind to gain distance at the expense of speed, or to lay off to gain the fastest point of sail. In sailing, you don't always get exactly where you meant to go. It is a question of balancing forces that are constantly changing, possibilities that continually transmute. Still there is that moment always hoped for, when everything conjoins and the boat leaps forward, creating its own wind, apparent wind exceeding true wind, drawing the boat forward.

Dozens of similar passages occur and are repeated, almost word for word, throughout the text. Not only is sailing a metaphor for life, it is also a metaphor for art; but Kenney, not unlike Susan Sontag before her, interweaves her thematic elements further by making Phil's illness and Sara's mother's illness in *In Another Country*, into a metaphor for the adventures of life and how people react to them and cope with life itself. To say that life itself is, for Kenney, a kind of illness would not be exactly correct, however. She portrays life rather as a struggle, an endless contest, between illness and health, living and death. It is in part the central role of the contest, the struggle, that gives Kenney's fiction its tragic, prophetic quality.

In *Sailing*, dreams, hallucinations and unusual states of consciousness (induced often by sedatives and painkillers) are woven into the narrative more systematically even than in *In Another Country*. These function to reveal the various levels of consciousness and subconsciousness across which the characters live out their present lives in the shadow of the traumas of their past: their childhood, their family relations. They also reveal the present as haunted by madness, loneliness, suffering and death. Phil's illness and Sara's mother's mental instability are the themes around which the demand of life is itself gathered. His and Sara's reactions imply the large issue of how to live life, how to respond to life and its terrors, to its ending in death. Yet, in the midst of these overwhelmingly depressing themes, Sara's existential and creative grasp on life, her determination to struggle – to concede nothing to chance or to incompetence, to subject everything to her will and to practical action – raises the narrative to an almost heroic pitch. Indeed, the final section of *Sailing*, with Phil's own experience alone out on the sea, his efforts to face death alone, and his final decision to turn back out of love for his family, represents Kenney's writing at its most impassioned and visionary.

Anne Tyler 1941–

Winner of the Pulitzer Prize in 1988 for *Breathing Lessons* (New York) and the National Book Critics Award in 1985 for *The Accidental Tourist* (New York), Anne Tyler has been publishing novels and short stories for thirty years. Born in

Minneapolis, she grew up in North Carolina and took a BA at Duke University before attending Columbia to study Russian. Her first novel, *If Morning Ever Comes* (New York, 1964), was admired, and *The Tin Can Tree* (New York, 1965) aroused further interest. Several novels followed, including *A Slipping-Down Life* (New York, 1970), *The Clock Winder* (New York, 1972), *Celestial Navigation* (New York, 1974 – her most complex plot), *Searching for Caleb* (New York, 1975), *Earthly Possessions* (New York, 1977) and *Morgan's Passing* (New York, 1980). With the 1982 publication of *Dinner at the Homesick Restaurant* (New York), Tyler's reputation was firmly established; it was then further confirmed by her two most recent novels, mentioned above. Short stories had appeared throughout the period, published in *Harper's*, *McCall's*, *Southern Review*, the *New Yorker*, *Cosmopolitan* and other magazines. An article by Tyler on Eudora Welty can be found in the *New York Times Book Review* 2 (November 1980), and see Tyler's piece, 'Still Just Writing', in *The Writer and Her Work*, ed. J. Sternburg (New York and London, 1981).

Tyler's novels, like Alice Munro's fiction, centre on the family and the domestic scene, but they do so in the way of Greek tragedy, namely, not to limit the scope of their formal, literary representation of human experience, but to examine it more thoroughly. Like Munro, Tyler is one of only a handful of contemporary novelists who have succeeded in fusing familiar post-modernist insights and reformulations with accessible literary forms. Both these writers demonstrate that overt experimentation with style, form, perspective, etc., is neither the only kind of post-modernism nor the only kind of experimentation possible. One of the great advantages of Tyler's (or Munro's) version of post-modernism is its much-needed ability to show how utterly applicable to human life post-modernist theory's insights are. Such insights are often accused of being airy-fairy theory, so utterly lacking any use or basis in daily life as to be almost meaningless. Tyler's novels knock the wind right out of such ignorant nonsense, and demonstrate with impressive clarity precisely how practical and applicable these insights are.

For example, each of her novels, without exception, is a systematic study of perspective, of focus, of point of view – with the intensity of a Henry James novel. Reality, we are constantly, endlessly reminded, is a projection from a point of view. It has no objective status, though it can be amplified by changing our focus. This central principle of Tyler's novels confronts the reader both as she reads the novel as a work of art and interprets it and its aesthetic effect on her, and as she applies the novel to her own life experiences – though these two aspects are of course a matter of emphasis only, and not a dichotomy. That is, Tyler's fiction constantly reminds the reader, first, that the meaning or significance depends on its narrative conventions, on, for example, the point of view from which it is read, and that there are many points of view; and second, that the meaning and significance of its topics – family, relationships, work, love, death, life itself – are also dependent on our focus, our view, our perspective. The consequence of such (much-maligned) 'relativity' is that the 'facts of reality' are disrupted. What is a happy family? What is a proper family? What is a family? Tyler's fiction raises many questions which set the reader wondering whether most of the categories, borderlines and oppositions we live by are not just useful illusions. Novels such as *Dinner at the Homesick Restaurant* bring intense focus to what all the earlier and later novels have mulled over: borders between inside/outside, family/strangers, intimacy/alienation, centre/margin, order/disorder. They show the way these borders are constantly crossed, so that each opposition is the life of its other. For example, families are created from 'outsiders' by marriage, adoption, birth and death – there is nothing 'pure' about the family. Its very essence involves outside 'impurities' coming in to dilute (invigorate) the family.

Similarly, Tyler has revealed how excessive purity, insideness, family, order, intimacy and so on lead to death or stasis. The order of family life, for example, is entirely dependent upon disruption and interruption of the purities, finalities and certainties which can become so obsessive as to make us miss the very interest or fulfilment that the implausible, unexpected and disruptive brings. More radically, Tyler's novels question these intellectual categories, and show them to be practical tools only, not absolute distinctions. Order is a familiar form of disorder;

other kinds of disorder may be possible and even more useful – and will come to seem like order with time. Or, what seems disorder to one person is another's routine. Putting it more humanely, Tyler has investigated the meaning of the concept of the family as well as of the happy family. She has shown both to be illusory fictions and also facts of life, paradoxically. In *Dinner*, outsiders are members of the family, while members of the family are the greatest strangers of all (the father has been absent for forty years). The family cannot be the repository of meaning since its very significance depends on 'significant others'. It cannot be a 'sign' for happiness, order, security or intimacy, since it is not only these things but also their opposites. The very notion of 'a happy family' is shown to be a fantasy, a partial truth at best, and a damaging one, since it simplifies complexities by offering misleading finalities, certainties and purities. Such finalities cause us to miss the detours, interruptions and surprises which, Tyler explained in 'Still Just Writing', not only enrich our lives but turn out to be its substance.

Tyler's use in her fiction of the literary conventions of reference to photography, diaries, rituals and numerous unfinished family dinners all serve to emphasize her insight into the central importance of appreciating perspective/focus/view. Her characters are often depicted as seeing each other narrowly as only their projections, rather than seeing each other from other viewpoints. These views are endlessly contrasted, not because the characters fail to see each other as they really are, or because they fail to remember some past event as it really was, or because they fail even to interpret some present occurrence as it really is, but because they fail even to be aware that there are other points of view. This adolescent mentality, this egotism, is portrayed to be the rule, not the exception, and the source of much grief. But Tyler has also exposed the numerous forms of 'phoney' tolerance which characters adopt; her clearest account is of the 'tolerance' which is just a passive opting out of a relationship, in order to avoid conflict. Yet her novels also remind us that a respect for the variety of points of view does not mean that 'anything goes', that there is no truth and hence no lying. Rather, while we cannot act on definites, certainties and absolutes, we can and do act on

well-informed, multiperspective opinion. For to act upon only a single-perspective opinion (our own view) constitutes adolescent egotism.

Ama Ata Aidoo 1942–

Playwright, poet and novelist, Aidoo was born near Dominase, in Ghana, and attended Ghana University, before studying further at Stanford and then returning to teach in Ghana, at the University's Cape Coast campus, and in Kenya and Tanzania. She was later appointed Minister of Education, but since 1983 she has been based in Zimbabwe; however, she has spent a considerable period of each year abroad lecturing, teaching and writing. Aidoo's fiction includes two novels, *Our Sister Killjoy: or Reflections from a Black-eyed Squint* (Harlow, 1977, 1988) and *Changes* (London, 1991), and a collection of eleven short stories, *No Sweetness Here* (Harlow, 1970; London, 1979, 1988). Her two plays are entitled *The Dilemma of a Ghost* (London, 1965) and *Anowa* (Harlow, 1970; London, 1980). She has also published a volume of poetry, *Someone Talking to Sometime* (Harare, 1985). Like Gayl Jones, Aidoo has addressed herself directly, in both her plays and *Changes*, to the extremely contentious issue of a woman's identity as not necessarily centred on the role of mother. Recognizing that however much lip service is paid to the freedom not to have any children, women are still pressured (especially by other women) to have them, Jones and Aidoo have both made this issue a central part of their literary thematics. Mother–daughter relationships (and mother–daughter-in-law) are also a central focus of the plays and early stories, as are the issues of men's revulsion from pregnant women, their jealousy towards their children, infidelity and other failures of relationship. Aidoo's essay, 'On Being a Woman' (in *Sisterhood is Global*, ed. R. Morgan, 1983), gives further information on her social attitudes and how to express them in literature, but it is in *Our Sister Killjoy* that Aidoo achieves her voice as a writer of compelling stature.

In this novel, Aidoo creates a fragmented, disrupted narrative surface of four apparently separate elements. Her techniques for unifying these thematically distinct sections involve, first, a powerful, all-pervasive irony – not merely satire, but an ironic consciousness which hovers over the whole and functions aesthetically to shock the reader into recognition of liberal prejudices which rationalize selfishness, greed and irresponsibility. Second, Aidoo uses a forceful image, the human heart, to unify all four sections of the text. Third, the character Sister Killjoy, or Sissie, is also a unifying element. Aidoo draws too upon another central feature, the act of eating – of food, of nourishment – and its metaphorical significance, to unify the novel with the constant question, 'What is it that nourishes the human spirit?' Throughout this novel, she makes use of a whole range of literary techniques associated with post-1960 literature (though many of them occurred during modernism as well). Her fragmentation of thematics, her avoidance of plot, her constant interruption of the narrative with poetry or non-fictional elements (newspaper articles, letters), her consequent mixing of genres and breaching of decorum, the intrusion of autobiographical elements – all these are familiar devices which she employs with skill to create a compelling artifact.

While Aidoo explores explicitly social and political themes of expatriation (especially to the richer Western countries), rejection of patriarchy and feminist separatism, greed, consumerism and materialism, along with issues of identity and decolonization, her fiction is finely constructed to prevent moralizing or didacticism. The ironic consciousness evident throughout *Our Sister Killjoy*, from the title to the subtitle to the first few sentences and the last pages, keeps the novel hovering amongst possibilities and moral issues, rather than preaching specific ideas. Further, Aidoo adapts the convention of the journey which also structures the novel and helps to unify the fragments: Sissie's story is told from her departure to her visit to Germany, then to England, and the book ends with her plane journey back and her gazing down on 'Africa – crazy old continent.' The central issue of this novel, as of much of her writing, is ironically symbolized in the image of the heart, grotesquely introduced explicitly only in section three, when one of her male friends grows ecstatic at the newspaper report of a heart transplant from a black man into a white man. The grotesqueness is a deliberate gesture of irony, reinforced in the scenes

of overeating and drinking in sections one and two, until people grow fat and nauseated, and lose their enjoyment of food because of its overabundance. Constant themes of the failure of Western society to nourish the heart, the soul, creep into the text, as Westerners and African immigrants are shown greedily collecting material goods and overeating – overconsuming generally – while neglecting their relationships, their spirits, their hearts. The longest section of the novel, 'The Plums', explores a friendship between Sissie and a young, lovely German mother, which ends abruptly when it becomes clear to Sissie that Marija needs an intensity of both emotional and physical involvement which Sissie cannot reciprocate. The novel ends with the almost post-modernist gesture of a long, detailed letter, which is never sent, but addressed to 'My Lost Heart', Sissie's lover, whom she leaves behind in England to return to Africa. The theme of spiritual nourishment is now expanded to include the issue of companionship and loneliness, which had also been explored in the section on Marija and Sissie's friendship.

In the final section of *Our Sister Killjoy*, it becomes evident that, for Sissie, there is no meaning in a journey which does not involve a return. A one-way journey means death to the spirit and exile from community, warmth and relationship. To 'live' abroad is only 'to learn how to die from a people whose own survival instincts have not failed them once yet'. In *Changes*, Aidoo never leaves Africa – her characters work at their lives on their own ground, and, while she still uses irony (in a milder way), the novel is much more conventional in structure, form and style. Yet her thematics are radical, as she writes of a woman who seeks a new kind of relationship with men, an equality which is genuinely realized in their practical lives rather than merely talked about. The woman never succeeds, however, though she refuses to concede defeat.

Rose Tremain 1943–

Playwright as well as novelist, Rose Tremain has written extensively for television and radio, and has had sixteen plays performed. Chosen as one of the Best of Young British Novelists in

1983, she has also won numerous other awards. For example, in 1979 she received a Creative Literary Fellowship, which she used to complete *The Cupboard* (London, 1981), her third novel. *The Swimming Pool Season* (London, 1985) won the Angel Literary Award, as did her recent novel *Restoration* (London, 1989), which also won the Sunday Express Book of the Year Award and was shortlisted for the Booker Prize. A volume of short stories, *The Colonel's Daughter and Other Stories* (London, 1984), won the Dylan Thomas Prize, and another collection of stories, entitled *The Garden of the Villa Mollini* (London), was published three years later. In 1984, Tremain became a Fellow of the Royal Society of Literature. Her first novel was *Sadler's Birthday* (London, 1976); her second, *Letter to Sister Benedicta* (London, 1979), was praised by Auberon Waugh as restoring his faith in the vitality of the English novel; and her most recent is *Sacred Country* (London, 1992). A collection of stories appeared in 1994, *Evangelista's Fan* (London).

Whether handling themes as various as an aged character of 87 taking control of her life and death, or a middle-aged woman confronting bereavement as she pores over her past life with her dying husband, or the love lives of young couples, Tremain's individuality is achieved in part through her marvellous humour, characterized by a generosity and pathos rather than any stringent or satirical strain. Throughout her meditations on love, life and death, 'in all this tragic scene' it is her wit which provides the focus for the unique voice of this imaginative writer. *Letter to Sister Benedicta* is an example of Tremain's skill in this respect, as she has explored the terrible trauma of a middle-aged woman, Ruby Constad, who, facing the gradual death of her husband, realizes that all her social roles are collapsing. Her children have recently left home and are asserting their independence, and we watch Ruby, who is searching for ways to cope with bereavement, succeed in creating a new life for herself.

Tremain has adopted a diary form for the novel, which interweaves first person narrative present events with past ones, in a Margaret Laurence-like effect, as Ruby gradually draws strength from her past – her childhood in India in a convent of Sister Benedicta's. It is not, however, religion which sustains her in her confrontations with the knowledge of her children's sibling incest and her husband's death, but a simple love of Sister Benedicta, which the old nun had reciprocated. Eventually, at the end of the novel, Ruby sells her flat and sets off for India, for her past, and for a new life in the present. The reader is left on the threshold of this journey, which functions as a symbol for Ruby's emergence from the cocoon of domination and dependence into maturity and independence. In *The Cupboard*, Tremain has experimented with more complicated formal structuring and narrative devices (which have probably influenced writers such as A.S. Byatt and Ruth Prawer Jhabvala). A novelist in her 80s, Erica, 'tells' the story of her life and times in a series of vivid and mordant interviews with a young American reporter. The past is enriched by Erica's present narrative, which has a profound effect upon the newspaperman, Ralph. Tremain has included, as well, diary entries and excerpts from Erica's novels, interspersed with events in Ralph's life. Erica's long narrative, which Ralph transcribes onto tapes, leads her to embrace a carefully planned death just before Ralph's return to America. Yet Ralph's experiences also constitute a vital part of the novel: he is Coleridge's 'Wedding Guest' who 'cannot choose but hear'. While the story Erica tells functions for her as the culmination of her life and her liberation into death, for Ralph (and the reader) it involves an awakening out of his mediocre life into larger possibilities. A description of one of Erica's characters, moreover, is also a description of what is happening to Ralph:

> He's very bad at expressing what he feels, yet he believes . . . he knows what the human spirit could be capable of – all the incredible possibilities – he senses their infinity. And he knows that the women from the ship have reached a higher plane of awareness, which is why he has to start living with one of them . . . his eyes are opened on the Possible.

Ralph has been drawn up to a 'higher plane' of life with Erica, and sacrifices his job, relationships and livelihood in order to begin to discover the possible. Strangely, then, and in a way full of significances for the reader, the character Erica created in fiction she also creates in life, through the effects of her charisma and affection for Ralph.

In her most recent novel, *Sacred Country*, Tremain has experimented with still different motifs, artistic formalities and narratives, adopting multiple subjective perspectives mixed with interspersed third person narratives. As in *The Cupboard* and *Letter to Sister Benedicta*, in *Sacred Country* Tremain's characters are once again portrayed as finding ways to overcome the artificial limitations placed upon them by social, biological and religious conventions. 'Mary' Ward, who has believed since the age of 7 that she is really a boy, dominates the novel, in her determined 'quest' to change her biology to fit her psychology and become 'Martin'. Other characters, such as her brother Timmy, shake off the crushing expectations of a father, while Walter discovers his homosexuality. Her mother finds temporary relief from the insanities of ordinary life in a mental hospital. Mary echoes the words of the fictional character Ralph, in *The Cupboard*, when she says:

> The things we learned in a single afternoon remind me that we live on a planet of the unexpected. I know now that a centipede can run faster than a cheetah. I know that in Peru there is a snake that milks cows. I know that the Giant Sequoia tree of California can live for fifteen hundred years . . . It gives me hope, to realize all this . . . [hope] in what is possible.

Later, the doctor helping Mary become Martin explains her euphoria at her change, in the following words: 'You may grow in spirit . . . It has to do with being always a little outside the world . . . soon, your two selves will be better integrated but your status will be a different status because you will have seen the world from two different perspectives . . . this isn't possible for most of us.' Tremain's imagination does make it possible – or, at least, she provides readers with the opportunity to imagine others' lives as though they were our own. Like Leslie Marmon Silko, Jane Bowles and Jean Rhys, amongst others, Tremain has drawn us into a world which convention and propriety discourage us from entering, and lead us to hate and fear. She has shown us, as did Flannery O'Connor, that the

real difference between people in these two worlds is, in the main, that the 'odd' ones are often a lot more human, diverse and individualized. Whether we see through Estelle's 'madness' or Mary–Martin's double perspective, or through the third person narrative with its unknown origin, we catch a glimpse of the possibility of a world of human diversity and interest which makes ordinary life look like endless repetitions, stereotypes and clichés. Tremain has revitalized language and the novel form, as she has unfurled her inventive imagination on page after page, creating characters and situations of extraordinary magic and fascination.

Buchi Emecheta 1944–

Ibo woman writer Emecheta was born near Lagos in Nigeria, where she grew up and married. She moved to London aged 17, to join her husband studying there, and graduated from London University with a degree in sociology, before taking up teaching, library work and social work. She has written scripts for radio, plays for television, adolescent and children's books and stories, and essays for various periodicals such as the *Times Educational Supplement* and the *New Statesman* (West Africa), but she is first of all both a mother and the author of over half a dozen novels, including *In the Ditch* (London, 1972), *Second-Class Citizen* (London, 1974, which continues the story of Adah from the first novel), *The Bride Price* (London and New York, 1976), *The Slave Girl* (London and New York, 1977, which won the Jock Campbell Prize), and *The Joys of Motherhood* (London and New York, 1979). *The Bride Price* was the first novel Emecheta wrote; it had to be completely rewritten many years later, since the first manuscript was destroyed by her husband. He had allegedly been outraged by the novel's feminist perspective and its criticism of some traditional Ibo practices, which Emecheta portrayed as oppressive to women. After this unfortunate event, Emecheta took herself and her five children away from her husband, finished her degree and continued her writing. Other novels include *A Kind of Marriage* (London, 1986), *The Family* (London, 1990), *Destination Biafra* (London and New York, 1982), *Double Yoke* (London and Ibuga,

1982) and several novels for teenagers. *Adah's Story* (London, 1983) is a reprint of the first and second novels in one volume.

Emecheta's fiction is often set in Nigeria (*In the Ditch* and *Second-Class Citizen* are the exceptions); it has been influenced by and has influenced a whole group of recent black African women writers, including Ifeoma Okoye and Flora Nwapa (Nigeria), Grace Ogot (Kenya), Miriam Masoli or Tlali (South Africa), Tsitsi Dangarembga (Zimbabwe) and Rebeka Njau (Kenya). Emecheta's success in combining the roles of mother and author (not wife, however) has been an inspiration to many women, both her contemporaries and those later writers of the late 1980s and early 1990s. Alice Walker drew attention to Emecheta's emphasis upon motherhood as not at odds with artistic production, and other critics and readers have seen the gradual fleshing out of a central metaphor in Emecheta's writings, namely motherhood as authorhood too. Suddenly, overtly domestic and mothering themes are seen as functioning aesthetically, because symbolic of creativity in all realms. Emecheta's novels, like those of the women listed above, take on a new and exciting significance and richness of meaning, as the portrayal and representation of mothers and their relations with their children become a covert statement about artists and their relation to their work.

Emecheta, Bessie Head, Nwapa and other African women writers have been exploring the extent to which this metaphor can release imaginative power. Yet what is most remarkable about it is not only that a cliché is utterly renewed and reinvigorated, exemplifying that essential process in art which Shelley called the revitalizing of 'dead metaphors'. Motherhood as a metaphor for artistic creativity makes it possible to go back to earlier texts by women detailing mothers and mother–child relations and re-read them symbolically in the light of this fresh emblem. Not only does this metaphorical equation deny the (sexist) notion that bearing children and creating art are conflicting, mutually exclusive activities; it also gives women a whole new language, a set of images and concepts, and a whole range of authentic experiences for articulating and portraying artistic creation. Rather than the mere allegory of art as giving birth, the creation of works of art is better understood as the longer

processes, which go beyond pregnancy and birth to the nurturing and parenting of the child into adulthood. The child, then, in any of these novels, can be read as an emblem for an artifact, a text, a poem. The portrayal of the mother–child relation is a direct symbolic rendering of the labour, nurturing and gradual progress of a novel's coming into being – into adulthood, one could say. *The Joys of Motherhood* most overtly develops this enriching dimension of apparently domestic, personal (therefore unimportant?) life as an allegory of creative art production. Yet *In the Ditch* and *Second-Class Citizen* are also fairly systematic in gaining aesthetic force from making the personal role of women as mother/artist into a vocation. There, the forces which try to destroy or at least obstruct the woman from becoming an artist are specifically analysed. These are portrayed as either husbands, poverty, discrimination or social pressures, all of which have literary reverberations and symbolic significances.

However, there is another aspect of this symbolic dimension of motherhood as a metaphor for artistic creativity, which further reveals its rich complexity. Many African women novelists, and certainly Emecheta, have portrayed – as either a main theme or a sub-theme – the relations of adult women with children to *their* mothers, an almost always problematic relationship. Sometimes supportive, sometimes undermining and alienating, but almost always fraught, mother–mother relationships provide yet a further rich metaphor for the artist's struggle, both to create and to create with a new and original voice. Thus, the issue of identity and self-development is tied up with the development of the artist in the struggle for authentic, original creation. Hence, no strict allegories are possible, as the young mothers are themselves portrayed in the novels as the children of older mothers. Labour, old age, exhaustion and suffering are, ironically, some of the 'joys' of motherhood. Unlike male novelists, who tend to idealize women by only portraying the beautiful, the idle and the young and sexy, these female novelists turn to a modern-day version of naturalism. Far from idealizing motherhood, however, they show the way forward for women whose womanhood has always been defined exclusively as motherhood: read 'motherhood' metaphorically instead of only literally; see it imaginatively, instead of through the eyes of men; redefine it, and the conflict between artistic creativity and bearing and rearing children collapses. The latter become a whole language and realm of experience for representing aesthetically specific artistic struggles, conflicts and achievements. To write of the personal, of children, of mothers, of cooking, etc., is to write symbolically, for these struggles are emblematic and symbolic (if read imaginatively) of precisely what one undergoes as an artist.

Alice Walker 1944–

Winner of the Pulitzer Prize and the national Book Award for *The Color Purple* (New York, 1982), her third and most impressive novel, Alice Walker is also one of America's best-known poets, and writes essays in a variety of genres, from literary history and criticism to political and social. Her first two novels, *The Third Life of Grange Copeland* (New York, 1970) and the remarkable *Meridian* (New York, 1976), were published contemporaneously with several volumes of poetry, namely, *Once* (New York, 1968), *Revolutionary Petunias* (New York, 1973), *Good Night Willie Lee . . .* (New York, 1979), *Horses Make a Landscape More Beautiful* (New York, 1984) and *Her Blue Body Everything We Know* (New York and London, 1991). Two powerful collections of short stories have also appeared, *In Love and Trouble* (New York, 1973) and *You Can't Keep a Good Woman Down* (New York, 1981). She has also published two wide-ranging volumes of essays, *In Search of Our Mothers' Gardens* (New York, 1983) and *Living by the Word* (New York and London, 1988). Her most recent novels are *The Temple of My Familiar* (New York and London, 1989) and *Possessing the Secret of Joy* (London and New York, 1992). This final novel takes a minor character from *The Color Purple*, the young African woman Tashi, who also appeared in *The Temple* (as did 'M'Lissa', another version of a character matrix), and explores, as two central themes, first the incapacitating sexism of Christianity as a meaningful religion for thinking women, and second the effects on Tashi of the ritual of female genital mutilation, practised clandestinely or openly all over the world, including the USA.

Even a cursory examination of Walker's fiction reveals it to be a series of developing experiments with narrative techniques and novelistic conventions, in an effort both for Walker to find a voice and style expressive of her individuality and experience, and to expand the familiar world of fiction, of what a novel can be and can do. One of the constant themes of all her novels, which is congruent with exploration of narrative voices and points of view, is the possibility for individual, personal growth and maturation, from her first novel, *Grange Copeland*, to her most recent one, *Possessing*. These novels suggest that growth comes about not merely through ageing or with the passage of time. Many characters are shown stunted and emotionally immature into their old age. Walker's portrayal of characters, both men and women, who succeed only rarely in learning from their experience (and thereby transforming themselves) reveals that even pain and suffering are not enough for maturation, contrary to popular myth. Often, then, her theme, reflected in her narrative techniques, especially in the later novels, involves the existential question of how it is that some individuals grow up and transform themselves into genuine adults, while most others, even though exposed to suffering, remain egotistically oriented and emotionally retarded. This question is reflected in Walker's growth as a novelist and poet, as she has searched out new forms and techniques to express new stages of her own development as a creative, thinking being. Analogously, her characters are shown, both through thematics and through narrative techniques, being tested by a whole variety of encounters with demanding emotional, moral and intellectual conflicts and complexities. These conflicts are the opportunity for the passage beyond egotism towards community and universality of experience. For this is the passage which must be made to achieve genuine maturity, though the question of why only a few people can find the way may be unanswerable.

Walker's title to her first novel, *The Third Life of Grange Copeland*, reflects the central conception in all of her fiction and poetry about this (almost mysterious) passage through various stages of life, until finally Copeland joyfully lays down his life to protect his granddaughter, and open up to her a future of possibility and freedom. The narrative technique of the novel is relatively conventional, but this first novel shows Walker already entirely in control of the conventions of traditional novel writing, including plot, sub-plot, use of narrative time in aesthetically powerful ways, characterization, conflict, encounter, the journey, context, and a clarity and unpretentiousness of language. After this controlled, successful first novel, she has moved out into much more original and experimental, innovative fiction.

By the writing of *Meridian*, Walker was beginning to want to experiment with more complex narrative strategies, more imaginative use of time, and more overt use of the 'supernatural' or at least of powerful spirituality. Here, she has adopted an effective fusion of the imaginative with the conventionally historical novel, without the trappings of the latter. That is, the figure of Meridian seems to be founded precisely upon Rebecca Cox Jackson (1795–1871), the nineteenth-century black spiritual leader from Philadelphia who experienced spiritual revelations and ecstasies which taught her radical departures from Christian sexist ideology. Meridian, this twentieth-century character who seems a spiritual daughter or even reincarnation of Jackson, is portrayed in the novel as undergoing similar enlightenment until her spiritual insights and powers capture the imagination of whole communities. The novel charts Meridian's early, utterly ordinary life, trapped in a typically deadened marriage, hindered in her personal development by the early birth of children while she is still a teenager, and also the way her powerful personal resistance to the demands of orthodoxy frees her to educate herself and eventually to take on Rebecca's spiritual characteristics. Central to Rebecca–Meridian's understanding of Christianity is the necessity to reject as nonsense the blasphemous notion that God is a male father figure. Further, we are confronted with the need to ask 'how Jesus could be a man as how can Jesus be a woman. God is spirit.' Meridian's 'agnostic' insights challenge the foundations of orthodox Christianity, with her insistence that resurrection occurs *in* life, not after it is over, through the experience of ecstasy and revelation, much as William Blake and other 'reprobates' had earlier proclaimed. Rebecca–Meridian lives the faith that the spirit of religion, of 'Christ'

as love, if you like, exists in the hearts and minds of human beings, an issue developed thoroughly toward the end of *The Color Purple*, when Celie writes, quoting Shug:

God is inside you and inside everybody else. You come into the world with God. But only them that search for it inside find it. And sometimes it just manifest itself even if you not looking, or don't know what you looking for. Trouble do it for most folks . . . Sorrow is feeling like shit. It? I ast.

Yeah. It. God ain't a he or a she, but a It. . . . Man corrupt everything. He try to make you think he everywhere . . . he God. But he ain't. But this hard work . . . He been there so long, he don't want to budge. He threaten lightning, floods and earthquakes. Us fight. I hardly pray at all. Every time I conjure up a rock, I throw it. Amen.

All Walker's novels are rich with this uncategorical rejection of sexist religion, of whatever name, as a first step towards personal maturation, since paternalistic religions discourage, precisely, emotional maturity and genuine individuality in their demand for unthinking obedience to, first, church, dogma, ritual and Big Daddy God, and, second, his earthly representatives, namely, a male Christ, male priests, husbands, fathers and brothers. Walker's novels make it clear that every woman (like every man) must liberate herself from such a personally crippling paternalistic apostasy as Christianity or Islam have become, if she is to be in a position to develop her humanity and maturity. Hence the centrality in the novels of a spirituality that is not, unlike Christianity, apostasy from humanity and decency. Indeed, these themes of exposing sexist religion (as the greatest obstacle to maturity and personal development for women and men), and Walker's creation of a new conception of spirituality and humanity, become more and more urgent and pervasive as her novels develop, thematically at least, from *Meridian* through *The Color Purple* and to her latest works. Her long-standing admiration for Flannery O'Connor reveals Walker's appreciation for this Georgian writer's spiritual insights as going so far beyond the sexist nonsense of Christianity as to make O'Connor read almost like a rather uniquely spiritual atheist to her audience, as Walker herself insisted.

While *Meridian*, then, brought into prominence the existential theme of personal maturation, which recurs throughout the novel, it also alerted the reader to one of the central stumbling blocks for both men and women of self-transformations from egotistical childishness to genuine adulthood, one which obstructs most people, namely orthodox or sexist, paternalistic religions. Such religions, moreover, are shown to be the single most powerful source of legitimacy for sexism and racism, and are exposed as uniquely responsible for the terrible pain and suffering which Walker's novels depict. Women are beaten, hammered, raped, abused and starved into submission, under the central Christian dogma of male God-given rights over women. While the quite conventional *Grange Copeland* was centred on a sympathetic exploration of, additionally, the victimization of male perpetrators, in her next four novels Walker has moved on not merely to understand both men and women as victims of specific injustices. (For this earlier task the more traditional narrative techniques, structures and conventions had been adequate.) By *Meridian*, Walker was trying to penetrate into a world deeper than the social realist world of *Grange Copeland*, that surface reality which O'Connor rejected. Walker needed to find new forms of expression for this new level of reality, this mystery of personal and communal spiritual resurrection and regeneration, in this life, and beyond sexist Christianity, or Islam, or Judaism. The narrative technique of shifting from present to past to present to intermediate past, from Meridian to Truman to Lynne, creates foils for the towering spirituality of Rebecca–Meridian herself, in the here and the now. For these sub-plots and 'other' times and places than the present and the here function essentially to frame Meridian's 'resurrection' *in* this life, her 'hereness' and 'nowness' and, more crucially, her recent state of utter ordinariness. Or, as Kierkegaard had argued, every human being has at least the *potentiality* to become such a figure, to achieve such a state of grace. What prevents this state of grace for most of us is made into a sub-plot of the novel. Part of that state of grace, Meridian makes clear, is not only to be spiritually transformed as an individual. Indeed, this is impossible: such transformation is never merely concerned with an individual. Meridian is 'resurrected' because she has 'seen' her essential humanity in terms of interconnection with a community. Her maturity, then, she first achieved by detachment from childish, egoistic, personal concerns. She achieved her spiritual transcendence when she transcended even her personal salvation for spiritual communion with humanity. This is another reef upon which all Western religions self-destruct: they privilege personal salvation over communal spirit. Like Martin Luther King, Meridian becomes fearless because she transcends her ego attachment. King, utterly fearless of personal death, lived and fulfilled his personal individuality, like Meridian, for humanity.

Later novels of Walker's after *The Color Purple* explore more overtly than ever powerful themes of religion, community, myths and storytelling, from Africa to South America, and reveal the dangers and the reward of moving cross-culturally. These later novels almost seem to be a thematic filling out and then an extension of and departure from the substantial section of *The Color Purple* written by Nettie to Celie, a section which, with its perspective both on and also from Africa, adds a dimension to the Georgia letters which remains deliberately and potently unintegrated into Celie and Shug's world. This fragment not only expresses Walker's respect for the vast difference between American blacks and African blacks after nearly 300 years of enforced separation; it is also a structural reflection of the thematic fact that Celie was denied access to Nettie's letters and her news from Africa for decades, this thematic element having social symbolism as well. Nettie reports the present destruction of black African villages and communal life by white imperialism, so that history is seen repeating itself in a terrible recurrence. But Walker's two final novels explore, in *The Temple of My Familiar*, especially, a new stage of religion, spirituality, community and individuality, and the forms this new life will take. Miss Lissie (related by opposition to M'Lissa in *Possessing*) is a literary variant of Meridian; she is the character who transcends individuality, albeit less spiritually, and thereby binds together the community through personal maturation, through spiritual development, and through releasing the power of myth, legend and story into her group. *The*

Temple proceeds through variations in the narrative from story-telling by characters and about characters, to omniscient, to first person, to diary entries and so on, creating a powerful network of points of view and distinct personalities, which by the end of the book are integrated into non-competitive, sharing relations.

In *Possessing the Secret of Joy*, on the other hand, Walker has studied the conflicts of Tashi, the African villager brought to America who is later accused of killing M'Lissa, the *tsunga* or woman who performed the traditional genital mutilation of Tashi and other girls. Far more fragmented and experimental than *The Temple*, *Possessing* is a triumph of experiment in point of view, use of narrative time, fragmentation of plot and choice of thematics, as Walker's text confronts the reader with Tashi's almost counter-ritual murder of the *tsunga*, Mama Lissa, who mutilated countless children. Indeed, as Tashi put it, 'I killed the woman who killed me years ago.' The novel begins with the startling but familiar literary convention, 'I did not realize for a long time that I was dead.' It ends with the ritual hanging execution of Tashi: 'There is a roar as if the world cracked open and I flew inside. I am no more. And satisfied.' The twice-dead Tashi, the main character of the story and the central narrator, makes death problematic, as she 'survives' according to the narrative voice, in acts of resistance to insane rituals which drive her insane and destroy her life. The exploration of the horrors of female mutilation, through the portrayal of the breakdown and resistance of a single character (rather than in a social realist or historical mode), turns out to be an effective means of bridging the ignorance of Walker's audience about the ghastly, life-long, physical, sexual and emotional traumas induced. Tashi's only joy is in courageously stopping the ritual mutilators, personified in M'Lissa.

Impressive thematically, at least, as Walker's most recent two novels are, neither *The Color Purple* nor *Meridian* can be said to be surpassed by them. Indeed, the former stands as one of her most unique and innovative novels. This is ironic, as the novel is based on the conventional epistolary form, so popular in the eighteenth century for emphasizing individual psychology over the external world or social context (the context which prevailed in the nineteenth cen-

tury). Through Nettie's African letters to Celie, a window on the world is explicitly given, of course, though Walker's portrayal of Celie through her letters achieves as well a fusion of private and public. Given the common nature of Celie's sufferings, we see the life of a people through her personal experience. Yet perhaps the most impressive innovation is Walker's uniquely successful use of the ungrammatical language of the uneducated to reveal the eloquence, grace and dignity of Shug and Celie's intellects and spirits. The language itself, freed from the polished, clichéd and stereotyped mediocrity of the educated version, verges on poetry, as it expresses the profound humanity, intelligence and breadth of mind of some of these supposedly 'simple, uneducated' country people. Yet it never once romanticizes the brutality of life in Georgia. It simply proclaims that grace of mind rarely occurs where convention teaches us to expect it.

Kathy Acker 1947–

Plagiarist, punk, nymphomaniac, kleptoparasite, murderess, artist and authoress, Acker was born and grew up in New York City and attended Brandeis University with Angela Davis and Larry Rivers. She was taught by Herbert Marcuse, and followed him to San Diego in 1967, where she finished a BA. Back in New York City, she met Burroughs, Kerouac and Jerome Rothenberg, and continued writing and working at odd jobs to support herself (her upper middle-class mother had disowned her and she never knew her father). Influenced by the Black Mountain poetry group while an adolescent, she later worked with rock groups and punk rockers to avoid the stultifying routine of the other robot jobs she had earlier had to do. In the mid-1970s, Sylvère Lotinger turned Acker on to post-structuralist, critical and cultural theorists such as Foucault, Deleuze, Derrida, Guattori and Lacan, who, she said, 'gave me a language with which I could speak about my work. Before that I had no way of discussing what I did.' Influenced further by the Marquis de Sade, Bataille, Genet, Artaud and Warhol, Acker continued her explosions of literary, social and personal conventions which have not been assimilated into post-modernism, post-structuralism or feminism. Her books are designed to shock and repel, and she explained her fondness for de Sade in words which describe her own effects: 'I always think when I read him . . . You're dealing with shock. To me nothing's interesting unless it's slightly shocking. Otherwise I am just dealing with my own habits. Lulled into habits again and again. It is good to be shocked.'

Acker's efforts to shock us out of deadening habits began with poems, but in 1973 she published her first major work, *The Childlike Life of the Black Tarantula* (New York), followed shortly by *I Dreamt I was a Nymphomaniac: Imagining* (San Francisco, 1974; New York, 1980). Then came *The Adult Life of Toulouse-Lautrec by Henri Toulouse-Lautrec* (New York, 1975); these three novels constituted a ribald examination of identity and the self: 'By "I", I mean an unknown number of individuals.' They were also a shocking exploration of sexuality and of exploitation by men, women and larger social forces of human sexual and emotional needs, in a Michel Foucault-like exposé of the dynamics of political and social power. *Kathy Goes to Haiti* (New York, 1978, 1989) consolidated these elements, but in a more conventional narrative form, though the thematic material is explicit and deliberately arousing and shocking. *Hello, I'm Erica Jong* (New York, 1982) might be described as a literary parody of a number of 'feminist' novels published during the 1970s. For Acker may have seen these as propping up the structures they alleged to challenge, by relying on the familiar conventions and languages of patriarchal authoritarianism and materialism. In rejecting in her own fiction the familiar literary conventions of plot, characterization, decorum, unity, coherent thematics, originality and so on, Acker adopted atraditional views of art ('Fuck art') as duplicity, crime, lies, impersonation, plagiarism, infamy, falsity and insincerity – the opposite of the virtually institutionalized view, which sees art as a sincere, true representation of a coherent, objective, comprehensible reality. Later texts, such as *Great Expectations* (New York, 1983), *Implosion* (New York, 1983) and *Blood and Guts in High School* (New York, 1984) developed these ideas of criminality, and especially plagiarism (not just intertextuality), much further: 'Everything has been said. These are not my writing.' Acker's

'appropriation' was described by her as 'decentralization', involving both life and literature: it included not only a rejection of genital sexuality as the primary sexuality, but also a subversion of autonomous identity and of notions of originality, ownership and property rights. (She fled England in the late 1980s, where she had lived for several years, out of fear of lengthy legal battles with publishers!)

This term 'decentralization' describes many of Acker's criminal activities, from the subversion of meaning, form and the phallus, as well as genre, to her challenge to the status quo and her exposure of its horrendously dehumanizing routine. The banality of ordinary life is rejected in favour of drugs, perverse sex, disobedience, anything which will help people to find some better reason for living than saving money for a new car or a bigger house. Acker's attacks on both the society of money-minded robots and the literary tradition of Great Art – which allegedly tyrannizes over experimentation, originality, and self-expression – have continued with the publication in 1984 of *My Death, My Life by Pier Paolo Pasolini* (London), then *Don Quixote: Which was a Dream* (New York and London, 1986) and *Empire of the Senseless* (New York and London, 1988). These were followed by *In Memoriam to Identity* (New York and London, 1990) and *Hannibal Lecteur, My Father* (New York, 1991). By 'rewriting' Cervantes, Shakespeare, Milton, Dickens, Nathaniel Hawthorne, Arthur Rimbaud, William Faulkner and so on, Acker 'put various texts next to each other to see how they work'. Like Jorge Luis Borges before her, she seemed to see texts as 'unique' not because of the way they are written so much as because of how we read them. This post-modernist emphasis on reading rather than writing – or, rather, writing as a kind of reinscription of what has already been written/read – is one aspect of Acker's Foucault-like political agenda of 'decentralizing' power, authority and acceptability or respectability. By drawing on punk techniques of rebellion against all normative behaviour in favour of liberating disobedience – those moments of Roland Barthes's *jouissance* – and by making use of dada and surrealism, Acker criminalized the phallocentric patriarchy of conventional materialistic society, politics, sex and phoney morality, in a Nietzschean reversal of all values: 'Good is bad. Crime is the only possible behaviour.' Further, 'money gives power to make change stop, to make the universe die, so everything in the materialistic society is the opposite to what it really is.'

Acker's agenda of 'decentralization' involves, then, a marginalization of literary convention, decorum and authorship; to use traditional techniques, language or themes is to fail at the outset, no matter how 'radical' the ideas expressed. In a Gertrude Stein-like gesture of emphasis upon the 'continuous present', the here and now, Acker's texts frustrate the reader's efforts to distance the material or appropriate it in traditional ways, that is, into traditional logic and ideas and meanings. The immediacy of the reading experience marginalizes the traditional response of reducing a text to familiar forms – which almost amounts for Acker to literary rape or castration. She flirts with the reader ('A narrative is an emotional moving'), and power is shared in a mutually shocking, liberating experience of 'I feel I feel I feel', celebrating release from the 'dullness of shit society': 'Any action no matter how off-the-wall – this explains punk – breaks through the deadness.' Acker also made exploitation of people an object of analysis; she used insights of Foucault's into power–money–politics relationships to expose the psychological motivations which constitute politics. People are used by each other to satisfy 'needs' which, ironically, turn out to be the socially engineered ones for money, power and objects, rather than love, sexual fulfilment or humane relationship. 'Decentralization' involves, then, not the effort of getting the bottom of the heap to the top or the top to the bottom, or merely equalizing wealth or power or ownership, or just reversing oppositions or hierarchies. As in her exposure of sexual and emotional exploitation, Acker has exploded the attraction of the prevailing 'needs' by revealing them to be spurious, unfulfilling and inhumane. Hence her celebration of sex, for example, or drugs, or violence – as a way out of the crippling proprieties of ordinary-life banalities, though not as an end. For, throughout her novels, the position of women, for example, is totally untenable, especially in sexual experiences: 'Women aren't just slaves. They are whatever their men want them to be. They are made, created by men. They are nothing without men.'

Acker's texts celebrate the existentialist possibility that, on the contrary, we can invent ourselves by breaking through the deadness of respectable life:

> Someday there'll have to be a new world. A new kind of woman. Or a new world for women because the world we perceive, what we perceive, causes our characteristics. In that future time a woman will be a strong warrior; free, stern, proud, able to control her own destiny, able to kick anyone in the guts . . .
> Unfasten chains, remove masks.

Acker's (initially) punk-inspired parodies of the 'literature of containment' (apparently radical content suppressed by its reliance on existing authorities of logic, law and meaning) has developed into a fiction of enormous vitality and passion. Her narrative techniques and her stylistics undermine the prevailing interpretations of the Great Tradition, with its elitist, sexist presuppositions, which Virginia Woolf, Djuna Barnes, Jean Rhys, Stein and others had challenged earlier. Like Leslie Marmon Silko's recent *Almanac of the Dead* (1991), Acker's frontal assault upon respectability, refinement and discretion functions by revealing the oppressiveness and, most of all, the inhumane banality of these 'values'. These restrictive cultural attitudes are mocked in Acker's fictional techniques, which express the Blakean-Nietzschean belief that 'only the road to excess leads to the palace of wisdom.' Like many other writers, from modernists through Borges to post-modernists, Acker has taken to an extreme the familiar devices of multiple narrative voices, autobiographical-fictional *mélanges*, and the breaking of narrative frames to create alternative ontological levels or 'metafictional loops'. She has also used Blakean devices of repeating the 'same' events and episodes from a different point of view; she has confused reality, fiction, fantasy and memory, as did Marguerite Young in the 1960s, and, like Ann Quin, she has proliferated interiorities and self-references so that there is no 'real story'. Her rejection of realists' notions of order, continuity or reality goes beyond most previous fictional experiments, as Acker is prepared to affirm existence without assigning it some meaning, affirm reality without separating it from fantasy, and affirm identity without distinguishing it from personas. Like Jacques Derrida or Young, Acker has actually created and expressed (rather than merely describing and invoking) disruption *and jouissance*, rebellion *and* fulfilment. As with those of Angela Carter, Henry Miller or Anaïs Nin, Acker's texts locate sexual repression as at the nexus of political-social-literary authoritarianism: 'At this point . . . in my life politics don't disappear but take place inside my body.'

In such texts as *In Memoriam to Identity* and *Empire to the Senseless*, Acker has proposed the 'emergence of radical otherness', which involves 'roaming' through unknown territories and as yet unimagined possibilities regarding multiple identity, role playing, sexuality and relationship. Acker's invocations of an ancient literary convention – the journey, travel, maps, roads, exotic lands – constitute a revitalizing of dead metaphors in a discourse which is not so much an anti-discourse or anti-literature as it is an ecstasy: a communal polymorphous perversity, which seeks to 'dephallocentrize the body' and sexuality, in order to roam into unknown, erogenous territory, where literature escapes the phallocentrism of determinate meaning.

Keri Hulme 1947–

Poet and short story writer as well as a novelist and painter, Keri Hulme, whose first and monumental novel *The Bone People* (Wellington, 1983) won the 1985 Booker Prize, was born and lives in New Zealand. Her first book, *The Silences Between: Moeraki Conversations* (Auckland, 1982) is a volume of mixed poetry and prose, and her stories have been published in *Te kaihau: The Windeater* (Wellington, 1986). She is also the author of *Lost Possessions* (Wellington, 1985), *Strands* (Auckland, 1992) and *Homeplaces* (Auckland and London, 1989), a collection of words by Hulme and pictures by Robin Morrison. Hulme explained, in a preface to the first edition, that *The Bone People* (her inspiring novel about a Maori boy, his father and a woman artist who befriends the autistic child) began as the short story 'Simon Peter's Shell'. Over twelve years, these three compelling characters haunted her, as she gradually began discovering/inventing their story together. When she was finally

able to finish the novel, she could not find a publisher; the book was rejected three times before she discovered the Spiral Collective, who published it to enormous critical acclaim. While Hulme wove the lives of her characters together, she created a tapestry of New Zealand Maori myth, legend and magic that takes in the whole of the country's life, culture and landscape.

Hulme's novel is remarkable for its language, its themes, its narrative techniques, its characters, its shape and unity, its use of landscape and description, its mastery of dialogue and its drama. Experimental in all these respects, *The Bone People* is not only a compelling and magical novel to enjoy; it also constitutes a unique achievement in the novel form, and can be studied closely with great advantage. Hulme pointed to the extent of her concern for the details and nuances of her poetic language, when she explained in her preface that words affect readers in a variety of ways: 'I think the *shape* of words brings a response from the reader – a tiny, subconscious, unacknowledged but definite response.' She gave two very straightforward examples, first 'okay' and 'o k' and second 'bluegreen' and 'blue-green', and then acknowledged the gratitude she felt to her editors at Spiral for respecting such nuances, which she called 'oddities'. Hulme emphasized that the novel was precisely, in part at least, a systematic effort to convey such unconscious but definite linguistic effects through 'experiments and eccentricities', which also constitute in part her voice as a writer. She then related a dream of a journey through the mountains on a train with a 'Club-Room', and concluded 'Kia ora koutou katoa' ('greetings to you all'), 'make of it what you will.' Thus begins for the reader a dream-like journey through Hulme's New Zealand landscape, the scene of imagination and love in all their complexities, oddities and eccentricities.

This novel, certainly 'passing strange' at first, becomes an addiction, all the more so if we heed Hulme's advice in the preface, which it is so easy to read over and forget – or almost forget, for perhaps it stays in our unconscious, helping us to appreciate the quite astonishing innovations and aesthetic effects which Hulme achieved. Part of the magic of the style arises from her free use of Maori words and phrases. Part of the ordinary yet legendary nature of the content is evident in the table of contents, with its mythic headings, 'Season of the Day Morn', 'The Sea Round' or 'Moonwater Picking', contrasted with the Janet Frame-like technique displayed in 'Feldapart Sinews, Breaken Bones' or the symbolic 'The End at the Beginning', 'Mirrortalk' and 'The Woman at the Wellspring of Death.' Indeed, the whole page is a poem, and is an important hint of how to read what is to follow, as is the prologue. The latter moves from a poem, to the poem restated in something more prose-like, to a related prose passage. Four short prose passages follow, from the points of view of a narrator and then of the three characters, establishing a central experience for each.

In addition to such symbolic and metaphorical devices, in addition to the careful, detailed uses of the resources of language for her style, Hulme experimented successfully with an unusual narrative technique, alternating between a relatively omniscient narrator and periodic narrative 'insets' in the immediate, subjective, first person voice of the main character, Kerewin Holmes. These insets jar dramatically with their context, which is the third person, detached, 'objective' voice, and draw the reader into an alert consciousness of Hulme's systematic questioning of the relationship between autobiography and fiction as well. Towards the end of the novel, Kerewin takes out her journal, called 'The Book of the Soul', 'a thousand pages of Oxford Indian paper', and describes the rebuilding of the Maori *marae* (a spiritual community gathering place), which mirrors her own miraculous recovery from illness. She then burns her journal, and returns to her tower by the sea, having completed a long journey of despair, illness and eventual reconciliation. Techniques of narration involving, for example, severe elision (as in the final pages) and carefully constructed gaps at crucial points (such as the gap in the action between the epilogue's beginning and the end of the previous section) have an almost modernist effect of de-emphasizing the plot, which throughout the novel provides only the most tenuous line. For the novel is made up of series of 'scenes', snapshots of events of a stark immediacy, deliberately disconnected from the previous and following scenes by sharp shifts in location, time and characters. These discrete scenes are characterized by a depth and dramatic intensity which

is denied to the plot. The reader is drawn into an almost painful participation in the text, as the intense immediacy of these events, sharply separated from each other in the surface, thematic dimension of the text, demands continuous imaginative acts of connection and integration by the reader.

The Bone People represents a genuine achievement in the revitalization of the novel in the late twentieth century. With its aesthetically effective experiments in language and style, in narrative techniques and in its explorations of possibilities for structure, unity and fragmentation, along with its attention to interfaces between autobiography and fiction, this book can be read as an innovation in the novel form. This is reflected in the thematic concern with the forms of love usually misunderstood by society. The characters, all 'oddities' and eccentrics, and their eccentric relations with each other function aesthetically to justify the oddities of Hulme's novelistic innovations as effective means of articulating and communicating to readers the inside of human experiences, which, when seen only from the outside, appear objectionable and indefensible.

Leslie Marmon Silko 1948–

Raised in the pueblos of Laguna, New Mexico, Leslie Marmon Silko studied and taught at the University of New Mexico. She received awards from the National Endowment of the Arts and a MacArthur Foundation fellowship. This made it possible for her to concentrate on her writing, which includes *Laguna Woman* (Greenfield Center, N.Y., 1974) and *Storyteller* (New York, 1981), both collections of poems, tales and stories, as well as the novels *Ceremony* (New York, 1977) and *Almanac of the Dead* (New York, 1991). *The Delicacy and Strength of Lace* (St Paul, Minn., 1986) is a collection of letters between Silko and James Wright, ed. Anne Wright.

One of the central themes of all Silko's marvellously impressive writings is the importance of stories, legends and myths in the lives of individuals as well as in the life of a society. Her own remarkable fiction is a demonstration of the role which stories play in the lives of her characters. When characters become disconnected from the stories of their cultural group, they are cut off from the sources of strength which make it possible to defeat the forces of illness, evil, destruction and death. Silko's novels and stories, then, like Patricia Grace's, constitute a profound rejection of the notion that stories, literature, art and culture generally are to be understood as a luxury or a dispensable element in human life. One of her central concerns is to show *how* stories function to make life endurable, and why they play such a profound and central role in human life. Her fiction is also an analysis of the forces which denigrate art, culture and the story – forces which try to deceive us into underestimating the value of story-telling and the value of preserving myths, legends and our cultural heritage. Silko's fiction explores the extent to which the very sanity of both individuals and societies is at stake when they are unable to draw on their culture for the strength they need to confront the demands of life.

Her stunning novel *Ceremony* is a complex narrative exploration of what happens to Tayo, the central character, when he is cut off from his cultural heritage and trapped amongst white people, who deny his very value as a human being, because they despise his 'identity'. Even after he returns to the Pueblo, he is so spiritually and physically ill that he becomes vulnerable to the destructive forces within his own tribe and cultural-social milieu. The novel portrays Tayo's gradual awakening to an understanding of how he can reconnect with his group's myths, so that these legends can strengthen and heal him:

I will tell you something about stories,
    . . .
They aren't just entertainment.
    Don't be fooled,
They are all we have, you see,
    all we have to fight off
    illness and death.
You don't have anything if you don't have
the stories.

Throughout her writings, Silko has not merely sought to restore, clarify and preserve specific stories, though she has done that; she has also sought to reveal to her readers why stories are so important to a culture, why story-telling is not merely entertainment or a luxury. One of the most difficult tasks a writer can set herself is to try to communicate to her readers what, essentially, can really only be 'witnessed' by each individual if it is to be genuinely grasped; hence Silko has often used supernatural, magical and legendary elements. That is, the psychological strength needed to survive the forces which threaten our health and our sanity is not derivable from the reason, as Gloria Naylor has also shown in her fiction. Reason can be our ally, but it needs the superior strength of human imaginative and supernatural powers to overwhelm negative elements, whether in nature, or in other people, or within our own psyches. Silko's writing shows why reason and rational measures, whether communal or individual, fail in the face of illness, fear, mental breakdown and death. Time and again, characters are shown having to tap into the more powerful communal resources of imaginative myths and legends which nourish, heal and restore the human spirit. Like many other writers, such as Willa Cather or Bessie Head, Silko is aware that the forces in human nature and the natural world can be either destructive or creative. Her novels and stories explore the human psyche in all its depths and complexities, but through universal forms rather than interior psychological portrayal. While Silko respects the power of reason and its creative effects in controlling destructive superstition, prejudice and ignorance, she has also sought to reveal the need to complete reason with intuition and art.

Silko's insight into the nature of human needs and the psychological importance of legend and story is evident in her narrative strategies. In *Ceremony*, the healing of Tayo's broken spirit is narrated, in the first half of the novel, by means of a skilful interweaving of the past horrors (which brought about his collapse) with the present. His adult experiences in war and in a prisoner-of-war camp, as well as childhood experiences, are intertwined with a present which, at first, is hazy and unfocused, as Tayo is shown swallowed up by his personal past. Neither hospitals and medication nor his family, friends and tribal medicine can help him out of his horrors. In the next, central section of the novel, the narrative begins to tap the fantastic energy of ritual, myth and legend, to focus almost exclusively on the present; Tayo emerges from his personal past and from his spiritual decay only after his extraordinary excursion to Gallup, and to the magical, gifted medicine man who reconnects him, by means of an elaborate, healing 'ceremony', to Tayo's spiritual past. The distinction between the destructiveness of the personal past and the liberating effects of the spiritual past and heritage is drawn both in the astonishing thematics and in the narrative technique, as the central excursion to Gallup and the subsequent, quite simply fantastic ceremony become the turning point in the story. The ceremony also becomes a metaphor of reading, and is a turning point for the reader, too. Tayo is sufficiently strengthened by the ceremony to return to the Pueblo and begin the 'task' of restoring his uncle's cattle (stolen by rich white ranchers).

This episode functions aesthetically in the story as the task of awakening him to a realization of the lies and deceits that white civilization has perpetrated. Tayo is spiritually aroused enough during this almost mythical quest to fulfil the previously incredible prophecies of the Gallup medicine man, with the help of the 'allies' he was advised to watch for. As predicted, a (legendary) female is encountered who nourishes and loves him, and later returns in the narrative to help him complete the restoration of his stolen livelihood, which is a simile for his stolen identity and heritage. This mysterious woman of unknown origins is later revealed to be a mythical figure of a supernatural kind whose very physical actuality is in question, but whose spiritual existence, wisdom and powers of healing are well-known, even legendary. 'She', this unnamed spirit of both the land and humanity, warns Tayo about the processes of dehumanization which threaten us all, and to which most people succumb. It becomes clear, by the end of the novel, that Tayo's illness is a result of his inability to dehumanize himself, while the 'sane' people succeed. The woman-spirit warns him that this dehumanization is far worse than death itself; these destructive forces annihilate both 'the feeling people have for each other' and that they have for themselves. They can destroy whole cultures, not just individuals.

Silko's narrative draws on familiar mythic forms itself, both from her own pueblo heritage and from universal, generic forms such as excursions, quests, passages, encounters, tasks and supernatural elements, all of which Silko has narrated effectively, precisely by tapping into the cultural heritages which are hers. These legends infuse the novel with a supernatural power only accessible through such a cultural accumulation of myth, ceremony, ritual and story. The novel itself becomes, then, not only the record of Tayo's spiritual recovery, but a vehicle for spiritual regeneration for Silko's people and her readers. Tayo's encounter with 'the woman' initiates a further self-referential episode in the preservation of the legend of her power (by which she empowers her people), for he then recounts this episode to the 'elders' of his community: 'It took a long time to tell them the story; they stopped him frequently with questions about the location and the time of day; they asked about the direction she had come from and the colors of her eyes ... you have seen her/we will be blessed again.' Only then, much later in the novel, does the reader realize with a profound shock that Tayo's encounter was with a spiritual ally, and not merely an ordinary woman. Moreover, we discover to our amazement that her companion, the hunter, is none other than the magical and mysterious mountain lion who had distracted the white ranchers from capturing Tayo when they caught him 'stealing' back his cattle. The old myth of the human being in the form of the lion – known all over the Americas and Africa – is used by Silko to release enormous imaginative energy into the story, as it was by Rachel Ingalls in *Binstead's Safari* (1983).

Further power spills into the prose from the fragmented narrative poems and the accompanying lyric songs, broken up and scattered throughout at crucial points, which 'tell the story' in apocryphal terms. Elemental forces of nature personified into friendly or hostile spirits characterize the narrative poetic 'commentary', with its vocative references to sunrise pitted against whirling darkness, and its legendary tales of the dangers of witchery, magic and superstition, along with drugs and drink, all of which entice people away from the ritual ceremonies, such as planting and harvesting, which express care and respect for nature and which constitute their livelihood and health.

The narrative poetic fragments reinforce the legendary episodes in the novel, such as the apocryphal ceremony with Betonie, the Gallup medicine man, which occurs at the exact centre of the novel, and which initiates all the other legendary episodes that follow, involving the woman, the lion and the mythically narrated recovery of the cattle, as well as the sacrificial murder which Tayo witnesses, and which brings him to his fullest spiritual development. Tayo resists the impulse for violence and revenge, so that the forces of evil (personified in his 'friends' as they murder and destroy each other) fail to claim him as another victim of darkness, another destroyer of feeling. As darkness fades and the dawn comes, Tayo connects with the energies of nature, of sun, stars, moon and mountains, through the songs recounting the ceremonies and rituals that remind him of this source of strength. He realizes his own naturalness, his belonging in the natural world as a blessed, loved, almost magical being in a magical world. But this connection with nature through a series of spiritual transitions (as narrated in the novel) is shown only to be possible through song, legend, ritual, ceremony, word and communality, passed from person to person and generation to generation by stories:

> The ear for the story and the eye for the pattern were theirs [the Native Americans']; the feeling was theirs: we came out of this land and we are hers . . . They had always been loved. He thought of her then; she had always loved him; she had never left him; she had always been there. He crossed the river at sunrise.

'She', the woman he encountered, his ally, is the incarnation and embodiment of nature herself, with all its healing and nourishing energies, and nature is then likened to story itself – as a growing natural plant. A story, like a plant, must grow and 'press out in all directions', and become 'strong and translucent as the stars'. Silko's novel is such a story, made as an offering to all people, who must share their stories and their heritage as they share their mixed parentage, if we are to resist the dehumanizing influences which deny the needs of the human spirit and pretend that stories are just stories. For without them, 'there will be a drought, and the people will starve.'

In *Almanac of the Dead: A Novel*, Silko has continued the questioning of the nature of

human fulfilment as involving art, imagination and love, rather than materialistic ends, power or prestige. She has also continued to present the individual as strong and developed when connected with her or his community and culture. In the apocalyptic epic narrative of this recent novel, predicting the demise of white civilization and the arrival soon of indigenous peoples from the south to retake their land, Silko has created a complex narrative and a huge canvas of related characters, places and events. She has portrayed the nature of the destructive forces in the human psyche, whether white or Native American, and the means of defeating them. Throughout the novel, Silko has interwoven ancient narratives of Native American legends, such as the giant stone snake facing south (Quetzalcoatl-like), the legend of the twin brothers and their northward advance, as well as many others, with a whole complex of stories about violence, materialism, drugs, consumption and the ruthless pursuit of money. She has also ripped the veil of propriety from judges, policemen and other examples of 'pillars of the community' to reveal the corruption of their hearts and minds by greed and inhumanity. She has interspersed with these accounts the stories of Zeta, Seese, Lecha and Yoeme, trying to re-establish connections with their past, their ancestors and their natural powers. The novel gradually builds up to a crescendo with the stunning prophecy, at the huge 'tribal' gathering of holistic healers, that the ancient predictions are about to be fulfilled: the indigenous peoples will take back the Americas from the White Europeans.

In the midst of this apocalyptic vision, indeed running throughout the novel, are constant references to the 'almanac of the dead'. The story of the almanac is told most explicitly a third of the way through this titanic novel, in about ten pages of continuous revelations about the incredible, magical powers of the almanac, in a chapter entitled 'The Journey of the Ancient Almanac'. It constitutes the heart of the entire 750 pages; Silko has tapped into the ancient literary and legendary convention of the journey as the context for this self-referential chapter. The story of the almanac ties Silko's own novel to ancient Egyptian and Sanskrit (as well as later Greek and European) myths about writings which not only tell the people 'who they are and where they had come from'; they also refer to and predict, even create, the future. The almanac has the power, that is, decisively to affect the present, for it is not merely a record of the past but a 'living' being. The survival of both the people and their almanac is at stake in Silko's novel, as she has narrated in these central ten pages the tale of the effort of a people, allegedly during a distant past – a time of slaughter and destruction – to save the manuscript, as people flee the south to escape the invaders. Now, past is present, time dissolves, and the almanac describes the here and the now.

The ancient almanac of the dead is, Silko's narrator explains, divided into four notebooks and sewn into the ragged garments of four children, who are sent north (the story goes) to seek survivors of their tribe, who will help them preserve the almanac and return someday to reclaim their heritage: 'The "book" [that the children] carried was the "book" of all the days of their people. These days and years were all alive, and all these days would return again. The "book" had to be preserved at all costs.' One of the grandmothers of Zeta and Lecha (the adult twins who have been entrusted with restoring the fading manuscript) reveals that, paradoxically, 'the story of their journey had somehow been included in these notebooks.' Through a stunning narrative, Silko has described how the children 'accidentally' ate a few pages of the almanac when they were starving, pages which predicted their failed journey and destruction at the hands of Death-Eye Dog's representative. The almanac's pages 'held many forces within them, countless spiritual properties to guide the people and make them strong ... You see, it had been the almanac that had saved them. That first night, if the eldest [child] had not sacrificed a page from the book, that crippled woman would have murdered them all right then.' Silko's own *Almanac of the Dead: A Novel* constitutes a section in the ancient legend of the almanac of the dead, and the entire novel becomes a self-referential prophecy for her people.

Gayl Jones 1949–

Professor of English literature at the University of Michigan, Gayl Jones was born in Lexington,

Kentucky, and took degrees from Brown University (MA and DA) and Connecticut College (BA). She is the author of several books, including *Corregidora* (New York, 1975), *Eva's Man* (New York, 1976) and a collection of short stories, *White Rat* (New York, 1977). Jones also writes plays and poetry; indeed, even her prose is written in both dramatic and poetic styles which overrun the borders between these genres. These writings include *The Hermit Woman* (Detroit, 1983) and *Song for Anninho* (Detroit, 1981). She has received a number of awards and grants for her poetry, plays and fiction, including the Mademoiselle Award for fiction in 1975. A number of published interviews as well as essays by Jones give helpful information about her intellectual, social and artistic commitments. One of the issues which comes up repeatedly is her emphasis upon character and relationships amongst characters. Nearly all her fiction explores the psychology of various types of people and the distinctive consequences of mutual exploitation – especially sexual exploitation. Violence is a central thematic concern, but Jones not only deals with overt violence; she also exposes the more subtle forms which are passed off as socially acceptable, but which do immense harm.

Language, diction and attitudes to language are portrayed as the origin of much conflict, as in the story 'White Rat'; the slow, laborious transformation from victim to genuine individuality is portrayed in her fiction as dependent upon overwhelming the distinctive, imprisoning aspects of language by its creative, liberating effects. Jones, like a number of other writers such as Flora Nwapa, Alice Walker, James Ngugi and Ama Ata Aidoo, has realized a means of combining written literature with the powers of direct speech and the oral tradition, by what she calls 'ritualized dialogue'. That is, she has steeped herself in the rhythms and structures of black speech and of the oral tradition of myth, legend and story-telling, and (instead of beginning with written language) has then condensed, transformed and selected elements of that ordinary speech, which becomes her central aesthetic device. One of its most powerful qualities is its musicality and sensuousness – its sexuality. This musical, sexual language is akin to the song, the incantation, and blues and jazz. Jones explained that 'I learned to write from listening to people talk' rather than from written literature.

This central aesthetic quality has several consequences in Jones's fiction. First, it allows her writing to plug into and gain strength from a powerful oral tradition and history, revealing this 'unwritten' history which is brought to life in her texts. Second, her 'written' narrative gains an immediacy and power from its directness of speech: the various intertwining tales of Ursa, Gram and Great Gram in *Corregidora*, for example, create the artistic illusion for the reader of being present in an active and engaged way. Indeed, this engagement with the reader is one of the most characteristic aesthetic achievements of Jones's work. The reader is goaded into reflection, into feeling, into response, and not allowed to remain passively submissive to a narrative authority. Indeed, in *Eva's Man*, Jones has stated overtly that 'the main thing I wanted to communicate is Eva's unreliability as the narrator of her story.' Eva is unable to escape the state of being a victim; her extreme violence is as destructive of her own humanity and individuality as it is harmful to others. She is trapped, Jones's narrative suggests, in silence, in the past, in her history. *Corregidora*, the close companion to this volume of 'otherness', charts the complex and difficult course by which Ursa first fails, and then gradually achieves regeneration and liberation from victimization.

At first, Ursa's acquiescent immersion in the literal level of the tales of her Gram and Great Gram trap her in a cycle of duty and passivity. For she does not reflect upon the stories; she does not retell them in her own terms; she does not 'reauthorize' them for her generation, her society and her changed circumstances. Gradually, her experiences galvanize her into rethinking her history, its legends and the stories, and she begins to question them and change them. For example, the stories tell her her first duty is to bear children to keep the history alive. Later, she comes to see that child-bearing is a choice, not a duty, and that there are other, perhaps better ways of revitalizing the past. This is a powerfully feminist gesture – for most women have as yet been unable to free themselves from the myth that the only real way to validate their identity and existence is as mothers. They may have careers and other activities, but childless they must not be. Jones's novel shows how this sexist attitude about the importance of children is as deeply embedded in the psyches of women as in those of men. Women victimize each other, then, the novel reveals, by being unable to accept their own or other women's childlessness.

Ursa turns to music and song, to blues singing, after the violence from her husband which damages her irretrievably for procreation; his rage at being made to feel a mere stud for her need for children is the origin of his outbreak. Yet her embracing of song and music is shown to be a means to an end, not the end itself, any more than her acquiescence in her ancestors' oral tradition was an end. If song, history and oral traditions are to heal, to regenerate, to liberate, they must not be repeated passively and submissively. They need to be resung and retold in new ways which involve genuine communication, not rote recitation. Narration and story-telling heal psychological and physical wounds only when they function communicatively – as establishing relationships between teller and listener so that a genuine dialogue is created. Calling up 'ancestral voices' and historical, legendary presences can release tremendous strength and give wisdom and articulacy. Orality embedded in written literature of Gayl Jones's kind creates the direct speech of dialogue between author and reader which is portrayed in the text between characters. By using family histories, myths and legends, dialogues, letters, memories, tales, and recitations of dreams and nightmares and fantasies, Jones orders her stories and attends to form, structure and style so that how things are told is as important as what is told. *Eva's Man* and *Corregidora* form two aspects of one major project: the exploration of ways of surviving and the reasons why failure so often occurs – with language and communication at the heart of that failure and that success.

Jamaica Kincaid 1949–

Born Elaine Potter Richardson in St John's, Antigua, Kincaid is one of the most prominent of Caribbean novelists to emerge in the 1980s. Presently living in New York and writer for the *New Yorker*, she is the author of two novels,

Annie John (London and New York, 1985) and *Lucy* (London, 1989). She has also written some boldly experimental short stories, published in the *New Yorker*, the *Paris Review* and *Rolling Stone* and now collected in *At the Bottom of the River* (London and New York, 1984). *A Small Place* (London, 1988) is a non-fictional, sharply sarcastic account of the exploitation of the Caribbean islands by Westerners, especially American and British invaders. Unlike novelists such as Erna Brodber, Merle Hodge (Trinidad) or Michelle Cliff (Jamaica), Kincaid attends to issues of national identity and ethnicity more through suggestion and analogy than directly through thematic issues. Her powerful, psychological character studies explore the processes of maturation and independence from the safety of childhood and parental care to the freedom and dangers of adulthood, but also as symbolic of the larger national quest for independence from colonial powers. The search for identity, whether personal or national, is described by Kincaid in an intensely subjective, intensely interior narrative voice in the novels, which nevertheless proceed in a fairly orderly, chronological way. The short stories, on the other hand, even dispense with this latter conventional aspect of narrative fiction. As a result, their reception by critics was even more mixed than the response to her novels, though this ambivalence has gradually waned in the face of growing appreciation of her works. In 1984, she was the recipient of the Morton Dauwen Zabel Award for fiction.

A number of the short fragments in *At the Bottom of the River*, such as 'My Mother', 'What I Have Been Doing Lately' or 'In the Night', could be read as anticipations or seeds of the two novels which followed. Several other stories strain deliberately at the order imposed upon them, arousing the reader to a consciousness of form, style and order which disrupts any possibility of passive acquiescence. For example, in 'The Girl', Kincaid has adopted the familiar post-modern device of a story made up entirely of extensive, unruly cataloguing of activities required of 'the kind of woman' who gains social approval, springing upon the reader a narrow, personal focus only in the final sentence/question, 'You mean to say that after all you are already going to be the kind of woman who the

baker won't let near the bread?' Suddenly the entire fragment is refocused in the light of this moral viewpoint. Dispensing with conventional plot or story form, Kincaid has woven her magic with a range of other techniques, too, drawing upon powerful psychological symbolism and imagery of the night, of darkness, of light, sun and shade, of obeah and other Caribbean folk traditions, of Caribbean flora and fauna (as Jean Rhys did before her), and of death. Kincaid has used descriptions of dream, hallucinations, illness and trance to further her narratives, instead of using plot. One of her stories proceeds around a series of questions asked of the narrator woman by her daughter, so that the constant shifting point of view of this 'descriptive dialogue' hardly prepares the reader for the lurch into a third person narrative of unknown origin at the end, which rhetorically repeats the question–answer mode. Other stories proceed by extreme fragmentation, setting up one segment next to another connected by imagery, incident or character, but rarely by plot.

Annie John and *Lucy* are much less fragmented, cataloguing and overtly experimental than these stories, but neither can be said to be conventional, either. The experimentation involves less narrative fragmentation than symbolism, indirection, analogy, intensity of interiority, subjectivity and style, though plot is still de-emphasized. *Annie John* has a superficially conventional chronological order, as it moves on several analogical thematic levels of varying overtness, through the childhood and adolescence of Annie until her escape from the confining protection of mother, home and island, to England, independence and adulthood. Kincaid has described *Lucy* as a novel 'about a girl who lives on an island and goes to a continent', and this is also true of *Annie John*, where the 'mother' of Annie is also the island, metaphorically speaking. Expatriation seems, in both novels, to be a precondition for independence, in various senses of the word. The intense emotional relationship between mother and daughter described in *Annie John*, which symbolizes colonialism as well, cannot be said to be atypical, for the intensity resides in large part in Kincaid's method of multilevel, symbolic narration rather than in the relationship per se. This distinction is not a mere formality, and is often overlooked, as though Kincaid's novel were about some special, unusual mother–daughter relationship. Rather, the intensely impassioned narrative is her method for revealing the strength of emotion hidden within all such familial relationships, however much it is denied at a surface level. The unconscious world of all of us is on display in these novels, then, namely that deeper realm of truth, which ignores the hypocrisies and pretence of detachment and control.

While *Annie John* is narrated from the point of view of the adolescent daughter, the narrative consciousness of the author is thoroughly and overtly interwoven throughout the text. This double perspective effect is extremely disturbing to the reader, for it disrupts, ruthlessly and systematically, any possibility of an uncritical, acquiescent acceptance of narrative authority or of simple overt thematics of mother–daughter relationships. The reader is further disturbed by the complete impossibility of ascertaining whether the novel is an autobiography or a fiction, and, therefore, what reading posture is to be adopted. Kincaid has exploited with considerable tact these disturbances of orders and genres, gradually establishing her political, social, psychological and emotional insights at several different levels; through implication and analogy, the author uses intense subjectivity, combined with an ironic consciousness, to achieve both a record of adolescent striving and a description of political, rational aspirations, which are both within and without the mentality – thus the psychological truth is expanded into more universal, social and political meanings. *Annie John* and *Lucy* are overtly novels about mothers and daughters, but they function through careful, intense analogy to create levels of meaning about colonialism, race and sexual exploitation. The colonization of land is an analogy for the colonization of women's bodies, as well. Kincaid's apparently simply, domestic novels are, on examination, psychologically insightful, complex multi-narratives, as death stalks emotional, sexual, political and personal maturation throughout them, and illness and depression play central roles, as if past selves and states of being, as well as familiar literary forms, must be allowed to die if we are to progress.

Michèle Roberts 1949–

Author of a play, 'The Journeywoman', and two books of poetry, co-editor of various collections of short stories, prose and poetry, and now author of numerous novels and one collection of stories, Michèle Roberts was born and lives in London. Her first novel, *A Piece of the Night* (London), published in 1978, was joint winner of the Gay News Book Award and was compared to novels by Colette. *The Visitation* (London, 1983) – a relatively conventional novel of the pains of love in a young woman writer's development – was shortly followed by *The Wild Girl* (London, 1984), one of Roberts's most imaginative and convincing novels. This was followed by *The Book of Mrs Noah* (London, 1987), an interesting experiment in fantasy, points of view and the rewriting of Biblical myths. *In the Red Kitchen* (London, 1990) continues the multiple narrative technique, this time, however, linked in the overarching consciousness of a spirit medium, Flora Milk, and in part based on a nineteenth-century controversy about a medium, Florence Cook. *Psyche and the Hurricane* (London) was published in 1991, and in 1992 *Daughters of the House* (London) appeared, and was shortlisted for the Booker Prize as well as winning the W.H. Smith Literary Award. Using, as Roberts often had previously, a narrative framework of the present, this time in order to present views of a mysterious past through two sisters, the author has explored the ambivalences of sibling relationships as well as the horror of a Nazi atrocity which haunts the communal consciousness of a small French town. *Flesh and Blood* (London, 1994) is Roberts's most recent book.

Roberts's novels share many thematic concerns as well as narrative strategies, the most obvious and central being her exploration of the sexism of much dogmatic Christianity and the implication that Christianity itself need not be interpreted this way. By 'rewriting' or reinterpreting Christian history, legend, myth and gospels, Roberts has created a female-friendly theology which is far more genuinely Christian than the sexist, priestly overlays of the last several centuries. Another central thematic concern in Roberts's fiction is the relations between siblings and close friends; *The Visitation*, like

Daughters of the House, is pre-eminently concerned with the emotional intensities, mysteries and complications of sibling relationships. Moreover, in each case there is some disturbing mystery, some immoral or obscene event which has been covered up, and which is gradually revealed in the course of the narration.

Mrs Noah and *The Wild Girl* constitute a genuine rewriting of Christian ideology and, like *Daughters of the House*, make use of different kinds of framework technique in order to 'set off' the 'past' events from ordinary life. In *Mrs Noah*, Roberts has invoked, first, a violent dream, then an ordinary scene of everyday life in Venice, disrupted, however, by the protagonist's hallucination of her grandmother. This vision leads her to 'dive into the wreck' of her unconscious (literally into a Venetian canal), and we are then launched on an incredible tale of Noah's Ark. The entire rest of the 275 pages of the text turns out to be the narration of what was a 'dream', resulting from a concussion in the water, a dream with five 'Sibyls' who tell their distinct stories of oppression and exploitation. The ark itself is portrayed as a vast library which represents the concretization of this oppression in the literature, the history and, generally, the discourse of Western civilization. The Sibyls do not write their stories, but when 'Mrs Noah' wakes up, she decides to write down her extraordinary experience in a gesture of 'survival' from the draining and undermining experiences of her marriage, her society and her religion.

Daughters of the House is another experiment in delving into the unconscious, this time not through dream or fantasy, however, but through excavating disturbing, never completely confronted memories and events from the past. After twenty years of absence in a convent, Thérèse returns to her inherited house in France, where her relation Leonie has lived with her husband Baptiste. She returns in order to rediscover her past, so that she can complete an autobiography which she entitles the 'Story of a Soul'. Leonie angrily resists this 'raking up of the past', for fear it will somehow expose things that are better forgotten. After the first 24 pages, the reader is plunged into this past, perhaps the very autobiography mentioned at first, which gradually, almost like a detective story, reveals over the course of 130 pages an unexpected but still am-

biguous parentage for Leonie and Thérèse. But the certain truth of Leonie's relationship with Thérèse as twin sister is also revealed, though the identity of their father is still left uncertain. The final 15 pages of the novel return to the present, out of the autobiography and into 'reality', and to the confrontation with the inevitable 'presence of the past' in the shapes of the two adult character 'doubles', Leonie and Thérèse. Distinct identities collapse, as Leonie finally enters into the chamber of the past: 'She twisted the handle of the door. She opened it. She paused in the doorway, then went in. The voices came from somewhere just ahead, the shadowy bit she couldn't see. She stepped forward, into the darkness, to find words.' Suddenly, the reader realizes that another novel is about to begin, the one that will tell the past from Leonie's point of view, as the previous 172 pages had told Thérèse's: 'Thérèse has begun writing it down. But I don't know that I'd want to rely on her memory alone. She'll have got half of it wrong.'

The rewriting of history, of religious history, is the explicit motivation of *The Wild Girl*, one of Roberts's most exuberant and imaginative novels. There, Roberts has exposed dogmatic Christianity: 'We have cut our God in two, and we have cast the female part out into the desert and have called it the devil, and we have tried to bind it and to forget it and to seal it in the abyss, where it has become dangerous.' Written in a first person narrative, *The Wild Girl* is 'framed' by a paragraph at the beginning and at the end; the first tells of this book as the Gospel of Mary Magdalene. The final paragraph refers to the book as exhumed from the place where it was buried by Mary until the time should come when her daughter's daughter could find it, copy it and send it out in the world, just as Mary finally went out into the world to spread the word after finding and burying her 'Book'. The book is written as a series of journeys away from the domination of men: 'I ran from the authority of the men of my own village only to encounter that of the men on the road.' After journeying to Alexandria and dressing herself as a boy, Mary finds refuge with Sibylla, who taught her much but eventually helped her return to her home on the Mount of Olives, to a new life as a disciple of Jesus. Wandering with crowds of followers, Mary goes to Galilee and to Jerusalem, but upon the death of Jesus she sets out with other women, once again to escape the domination of sexist disciples. In addition to these journeys, the narrative proceeds by a series of dreams of Mary, some long and elaborate, some short and prophetic, in which great battles take place between Ignorance (sexism) and 'women full of light'. The dream tells, albeit in mythic proportions, the reality of Mary's everyday struggle with Peter and other sexist disciples who try to marginalize and dominate the women.

Eventually, the women escape to Massilia, on the far shores of the Mediterranean, and set up a religious community where they thrive for some fifteen years, until Mary's daughter grows up in freedom and Mary writes her book as an expression of her 'need to bear witness to God . . . the need to go inwards'. The last thirty pages of the novel describe first the struggle to find the truth in words which Mary had thought would be easy; moreover, recording the truth 'has increased my doubts and confusion rather than lessening them'. In the midst of this description of the writing of the book, a series of horrific, nightmarish dreams symbolize and consolidate Mary's past as well as predicting the terrible struggles of the future of women trying to fight against the ignorance or sexism in the church.

Gloria Naylor 1950–

Often compared with Toni Morrison, Naylor was born in New York City, where she took a BA from Brooklyn College before going to Yale for her MA. Her first book, a 'novel' composed of seven connecting stories, entitled *The Women of Brewster Place* (New York, 1982), won the American Book Award for first fiction. Guggenheim and other fellowships followed in 1985 and 1988. In 1985, *Linden Hills* was published (New York), another novel which uses allegorical and symbolical methods to enrich its surface thematics with religious, moral and aesthetic reverberations. Three years later Naylor's most accomplished work appeared, *Mama Day* (New York, 1988), a novel alternating between the gritty, inhumane world of New York and the magical, timeless place called Willow Springs. Her fourth novel, *Bailey's Café*, appeared in 1992 (New York).

In these novels, Naylor has used to great effect the literary device of making a geographical place into an allegory for the human spirit, so that the events which occur, whether in Linden Hills or Willow Springs, take on a universal significance, which exceeds their overt reference to American, or black, or female or male experience. In addition, what is past – or history – and what is present or in the future are woven into a pattern. This is not only to reveal that history is constantly recurring in disguised forms. Naylor has also suggested that one way of turning the past into an energizing force, instead of an imprisoning element, is to make it conscious: to know it, to study it, to write about it, to tell stories about it, and thereby to harness it for personal and social uses. The energizing of the past is made also to function as a metaphor for the process of making the unconscious conscious, and gaining control over the obsessions, desires, fears and needs which otherwise defeat the individual's will.

The use of place and time as allegorical is the central literary device around which Naylor gathers her other powers as a novelist – her finely crafted prose, rich yet unpretentious, her construction of compelling characters and situation, which flesh out plots of quite surprising simplicity, and her ability to subordinate without sacrifice her intellectual, moral and social dimensions to the demands of a work of art. *Linden Hills* begins explicitly with Naylor's central artistic, unifying principle of geographical place as a symbol for moral and spiritual 'place': 'There had been a dispute for years over the exact location of Linden Hills.' Like Dante's rings around hell in the *Inferno*, and like the landscape of *Purgatories*, Linden Hills is made up of a series of crescent drives of residential homes which gradually lead down to the bottom of the hills, to a cemetery and to the house of Luther Nedeed, an undertaker who became vastly rich and built up Linden Hills for aspiring, wealthy black people. Luther, a kind of devil's advocate, is described in the first, historical section of the novel as an impersonal figure who is the reproduction, exactly, of his father, his grandfather, and his great-grandfather. Naylor has thus escaped the confines of both specific time and place by using the here and the now as mystical representations of the battles within the human psyche, of every individual, between the forces of humaneness

303

and of hellish greed and selfishness. Racism takes centre stage, as Luther Nedeed virtually buries his wife and son alive in the depths of his infernal house, because his black wife has produced a white-skinned albino son whom he disowns as not possibly of his seed. The novel plots the fantastic process of two young black adolescents, a pair of aspiring poets (Willie and Lester, like Dante and Virgil), working their way downwards, until, on Christmas Eve, they are the inadvertent 'liberators' of Willa and her dead son from her coffin-basement and her nameless, faceless existence as Nedeed's wife. But the heart of Linden Hills is engulfed accidentally in an infernal conflagration and the death, finally, of the long line of Nedeeds.

Throughout *Linden Hills*, Naylor has adopted a parallel narrative to that of the descent of the poets in the normal world of everyday life, down the hills towards Nedeed's house. Willa Nedeed, the buried wife, begins to explore the boxes of books and photographs, hidden in the basement, after her son's death from pneumonia. Beginning with a Bible annotated by an earlier wife of an earlier Luther Nedeed, Willa discovers a whole history of the sufferings of nameless Nedeed wives. Eventually, while poring over a series of photograph albums, she discovers the face of one of the wives gradually disappearing from the pictures, until she is completely 'effaced', left only with a body, by her husband and son. These explorations eventually galvanize Willa into action, into an obsessive cleaning of the basement; when she finishes, she heads up the stairs to begin her work on cleaning out the rest of the house, from top to bottom, all the time carrying her dead child wrapped around her body. This narrative is presented to the reader in constant alternation with that of the story of Willie and Lester until they finally collide in the final pages of the novel.

In *Mama Day*, Naylor has achieved similar effects of using specific times and places as allegories, but her methods have been rather different. *Mama Day* progresses by shifting between Willow Springs and New York City, the two places where Cocoa (Ophelia), the granddaughter of Mama (Miranda) Day lives her tempestuous life. Naylor has complicated the narrative further by alternating between first person points of view for Cocoa and her husband George, and

a third person narrative of most of the events in Willow Springs. She has also made the location of Willow Springs an issue, as was that of Linden Hills: an island off the coast of Georgia and South Carolina, 'Willow Springs ain't in no state.' Moreover, it is connected to the mainland USA only by a fragile bridge, which collapses when the hurricane described at the end of the novel hits the island, a natural disaster functioning aesthetically as an external dramatization for the madness engulfing Cocoa, apparently due to a voodoo magic of one of the island women. Further, the meaningfulness of present events is mythologized, as Naylor has infused them with constant references to the legendary Sapphira Wade, great-grandmother of Mama Day, who wrested from her white master-husband not only her freedom but also the deeds to all of Willow Springs island. Hence, the island is the property of its black inhabitants and their children's children, and can never be sold. It is not America: 'America ain't even entered into the question at all when it come to our land.'

Mama Day is almost a reincarnation of Sapphira, that legend 'everybody knows but nobody talks about . . . Sapphira Wade don't live in the part of our memory we can use to form words.' The knowledge of the slave woman who 'brought a whole new meaning to both them words' permeates the lives of all in Willow Springs, yet 'the *name* Sapphira Wade is never breathed out of a single mouth.' Mama Day is a present-day legend, with her wisdom, her medicinal abilities, her soul-healing powers and her moral character. The novel explores concurrently the battle between the sexes, as Cocoa and George try to build a loving relationship, and the battle between reason and imagination, as Naylor explores the mystical regions of belief, superstition, voodoo and the powers of art and faith. Mama Day and George, at first fast friends and mutual admirers, become locked in a battle of belief as Cocoa's sanity is destroyed and they quarrel about both the cause of the illness and its cure. Naylor has skilfully used the power of place and setting to narrate her story, as Mama Day's pilgrimages to the ancient, dilapidated country house in the backwoods become a source of past wisdom and knowledge, through memory and intuition. George's reason is not enough; it leads to his death.

Jayne Anne Phillips 1952–

Phillips was born in that mountainous border state between North and South, namely West Virginia. She began publishing short story collections in limited editions, including *Sweethearts* (Short Beach, Conn., 1976; and later St Paul, Minn., 1976) and *Counting* (New York, 1978), shortly followed by *Fast Lanes* (New York, 1986). Wider recognition was suddenly achieved with *Black Tickets* (New York, 1979), which won the Sue Kaufman Prize for first fiction, and which Nadine Gordimer praised as follows: 'Jayne Anne Phillips blasted the American short story out of suburbia and restored it to its former glory. An exquisite and terrible insight in the hands of one who fakes nothing: the best short-story writer since Eudora Welty.' Phillips was awarded a Guggenheim Fellowship and a National Endowment for the Arts Award, and has recently taught at New York University and Harvard. Also described as 'a sort of female equivalent of . . . Ian McEwan', Phillips has been praised for her powerful originality, her passionate but acute feeling for words, and her penetrating grasp of small-town American life and the psychological effects on its inhabitants of war, the Great Depression, and more war in Vietnam, as exemplified in her novel *Machine Dreams* (London and New York, 1984), nominated for the National Book Critics Circle Award.

The short story collection *Black Tickets* (twenty-seven 'stories' of greatly varying length, from less than a page to over twenty pages) is overtly and deliberately experimental in style, structure and thematics. Indeed, there is not much that we normally associate with the short story (or 'short short', as they are sometimes referred to) which Phillips has not experimented upon in these examples. The first 'story' is a disturbing verbal 'description' (interpretation, memory, fantasy?), two-thirds of a page long, entitled 'Wedding Picture', which introduces, in a manner of speaking, several of the characters who later recur in these often linked stories, including the describer-observer of the photograph. 'Home', the next story, jolts the reader out of this first shock into a more familiar literary landscape, a realm fully developed in Phillips's novel *Machine Dreams*. Plotless, fragmentary, and a mixture of dream, memory, photograph-description, conversation and narrative description of events in turn, 'Home' shatters sentimentality and complacency as it, itself, proceeds by photographic, episodic jerks to give the reader a clarity of vision about American family life in the 1960s. More overtly macabre elements intrude in the next fragment, 'Blind Girls', based on an almost universally known teenage apocryphal horror story about the hook of a crazed amputee, found in the doorhandle of the car by a necking couple when they get home. 'Lechery' departs completely from its full-length predecessor 'Home'; by using a first person narrative as in 'Home' and by starting the story with a line from that story's female narrator, Phillips has achieved continuity and shock simultaneously. The narrator of 'Lechery' is a 15-year-old male prostitute, and suddenly we are drawn into a world normally shunned and religiously avoided by conventional people. More stories of 'underworld' life follow, of prison inmates, drug addicts, murderers – but all portrayed as individuals rather than types.

'El Paso' constitutes a new complexity for these short stories. Phillips has handled astutely the alternating narrative point of view, as Dude, Rita, Bimp, The Blonde and 'Watching' create Texas in the 1960s, while '1934' connects back with 'Home', and 'The Heavenly Animal' explores father–daughter relationships to contrast with the mother–daughter emphasis in 'Home' and in 'Souvenir'. Other stories describe with disturbing insights the mind of a shell-shocked ex-soldier, or blind parents whose children also go blind in adolescence, interspersed with the fragmentary narrative blasts of a page or less which keep shattering the reader's expectations.

Machine Dreams is less obviously experimental than *Black Tickets*; in theme it is a relatively conventional chronicle of the life of a small-town American family from the 1930s to the 1960s. But the skilful alteration of point of view amongst the various characters establishes a psychological richness and completeness at which the stories could only hint. Through a carefully varied combination of first person, autobiographical reminiscences, 'war' letters, first from Mitch (1942–5) then, a generation later, from his son Billy (1970), distributed amongst chapters from the viewpoints of Jean and Mitch (the parents) and Danner and Billy (siblings), a remarkable verbal construction unfolds before the reader, communicating almost subconsciously the profound, long-lasting effects of war on ordinary Americans, whether male or female, young or old. Indeed, the novel seems to suggest that while the Hampson family have been able to survive illness, tragic accidents, the poverty consequent upon a failed business, divorce, a drug-busting and other not uncommon demands, it is the US government's silence in the 1960s' Vietnam War which finally defeats them. Billy is drafted and goes missing, and the government and army will not tell 'what happened'. The novel ends with the futility of Danner, Mitch or Jean trying to find out the authoritative 'truth' of Billy's final assignment, except for a hotly disputed eyewitness account in a personal letter from one of the survivors. For a novel as realist in style if not method as this one, such an ending is all the more effective for portraying the tenacity of the craving for 'authorized', objective versions.

Other books by Phillips include *How Mickey Made It* (St Paul, Minn., 1981) and *Hometown* (Iowa City, 1980), as well as *The Secret Country* (Chapell Hill, N.C., 1982).

Amy Tan 1952–

Born and brought up in California, Amy Tan is the author of three immensely successful books, *The Joy Luck Club* (New York, 1989), *The Kitchen God's Wife* (New York, 1991) and *The Moon Lady* (New York, 1992). Most recently she has published the novel *The Hundred Secret Senses* (New York, 1996). In these books, Tan has constructed a narrative which is based overtly on the lives and experiences of her parents and relatives. In *The Joy Luck Club*, she has focused on the tales her protagonist's mother's friends related at their weekly meeting, to which the daughter delighted to listen. *The Kitchen God's Wife* and *The Joy Luck Club* are sophisticated novels in terms both of structure, narrative point of view, and lively, imaginative, fantastic and grotesque tales within tales.

In *The Joy Luck Club*, Tan's central formal convention is a carefully structured set of alternating narrative points of view, which give contradictory accounts of the 'same' events. There is minimal plot, and characterization is not highly

developed. Rather, the latter is used aesthetically to express continuity, communality and identity, understood as primarily a social event and not an individual, personal, egotistical one. Both novels function further as cultural documents, like the novels of Patricia Grace, Leslie Marmon Silko and Paule Marshall, for example. That is, the texts function to preserve legends, stories and rituals which are threatened and otherwise might be lost. For all these authors, one's 'identity' and strength, indeed one's very survial, depend upon keeping alive the cultural specificity of a people.

In her second novel, *The Kitchen God's Wife*, Tan has again adopted a traditional story-teller's framework technique: the present functions as a many-latticed window to focus and tame the wild adventures which were the narrator's mother's life. Pearl, a daughter of about 40 who is dangerously ill from an unpredictable case of multiple sclerosis, dominates the framework of the present along with her husband and children, especially in her problematic relationship with her mother and other relatives. The central rhetorical figure in the thematics of this section of the novel is the lies, deceits and secrets the characters hide from each other. Pearl cannot bring herself to tell her mother about her possibly fatal illness; her mother keeps an equally powerful secret from her daughter, which is only revealed at the end: Pearl's father was probably not her biological father. All these and many, many other secrets come out only because Aunt Helen, who thinks she knows (almost) all, mistakenly believes she is dying of a brain tumour, and threatens to tell mother and daughter some of their secrets if they do not tell each other. (Aunt Helen does not know about Pearl's paternity, however.) Hence, after about 60 pages, the reader is unexpectedly launched on a 300-page Odyssey back in time, back to mainland China, back to youth, via the most amazing, colourful, adventurous digression a narrator has achieved since *Tristram Shandy*.

Tan's novel is complicated further by the fact that the strength of the first person narrator of the frame, Pearl, is so great that it takes the reader some time – 300 pages, in fact! – to realize that the novel is not going to be Pearl's and her partner Phil's life or story, but her mother's. The deferral of the realization that the digression into the past is not a digression at all creates a gradually dawning surprise. This technique achieves several artistic and psychological effects: first, the absolute distinction between Pearl and her mother disintegrates, as identities and lives merge into a continuous, rushing stream of life. Second, prejudice is overcome as the reader has to make a tremendous effort to realize that Winnie is going to be the heroine of the novel, not Pearl. For Winnie is portrayed in the frame as a rather silly, negligible, fussy old superstitious grandmother. Suddenly, she is transformed into a deserted child and then a highly desired, beautiful young woman and then wife.

Some of Tan's thematic interests are finely reflected in these narrative devices. She has exposed the tragic prejudice of the young towards elderly people. The force of the past in the present is one way of describing this dilemma; we cannot allow the past to dominate, yet it does so precisely if we deny it, both historically and in terms of personal psychology. Tan has sought in her novel to depict ways of reconciling the past with the present. This struggle is also describable as Pearl's efforts to negotiate the demands her relatives make on her to participate in family rituals and to fulfil her duties as a daughter, while trying to establish the claims of her husband and of her children and their role in this extended family. In the frame, these issues are brought to the fore, as an engagement party, a family reunion and, finally, the funeral of an aunt in her 90s are the material of the first sixty pages, material which acts as the vehicle for issues of telling versus not telling, of what to tell, of what truth *is*, anyway. The strange indeterminacy of Pearl's illness, the uncertainty of who her father is, and Aunt Helen's mistaken notion about her brain tumour, along with the collapse of the rituals which structure social life, all function to reinforce confusion as digression becomes substance and point of view shifts dramatically.

Before the reader is launched into the historical digression which becomes the substance, however, the first person narrator changes from Pearl to Pearl's mother; for about thirty pages the time frame of the present continues, as Aunt Helen and Winnie argue about the 'lies' of Winnie and Helen's past, the multiple deceptions perpetrated to gain entry to America as immigrants and then continued out of embarrassment

and fears. Finally, Winnie decides to risk hurting her daughter by telling her the whole, long, complicated and tragic story of her mother's extraordinary life during the terrific upheavals in China in the 1930s, 1940s and 1950s. With quite simply exuberant wit and vivacity, a complicated story of hilarious, blood-curdling and astonishing intricacy is woven, as Tan has drawn on various novel forms, from the historical to romance and to picaresque adventure genres. As with *The Joy Luck Club*, Tan has forcefully revitalized and invigorated the novel in numerous aspects, showing that as a form of human expression it is as inexhaustible as the variety of human experience itself. And, by the end of the novel, Tan has offered a clear and convincing way forward to many of the impasses and conflicts discussed above, such as, first, the role of the past and present and, second, the way to cope with fear, illness and death. Winnie finds a previously unnamed goddess (a factory error!) to go in the altar Grand Auntie Du had left Pearl in her will, and explains simply, but eloquently:

> You should tell her everything . . . When you are afraid, you can talk to her. She will listen . . . See her name: Lady Sorrowfree, happiness winning over bitterness, no regrets in this world . . . Of course, it's only superstition, just for fun. But see how fast the smoke rises – oh, even faster when we laugh, lifting our hopes higher and higher.

Tan's novel sumptuously expresses this philosophy, so concisely articulated by W.B. Yeats in these lines from 'Lapis Lazuli', which catch the flavour of Tan's fiction to perfection as it describes a work of art:

> And I
> Delight to imagine them seated there;
> There, on the mountain and the sky,
> On all the tragic scene they stare.
> One asks for mournful melodies;
> Accomplished fingers begin to play.
> Their eyes mid many wrinkles, their eyes,
> Their ancient, glittering eyes, are gay.

Louise Erdrich 1954–

Of Chippewa and German American descent, Louise Erdrich, a member of the Turtle

Mountain Band of Chippewa, was born in Little Falls, Minnesota, the eldest of seven siblings. Having attended Dartmouth College from 1972, she returned to North Dakota to teach poetry in schools, until taking a master's degree at Johns Hopkins in 1979. She spent time in Boston as editor of a newspaper, a year in New Hampshire at the McDowell Colony, and another year at Dartmouth as writer in residence. Her first book was a collection of poems entitled *Jacklight* (1984), followed immediately by *Love Medicine* (New York, 1984), the first in a series of related novels, including *The Beet Queen* (New York, 1986; London, 1987), *Tracks* (New York, 1988) and *The American Horse*.

Erdrich's novels seem to have taken shape as short stories, which appeared in such magazines as the *Atlantic Monthly, Ms*, the *Georgia Review*, the *Kenyon Review, Esquire, Harper's* and others. She won several awards for these stories, and was included in various prize anthologies of stories such as the *O. Henry* and *Best American Short Story* volumes. Erdrich's novels have been greeted with considerable praise. Angela Carter described *The Beet Queen* as imparting its 'freshness of vision like an electric shock'. Philip Roth said Erdrich was 'the most interesting new American novelist to have appeared in years'. Toni Morrison commended her 'devastating power' with its saving beauty. *The Beet Queen* and *Love Medicine* won the Critics Circle Award for Fiction (1985), and *The Beet Queen* won the Los Angeles Times award for best novel in the same year. Numerous other prizes have also been awarded to these novels. John Berger predicted Erdrich could be 'by the end of this century, a great world writer of whom the Chippewas can be proud'.

Erdrich's novels tend to take the form of what one might call a tissue of interwoven narratives with multiple points of view; each novel is interrelated to the others by means of characters who reappear from one book to another. Thus, from both within and without, these novels problematize notions of unity and autonomy: they are constructed out of stories which appeared as separate entities, and they expand and develop beyond the boundaries of each 'novel'. Boundaries are eroded further, first as Erdrich's novels merge into a tribal document of Chippewa life in twentieth-century USA, and second as the recent history of a land and a people crowds into the fiction. In the final section of *Tracks*, the felling of the trees is symbolic of a whole wilderness and way of life falling to civilization. The white man's aggression is portrayed as a destructive will both in physical nature and in the realm of the spirit, as the Chippewa woman, Fleur Adcock, engineers her almost incredible spiritual rebellion against white material progress desecrating her natural world. Erdrich's novels constitute a rewriting of twentieth-century American history, as 'reality' is seen through the eyes of Chippewa individuals. Yet she never romanticizes or idealizes; her characters are drunkards, murderers, debauched men and wild women, but their essential humanity is, as happens in Jean Rhys's novels, explored and revealed with insight and conviction.

Whatever horrors her characters may have perpetrated, and they are many, Erdrich convinces the reader that these are ordinary people, with ordinary passions and needs, often driven, however, by extraordinary frustrations. These may arise from natural disasters, such as illness and drought, or from personal circumstances; but they often come from the paternalistic, interfering and petty cruelty of the American government towards its Indian inhabitants. Erdrich shows these historical-social-economic conflicts, while she also rips away the stereotypes and classifications which blind people to the humanity of others. Her characters, moreover, are so individualistic that they border on the eccentric; but it is in part their eccentricity which devolves a profoundly interesting individuality upon them. The tone of the novels is congruent with this eccentric originality, and Erdrich uses comedy and absurdity to convey the trials of ordinary living, from the agony of adolescence to the extreme frustration of old age. Loss, illness, madness, death and the destruction of an entire culture are charted with so much imaginative detachment that we laugh without restraint as Erdrich infuses events with the quality of controlled folly characteristic of wise men and gurus throughout the ages, who are able to maintain gaiety in the face of great misfortune.

Time stalks through Erdrich's stories like the grim reaper, while its very structure is often ripped away in the gaps and spaces that are the substance of our lives. The ultimate betrayer is not so much death (though it *can* be) as love: again and again, characters struggle with the conflicting needs of intimacy with others versus solitude and self-definition. Erdrich never seems to bother with people who abjure intimacy for a life of peace; her characters are those who have the courage to face the conflicts arising inevitably from the differences amongst people, and who try in the midst of that tragic conflict to create bonds which, nevertheless, give depth and intensity to life. Time and again her stories relate the inordinate determination of highly individualized people to accept discord, both for the sake of intimate relationship and out of the knowledge that harmony without clash is almost always bought at the price of intimacy. Unlike many English novelists, then, Erdrich rarely attends to the concealed destructiveness of 'contractual' relationships so common in much British life. Her characters are those who explore the extremes of love and hate, and are far more alive because of it than those who walk through life on eggshells. Consequently, we find ourselves in the presence of people who, for all their unpleasantness, violence, verbal abuse, promiscuity and drunkenness, are courageously loving and vigorously alive as individualities.

For Erdrich, as for many writers, the place or location of her fiction (in her case North Dakota) is the point of view of all her narratives. The feeling her novels portray emanates from the vividness of her depiction of the locale, which is part of the very life of these stories. In *The Beet Queen*, for example, the little town of Argus, North Dakota, is as original as the amazing characters of that novel, as original as the absurd yet utterly real events; Argus is the distinctive crossroad of circumstance, the gateway to reality. Distinctness of location becomes a metaphor for the fact that reality can be found not in the typical or average or stereotyped, but in particularity; in the concrete alone, for Erdrich, is universality to be experienced, in contrast to abstraction and generality. Her towns and reservations create the effect of unfolding around the reader to reveal a whole world of plain, ordinary life as a cornucopia of comedy, tragedy and absurdity, and infinitely interesting.

One of the central themes which structure Erdrich's novels is the natural world as a symbol or even metonym for the human spirit. This is particularly central to her third novel, *Tracks*, which takes on William Faulkner-like dimensions in exploring the relationship between the demise of the wilderness and the dehumanization of civil life. The rape of nature by white Americans is explored as self-mutilation of the human spirit and imagination: the possession of dead objects takes precedence in life over experience, relationship and fulfilment of genuine human needs. Erdrich's novels explore the alternative to consumerism and competition, namely, the cooperation and conservation characteristic of humans pitted against a nature so threatening that non-cooperation means death. These novels reveal competition to be an immature form of social relationship, and consumerism a perversion and extreme form of the natural need to store goods for a winter or a drought. Yet Erdrich shows no nostalgia or idealization of the Chippewa, as individuals; many of them are as immature and selfish as the white people. If there is a difference, it lies not in some sentimental notion that American Indians are less corruptible than others, but in the implicit suggestion that immature competitiveness and selfish consumerism have not been institutionalized in Chippewa social structure as they have in white American society. This may be because the divorce between nature and society has been delayed amongst Indians by the demands of survival in an environment different from the white American one.

Erdrich's novels reinforce the careful balance between community and individual, social and natural; they unfold as that interlocking tissue of narratives about (and narrated by) an interlocking complex of individuals. Unlike many novels and short stories, which take a single individual and explore her or his experiences, character or moral transformation, Erdrich's texts place individuals within a whole nest of relationships, so that the novels are about a whole community. Individuality is neither sacrificed to nor subsumed under the force of the communal: the two are finely balanced, as intensely individualistic, even eccentric characters are sharply focused and realized, but within a context of communal life. Erdrich develops the idea that the social and the individual are themselves interlocking entities (like her stories), totally incapable of existing without each other: the notion of the absolutely individual, primitive, asocial human is absurd. Society – and its condition, language – are part of human individuality, and this interdependence is realized in the structure of her novels, as Erdrich has created a genre quite different from that of the traditional novel, though not without precedents.

This is not to suggest that individuals do not play large roles, indeed at times heroic ones. Put another way, Erdrich does not achieve her integration by pitting a hero or heroine against a Greek chorus or a society. Rather, she takes the individual chorus members or social individuals and reveals the heroic dimensions of their existence, as they battle for survival and fulfilment, yet without privileging any one individual. The lives of her characters are so utterly interwoven with each other for their very significance that, even when a character steps forward briefly to have her or his say, she or he drags the whole community with her or him. Individuality cannot appear, unlike in so much of the European novel tradition, without its interconnection to other individuals. That Erdrich has realized this thematic content in the structure of her novels is part of their power as artistic achievements. It may also be an aspect not only of an American Indian point of view, but of a certain female point of view, this tendency towards balance, integration and realization of individual fulfilment through cooperation and communality, as opposed to competitiveness and self-development at the expense of others. Yet Erdrich's novels never oversimplify: they explore the dilemma that while self-development must occur if a group is to survive, rampant individualism will destroy the group and the individual as much as the stifling of individuality ensures the society's demise. Perhaps her writing can be said to analyse the forms which the obstacles to this necessary balance take, and the ways people find of overcoming them, as well as the reasons why we often fail to do so.

Jeanette Winterson 1959–

A graduate in English literature from Oxford, Winterson was born in Lancashire and now lives in London. Author of numerous novels, she has also written a guide for fitness and health, *Fit for the Future* (London, 1986). Her first novel, *Oranges Are Not the Only Fruit* (London, 1985), won the Whitbread Award. Made into a BBC television adaptation (for which she won a BAFTA award for best drama), *Oranges* deals with religious obsession and an adolescent girl's escape from the sexist dogmas of Christianity into a lesbian romance. In the same year she published a comic novel about Doris, Gloria, Noah and a flood, entitled *Boating for Beginners* (London, 1985). Her next novel, *The Passion* (London, 1987), winner of the John Llewellyn Rhys prize, is set in Napoleonic times, and continues the parody of the historical romance begun in *Boating*, as well as Winterson's own variation on 'magic realism'. Winner of the E.M. Forster award, *Sexing the Cherry* (London, 1989) develops further her narrative style of historical fantasy and farce, set as it is in a picaresque, notional, seventeenth-century England. As in *The Passion*, multiple narrative perspectives are used to create a legendary, mythical – yet historical – past, which ends in an imaginative leap into the present, as did *Boating*. Another recent novel, *Written on the Body* (London, 1992), returns to techniques and times more similar to those of *Oranges Are Not the Only Fruit* than the 'picaresque realism' of the middle three novels. Its continuous, unified, first person narrative, its theme of love, responsibility, guilt and illness, and its setting in the England of the 1980s do not obscure its originality, as Winterson's characteristic wit and playfulness are evident in the intricacy and virtuosity of her handling of both style and thematic elements, both in this and in her most recent novel, *Art and Lies* (London, 1994).

In a 1991 'introduction' to *Oranges Are Not the Only Fruit*, Winterson made several remarks which help readers to come to grips with her innovations. She first explained that while she could tolerate cold, poverty, discomfort, hunger and trauma (all of which she experienced in London in the early 1980s), she could not tolerate 'dinginess': 'Dinginess is death to a writer . . . dinginess, the damp small confines of the mediocre and the gradual corrosion of beauty and light.' These statements are 'echoes' of Willa Cather's passionate outcry against mediocrity as the true enemy of the spirit; they help to account to some degree for the vibrant colour and fresh imagery of Winterson's style. Indeed, the often apparently gratuitous adventurousness of these novels – their whimsical thematic gestures, the 'boiling over' of the fantastic, and the almost bizarre inventiveness of the situations, characters, dialogue and events – is a large gesture which 'staves off that dinginess of soul that says that everything is small and grubby and nothing is really worth the effort'. Like Susan Glaspell in, for example, *Trifles*, Winterson has attacked with Cather-like, primitive energy the destructive forces of depression and its close relative, passivity, which earlier writers like Blake and Nietzsche abhorred.

Winterson went on to explain that *Oranges* was neither an accident, nor an experiment, nor a whim: 'it was a downstream force by a high wind . . . as though the book was already written.' She argued for its originality in structure, style and content, explaining that she wanted to write an 'anti-linear' narrative. This 'complicated narrative structure, described as a simple one', can be read, she proposed, 'in spirals' – like Shelley's 'Adonais', which invokes the spiralling movement as an image of imaginative progression versus discursive, logical, linear progression. Like many other writers of the twentieth century, Winterson has sought to break out of the arbitrary order of realist, forward-moving plots, though of course the best realist novels have the same kind of networking, spiralling, or resonating effect as does non-realist fiction. For, as Winterson has argued, our thinking and our language do not go along in straight lines – they are more like a maze, a labyrinth, 'every turning yielding another turning, not symmetrical, not obvious. Not chaos either.'

Nearly all of Winterson's novels give us a fresh, new look at a lot of old structures, institutions and attitudes. She has made her themes the exposure of the sanctity of the family by revealing the rot within it; she has exposed the pretensions of the church by revealing their inherent sexism as a contradiction in the fundamentals of faith; and she has revealed the perversity of conventional sexual behaviour and attitudes by showing romantic love as a 'chamber of horrors', to use Angela Carter's phrase. Winterson has indirectly examined the literary

tradition, too, and proceeded to disrupt and disturb with her originality as described above.

Sexing the Cherry is one of her most accomplished novels, with its picaresque and extravagant method of exploring the very nature of time and place, fact and fiction. And explore it she does, as her characters are portrayed journeying through history, across the world, and over the boundaries of fact, into fairy tale and legend, memory, fantasy, dream and desire. No borders are respected, as Winterson has written in Jorge Luis Borges-like parables about journeys within journeys, futures within pasts, time and space as meaningless, and the self as merely the intersection of a time and place wherein it might catch a glimpse of itself vanishing through a door. Like Borges, Winterson has explored these paradoxes, and revealed to us the contamination of reality by dreams, the nature of the self as an unknowable, fictional double, the nature of artifacts as always eluding the grasp of the reader, and the nature of life itself as nothing so much as a story.

On the first page of *Sexing the Cherry*, we find: 'Every journey conceals another journey within its lines: the path not taken and the forgotten angle. These are journeys I wish to record. Not the ones I made, but the ones I might have made, or perhaps did make in some other place or time.' These three sentences are an apt emblem of the novel itself, as the borderline between reality and fantasy, present and past, memory and perception is erased. As readers, we are presented with a Marguerite Young-like reality, made up of nothing so much as dreams, desires, fantasies, inaccurate memories and fictions of the present. For Winterson, as for Young, the most real thing about reality is how fictional it is. The journey metaphor – that ancient literary convention for imaginative states of consciousness – becomes one of the central motifs of Winterson's novels, as she has explored the Kantean categories of time and space and in her own unique way created a Borges-like fiction: 'Time has no meaning, space and place have no meaning, on this journey. All times can be inhabited, all places visited. In a single day the mind can make a millpond of the ocean . . . The journey is not linear, it is always back and forth, denying the calendar.' Later, Winterson has described the human self as only 'in the intersection of moment and place', and, like the meaning of the novel for the reader, the self too can only be seen for a moment, 'vanishing through a door, which disappears at once'.

Moreover, she has explained that the self and one's own life are 'squashed between the facts', and that one's life is written invisibly, hidden between the visible lines, as in the following image of the human self as a letter: 'For the Greeks, the hidden life demanded invisible ink. They wrote an ordinary letter and in between the lines set out another letter, written in milk. The document looked innocent enough until one who knew better sprinkled coal-dust over it.' Life as a letter, with a concealed document between its lines, functions as a powerful metaphor on several further levels. Winterson has implicated her novel as just such a document, and even equated the human mind, language and art generally with such an emblem, drawing upon modern theories of autobiography, Roland Barthes's idea of desire as meaning, Jacques Derrida's emphasis upon the trace, and Jacques Lacan's image of the vanishing self, the self as site where events occur, not as substance.

In *Sexing the Cherry*, Winterson has been at her most provocative; the novel, with its sudden collapse at the end into a present, contemporary framework portrayed as a double exposure (as characters, themes and events of the past keep intruding), suggests an alternative novel, just as the tales, dreams and fantasies of the characters Jordan and Dog-Woman keep veering off into paths that might have been taken. Sometimes Jordan seems like a fantasy of Dog-Woman, his foster mother, sometimes she an invention of his. Everywhere unities are broken up and certainties collapse, as Winterson's novel tells the story of a labyrinthine narrative which is life itself; meaning for the reader vanishes 'through a door, which disappears at once'. The novel is about nothing so much as the reality of fiction as our most real 'reality'.

A.L. Kennedy 1960?–

Winner of the John Llewellyn Rhys Prize for her collection of short stories (her first book),

Night Geometry and the Garscadden Trains (Edinburgh, 1990), Kennedy was born in Dundee and lives in Glasgow. Her story collection also won the Scotsman Saltire Award, and was soon followed by her novel *Looking for the Possible Dance* (Edinburgh, 1993), which gained her selection as one of the Best British Novelists under 40. Described further as one of the most promising of recent Scottish writers, praised by her critics for her warmth and humanity, and said to have an austere and intense talent, Kennedy has explored truth, lies, deceit, honesty and love in characters' efforts to escape their fear that 'Nothing of what we did was ever new.' She has explored ways of articulating the paradox that while we repeat the roles of wife, mother, lover, 'wounded wife, wicked wife', at that very moment we can feel most ourselves, and never even notice the stereotypes and clichés into which we have fallen. Her stories scrutinize the way stereotyped role playing destroys originality and character. Her recent publications *Now That You're Back* (London, 1994) and *So I am Glad* (London, 1995) confirm Kennedy as a major new writer of fiction in the 1990s.

The stories in *Night Geometry* are overtly concerned with showing fiction as valuable not because it is mimetic of reality or a record of the truth or even historically accurate:

> This is no more than a story about Grandmother, because it cannot be the truth . . . Time divides me from my mother and her mother and her mother and beyond them there are lines and lines of women who are nothing more than shadows in my bones. As you read this, I am somewhere else, so this is a story.

This theme is carried throughout Kennedy's writings, as she has struggled with the paradox that 'nothing is less believable than the truth.' Moreover, her fiction sets itself the deliberate task of writing about 'the people who are too small to record. They disappear and leave the past inhabited only by murderesses and prodigies and saints.' In 'The Role of Notable Silences in Scottish History', Kennedy's first person narrator tells the story of her obsession with writing obituaries of ordinary, living people.

One of these, a man who becomes her friend, is murdered in a bar, and she remarks at the end of the story: 'Our city and us inside it and time and me inside us. I should write descriptions of them all, but everyone knows I lie too much . . . My only contribution on the subject is already here: the obituary I wrote him before we first met. It is inaccurate.'

This story is Kennedy's most explicit and systematic experiment with post-modernist techniques. She has made typical post-modernist gestures of self-referentiality, constantly discussing writing and reading as forms of deceit, lying or plagiarism. Her first person narrator is a typical figure in both modernism and post-modernism (comparable to the narrator in, for example, Katherine Mansfield's short story, 'Je Ne Parle Pas Français'), obsessed with the impossibility of telling the truth, with an acute self-consciousness, and with writing 'false' obituaries – that is, fictional accounts of the deaths of acquaintances. Sometimes they come true. Genre violations occur, as the story passes itself off as an autobiographical account, while the 'author' is the author of this book as well. Thus, fact intrudes into fiction and ontological levels are confused, leading to the radical instability for the reader of any fixed, 'true' account. Moreover, the subject matter of the story is reading and writing; it is about words and meaning, with writing being implied to be simply a reinscription of what has already been read. Kennedy has used the post-modernist device of mixing into her fictional narrative long, non-fiction, disruptive passages 'excerpted' from, say, her work for the transport authority or from the work of other writers about, for example, murder, slaughter and Scottish history. Other stories, like 'The Seaside Photographer', 'Night Geometry', and 'Translations', exhibit her ability to make such devices function in the service of less obviously self-referential themes, themes of love, infidelity and efforts to express ordinary people. Yet she has never ceased to scrutinize the meaning of basic concepts, and their instability in the face of such scrutiny.

In her second book, *Looking for the Possible Dance*, Kennedy has adopted traditional literary and thematic conventions, such as journeys and celebrations, as the structure of her texts, in a strikingly original and compelling novel focused upon the efforts of a man and woman, Colin and Margaret, to build a meaningful relationship, without resorting to the stifling roles and stereotypes which make human differences bearable. After a brief narrative of a significant event in Margaret's childhood involving her father, Kennedy has introduced the metaphor of a train journey south from Scotland to London, and this journey of Margaret's, which runs all the way to the end of the book, structures, unifies and enriches the narrative. The complexity of the novel is notable: it proceeds overtly on several narrative levels. First, the train journey itself is a significant thematic element, involving a disabled, autistic child with whom Margaret communicates in an emotionally charged series of numerous, discrete but progressive scenes. It is repeatedly interrupted by other levels of narration. A second level is the story of Colin and Margaret, presented by Kennedy in a series of passages which do not respect progressive time order, so that the reader often has to struggle with 'placing' these events in some chronology. Indeed, at this thematic level, an early scene is repeated almost word for word nearly two hundred pages later. As with the first thematic level, the subtext is also self-referential; that is, communication, words, language, speech, writing and reading are its subject matter. The third thematic structure which dominates and shapes the novel, along with these other two complex ones, is Margaret's relationship with her father, especially as a young child, but also as a young adult. Reading this novel, one almost has the sense of reading three novels at once, beautifully interwoven yet also impressively autonomous.

A further symbolic rather than specifically narrative, thematic or structural element is the metaphor of the dance. It recurs throughout the novel and gains strength from its allusion to longstanding metaphoric associations, such as W.B. Yeats used in his 'Among School Children'. Kennedy has used the emblem of the dance to draw together life and art, as imaginative loving is metaphorized in the figure of an art form. The further motif in the novel, of the quest or journey for imaginative, loving relationships, enriches her account as the dance metaphor is reversed, so that imaginative loving becomes the figure for the writing of fiction. Analogously, the quest of

Kennedy, the author, for an 'original' voice and an artifact of beauty is 'written in' to the theme of the novel through the metaphor and emblem of the dance, then, as a figure both of writing imaginatively and of loving imaginatively. That is, the dance draws all three independent yet related narratives together, into a powerful, symbolic complex of great emotional force as well. Indeed, by the end of the novel, what is only implicit in the figure of the dancing father is made explicit in the last words of the text, namely, that life itself, as lived imaginatively, is figured in the dance. In Kennedy's case, it is the dance made possible by words:

> The late sun outside the station is very strong and from a distance its doorways seem white, more like curtains of white than ways made through walls and into light. Margaret walks to one door and sinks into brilliant air, becoming first a moving shadow, then a curve, a dancing line.

Part V

Theory, Further Reading and Research

Chapter 13

Feminist Theory and Feminist Writing

In addition to the transformation of English literature by the new international literatures in Englishes, feminist theory (along with post-structuralism) has been another major post-war development. It shares with international English literature many issues and debates, often sharpening these further in the process of focusing them specifically on women's writings and writing about women. The two dominant strains of recent feminist theory, Anglo-American and Continental (especially French), share a number of concerns, which include, for example, examining how women have been represented in literature. The effects of long-unquestioned stereotypes, whether portrayed by male or by female authors, are shown to be literary, social, moral and political – and personal. The influence of much literature which has uncritically accepted sexist stereotypes of women has been exposed in feminist theory to be far-reaching and effective in perpetuating social injustice, domestic exploitation and poor self-images. This scrutiny of the 'literary representation of women' constituted an early (and continuing) stage of feminist literary criticism, and was soon complemented by the more radical insistence on recovering and analysing texts by women, as well as about them. For the former exercise perpetuated the giving of exclusive attention to male writers, in the main, restricting itself in general to canonical works. The new stage, of recovering and reassessing literatures by women, marked a genuine advancement of feminist theory. Its results were decisive, as it challenged male

dominance of the canon and of critical theory. Later still, feminists began challenging the idea of the canon itself as a categorization demonstrably based on prejudice, from sexism to racism and homophobia, and quite inappropriate in professional study. The argument for a canon based on 'purely literary' considerations, while questionable even in theory, has certainly never worked in practice, as the recovery of dozens of works of literature by women, equal to male writings even in their own 'purely literary' terms, proves. Both post-structuralist theory and international English literatures show that 'literary' traits are always applied in politicized and partial ways, and not objectively, as early critics pretended.

As literary justifications for a canon of masterpieces were exposed as the subjectively applied preferences of certain classes of people, the canon not only grew to include previously marginalized texts. It has now, in recent years, begun to collapse under the pressure of inclusiveness, and is looking more than ever like an unnecessary prejudice. There is no substitute for wide-ranging reading, no possibility that reliance on academic or critical authorities can be an alternative to educating oneself, and no need for the lover of literature to bow in obedience to other's preferences. Texts can be valued and even evaluated, but never in an objective, purely literary realm. Texts are valuable within specific contexts and in different but equally relevant ways, even within the relative category of the literary or the aesthetic. The more widely one reads, the more one becomes aware of the range of literary forms and practices which make texts valuable for a diversity of aesthetic and social purposes. For the aesthetic is tied up within all our communal activities.

Another aspect of the feminist examination of canon has been an almost revolutionary re-evaluation of women authors, many of whom, it turns out, were highly regarded in their own time before being consigned to oblivion. Many of their less gifted male contemporaries were kept in circulation by male reviewers, critics, publishers, editors, academics and readers. Along with this revaluation of earlier women writers has come the exposure of prejudices about what makes good literature. Prejudices about thematics, characterization, genre, style, structure and diction – in short, practically all aspects of writing – have been shown up as the non-literary partialities, in practice at least, of a small group of men with considerable influence over what counts as 'literature'. These latter have put into question the value of literature which attends preeminently to emotional life, domestic life and women heroines who do not fit stereotypes, and which does not attend enough to war, politics and the public events of the time; of literature which draws overtly on autobiographical elements, or which uses genres of the diary, the journal and other kinds of 'personal' writing not 'transformed by superior powers of imagination'; and so on. (See Joanna Russ for a few dozen techniques for suppressing women's writing!)

Results of these feminist criticisms have included the emphasis upon the authority of women's experience, as not mere subjectivity, emotionalism, hysteria or personal notions, while men's experience is no longer characterized as more objective, rational, tasteful and imaginative, the material of true genius. While women have been learning to value more highly their own experiences and have been learning to see the world and themselves differently, they began quickly to realize that few gains could be made by setting up female experience as objective, and reversing privileges from male to female. This reversal could be called the 'feminism of difference', but it seemed that another solution might be to argue for equal rights for women to social opportunities and commodities previously held mainly by men. This second alternative we could call the 'feminism of equality'. Yet the hollowness of this goal has also begun to reveal itself, as women discover the drawbacks of male values, male ways of living or working, and male ways of interacting. That is, women, recent theorists have suggested, cannot gain control of their lives and escape stereotypes which imprison them into often inappropriate and even maddening roles until they refuse to see either themselves or the world through the eyes of men. They must learn to disassemble the views which are passed off as nature, fact and truth, and explore what they and the world are capable of beyond these limited partialities.

The first set of truths they must confront is that bequeathed to them by their fathers, often verified by their mothers. This could be called a 'feminism of community', the third stage of theory and practice beyond feminisms of difference and of equality, which yet draws upon them and uses them in appropriate contexts. This third analysis has much in common with existentialist projects, since it involves the potent idea of self-fashioning, and rejects notions of a prior human nature. Thus, women were learning not only to reject male views of themselves, and male representations of 'woman'; they later learnt to reject male views of the world, society, literature and values generally. Feminist theorists realize, moreover, that women need to liberate themselves not only from sexist notions; they must forge new, humane, communal values and realities different from those presented by the fathers.

Parallel to these developments were the insights into art and literature which they implied. No longer were women coerced into trying to write like men, adopting their themes, styles and practices. One issue which dominated feminist thinking in the early part of the century was whether women had a language or style of writing distinct from a male one. Was there a feminine (or masculine) sentence, and if so, what were its characteristics? While numerous feminists mused about this 'characteristic feminine style', Virginia Woolf suggested that writing is better understood as androgynous, using the male/female aspects within every psyche. Woolf's idea of androgyny is at the basis of much liberating thinking about gender, sexuality and social/literary/political issues today, for it began the twentieth-century project of unravelling the sacred dualisms which shore up most prejudices. That is, while literary canons have been attacked, while male and female text evaluations have been radically reconstrued, and while stereotypes of women and literary prejudices have been brought to light as untenable, feminist theory has kept moving into new debates opened up by the spur of androgyny. Gender, sexuality, identity, the status of the subject as unitary or split, the nature of the self, the relations of author, reader, critic and text – all these issues have been rewritten into feminist theory, once androgyny revealed the opposition within every concept as its very substance. Nothing is homogeneous and seamless, no one is just male or female, just author or reader, just self or other, just heterosexual or gay, just creative or uncreative, just exploiter or victim, and so on. While post-structuralist writers were theorizing this exposure of the falsity of a literal interpretation of dualistic categories, feminists and internationalists were – in a continuous drawing upon psychological, modernist and pragmatist insights of the early twentieth century – revealing the functional and relative nature of all dualisms. Not only are all concepts intelligible only in relation to their opposites, but the tension between opposites is the only substantive meaning of any concept.

These and other theorizings about language and psychology provided the powerful tool for feminism and internationalist literary theory mentioned in previous sections. Namely, concepts and attitudes passed off as natural and factual, biological and true, are mere social constructs, and these constructions can be changed. The 'natural attitude', as we named it, which pretends that works of social art are nature-independent, must be dismantled and shown to be illusion. No truth, value, belief or thing is exempt from scrutiny and from change; our most cherished ideals and our most closely guarded beliefs may turn out to be damaging clichés in need of replacement. The early Woolfian insight that all dualisms are relational does not mean, however, that there is a substantive essence or *tertium aliquid* of which they are the poles. Feminist criticism has still been struggling with this idea of essentialism, found in the early twentieth-century musings about the feminine sentence, for example. French theorists in particular, such as Hélène Cixous and Luce Irigaray, have been encumbered by a fascination with the idea of some essential womanliness which constitutes our identity. This had its counterpart in internationalist debates about ethnicity and nationhood, with essentialist ideas about these aspects of identity emerging repeatedly in the effort to preserve the differences between people which are valued.

These recurring essentialist notions, which apply to the nature of identity and the status of the subject, have taken the form of puzzling questions in femininist theory such as 'Does woman exist?' and 'What is woman, and what does she want?' Freud had posed the latter question, while half a century later Julia Kristeva was suggesting the answer 'No' to the first one. Contemporaneously, Michel Foucault was positing that sexuality and gender have been allowed to dominate this century's conception of the self and of identity too unquestioningly, as nationhood and tribalism, or religion and race, had done in the past. Kristeva has repeatedly insisted that we need to examine our concept of identity more articulately, while avoiding essentialisms. Even in her writings there is a tendency, however, to emphasize the aspect of identity signified by the word 'individuality', with a neglect of identity as conceived in its social, communal participation. We can hardly 'deconstruct sexualized binary thought' or 'patriarchal metaphysics' by deconstructing identity, if we forget or repress the fact that identity is not individuality only, but also participatory relationship. This has as an analogy the insistence by Juliet Mitchell that we need to accept the idea of the unconscious as an undeniable meaning of consciousness.

Feminist theory has opened up other fascinating areas of debate in recent decades. One of the most productive has been theorizing about autobiographical writings, and how they relate to exclusive definitions of 'literature'. Because many women have written letters, diaries, journals, memoirs, autobiographical fiction, *romans-à-clef* and other 'inferior' writings not usually accorded the status of literature, women critics have begun to insist upon a reassessment of what constitutes literature, who decides, and why. With post-structuralists attacking the 'law of literature' in similar ways if for different immediate purposes, feminist theorists have initiated a fascinating area of discussion of the role of autobiography in all writings, whether well-disguised fiction and criticism or openly self-revealing texts. Texts are now being included in the category 'literature' which were excluded before, such as the magnificent diaries of Alice James, Anaïs Nin and Woolf, the autobiographies of Dora Russell, Maya Angelou, Vera Brittain, Sylvia Plath, Simone de Beauvoir, Sally Morgan and Mary E. Wilkins Freeman, the travel writings of Mary Kingsley, Isabella Bird, Gertrude Bell, Beryl Markham and Edith Wharton, the political writings of Rebecca West and Susan Sontag, the (few surviving) letters of Jane Austen, Charlotte Brontë, Anne Stevenson and Emily Dickinson, the autobiographical fiction of H.D., Antonia White, Agnes Smedley and Elizabeth Smart, the alleged autobiographical fiction of Jean Rhys, Zelda Fitzgerald, Dorothy Richardson and Kay Boyle, the parodic 'autobiography' of Alice B. Toklas, the journals of Dorothy Wordsworth, Mary Shelley, Sylvia Ashton-Warner and Katherine Mansfield, and the memoirs of Rosamond Lehmann, Elizabeth Hardwick, Lillian Hellman and Ellen Glasgow, to name only a few. This debate about the relation of autobiography and fiction and the resulting questioning of the exclusion of such non-fiction from 'literature' may tell us something about the prejudices of our own times. For the concept of 'letters' always included a wide variety of writing, and did not privilege fiction, drama and poetry in the way that twentieth-century critics have done, to the detriment of 'non-fiction'.

This feminist challenge to the concept 'literature' has been characterized by a blurring of the boundary between imaginative writing and non-fiction, as well as the above-noted re-evaluation of the intrinsic literary merit of non-fictional writings. Like post-structuralist theory, feminist theorists have debunked the purity of literature and imaginative writings, and shown it to be stratified with autobiography, criticism and non-fiction. This hybridity and heterogeneity has come to be seen as not a mere supplement to but a fundamental characteristic of 'literature' or 'écriture'. Such border crossings between genres, such transgressions of boundaries, are designed not merely to produce hybrid results, then, but to show the hybridity and impurity of all writings. The most apparently pure poetry or fiction

can be shown to be a mosaic or patchwork of personal, biographical and historical material, as well as including critical dimensions which refer to the text itself and to its reader.

Another intensely interesting area of feminist literary criticism has been the re-reading of texts to reveal possibilities for subversive interpretations which had been denied or repressed. Where specific texts are concerned, however, it is striking that only a few women critics have challenged prevailing readings as far as they could. In the case of such mainstream writers as Austen, Charlotte Brontë and Willa Cather, for example, the sheer power of prior interpretations and prior attitudes may be the limiting factor in much revisionary reading. Once a view of Austen, for example, as a certain type of woman (obedient and well behaved) is established, certain readings of her texts emerge which strictly enforce limits to the extent to which her irony can operate, her sarcasm can be acknowledged or her texts' rejection of marriage can be countenanced. Presented as acquiescing, basically, in the social system she described in her novels, Austen, then, cannot be the author of texts which go very far in the criticism of her times. Yet, a fresher reading of her novels not based on such questionable, unsubstantiated biographical material reveals an irony, if we choose to see it, which is scathingly explosive of the marriage contracts, the treatment of women as commodities of exchange and pieces of property, the nonsense pedalled about romance and infatuation as able to provide the basis for life-long relationships, or the institutionalized restriction of women's talents to domestic, non-intellectual activities. Otherwise we not only ignore contextual information which challenges these views (Austen never married; she devoted her life to writing novels; she wrote some very acerbic and critical letters which so tarnished the image of the nice lady that the worst were burnt, but what remains is very telling, and certainly not from the pen of the obedient conformist she has been made out to be); we also ignore the evidence of the texts, for when Austen's irony is not shrunk into the allowable sphere of merely local elements, events or characters, it expands into the whole of the novels, and the texts become a scathing indictment of the sexism, snobbery and preoccupation with money of male–female relations.

Charlotte Brontë's *Jane Eyre* is supposed to be another one of those anti-feminist texts written by a brainwashed genius. Often appropriated by various critics for nearly a hundred and fifty years as a purveyor of male notions of how devoted women should behave, women have been slow in revising these establishment readings. For those who see the text as profoundly, suggestively subversive, what does it say about the power to endure of patriarchal appropriations of such texts that this novel has not been clearly revealed as yet another ruthlessly critical anti-colonialist, anti-patriarchal, anti-missionary text? *Must* one really read Bertha's incarceration as a mad woman in the attic as Brontë approving of colonialism and woman hatred? *Must* one discount Brontë's early description of Jane Eyre's ghastly, orphaned childhood as an effort to explain how women can become so desperate for romantic protectors? *Must* one interpret Jane's courageous rejection of the egotist St John Rivers and the missionary servitude he offered her as weakness originating in foolish infatuation for Rochester? The last quarter of the novel, devoted as it is to the Rivers scenario, establishes clearly the difference between a loveless marriage of servitude and an alternative of companionship with the disabled husband. Apparently, *Jane Eyre* was subversive enough to inspire Rhys's *Wide Sargasso Sea* (1966), but is the latter more subversive and critical? Or can it not be read as revealing a dimension of Charlotte Brontë's text previously obscured by critical blindness? At the same time, Emily Brontë was writing a remarkably subversive, unfeminine text, with another colonial representative, another Bertha figure, Heathcliff. These figures of the 'Other' are woven into the texts so intimately that they suggest the otherness *within* the identity of Englishness, much as Joseph Conrad was to do fifty years later. (Yet Edward Said and other readers cannot see the criticism of imperialism written into every line of *Heart of Darkness* (1902), *Lord Jim* (1900) and *Victory* (1915).)

Feminist theory, post-colonial literary theory, ethnic and race theory, post-structuralist theory and queer theory interact in creative ways to reinforce each other's projects, even as they focus on the specifics of their particular interests. In addition to recovering texts, re-reading texts, and revising evaluations, canons and principles of literary criticism, each of these areas seeks to theorize about what constitutes literariness and literary excellence, and how their specific identity issues can best be formulated. One of the other central issues for all these groups is the question of how one writes freely in the language which has marginalized some and centred others. Ideas about how to use this language against itself for creative purposes involve heteroglossia, distanciation, defamiliarization and estrangement, combined with irony, parody and mimicry as well as pastiche, mosaic and collage, including indecorous mixtures of tone, genre, style and diction. Feminist theorists have been particularly interested in parody and mimicry (as have post-colonialists) as a means of escaping from the confines of the language used for oppression and silencing. Heteroglossia is also useful for women writers; culture is seen as inherently a multitude of diverse verbal and ideological systems, of the conflicting values of various groups within a non-unitary, inharmonious 'centre'. Culture is not a single, determinant, dominant voice, according to this theory; the rejection of language as a monolithic, homogeneous entity belonging to one class of people reduces the 'problem' of how to write in patriarchal language to a pseudo-problem. For the language is not inherently patriarchal; it is only constructed as such in part, and those parts can be disassembled to promote new perspectives. One uses the language of the centre to escape its domination, because the language never belonged to the centre alone. Women are discovering that they never have been silent: they do not have to learn to speak, because they have always already written and spoken. Perhaps they need to learn to read their own literature and listen to each other more, instead of believing the fictions they are told, that women have only a little literature worth reading and a little worth saying.

Distanciation and irony are means of attending to the performative aspect of literary criticism as well, revealing that the content is often rhetorical obfuscation. That is, much literary criticism is a mass of performance designed to obscure the privileging norms and excluding ideologies which further patriarchy. (Similarly, much psychoanalysis is an obfuscation of the profound fear men have of the creative powers

321

of women's bodies to produce children, whose father, moreover, is unknown. Perhaps patriarchy and the exchange of women have their basis in this problem of paternity, and in the miracle of child-bearing.) Reading strategies, interpretative practices and writing strategies are all under scrutiny, then, and one of the most vigorous debates in feminist theory has been about the extent to which sexuality as well as gender is constructed and hence alterable. While most writers accepted long ago the social relativity and arbitrariness of gender roles, and much literature by women thematized this, sexuality has been a more contentious issue. Numerous theorists have argued that our identity is not stable regarding sexual behaviour. Homosexuality and heterosexuality are relative and constructed. Queer theory and feminist writing have explored the question of biology and bodily differences. Even the body can be read as a text, it is argued, not merely a natural reality, for sex differences become meaningful and have consequences only when social attitudes and established practices come into play. The act of 'worlding' or 'authoring', as some critics have described perception and evaluation both, applies to the body in its most basic traits. Differences must first be selected as significant for certain ends to become 'real'. They accrue value as weaknesses or strengths, facilitating or obstructing characteristics, only as they are interpreted from a point of view.

Further reading

Belsey, C. and Moore, J., eds. *The Feminist Reader*. London, 1989.

Butler, Judith. *Gender Trouble*. London, 1990.

Christian, Barbara. *Black Feminist Criticism*. New York and Oxford, 1985.

Coward, Rosalind. *Patriarchal Precedents*. London, 1983.

Faludi, Susan. *Backlash*. New York, 1991.

Felski, Rita. *Beyond Feminist Aesthetics*. New York, 1990.

Gilbert, S.M. and Gubar, S. *No Man's Land*. 3 vols. New Haven, 1988, 1989, 1994.

Greene, Gayle and Kahn, Coppelia, eds. *Making a Difference*. London, 1985.

Humm, Maggie. *A Reader's Guide to Contemporary Feminist Criticism*. New York and London, 1994.

Humm, Maggie. *The Dictionary of Feminist Theory*. Rev. edn, New York and London, 1995.

Jacobus, Mary. *Reading Women*. London, 1986.

Jardine, Alice. *Gynesis*. Ithaca, N.Y., 1985.

Kaplan, Cora. *Sea Changes*. London, 1986.

Lovell, Terry, ed. *British Feminist Thought: A Reader*. Oxford, 1990.

Moi, Toril. *Sexual/Textual Politics*. London and New York, 1985.

Monteith, Moira, ed. *Women's Writing*. Brighton, 1986.

Rose, Jacqueline. *Sexuality in the Field of Vision*. London, 1986.

Sellers, Susan, ed. *Feminist Criticism*. Brighton, 1991.

Spacks, Patricia. *The Female Imagination*. London, 1976.

Chapter 14

More Women Writers World-Wide

As is evident from the preceding three hundred pages, the wealth of literature, and of information about this literature, is great enough to daunt even the most energetic explorer. The present critical guide being only an introduction to this vast country, one must conclude by directing the reader to more of the fascinating writers she or he will perhaps wish to explore, and to some of the innumerable research resources available to aid that exploration.

This chapter is geographically arranged and, by dealing last with Britain, Ireland and America, deliberately foregrounds what is usually marginalized. It gives the authors' dates of birth, with place and date of publication, wherever these have been reasonably accessible. Chapter 15 and section II of the bibliography use the same geographical divisions as this chapter, but place them in alphabetical order.

Africa

For example, a brief glance at the African continent reveals a number of novelists writing in English, such as the prolific Flora Nwapa (b. 1931), West African, Nigerian novelist of *Efuru* (London, 1966) and *Idu* (London, 1970), with her innovative use of 'choric language' and a highly verbalized narrative technique, in order to evoke the everyday, communal and collective reality of women's lives in Ibo villages. Through conversation and verbal self-representation, rather than through descriptive or objective

narrative authority, Nwapa has conveyed the lived reality of women as not marginal or trivial to their society, but the very ground and centre of lived existence. Her rejections of realist conventions of plot, description and causal narrative representation constitute not a flaw, not a 'failure of narrative complexity', but a decision on how best artistically to verbalize experiences different from those of male perceptions. Other Nigerian writers include Simi Bedford (b. 1942), with her *Yoruba Girl Dancing* (London, 1991), and Hauwa Ali with *Victory* (1989), which portrays the experience of Nigerian Muslims. Catherine Acholonu (b. 1951) and Funmilayo Fakunle may use more traditional narrative practices, but still achieve unusual effects, as when mixing present and past through powerful memory sequences and transcending time. Ifeoma Okoye's *Behind the Clouds* (Harlow, 1982) and *Men Without Ears* (London, 1984) and Zaynab Alkali's *The Stillborn* (Harlow, 1984) and *A Virtuous Woman* (Harlow, 1987) add to the variety of Nigerian writing appearing in recent decades. Both novelists explore the lives of girls and women through interesting, often non-linear narratives. Guyanese-born Karen King-Aribisala, who now lives in Lagos, is the author of *Our Wife* (Lagos, 1980), a collection of short stories.

From Kenya, Miriam Were (b. 1940), with *The Eighth Wife* (1972), and Marjorie Macgoye (b. 1928), with the prize-winning *Coming to Birth* (London, 1986), have explored the painful process of self-creation and nationhood. Another Kenyan, Evelyn Ayoda (b. 1956), who now lives in the USA, has published numerous stories in the East African magazine *Drum*, as has Barbara Kimenye (b. 1940), whose stories are collected in *Kalasanda* (London and Nairobi, 1965) and *Kalasanda Revisited* (London and Nairobi, 1966). Her other fiction includes *The Gem-Stone Affair* (Sunbury-on-Thames, 1978) and *The Scoop* (Sunbury-on-Thames, 1978). Their fellow countrywomen, Rebeka Njau (b. 1932) and Grace Ogot (b. 1930), must also be mentioned. Njau's *Ripples in the Pool* (1975; London, 1978) charts, through powerful symbolism and even mystical imagery, the disintegration of traditional life in the breakdown of one (barren) woman. Ogot's *The Promised Land* (Nairobi, 1966) and her short story collections, *Land Without Thunder* (Nairobi, 1968) and *The Other Women* (Nairobi, 1976, 1992), constitute another major contribution from Kenya, with Ogot's use of traditional folk tales, fantasy and traditional rituals, such as witchcraft.

Other recent African fiction writers include women such as the exiled South African Lauretta Ngcobo (b. 1932), best known for *Cross of Gold* (London, 1981) and *And They Didn't Die* (London, 1990), and editor of the anthology, *Let it Be Told* (London, 1987, 1988). Sindiwe Magona's short story collection, *Living, Loving, and Lying Awake at Night*, appeared in 1992 (London). E.M. Macphail's fiction includes the novel *Mrs Chud's Place* (Johannesburg, 1992) and *Phoebe and Nio* (Johannesburg, 1987). Another South African writer, Menan du Plessis (b. 1952), has written two novels, *Longlive!* (Cape Town, 1989), a novel of considerable interest, and her prize-winner *A State of Fear* (1983; London, 1987). In both, she has experimented with narrative point of view, exploring the range from extreme subjectivity to relative objectivity. Beverley Naidoo's *Chain of Fire* (London, 1989) and Agnes Sam's *Jesus is Indian* (London, 1989) add to the vigorous tradition of southern African writing by women. Gcina Mhlope's (b. 1958) *Sometimes When it Rains* (1987), a collection of short stories, is also a fascinating narrative achievement. Ellen Kuzwayo's (b. 1914) stories were collected in *Sit Down and Listen* (London, 1990), and her *Call Me Woman* (London, 1985, with a preface by Nadine Gordimer and a foreword by Bessie Head) won the Central News Agency Prize; she was the first black novelist to receive it. Kuzwayo also taps into the power of oral traditions for her narrative techniques. Another collection of prize-winning short stories, *Outside Life's Feast* (Johannesburg, 1975), and *This Time of Year* (1983) are by the South African Sheila Roberts (b. 1942), who has written numerous novels as well, such as *He's My Brother* (Johannesburg and London, 1977). Another South African, Elleke Boehmer (b. 1961), has written two novels, *Screens Against the Sky* (London, 1990) and the remarkable *An Immaculate Figure* (London, 1993).

Further African writers from the 1970s and 1980s include Yvonne Burgess (b. 1936) from Pretoria, Jillian Becker (b. 1932) from Johannesburg and Rose Zwi (b. 1928), whose *Exiles* (1984) charts the lives of Jewish people in South Africa struggling to survive. Her *The Umbrella Tree* appeared in 1990 (New York and Ringwood, Victoria). Somewhat earlier, Mary Benson (b. 1919) published *At the Still Point* (1969; London, 1988), described by Nadine Gordimer as 'a live nerve of a novel'. The work of Violet Lannoy (b. 1925) from Mozambique was published only posthumously. Additionally, from Uganda is the writer Daisy Kabagarama (b. 1951), who has published poetry, plays and fiction. Tsitsi Dangarembga (b. 1959) is one of the best-established of these recent African novelists. From Zimbabwe, Dangarembga published *Nervous Conditions: A Novel* (London, 1988), won several prizes, and has now also written plays and short stories. *Nervous Conditions*, winner of the African section of the Commonwealth writers Prize in 1989, traces poignantly the adolescence of Nyasha, and the painful adjustment she has to make to move from village life to urban existence. Jean Marquand, from South Africa (b. 1942), wrote short stories and was a highly regarded academic critic on African women novelists. Also from South Africa, Zoë Wicomb (b. 1948) has written a cycle of short stories, *You Can't Get Lost in Capetown* (London, 1987), often revealing life's absurdities by using the point of view of children in an ironic, witty vein. Other novelists from South Africa include Sheilah Fugard (b. 1932), who handles large issues of war, revolution and racism through representation of small, personal events of love, hate and infidelity, as in the prize-winning *Castaways* (London, 1972), *Rite of Passage* (1976) and *A Revolutionary Woman* (Johannesburg, 1983;

London, 1984). Farida Karodia (b. 1942) has published two novels, *A Shattering of Silence* (Oxford, 1993) and *Daughters of the Twilight* (London, 1986), and a collection of stories, *Coming Home and Other Stories* (London, 1988). Born in South Africa, she emigrated to Canada, where she now lives. But her 'chronicles' or fictional reconstructions of such events as the tragic episodes of the war in Mozambique have gained her much regard and a place on the shortlist for the Fawcett Prize.

Earlier novelists who provided a tradition for these women writers include the South African Daphne Rooke (b. 1914), who wrote *The Sea Hath No Bounds* (London, 1946); Florence E. Mills Young, called the Katharine Susannah Prichard of South Africa, who wrote of the gold-mine strikes; and Mary E. Martens, whose early feminist novels *A Daughter of Sin* (London, 1915) and *A Woman of Small Account* (London and Felling-on-Tyne, 1911) set a standard of protest rarely surpassed in later fiction. Earlier novelists, such as Dorothea Fairbridge (b. 1862) in *Piet of Italy* (London, 1913) and *The Torch Bearer* (London, 1915), argued for an abandonment of European liberal notions in favour of a recognition that Cape Malay culture was as valuable as European. And, last but not least, Sarah G. Millin's (b. 1888) early novel, *God's Stepchildren* (London, 1924), dealt in traditional but interesting ways with the acceptability of miscegenation as early as 1924.

A number of books on women African novelists are essential sources of further information. See the sections on Africa in chapter 15 and section II of the bibliography, as well as bibliography section I.

Australia, New Zealand and the Pacific Region

Australian fiction by women has been recovered and reinscribed into the literary landscape most fully by Dale Spender, whose extensive research has inspired others to attend to this rich trove of women novelists. From the time of early writers, such as Ada Cambridge (b. 1844), Jessie Couvreur ('Tasma', b. 1848) and Rosa Praed (b. 1851), novelists have experimented with a whole range of types of fiction, and adapted them

to life in an Australian world. Cambridge's most admired novel is probably *A Marked Man* (London, 1890), which displays considerable sophistication in such narrative techniques as characterization, formal shape and artistic handling of human emotions and other themes, often through irony and satire. Making use of the genre of the romance, Cambridge also achieved an epic scope for her novel which sets the romance within an enriching social context. Couvreur's fiction displays its own particular strengths, such as presentation of character through other characters' points of view, converging sets of characters, the journey motif, sharp satire and antitheses between rural and urban life, as in *Uncle Piper of Piper's Hill* (London, 1889). Praed was a prolific writer and popular in her own day. She displayed a variety of types of fiction in her fifty-odd books, from romance, historical and adventure novels to social satires, the occult and travel fiction. Such novels as *Outlaw and Lawmaker* (London, 1893) or *Lady Bridget in the Never-Never Land* (London, 1915), the latter with its alternating narrative points of view, show Praed's central literary device to be a successful fusion of personal with larger social and political issues, which intruded into the lives of ordinary women and men at every moment.

Mary Gaunt (b. 1861) based much of her fiction on the experiences gained from extensive travels to Africa, China and Europe. Such collections of short stories as *The Moving Finger* (London, 1895), and the novel *The Mummy Moves* (London, 1910), established her as a figure of great talent in the literary world. Her stories are often powerfully effective in shocking the reader by their artistically successful rendering of racism, sexism and materialism. Ironic and critical of such prejudice, Gaunt nevertheless subjected her thematic material to rigorous artistic shaping; her endings are often an ironic mockery of the romantic illusions and sentimentality which block perception of unpalatable truths. Molly Skinner (b. 1876), friend of D.H. Lawrence, with whom she co-authored *The Boy in the Bush* (London, 1924), turned the exercise of her nursing skills in World War I into an articulate and impressive work, *The Letters of a V.A.D.* (London, 1918). Her seven works of fiction, including short stories and an autobiography, *The Fifth Sparrow* (Sydney, 1972), testify

325

that Lawrence's great admiration for her was well deserved. Dorothy Cottrell (b. 1902), artist, journalist and writer of numerous novels and short stories, is best known for her *Singing Gold* (Boston, 1928), serialized in the *Ladies Home Journal*, and *The Silent Reefs* (London, 1954), which was made into a film. Sarah Campion (Mary Coulton, b. 1906) is famous for her *Mo Burdekin* trilogy (London, 1941, 1942, 1944), which is recognized as a brilliant account of North Queensland life, with its striking contrasts between the power of nature and the landscape on the one hand and the transient and pitiful weakness of humans on the other. *All the Rivers Run* (London, 1958) is another trilogy, by the social realist Nancy Cato (b. 1917), who also wrote *Green Grows the Vine* (London, 1960) and *Brown Sugar* (London, 1974). Her family sagas and historical fiction attend to human relationships, but always within the context of political and social issues of racism, sexism and pacifism.

Faith Bandler (b. 1918) is a Kanaka, daughter of a Pacific Islander impressed into work on sugar plantations. Her numerous works of fiction are passionate challenges to the outrages against the native peoples of Australia and nearby islands. *The Time was Ripe* (Sydney, 1983) and *Welou, My Brother* (Sydney, 1984) complement *Wacvie* (Adelaide, 1977) and *Marani in Australia* (Adelaide, 1956), those fictional renderings of the stories of her father, of slavery and of life in the canefields. Nene Gare (b. 1919) is also concerned with artistic representation of aboriginal experience, culture and values, and has become greatly admired for such novels as *Green Gold* (London, 1963) and *An Island Away* (Melbourne, 1981). *Bend to the Wind* (Melbourne, 1978) is a collection of her short stories. In a quite different thematic vein, Olga Masters (b. 1919) made her name late in life with the publication of the remarkable *The Home Girls* (St Lucia, Queensland, 1982), a prize-winning novel about the trials and tribulations of girls and women. This was followed shortly by *Loving Daughters* (St Lucia, Queensland, 1984) and *A Long Time Dying* (St Lucia, Queensland, 1985). Another short story writer is Jean Bedford (b. 1946), whose *Country Girl Again and Other Stories* (Melbourne, 1985) and the novel *Sister Kate* (Melbourne, 1982) explore, using traditional realist narrative techniques, life in the bush as well as urban life.

Other, more recent writers in Australia include Jessica Anderson (b. 1923), with her marvellous *Tirra Lirra by the River* (London, 1978), a spirited account of voyaging, and *The Impersonators* (Melbourne, 1980), which is on expatriation. Thea Astley (b. 1925) is one of Australia's best-known writers and the author of some twelve novels, including *It's Raining in Mango* (New York, 1987), *The Acolyte* (Sydney, 1968), *A Kindness Cup* (Melbourne, 1974) and *Reaching Tin River* (London, 1990). Her witty and ironic narrative viewpoint adds a powerful dimension to these fictions, recently added to by her latest novel, *Coda* (London, 1995). Elizabeth Harrower (b. 1928) is author of the widely acclaimed *The Catherine Wheel* (London, 1960), as well as *The Watch Tower* (London, 1966), while June Factor (b. 1936) is a Polish immigrant to Australia whose fiction also constitutes an important new viewpoint in Australian writing. And we must mention Barbara Hanrahan (b. 1939), whose fantastic short stories (with their highly visual imagery) in the collection *Dream People* (London, 1987), as well as her *Annie Magdalene* (London, 1985), are concerned with the heroism of everyday, ordinary life, as it presents the dilemmas and conflicts which must somehow be lived through. Additionally, Glenda Adams's (b. 1939) experimental stories and novels, such as *Dancing on Coral* (New York and North Ryde, New South Wales, 1987) or *Longleg* (1990), and Marion Campbell's (b. 1948) experiments with disruptions of realism in *Not Being Miriam* (1989) and *Lines of Flight* (Fremantle, 1985), testify to the vigour and originality of Australian women's fiction. Two other prize-winning fiction writers are Kate Grenville (b. 1950) and Helen Garner (b. 1942). Grenville's *Lilian's Story* (Sydney and London, 1986), the stories *Bearded Ladies* (St Lucia, Queensland, 1984), and *Joan Makes History* (London, 1988) take experimentation into further levels of originality. More recently, Grenville's *Dark Places* (London, 1994) appeared. Garner's *Monkey Grip* (Melbourne, 1977) and *Postcards from Surfers* (Melbourne, 1985) are also noted recent achievements, as are Gillian Mears's (b. 1964) *Ride a Cockhorse* (Fairfield, 1988) and *Fineflour* (St Lucia, Queensland, 1990). Her first novel is *The Mint Lawn* (Sydney, 1991).

Marian Halligan is another contemporary fiction writer whose novels and stories have won numerous prizes. *Lover's Knots* (London, 1992) took several awards, and other novels include *Self-Possession* (St Lucia, Queensland, 1987) and *Spider Cup* (Harmondsworth, 1990), while Halligan published two collections of short stories in 1991 and 1993. Beverley Farmer (b. 1941) is the author of *A Body of Water* (St Lucia, Queensland, 1990), an interesting experiment in mixed genres, and *Milk* (Harmondsworth and Ringwood, Victoria, 1983), which is a moving collection of stories about life in a tiny Greek village. One of Australia's most experimental writers is Kathleen Mary Fallon (b. 1951); her *Working Hot* (Melbourne, 1989) and forthcoming *Staff of Life* are complemented by numerous plays. Other new Australian writers are Susan Hampton, with the collection of stories *Surly Girls* (1989), and Finola Moorhead (b. 1947), with the novel *Remember the Tarantella* (1987; London, 1994) as well as *Quilt* (Melbourne, 1985) and *A Handwritten Classic* (Melbourne, 1985). All these last three writers deal with lesbian experiences as well.

Ania Walwicz's *red roses* (St Lucia, Queensland, 1992) is a borderline autobiographical/fictional work of extraordinary originality and experimentation. Through subtle use of the ancient 'journey' motif, Walwicz examines notions of memory, history, identity, gender, ethnicity and authorship in a compelling collage, portraying the 'constructedness' of these concepts through language. Walwicz is one of Australia's most experimental, post-modern novelists; she uses ideas from Mikhail Bakhtin, such as heteroglossia, to concoct 'wordy salads' and to disestablish any prevailing essentialisms. The reader is seduced into a self-conscious exile, a wandering and displacement which supplant any stable dwelling in meaning or in text. Collage, the structure of the novel on numerous levels, becomes a metaphor for experience itself; all our stable concepts are results of patchwork, stuck together according to desire rather than reality principles. Walwicz has also published *Boat* (North Ryde, New South Wales, and London, 1989).

For further information, see section I of the bibliography and chapter 15. In addition to the numerous ground-breaking works by Dale Spender and, later, Debra Adelaide, there are a number of helpful histories, critical works and anthologies. The *Australian Women's Library*

Series is republishing books by women, many long out of print, while numerous journals and periodicals are now more attentive to women writers, or attend exclusively to them.

Fiction appeared quite early on the New Zealand scene, with the writers G.B. Lancaster (Edith Lyttleton, b. 1873), Jane Mander (b. 1877) and Mary Scott (b. 1888). Lancaster is the author of a Tasmanian historical family saga published between 1933 and 1943, the first volume of which is entitled *The Pageant* (London, New York and Sydney, 1933). *The Law-Bringers* (London and New York, 1913) had already established her in England and New Zealand as a mistress of plot, picaresque action and romance, while later novels, infused with an ironic scepticism, were freer of traditional narrative practices. In *Promenade* (Sydney, New York and London, 1938), for example, characterization is the predominant focus, and incident and theme are subordinated to it. Mander, by contrast, was an extremely talented realist of setting and place. This is most evident in her final novel, *Allen Adair* (London, 1925; Auckland, 1971), but *The Story of a New Zealand River* (London and New York, 1920) is also an example of this regional realism, successfully deployed in the service of a *Bildungsroman*. Scott began writing fairly late in her life, though an early novel, *The Unwritten Book* (not published until 1957, Wellington and London), is her most serious; the rest have a lighter, more ironic touch, and many are rich in intertextual allusions, as well as self-conscious dialogues between 'high' culture and 'popular' literature.

Syvia Ashton-Warner (b. 1908) is also a novelist of character; *Spinster* (London, 1958), *Three* (London and Christchurch, 1971) and *Bell Call* (New York, 1964; Christchurch, 1971) all present strong female protagonists in conflict with their worlds, often through commitment to excellence and passion. Helen Shaw (b. 1913) is a short story writer whose two collections are *The Orange Tree and Other Stories* (Auckland, 1957) and *The Gipsies* (Wellington, 1978). Shaw makes use of the motif of the house in many of her stories as a symbol of traditional values, now lost in the consumerism and materialism of modern life. Yvonne du Fresne (b. 1929) is author of the collection of short stories *The Growing of Astrid Westergaard* (Auckland, 1985), and she has also published novels. Jean Watson (b. 1935) has perfected the short, anecdotal style in *The Balloon Watchers* (Palmerston North, 1975). In *Address to a King* (Wellington, 1986), she has developed a complex, reflective narrative of a woman who takes eight weeks off work to think about time. This novel, experimental in theme and practices, captures the reader in a spiral of self-referentiality.

Other novelists include Marilyn Duckworth (b. 1935), sister of the poet Fleur Adcock and winner of the Katherine Mansfield Award. Both realist and science fiction genres are explored by Duckworth; *Over the Fence is Out* (London, 1969) is one of her more interesting works. And see Fiona Kidman (b. 1940), the author of *A Breed of Women* (Sydney, 1979) and *The Book of Secrets* (Auckland, 1987), for the second of which she won the New Zealand Book Award. Kidman tends to keep in central position a single female character, up against forces of prejudice and stereotyped notions which inhibit her self-realization. Joy Cowley (b. 1936) and Sue McCauley (b. 1941), as well as Rachel McAlpine (b. 1940) and Elizabeth Smither (b. 1941), are other recent novelists, whose accomplishments have created a fresh, vigorous and diverse world of fiction from New Zealand. Cowley's novels include *The Growing Season* (Garden City, N.Y., 1978) and *The Mandrake Root* (Garden City, N.Y., 1978), while McAlpine's *The Limits of Green* appeared in 1985 (Auckland). McCauley, winner of awards for *Other Halves* (Auckland, 1982), is also the author of *Bad Music* (Auckland, 1990). Her novels often deal with the charged issue of single parenthood. Smither's *First Blood* (Auckland, 1983) and *Brother-Love Sister-Love* (Auckland, 1986) have also contributed to the flourishing New Zealand novel, as has Lauris Edmond (b. 1924) who, while primarily a poet, has published the novel *High Country Weather* (Wellington, 1984), plays and the autobiography, *Hot October* (Wellington, 1989).

Amongst Maori writers contributing to the process of creating a voice for the indigenous people, in addition to those discussed in the entries, are Katerina Mataira (b. 1932), Arapera Blank (pseudonym 'Hineira'), Rora Paki-titi, Sally Morgan (b. 1951) – with *My Place* (Fremantle, Western Australia, 1987) and *The Flying Emu* (1992) – Rose Denness, and J.C. Sturm. Blank won the Katherine Mansfield Memorial Award, and the other women mentioned here have published stories in the journal *Te Ao Hou*. In Oceania – or the Pacific region – recent women's fiction by Tili Peseta, Vanessa Griffin (b. 1952) and Marjorie Crocombe has appeared in *Mana* and other journals. Crocombe's stories have been published in *Lali: A Pacific Anthology*, ed. Albert Wendt (Auckland, 1980). See chapter 15 and section I of the bibliography for further information. And there are numerous anthologies, sometimes grouping Australian and New Zealand and Pacific women's writing together (see section II of the bibliography). Journals such as *Pacific Islands Monthly* and *Mana* can be consulted, in addition to the usual ones such as *Kunapipi*, *Wasafiri*, the *Journal of Commonwealth Literature* and so on.

India and South Asia

South Asian literature has also exhibited a flourishing tradition of fiction in the English language. Nayantara Sahgal (b. 1927), the niece of Nehru, has used in *Rich Like Us* (London, 1985) a complex and effective alternating narrative, to give both a personal and a more public view of the crisis in democracy in India in the 1970s. The first point of view is provided by Sonali, in the first person, as she watches her job and her freedoms, and those of others, evaporate in the government decrees. Half-way through the novel, Sonali finds and presents to the reader a manuscript of her grandfather's, written some sixty years earlier, which raises issues about suttee and satyagraha, and generally treats writing as a means of finding what the questions are which we must learn to pose in order to achieve a more civilized society. The second narrative is of Rose, an English woman married to an Indian. In *Rich Like Us*, Sahgal has deftly marshalled complex use of memory, myth, past times and Indian legend to create a wonderfully effective novel of immense force and compelling reading. Other recent novels include *Mistaken Identity* (London, 1988) and *Plans for Departure* (London, 1986), and Sahgal is also author of *The Day in Shadow* (New York, 1971), *A Time to be Happy* (New York, 1958), *This Time of*

Morning (New York, 1965) and *Storm in Chandigarh* (Delhi, 1970).

Another major Indian writer, in a completely different vein, is Suniti Namjoshi (b. 1941), well known for her poetry, but also a writer of fables and innovative short fictions. *Aditi and the One Eyed Monkey* (London, 1986) is a story of a quest, and is not only a book for children, while *The Conversations of Cow* (London, 1985) is a wonderfully witty and trenchant examination of our sexual and social relationships and attitudes, by means of a long dialogue between a cow-man-goddess and Suniti. Other short fiction-fables of Namjoshi's include *The Blue Donkey* (London, 1988) and *Feminist Fables* (London, 1981). Under the guise of literature for children, Namjoshi is rewriting the socializing influences which create homophobia and other 'isms'. Other Indian women living outside India include authors such as Meena Alexander.

More recent Indian women writers such as Rukhsana Ahmad (editor of *Flaming Spirits: Stories from the Asian Women Writers Collective* (London, 1994)), Shama Futehally (b. 1952) and Anjana Appachana (with *Incantations* (London, 1991)) have published short stories in various literary magazines, while V.L. Iyengar (b. 1958) also writes plays and poems as well as short fiction. Padma Hejmadi, from Madras, has collected her stories in *Birthday Deathday* (1985), while somewhat earlier, Santha Rama Rau (b. 1923) and Attia Hosain (b. 1913) wrote several notable novels. Rau's fiction, including *Remember the House* (London, 1956) and *The Adventuress* (New York, 1970), treats the problems occurring in the encounter of East and West, while Hosain's *Sunlight on a Broken Column* (London, 1961; reissued London, 1992 with an introduction by Anita Desai) weaves past and present, political and intellectual, independence and community, revolution and tradition into a beautifully designed sari of many colours and patterns. Hosain's short stories have been collected in the volume *Phoenix Fled* (London, 1953), and in all her fiction the struggle of women for independence and equality is a central theme, conveyed in evocative language which is itself a testimony to women's intellectual and creative spirit. Other writers include Mrinal Pande (b. 1946), whose autobiographical fiction *Daughter's Daughter* (New Delhi and London, 1993) is an example of recent efforts to question the relation of these two genres.

As well as writers in English in India, Bapsi Sidhwa (b. 1938) from Pakistan has written several novels, including *The Crow Eaters* (Lahore, 1978), *The Bride* (London, 1983), The *Ice-Candy-Man* (London, 1988) and *Cracking India* (Minneapolis, 1991). Much earlier, Kerima Poloton Tuvera (b. 1925) published, in 1962, the novel *The Hand of the Enemy*; and Sunetra Gupta (b. 1965), with the novels *Memories of Rain* (London, 1992) and *Glassblowers' Breath* (London, 1993), should also be mentioned in any survey. Bharati Mukherjee (b. 1940), author of *Jasmine* (New York, 1989) and many other novels and pieces of non-fiction, now lives in the USA. Her *Middleman and Other Stories* (New York, 1988) was the winner of the National Book Critics Circle Award. Githa Hariharan also lives in the United States; she is author of the prize-winning *Thousand Faces of Night* (Delhi, 1992) and of *The Art of Dying* (Delhi and London, 1993). Numerous other Pakistani and Indian women have left their lands of birth to live and write in Europe, Japan, America and Australia, for example.

Linda Ty-Caster, PEN prize-winner, Edith Lopez Tiempo (b. 1919, Filipina) and Jessica Hagedorn (born in the Philippines, but now living in the States, whose *Dogeaters* appeared in 1990) add to the variety of international literatures in English. From Malaysia, Shirley Geoklin Lim (b. 1944) has written *Another Country*, a collection of short stories. She has co-edited an anthology, *The Forbidden Stitch: An Asian American Women's Anthology* (Corvallis, Oreg., 1989), and has published *Nationalism and Literature: English-Language Writing from the Philippines and Singapore* (Quezon City, 1993).

Other writers, including Minfong Ho (b. 1954) – whose *Sing to the Dawn* (New York, 1975) was one of the first novels in English by a Malaysian woman – and Catherine Lim (b. 1942) – with her immensely popular stories *Little Ironies* (London, 1978) and numerous other novels and stories – have contributed to fiction published in journals and anthologies. Lim's other collection, *Or Else, the Lightning God* (Singapore, 1980), and her novel *The Serpent's Tooth* (Singapore, 1982) have been followed by several new volumes, and she is now the best-established woman fiction writer in the region. Suchen Christine Lim's *Gift from the Gods* (Singapore, 1990) and *A Fistful of Colours* (Singapore, 1993) are also important additions to Singapore women's fiction. One should not overlook Ovidia Yu (with *Miss Moorthy Investigates* (Singapore, 1990)), Wee Kiat, Liao San and Shirley Lau, however. San's semi-autobiographical fiction traces the life of heroine Lienhwa through cultural clashes and sexual prejudices, while Wee Kiat portrays in her fiction the problems and joys of female friendship. Rebecca Chua and Stella Kon, the latter the author of *The Scholar and the Dragon* (Singapore, 1986), are both included in the helpful anthology *The Sun in her Eyes: Stories by Singapore Women*, ed. Geraldine Heng (Singapore, 1976). *How to Hook a Husband and Other Stories*, ed. Fadzilah Amin (1982), is another useful anthology for writers of this region.

Women are also writing in English in Sri Lanka; recent writers include, for example, Jean Arasanayagam, whose poetry, drama and fiction include the collection of stories *Fragments of a Journey* (Colombo, 1992) and *The Cry of the Kite* (Colombo, 1984). Sri Lanka's best-known English-language novelist is probably Punyakante Wijenaike, who has written several novels and collections of short stories, such as *The Rebel* (Colombo, 1979), *Yukthi and other Stories* (Colombo, 1991), the family saga *A Way of Life* (Colombo, 1987) and *The Third Woman* (Colombo, 1963). Her most recent novel, *Amulet* (Colombo, 1994), together with the earlier novel *Giraya* (Colombo, 1971), has established her as a major writer in English in Sri Lanka. Sita Kulatunga, in her novel *Dari the Third Wife* (Colombo, 1993), looks at polygamy through a fascinating and deft use of the epistolary form. *Moth and Other Stories* (London, 1993) by Chandani Lokugé exposes the prejudices and stereotypes which confine both women and men in the context of a Buddhist cultural-ethical system, and which lead to violence and disruption.

Other writers include Maureen Seneviratne, whose collections of short fictions, *Mists on a Lake* (1984), *The Fleeting Emptiness* (1986) and *Leaves from As'vattha* (1991), contribute to a flourishing Sri Lankan fiction in English. L.K. Witanachchi's short stories, *The Wind Blows Over the Hills* (1993), and S. Karunaratna's well-known collections have now been complemented by the latter's novel, *Lake Marsh* (1993). The critic Yasmine Gooneratne has now published *Relative Merits* (London, 1986), a 'novel' (memoir) of a family over several generations. Other writers who must be mentioned are Lolita Subasinghe, Nafeela Muktha, and Vijita Fernando, all of whom have recently published book-length fiction.

Caribbean

In the Americas, the Caribbean is also rich in women's writing; indeed, from Jamaica alone a number of distinguished novels have appeared in recent decades. Joan Riley's (b. 1958) four novels, often about racism, the sexual abuse and incest children suffer, and immigration, include *A Kindness to the Children* (London, 1992) and *The Unbelonging* (London, 1985). In *Romance* (London, 1988), Riley has engaged in a metafictional commentary on the damage the genre of romance novels can do in perpetuating destructive stereotypes, such as that 'love is the only thing in the world.' Olive Senior's (b. 1943) short stories include the collection, *Summer Lightning* (London, 1986), a Commonwealth prizewinner, and *The Arrival of the Snake Woman* (London, 1989); in all her stories, language, mother-tongue, dialect and speech are, in part, the thematic material as well as the medium. Senior has experimented with establishing character and character relations through analysis of the role of language and speech habits in establishing power. *The Discerner of Hearts* (Toronto, 1995) is Senior's newest collection of stories. Another Jamaican, Patricia Powell (b. 1966), has also experimented with the 'power of speech' and with letting her characters 'tell their own stories', albeit in a different way, in her notable novel *Me Dying Trial* (Oxford, 1993); the novel charts Gwennie's determined but fateful escape from poverty and subservience. Powell's second novel is *A Small Gathering of Bones* (Oxford, 1994). Michelle Cliff's (b. 1946) four novels include *No Telephone to Heaven* (New York, 1987) and *Abeng* (1984); she has also published the stories *Bodies of Water* (London, 1990). Opal Palmer Adisa (b. 1954) has published the imaginative *Bake-Face and Other Guava Stories* (London, 1989).

Erna Brodber (b. 1940), a sociologist (and author of several books on children and women), is one of the best known of Jamaican women novelists; she won a Commonwealth literature prize for the novel *Myal* (London, 1988), and she has published *Jane and Louisa Will Soon Come Home* (London, 1980). *Myal* is constructed in parallel plots which focus upon the 'possessed'/dispossessed woman. Voodoo, obeah and therapeutic *myal* (or healing of spirit theft) become symbols of the destructive effects of European culture which robbed people of their identity. Brodber's fiction is also a meta-fictional writing, examining the effects of 'white' reading, from primary school onwards, on the native spirit, and zombification as a symbol of the process of oppression. Sylvia Wynter's (b. 1928) novel *Hills of Hebron* (London, 1962) is an earlier exploration of dispossession, especially by men of women's identity, and Sybil Seaforth (b. 1932) continued the exploration of identity in *Growing up with Miss Milly* (1988).

From Trinidad, Rosa Guy (b. 1928) is a prolific and admired novelist of adult and adolescent fiction. *Bird at My Window* (New York, 1966) is a moving fictional account of her own experiences growing up in Harlem, where she was raised after leaving Trinidad. Other novels include *A Measure of Time* (New York, 1983) and *My Love, My Love* (New York, 1985), the latter a tragic but ironic fable of doomed love and the fickleness of men. Merle Hodge's (b. 1944) *Crick Crack Monkey* (London, 1970, 1981) is seen as a key text in Caribbean literature, judging from a number of recent publications. Amryl Johnson (b. 1955) is also Trinidadian; mainly a poet, she has recently written fiction, including a book of short stories set in the Caribbean and drawing on her childhood experiences. *Sequins for a Ragged Hem* (London, 1988) is a memoir of her return to Trinidad after an absence of some time, and *Long Road to Nowhere* (Oxford) was published in 1982. Another Trinidad writer, Marion Patrick Jones (b. 1934), has written two highly regarded novels, *Pan Beat* (Port of Spain, 1973) and *J'Ouvert Morning* (Port of Spain, 1976). Valerie Belgrave (b. 1945) has been much praised for her remarkable historical novel *Ti Marie* (London, 1988), set in sixteenth-century Trinidad and examining the origins of the exploitation and racism of the present, through an analysis

of the distant past. Clara Rosa de Lima has written five novels to date, including *Countdown to Carnival* (Ilfracombe, 1978), *Kilometre Nineteen* (Ilfracombe, 1980) and *Tomorrow Will Always Come* (1965).

From Belize, the Fawcett Society prize-winner, Zee Edgell (b. 1940) has written *Beka Lamb* (London, 1982), while, from Guyana, Janice Shirebourne (b. 1947) has published two novels and a short story collection; this fiction includes the book *Timepiece* (Leeds, 1986). Another Guyanese writer, Grace Nichols (b. 1950), now lives in Britain, and is both a prize-winning poet and a novelist. In *Whole of A Morning Sky* (London, 1986), Nichols's fluency with dialect, with speech in general and with a language of imagery and lyricism has created a novel of powerful intensity, as transient political disruption in Charlestown is contrasted with the permanence of natural scenery. Phyllis Shand Allfrey (b. 1915) is another novelist who used symbol, imagery and metaphor to enrich her fictional language, as in her fine novel *The Orchid House* (London, 1953, 1982). Merle Collins, from Grenada, has published *Angel* (London, 1987) and a collection of stories, *Rain Darling* (London, 1990). *Angel* depicts three generations of women surviving violence, revolution and family pressures. Other women fiction writers include Velma Polland, *Considering Woman* (London, 1989), Vernella Fuller, *Going Back Home* (London, 1992), and Pauline Melville, *Shapeshifter* (London, 1990).

For further information, see the numerous works of secondary reference on the Caribbean in chapter 15. Section I of the bibliography specifies some of these as well, while information about anthologies for this region is in section II of the bibliography.

Canada

Another major scene of women's writing in the Americas is Canadian fiction. As in the Caribbean, women writers in Canada experiment with form, style and language, and also find new ways of utilizing familiar conventions of plot, characterization and other narrative practices. Australian-born Janette Turner Hospital (b. 1942) is one of the most recent of Canada's writers to experiment with post-modernist devices. Recipient of numerous prizes and much acclaim, Turner Hospital has recently published, amongst other notable novels, *Borderline* (London, 1985), *The Ivory Swing* (Toronto, 1982) and *The Last Magician* (London, 1992); this final novel is a fascinating example of artifice displayed in the service of feminist ideals. Audrey Thomas (b. 1935), with *Munchmeyer and Prospero in the Island* (Vancouver, 1971), had achieved much earlier some very effective experimentation with language, gender and fiction itself. These two interlocking novellas, which depict the careers of two aspiring young writers, one male, the other female, were followed some years later by *Blown Figures* (Vancouver, 1974), an analysis of colonialism. Susan Kerslake's *Penumbra* (1984) is experimental in its intensely poetic and impenetrable language, and Kerslake has published two collections of short stories, including *Blind Date* (Potters Lake, 1989). Sheila Watson (b. 1909) is another experimentalist; written almost entirely in dialogue, with its bare, austere prose, her most famous innovative novel *The Double Hook* (Toronto, 1959) engages in a dialogue between an isolated (Indian?) community and T.S. Eliot's *The Wasteland*. The poet Daphne Marlatt (b. 1942) has also written an experimental post-modern novel, entitled *Ana Historic* (London, 1988), which plays on words and shows that Ana, everywoman, is not without her history, her story or her voice in fiction.

Other novelists, such as Aritha van Herk (b. 1954) in *Places Far From Ellesmere* (1990), offers us a rewriting and a re-reading of Tolstoy's *Anna Karenina*, in what the author has described as a 'geografictione'. Other novels include *No Fixed Address* (Toronto, 1986) and *Judith* (London, 1978). Maria Campbell (b. 1940), with Linda Griffiths, created another genre-busting metafictional play/novel/memoir, called *The Book of Jessica* (Toronto, 1989). Here the author and actress explore how a writer can possibly depict Native American consciousness in the English language. This concern is indirectly expressed in Campbell's *Halfbreed* (Toronto, 1973), a semi-autobiographical account of the clash of Native American and white cultures. Joy Kogawa (b. 1935), on the other hand, has written a subtle analysis of the negotiation of cultures in *Obasan*

(Boston, 1982). Primarily a poet, Kogawa won a number of prizes for this novel of the incarceration of the Japanese Canadians during World War II, but the novel also engages in a fascinating intertextual dialogue with the twentieth-century forms and development of the novel itself. The prolific Anne Cameron (b. 1938) with her *Stubby Amberchuck* (Madeira Park, BC, 1987), *Dreamspeaker* (1978) and *Daughters of Copper Woman* (Vancouver, 1981), Beatrice Culleton with *In Search of April Raintree* (1983), and Jeannette Armstrong (grand niece of Mourning Dove or Hum ishu ma) with *Slash* (1985) also explore white acculturation of Native Americans. The mixed marriage in Joan Crate's (b. 1953) *Breathing Water* (Edmonton, 1989) takes up this theme again, and successfully depicts the contradictions involved in such cross-cultural identity situations. A new novel, *Night Terrors*, is about to be published.

Other novelists, such as Susan Swan in *Biggest Modern Woman in the World* (London, 1983), have explored another major conflict in Canadian experience, that between Canada and the United States' encroachment or appropriation. Ann Rosenberg, in her marvellous and inventive *Bee Book* (Toronto, 1981), has explored instead our common humanity, or the 'beeing-ness' of being human, as we busy our ways through life and time in a hive of mindless activity. Jane Urquhart (b. 1949) in *Changing Heaven* (London, 1990), Joan Barfoot (b. 1946) in *Plain Jane* (London, 1992) and *Gaining Ground* (London, 1980), Carol Shields (b. 1935), Pulitzer Prize winner, Miranda Archer in her best-known novel *Intertidal Life* (1984), and Isabel Huggan (b. 1943) in *The Elizabeth Stories* (New York, 1984) and *You Never Know* (Toronto, 1993), all add to this rich tradition, which had long been established by earlier writers. Among these were the redoubtable Nellie McClung (b. 1873), Emily Murphy (b. 1868), Ethel Wilson (b. 1888), and the unforgettable Lucy Maud Montgomery (b. 1876), whose *Anne of Green Gables* (London, 1908) was a world-wide best-seller. With McClung's *Sowing Seeds in Danny* (1908) and Wilson's feminist manifesto and arguably her best novel, *Swamp Angel* (London, 1954), Canada has a fiction by women in English which cannot be ignored by any reader interested in the novel's development in this century.

For further information and secondary criticism on Canadian fiction, see chapter 15 and sections I and II of the bibliography.

Britain and Ireland

With the appearance of Sarah Grand's (b. 1854) *The Beth Book* (New York) in 1897, the feminist movement in literature was well launched in Britain. The book anticipates the issues of feminism for the whole of the twentieth century, dealing as it does with the theme of liberation in every aspect. Grand's *The Heavenly Twins* (London and New York, 1893) also achieved recognition with its treatment of the problems of sex in marriage and venereal disease. Mary Cholmondeley (b. 1859) dealt more with general social pretentiousness and snobbery than with feminism per se. In her delightful and astute novel *Red Pottage* (1898), she used a pervasive irony which is tempered by much comedy and wit. She also wrote very self-consciously of the act of writing and reading, anticipating her audience's response. Elizabeth von Arnim's (b. 1866) *Elizabeth and Her German Garden* (London, 1898) was another immensely popular book of the period, while a decade later saw the appearance of the *Little Ottleys* trilogy (London, 1908, 1910, 1916) by Ada Leverson (b. 1862), the friend of Oscar Wilde. This and Leverson's other delightful comedies of manners in Edwardian England are constructed out of black comedy, absurd as well as ordinary characters, and witty incident.

F.M. Mayor's (b. 1872) *The Rector's Daughter* (London, 1924) is a technically accomplished, elegant and dramatic novel about a woman suffering from limited opportunities, and it constitutes a statement in a different tone of a woman's efforts to come to terms with love for a father, a lover and herself. Mayor's skill is also reflected in the beautiful shape of the novel, and in her sense of timing of scene and event. In a contrasting theme, Sheila Kaye-Smith (b. 1887) in *Joanna Godden* (London, 1921) traced a young woman's efforts to run a farm on her own, while E.H. Young (b. 1880), in *Miss Mole* (London and New York, 1930) and *William* (London and New York, 1925), displayed great skill in characterization, plot and realist technique generally.

These two powerful novels show Young at her most successful, though numerous other novels are also compelling reading of provincial life in Bristol. Witty and insightful of the nature of human relationship, Young's subtle humour lightens even her more serious novels, such as *William*. Other writers, such as Mary Webb (b. 1881), wrote regional novels of Shropshire, the most admired of which is probably *Precious Bane* (London, 1924), which received the Prix Feminina Vie Heureuse. All her novels evoke the 'power of place' in an intense and lyrical style, which caused Webb to be described as a 'strange genius' and to be admired by contemporaries like Rebecca West and Arnold Bennett.

Other novelists who built upon this tradition include the political activist Ivy Litvinov (or Ivy Low, b. 1899), the friend of Catherine Carswell, the poet Alice Meynell, and Lawrence. *She Knew She Was Right* (London, 1971) is a collection of short stories, while *His Master's Voice* (London, 1930) is her final novel. A mistress of the economical style, Litvinov wrote fiction infused with her intellectual sophistication and commitment to political awareness. Meanwhile, Phyllis Bentley (b. 1894) wrote *The World's Bane and Other Stories* (London, 1918) and *Life Story* (London, 1948), and G.B. Stern (b. 1890) published historical family sagas of Jewish life in London in *The Rakonitz Chronicles* (London, 1924, 1926, 1930). Another novelist of the period, Angela Thirkell (b. 1890), wrote over thirty-five books of fiction, including the popular *Pomfret Towers* (London and New York, 1938) and *Trooper to the Southern Cross* (London, 1934), as well as *Wild Strawberries* (London and New York, 1934). Known for her humour and satire on the social manners of the British, the Australians and others, Thirkell spent over a decade in Australia.

Vera Brittain (b. 1893) was not only the famous biographer of Winifred Holtby; her *Dark Tide* (London, 1923) is a testimony to her deeply held political and social beliefs. Vita Sackville-West (b. 1892) is perhaps best known for *The Edwardians* (London and Garden City, N.Y., 1930), but she achieved her most remarkable work in *All Passion Spent* (London and Garden City, N.Y., 1931), a passionate novel about the independence of an extremely elderly widow who seeks to shake off the tyranny of her children and live for herself after seven decades of self-sacrifice. Psychological studies were carried into the realm of madness by other novelists following Sackville-West, such as Antonia White's (b. 1899) final, most accomplished novel of a quartet, *Beyond the Glass* (London, 1954). Having traced Clara Batchelor through adolescence into marriage and then infidelity, White produced this insightful and compassionate study of madness as a process of healing and development. Her predecessor Edith Olivier (b. 1879) had already published a remarkable study of madness in *The Love Child* (London, 1927), a minor classic of the insanity produced in a woman unable to bear children. In 1930, Emily Holmes Coleman (b. 1899) published *The Shutter of Snow* (London, 1930), a novel of her own experiences in an insane asylum after the birth of her son. Her only novel (though she published poetry), this book is an inspired and insightful account of life from the point of view of a witty and intelligent inmate, whose view of the doctors and nurses is not deferential. Jennifer Dawson (b. 1929) also explored mental illness in *The Ha-Ha* (London, 1961), a novel of thematic and technical skill, and winner of the James Tait Black Memorial Prize. Dawson wrote several other novels as well as publishing poetry.

The several different explorations of the world beyond the normal were extended in the writings of Rumer Godden (b. 1907) to explore exotic lands and unknown societies and cultures. Whether exploring love in India in *Breakfast with the Nikolides* (London and Boston, 1942), or the love of God in the convent of *In this House of Brede* (London and New York, 1969) or *Black Narcissus* (London and Boston, 1939), Godden's powers as a novelist carry the reader over any reservations or hesitations into realms we might never otherwise have wished or dared to enter. Daphne du Maurier's (b. 1907) *Rebecca* (London and New York, 1938) and *Jamaica Inn* (London and Garden City, N.Y., 1936) may both be set in Cornwall but they take us into terrifying regions of murder and mystery, yet in the genre of the historical romance. In *Saraband* (London, 1931) and *Luminous Isle* (London, 1934), Eliot Bliss (b. 1903) infused lyricism and even exoticism into the lives of two young women quietly striving to escape stereotyped roles, one in a Berkshire village and the other in Jamaica. In a modernist gesture of dispensing with plot, Bliss

developed the characters of her two determined young women in a lyrical atmosphere of quiet passion, as the women pour their energies into affection for each other, and there is a strong suggestion of homosexuality in the men's relations, too. A few years later Dorothy Bussy (pseudonym 'Olivia'), sister of Lytton Strachey, published *Olivia* (London, 1949), a novella of a young girl's intensely emotional feelings for her female teacher. E. Arnot Robertson (b. 1903) returned us to more common life, in *Ordinary Families* (London, 1933), but her moving descriptions of nature and the beauty of the Suffolk coast enrich her writing and imbue it with an elemental energy and drama which are greatly rewarding. Much admired in her own time, she showed how truly extraordinary is the ordinary, how unique and particular experience can be.

In Pamela Frankau (b. 1908) we find a prolific novelist of some thirty books, the best known being *The Willow Cabin* (London, 1949) and *A Wreath for the Enemy* (London, 1954). In the former, Frankau anatomized an obsessive love affair eventually overcome by understanding of the excluded wife, and in the latter she explored growing up on the French Riviera. Her witty language, wonderful dialogue and deft use of maxims give her novels a fluency and humour which are a delight for the reader. Barbara Comyns (b. 1909?) is another writer of great wit, but one who has veered towards a fascinating eccentricity and inventiveness in such novels as *The Skin Chairs* (London, 1962) and *Who was Changed and Who was Dead* (London, 1954). Elizabeth Jenkins (b. 1915) takes us back to the world of women's conflicts and struggles to deal with tragedy and loss in personal and public life. Her most admired novel, *The Tortoise and the Hare* (London, 1954), is an elegant and impassioned account of the self-construction of a woman after the collapse of her marriage and desertion of her husband in middle life, a novel many women will read with horror and identification.

Elizabeth Taylor (b. 1912), a prolific and popular novelist of middle-class life in the south of England, is known for her precise description and shrewd observation; her self-mocking, ironic view is most evident in *Angel* (London, 1957), a novel of a young girl aspiring to be a famous writer. Other novels include *A Wreath of Roses* (London, 1950) and *The Soul of Kindness* (London, 1964). Taylor's contemporary, Sybille Bedford (b. 1911), is known for her novels *A Legacy* (London, 1956) and *A Favourite of the Gods* (London, 1963), as well as *A Compass Error* (London, 1968); in addition to domestic scenes, Bedford wrote of political and anti-fascist issues in a dramatic style. Brigid Brophy (b. 1929) wrote daringly explicit novels of female sexuality, while Olivia Manning's (b. 1908) novels also combine domestic scenes with war and intrigue, exile and tragedy, as in *The Balkan Trilogy* (London and Garden City, N.Y., 1960, 1962, 1965). Nina Bawden (b. 1925) focused in numerous novels on marriage and family conflict, in the main, and dealt with infidelity as well as the adult world seen through the eyes of children. Penelope Mortimer (b. 1918) carried the domestic novel into a new, lighter style, with *The Pumpkin Eater* (London, 1962), *The Handyman* (London 1983), *Long Distance* (London, 1974) and others, exploring family life from hilarity to tragedy and attending to breakdown, love and betrayal at the same time. Elizabeth Jane Howard (b. 1923) is also a sharp observer and recorder of personal and social relations; her first novel, *The Beautiful Visit* (London, 1950, 1990), won the Rhys Prize and *Getting It Right* (London, 1982) won the Yorkshire Post Novel award.

More recent novelists include Sara Maitland (b. 1950), Valerie Miner (b. 1947) and Zoë Fairbains (b. 1948), as well as the inimitable Beryl Bainbridge (b. 1934): *The Bottle Factory Outing* (London, 1974) is a novel typical of Bainbridge's comi-tragic, inventive bizarreries and grotesqueries. Her novels show considerable originality and stylistic accomplishment. Like Bainbridge, Penelope Fitzgerald's (b. 1916) novels are funny, bizarre and stylistically impressive in their originality and wit. Her *Offshore* (London, 1979) won the Booker Prize; it sets its characters in houseboats on the Thames and uses the images of drifting, flux and rootlessness to complex artistic effect. Berenice Rubens (b. 1928) has provided a marked contrast to Bainbridge and Fitzgerald's witty elegances; she has explored life as a frustrating, victimizing and sinister experience, in a spare, relentlessly direct mode. Elaine Feinstein's (b. 1930) novels are also concerned with fear, insecurity and the horrors of life, but in a more supernaturally fantastic vein, as in *The Shadow Master* (London, 1978). This is a bold and apocalyptic tale of reality overturned completely by mythic events.

Susan Hill (b. 1942) established herself as a writer of craft and imagination with *Strange Meeting* (London, 1971) and *In the Springtime of the Year* (London, 1974), while Janice Elliott (b. 1931) has also produced varied and interesting works, from the intertextual experiment of *The Italian Lesson* (London, 1985) to *Dr Gruber's Daughter* (London, 1986). Michelene Wandor's (b. 1940) *Guests in the Body* (London, 1986) is another exploration of the supernatural. In this collection of seventeen tales about a dybbuk, this Jewish spirit invades the souls of a range of characters, which Wandor has portrayed in parables and riddles. Other recent writers, such as Marina Warner (b. 1945) in *The Lost Father* (London, 1988), Verity Bargate in *No Mama No!* (London, 1978) and *Tit for Tat* (London, 1981), Anna Wilson (b. 1954) in *Cactus* (London, 1980), and Maggie Gee (b. 1948) in *Grace* (London, 1988) and *Light Years* (London, 1985), as well as in *The Burning Book* (London, 1983), explore and push beyond the familiar limits of fiction. Gee's writing is particularly interesting for its experimentation with formal conventions and the novel genre.

Britain has a strong tradition of world-famous crime fiction, too, from P.D. James (b. 1920) to Nancy Mitford (b. 1904), Dorothy L. Sayers (b. 1893) and Agatha Christie (b. 1890). James's 'Adam Dalgliesh' novels are her most famous, as in *Death of an Expert Witness* (London, 1977), while Mitford's *Christmas Pudding* (London, 1932) and Sayers's *Strong Poison* (London and New York, 1930) are favourites, as is Gillian Slovo's (b. 1952) *Death by Analysis* (London, 1986). Immigrant writers in addition to Slovo include Leena Dhingra (b. 1940?) and Ravinder Randhawa (b. 1953), whose novels *Amritvela* (London, 1988), on the one hand, and *A Wicked Old Woman* (London, 1987), on the other, deal with issues of racism, difference and self-construction through collective action.

In addition to the Scottish women discussed in the entries, Jane and Mary Findlater (b. 1866 and b. 1865) collaborated on novels, short stories, poems and non-fiction, though each wrote alone as well. Their collaboration brought them the most fame, with *Crossriggs* (London, 1908) and *Beneath the Visiting Moon* (London, 1923) being two of their most noted novels. *Crossriggs* portrays life in a small Scottish village, but in the process it touches upon the most pressing of spiritual and moral themes in a sophisticated and detached manner. Naomi Mitchison is another prolific Scotswoman: born in 1897, she has written some seventy-two books in her long life, from novels and historical novels to short stories, poetry, children's books, travel, autobiography and history. Her wonderful tales evoke the lives of corn kings and spring queens, of Halla and All-Father in the fabled city of Micklegard, and other myths of strange and fabulous events, involving creatures such as unicorns and dragons, magical horses and flying black bears. Whether we read *Travel Light* (London, 1952), a fable of moral and spiritual meaning, or *Early in Orcadia*, a mythical reconstruction of island peoples thousands of years ago, Mitchison has transported her reader into the timeless mists of antiquity, legend and universality.

Another writer of magical prose, Jessie Kesson (b. 1916), is the author of *The White Bird Passes* (London, 1958), *Glitter of Mica* (London, 1963) and *Another Time, Another Place* (London, 1983), as well as short story collections and poetry, drama and journalism. Kesson has transmuted the ordinary into the glitter of mica, as she has woven tales of a small farming community struggling with passion, illicit love affairs, and tragic marriages. *The White Bird Passes* traces the life of the indomitable young girl Janie, growing up in the back streets of a city, facing poverty alone with a sick mother. In a rich tapestry of characters, Kesson sets the stage for the novel's sequel, *Another Time, Another Place*. Married now, Janie, isolated on a distant farm, comes into contact with Italian prisoners of war, and her life is shattered. Kesson has handled her thematic material with subtlety and humour, and her prose burns with a warmth and liveliness all her own.

Elspeth Davie (b. 1920) is the author of novels and stories, including *Creating A Scene* (London, 1971), *Providings* (London, 1965) and *The Spark* (London, 1968). The first book is an exploration both of obsession and of the relation of objects to life, as materials swamp our emotions and influence our human relationships.

Markedly individual in style, imagery and situation, Davie's fiction brings the inanimate alive and anatomizes the conflicts that arise when we allow ourselves to be overtaken by materiality. Agnes Owens (b. 1926) is the author of two story collections, *Gentlemen of the West* (Edinburgh, 1984) and *Like Birds in the Wilderness* (London, 1987). She has also published stories in *Lean Tales* (London, 1985), which includes stories by several authors. However serious her themes, they are always infused with a sense of the folly of human endeavour.

Amongst Irish writers, Katherine Cecil Thurston (b. 1875) is the author of six novels; her best-seller *John Chilcote, MP* (Edinburgh and London, 1904) was made into a play and a film, and *The Gambler* (Toronto, 1905; London, 1906) was serialized in *Harper's Weekly*. *The Fly on the Wheel* (Edinburgh and London, 1908; London, 1987) is a psychological/sociological study of middle-class marriage which ends in tragedy and misunderstanding. Mary Lavin (b. 1912) has achieved her most outstanding work in the novella and short story form, though *Mary O'Grady* (London, 1950) and *The House in Clewe Street* (London, 1945) are also substantial works of fiction. Lavin has won numerous prizes and awards, from the James Tait Black Memorial Prize in 1943 for the collection *Tales From Bective Bridge* (London, 1943) to the Katherine Mansfield Prize and the Eire Society Gold Medal and Gregory Medal, and has been praised as one of the finest living writers of the short story by numerous readers and critics. Her other collections include *A Single Lady* (London, 1951) and *The Great Wave* (London, 1961); *Selected Stories* was published in 1981 (Harmondsworth).

Maura Laverty (b. 1906) achieved acclaim in 1942 with the publication of her first novel, *Never No More* (London), followed by three others, all of which were banned in Ireland until the 1960s. In *Never No More*, the young Delia grows up with her grandmother on a farm; Laverty filled the novel with the magnificence of the rich Irish countryside and the meaningfulness of the seasonal cycle of planting and harvesting, as Delia reaches maturity herself. Betty Miller (b. 1910) is the author of seven novels, including *On the Side of the Angels* (London, 1945) and *The Death of the Nightingale* (London, 1949). In the former, Miller took up the topical theme of the psychological damage of war and its after-math, as the effects seep deep into personal lives, marriage and other (homosexual) relationships. Katherine Keane's *Who Goes Home?* (Dublin, 1947) is a historical novel which draws upon events involving Parnell and others, as it charts the recovery of a young woman from a failed love affair to independence and freedom from conventional, restrictive roles.

Born in the same year as her more famous countrywoman Edna O'Brien, Julia O'Faolin (b. 1932) is the author of the remarkable *Woman in the Wall* (London, 1975) as well as other novels and collections of short stories, including *Daughters of Passion* (Harmondsworth, 1982). Based on chronicles and letters from sixth-century Gaul, *Woman in the Wall* is a dramatic reconstruction of life in a convent, and of fanaticism, sainthood and the eventual, terrible collapse of this sanctuary. The narrative alternates between the intensely subjective monologue of an anchoress and a more objective, third person perspective, involving political intrigue; the latter is set against the anchoress's religious reflections, walled up as she has been for months in her tiny narrow space. Other works of O'Faolin's include *The Obedient Wife* (London, 1982) and the collection of stories *Melancholy Baby* (Dublin, 1978).

For further information on British and Irish writers, see sections I and II of the bibliography on anthologies, general works and criticism, and geographically organized criticism in chapter 15. For example, on Irish women writers, an area badly neglected until quite recently, see Ann Owens's *Irish Women Writers: An Uncharted Tradition*, and *Wildish Things: An Anthology of New Irish Writing*, ed. A. Smyth. For British writers, see Janet Todd's excellent collection, and see *The Norton Anthology of Literature by Women*. See also, for example, books by David Lodge and Malcolm Bradbury, S. Robinson's *Engendering the Self*, L. Anderson's *Plotting Change*, and B.K. Bowers and B. Brothers's *Reading and Writing Women's Lives*, amongst many, many others listed in section I of the bibliography.

For more British lesbian works, see the end of the 'America' section below (p. 343), devoted to specifically 'radical' or 'separatist' feminist/lesbian writing.

America

American women novelists of the twentieth century have also been numerous, so that one can only give a further sampling of their achievements, as with writers from the other geographical areas mentioned. One of the predominant forms of writing in the 1890s and early 1900s was regionalism, with a tendency towards realist conventions structuring this local-colour literature. This is not surprising, since with nature playing such an obviously enormous role in the lives of Americans beyond the East coast, the landscape and other regional features of a less urbanized, more socially diverse society took on a distinct particularity. In many regions, people were still grappling in basic ways with a wild and underdeveloped land. Hence themes of the frontier – as a symbol of limits and obstacles and opportunities – and the wilderness took on powerful metaphorical and legendary meanings in the writings of many novelists. Nevertheless, as far as California and the Pacific coast generally, fiction was a vigorous and important element in the lives of these early twentieth-century people.

Mary Austin (b. 1868) was one of the most accomplished of the California regionalists, writing of her love of the land in *The Land of Little Rain* (Boston and New York, 1903), but also of women's struggles against oppression in *A Woman of Genius* (Garden City, N.Y., 1912). Austin's love of California and her feeling of the importance of a rootedness in the land were reflected in her often mythic and primitive imagery, and in her almost mystical celebration of nature. She was also a close and sympathetic observer of Native American Indians. Her love of California was shared by the accomplished writer Gertrude Atherton (b. 1857), in such novels as *Before the Gringo Came* (New York, 1894) and *The Californians* (London and New York, 1898). Atherton also wrote other sorts of novel, such as *Black Oxen* (London and New York, 1923), which was her most famous. Dorothy Scarborough (b. 1877) in Texas continued this regional realism, as did later Western novelists such as Virginia Sorensen (b. 1912), who studied Mormon life in *Kingdom Come* (New York, 1960). Ruth Suckow (b. 1892) depicted life in the harsh but fertile Iowa country in

Country People (New York, 1924), while Mari Sandoz (b. 1896) not only wrote of life on Nebraska farms and ranches in Slogum House (Boston, 1937); she was also the author of the acclaimed The Battle of the Little Big Horn (Philadelphia, 1966), a historical/fictional reconstruction of Custer's last stand, and wrote Crazy Horse (New York, 1942), the 'biography' of a Sioux chief, and The Buffalo Hunters (New York, 1954). Sandoz's prose challenged the boundary between fiction and history in a way that was rarely surpassed for its demonstration of the fictionality of all writing. Love Song to the Plains (New York, 1961) is another challenge to notions of narrative and historical objectivity, as Sandoz produced a beautiful account of the inspiration of the land and its history. Much later, writers such as Diane Johnson (b. 1934) wrote of the disintegration of Californian life through decadence and wealth, in, for example, The Shadow Knows (New York, 1974) or Lying Low (New York, 1978).

Midwestern novelists shared some of the concerns of the Western novelists discussed, but there were also differences due to greater urban development, which provided some protection from the naked forces of nature met with in the West. This led to thematic and formal differences. For example, realism in Western writers was often (though not always) tempered by the mystical force of nature, and the lyricism that resulted from close contact with land, sun, sky and other entities with primitive power, such as the cycle of the seasons, planting and harvesting of crops, and sources of water, as life–giving elements. This power of the 'natural' led to evocations of the supernatural, the mystical and the legendary. By contrast, in the writing of the more urban Midwest, the tendency of realist writing could often be towards a rather bare naturalism, though there were exceptions.

Thus, for example, Mary Watts (b. 1868), an Ohio novelist, wrote of the rise of a slum girl fighting for her humanity in the face of poverty and social obstructions, in The Rise of Jenny Cushing (New York, 1914). Janet Fairbanks's (b. 1879) Chicago novels, such as Rich Man Poor Man (1936), thematize the struggle of women for the right to vote. Zoë Akins (b. 1886) turned her Missouri eye to characterizing life in a girls' school in Forever Young (1941). Two of the most outstanding novels of the Midwest were the

lyrical Now in November (1934; London, 1935) by Josephine Johnson (b. 1910), which won a Pulitzer Prize, and The Dollmaker (New York, 1954) by Harriette Arnow (b. 1908). These two novels exemplify the two different tendencies described above. Now in November, about the harsh farming life of a Missouri family, moves away from the harsh naturalism of Arnow's tragic story of Chicago factory life. Johnson's poetic prose is infused with the lyricism and mysticism of Tillie Olsen's writing, as the power of the place, of the land and of nature is evoked in a quite splendid novel of great beauty and style. Johnson is also the author of other notable works, such as Winter Orchard (1935), a collection of short stories, and the novels Jordanstown (1937), Wildwood (1946) and The Dark Traveler (1963), as well as poetry and non-fiction including The Inland Island (1969) and Seven Houses (1973). Now in November is her crowning achievement, however, and is too important a work of art to continue to be ignored. While Arnow also wrote other novels, such as Hunter's Horn (New York, 1949), The Weedkiller's Daughter (New York, 1970) and Old Burnside (Lexington, Ky., 1977), The Dollmaker is her most remarkable work, and has recently been made into a film. However, Johnson's Now in November can be said to mark something of a departure from the regional realism of much fiction of the early part of the century, in its greater attention to style and form. Unlike some other Pulitzer Prize winners, this novel utterly transcends its time and locale, by means of a lyricism and universality characteristic of Olsen's and Bessie Head's prose, to achieve a firm place in the history of American fiction.

Southern writing from Kentucky to Florida was also dominated by attention to forces of nature and place, though exceptions like the work of Amelia Rives (b. 1863) are not very unusual. The Virginian Rives, who lived for a time in England, made use of impressionist techniques for her psychological studies and romances, such as The Quick or the Dead? (1888) and its sequel, Barbara Dering (London, 1892). Later novels, which continued until 1930, veered towards romance, and are far removed from the writings of the Kentuckian Olive Dargan (b. 1869), who wrote movingly of Kentucky mountain life in such novels as Highland Annals (1925), and of textile mill workers in the famous Call Home the

Heart (1932). Another well-known Kentuckian, Elizabeth Madox Roberts (b. 1881), is much admired for her remarkable recreations of folk culture and speech in, for example, *Jingling in the Wind* (New York, 1928). Her *My Heart and My Flesh* (New York, 1927) deals with a woman's madness, while *He Sent Forth a Raven* (New York, London and Toronto, 1935) is again about Kentucky farming life. Roberts is probably one of the most accomplished of the writers of this region and period; *The Great Meadow* (London and New York, 1930) and *A Buried Treasure* (New York, 1931) display her versatility.

With Marjorie Kinnan Rawlings (b. 1896) we enter an entirely different world, the almost jungle-like, swampy wilderness of north Florida in the early part of the century. *The Yearling* (New York and London, 1938), also a Pulitzer Prize winner, is a remarkably powerful novel, written from the point of view of a young boy watching his parents hack out an existence in the face of an intractable nature. The fine portrayal of the survival of innocence and love in the face of calamity and destruction makes the novel much more than a regional realist fiction. *South Moon Under* (London and New York, 1933) and *Golden Apples* (New York, 1935), as well as the non-fiction *Cross Creek* (New York, 1942), are other works of the sophisticated Rawlings, born in Washington, D.C., who decided to leave the decadence of urban life and make her home in the 'vanishing frontiers'.

Lillian E. Smith (b. 1897), Caroline Gordon (b. 1895) and Shirley Ann Grau (b. 1926) are other notable Southern writers. Smith's *Strange Fruit* (New York, 1944) and her non-fiction *Killers of the Dream* (1946) treat of racism in the South, and of the mixed-race love affair of a couple who were torn between two worlds. *Strange Fruit* is a powerful novel combining techniques of romance and documentary/historical fiction in an impressive fusion, as is Smith's other novel, *One Hour* (London and New York, 1960). Other non-fiction includes *The Journey* (1954), *Now is the Time* (1955) and *Our Faces, Our Words* (1964), all indictments of racism and segregation. Somewhat later, Grau's *The Keepers of the House* (London and New York, 1964; Pulitzer Prize 1965) depicted a plantation family in Louisiana and the gradual coming to terms with the violent consequences of racism

over several generations. Gordon's fiction moved in a different direction, to war and historical novels, such as *None Shall Look Back* (New York, 1937), which is about the effects of the Civil War on a Kentucky family, *The Malefactors* (New York, 1956) and *The Women on the Porch* (1944), which is an interiorized, psychological study of the life of a woman. Finally, Margaret Mitchell's (b. 1900) *Gone With the Wind* (New York and London, 1936), her only novel (which she took ten years to write), was also a Pulitzer Prize winner and is said to have made publishing history for the speed and size of its sales. This historical romance, in the genre of *War and Peace*, has never achieved the critical estimation which it deserves; it is not only a popular but also an accomplished novel of scope and intelligence.

Edna Ferber (b. 1887) was a Michigan-born writer whose most notable novel is *So Big* (Garden City, N.Y., and London, 1924), the moving study of Selina, a woman who built up a life for her feckless son out of relentless labour and self-sacrifice. After the death of her incompetent but well-meaning husband, Selina takes over the running of her Midwestern farm, and makes an unexpected success of what, until her capable management, had been an unnecessary failure. The theme is much like that of Glasgow's *Barren Ground* (1925), but Ferber's style is not the unrelieved realism of Glasgow's heroic novel. Martha Ostenso (b. 1900) was another novelist fascinated by the theme of 'making it' in America; she and other immigrants give us a different perspective from the American-born Ferber. Ostenso's prize-winning *Wild Geese* (New York and Toronto, 1925) charted the almost incredible battle with nature of settlers in the northern wilds of Canada, while Mary Antin (b. 1881) wrote *The Promised Land* (London and Cambridge, Mass., 1912), a novel of the struggle of poor Jewish immigrants to establish themselves in America. The Native American Hum ishu ma (b. 1886) or Mourning Dove, in *Cogewea* (Boston, 1927; reprinted Lincoln, Nebr., 1981) and *Coyote Stories* (Caldwell, Idaho, 1933; reprinted New York, 1977), kept alive knowledge of the stories and fables of the Okanogan American Indian tribe, fighting for survival against invading, ruthless European hordes. Mourning Dove was probably the first American Indian to write down in English the legends and stories of the indigenous population from its own perspective.

Northeasterners tended to write a fiction often markedly different from their fellow countrywomen of the West and South. For instance, the intellectualized and polished writings of Ann D. Sedgwick (b. 1873), who was born in New Jersey but resided abroad for most of her life, are in complete contrast to the regional realism of Austin, Johnson and Rawlings, for example. Sedgwick's numerous novels, in the style of Edith Wharton, concern more often than not the differences between English and American and between English and French consciousness, which so fascinated Wharton and Henry James. Sedgwick's short story collection *Christmas Roses* (New York, 1920), and novels such as *A Fountain Sealed* (New York, 1907), which is about mother–daughter tensions, and *Adrienne Toner* (London and New York, 1921), also deal with the anatomy of social relations and the forms which violence and tyranny can take under the cloak of social acceptability. The Pennsylvanian Margaretta Deland (b. 1857) is a mistress of the genre of character study, but her talents are great and extend beyond even this achievement to a truly impressive ironic sophistication and detachment, which she wrote about in a preface to *Dr. Lavendar's People* (London and New York, 1903). This is a fine collection of short stories of the trivialities and tragedies of civilized life in a Pennsylvania town, from the point of view of a mind of great refinement and wit, as Deland portrayed her characters' foibles and strengths, their compassion and selfishness, with a quite stunning humanity and perceptiveness. Her novels, from *The Awakening Of Helena* (New York and London, 1906) to *The Vehement Flame* (New York and London, 1922), from *The Iron Woman* (New York and London, 1911) to *The Kays* (New York and London, 1926), display an artistic accomplishment too great to be forgotten.

Another major figure of the region and period is the inimitable Elinor Wylie (b. 1885), the poet and author of a fantastically mannered fiction, in the genre of Rebecca West's *Harriet Hume* (1929). A New Jersey writer, Wylie began publishing poetry before she turned to her wonderfully original and witty novels of artifice and satire, including the formal style of *Jennifer Lorn: A Sedate Extravaganza* (New York, 1923), *The Orphan*

Angel (New York, 1926), which is the fictional tale of Shelley saved from death by drowning and carried off to America, and *The Venetian Glass Nephew* (New York, 1925), again in a style as formal as a porcelain vase. Contemporaneously, Nella Larsen's (b. 1891?) two novels *Passing* (New York and London, 1929) and *Quicksand* (New York and London, 1928) appeared, the latter portraying the sophisticated consciousness of Helga Cane, a middle-class black American. Helga's awareness of the complex nature of the issues of gender, class and race are depicted by Larsen as an effort to grasp the control of the representation of black people and women from the control of white people and males. *Passing* explored the further issue of people of one race (or religion, for that matter) 'passing' for another, and the moral and psychological consequences of this phenomenon. This theme in fiction has fascinated readers throughout the century, whether male or female, black or white, Christian, Muslim, Jewish or whatever, for it traces the fascination each of us has with the unknown, the forbidden and the 'Other'.

The post-war period displays a new approach in theme, style and tone, reflecting the enormous if gradual changes in American society and life. This approach came only after the regionalism, communalism and proletarianism of many novels of the pre-war period, such as Pearl S. Buck (b. 1892) with, amongst many other novels, *The Good Earth* (New York and London, 1931) or Fannie Hurst (b. 1889) with the notable novel *Song of Life* (London and New York, 1927). The contemporaneous, remarkable fiction and non-fiction of Agnes Smedley (b. 1892?), including such books as *Daughter of Earth* (New York, 1929) and a few scattered short stories, testify to the power of the faith in human beings to change the intolerable, grinding existence of their fellow women and men, and to find a literary form in which to express this inspiration. Smedley's classic non-fiction books, such as *Chinese Destinies* (1933), *China Fights Back* (London, 1938) and *Battle Hymn of China* (London, 1943), are remarkable documentary-historical-personal accounts of the Chinese revolution in its earlier stages, while *The Great Road* (London, 1958) is a biography of Chu Teh, commander-in-chief of the Red Army, whom she knew well. Smedley was one of the most remarkable political activists of the 1930s and 1940s; her books on China constitute an invaluable resource for first-hand knowledge of this period in the struggle of the Chinese against Japan and against international capitalism. *Daughter of Earth*, on the other hand, is a notable work of fiction about the early life of an adolescent in poverty-stricken Missouri, where constant work and diligence led only to sickness and loss. (See the *Bulletin of Concerned Asian Scholars*, Winter, 1975, for further information about Smedley.)

After Smedley's writings, and those of her friend Emma Goldman (b. 1869), a new individualism and urbanism set in. Novels such as Ayn Rand's (b. 1905) *The Fountainhead* (Indianapolis, 1943), whose protagonist was modelled on Frank Lloyd Wright, and *Atlas Shrugged* (New York, 1957) celebrate a concept of radical individualism and have a utopian dimension, later expounded upon in Rand's non-fiction, *The Romantic Manifesto* (1969) and *For the New Intellectual* (New York, 1961). In a quite different style, Betty Wehner Smith's (b. 1904) immensely popular *A Tree Grows in Brooklyn* (1943) and, much later, *Joy in the Morning* (London and New York, 1963) explored the poverty trap of a working-class family in the tenements of New York City, and their almost incredible efforts to work themselves into a better way of life for their children.

Other mid-century writers such as Mary McCarthy (b. 1912) in *The Group* (New York and London, 1963), and May Sarton (b. 1912) in *Faithful are the Wounds* (New York and London, 1955), wrote of Eastern intellectual life and its moral dilemmas and social frustrations. Both these writers were prolific, and were highly regarded for the sophistication of their themes and the satiric and detached narrative view they often adopted. Dorothy West (b. 1921) was another New Yorker, who became active in the Harlem Renaissance and founded the literary magazine *Challenge* in 1934. *The Living is Easy* (Boston, 1948), her only novel, uses traditional narrative techniques to analyse the effects of racism upon black women and men, and traces the tragic obsession of a young, light-skinned black woman to gain respectability at any price. West has also written innumerable short stories, which may be published in a collected volume soon. Later, Alice Childress (b. 1920), playwright

and novelist, took up similar themes but different narrative techniques in her fiction.

With the more recent writings of Joan Didion (b. 1934), a regionalism similiar to that of the early part of the century was revived to some extent, but with a strong intellectual strain balancing it, as Didion has written of psychological and social disintegration in California. *Play it as it Lays* (New York, 1970) and *Run River Run* (New York, 1963), along with *A Book of Common Prayer* (New York and London, 1977), are notable amongst her distinguished oeuvre, and have much in common thematically with Diane Johnson's work (see above, p. 338). Contemporaneously, Marilyn French (b. 1929) with *The Women's Room* (New York, 1977), Marilynne Robinson (b. 1944) with her splendid novel *Housekeeping* (New York, 1980), Erica Jong (b. 1942) with *Fear of Flying* (New York and Chicago, 1973) and Rita Mae Brown (b. 1944) with the inimitable *Rubyfruit Jungle* (Plainfield, 1973) initiated a new explicitness and outspokenness into women's fiction. This gave a tremendous boost to the articulation of exploitation and sexism, at the same time as it necessarily shocked and disturbed many readers out of their traditional notions of propriety and literary decorum. Joyce Carol Oates (b. 1938), a New Yorker, has depicted, in her ruthlessly analytic, psychological portrayals, the frustrated lives of people obstructed both from within and from without, as in *Them* (New York, 1969) and *The Assassins* (New York, 1975), to mention only two of her many novels. She also writes short stories, essays and poetry. Her fiction is characteristic of the direction in fiction of the second half of the twentieth century towards psychological, intellectual and social themes; but in style, form and narrative practices, this writing is extremely varied, as is evident from the individual author entries.

Numerous recent writers have been experimenting both with the novel form and with the possibilities the short story offers for articulating experience, from Marge Piercy (b. 1936) to Ellen Gilchrist (b. 1945), Lydia Davis (b. 1947) and Maxine Chernoff (b. 1952). Piercy's best-known novel is probably *Woman on the Edge of Time* (New York, 1976), a marvellously inventive, futuristic fiction about a woman driven 'mad' by social prejudice; the book moves from present to future to chart the utopian possibilities of self-construction. Her *Fly Away Home* (New York and London, 1984) is another novel of women having to build a foundation for their lives which does not rely on men. With humour, inventiveness and vigour, Piercy deals with the perennial problem of the construction of female independence after a life of socialized dependence. Gilchrist's *The Annunciation* (Boston, 1983) and her other novel *The Anna Papers* (Boston and Toronto, 1988) are accompanied by five collections of short stories, including the acclaimed *In the Land of Dreamy Dreams* (Fayetteville, Ark., 1981). Grotesque and elegant, her 'Rhoda' stories are especially biting, witty and compelling tales of the spoiled and decadent but nevertheless human inhabitants of rich New Orleans. The recurring appearance of Rhoda, her most compelling character, at unexpected moments, at different ages and in utterly different comic situations creates a network of tales which proves utterly irresistible to the reader. Davis's minimalism and defamiliarization in *Story and Other Stories* (Great Barrington, Mass., 1983) and in *Break it Down* (New York, 1986) are impressive experiments in fiction, while Chernoff's *New Faces of 1952* (Ithaca, N.Y., 1985) has been described as consisting of experimental 'hermeneutic parables' which only appear realist in their narrative practices. Anne Beattie (b. 1947), has established herself as a writer of wit and sharp satire with *Love Always* (London and New York, 1985) and *Picturing Will* (London and New York, 1989). Anne Redmon's (b. 1943) character study *Emily Stone* (London, 1974) and her next novel, *Music and Silence* (London and New York, 1979), show her to be a versatile writer; the first is a display of wit and sharp observation, the second a tragedy in a melodic, bass tone of fugal structure and complexity.

Other recent novelists include the experimental Joy Williams (b. 1944), whose meta-fictional *Taking Care* (1982) and *Escapes* (London, 1990) are notable contributions to the exploration of the limits of traditional narrative practice. Similarly, Barbara Guest's (b. 1920) anti-narrative novels *Bop* (1986) and *Seeking Air* (Santa Barbara, Calif., 1978) add enormously to our sense of what narrative practices are possible. In a more traditional vein, Mary Gordon (b. 1949) and Judith Guest (b. 1937), as well as Monica Stone,

should be mentioned. Lucha Corpi's (b. 1945) *Delia's Song* (Houston, 1989) is characteristic of themes of struggle for identity which run right through the twentieth century, while Susan Power's (b. 1961) remarkable first novel, *The Grass Dancer* (London, 1994), adds to the increasing body of accomplished literature by Native American women. This novel is the tale of Anna Thunder, a Sioux Indian misusing ancestral powers for her own emotional greed. In this example of almost magical potency, Power uses images of the dance and alternating narratives, to create an incredible story of imaginative intensity comparable to Leslie Marmon Silko's *Ceremony* (1977).

Further challenges come from other Native Americans such as Paula Gunn Allen (b. 1939), whose novel *The Woman Who Owned the Shadows* (San Francisco, 1983), like Silko's *Ceremony*, explores the strength of oral narratives, tales and tribal traditions to fend off powerlessness, illness and despair in the face of a hostile American-European environment. Other works of Allen's are *Sacred Hoop* (Boston, 1986) and *Studies in American Indian Literature* (New York, 1983). She has also edited an anthology of Native American women writers' stories, *Spiderwoman's Granddaughters* (London, 1990). Linda Hogan's (b. 1947) historical novel *Mean Spirit* (New York and Toronto, 1990) rewrites American 'history' to reveal the fictionality of 'white' versions, while *Seeing through the Sun* (Amherst, Mass., 1985) celebrates tribal values of the unity of human life and nature.

Latina American writers such as Sandra Cisneros (b. 1955) and Denise Chavez (b. 1948) have shown a strong sense of ethnic and gender consciousness. Cisneros's *Woman Hollering Creek and Other Stories* (New York, 1991) and *House on Mango Street* (Houston, 1984) and Chavez's linked short stories *The Last of the Menu Girls* (Houston, 1986) express the means of escape which are available to women from the oppressive roles and images traditionally assigned to them as abused wives, daughters or houseservants. Ana Castillo (b. 1953) in the *Mixquiahuala Letters* (Binghamton, N.Y., 1986), for example, represents women's experiences of the erotic in new terms, different from those male ones of power, pain, domination and penetration that are familiar in earlier fiction. Gloria

Anzaldua (b. 1942) mixed genres in her remarkable, symbolic and accomplished *Borderlands/ La Frontera: The New Mestiza* (San Francisco, 1987), a bilingual experiment redefining reality as multiple identities and constant border crossings of all kinds – sexual, social, literary, linguistic and geographical. Helen Viramontes (b. 1954) is the author of *The Moths and Other Stories* (Houston, 1985), an experiment in analysing the patriarchal forces of the church, the family and authority generally, which impose images and views of women, designed to oppress and entrap them.

In the novels of these imaginative and accomplished Latina writers, there is a constant sophistication about the power of the gaze, the 'camera', the notion of the 'natural attitude', and the necessity of exposing this 'nature' as a construct with specific, damaging, ideological aims. If women can learn to see themselves in new ways and with unlimited possibilities, if women can stop seeing themselves and each other through the 'eyes' of conventional notions, they may be able to stop imprisoning themselves and each other in sexual jealousy, victimization and hate. These novelists employ comedy, irony, tragedy, the fabulous and the grotesque, as well as a quite astonishing inventiveness fused with traditional cultural and literary devices, to shock and to expose to women and men the idiocy of falling for the 'natural attitude', whether regarding literature, life generally or women and men. Their fiction constitutes an unmitigated rejection of nature and of notions of women, men and society as anything but cultural constructs, *which can be changed*. And change them they do; these changes, if ignored, deprive us of the chance to experience imaginative living.

British and American feminist and lesbian writing has also invigorated recent fiction and given narrative practices a jolt, as in May Sarton, Rita Mae Brown, and other writers discussed in the individual author entries. As early as 1953, Claire Morgan's *Price of Salt* was published (reissued

Tallahassee, Fla., 1984), while Jane Rule's (b. 1931) *Desert of the Heart* (1964; reissued London, 1986) and *This is Not for You* (1970; reissued London, 1987) appeared shortly after. Anna Wilson's *Cactus* (London, 1980), Barbara Deming's *A Humming Under My Feet: A Book of Travail* (London, 1985) and other novels continued this well-established exploration of the narrative means of representing and exposing the gratuitous difficulties a homophobic society creates for gay people. Barbara Burford's (b. 1946) *The Threshing Floor* (London, 1986) is another contribution, including a novella and several stories, which combine attacks on racism and homophobia with deft narrative power and humour. *Relatively Norma* (London, 1982) and *Bulldozer Rising* (London, 1988), by Anna Livia, take disruptive narrative devices further, as comedy and intertextuality intrude, especially in *Accommodation Offered* (London, 1985), while Barbara Wilson (b. 1951) and Valerie Miner (b. 1947) use traditional genre fictional forms, such as detective fiction (see above, p. 335), as a means of articulating lesbian and feminist experiences and points of view in a mixture of conventional and innovative literary practices. Utopian fiction by lesbian and feminist writers has also proven to be a rich genre for exploding homophobic myths lurking in language, literature and psychology, for Marge Piercy and Joanna Russ, as well as Sally Gearheart Miller (b. 1931) in *Wanderground* (1979; London, 1985), and for Jane Palmer, Caroline Forbes and Aileen La Tourette (b. 1946), as in La Tourette's *Cry Wolf* (London, 1986). Finally, Suzette Haden Elgin (b. 1936), Isabel Miller and others have found literary means of articulating representations of separatist communities in such novels as Elgin's *Native Tongue* (1984; London, 1985) and Miller's *Patience and Sarah* (London, 1979).

For further information on American women novelists, see the section on America in chapter 15, and see sections I and II of the bibliography. *The Columbia History of the American Novel* is also highly recommended.

Chapter 15

Selected Research Resources for the
Twentieth-Century Novel by Women

After the introductory section on general sources, this chapter uses the same geographical divisions as chapter 14 and section II of the bibliography, in alphabetical order.

Readers and students of the novel of this period will find numerous resources at hand for extending their knowledge. These are of a wide and various kind, from bibliographies of secondary and primary material to, at the other end of the spectrum, highly readable critical and interpretative accounts organized in various ways. For the student working on a particular novelist and wishing to find secondary criticism, the *Modern Language Association (MLA) International Bibliography of Books and Articles on the Modern Languages and Literatures* (MLA, New York, 1922– , published annually), available on CD-ROM in many libraries for publications since the early 1980s, is an excellent source, at least in the case of most writers. The CD-ROM is updated every few months. The *Annual Bibliography of English Language and Literature* (Modern Humanities Research Association (MHRA), London, 1921– , published annually) is another major source of secondary literature. It is organized first into periods, then into sections of general, theory and so on, and finally into alphabetical listings for individual authors.

These two major bibliographies are supplemented by a wide range of more specific books or journal bibliographies, such as *Current Contents*, a quarterly journal with annual cumulation, starting in 1976, which is invaluable in helping to bring the above two resources up to date. (Their preparation for publication means that they are behind by about two to three years, except in the case of the CD-ROM MLA version.) *Current Contents: Arts and Humanities* is a part of the *American Humanities Index* (AHI, Troy, Mich., 1979–), and is devoted in its entirety to listing recent journal publications, which the student working on contemporary authors will find particularly helpful. Another resource for updating secondary criticism is the *Literary Criticism Register: A Monthly Listing of Studies in English and American Literature* (Literary Criticism Register, 1983– , Deland, monthly). It lists journal articles from over 300 journals, as well as dissertations and books, and contains two helpful indexes.

Other extremely useful bibliographies include the invaluable *American Literature, English Literature, and World Literatures in English. An Information Guide Series*, series ed. T. Greider, assoc. ed. D. Devries (Gale Research, Detroit, Mich.). These dozens of volumes were published starting in the early 1970s, and often document secondary literature on writers who were not at that time included in other bibliographies, or not thoroughly recorded. The volumes are usually devoted to writers of specific geographical or ethnic backgrounds, and include Indian, African, Afro-American and so on. This constitutes an important supplement to the resources mentioned above. The *Cumulative Book Index: A World List of Books in the English Language* (CBI, New York, 1898– , quarterly, annual and larger cumulations) can always be turned to for information on an author or a book.

For a readable, accessible and excellently

presented resource, *The Year's Work in English Studies* (Blackwell, Oxford and Atlantic Highlands, N.J., 1921– , annual) cannot be bettered. It covers all literatures in the English language and is organized first into periods and then geographically. Within the latter, the material is divided into general, reference, anthology, theory and so on. While not always as inclusive as the MLA or MHRA bibliographies, *The Year's Work* is more informative and evaluative. Indeed, the sections function as annotated bibliographical essays which it is possible to read through as a whole. One can thus often gain some information about the context within which a writer is working. These volumes are a resource which can help to keep readers up to date on both primary and secondary literature and criticism, on available new anthologies and editions, and on other research resources recently published as well. It cannot be recommended highly enough.

There are numerous bibliographies of primary and secondary literature which are organized geographically or according to political bodies, such as the *Critical Writings on Commonwealth Literatures: A Selective Bibliography to 1970* (W.H. New, University Park, Pa., and London, 1975). Or there is the invaluable *Journal of Commonwealth Literature Annual Bibliography* (1964–), with selected authors and primary and secondary literature. All these bibliographies become more inclusive with time, whereas most of their earlier volumes excluded many women writers; hence the need to supplement them with bibliographies specifically devoted to women or to small regions. Before proceeding to these 'regional' bibliographies, one should note such resources as the *Articles on Women Writers: A Bibliography 1960–84*, 2 vols (N.L. Schwartz, Santa Barbara, 1977–86) and the *Bibliography of Women and Literature: Articles and Books 1974–81 by and about Women 600–1975*, 2 vols (Florence Boos, New York, 1988). V.S. Gilbert and D.S. Tatla have prepared *Women's Studies: A Bibliography of Dissertations 1870–1982* (Blackwell, Oxford, 1985), while S.E. Searing has published the more general *Introduction to Library Research in Women's Studies* (Boulder, Col., 1985). James Harner's *Literary Research Guide: A Guide to Reference Sources for the Study of Literature in English and Related Topics* (New York, 1989) is more general, but a real aid to research, with which all students should be familiar.

Amongst the numerous journals which are also available for research and reading in women and literature, the student should not forget to consult, for example, *The Feminist Review, Women's Studies: An Interdisciplinary Journal* (1972–), *Signs: Journal of Women in Culture and Society* (1975– , quarterly), *Spare Rib, Tulsa Studies in Women's Literature* (1982–) and other journals which do not exclude women as much as often happens, such as *Kunapipi* (international, ed. Anna Rutherford), *Manushi* (Indian), numerous Canadian journals such as *Tessara*, and African journals such as *Researches in African Literatures* or the *Zimbabwe Women Writers Group* and the Ghana mazagine *Obaa Sima*, ed. Kate Abbam. (Many other small magazines and journals have flourished at times. These can be traced in the references of books mentioned for specific geographical areas, or in the secondary criticism for each individual author.) The *Journal of Commonwealth Literature* and several Australian journals cover women writers. *SPAN* is the newsletter of the South Pacific Association, while *Ariel* and *World Literatures Written in English* are other useful journals.

For bibliographies of primary and secondary literature organized by geographical area, see for example the *Bibliography of African Women Writers and Journalists*, by B. Berrian (Washington, D.C., 1985) or B. Richter and S. Kotze's *Bibliography of Criticism of Southern African Literature in English* (Bloemfontein, 1983). (These bibliographies on Africa – and the following ones on other regions – can be supplemented by the histories, guides, reviews and studies discussed below.) The volume on Africa in the Gale Research *Information Guide Series* mentioned earlier should also be consulted for writing on this region. For Australia, Debra Adelaide's *Bibliography of Australian Women's Literature, 1795–1990* (Sydney, 1991) is a selected, alphabetically arranged volume with some additional information. The yearly *Australian Literary Studies Bibliography* is also much more inclusive of women writers than it used to be. And see Margaret Murphy, *Women Writers and Australia: A Bibliography, Nineteenth Century to 1987* (Parkville and Melbourne, 1988).

Beryl Berrian has also published a *Bibliography of Women Writers from the Caribbean* (Washington, D.C., 1989), which can be used in conjunction with M.J. Fenwick's two-volume *Writers of the Caribbean Area. A Bibliography* (New York, 1991). D. Cumber Dance's *Fifty Caribbean Writers: A Bio-Bibliographical Sourcebook* (Westport, Conn., 1986) also includes a large number of women novelists in the alphabetical entries, with much useful biographical material as well. For other regions outside Britain and North America, the Gale Research *Information Guide Series* is again a vital resource, but so are regional journals (which frequently publish individual author bibliographies from time to time or annually), such as *Canadian Literature*, the *Journal of New Zealand Literature*, and other Canadian, Australian, Indian, etc., journals, as well as the more general *Bulletin of Bibliography*, the *Journal of Commonwealth Literature, World Literature Written in English* and so on. Useful bibliographies can also be found in such volumes as *The Oxford History of New Zealand Literature in English* ed. T. Sturm (Auckland and Oxford, 1991) and other histories, though *The Oxford History* is particularly worthy of mention for its completeness and accessibility.

For Britain and North America, there are innumerable bibliographical resources on women writers, many of them quite recent and up to date. For American women writers, both the *American Women Writers: Bibliographical Essays*, eds M. Duke, J.R. Bryer and M. Thomas Inge (Westport, Conn., and London, 1983), and *Facts on File: Bibliography of American Fiction 1919–1988*, eds M.J. Bruccoli and J.S. Baughman, 2 vols (New York and Oxford, 1991), are most informative and readable. There is also an earlier *Facts on File* for the period 1850–1918. The somewhat dated but still indispensable compilation by L. Leary, *Articles on American Literature 1900–1976*, 3 vols (Durham, N.C., 1954, 1970, 1979) is remarkable for its inclusion of articles on women writers often excluded from other bibliographies of the era. L.D. Rubin's *Bibliographical Guide to the Study of Southern Literature* (Baton Rouge, La., 1969) is helpful on a more limited regional range, but should not be ignored, while B.A. White's *American Women Writers: An Annotated Bibliography of Criticism* (New York, 1977) is obviously more targeted

on women. *Black American Women in Literature: A Bibliography: 1976–87*, by Ronda Glikin (Jefferson, N.C., 1989), is a thorough resource, albeit for a short period, and will in due course, one hopes, be joined by more extensive bibliographies of black women writers. *American Indian Novelists: An Annotated Critical Bibliography*, by Tom Colonnese and Louise Owen (New York and London, 1985), fills part of another void; this area is in great need of extension and updating.

For Britain, there are also considerable bibliographic resources on women writers, though they often tend to be contained in other works, such as *Scottish Women Writers to 1987*, by K.A. Stewart (Glasgow, 1987) or the *Dictionary of British Women Writers*, ed. Janet Todd (London, 1989), a quite invaluable reference book, with essays on individual authors of biographical and thematic content, and shortened primary and secondary bibliographical information. Indeed, this brings us to the most extensive and reliable bibliographic aid for British and American women writers, apart from the MLA and MHRA volumes, namely, the *Dictionary of Literary Biography*, which now amounts to more than 145 volumes published from the 1970s to the present day, and which will be discussed more fully below. Perhaps the most famous bibliography for English literature researchers, *The New Cambridge Bibliography of English Literature*, 5 vols, eds George Watson, I.R. Williams and J.D. Pickels for the index (Cambridge, 1974–7), is more helpful for earlier writers in the first half of the century. (See also *The Shorter New Cambridge Bibliography of English Literature*, again ed. George Watson, Cambridge, 1981). L.B. and S. Corse's *Articles on American and British Literature 1950–1977* (Athens, Ohio, 1981) fills gaps in unexpected ways. *English Novel Explication*, plus supplements I, II, III and IV, compiled by various editors (London and Hamden, Conn., 1972–90), is a bibliography of secondary criticism on the English novel, but its coverage of (until now) less well-known women authors is patchy. This lack makes a number of other bibliographies of English (and, even more so, Irish) literature less useful than they might at first appear.

As has been indicated already above, many extremely useful, more highly focused bibliographies will be found in works of biographical or critical emphasis, such as the *Dictionary of Literary Biography*, general eds M.J. Bruccoli, R. Layman et al., 146 vols (with *Yearbooks* from 1980 updating previous volumes, and the *Documentary Series*, Gale Research Centre, Detroit, Mich., 1978–94) for American and British writers, and such volumes as the *Encyclopedia of Post-Colonial Literatures in English*, eds Eugene Benson and L.W. Conolly, 2 vols (London, 1994). These two works, along with *International Literature in English: Essays on the Major Writers*, ed. R.L. Ross (New York and London, 1991), are volumes of essays on individual writers, with biographical, some critical and much thematic information, and in a few cases very full bibliographical data. One of the most impressive of such recent volumes of essays on individual writers is *Post-War Literatures in English: A Lexicon of Contemporary Authors*, eds H. Bertens, T. D'haen, L. Herman and R. Todd (Houten and Groningen, 1988–). This work is constantly being updated with new articles, which are to be added to a loose-leaf notebook, or set of notebooks, in alphabetical order. These essays are of a generally high quality, and are primarily interpretative rather than biographical or thematic, though they contain biographical material too. For post-war novelists, there is hardly a better critical-reference work available, and the imaginative format makes it possible to keep the volumes up to date on both new authors and re-evaluated older authors previously excluded from most secondary consideration.

Before turning to other research resources, one must mention Hal May's *Contemporary Authors: A Bio-Bibliographical Guide to Current Writers*, updated by A. Evory and L. Metzger as *Contemporary Authors New Revision Series* (Gale Research, Detroit, Mich., 1962–88). Along with this there is *The Writers' Directory*, a biennial compilation (published in Chicago since 1973). *The Twentieth Century Novel in English: A Checklist*, ed. E.C. Bufkin (Atlanta, Ga., 1985, revised from 1967), provides a useful companion to these other two, from the perspective, however, of the text rather than the author.

If we move now to other sorts of research resources, which of course often contain bibliographical material, we find a whole range of guides, companions, dictionaries and encyclopedias, which are of real value for basic informa-

tion. For twentieth-century women novelists writing in English, some of the most obvious, though wider ranging, are *The Bloomsbury Guide to Women's Literature from Sappho to Atwood*, ed. C. Buck (London, 1992). The long essays at the beginning of this reference book, organized around geographical regions all over the world, are its real distinguishing strength over other such works, as, for example, *The (Batsford) Feminist Companion to Literature in English*, eds V. Blair, P. Clements and E. Grundy (London, 1990). Different writers are to be found in the two books, due in part to the difference in scope, and hence both are most helpful groundbreakers in their aims. James Vinson's *Contemporary Novelists* (London, 1972, revised with D.L. Kirkpatrick, 1981, 1986) and his *Novelists and Prose Writers* in the series *Great Writers of the English Language* (London, 1979) are not to be overlooked; they contain short but sometimes extremely insightful essays. *The Cambridge Guide to Literature in English*, ed. I. Ousby (Cambridge, 1993), is useful for its internationalism, as is *The Macmillan Dictionary of Women's Biography* (London, 1982; New York, 1989).

Guides to specific regions often offer much more information than the works mentioned directly above; they may be in the form of histories, surveys and other kinds of review and study, which begin to move away from biographical, bibliographical or thematic emphases into critical and interpretative writing, while still offering some of this type of scholarly-academic material.

Africa

African writing is quite well served for some regions, though only recently have women writers been included systematically in these sorts of research resource, as with works on other regions. For example, O. Owolmoyela has compiled *A History of Twentieth Century African Literatures* (Lincoln, Nebr., 1993), while L. Brown published over a decade earlier the more specific *Women Writers in Black Africa* (Westport, Conn., 1981). Oladele Taiwo's *Female Novelists of Modern Africa* (New York and Basingstoke, 1984) and Eldred Jones's *Women in African*

Literature Today: A Review (London and Trenton, N.J., 1987) complement these other works with their critical surveys. Several collections of critical essays have recently appeared to revise and expand the 'canon', from Gina Wisker's recent *Black Women's Writing* (Basingstoke, 1993) to Abdulrazak Gurnah's *Essays on African Writing: A Re-evaluation* (Oxford, 1993), Robin Morgan's earlier collection *Sisterhood is Global* (New York, 1984), and *Ngambika: Studies of Women in African Literature*, eds. C.B. Davies and A.A. Graves (Trenton, N.J., 1986). A special issue of the journal *Matutub*, ed C.B. Davies and called *Black Women's Writing: Crossing the Boundaries* (Frankfurt, 1989), collects essays on numerous writers. Gay Wilentz has written *Binding Cultures: Black Women Writers in Africa and the Diaspora* (Bloomington, Ind., 1992), which adds to this already flourishing field of preliminary studies in women writers.

South African writing has received still more attention in these early years of the recovery of women's writing and the re-evaluation of already known texts. For example, U.A. Barnett's *Black South African Writing 1914–80* (London, 1983) attends in considerable detail to female as well as male writers, and has some insightful pages on numerous women novelists. A helpful companion to this is *Black South African Women Writers in English: A Preliminary Checklist*, ed. A. House (Evanston, Ill., 1980); J.M. Coetzee's *White Writing* (New Haven, 1985) is also reasonably attentive to South African women. *The South African Novel in English: Essays in Criticism and Society*, ed. Kenneth Parker (London, 1978), complements the anthology by Nadine Gordimer and L. Abrahams, *South African Writing Today* (Harmondsworth, 1967). *Nigerian Female Writers: A Critical Perspective*, eds H. Otukunefor and O. Nwodo (Lagos, 1989), is, one can only hope, the precursor of many such volumes to come on other African women writers.

For more wide-ranging studies or collections, see *Motherlands: Black Women's Writing from Africa, the Caribbean, and South Asia*, ed. Susheila Nasta (London, 1991), which, in addition to some very fine articles, has information on primary and secondary literature to some extent. And see *Unheard Words: Women and Literature in Africa, the Arab World, Asia, the Caribbean, and Latin America*, ed. Mineke Schipper (London and New York, 1985). Both these volumes are a reminder of the extensive international range of writing in English, which reaches into the Middle East, Southeast Asia and South America.

America

For some very general but nevertheless often helpful reference texts, works such as *American Writers*, ed. Leonard Unger, 8 vols (New York, 1974–), can be useful, though the number of women included is somewhat small. The *Reader's Encyclopedia of American Literature*, eds M.J. Herzberg et al. (New York, 1962) is a little dated, but still a useful source of elusive information on many occasions. *The Oxford Companion to American Literature*, ed. James D. Hart (Oxford, 1983), has recently been supplanted for our purposes by the *Oxford Companion to Women's Writing in the United States*, ed. C.N. Davidson (Oxford, 1995). Other works which are targeted at specific geographical areas are *Fifty Western Writers: A Bio-Bibliographical Sourcebook*, eds F. Erisman and R.W. Etulain (Westport, Conn., 1982), and *Fifty Southern Writers after 1900: A Bio-Bibliographical Sourcebook*, eds J.M. Flora and R. Bain (New York, 1987). These two, and *A History of Southern (American) Writers. A Biographical Dictionary*, eds R. Bain, J.M. Flora and L.D. Rubin, Jr. (Baton Rouge, La., and London, 1979), contain reasonably substantial entries, full of a range of information and some critical observations on the literature, though the last of these volumes needs updating. They can be read for material about an individual writer, or browsed through to familiarize the reader with writers she or he may not yet know. Rubin has also edited, along with others, the companion to this last volume, namely, *A History of Southern (American) Literature* (Baton Rouge, La., and London, 1985), which is a readable and intelligent critical-historical work of real value. Further books on these regions include *Tomorrow is Another Day: The Woman Writer in the South 1859–1936*, by A.G. Jones (Baton Rouge, La., 1981), and *Women and Western American Literature*, eds H. Stauffer and S. Rosowski (Troy, N.Y., 1982). The latter overlaps only in part with *Women, Women Writers and the West*, eds L. Lee and M. Lewis (Troy, N.Y., 1980). See also *The Oxford Companion to Women's Writing in the United States*, eds C.N. Davidson and L. Wagner-Martin (New York and Oxford, 1995).

There is an already substantial secondary and reference literature focused on ethnic groupings such as Native Americans, Afro-Americans, Chinese Americans and so on, and there are works devoted to lesbian writers. Some of the most useful of these are, for example, *The Safe Sea of Women: Lesbian Fiction, 1969–1989*, by B. Zimmerman (Boston, 1990), and Patricia Duncker's wide-ranging survey, *Sisters and Strangers: An Introduction to Contemporary Feminist Fiction* (Oxford, 1992), which is not restricted to American fiction by any means. Barbara Christian's groundbreaking *Black Women Novelists: The Development of a Tradition 1892–1976* (London and Westport, Conn., 1980) was shortly followed by Sandi Russell's *Render Me My Song: African American Women Writers from Slavery to the Present* (London, 1990). *Invented Lives: Narratives of Black Women, 1860–1960*, by M. Washington (Garden City, N.Y., 1987), and *Prologue: The Novels of Black American Women 1891–1965*, by C.M. Watson (New York, 1985), cover somewhat similar ground, but have varied approaches and emphases which make each of these four works an important complement to the others. Hazel Carby's *Preconstructing Womanhood: The Emergence of the Afro-American Woman Novelist* (New York, 1987) offers still another historical slant (but see section I of the bibliography for more books on Afro-American women writers).

Further work on writers organized around ethnicity includes *Pocahontas's Daughters: Gender and Ethnicity in American Culture*, by M.V. Dearborn (New York, 1986), which includes a whole range of writers from non-European or non-white American backgrounds. *Between Worlds: Women Writers of Chinese Ancestry*, by Amy Ling (New York, 1990), and *Three American Literatures: Essays in Chicano, Native American, and Asian-American Literature for Teachers of American Literature*, ed. H.A. Baker (New York, 1982), are both excellent guides and informative sources, as is *Asian American Literature: An Introduction to the Writings and Their Social Context*, by E.H. Kim (Philadelphia, 1982). R. Fleck's collection of critical essays, *Critical Perspectives on Native American Fiction* (Washington, D.C., 1993), is pre-eminently an interpretative

work, but is of course informative about this ethnic group for readers who need an introduction to this superb body of emerging literature, as is the earlier *American Indian Fiction*, by C.R. Larson (Albuquerque, 1978). A more recent guide is Kenneth Lincoln's *Native American Renaissance* (Berkeley, Calif., 1983). Further works on Asian American writers, on the other hand, include A.R. Lee's collection of essays by different authors, *A Permanent Etcetera: Cross Cultural Perspectives on Post-War America* (London, 1993), and the edition by S. Geok-lin Lim, *Reading the Literatures of Asian America* (Philadelphia, 1992). *Reading Asian American Literature*, by Sau-Ling Cynthia Wong (Princeton, N.J., 1993), is one of the most recent works to appear on this area. (Section I of the bibliography should be consulted for further works on these ethnic writings.)

Books of reference and criticism on other specific groups of writers include L. Fried et al., *A Handbook of American Jewish Literature* (Westport, Conn., 1988), and the reader interested in Jewish fiction should not forget the journals devoted to Jewish and Jewish American writing. *The Three Worlds: Minority Women Writers in the United States*, ed. Dexter Fisher (Boston, 1980), is more general and looks at a whole range of minorities, while Maria Herrera-Sobek has edited *Beyond Stereotypes: The Critical Analysis of Chicana Literature* (Binghampton, N.Y., 1985). For a more general, theoretical discussion of the concept of ethnicity, see Werner Sollors, ed., *The Invention of Ethnicity* (New York, 1989). For one of the best of its kind, see, finally, *The Columbia History of the American Novel*, ed. Emory Elliott (New York, 1991). This is a most successful collection of essays about periods, regions, ethnicity, post-modernism, magic realism and so on. It is an excellent sourcebook and introduction to the novel in North America, and is most readable.

Australia, New Zealand and the Pacific Region

The pioneering and determined work of such women as Dale Spender and Debra Adelaide, amongst others, has transformed the Australian literary landscape, which is now being further revised and reinvented both by reassessments of women novelists of the past and by the greater appreciation of contemporary contributions to the genre by women. Spender's anthology of women writers was accompanied by her *Writing a New World: Two Centuries of Australian Women Writers* (London, 1988), backed up by D. Adelaide's bibliography mentioned above. Pam Gilbert contributed to this new awareness with her *Coming Out from Under: Contemporary Australian Women Writers* (London and North Sydney, 1988). In the same year, Margaret Murphy published *Women Writers and Australia* (Melbourne, 1988). Earlier, Drusilla Modjeska had anticipated and perhaps even in part stimulated these later books with *Exiles at Home: Australian Women Writers, 1925–45* (London, 1981), as had Carole Ferrier, who edited *Gender, Politics and Fiction: Twentieth Century Australian Women's Novels* (St Lucia, Queensland, 1985). Republication by Virago and in other series of earlier texts, along with a growing number of anthologies of Australian women writers, has led to a huge increase in appreciation and a large and informative body of literary criticism, especially in journals but also in book form. For more basic information, see Ken Goodwin's *A History of Australian Literature* (London, 1986), which includes a number of women, as does G. Dutton's *The Literature of Australia* (Harmondsworth, 1976). *The Oxford History of Australian Literature*, ed. L. Kramer (Oxford and New York, 1981), may be less informative about women writers than one could have expected.

There is probably no better basic guide to New Zealand literature than the remarkable *Oxford History of New Zealand Literature in English*, ed. T. Sturm (Auckland and Oxford, 1991), which sets a standard for histories of literature rarely attained. It is not only critically astute, historically adept and rich in biographical and bibliographical (secondary and primary) material; it is also unusually inclusive, whether of women or of native writers. Other books of a general kind include the useful *Biography in New Zealand*, ed. J. Phillips (Wellington, 1985), *New Zealand Novels and Novelists, 1861–1979*, by James Burn (Auckland, 1981), and *New Zealand Fiction*, by J. and J. Jones (Boston, 1984). Other books providing a background to the woman writer include *Barbed Wire and Mirrors: Essays*

on New Zealand Prose, by Lawrence Jones (Dunedin, 1987), *Critical Essays on the New Zealand Short Story*, ed. Cherry Hankin (Auckland, 1982), and *The New Zealand Novel, 1860–1965*, by Joan Stevens (Wellington, 2nd rev. edn, 1966). Collections by C.K. Stead include *In the Glass Case: Essays on New Zealand Literature* (Auckland, 1981) and *Answering to the Language: Essays on Modern Writers* (Auckland, 1989). *Leaving the Highway: Six Contemporary New Zealand Novelists*, by Mark Williams (Auckland, 1990), and *Talking about Ourselves*, by Harry Ricketts (Wellington, 1986), provide much insight into the region's writers.

For books specifically on women writers, however, M. Hayward and J. Cowley's *Women Writers of New Zealand 1932–82* (Wellington, 1982) provides a good introduction, followed by, say, *Where Did She Come From? New Zealand Women Novelists 1862–1987*, by Heather Roberts (Wellington, 1989). Joan Stevens's *New Zealand Women in Literature* (Wellington, 1972) is an earlier survey, while Sue Kedgely's more recent *Our Own Country* (Auckland, 1989) should be consulted. Gail Pittaway's article in the *Journal of New Zealand Literature* 6 (1987) on recent fiction by women needs to be updated shortly, and a reading of recent issues of the journal itself is instructive of recent fiction. Maori journals must also be consulted (see the individual author entries on Patricia Grace and Keri Hulme for further detailed information). James Vinson and D.L. Kirkpatrick's *New Zealand Contemporary Novelists* (London 4th edn, 1986) is still indispensable for a number of very competent short articles on women novelists who are still not receiving enough attention today.

A Sense of Exile: Essays in the Literature of the Asia-Pacific Region, ed. Bruce Bennett (Nedlands, Western Australia, 1988), is another wide-ranging collection which will provide the reader with basic information and critical interpretation, as does *South Pacific Literature: From Myth to Fabulation*, ed. Subramani (Suva, 1985). One must not forget how useful the *Encyclopedia of Post-Colonial Literatures in English*, eds Benson and Conolly (1994), mentioned in an earlier section (p. 347), can be, with its often full and intelligent essays. Alongside this is Ross's *International Literature in English: Essays on the Major Writers* (1991), also mentioned earlier (p. 347).

Fewer women are included, probably, than by Benson and Conolly, but the articles are frequently more thorough, thanks to the greater space allowed (for fewer writers, though). In addition, books such as *Crisis and Creativity in the New Literatures in English*, eds G. Davis and M. Maes-Jelinek (Amsterdam, 1990), and T. D'haen and C. Barfoot's collection *Shades of Empire: Studies in Colonial and Post-Colonial Literatures* (Amsterdam and Atlanta, 1993) are really informative both on this region and on the wider scene within which internationalist women's writing is occurring. Thelma Kintanar's collection of essays, *Women Novelists of Southeast Asia* (forthcoming), will be a great addition to secondary literature about this region, and see *Essays on Literature and Society in Southeast Asia*, ed. Tham Seong Chee (Singapore, 1981). *Commentary: Journal of the National University of Singapore Society* is another source of secondary information, as is Koh Tai Ann's essay 'The Sun in her Eyes: Writing in English by Singapore Women', in *Into the Nineties: Post-Colonial Women's Writing*, eds A. Rutherford, L. Jensen and S. Chew (Armidale, New South Wales, 1994).

Britain and Ireland

Margaret Crosland's early survey of women novelists, *Beyond the Lighthouse: English Women Novelists in the Twentieth Century* (London, 1981), is more an annotated primary bibliography than a critical work, and is extremely informative for being so, as an introduction to the sheer extent of previously appreciated but lately ignored writers. The next year, Elaine Showalter's *A Literature of their Own: British Women Novelists from Bronte to Lessing* (London, 1982) took a more selective and critical-interpretative approach, though many of her questionable evaluations caused concern amongst literary critics. Earlier than both of these, however, were J.I. Biles's *The Female Novelist in Twentieth Century Britain* (Atlanta, Ga., 1978), more selective again than Crosland but also more interpretative, and Janet Kaplan's exceptionally insightful *Feminine Consciousness in the Modern British Novel* (Urbana, Ill., 1975). Here Kaplan examined about half a dozen women writers, including, for example, the then little-known May Sinclair and Rosamond

Lehmann; she focused her book on the typically modernist representation of consciousness as a stream. Malcolm Bradbury and David Perkins's collection of essays, *The Contemporary English Novel* (London, 1979), dealt with more women than the usual token one, in some fine articles on a range of British writers including Iris Murdoch, Barbara Pym and Margaret Drabble. As mentioned above under 'America', *Sisters and Strangers: An Introduction to Contemporary Feminist Fiction* by Patricia Duncker (Oxford, 1992), is a thorough survey of lesbian and feminist fiction, not restricted to Britain but focused on it, while *The British Novel since the Thirties: An Introduction*, by Randall Stevenson (London, 1986), is also more inclusive of women than was usual until recently. For more basic data, reference works such as *The Oxford Guide to British Women Writers*, ed. Joanne Shattock (Oxford, 1993), is useful, while *An Encyclopedia of British Women Writers*, by P. and J. Schleuter (London and New York, 1988), can also be consulted. *The Oxford Companion to English Literature*, ed. M. Drabble (Oxford, 1985), leaves out more women than it includes, sadly, while *The Columbia History of the British Novel*, ed. John Richetti (New York, 1994), cannot but disappoint both critically and for its extreme male bias, especially if one is familiar with the immensely more successful and inclusive American volume in that series. The most reliable and extensive work is Janet Todd's *Dictionary of British Women Writers* (London, 1989), a collection of hundreds of essays with useful basic (if necessarily extremely limited) biographical and bibliographical information, and descriptions of the thematics of novels.

Turning to books specifically on Scottish writers, one finds K.A. Stewart's *Scottish Women Writers to 1987* (Glasgow, 1987), the best available for Scotland, supplemented only for basic information by *The Macmillan Companion to Scottish Literature*, ed. Trevor Royle (London, 1983).

For Irish writers, there is also a *Macmillan Dictionary of Irish Literature*, ed. R. Hogan (London, 1979), but see Ann Owens Weekes's *Irish Women Writers: An Uncharted Tradition* (Lexington, Ky., 1990), for the first real attention to the value of women novelists in Ireland, with the rare exceptions of some articles in journals and collections. See also the collection *The British and Irish Novel since 1960*, ed. James Acheson (Basingstoke, 1991).

R.E. Horner's collection of essays, *Contemporary British Women Writers* (London, 1992), is another helpful source of critical and bibliographical material, as is Olga Kenyon's earlier *Women Novelists Today: A Survey of English Writing in the Seventies and Eighties* (Brighton, 1988). Many other collections, which include British women amongst other nationalities, have been edited by Nicola Beauman, Laura Doan, Rachel Blau DuPlessis, E.G. Friedman and M. Fuchs, Mary Jacobus, Sue Roe, Patricia Spacks, Marlene Springer, Thomas Staley, and others; these re-evaluate earlier writers and introduce new women writers. Books by Ellen Moers, Paulina Palmer, Lorna Sage, Kate Fulbrooke and other women provide wide surveys with intelligent critical approaches, and can furnish much helpful information to both beginners and experts. (See section I of the bibliography for details.)

Canada

Canadian women writers have been well served already by critical essay collections, surveys and interpretative books, as well as having a vigorous journal-article resource, some of which is shared with Australia or Britain in journals devoted to both nationalities. For the most basic and general information, the reader and student can of course consult *The Oxford Companion to Canadian Literature*, ed. William Toye (Toronto and Oxford, 1983), W.J. Keith's *Canadian Literature in English* (Toronto and New York, 1985) or *A Reader's Guide to the Canadian Novel*, by J. Moss (2nd edn, Toronto, 1987). But there are a number of works specifically about women, such as Lorna Irvine's *Sub/Version: Canadian Fiction by Women* (Toronto, 1986), *A Mazing Space: Writing Canadian Women Writing*, eds S. Neuman and Smaro Damboureli (Edmonton, 1986), *Language in her Eye*, eds L. Scheier, S. Sheard and E. Wachtel (Toronto, 1990), or C.A. Howells's *Private and Fictional Worlds: Canadian Women Novelists of the 1970s and 1980s* (London, 1987). Howells edited, with L. Hunter, *Narrative Strategies in Canadian Literature* (Buckingham and

Philadelphia, 1991), while Elizabeth Thompson's *The Pioneer Woman: A Canadian Character Type* (Montreal, 1991) looks at Canadian representations of women in a range of novels. *Writing in the Feminine: Feminism and Experimental Writing in Quebec*, by Karen Gould (Carbondale, Ill., 1990), and *The Canadian Postmodern: A Study of Contemporary English-Canadian Fiction*, by Linda Hutcheon (Toronto, 1988), provide more specific critical attention to narrative practices and strategies. Penny Petrone has recently published *Native Literature in Canada: From the Oral Tradition to the Present* (Toronto, 1990), which is one of several studies of Native American literature. And see the journals *Tessara, A Room of One's Own, Atlantis* and *Fireweed*, all devoted to women writers. Section I of the bibliography gives further information, especially on books dealing with several nationalities.

Caribbean

Several extremely informative works, some specifically about women writers of this region, provide excellent introductory data about novels by women in English. For example, Selwyn Cudjoe's *Caribbean Women Writers* (Ithaca, N.Y., 1991) is a very useful source, especially when placed alongside *Women of the Caribbean*, by Pat Ellis (London, 1986), and *Out of the Kumbla: Caribbean Women and Literature*, eds C.B. Davies and E.S. Fido (Trenton, N.J., 1990). Several books not exclusively women-writer oriented are helpful, such as *Tbisi: Caribbean Writers and Critics*, ed. Maggie Butcher (Mundelstrup, 1989), and Michael Gilkes's *The West-Indian Novel* (Boston, 1981). *Whispers from the Caribbean: I Going Away, I Going Home*, by Wilfred Cartey (Los Angeles, 1991), on the English-language novel in the Caribbean, provides much contextual material, and see Selwyn Cudjoe's *Resistance and Caribbean Literature* (Athens, Ohio, 1980) for a different contextual emphasis. *Fifty Caribbean Writers: A Bio-Bibliographical Sourcebook*, ed. D. Cumber Dance (Westport, Conn., 1986), mentioned in the bibliographical section, should also be made use of for essential information. Susheila Nasta, in her collection *Motherlands* (London, 1991), has several essays devoted to the Caribbean woman writer, as does *Unheard Words*, ed.

M. Schipper (London and New York, 1985); both these latter books cover a wider geographical range, however.

India and South Asia

Both *Unheard Words* and *Motherlands*, mentioned directly above, cover this area, if only regarding a few writers, but William Walsh in *Indian Literature in English* (London, 1990) includes numerous women authors, and see also the collection of essays edited by Madhusudan Prasad, *Indian English Novelists* (New Delhi, 1982). *Twice Born Fiction: Themes and Techniques of the Indian Novel in English*, by M. Mukherjee (New Delhi, 1971), is finely updated by *The New Indian Novel in English: A Study of the 1980s*, ed. Viney Kirpal (New Delhi, 1990). G.S.B. Gupta edited another collection of critical essays, *Studies in Indian Fiction in English* (Gulbarga, 1987), and see also that edited by D. MacDermott and S. Ballyn, *A Passage to Somewhere Else* (New Delhi, 1986). *Women Writing in India: 600 B.C. to the Present*, eds E. Tharu and K. Lalita, 2 vols (New York, 1991) is an anthology of mainly non-English-language writers, but anyone interested in writing in English in this region should know about this tradition, which provides the context for the other. Most importantly, the feminist journal *Manushi* and the collection *Recasting Women: Essays in Colonial History*, eds K. Sangria and S. Vaid (Delhi, 1989), add to the critical tradition, while Kali for Women has now published several volumes of anthologies of short stories by women in the Kali collective.

The Writer's Sense of the Past: Essays on Southeast Asian and Australasian Literature, ed. Kirpal Singh (Singapore, 1987) is helpful for providing awareness of the larger region adjoining India, while 'Philippine Women Writers: A Room Shared', by L.T. Caspar, *Pilipinas* 9 (1987), opens up fields even further beyond the usual Anglo-American preoccupations, which so narrow our conceptions and blind us to possibilities for what fiction can do.

Select Bibliography

I General Works and Criticism

Albinski, N.M. *Women's Utopias in British and American Fiction*. London, 1988.

Alexander, Flora. *Contemporary Women Novelists*. London, 1989.

Allen, P.G. *The Sacred Hoop: Recovering the Feminine in American Indian Traditions*. Boston, 1986.

Ammons, Elizabeth. *Conflicting Stories: American Women Writers at the Turn into the Twentieth Century*. New York, 1991.

Anderson, L., ed. *Plotting Change: Contemporary Women's Fiction*. London, 1990.

Armitt, Lucie, ed. *Where No Man Has Gone Before: Women and Science Fiction*. London and New York, 1991.

Auchincloss, Louis. *Pioneers and Caretakers: A Study of Nine American Women Novelists*. Minneapolis, 1961.

Awkard, Michael. *Inspiring Influences: Tradition, Revision, and Afro-American Women's Novels*. New York, 1991.

Baker, H.A. *The Workings of the Spirit. The Poetics of Afro-American Women's Writing*. Chicago, 1991.

Barbour, James and Quirk, Tom, eds. *Writing the American Classics*. Chapel Hill, N.C., 1991.

Bataille, G.M. and Sands, K.M. *American Indian Women: Telling their Lives*. Lincoln, Nebr., 1984.

Beauman, Nicola. *A Very Great Profession: The Woman's Novel 1914–39*. London, 1983.

Bell, R.P., Parker, B.J. and Guy-Shefftall, B., eds. *Sturdy Black Bridges. Visions of Black Women in Literature*. Garden City, N.Y., 1979.

Benstock, Shari. *Women of the Left Bank: Paris, 1900–1940*. London, 1987.

Bjorhorde, Gerd. *Rebellious Structures: Women Writers and the Crisis of the Novel 1880–1900*. Oxford, 1987.

Blaber, M. and Gilman, M. *Roguery: The Picaresque Tradition in Australian, Canadian and Indian Fiction*. Butterfly, 1990.

Bowers, B.K. and Brothers, B., eds. *Reading and Writing Women's Lives: A Study of the Novel of Manners*. Ann Arbor, Mich., and London, 1990.

Boyle, Kay. *Words That Must Somehow be Said. Selected Essays 1927–1984*. Ed. E.S. Bell. London, 1985.

Braxton, J.M. and McLaughlin, A.N., eds. *Wild Women in the Whirlwind: The Afro-American Contemporary Literature Scene*. New Brunswick, N.J., 1990.

Broe, M.L. and Ingrum, A. *Women's Writing in Exile*. Chapel Hill, N.C., 1989.

Bruck, Peter and Karrer, Wolfgang, eds. *The Afro-American Novel since 1960*. Amsterdam, 1982.

Brunt, R. and Coward, R., eds. *Feminism, Culture, and Politics*. London, 1982.

Bruss, Elizabeth. *Beautiful Theories: The Spectacle of Discourse in Contemporary Criticism*. Baltimore, 1982.

Burridge, Christine, ed. *Autobiographies*. Vancouver, 1987.

Butler-Evans, E. *Race, Gender and Desire*. Philadelphia, 1989.

Byerman, K.E. *Fingering the Jagged Grain. Tradition and Form in Recent Black Fiction*. Athens, Ga., 1986.

Carpenter, Lynette and Kolmar, W.K., eds. *Haunting the House of Fiction*. Knoxville, Tenn., 1991.

Christ, Carol. *Diving Deep and Surfacing: Women Writers on Spiritual Quest*. Boston, 1980.

Clark, G., ed. *The New American Writing: Essays on American Literature since 1970*. London, 1990.

Cruikshank, M. *Lesbian Studies Present and Future.* New York, 1982.

Davis, G. and Maes-Jelinek, M., eds. *Crisis and Creativity in the New Literatures in English.* Amsterdam, 1990.

D'haen, T. and Barfoot, C., eds. *Shades of Empire: Studies in Colonial and Post-Colonial Literatures.* Amsterdam and Atlanta, 1993.

Dipple, Elizabeth. *The Unresolvable Plot: Reading Contemporary Fiction.* London, 1988.

Doan, L.L., ed. *Old Maids to Radical Spinsters. Unnamed Women in the Twentieth Century Novel.* Chicago, 1991.

Donovan, Josephine. *New England Local Color Literature.* New York, 1983.

Duplessis, Rachel Blau. *Writing Beyond the Ending: Narrative Strategies of Twentieth-Century Women Writers.* Bloomington, Ind., 1984.

Eckstein, Barbara J. *The Language of Fiction in a World of Pain: Reading Politics as Paradox.* Philadelphia, 1990.

Edel, Leon. *The Modern Psychological Novel 1900–1950.* New York, 1955.

Evans, Mari. *Black Women Writers 1950–1980: A Critical Evaluation.* Garden City, N.Y., 1984.

Ferrier, Carole, ed. *Gender, Politics, and Fiction: Twentieth Century Australian Women's Novels.* St Lucia, Queensland, 1985.

Fiedler, Leslie. *Love and Death in the American Novel.* London, 1967.

Fisher, Dexter, ed. *The Three Worlds: Minority Women Writers in the United States.* Boston, 1980.

Fried, L. et al., eds. *A Handbook of American Jewish Literature.* Westport, Conn., 1988.

Friedman, E.G. and Fuchs, Miriam, eds. *Breaking the Sequence: Women's Experimental Fiction.* Princeton, N.J., 1989.

Fulbrook, Kate. *Free Women. Ethics and Aesthetics in Twentieth Century Women's Fiction.* Hemel Hempstead, 1990.

Gates, H.L. *The Signifying Monkey. A Theory of Afro-American Literary Criticism.* New York, 1988.

Gelphant, B.H. *Women Writers in America: Voices in Collages.* Hanover, N.H., 1984.

Gerrard, Nicci. *Into the Mainstream: How Feminism has Changed Women's Writing.* London, 1989.

Gilbert, S.M. and Gubar, S. *No Man's Land: The Place of the Woman Writer in the Twentieth Century.* 3 vols. London and New Haven, 1988–94.

Girgus, S.B. *Desire and the Political Unconscious.* Basingstoke, 1990.

Goldsmith, E. *Writing the Female Voice: Essays on Epistolary Literature.* London, 1989.

Grove, Valerie. *The Compleat Woman: Marriage, Motherhood, Career.* London, 1988.

Gullette, M.M. *Safe at Last in the Middle Years: The Invention of the Midlife Progress Novel.* Berkeley, Calif., 1988.

Halperin, Daniel, ed. *Antaeus on Nature.* London, 1989.

Hanscombe, Gillian and Smyers, Vivien. *Writing for their Lives: The Modernist Women, 1910–1940.* London, 1987.

Hanson, Clare. *Short Stories and Short Fictions 1880–1980.* London, 1985.

Hardwick, Elizabeth. *Seduction and Betrayal.* London, 1974.

Heath, Stephen. *The Nouveau Roman: A Study of the Practice of Writing.* London, 1972.

Hernton, C.C. *The Sexual Mountain and Black Women Writers.* New York, 1987.

Herrera-Sobek, Maria, ed. *Beyond Stereotypes: The Critical Analysis of Chicana Literature.* Binghampton, N.Y., 1985.

Hobson, R. *The Southern Writer in the Postmodern World.* Athens, Ga., 1991.

Hornby, Nick. *Contemporary American Fiction.* London, 1992.

Horner, Avril and Zlosnik, Sue. *Landscapes of Desire: Metaphors in Modern Women's Fiction.* Hemel Hempstead, 1990.

Hosmer, R.E., ed. *Contemporary British Women Writers.* London, 1992.

Howells, C.A. *Private and Fictional Worlds; Canadian Women Novelists of the 1970s and 1980s.* London, 1987.

Howells, C.A. and Hunter, L., eds. *Narrative Strategies in Canadian Literature.* Buckingham and Philadelphia, 1991.

Humm, Maggie. *Border Traffic: Strategies of Contemporary Women Writers.* Manchester, 1991.

Humm, Maggie. *A Reader's Guide to Contemporary Feminist Criticism.* New York and London, 1994.

Humm, Maggie. *The Dictionary of Feminist Theory.* Rev. edn, New York and London, 1995.

Hutcheon, Linda. *The Politics of Postmodernism.* London, 1989.

Jackson, R. *Fantasy: The Literature of Subversion.* London, 1981, rev. 1991.

Jacobus, Mary, ed. *Women Writing and Writing about Women.* London, 1979.

James, Adeola, ed. *In their Own Voices: African Women Writers Talk.* London, 1990.

Jay, K. and Glasgow, J., eds. *Lesbian Texts and Contexts.* New York, 1990.

Jones, S.W., ed. *Writing the Woman Artist: Essays on Poetics, Politics, and Portraiture.* Philadelphia, 1991.

Josipovici, Gabriel. *The World and the Book.* London, 1971.

Jump, H.D., ed. *Diverse Voices. Essays on Twentieth*

Century Women Writers in English. Hemel Hempstead, 1991.

Kappeler, Susanne. *The Pornography of Representation*. London, 1986.

Kenyon, Olga. *Women Novelists Today. A Survey of English Writing in the Seventies and Eighties*. Brighton, 1988.

Kenyon, Olga. *Writing Women: Contemporary Women Novelists*. London, 1991.

Killam, G.D., ed. *The Writing of East and Central Africa*. London, 1984.

King, B., ed. *The Commonwealth Novel Since 1960*. Basingstoke, 1991.

Klein, Kathleen. *The Woman Detective: Gender and Genre*. Urbana, Ill., 1988.

Klinkowitz, Jerome. *Structuring the Void: The Struggle for Subject in Contemporary American Fiction*. Durham, N.C., 1991.

Labovitz, E.K. *The Myth of the Heroine. The Female Bildungsroman in the Twentieth Century*. New York, 1986.

Larson, Wendy. *Literary Authority and the Modern Chinese Writer*. Durham, N.C., 1991.

Lee, A.R., ed. *A Permanent Etcetera: Cross Cultural Perspectives on Post-War America*. London, 1993.

Lim, S. Geok-lin, ed. *Reading the Literatures of Asian America*. Philadelphia, 1992.

Ling, Amy. *Between Worlds: Women Writers of Chinese Ancestry*. New York, 1990.

Lodge, David. *The Language of Fiction*. London, 1966.

Lodge, David. *The Modes of Modern Writing*. London, 1977, 1979.

McCullers, Carson. *The Mortgaged Heart and Other Essays*. Harmondsworth, 1985.

McHale, Brian. *Constructing Postmodernism*. London, 1992.

McHale, Brian. *Postmodernist Fiction*. London, 1988.

Mansfield, Katherine. *The Critical Writings of Katherine Mansfield*. Ed. Clare Hanson. London, 1987.

Mickelson, Anne Z. *Reaching Out: Sensitivity and Order in Recent American Fiction by Women*. Metuchen, N.J., 1979.

Miles, Rosalind. *The Female Form: Women Writers and the Conquest of the Novel*. London and New York, 1987.

Miller, Karl. *Authors*. Oxford, 1989.

Minh-ha, T.T. *Women, Native, Other*. Bloomington, Ind., 1989.

Moers, Ellen. *Literary Women: The Great Writers*. London, 1977.

Mogen, D., Busby, M. and Bryant, P., eds. *The Frontier Experience and the American Dream: Essays on American Literature*. College Station, Tex., 1990.

Moi, Toril. *Sexual/Textual Politics: Feminist Literary Theory*. London, 1985.

Monteith, M. *Women's Writing: A Challenge to Theory*. Brighton, 1986.

Moraga, Cherrie and Anzaldua, Gloria, eds. *This Bridge Called My Back: Writings by Radical Women of Color*. New York, 1981.

Morrison, Toni. *Playing in the Dark*. London and Cambridge, Mass., 1990.

Murray, David. *Forked Tongue: Speech, Writing, and Representation in North American Indian Texts*. London, 1991.

New, W.H. *Dreams of Speech and Violence. The Art of the Short Story in Canadian and New Zealand Literature*. Toronto, 1987.

Nin, Anaïs. *A Woman Speaks*. London, 1982.

Nischik, R.M. and Korte, B., eds. *Modes of Narrative*. Wurzburg, 1990.

O'Connor, Flannery. *Mystery and Manners: Occasional Prose*. London, 1972.

Ostriker, Alicia. *Writing Like a Woman*. Ann Arbor, 1983.

Palmer, Paulina. *Contemporary Women's Fiction: Narrative Practice and Feminist Theory*. Hemel Hempstead, 1989.

Pearlman, M. and Henderson, K.U., eds. *Inter/Views*. Lexington, Ky., 1990.

Perry, Ruth. *Women, Letters and the Novel*. New York, 1980.

Prasad, Madhusudan, ed. *Indian English Novelists*. New Delhi, 1982.

Pryse, M. and Spillers, H.J., eds. *Conjuring: Black Women, Fiction, and Literary Tradition*. Bloomington, Ind., 1985.

Radford, Jean, ed. *The Progress of Romance: The Politics of Popular Fiction*. London and New York, 1986.

Rainwater, C. and Scheik, W.J., eds. *Contemporary American Women Writers*. Lexington, Ky., 1985.

Robinson, S. *Engendering the Subject: Gender and Self-Representation in Contemporary Women's Fiction*. Albany, N.Y., 1991.

Roe, Sue, ed. *Women Reading Women's Writing*. Brighton, 1987.

Rossum-Guyon, F. van, ed. *Femmes Frauen Women*. Amsterdam, 1990.

Rule, Jane. *Lesbian Images*. Garden City, N.Y., 1975.

Sage, Lorna. *Women in the House of Fiction. Post-1945 Novelists*. London, 1992.

Sellars, S., ed. *Feminist Criticism: Theory and Practice*. Hemel Hempstead, 1991.

Showalter, Elaine, ed. *Sister's Choice: Tradition and Change in American Women's Writing*. Oxford, 1991.

Siegle, Robert. *Suburban Ambush: Downtown Writing and the Fiction of Insurgency*. Baltimore, 1989.

Smith, Valerie. *Self-Discovery and Authority in Afro-American Narrative*. Cambridge, Mass., 1987.

Smith, V., Baechler, L. and Litz, A.W., eds. *African American Writers*. New York, 1991.

Sollors, Werner, ed. *The Invention of Ethnicity*. New York, 1989.

Sontag, Susan. *A Reader*. Intro. Elizabeth Hardwick. Harmondsworth, 1983.

Spacks, Patricia. *The Female Imagination*. London, 1976.

Spacks, Patricia, ed. *Contemporary Women Novelists*. New Brunswick, N.J., 1977.

Spilka, Mark and McCracken-Flesher, Caroline, eds. *Why the Novel Matters: A Postmodern Perplex*. Indianapolis, Ind., 1990.

Springer, Marlene, ed. *What Manner of Woman: Essays on English and American Literature*. New York, 1977.

Staley, Thomas, ed. *Twentieth Century Women Novelists*. London, 1982.

Stubbs, Patricia. *Women and Fiction: Feminism and the Novel 1880–1920*. Brighton, 1979.

Suleiman, Susan. *Authoritarian Fictions: The Ideological Novel as Literary Genre*. New York, 1983.

Suleiman, Susan. *Subversive Intent. Women, Men and the Avant-Garde*. Cambridge, Mass., 1990.

Swann, B. and Krupat, A., eds. *Recovering the Word: Essays on Native American Literature*. Berkeley, Calif., 1987.

Tanner, Tony. *City of Words: American Fiction 1950–1970*. London, 1971.

Tate, Claudia, ed. *Black Women Writers at Work*. New York, 1983.

Thompson, Elizabeth. *The Pioneer Woman: A Canadian Character Type*. Montreal, 1991.

Walker, Melissa. *Down From the Mountaintop: Black Women's Novels in the Wake of the Civil Rights Movement 1966–89*. New Haven, 1991.

Walker, N. *Feminist Alternatives: Irony and Fantasy in the Contemporary Novel by Women*. Jackson, Miss., 1990.

Wandor, Michelene, ed. *On Gender and Writing*. London, 1983.

Ward, David. *Chronicles of Darkness*. London, 1989.

Watson, Daphne. *Their Worst Enemies: Women as Writers of Popular Fiction*. London, 1992.

Watts, Jane. *Black Writers from South Africa: Towards a Discourse of Liberation*. Basingstoke, 1989.

Waugh, Patricia. *Feminine Fictions: Revisiting the Postmodern*. London, 1989.

Weever, Jacqueline de. *Mythmaking and Metaphor in Black Women's Fiction*. Basingstoke, 1991.

Wheeler, Kathleen M. *'Modernist' Women Writers and Narrative Art*. Basingstoke, 1994.

Wilentz, Gay. *Binding Cultures: Black Women Writers in Africa and the Diaspora*. Bloomington, Ind., 1992.

Willes, Susan. *Specifying: Black Women Writing the American Experience*. London and Madison, 1987.

Williams, Merryn. *Six Women Novelists*. London, 1987.

Wilt, J. *Abortion, Choice, and Contemporary Fiction*. Chicago, 1990.

Wong, S.C. *Reading Asian American Literature*. Princeton, N.J., 1993.

Yaeger, Patricia, ed. *Refiguring the Father: New Feminist Readings of Patriarchy*. Carbondale, Ill., 1989.

Zeman, Anthea. *Presumptuous Girls: Women and their World in the Serious Woman's Novel*. London, 1977.

II Anthologies

This section uses the same geographical divisions as chapters 14 and 15, in alphabetical order, after an initial 'general' list.

General

Adams, B. and Tate, T., eds. *That Kind of Woman: Stories from the Left Bank and Beyond*. London, 1991.

Arkin, M. and Shollar, B., eds. *The Longman Anthology of World Literature by Women 1875–1975*. London, 1989.

Bulkin, E., ed. *Lesbian Fiction: An Anthology*. Watertown, Mass., 1981.

Carter, Angela, ed. *Wayward Girls and Wicked Women*. London, 1986.

Gilbert, S.M. and Gubar, S., eds. *The Norton Anthology of Literature by Women*. New York, 1985.

Lee, Hermione, ed. *The Secret Self*. 2 vols. London, 1985, 1987.

Park, C. and Heaton, C., eds. *Close Company. Stories of Mothers and Daughters*. London, 1987.

Rutherford, Anna et al., eds. *Into the Nineties: Post-Colonial Women's Writing*. Armidale, New South Wales, 1994.

St Aubin de Teran, L., ed. *Indiscreet Journeys: Stories of Women on the Road*. London, 1989.

Africa

Brown, Susan et al., eds. *LIP from Southern African Women*. Johannesburg, 1983.

Bruner, Charlotte H., ed. *Unwinding Threads*. London, 1983.

Bruner, Charlotte H., ed. *African Women's Writing*. Oxford, 1993.

Clayton, C., ed. *Women and Writing in South Africa: A Critical Anthology*. Johannesburg, 1989.

Mabuze, Lindiwe, ed. *One Never Knows: An Anthology of Black South African Women Writers in Exile*. Braamfontein, 1989.

Oosthuizen, Ann, ed. *Sometimes When it Rains: Writings by South African Women*. London, 1987.

America

See also the 'general' section above.

Lim, S.C. et al., eds. *The Forbidden Stitch: An Asian American Women's Anthology*. Corvallis, Oreg., 1989.

McKay, Nellie, ed. *Norton Anthology of Afro-American Literature*. New York and London, forthcoming.

Australia, New Zealand and the Pacific Region

Burns, C. and McNamara, M., eds. *Eclipsed: Two Centuries of Australian Women's Fiction*. London, 1988.

Burns, C. and McNamara, M., eds. *Feeling Restless: Australian Women's Short Stories 1940–1969*. London, 1989.

Davis, S. and Haley, R., eds. *Contemporary New Zealand Short Stories*. Harmondsworth, 1989.

Dunsford, C. and Hawthorne, S., eds. *The Exploding Frangipangi: Lesbian Writing from Australia and New Zealand*. London and Auckland, 1990.

Gibbs, Anna and Tilson, Alison, eds. *Frictions: An Anthology of Fiction by Women*. Melbourne, 1982.

Gunew, Sneja and Mahyuddin, Jan, eds. *Beyond the Echo: Multicultural Women's Writing*. St Lucia, Queensland, 1988.

Hooton, Joy, ed. *Stories of Herself When Young*. Oxford, 1990.

Modjeska, Drusilla, ed. *Inner Cities*. Ringwood, Victoria, 1989.

Spender, Dale, ed. *The Penguin Anthology of Australian Women Writers*. Ringwood, Victoria, and London, 1988.

Waten, J. and Murray-Smith, S., eds. *Classic Australian Short Stories*. Melbourne, 1974.

Webby, E. and Wevers, L., eds. *Happy Endings: Stories by Australian and New Zealand Women 1850s–1930s*. North Sydney, 1987.

Webby, E. and Wevers, L., eds. *Goodbye to Romance: Stories by New Zealand and Australian Women Writers 1930–1988*. London, 1989.

Wendt, Albert, ed. *Lali: A Pacific Anthology*. Auckland, 1980.

Whitlock, Gillian, ed. *Eight Voices of the 1980s*. St Lucia, Queensland, 1989.

Britain and Ireland

See also the 'general' section above.

Smyth, Ailbhe, ed. *Wildish Things: An Anthology of New Irish Writing*. Dublin, 1989.

Canada

Atwood, Margaret and Weaver, R., eds. *The Oxford Book of Canadian Short Stories in English*. Toronto, 1986.

Campbell, S. and McMullen, L., eds. *New Women: Short Stories by Canadian Women*. Ottawa, 1991.

Richler, M., intro. *Canadian Writing Today*. Harmondsworth, 1970.

Sullivan, Rosemary, ed. *Stories by Canadian Women*. Toronto, 1984.

Sullivan, Rosemary, ed. *More Stories by Canadian Women*. Toronto, 1987.

Tell It Book Collective, ed. *Telling It: Women and Language Across Cultures*. Vancouver, 1990.

Caribbean

Mordecai, E.P. and Wilson, B., eds. *Her True True Name: An Anthology of Women's Writing from the Caribbean*. London, 1989.

Paravisini, L. and Esteves, C.C., eds. *Green Cane and Juicy Flotsam: Short Stories*. New Brunswick, N.J., 1991.

India and South Asia

Amin, F., intro. *How to Hook a Husband and Other Stories*. Singapore Women Writers series. Singapore, 1982.

Heng, Geraldine, ed. *The Sun in her Eyes: Stories by Singapore Women*. Singapore, 1976.

Holmstrom, L., ed. *The Inner Courtyard: Stories by Indian Women*. London, 1990.

Kali for Women, ed. *Truth Tales. Contemporary Writing by Indian Women*. New Delhi, 1986; London, 1987.

Kali for Women, ed. *The Slate of Life*. New Delhi, 1990.

Kali for Women, ed. *In Other Worlds*. New Delhi, 1992.

III Secondary Criticism on Individual Women Authors

This section is listed alphabetically by woman writer's name. It covers all authors on whom there are individual author entries in parts I–IV. The 'Books' category includes book-length studies such as Ph.D. theses and special issues of journals. Bibliographies, checklists, etc., are listed after articles.

Kathy Acker

Books

Brennan, K.M. 'Hysteria and the Scene of Feminine Representation'. Ph.D., University of Arizona, 1990.

Griggers, C.J. 'Reinventing the Popular: Inscriptions of the Feminine Subject in Postmodern Genres'. Ph.D., University of Florida, 1989.

McHale, Brian. *Constructing Postmodernism*. London, 1992.

Miller, Karl. *Authors*. Oxford, 1989.

Review of Contemporary Fiction. Special Issue: Kathy Acker, Christine Brooke-Rose and Marguerite Young. 9 (1989).

Ruddick, N., ed. *The State of the Fantastic*. Westport, Conn., 1992.

Siegle, Robert. *Suburban Ambush: Downtown Writing and the Fiction of Insurgency*. Baltimore, 1989.

Articles

Interview. *Over Here: An American Studies Journal* 6 (1986).

Interview. *Textual Practice* 6 (1992), 371–82.

Benson, Steve. 'Approaches to Kathy Acker'. *L=A=N=G=U=A=G=E* 4 (1982), 77–82.

Brennan, K. 'Hysterical Pastiche in Acker'. *Boundary* 2: 21 (1994), 243–68.

Brown, T. 'Acker and the Politics of Pain'. *Literature Interpretation Theory* 2 (1987), 167–77.

Ellis, R.J. 'Kathy Acker'. In *Post-War Literatures*. Eds H. Bertens et al. Houten and Groningen, 1992.

Englebrecht, P.J. 'Re/Viewing Acker'. *Trivia* 21 (1993), 30–41.

Friedmann, Ellen G. 'An Introduction to the Works of Acker'. *Review of Contemporary Fiction* 9 (1989), 37–47.

Harper, G.A. 'The Subversive Power of Sexual Difference in the Work of Kathy Acker'. *SubStance* 16 (1987).

Hulley, Kathleen. 'Transgressing Genre: Kathy Acker's Intertext'. In *Intertextuality and Contemporary American Fiction*. Eds P. O'Donnell and R. Con Davis. Baltimore, 1989, 171–90.

Jacobs, N. 'Acker and the Plagiarized Self'. *Review of Contemporary Fiction* 9 (1989), 10–15.

McCaffery, Larry. 'The Artist of Hell: Kathy Acker and Punk Aesthetics'. In *Breaking the Sequence*. Eds E.G. Friedman and M. Fuchs. Princeton, N.J., 1989, 215–30.

Noise, R. 'Shock Treatment'. *Strange Things are Happening* 1 (1988), 35–7.

Redding, A.F. 'Masochism and Acker'. *Contemporary Literature* 35 (1994), 281–304.

Sciolino, M. 'Acker and the Postmodern Subject of Feminism'. *College English* 52 (1990), 437–45.

Siegle, Robert. 'On the Subject of Walter Abish and Kathy Acker'. *Literature and Psychology* 33 (1987), 38–58.

Walsh, Richard. 'The Quest for Love and the Writing of Female Desire in Kathy Acker's *Don Quixote*'. *Critique* 32 (1991), 149–68.

Ama Ata Aidoo

Books

Bardolph, Jacqueline, ed. *Short Fiction in the New Literatures in English*. Nice, 1989.

Brown, L.W. *Women Writers in Black Africa*. Westport, Conn., 1981.

Davies, C.B. and Graves, A.A., eds. *Ngambika: Studies of Women in African Literature*. Trenton, N.J., 1986.

James, Adeola, ed. *In Their Own Voices: African Women Writers Talk*. London, 1990.

Killam, G.D., ed. *The Writing of East and Central Africa*. London, 1984.

Nasta, Susheila, ed. *Motherlands*. London, 1991.

Articles

Adelugba, Dapo. 'Language and Drama: Ama Ata Aidoo'. *African Literature Today* 8 (1976), 72–84.

Berrian, B.B. 'African Women in Flora Nwapa and Aidoo'. *College Language Association Journal* 25 (1982), 331–9.

Booth, James. 'Sexual Politics in Aidoo'. *Commonwealth Essays and Studies* 15 (1993), 80–96.

Chetin, Sara. 'Interview'. *Wasafiri* 6/7 (1987).

Chetin, Sara. 'Reading from a Distance: Aidoo's *Our Sister Killjoy*'. In *Black Women's Writing*. Ed. Gina Wisker. Basingstoke, 1993, 146–59.

Conde, Maryse. 'Three Female Writers in Modern Africa: Nwapa, Aidoo, and Ogot'. *Presence Africaine* 82 (1972), 132–43.

Cooper, B. 'Aidoo'. *English in Africa* 12 (1985).

Coussey, Denise. 'Is Life Sweet? The Short Stories of Aidoo'. In *Short Fiction in the New Literatures in English*. Ed. J. Bardolph. Nice, 1989, 285–90.

Dunton, C. '"Wheting Be Dat?" The Treatment of Homosexuality in African Literature'. *Research in African Literature* 20 (1989), 422–48.

Eko, Ebele. 'Beyond the Myth of Confrontation'. *Ariel E* 17 (1986), 139–52.

Elder, Arlene. 'Aidoo and the Oral Tradition: A

Paradox of Form and Substance'. *African Literature Today* 15 (1987), 109–18.

Frank, Katherine. 'Women Without Men: The Feminist Novel in Africa'. In *Women in African Literature Today*. Eds E.D. Jones et al. London, 1987.

Hill–Lubin, Mildred. 'The Relationship of African-American and African in Aidoo'. *Presence Africaine* 124 (1982), 190–201.

Hill–Lubin, Mildred. 'The Storyteller and the Audience in the Works of Aidoo'. *Neohelicon* 16 (1989), 221–45.

McCaffrey, K. 'Images of the Mothers in Aidoo'. *Africa Women* 23 (1979), 40–1.

Nwanko, Chimalum. 'Feminist Impulse and Social Realism in Aidoo'. In *Ngambika*. Eds C.B. Davies et al. Trenton, N.J., 1986, 151–9.

Ogunyemi, C.O. 'Womanism: The Dynamics of the Contemporary Black Female Novel in English'. *Signs* 11 (1985), 63–80.

Okafor, C.G. 'Ama Ata Aidoo: *Anowa*'. *Okike Educational Supplement* 4 (1985), 137–46.

Owusu, Kofi. 'Canons Under Siege: Blackness, Femaleness, and Aidoo'. *Callaloo* 13 (1990), 341–63.

Rooney, Caroline. 'Are We in the Company of Feminists? A Preface for Bessie Head and Aidoo'. In *Diverse Voices*. Ed. H.D. Jump. Hemel Hempstead, 1991.

Sackey, Edward. 'Oral Tradition and the African Novel'. *Modern Fiction Studies* 37 (1991), 389–407.

Wilentz, Gay. 'The Politics of Exile: Aidoo's *Our Sister Killjoy*'. *Studies in Twentieth Century Literature* 15 (1991), 159–73.

Margaret Atwood

Books

Beran, Carol. *Living over the Abyss: Atwood's 'Life Before Man'*. Toronto, 1993.

Bouson, J.B. *Brutal Choreographies*. Amherst, Mass., 1993.

Davey, Frank. *Margaret Atwood: A Feminist Poetics*. Vancouver, 1984.

Davidson, E.E. and Cathy, N., eds. *The Art of Margaret Atwood: Essays in Criticism*. Toronto, 1981.

Fee, Margery. *The Fat Lady Dances: Atwood's 'Lady Oracle'*. Toronto, 1993.

Frederick, B. et al., eds. *Women and the Journey*. Pullman, Wash., 1993.

Fulbrook, Kate. *Free Women*. Hemel Hempstead, 1990.

Gibson, Graeme. *Eleven Canadian Novelists* (Interviews). Toronto, 1973.

Grace, Sherrill. *Violent Duality: A Study of Atwood*. Montreal, 1980.

Ingersoll, Earl and Howard, P., eds. *Margaret Atwood: Conversations*. Princeton, N.J., 1990.

Irvine, Lorna. *Collecting Clues: Atwood's 'Bodily Harm'*. Toronto, 1993.

Keith, W.J. *A Sense of Style: Studies in the Art of Fiction in English-Speaking Canada*. Toronto, 1989.

Keith, W.J. *Introducing Atwood's 'The Edible Woman': A Reader's Guide*. Downsview, Ontario, 1989.

McCombs, Judith, ed. *Critical Essays on Atwood*. Boston, 1988.

Mendez-Egel, B., ed. *Margaret Atwood: Reflection and Reality*. Edinburgh, 1987.

Nischik, R.N. *A Theory of Mind Style*. Tübingen, 1991.

Rigney, B.H. *Margaret Atwood*. Basingstoke, 1987.

Rosenberg, J.H. *Margaret Atwood*. Boston, 1984.

Sandler, Linda, ed. *Margaret Atwood: A Symposium*. Victoria, 1977.

VanSpanckeren, K. and Castro, J.G., eds. *Margaret Atwood: Vision and Forms*. Carbondale and Edwardsville, Ill., 1988.

Weir, L. and Grace, S., eds. *Margaret Atwood: Language, Text, and System*. Vancouver, 1983.

Woodcock, G. *Introducing Atwood's 'Surfacing'*. Canadian Fiction Studies Series. Downsview, Ontario, 1989.

Articles

Banerfee, Chinmay. 'Alice in Disneyland: Criticism as Commodity in *The Handmaid's Tale*'. *Essays in Canadian Writing* 41 (1990), 74–92.

Beran, D.L. 'Intertexts in *Life Before Man*'. *American Review of Canadian Literature* 22 (1992), 199–214.

Bergman, Harriet. 'Teaching them to Read: A Fishing Expedition in *The Handmaid's Tale*'. *College English* 51 (1989), 847–54.

Bouson, J.B. 'The Anxiety of Being Influenced: Character in *The Edible Woman*'. *Style* 24 (1990), 228–41.

Cowart, David. 'Bridge and Mirror: Replicating Selves in *Cat's Eye*'. In *Postmodern Fiction in Canada*. Eds T. D'haen and H. Bertens. Amsterdam, 1992, 125–36.

Deer, Glenn. 'Rhetorical Strategies in *The Handmaid's Tale*'. *English Studies in Canada* 18 (1992), 215–33.

Devine, Maureen. 'The Dilemma of I'. In *Women in Search of Literary Space*. Eds M. Divine and G.M. Gruber. Tübingen, 1992, 28–41.

Ingersoll, E.G. 'Margaret Atwood's *Cat's Eye*'. *Ariel E* 22 (1991), 18–27.

Klarer, Mario. 'The Gender of Orality in *The Handmaid's Tale*'. *Arbeiten aus Anglistik und Amerikanistik* 15 (1990), 151–70.

Lancashire, Ian. 'Computer-Assisted Critical Analysis: A Case Study of *The Handmaid's Tale*'. In *The Digital Word*. Eds G.P. Landon and P. Delany. Cambridge, Mass., 1993, 293–318.

McCombs, Judith. 'Contrary Rememberings: The Creating of Self and Feminism in *Cat's Eye*'. *Canadian Literature* 129 (1991), 9–23.

Murray, Shauna. 'Narrative Strategies in *Bluebeard's Egg*'. *British Journal of Canadian Studies* 5 (1990), 127–40.

Osborne, Carol. 'Constructing the Self through Memory: *Cat's Eye*'. *Frontiers* 14 (1994), 95–112.

Patton, Marilyn. '*Lady Oracle*: The Politics of the Body'. *Ariel E* 22 (1991), 29–48.

Rao, Eleonora. 'Atwood's *Lady Oracle*: Writing Against Notions of Unity'. *British Journal of Canadian Studies* 4 (1989), 136–56.

Staels, H. 'Margaret Atwood'. *Post-War Literatures*. Eds H. Bertens et al. Houten and Groningen, 1988.

Strobel, Christina. 'On the Representation of Representation in *Surfacing*'. *Zeitschrift fur Anglistik und Amerikanistik* 40 (1992), 35–43.

York, L.M. 'The Habits of Language: Uniformity, Transgression, and Atwood'. *Canadian Literature* 126 (1990), 6–19.

Bibliography and reference
McCombs, J. and Palmer, C.L. *Margaret Atwood: A Reference Guide*. Boston, 1991.

Toni Cade Bambara

Books
Bell, R., Parker, B. and Guy-Sheftall, B., eds. *Sturdy Black Bridges: Visions of Black Women in Literature*. Garden City, N.Y., 1979.

Braxton, J.M. and McLaughlin, A.N., eds. *Wild Women in the Whirlwind*. New Brunswick, N.J., and London, 1990.

Butler-Evans, E. *Race, Gender, and Desire: Narrative Strategies in the Fiction of Bambara, Morrison, and Walker*. Philadelphia, 1989.

Byerman, Keith. *Fingering the Jagged Grain*. Athens, Ga., 1985.

Cudjoe, S.R. *Caribbean Women Writers*. Wellesly, Calaloux, 1990.

De Weever, Jacqueline. *Mythmaking and Metaphor in Black Women's Fiction*. Basingstoke, 1991.

Evans, Mari, ed. *Black Women Writers*. London and Sydney, 1985.

Koenen, Anne. *Zeitgenossische Afro-Amerikanische Frauenliteratur: Morrison, Bambara, und Jones*. Frankfurt and New York, 1985.

Pearlman, Mickey, ed. *American Women Writing Fiction*. Lexington, Ky., 1989.

Pryse, M. and Spillers, H.J., eds. *Conjuring: Black Women, Fiction and Literary Tradition*. Bloomington, Ind., 1985.

Russell, Sandi. *Render Me My Song*. London and Sydney, 1990.

Smith, Barbara, ed. *Home Girls*. New York, 1983.

Tate, Claudie, ed. *Black Women Writers at Work*. New York, 1983.

Willis, Susan. *Specifying: Black Women Writing*. Madison, Wis., 1987.

Articles
Byerman, K.E. 'Healing Arts'. *Postscript* 5 (1988), 37–43.

Carby, H.V. 'Reinventing History, Imagining the Future'. *Black American Literature Forum* 23 (1989), 381–7.

Dance, D.C. 'Go eena Kumbla'. In *Caribbean Women Writers*. Ed. S.R. Cudjoe. Wellesley, Mass., 1990, 169–84.

Deck, A.A. 'Toni Cade Bambara'. *Dictionary of Literary Biography* 38 (1985), 12–22.

Gidley, Mick. 'Reading Bambara's "Raymond's Run"'. *English Language Notes* 28 (1990), 67–72.

Hargrove, N.D. 'Youth in Toni Cade Bambara'. In *Women Writers of the Contemporary South*. Ed. P.W. Prenshaw. Jackson, Miss., 1984, 215–32.

Kelley, M.A. 'Modes of Access to *The Salt Eaters*'. *African American Review* 27 (1993), 479–93.

Lyles, L.F. 'Time, Motion, Sound and Fury in *The Sea Birds are Still Alive*'. *College Language Association Journal* 36 (1992), 134–44.

Bibliography and reference
Glikin, Ronda. 'Toni Cade Bambara' (a bibliography of primary and secondary literature). In *Black American Women in Literature 1976–87*. Jefferson, N.C., and London, 1989, 8–10.

Marjorie Barnard

Books
Giuffre, Giulia, ed. *A Writing Life: Interviews with Australian Women Writers*. Boston and Sydney, 1990.

Hickey, B. *Lines of Implication*. Venice, 1985.

Modjeska, Drusilla. *Exiles at Home*. St Lucia, Queensland, 1985.

Rorabacher, L.E. *Marjorie Barnard and M.Barnard Eldershaw*. Boston, 1973.

Articles

Barnard, Marjorie. 'How Tomorrow and Tomorrow Came to be Written'. *Meanjin* 29 (1970), 328–37.

Burns, R. 'Flux and Fixity: Marjorie Barnard'. *Meanjin* 29 (1970), 320–7.

Carter, David. 'Barnard Eldershaw'. *Australian Literary Studies* 14 (1989), 174–87.

Dever, Marilyn. 'No Time is Inopportune for a Protest'. *Hecate* 17 (1991), 9–21.

Holt, P., ed. 'Introduction'. *A City in the Mind: Sydney Imagined by its Writers*. North Sydney, 1984.

Palmer, Vance et al. 'Tributes to Eldershaw'. *Meanjin* 15 (1956), 390–4.

Roe, Jill. 'Barnard Eldershaw's *Tomorrow and Tomorrow and Tomorrow*'. *Meanjin* 43 (1984), 241–52.

Roe, Jill. 'Foreword'. In *Miles Franklin*. By Marjorie Barnard. St Lucia, Queensland, 1989.

Saunders, Ian. 'The Texts of *Tomorrow and Tomorrow and Tomorrow*'. *Southern Review* 26 (1993), 239–61.

Djuna Barnes

Books

Benstock, Shari. *Women of the Left Bank. Paris 1900–1940*. Austin, Tex., 1986.

Broe, M.L., ed. *Silence and Power: A Re-Evaluation of Djuna Barnes*. Carbondale, Ill., 1991.

Field, A. *Djuna: The Life and Times of Djuna Barnes*. New York, 1983. (Published as *The Formidable Miss Barnes*. London, 1983.)

Friedman, Melvin. *Stream of Consciousness: A Study in Literary Method*. New Haven, 1955.

Fulbrook, Kate. *Free Women*. Hemel Hempstead, 1990.

Gildzen, Alex, ed. *Djuna Barnes*. Kent, Ohio, 1972.

Hanscombe, G. and Smyers, V. *Writing for Their Lives*. London, 1987.

Jay, Karla and Glasgow, Joanne, eds. *Lesbian Texts and Contexts*. New York, 1990.

Kaivola, Karen. *All Contraries Confounded. The Lyrical Fiction of Woolf, Barnes, and Duras*. Iowa City, 1991.

Kannenstein, Louis F. *The Art of Djuna Barnes: Duality and Damnation*. New York, 1977.

Plumb, C.J. *Fancy's Craft. The Early Works of Barnes*. Selingrove, Pa., 1986.

Review of Contemporary Fiction. Special Issue 13 (1993).

Scott, James B. *Djuna Barnes*. Boston, 1976.

Singer, Alan. *A Metaphorics of Fiction*. Tallahassee, Fla., 1983.

Spencer, Sharon. *Space, Time and Structure in the Modern Novel*. New York, 1971.

Articles

Allen, Carolyn, 'The Erotics of Nora's Narrative'. *Signs* 19 (1993), 177–200.

Baxter, Charles. 'A Self-Consuming Light: *Nightwood* and the Crisis of Modernism'. *Journal of Modern Literature* 3 (1974), 1175–87.

Bronfen, Elizabeth. 'Death, Narration, and Gender in *Nightwood*'. *American Studies* (Amerikastudien) 33 (1988), 167–77.

Burke, Kenneth. 'Version, Con-, Per-, and In-'. In *Language as Symbolic Action*. Berkeley, Calif., 1968.

DeVore, Lynn. 'The Background of *Nightwood*'. *Journal of Modern Literature* 10 (1983).

Fuchs, Miriam. 'Barnes and Eliot'. *Tulsa Studies in Language and Literature* 12 (1993), 289–313.

Gerstenberger, Donna. 'The Radical Narrative of Djuna Barnes's *Nightwood*'. In *Breaking the Sequence*. Eds E.G. Friedman and M. Fuchs. Princeton, N.J., 1989, 129–39.

Greiner, D.J. 'Djuna Barnes's *Nightwood* and the American Origin of Black Humor'. *Critique* 17 (1975), 41–54.

Gunn, Edward. 'Myth and Style in Djuna Barnes's *Nightwood*'. *Modern Fiction Studies* 19 (1973–4), 545–55.

Johnson W.A. 'Modern Women Novelists: *Nightwood* and the Novel of Sensibility'. *Bucknell Review* 21 (1973), 15–28.

Michel, Frann. 'Displaying Castration: *Nightwood, Ladies Almanack*, and Feminist Writing'. *Contemporary Literature* 29 (1989), 33–58.

Morrison, J.E. 'The Preface as Criticism: T.S. Eliot on *Nightwood*'. *Centennial Review* 32 (1988), 414–27.

Nadeau, R.L. '*Nightwood* and the Freudian Unconscious'. *International Fiction Review* 2 (1975), 159–63.

Nimeiri, Ahmed. 'Djuna Barnes' *Nightwood* and "the Experience of America"'. *Critique* 34 (1993), 100–12.

Pochada, Elizabeth. 'Style's Hoax: A Reading of Djuna Barnes's *Nightwood*'. *Twentieth Century Literature* 22 (1976), 179–91.

Schehr, L.R. 'Barnes' *Nightwood*'. *Style* 19 (1985), 36–49.

Bibliography and reference

Messerli, Douglas. *Djuna Barnes: A Bibliography*. Rheinbeck, N.Y., 1975.

Stephens, Jamie. 'Barnes: An Updated Bibliography'. *Review of Contemporary Fiction* 13 (1993), 201–4.

Barbara Baynton

Books

Hackforth-Jones, Penne. *Barbara Baynton: Between Two Worlds: A Biography*. Ringwood, Victoria, 1989.

Niall, B. *Martin Boyd*. Oxford and Melbourne, 1977.

Walker, Shirley, ed. *Who Is She?* New York, 1983.

Articles

Colmer, John. 'Barbara Baynton'. In *The Story Must Be Told: Short Narrative Prose in the New English Literatures*. Ed. P.O. Stummer. Würzburg, 1986.

Gullett, H.B., ed. 'Memoir'. In *Bush Studies*. Sydney, 1965, 1–27.

Iseman, Kay. '[Baynton]'. *Australian Literary Studies* 11 (1983), 25–37.

Kirkby, Joan. 'Barbara Baynton: An Australian Jocasta'. *Westerly* (1989), 114–24.

Linsday, Jack. 'Barbara Baynton: A Master of Naturalism'. *Meanjin* 25 (1966), 345–8.

Matthews, Brian. 'Directions in Recent Fiction'. *Island* 33 (1986).

Moore, Rosemary. 'The Enigma of Women: Baynton's *Human Toll*'. *Australian Fiction Studies* 12 (1990), 83–93.

Phillips, A.A. 'Baynton and the Dissidence of the Nineties'. *Overland* 22 (1961–2), 15–20.

Phillips, A.A. 'Baynton's Stories'. In *Bush Studies*. Sydney, 1965, 27–45.

Rowley, Sue. 'The Representation of Motherhood in Bush Mythology'. *Westerly* 33 (1989), 76–95.

Sheridan, Susan. 'Gender and Genre in Baynton's *Human Toll*'. *Australian Literary Studies* 14 (1989), 66–77.

Walker, Shirley. 'Barbara Baynton's *Human Toll*: A Modernist Text?' *Southerly* 48 (1989), 131–48.

White, Robert. 'Grim Humour in Short Stories of the 1890s'. *Aspects of Australian Fiction* 1 (1990), 17–39.

Elizabeth Bowen

Books

Austin, Allen E. *Elizabeth Bowen*. New York, 1971.

Bennett, Andrew and Royle, Nicholas. *Elizabeth Bowen and the Dissolution of the Novel: Still Lives*. London, 1995.

Blodgeatt, Harriet. *Patterns of Reality: Elizabeth Bowen's Novels*. The Hague, 1975.

Brooke, Jocelyn. *Elizabeth Bowen*. London, 1952.

Dawe, Gerald and Longley, Edna, eds. *Across a Roaring Hill*. Belfast, 1985.

Glendinning, Victoria. *Elizabeth Bowen: Portrait of a Writer*. London, 1977.

Heath, W. *Elizabeth Bowen: An Introduction to her Novels*. Madison, 1961.

Hildebidle, J., ed. *Five Irish Writers*. Cambridge, Mass., 1990.

Jordan. H.B. *Bowen and the Landscape of War*. Ann Arbor, 1992.

Kenney. E.T. *Elizabeth Bowen*. Lewisburg, Pa., 1975.

Lassner, Phyllis. *Elizabeth Bowen*. Basingstoke, 1990.

Lassner, Phyllis. *Elizabeth Bowen: A Study of the Short Fiction*. New York, 1991.

Lee, Hermione. *Elizabeth Bowen: An Estimation*. London, 1981.

Reed, Toni. *Demon-Lovers and their Victims in British Fiction*. Lexington, Ky., 1988.

Articles

Bates, Judith. 'Undertones of Horror in Elizabeth Bowen'. *Journal of the Short Story in English* 8 (1987), 81–91.

Coates, John. 'The Rewards and Problems of Rootedness in Bowen's *Heat of the Day*'. *Renascence* 39 (1987), 484–501.

Coates, John. 'The Recovery of the Past in *A World of Love*'. *Renascence* 40 (1988), 226–46.

Daiches, David. 'The Novels of Elizabeth Bowen'. *English Journal* 38 (1949), 305–13.

Dorenkamp, A.G. 'Bowen's *The Heat of the Day*'. *Critique* 10 (1968), 13–21.

Hardwick, Elizabeth. 'Elizabeth Bowen's Fiction'. *Partisan Review* 16 (1949).

Heinemann, Alison. 'The Indoor Landscape in *Death of the Heart*'. *Critique* 10 (1968), 5–12.

Jarrett, Mary. 'The Short Stories of Bowen'. *Journal of the Short Story in English* 8 (1987), 69–79.

Johnson, T. O'Brien. 'Bowen's Irish Novels'. *Ariel* 18 (1987), 47–62.

Lassner, Phyllis. 'Language and History in Bowen'. *Perspectives on Contemporary Literature* 14 (1988), 30–8.

Shaw, L. 'The Uncertain "I": A Study of Elizabeth Bowen's Fiction'. *Western Humanities Review* 4 (1950).

Van Duyn, Mona. 'A Reading of *The Death of the Heart*'. *Critique* 4 (1961), 52–66.

Wagner, G. 'Elizabeth Bowen and the Artificial Novel'. *Essays in Criticism* 13 (1963), 155–63.

Weatherhead, A.K. 'Bowen: Writer in Residence'. *CEA Critic* 50 (1987–88), 35–44.

Bibliography and reference

Sellery, J'nan and Harris, W.O. *Elizabeth Bowen: A Bibliography*. Austin, Tex., 1981.

SELECT BIBLIOGRAPHY

Jane Bowles

Books

Dillon, Millicent. *A Little Original Sin: The Life and Work of Jane Bowles*. New York, 1981.

Articles

Bassett, M.T. 'Imagination, Control and Betrayal in Jane Bowles'. *Studies in Short Fiction 24* (1987), 25–9.

Dillon, Millicent. 'Jane Bowles: Experiment as Character'. In *Breaking the Sequence*. Eds E.G. Friedman and M. Fuchs. Princeton, N.J., 1989, 140–7.

Gray, Francine de Plessix. 'Introduction'. In *Two Serious Ladies*. By Jane Bowles. London 1979.

Hoefer, Jacqueline. 'Jane Bowles'. In *Contemporary Novelists*. Ed. J. Vinson. London and New York, 1972.

Kraft, J. 'Jane Bowles as Serious Lady'. *Novel* 1 (1968), 273–7.

Lakritz, A.M. 'Jane Bowles' Other World'. In *Old Maids to Radical Spinsters*. Ed. L.L. Doan. Bloomington, Ind., 1991, 213–34.

Lougy, R.E. 'The World and Art of Jane Bowles'. *CEA Critic* 49 (1986–7), 157–73.

Roditi, Edouard. 'The Fiction of Jane Bowles'. *Review of Contemporary Fiction* 12 (1992), 182–94.

Roscoe, Patrick. 'Influence'. *New Quarterly* 13 (1993), 6–11.

Wheeler, K.M. 'Jane Bowles: That Modern Legend'. In *'Modernist' Women Writers and Narrative Art*. Basingstoke, 1994, 162–81.

Kay Boyle

Books

Bell, E.S. *Kay Boyle: A Study of the Short Fiction*. New York, 1992.

Benstock, Shari. *Women of the Left Bank: Paris 1900–1940*. London, 1987.

Crosby, Caresse. *The Passionate Years*. New York, 1953.

Ford, H.D. *Four Lives in Paris*. San Francisco, 1987.

Spanier, S.W. *Kay Boyle: Artist and Activist*. Carbondale and Edwardsville, Ill., 1986.

Twentieth Century Literature. Special issue 34 (1988).

Articles

These do not include special issues.

Bell, E.S. 'Kay Boyle'. *Dictionary of Literary Biography Yearbook 1993*, 261–9. (See also vols 4, 9, 48 and 86 for further information.)

Carpenter, R.C. 'Kay Boyle'. *English Journal* 42 (1953), 425–30.

Carpenter, R.C. 'Kay Boyle: The Figure in the Carpet'. *Critique* 7 (1964–5), 65–78.

Centing, R.R. 'Kay Boyle: The Cincinnati Years'. *Ohioana Quarterly* 15 (1972), 11–13.

Davis, Margo. 'Kay Boyle'. In *Women Writers of the West Coast*. Ed. M. Yalom. Santa Barbara, Calif., 1983, 105–20.

Grumbach, D. 'Afterword'. In *My Next Bride*. By Kay Boyle. London, 1986.

Grumbach, D. 'Afterword'. In *Year Before Last*. By Kay Boyle. London, 1986.

Harter, Evelyn. 'Kay Boyle: Experimenter'. *Bookmarket* 75 (1932), 249–53.

Hawkins, A.D. 'Death of a Man'. *Critic* 27 (1937), 498–501.

Madden, C.F., ed. 'Interview'. In *Talks with Authors*. Carbondale and Edwardsville, Ill., 1968, 215–38.

Mesher, D.R. 'Interview'. *Malahat Review* 65 (1983), 82–95.

Meyer, Martin. 'Boyle's Postwar Germany'. In *Germany and German Thought in American Literature*. Ed. P. Freese. Essen, 1990, 205–29.

Spanier, S.W. 'Introduction'. In *Life Being the Best and Other Stories*. By Kay Boyle. New York, 1990.

Spanier, S.W. 'Kay Boyle: In a Woman's Voice'. In *Faith of a (Woman) Writer*. Ed. A. Kessler-Harris et al. Westport, Conn., and London, 1988, 59–70.

Bibliography and reference

Anon. 'A Selected Bibliography: Books by Kay Boyle'. *Twentieth Century Literature* 34 (1988), 392–4.

Sharp, R. 'A Bibliography of Kay Boyle'. *Bulletin of Bibliography* 35 (1978), 180–9.

Christine Brooke-Rose

Books

Birch, Sarah. *Christine Brooke-Rose and Contemporary Fiction*. Oxford, 1994.

Review of Contemporary Fiction. Special issue 9 (1989).

Articles

These do not usually include the *Review of Contemporary Fiction* special issue.

Caserio, R.L. 'Mobility and Masochism: Christine Brooke-Rose and J.G. Ballard'. *Novel* 21 (1988), 192–310.

Friedman, E.G. 'Utterly Other Discourses: The Anticanon of Experimental Women Writers from Dorothy Richardson to Brooke-Rose'. *Modern Fiction Studies* 34 (1988), 353–70.

364

Hawkins, S.E. 'Innovation/History/Politics: *Amalgamemnon*'. *Contemporary Literature* 32 (1991), 58–74.

Little, Judy. 'Humoring the Sentence: Women's Dialogic Comedy'. In *Women's Comic Visions*. Ed. J. Sochen. Detroit, 1991, 19–32.

Martin, Richard. '"Just Words on a Page": The Novels of Brooke-Rose'. *Review of Contemporary Fiction* 9 (1989), 110–23.

Martin, Richard. 'Redundancy and Generation in *Amalgamemnon*'. In *Breaking the Sequence*. Eds E.G. Friedman and M. Fuchs. Princeton, N.J., 1989, 177–87.

Rimmon-Kenan, S. 'Ambiguity and Narrative Levels: Brooke-Rose's *Thru*'. *Poetics Today* 3 (1982), 21–32.

Seed, David. 'Interview'. *Textual Practice* 7 (1993), 247–57.

Anita Brookner

Books

Alexander, Flora. *Contemporary Women Novelists*. London, 1989.

Hall, S.K., ed. *Contemporary Literary Criticism*. Special issue 34 (1985).

Kenyon, Olga. *Women Novelists Today*. Brighton, 1988.

Ricks, C. and Michaels, L., eds. *The State of the Language*. Berkeley, Calif., and London, 1980.

Skinner, John. *The Fiction of Anita Brookner: Illusions of Romance*. London, 1992.

Spacks, Patricia. *The Female Imagination*. New York, 1976.

Watson, Daphne. *Their Worst Enemies: Women as Writers of Popular Fiction*. London, 1992.

Waugh, Patricia. *Feminine Fictions: Revisiting the Postmodern*. London, 1989.

Articles

Bawer, Bruce. 'Doubles and More Doubles'. *New Criterion* 7 (1989), 67–74.

Baxter, G.M. 'Clothes, Men, and Books'. *English* 42 (1993), 125–39.

Burchfield, Robert. 'Two Kinds of English'. In *The State of the Language*. Eds C. Ricks and L. Michaels. Berkeley, Calif., 1990, 356–66.

Guppy, Sasha. 'The Art of Fiction'. *Paris Review* 104 (1987), 146–69.

Hosmer, R.E. 'Paradigm and Passage in Brookner'. In *Contemporary British Writers*. Ed. R.E. Hosmer. New York, 1993, 26–54.

Kurz, Helga. 'The Impossibility of Female Friendship: A Study of Brookner's Female Characters'.

Arbeiten aus Anglistik und Amerikanistik 15 (1990), 13–25.

Plimpton, George. 'Interview'. In *Writers at Work*, vol. 8. Harmondsworth, 1988, 323–42.

Stetz, M.D. 'Anita Brookner: Woman Writer as Reluctant Feminist'. In *Writing the Woman Artist*. Ed. S.W. Jones. Philadelphia, 1991, 96–112.

Wyatt-Brown, A.M. 'Creativity in Mid-Life'. *Journal of Aging Studies* 3 (1989), 175–81.

A.S. Byatt

Books

Alexander, Flora. *Contemporary Women Novelists*. London, 1989.

Gerrard, Nicci. *Into the Mainstream*. London, 1989.

Hosmer, R.E. *Contemporary British Women Writers: Narrative Strategies*. New York, 1993.

Kenyon, Olga. *Women Novelists Today*. Brighton, 1988.

Taylor, D.J. *After the War: The Novel and English Society Since 1945*. London, 1993.

Articles

Alexander, Flora. 'A.S. Byatt'. In *Post-War Literatures*. Eds H. Bertens et al. Houten and Groningen, 1992.

Ashworth, Ann. 'Fairy Tales in *Possession*'. *Journal of Evolutionary Psychology* 15 (1994), 93–4.

Campbell, Jane. 'The Hunger of the Imagination in A.S. Byatt's *The Game*'. *Critique* 19 (1988), 147–62.

Campbell, Jane. 'Fact, Fiction, and Intertextuality in "Precipice Encurled"'. *Studies in Short Fiction* 28 (1991), 115–23.

Creighton, J.V. 'Sisterly Symbiosis: Margaret Drabble and A.S. Byatt'. *Mosaic* 20 (1987), 15–29.

Dusinberre, Juliet. 'Forms of Reality in A.S. Byatt's *The Virgin in the Garden*'. *Critique* 24 (1982), 55–62.

Kelso, Sylvia. 'The Matter of Melusine: A Question of Possession'. *Literature in North Queensland* 19 (1992), 134–44.

Musil, C. McTighe. 'A.S. Byatt'. *Dictionary of Literary Biography* 14 (1983), 194–205.

Yelin, Louise. 'Cultural Cartography: A.S. Byatt's *Possession*'. *Victorian Newsletter* 81 (1992), 38–41.

Hortense Calisher

Books

Snodgrass, Kathleen. *The Fiction of Hortense Calisher*. Newark, N.J., 1993.

Articles

Garganus, Allan et al. 'The Art of Fiction'. *Paris Review* 105 (1987), 156–87.

Hahn, Emily. 'In Appreciation of Hortense Calisher'. *Wisconsin Studies in Contemporary Literature* 6 (1965), 243–9.

Ingersoll, E. and Marchant, P. 'Conversation'. *Southwest Review* 7 (1986), 186–93.

Kirky, D.K. 'The Princess and the Frog: The Modern American Short Story as Fairy Tale'. *Minnesota Review* 4 (1973), 145–9.

Matalene, Carolyn. 'Hortense Calisher'. *Dictionary of Literary Biography* 2 (1978).

Snodgrass, Kathleen. 'Coming Down from the Heights: Three Novels of Hortense Calisher'. *Texas Studies in Literature and Language* 31 (1989), 554–69.

Snodgrass, Kathleen. 'Hortense Calisher: "A Beginning Animal"'. *Confrontation* 41 (1989), 63–79.

Bibliography and reference

Snodgrass, Kathleen. 'Hortense Calisher: A Bibliography'. *Bulletin of Bibliography* 45 (1988), 40–50.

Dorothy Canfield (Fisher)

Books

Frost, Robert. *Dorothy Canfield Fisher. In Memoriam.* 1958.

McCallister, L. 'Dorothy Canfield Fisher: A Critical Study'. Ph.D., Case Western Reserve University, 1969.

Overton, Grant. *The Women Who Make our Novels.* Freeport, N.Y., 1967; reprinted from 1928.

Quinn, A.H. *American Fiction.* New York, 1936.

Washington, I.H. *Dorothy Canfield Fisher: A Biography.* Shelburne, 1982.

Williams, B.C. *Our Short Story Writers.* New York, 1920.

Yates, E. *Pebble in a Pool: The Widening Circles of Dorothy Canfield Fisher's Life.* New York, 1958.

Articles

Boynton, P.H. 'Two New England Regionalists'. *College English* 1 (1940), 291–9.

Firebaugh, J.J. 'Dorothy Canfield and the Moral Bent'. *Educational Forum* 15 (1951), 283–94.

Goldman, Dorothy. 'Introduction'. In *Her Son's Wife.* By Dorothy Canfield (Fisher). London, 1986.

Goldman, Dorothy. 'Introduction'. In *The Brimming Cup.* By Dorothy Canfield (Fisher). London, 1987.

Madigan, M.J. 'Dorothy Canfield Fisher'. *Legacy* 9 (1992), 49–58.

Mann, D.L. 'Dorothy Canfield: The Little Vermonter'. *Bookman* 65 (1927), 695–701.

Phelps, W.L. 'Dorothy Canfield Fisher'. *English Journal* 22 (1933), 1–8.

Pottle, F.A. 'Catharsis'. *Yale Review* 40 (1951), 621–41.

Schroeter, J.G. 'Crises, Conflict and Constituting the Self: A Lacanian Reading of *The Deepening Stream*'. *Colby Library Quarterly* 27 (1991), 148–60.

Smith, Bradford. 'Dorothy Canfield Fisher'. *Atlantic* 203 (1959), 73–7.

Wyckoff, E. 'Dorothy Canfield': A Neglected Bestseller'. *Bookman* 74 (1931), 40–4.

Bibliography and reference

Schroeter, J. 'A Revised Bibliography'. *Analytical and Enumerative Bibliography* 4 (1990), 169–70.

Leonora Carrington

Books

Chadwick, Whitney. *Women Artists and the Surrealist Movement.* London, 1986.

Helland, Janice. 'Daughter of the Minotaur: Leonora Carrington and the Surrealist Image'. Ph.D., University of Victoria, British Columbia, 1984.

Kaplan, Janet. *Unexpected Journeys: The Art and Life of Remedios Varo.* London, 1988.

Suleiman, Susan. *Subversive Intent. Women, Men and the Avant-Garde.* Cambridge, Mass., 1990.

Articles

Assa, Sonia. 'Carrington in the Kitchen'. *Studies in Twentieth Century Literature* 15 (1991), 213–27.

Byatt, Helen. 'Introduction'. In *The Hearing Trumpet.* By Leonora Carrington. London, 1991.

Christensen, P.G. 'The Flight From Passion'. *Dada/Surrealism* 18 (1990), 148–58.

Cootenet-Hage, M. 'The Body Subversive'. *Dada/Surrealism* 18 (1990), 76–95.

Hubert, R.R. 'Carrington and Ernst'. *New Literary History* 22 (1991), 715–45.

Orenstein, G.F. 'The Methodology of the Marvelous'. *Symposium* 42 (1989), 329–39.

Warner, Maria. 'Introduction'. In *House of Fear.* By Leonora Carrington. London, 1989.

Warner, Maria. 'Introduction'. In *The Seventh Horse.* By Leonora Carrington, London, 1989.

Catherine Carswell

Books

Crosland, Margaret. *Beyond the Lighthouse: English Women Novelists in the Twentieth Century.* London, 1981.

Articles

Carswell, Ianthe. 'Introduction'. In *The Camomile*. By Catherine Carswell. London, 1987.

Carswell, John. 'Introduction'. In *Open the Door!*. By Catherine Carswell. London, 1986.

Kemnitz, C. and Farmer, D. 'Catherine Carswell'. *Dictionary of Literary Biography* 36 (1985), 20–3.

Angela Carter

Books

Alexander, Flora. *Contemporary Women Novelists*. London, 1989.

Anderson, L., ed. *Plotting Change: Contemporary Women's Fiction*. London, 1990.

Cornwell, Neil. *The Literary Fantastic: From Gothic to Postmodernism*. Hemel Hempstead, 1990.

Humm, Maggie. *Border Traffic: Strategies of Contemporary Women Writers*. Manchester, 1991.

Hutcheon, Linda. *The Politics of Postmodernism*. London, 1989.

Jackson, R. *Fantasy: The Literature of Subversion*. London, 1981; rev., 1991.

Kappeler, Susanne. *The Pornography of Representation*. London, 1986.

Kenyon, Olga. *Writing Women. Contemporary Women Novelists*. London, 1991.

McHale, Brian. *Postmodernist Fiction*. London, 1988.

Marowski, D.G. and Matuz, R., eds. *Contemporary Literary Criticism*. Detroit, 1987.

Palumbo, Donald, ed. *Erotic Universe: Sexuality and Fantastic Literature*. New York, 1986.

Robinson, Sally. *Engendering the Subject*. New York, 1991.

Sage, Lorna. *Women in the House of Fiction: Postwar Women Novelists*. Basingstoke, 1992.

Sage, Lorna. *Angela Carter*. Plymouth, 1994.

Sage, Lorna, ed. *Flesh and the Mirror: Essays on the Art of Angela Carter*. London, 1994.

Articles

Alvarez, Antonia. 'On Translating Metaphors'. *META* 38 (1993), 479–90.

Bell, Michael. 'Narration as Action'. *German Life and Letters* 45 (1992), 16–32.

Bono, Paola. 'The Passion for Sexual Difference'. *Tessera* 11 (1991), 31–46.

Bryant, Sylvia. 'Reconstructing Oedipus through "Beauty and the Beast"'. *Criticism* 31 (1989) 439–53.

Clarke, Robert. 'Angela Carter's Desire Machine'. *Women's Studies* 14 (1987), 147–61.

Duncker, Patricia. 'Re-Imaging Fairy Tales'. *Literature and History* 10 (1984), 3–14.

Farrell, Robyn. 'Carter and the Uncanny'. In *The Illusion of Life*. Ed. A. Cholodenko. Sydney, 1991, 131–44.

Fowl, M.G. 'Angela Carter's *The Bloody Chamber* Revisited'. *Critical Survey* 1 (1991), 71–9.

Hanson, Clare. 'Each Other: Images of Otherness'. *Journal of the Short Story in English* 10 (1988), 67–82.

Jordan, E. 'The Dangers of Angela Carter'. In *New Feminist Discourses*. Ed. I. Armstrong. London and New York, 1992, 119–31.

Jordan, Elaine. 'Enthralment: Angela Carter's Speculative Fiction'. In *Plotting Change*. Ed. L. Anderson. London, 1990, 18–40.

Kendrick, William. 'The Real Magic of Carter'. In *Contemporary British Women Writers: Narrative Strategies*. Ed. R.E. Hosmer. New York, 1993, 66–84.

LeWallen, Avis. 'Female Sexuality in Carter's *Bloody Chamber*'. In *Perspectives on Pornography*. Eds Gary Day and Clive Bloom. New York, 1988, 144–58.

Linkin, H.K. 'Carter's Bloody Revision'. *Contemporary Literature* 35 (1994), 305–23.

Lokke, K.E. 'The Grotesque of Self-Parody and Self-Assertion'. *Frontiers* 10 (1988), 7–12.

Matus, Jill. 'Blonde, Black, and Hottentot Venus: *Black Venus*'. *Studies in Short Fiction* 28 (1991), 467–76.

Palmer, Paulina. 'From Coded Mannequin to Bird Woman: Angela Carter's Magic Flight'. In *Reading Women's Writing*. Ed. Sue Roe. Hemel Hempstead, 1987, 179–208.

Patten, Eve. 'Angela Carter'. In *Post-War Literatures*. Eds H. Bertens et al. Houten and Groningen, 1993.

Punter, David. 'Angela Carter: Supersessions of the Masculine'. *Critique* 25 (1984), 109–22.

Rubenstein, Roberta. 'Intersexions: Gender Metamorphosis in Carter'. *Tulsa Studies in Women's Literature* 12 (1993), 103–18.

Sage, Lorna. 'Female Fictions: The Women Novelists'. In *The Contemporary English Novel*. Eds M. Bradbury and D. Palmer. London, 1979, 67–88.

Schmidt, Ricarda. 'The Journey of the Subject in Carter's Fiction'. *Textual Practice* 5 (1989), 56–75.

Todd, Richard. 'Convention and Innovation in British Fiction 1981–1984: The Contemporaneity of Magic Realism'. In *Convention and Innovation in Literature*. Eds T. D'haen et al. Amsterdam and Philadelphia, 1989, 361–88.

Turner, R.P.B. 'Subjects and Symbols in *Nights at the Circus*'. *Folklore Forum* 20 (1987), 39–60.

Wilson, R.R. 'SLIP PAGE: Carter In/Out/In the Post-modern Nexus'. In *Past the Last Post*. Eds I. Adam and H. Tiffin. Hemel Hempstead, 1991, 109–23.

Willa Cather

Books

Ambrose, Jamie. *Willa Cather: Writing at the Frontier*. Leamington Spa, 1989.

Ammons, Elizabeth. *Conflicting Stories*. New York and Oxford, 1991.

Barbour, James and Quirk, Tom, eds. *Writing the American Classics*. Chapel Hill, N.C., 1991.

Brown, E.K., completed by Leon Edel. *Willa Cather: A Critical Introduction*. New York, 1951, 1962.

Cather Studies 1992– .

Dekker, George. *The American Historical Romance*. Cambridge, 1987.

Fryer, Judith. *Felicitous Space: The Imaginative Structures of Wharton and Cather*. Chapel Hill, N.C., 1986.

Gerber, Philip L. *Willa Cather*. Boston, 1975.

Harrell, David. *From Mesa Verde to 'The Professor's House'*. Albuquerque, N. Mex., 1992.

Jump, H.D., ed. *Diverse Voices: Essays on Twentieth Century Women Writers in English*. Hemel Hempstead, 1991.

Kaye, Frances W. *Isolation and Masquerade: Cather's Women*. New York, 1992.

Lee, Hermione. *Willa Cather: A Life Saved Up*. London, 1989.

Lee, Hermione. *Willa Cather: Double Lives*. New York, 1990.

Lewis, Edith. *Willa Cather Living*. New York, 1953.

Meyering, S.L. *A Reader's Guide to the Short Stories of Cather*. New York, 1994.

Middleton, Jo Ann. *Willa Cather's Modernism*. Rutherford, N.J., 1990.

Modern Fiction Studies. Special issue on Willa Cather 36 (1990).

Murphy, J.J., ed. *Critical Essays on Willa Cather*. Boston, 1984.

Nelson, R.J. *Willa Cather and France*. Champaign, Ill., 1988.

O'Brien, Sharon. *Willa Cather: The Emerging Voice*. New York, 1987.

Quirk, Tom. *Bergson and American Culture: The Worlds of Willa Cather and Wallace Stevens*. Chapel Hill, N.C., 1990.

Robinson, Phyllis C. *Willa: The Life of Willa Cather*. New York, 1983.

Rosowski, S.J. *The Voyage Perilous: Cather's Romanticism*. Lincoln, Nebr., 1986.

Schroeter, James, ed. *Willa Cather and her Critics*. Ithaca, N.Y., 1967.

Sergeant, Elizabeth. *Willa Cather: A Memoir*. Philadelphia, 1953; Athens, Ohio, 1992.

Skaggs, M.M. *The Later Novels of Willa Cather*. Charlottesville, 1990.

Slote, Berenice. *Willa Cather: A Pictorial Memoir*. Lincoln, Nebr., 1986.

Slote, B. and Faulkner, V., eds. *The Art of Willa Cather*. Lincoln, Nebr., 1974.

Stouck, David. *Willa Cather's Imagination*. Lincoln, Nebr., 1975.

Thomas, Susie. *Willa Cather*. Basingstoke, 1989.

Van Ghent, Dorothy. *Willa Cather*. Minneapolis, 1964.

Wasserman, Loretta. *Willa Cather: A Study of the Short Fiction*. Boston, 1991.

Welsh, R.L. and L.K. *Cather's Kitchens*. Lincoln, Nebr., 1988.

Woodress, James. *Willa Cather: Her Life and Art*. Lincoln, Nebr., 1970.

Woodress, James. *Willa Cather. A Literary Life*. Lincoln, Nebr., 1988.

Articles

Arnold, Marilyn. 'The Function of Structure in *The Professor's House*'. *Colby Library Quarterly* 11 (1975), 169–78.

Arnold, Marilyn. 'Cather's Artistic "Radicalism"'. *CEA Critic* 51 (1989), 2–10.

Byatt, Antonia. 'Introduction.' In *A Lost Lady*. By Willa Cather. London, 1980.

Byatt, Antonia. 'Introduction'. In *The Professor's House*. By Willa Cather. London, 1981.

Byatt, Antonia. 'Introduction'. In *My Mortal Enemy*. By Willa Cather. London, 1982.

Dinn, J.M. 'A Novelist's Miracle: Structure and Myth in *Death Comes for the Archbishop*'. *Western American Literature* 7 (1972), 39–46.

Fulbrook, Kate. 'Willa Cather: Folktale, Parable and the Heroic Mode'. In *Free Women*. London, 1990.

Hart, Clive. '*The Professor's House*: A Shapely Story'. *Modern Language Review* 67 (1972), 271–81.

Ikuta, Toshito. '*A Lost Lady*: The Problem of Point of View'. *Kyushu American Literature* 15 (1974), 85–7.

Leddy, M. '*The Professor's House*: The Sense of an Ending'. *Studies in the Novel* 23 (1991), 443–51.

Leddy, M. '*The Professor's House* and the Professor's House'. *Modern Fiction Studies* 38 (1992), 444–54.

McElhiney, A.B. 'Tripartite Narrative Point of View in *My Ántonia*'. *CEA Critic* 56 (1993), 65–76.

Murphy, M. 'The Complex Past in *A Lost Lady* and *The Professor's House*'. *South Dakota Review* 28 (1990), 113–25.

Oehlschlaeger, F. 'Indisponibilité and the Anxiety of Authorship in *The Professor's House*'. *American Literature* 62 (1990), 74–86.

Stineback, D.C. 'Willa Cather's Ironic Masterpiece'. *Arizona Quarterly* 29 (1973), 317–30.

Stouck, David. 'Perspective as Structure and Theme in *My Ántonia*'. *Texas Studies in Language and Literature* 12 (1970), 285–94.

Wheeler, K.M. 'Excavating Meaning in Willa Cather's Novels'. In *'Modernist' Women Writers and Narrative Art*. Basingstoke, 1994, 19–50.

Yukman, C. 'Frontier Relationships in Willa Cather'. *Pacific Coast Philology* 23 (1988), 94–104.

Bibliography and reference

Arnold, M. *Willa Cather: A Reference Guide*. Boston, 1986.

Crane, Joan. *Willa Cather: A Bibliography*. Lincoln, Nebr., 1982.

Kate Chopin

Books

Ammons, Elizabeth. *Conflicting Stories*. New York and Oxford, 1991.

Bloom, H., ed. *Kate Chopin*. New York, 1986.

Bonner, Thomas. *The Kate Chopin Companion*. New York, 1988.

Boren, L.S. and Davis, S., eds. *Kate Chopin Reconsidered*. Baton Rouge, La., 1992.

Culley, M. *The Awakening: An Authoritative Text, Contexts, Criticism*. New York, 1976 (contains numerous critical essays).

Dyer, Joyce. *The Awakening: A Novel of Beginnings*. New York, 1993.

Ewell, Barbara. *Kate Chopin*. New York, 1986.

Girgus, S.B. *Desire and the Political Unconscious*. Basingstoke, 1990.

Hoder-Salmon, Marilyn. *Kate Chopin's 'The Awakening'*. Gainesville, Fla., 1992.

Horner, A. and Zlosnik, S., eds. *Landscapes of Desire*. Hemel Hempstead, 1990.

Keesey, Donald, ed. *Contexts for Criticism*. Mountain View, Calif., 1994.

Koloski, B., ed. *Approaches to Teaching 'The Awakening'*. New York, 1988.

Louisiana Literature. Special issue 11 (1994).

Martin, W., ed. *New Essays on 'The Awakening'*. Cambridge, 1988.

Papke, M.E. *Verging on the Abyss: The Social Fiction of Chopin and Wharton*. New York, 1990.

Rankin, D.S. *Kate Chopin and her Creole Stories*. Philadelphia, 1932.

Seyersted, Per. *Kate Chopin: A Critical Biography*. Baton Rouge, La., 1969.

Skaggs, Peggy. *Kate Chopin*. New York, 1985.

Taylor, Helen. *Gender, Race, and Region*. Baton Rouge, La., 1989.

Toth, Emily. ed. *Kate Chopin Newsletter* (now known as *Regionalism and the Female Imagination*) 1975–9.

Toth, Emily. *Kate Chopin*. New York, 1990.

Walker, Nancy A., ed. *Kate Chopin: 'The Awakening'*. (*Case Studies in Contemporary Criticism*) New York, 1993. (Text and critical essays).

Articles

See the *Kate Chopin Newsletter* 1975–9.

Apthorpe, E.S. 'Revisioning Creativity: Cather, Chopin, Jewett'. *Legacy* 9 (1992), 1–22.

Bell, P.K. 'Kate Chopin and Sarah Orne Jewett'. *Partisan Review* 55 (1988), 238–53.

Cutter, M.J. 'Resistance to Patriarchal Discourse'. *Legacy* 11 (1994), 17–36.

Kearns, K. 'The Nullification of Edna Pontellier'. *American Literature* 63 (1991), 62–88.

Louisiana Studies. A Special Kate Chopin issue 14 (1975).

Peel, Ellen. 'Semiotic Subversion in "Desirée's Baby"'. *American Literature* 62 (1990), 223–37.

Rocks, J.E. 'Kate Chopin's Ironic Vision'. *Louisiana Review* 1 (1972), 110–20.

Seidel, Kathryn. 'Art and Mme Reisz'. *Mississippi Quarterly* 46 (1993), 199–214.

Shaw, Pat. 'Psychosexuality and Perspective Shifts in *The Awakening*'. *American Literary Realism* 23 (1990), 61–9.

Stange, Margit. 'Personal Property: Exchange Value and the Female Self in *The Awakening*'. *Genders* 5 (1989), 106–19.

Sullivan, R. and Smith, S. 'Narrative Stance in Kate Chopin's *The Awakening*'. *Studies in American Fiction* 1 (1973), 62–75.

Wheeler, K.M. 'Kate Chopin: Ironist of Realism'. In *'Modernist' Women Writers and Narrative Art*. Basingstoke, 1994, 51–76.

Wheeler, Otis B. 'The Five Awakenings of Edna Pontellier'. *Southern Review* 11 (1975), 118–28.

Bibliography and reference

Bonner, T. 'Bibliographic Essay'. In *The Kate Chopin Companion*. New York, 1988, 233–45.

Ewell, B.C. 'Kate Chopin and the Art of Fiction'. *Louisiana Literature* 11 (1994), 157–71.

Springer, Marlene. *Edith Wharton and Kate Chopin: A Reference Guide*. Boston, 1976.

Ivy Compton-Burnett

Books

Baldenza, F. *Ivy Compton-Burnett*. New York, 1964.

Bhagyalaskshmi, J. *Ivy Compton-Burnett and her Art*. New Delhi, 1986.

Biles, Jack. *British Novelists since 1900*. New York, 1987.

Blake, Nevius. *Ivy Compton-Burnett*. New York, 1970.

Burkhart, Charles. *Ivy Compton-Burnett*. London, 1965.

Burkhart, Charles, ed. *The Art of Ivy Compton-Burnett: A Collection of Critical Essays*. London, 1972.

Gentile, K.J. *Ivy Compton-Burnett*. Basingstoke, 1991.

Greig, Cicely. *Ivy Compton-Burnett. A Memoir*. London, 1972.

Gryll, R. Glynn. *Ivy Compton-Burnett*. Harlow, 1971.

Johnson, Pamela Hansford. *Ivy Compton-Burnett*. London, 1951.

Liddell, Robert. *The Novels of Ivy Compton-Burnett*. London, 1955.

Liddell, Robert. *Elizabeth and Ivy*. London, 1986.

Lilly, Mark, ed. *Lesbian and Gay Writing*. Basingstoke, 1991.

Miles, Rosalind. *The Female Form. Women Writers and the Conquest of the Novel*. London, 1987.

Powell, Violet. *A Compton-Burnett Compendium*. London, 1973.

Ramakrishnarao, V. *Ivy Compton-Burnett: A Critical Study*. Waltair, 1974.

Sarkor, R.N. *Ivy Compton-Burnett: A Trend in English Fiction*. Calcutta, 1979.

Sprigge, Elizabeth. *The Life of Ivy Compton-Burnett*. New York, 1973.

Spurling, Hilary. *Ivy When Young, 1884–1919*. London, 1974.

Spurling, Hilary. *The Secrets of a Woman's Heart: The Later Life of Ivy Compton-Burnett, 1920–1969*. London, 1984.

Eleanor Dark

Books

Devanny, Jean. *Bird of Paradise*. Sydney, 1945.

Eldershaw, M. Barnard. *Essays in Australian Fiction*. Melbourne, 1938.

Gross, K. and Klooss, W., eds. *English Literature of the Dominions*. Würzburg, 1981.

Grove-Day, A. *Eleanor Dark*. Boston, 1977.

Hergenhan, L. *Unnatural Lives: Studies in Australian Fiction*. St Lucia, Queensland, 1983.

Thomson, A.K. *Understanding the Novel 'The Timeless Land'*. Milton, Queensland, 1966.

Articles

Giuffre, Giulia. 'An Interview with Eric Dark about Eleanor'. *Southerly* 48 (1987), 83–93.

Lowe, Eric. '[The Novels of Eleanor Dark]'. *Meanjin* 10 (1951), 341–8.

McKellar, John. 'The Black and the White'. *Southerly* 9 (1948), 92–8.

McQueen, H. 'Introduction'. In *The Timeless Land*.
By Eleanor Dark. London and North Ryde, New South Wales, 1990.

McQueen, Humphey. '[The Novels of Eleanor Dark]'. *Hemisphere* 17 (1973), 38–41.

Modjeska, Drusilla. 'Introduction'. In *Waterway*. By Eleanor Dark. London and North Ryde, New South Wales, 1990.

O'Reilly, H. '[Eleanor Dark's Fiction]'. *Outrider* 21 (1989).

Scheckler, John. 'Australia Lost and Found'. *ACLALS Bulletin* 6 (1982), 27–41.

Tennant, Kylie. 'Interview with Eleanor Dark'. *Sydney Morning Herald* (14 February 1974).

Anita Desai

Books

Afzal-Khan, Fawzia. *Cultural Imperialism and the Indian-English Novel*. University Park, Pa., 1992.

Aneja, Anu. 'Feminine Discourses of Love: Cixous, Das, and Desai'. Ph.D., Pennsylvania State University, 1989.

Bande, Usha. *The Novels of Anita Desai*. New Delhi, 1988.

Belliappa, Meena. *Anita Desai: A Study of her Fiction*. Calcutta, 1971.

Gupta, G.S. Balarama, ed. *Studies in Indian Fiction in English*. Gulbarga, 1987.

Jain, Jasbir. *Stairs to the Attic: The Novels of Anita Desai*. Jaipur, 1987.

King, B., ed. *The Commonwealth Novel since 1960*. Basingstoke, 1991.

Kirpal, Viney, ed. *The New Indian Novel in English: A Study of the 1980s*. New Delhi, 1990.

Nasta, Susheila, ed. *Motherlands: Black Women's Writing*. London, 1991.

Pathania, Usha. *Human Bonds and Bondage: The Fiction of Anita Desai and Kamala Markandaya*. Delhi, 1992.

Paul, S.L. *A Critical Study of Anita Desai's 'Cry, the Peacock'*. New Delhi, 1988.

Pradhan, N.S., ed. *Major Indian Novels*. Atlantic Highlands, N.J., 1986.

Prased, M., ed. *Indian English Novelists*. New Delhi, 1982.

Rao, B. Ramachandra. *The Novels of Mrs. Anita Desai: A Study*. New Delhi, 1977.

Sharma, R.S., ed. *Anita Desai*. New Delhi, 1981.

Srivastava, R.K. *Perspectives on Anita Desai*. Ghaziabad, 1984.

Articles

Bliss, C.D. 'Conversation'. *Massachusetts Review* 29 (1988), 521–37.

Chellappan, K. 'Being and Becoming in Desai's "Where Shall We Go This Summer?"'. In

Subjects Worthy Fame: Essays on Commonwealth Literature. Ed. A.L. McLeod. New Delhi, 1989, 10–16.

Kher, I.N. 'Madness as Discourse in *Cry, the Peacock*'. *Commonwealth Novel in English* 5 (1992), 16–25.

Kirpal, Viney. 'An Image of India'. *Ariel* 17 (1986), 127–38.

Knapp, B.L. '*Fire on the Mountain*: A Rite of Exit'. *Journal of Evolutionary Psychology* 8 (1987), 223–37.

Libert, Florence. 'Interview'. *World Literature Written in English* 30 (1990), 47–55.

Libert, Florence. 'Discrepancy Between Inner Being and Outside World'. In *International Literature in English*. Ed. R.L. Ross. London, 1991, 571–82.

Maini, D.S. '*Cry the Peacock* as Poetic Novel'. In *Indian Literature of the Past Fifty Years: 1917–67*. Ed. C.D. Narasimhaiah. Mysore, 1970, 225–34.

Nayak, P.M. and Swain, S.P. 'The Outsider in *Baumgartner's Bombay*'. *Commonwealth Novel in English* 6 (1993), 112–20.

Newman, Judie. 'History and Letters: Desai's *Baumgartner's Bombay*'. *World Literature Written in English* 30 (1990), 37–46.

Pathania, Usha. 'Self-Concept and Interpersonal Interaction'. *Aligarh Journal of English Studies* 15 (1993), 73–86.

Phillips, K.J. 'Ambiguous Tragic Flaw in *Fire on the Mountain*'. *International Fiction Review* 17 (1990), 3–8.

Ramanathan, Geetha. 'Sexual Violence/Textual Violence'. *Modern Fiction Studies* 39 (1993), 17–35.

Sequet, P. 'Interview'. *Commonwealth Essays and Studies* 10 (1988), 43–50.

Sharrad, Paul, 'Tradition and Tragedy'. *Commonwealth Review* 2 (1990–1), 181–92.

Taneja, G.R. '*Baumgartner's Bombay*: A Note'. *Journal of English Studies* (1990), 163–73.

Uma, Alladi. 'I Have Had My Vision'. *Literary Criterion* 22 (1987), 73–7.

Valentine, T.M. 'Cross-sex Conversation in Indian English Fiction'. *World Englishes* 4 (1985), 319–32.

Shashi Deshpande

Books

Dhawan, D.K., ed. *Indian Women Novelists*. Bombay, 1991.

Gupta, G.S.B., ed. *Studies in Indian Fiction in English*. Gulbarga, 1987.

Nasta, Susheila, ed. *Motherlands*. London, 1991.

Sandhu, S.K. *The Novels of Shashi Deshpande*. New Delhi, 1991.

Walsh, William. *Indian Literature in English*. London, 1990.

Articles

D'Cruz, Doreen. 'Deshpande's Fiction'. *SPAN* 36 (1993), 452–70.

King, Adele. 'Shashi Deshpande'. In *The New Indian Novel in English*. Ed. V. Kirpal. New Delhi, 1990, 159–68.

Mukherjee, Meenakshi. 'Towards Liberation'. *Westerly* 28 (1983), 66–72.

Rajan, R.S. 'The Feminist Plot and the Nationalist Allegory'. *Modern Fiction Studies* 39 (1993), 71–92.

Ramarao, V. 'Shashi Deshpande'. In *The Encyclopedia of Post-Colonial Literatures in English*. Eds E. Benson and L.W. Conolly. London and New York, 1994, 357–8.

Jean Crook Devanny

Books

Cvitanovich, Lynley. *Breaking the Silence*. Palmerston North, 1985.

Ferrier, Carole. *Gender, Politics and Fiction*. St Lucia, Queensland, 1985.

Modjeska, Drusilla. *Exiles at Home*. Sydney, 1981.

Articles

Ferrier, Carole. 'Devanny's Queensland Novels'. *Literature in North Queensland* 8 (1980), 11–30.

Ferrier, Carole. '*Sugar Heaven* and the Reception of Working-Class Texts'. *Hecate* 11 (1985), 19–25.

Ferrier, Carole. 'Introduction'. In *Cindie*. By Jean Crook Devanny. London, 1986.

Ferrier, Carole. 'Constructing and Deconstructing Devanny'. *Australian Feminist Studies* 16 (1992), 144–57.

Modjeska, Drusilla. 'Jean Devanny's New Zealand Novels'. *Hecate* 6 (1980).

Stove, R.E. and Anderson, R. 'Jean Devanny: A Biographical and Bibliographical Note'. *Australian Academic Research Libraries* 1 (1970).

Syson, Ian. 'Towards a Poetics of Working-Class Writing'. *Southern Review* 26 (1993), 86–100.

Bibliography and reference

Daniels, K. et al. *Women in Australia: An Annotated Guide to Records*. Canberra, 1977.

Isak Dinesen

Books

Aiken, S.H. *Isak Dinesen and the Engendering of Narrative*. Chicago, 1990.

Hannah, Donald. *'Isak Dinesen' and Karen Blixen: The Mask and the Reality*. London, 1971.

Horton, S.R. *Difficult Women, Artful Lives: Olive Schreiner and Isak Dinesen*. Baltimore and London, 1995.

Johannesson, E.O. *The World of Isak Dinesen*. Seattle, 1961.

Langbaum, R.W. *The Gayety of Vision*. London, 1964 (revised, 1975, as *Isak Dinesen's Art*, Chicago).

Lasson, Frans, ed. *The Life and Destiny of Isak Dinesen*. London, 1970.

Pamenia, Migel. *Titania*. London, 1968.

Pelensky, O.A., ed. *Isak Dinesen: Critical Views*. Athens, Ohio, 1993.

Stambaugh, Sara. *Dinesen: A Feminist Reading*. Ann Arbor, 1988.

Svendesen, Clara. *Isak Dinesen: A Memorial*. Copenhagen, 1965.

Thurman, Judith. *Isak Dinesen: The Life of Karen Blixen*. Harmondsworth, 1984, rev. from 1982 edn.

Wamberg, Botil, ed. *Out of Denmark: Isak Dinesen*. Copenhagen, 1985.

Ward, David. *Chronicles of Darkness*. London, 1989.

Whissen, R.R. *Isak Dinesen's Aesthetics*. Port Washington, N.Y., 1973.

Articles

Aiken, S.H. 'The Uses of Duplicity: Dinesen and Questions of Feminist Criticism'. *Scandinavian Studies* 57 (1985), 400–11.

Blackwell, Marilyn. 'The Transforming Haze: Identity and Sexuality in Dinesen'. *Scandinavian Studies* 63 (1991), 50–65.

Bogan, Louise. 'Isak Dinesen'. In *Selected Criticism*. New York, 1955, 231–4.

Davenport, John. 'A Noble Pride: The Art of Karen Blixen'. *Twentieth Century* (1956), 264–74.

Kirss, Tina A. 'The Role of the Female Storyteller in *Seven Gothic Tales*'. In *Essays in European Literature*. Eds A.N. Benson and M.C. Olds. Lincoln, Nebr., 1990.

Knafo-Setton, Ruth. 'The Dream World of Isak Dinesen'. *Journal of the Short Story in English* 10 (1988), 83–91.

Larsen, S.E. 'Spaces in Dinesen'. In *Space and Boundaries in Literature*, vol. 3. Eds R. Bauer et al. Munich, 1990, 86–91.

Lee, Judith. 'The Mask of Farm in *Out of Africa*'. *Prose Studies* 8 (1985), 45–59.

Richter, D.H. 'Covert Plot in "Sorrow-Acre"'. *Journal of Narrative Technique* 15 (1985), 82–90.

Riechel, D.C. 'Isak Dinesen's "Roads round Nietzsche"'. *Scandinavian Studies* 63 (1991), 326–50.

Stafford, Jean. 'Isak Dinesen: Master Teller of Tales'. *Horizon* (1959), 111–12.

Thorkild, B. 'Who am I? The Story of Dinesen's Identity'. *Scandinavian Studies* 57 (1985), 363–78.

Walter, Eugene. 'Isak Dinesen' (Interview). *Paris Review* (1956), 43–59.

Yacobi, Tamar. 'Dimensions of Space: Dinesen'. In *Space and Boundaries in Literature*, vol. 3. Eds R. Bauer et al. Munich, 1990, 79–85.

Bibliography and reference

Jørginsen, Aage. *Karen Blixen/Isak Dinesen: A Select Bibliography*. Aarhus, 1985.

H.D.

Books

Benstock, Shari. *Women of the Left Bank. Paris 1900–1940*. London, 1987.

Buck, Claire. *Bisexuality and a Feminine Discourse*. Hemel Hempstead, 1991.

Contemporary Literature. Special issue on H.D. 10 (1969).

Contemporary Literature. Special issue on H.D. 27 (1986).

Duplessis, Rachel Blau. *H.D.: The Career of That Struggle*. Bloomington, Ind., 1986.

Ellerman, Winifred (Bryher). *The Heart to Arlem's: A Writer's Memoirs*. New York, 1962; London, 1963.

Friedman, S.S. *Penelope's Web: Gender, Modernity, H.D.'s Fiction*. Cambridge, 1990.

Friedman, Susan S. *Psyche Reborn: The Experience of H.D.* Bloomington, Ind., 1981.

Friedman, S.S. and Duplessis, R. Blau, eds. *Signets: Reading H.D.* Madison, 1990.

Goldman, Dorothy, ed. *Women and World War I*. New York, 1993.

Guest, Barbara. *Herself Defined. The Poet H.D. and her World*. New York, 1984.

Hughes, Glenn. *Imaginism and the Imagists*. Stanford, 1931.

Iowa Review. Special issue on H.D. 16 (1986).

Jones, S.W. *Writing the Woman Artist*. Philadelphia, 1991.

Kloepfer, D.K. *The Unspeakable Mother: Forbidden Discourse in Jean Rhys and H.D.* Ithaca, N.Y., and London, 1989.

Ostriker, Alicia. *Writing like a Woman*. Ann Arbor, 1983.

Quinn, Vincent. *Hilda Doolittle*. New York, 1967.

Robinson, Janice S. *H.D.: The Life and Work of an American Poet*. Boston, 1982.

Smith-Rosenberg, Carroll. *Disorderly Conduct*. New York, 1985.

Swann, Thomas B. *The Classical World of H.D.* Lincoln, Nebr., 1962.

Articles

Bryher, J.R. 'H.D.: A Note on her Critical Reputation'. *Contemporary Literature* 10 (1969), 627–31.

Collecott, Diana. 'A Double Matrix: Rereading H.D.'. In *Women Reading Women's Writing*. Ed. Sue Roe. Brighton, 1987, 140–78.

Dembos, L.S. 'H.D.: A Reconsideration'. *Contemporary Literature* 10 (1969), 435–75.

Duplessis, Rachel Blau. 'Romantic Thralldom in H.D.'. *Contemporary Literature* 20 (1979), 178–203.

Duplessis, Rachel Blau, and Friedman, S.S. '"Woman is Perfect": H.D.'s Debate with Freud.' *Feminist Studies* 7 (1981), 417–29.

Friedman, Susan S. 'Who Buried H.D.?'. *College English* 36 (1975), 801–14.

Fuchs, Miriam. 'H.D.'s Self-Inscription: *The Gift*'. *Southern Review* 26 (1990), 542–54.

Greenwood, E.B. 'H.D. and the Problem of Escapism'. *Essays in Criticism* 21 (1971), 365–76.

Lucas, Rose. 'Memory and Desire in H.D.'. *Literature and Psychology* 39 (1993), 28–64.

Rainey, L.S. 'Canon, Gender, Text'. In *Representing Modernist Texts*. Ed. G. Borstein. Ann Arbor, 1991, 99–124.

Riddel, J.N. 'H.D. and the Poetics of Spiritual Realism'. *Contemporary Literature* 10 (1969), 447–73.

Wagner-Martin, Linda W. 'H.D.'s Fiction: Convolutions to Clarity'. In *Breaking the Sequence*. Eds E.G. Friedman and M. Fuchs. Princeton, N.J., 1989, 148–60.

Watts, H.H. 'H.D. and the Age of Myth'. *Sewanee Review* 56 (1948), 287–303.

Weatherhead, A.K. 'Style in H.D.'s Novels'. *Contemporary Literature* 10 (1969), 537–56.

Bibliography and reference

Bryher, J.R. and Robyn, Pamela. 'H.D.: A Preliminary Checklist'. *Contemporary Literature* 10 (1969), 632–75.

Margaret Drabble

Books

Acheson, James, ed. *The British and Irish Novel since 1960*. New York, 1991.

Creighton, J.V. *Margaret Drabble*. London, 1985.

Gullette, M.H. *Safe at Last in the Middle Years*. Berkeley, Calif., 1988.

Hannay, John. *The Intertextuality of Fate: A Study of Margaret Drabble*. Columbia, Mo., 1986.

Higdon, D.L. *Shadows of the Past in Contemporary British Fiction*. London, 1984.

Humm, Maggie. *Border Traffic: Strategies of Contemporary Women Writers*. Manchester, 1991.

Moran, M.H. *Margaret Drabble: Existing within Structures*. Carbondale, Ill., 1983.

Myer, V.G. *Margaret Drabble: Puritanism and Permissiveness*. London, 1974.

Rose, E.C. *The Novels of Margaret Drabble: Equivocal Figures*. London, 1980.

Rose, E.C., ed. *Critical Essays on Margaret Drabble*. Boston, 1985.

Sadler, L.V. *Margaret Drabble*. Boston, 1986.

Schmidt, Dorey, ed. *Margaret Drabble: Golden Realms*. Edinburgh, 1982.

Sizemore, C.W. *A Female Vision of the City: London in the Novels of Five British Women*. Knoxville, Tenn., 1989.

Takamo, Fumi, ed. *Margaret Drabble in Tokyo*. Tokyo, 1991.

Walker, N. *Feminist Alternatives: Irony and Fantasy in the Contemporary Novel by Women*. Jackson, Miss., 1990.

Articles

Alexander, Flora. 'Margaret Drabble'. In *Post-War Literatures*. Eds H. Bertens et al. Houten and Groningen, 1990.

Boch, G.G. 'Survival in a Dying Tradition: The Novels of Drabble'. In *Essays on the Contemporary British Novel*. Eds H. Boch and A. Wertheim. Munich, 1986, 245–61.

Bromberg, P.S. 'The Development of Narrative Technique in Margaret Drabble's Novels'. *Journal of Narrative Technique* 16 (1986), 179–91.

Campbell, Jane. 'Humor as Narrative Strategy in Drabble's Fiction'. *Contemporary Literature* 32 (1991), 75–99.

Cunningham, Gail. 'Patchwork and Patterns: The Condition of England in Drabble's Later Novels'. In *The British and Irish Novel since 1960*. Ed. J. Acheson. Basingstoke, 1991.

Rose, E.C. 'The Sexual Politics of Narration: Drabble's Feminist Fiction'. *Studies in the Novel* 20 (1988), 86–99.

Rubenstein, Roberta. 'Fragmented Bodies/Selves/Narratives: Drabble's Postmodern Turn'. *Contemporary Literature* 35 (1994), 136–55; and see 30 (1989), 95–112.

Stovel, N.F. 'From Wordsworth to Bennett: The Development of Drabble's Fiction'. *International Fiction Review* 15 (1988), 130–40.

Todd, J. and Parker, G. 'Margaret Drabble'. *Women Writers Talking*. Ed. J. Todd. New York, 1983, 160–78.

Wyatt, Jean. 'Escaping Literary Designs: The Politics of Reading and Writing in Drabble's *The*

Waterfall'. *Perspectives on Contemporary Literature* 11 (1985), 37–45.

Bibliography and reference
Packer, J.G. *Margaret Drabble: An Annotated Bibliography*. New York, 1988.

Alice Dunbar-Nelson

Books
Ammons, Elizabeth. *Conflicting Stories. American Women Writers at the Turn into the Twentieth Century*. New York and Oxford, 1991.
Brown, D.H., ed. *Louisiana Women Writers: New Essays*. Baton Rouge, La., 1992.
Hull, Gloria T. *Color, Sex, and Poetry: Three Women Writers of the Harlem Renaissance*. Bloomington, Ind., 1987.
Russell, Sandi. *Render Me My Song: African-American Women Writers from Slavery to the Present*. London, 1990.
Toth, Emily, ed. *Regionalism and the Female Imagination*. New York, 1985.
Walker, Alice. *In Search of Our Mother's Gardens*. London, 1984.

Articles
Bryan, V.H. 'The Myth of New Orleans: Dunbar-Nelson and Grace King'. *Publications of the Mississippi Philological Association*. (1987), 185–96.
Hull, G.T. 'Researching Dunbar-Nelson'. *Feminist Studies* 6 (1980), 314–20.
Hull, G.T. 'Dunbar-Nelson. A Regional Approach'. In *Teaching Women's Literature from a Regional Perspective*. Eds C. Hoffman et al. New York, 1982, 64–8.
Hull, G.T. 'Dunbar-Nelson and the Black Creole Experience'. *New Orleans Review* 15 (1988), 34–7.
Hull, G.T. 'Introduction'. In *The Works of Alice Dunbar-Nelson*. 3 vols. Oxford and New York, 1988.
Johnson, A. 'Writing Within the Script: *Ellen Fenton*'. *Studies in American Fiction* 19 (1991), 165–74.
Moreland, A. 'Introduction'. In *An Alice Dunbar-Nelson Reader*. Ed. R.O. Williams. Washington, D.C., 1978.

Bibliography and reference
Williams, Ora. 'Alice Moore Dunbar-Nelson'. In *Dictionary of Literary Biography* 50 (1986), 225–33.
Williams, R.O. 'Works by and about Alice Ruth (Moore) Dunbar-Nelson. A Bibliography'. *College Language Association Journal* 19 (1976), 322–6.

George Egerton

Books
Bjørhorde, Gerd. *Rebellious Structures: Women Writers and the Crisis of the Novel, 1880–1900*. Oxford, 1987.
Cunningham, Gail. *The New Woman and the Victorian Novel*. London, 1978.
Pollard, Arthur, ed. *The Victorians*. London, 1987.
Stubbs, Patricia. *Women and Fiction: Feminism and the Novel 1880–1920*. Brighton, 1979.

Articles
Harris, W.V. 'Fiction of the 1890s'. *PMLA* 83 (1968) 1407–13.
Harris, W.V. 'Egerton: Forgotten Realist'. *Victorian Newsletter* 35 (1968), 31–5.
Moss, Anita. 'George Egerton'. *Dictionary of Literary Biography* 135 (1994), 106–15.
Stutfield, H. 'Tommyrotics'. *Blackwood's* 157 (1895), 833–45.
Vicinus, Martha. 'The Stories of George Egerton'. In *Feminist Revisions*. Eds L. Tilly and V. Patraka. Ann Arbor, 1982, 12–25.
Vicinus, M. 'Introduction'. In *Keynotes and Discords*. London, 1983.

Alice Thomas Ellis

Books
Alexander, Flora. *Contemporary Women Novelists*. London, 1989.
Grove, Valerie. *The Compleat Woman*. London, 1987.
Kirkpatrick, D.L., ed. *Contemporary Novelists*. London and Chicago, 1986 (4th edn).
Woodman, Thomas. *Faithful Fictions: The Catholic Novel in British Literature*. Buckingham and Philadelphia, 1991.

Articles
Ackroyd, Peter. 'Out of Sight'. *Spectator* 239 (29 December 1977).
Alexander, Flora. 'Alice Thomas Ellis'. *Post-War Literatures*. Eds H. Bertens et al. Houten and Groningen, 1992.
Coe, Jonathan. 'Conversions'. *London Review of Books* 12 (13 September 1990), 15–16.
Gertler, T. 'Arms and the Men'. *New York Magazine* 17 (15 October 1984).
Kenyon, Olga. 'Interview'. *Women Writers Talk*. Oxford, 1989.
Kurz, Helga. 'Alice Thomas Ellis' *The Clothes in the Wardrobe*'. In *Women in Search of Literary Space*. Eds G.M. Grabber and M. Devine. Tübingen, 1992, 85–112.

Mills, Sara. 'Alice Thomas Ellis'. In *Dictionary of British Women Writers*. Ed. J. Todd. London, 1989, 220–1.

Treglown, J. 'A Handful of Dust'. *New Statesman* 94 (16 December 1977).

Buchi Emecheta

Books

Acheson, James, ed. *The British and Irish Novel since 1960*. Basingstoke, 1991.

Brown, Lloyd. *Women Writers in Black Africa*. Westport, Conn., 1981.

Davies, D.B. and Graves, A.A. *Njambika: Studies of Women in African Literature*. Trenton, N.J., 1986.

Davis, G.V. and Maes-Jelinek, H., eds. *Crisis and Creativity in the New Literatures in English*. Amsterdam, 1990.

Jones, E.D. *Women in African Literature Today*. London, 1987.

Nasta, Susheila, ed. *Motherlands*. London, 1991.

Otunkunefor, H. and Nwodo, O., eds. *Nigerian Female Writers: A Critical Perspective*. Lagos, 1989.

Research in African Literature. Special issue 19 (1988).

Taiwo, Odalele. *Female Novelists of Modern Africa*. London, 1984.

Articles

Andrade, S.Z. 'Rewriting History, Motherhood, and Rebellion'. *Research in African Literatures* 21 (1990), 91–110.

Barthelemy, Anthony. 'Western Time, African Lives: Time in the Novels of Buchi Emechta'. *Callaloo* 12 (1989), 559–74.

Bazin, N.T. 'Feminism in the Literature of African Women'. *World Literature Written in English* 25 (1985), 183–97.

Bazin, N.T. 'Bessie Head and Emecheta'. In *The Tragic Life*. Ed. Cecil Abrahams. Trenton, N.J., 1990, 45–58.

Birch, E.L. 'Autobiography: The Art of Self-Definition'. In *Black Women's Writing*. Ed. G. Wisker. Basingstoke, 1993, 127–45.

Bruner, Charlotte. 'The Other Audience: Children and the Example of Buchi Emecheta'. *African Studies Review* 29 (1986), 129–40.

Davis, Christina. 'Mother and Writer: Means of Empowerment in the Works of Buchi Emecheta'. *Commonwealth Essays and Studies* 13 (1990), 13–21.

Daymond, M.J. 'Emecheta, Laughter, and Silence'. *Journal of Literary Studies* 4 (1988), 64–73.

Emenyonu, E.M. 'Technique and Language in Buchi Emecheta'. *Journal of Commonwealth Literature* 23 (1988), 130–41.

Ezeigbo, T.A. 'Traditional Women's Institutions in Igbo Society'. *African Languages and Cultures* 3 (1990), 149–65.

Flewellen, E.C. 'Assertiveness vs Submissiveness in Selected Works by African Women Writers'. *Ba Shiru* 12 (1985), 3–18.

Frank, Katherine. 'African Womanhood in Emecheta'. *World Literature Written in English* 21 (1982), 476–97.

Katract, K.H. 'Womanhood/Motherhood: Selected Novels of Buchi Emecheta'. *Journal of Commonwealth Literature* 22 (1987), 159–70.

Kemp, Yakini. 'Romantic Love and the Individual'. *Obsidian II* 3 (1988), 1–16.

Nwankwo, Chimalum. 'Emecheta's Social Vision: Fantasy or Reality?'. *Ufahamu* 17 (1988), 35–44.

Ogunyemi, C.O. 'Buchi Emecheta: The Shaping of a Self'. *Komparatistische Hefte* 8 (1983), 65–77.

Ojo-Ade, Femi. 'Female Writers, Male Critics'. *African Literature Today* 13 (1983), 158–79.

Ojo-Ade, Femi. 'Women and the Nigerian Civil War: Emecheta and Nwapa'. *Etudes Germano-Africaines* 6 (1988), 75–86.

Petersen, K.H. 'Unpopular Opinions: Some African Women Writers'. *Kunapipi* 7 (1985), 107–20.

Porter, A.M. '*Second Class Citizen*: The Point of Departure'. *International Fiction Review* 15 (1988), 123–9.

Solberg, Rolf. 'The Women of Black Africa: Emecheta'. *English Studies* 64 (1983), 247–63.

Stratton, Florence. 'Archetypes of Female Experience in African Fiction'. *Research in African Literatures* 19 (1988), 143–69.

Ume, David. 'Interview'. *Ba Shiru* 12 (1985), 19–25.

Ume, M.A. 'African Women in Transition in Emecheta'. *Presence Africaine* 116 (1980), 190–9.

Ume, M.A. 'The Idea of Motherhood in two Third World Novels'. *College Language Association Journal* 31 (1987), 31–43.

Ward, Cynthia. 'What They told Emecheta: Oral Subjectivity and the Joys of "Otherhood"'. *PMLA* 105 (1990), 83–97.

Louise Erdrich

Books

Allen, P.G. *The Sacred Hoop: Recovering the Feminine in American Indian Traditions*. Boston, 1986.

Clarke, Graham, ed. *The New American Writing*. New York and London, 1990.

Pearlman, M., ed. *American Women Writing Fiction*. Lexington, Ky., 1989.

Pearlman, M. and Henderson, K.U., eds. *Inter/Views*. Lexington, Ky., 1990.

Schirer, T.E., ed. *Entering the 90s: The North American Experience*. Sault Ste Marie, 1991.

Sollors, Werner, ed. *The Invention of Ethnicity*. New York, 1989.

Swann, B. and Krupat, A., eds. *Recovering the Word: Essays on Native American Literature*. Berkeley, Calif., 1987.

Versluys, K., ed. *Neo-Realism in Contemporary American Fiction*. Amsterdam, 1992.

Vizenor, G., ed. *Postmodern Discourse on Native American Indian Literatures*. Albuquerque, N.Mex., 1989.

Woodward, P.G. 'New Tribal Forms: Community in Louise Erdrich's Fiction'. Ph.D., Tufts University, 1991.

Articles

Barry, N. and Prescott, M. 'The Triumph of the Brave: *Love Medicine*'s Holistic Vision'. *Critique* 30 (1989), 123–38.

Castillo, S.P. 'Postmodernism, Native American Literature, and the Real: The Silko–Erdrich Controversy'. *Massachusetts Review* 32 (1991), 285–94.

Castillo, S.P. 'The Construction of Gender and Ethnicity in the Texts of Silko and Erdrich'. *Yearbook of English Studies* 1994, 228–36.

Clarke, J.A. 'Transformation and Oral Tradition in *Tracks*'. *Journal of the Association for the Study of American Indian Literatures* 4 (1992), 28–48.

Cornell, D. 'Revis(ion)ing Pauline's Subject Position in *Tracks*'. *Studies in American Indian Literatures* 4 (1992), 49–64.

Flavin, Louise. 'Erdrich's *Love Medicine*: Loving over Time and Distance'. *Critique* 31 (1989), 55–64.

Gleason, W. 'Humor in *Love Medicine*'. *American Indian Culture and Research Journal* 11 (1987), 51–73.

Larson, S. 'Fragmentation of a Tribal People in *Tracks*'. *American Indian Culture and Research Journal* 17 (1993), 1–13.

Matchie, Thomas. '*Love Medicine*: A Female *Moby Dick*'. *Midwest Quarterly* 30 (1989), 478–91.

Meisenhelder, S. 'Race and Gender in *The Beet Queen*'. *Ariel* 25 (1994), 45–57.

Portales, Marco. 'People with Holes in Their Lives'. *New York Times* (23 December 1984), 6. (Review of *Love Medicine*).

Rainwater, Catherine. 'Reading Between Worlds: Narrativity in the Fiction of Louise Erdrich'. *American Literature* 62 (1990), 405–22.

Ruppert, J. 'Meditation and Multiple Narrative in *Love Medicine*'. *North Dakota Quarterly* 59 (1991), 119–41.

Sanders, S.R. 'Comments on the Art of Louise Erdrich'. *Studies in American Literature* 9 (1985).

Schultz, L.A. 'Fragments and Ojibwe Stories:

Narrative Strategies in Erdrich's *Love Medicine*'. *College Literature* 18 (1991), 80–95.

Sergei, Jennifer. 'Storytelling: Tradition and Preservation in Erdrich's *Tracks*'. *World Literature Today* 66 (1992), 179–82.

Smith, J. 'Transpersonal Selfhood in *Love Medicine*'. *Studies in American Indian Literatures* 8 (1991), 13–26.

Towery, M. 'Characters in Erdrich's Fiction'. *American Indian Culture and Research Journal* 16 (1992), 99–122.

Jessie Redmon Fauset

Books

Addison, Gayle. *The Way of the New World: The Black Novel in America*. Garden City, N.Y., 1976.

Ammons, Elizabeth. *Conflicting Stories*. Oxford and New York, 1991.

Black World. Special issue 20 (1970).

Byerman, K.E. *Fingering the Jagged Grain. Tradition and Form in Recent Black Fiction*. Athens, Ga., 1986.

Christian, Barbara. *Black Women Novelists*. Westport, Conn., 1984.

Dearborn, Mary V. *Pocahontas's Daughters: Gender and Ethnicity in American Culture*. Oxford and New York, 1986.

Hemenway, Robert, ed. *The Black Novelist*. Columbus, Ohio, 1970.

McDade, G.L. 'The Novels of Jessie Redmon Fauset'. Ph.D., University of Washington, 1987.

Noble, Jeanne. *Beautiful, Also, Are the Souls of My Black Sisters*. Englewood Cliffs, N.J., 1978.

Pryse, M. and Spillers, H.J., eds. *Conjuring: Black Women, Fiction, and Literary Tradition*. Bloomington, Ind., 1986.

Sylvander, C.W. *Jessie Redmon Fauset*. Troy, N.Y., 1981.

Articles

Ammons, Elizabeth. 'New Literary History: Wharton and Fauset'. *College Literature* 14 (1987), 207–18.

Condé, Mary. 'Passing in the Fiction of Jessie Redmon Fauset and Nella Larsen'. In *Yearbook of English Studies* 24: *Ethnicity and Representation*. Ed. A. Gurr. Leeds, 1994, 94–104.

deCille, Ann. 'Blues Notes on Black Sexuality: Fauset and Larsen'. *Journal of the History of Sexuality* 3 (1993), 418–44.

Feeney, J.J. 'Greek Tragic Patterns in a Black Novel: Jessie Fauset, *The Chinaberry Tree*'. *College Language Association Journal* 17 (1974), 211–15.

Feeney, J.J. 'A Sardonic, Unconventional Fauset'.

College Language Association Journal 22 (1979), 365–82.

Johnson, A.A. 'Literary Midwife: Fauset and the Harlem Renaissance'. *Phylon* (1978), 143–53.

Lewis, V.C. 'Mulatto Hegemony in Fauset'. *College Language Association Journal* 35 (1992), 375–86.

Lupton, M.J. 'Fauset's *The Chinaberry Tree*'. *College Language Association Journal* 27 (1984), 383–92.

Lupton, M.J. 'Black Women and Survival'. *Zora Neale Hurston Forum* 1 (1986), 38–44.

Lupton, M.J. 'The Cinderella Story in Fauset, Walker, and Morrison'. *Black American Literature Forum* 20 (1986).

McCoy, V.C. 'Mulatto Hegemony in Fauset'. *College Language Association Journal* 35 (1992), 375–86.

McDowell, D.E. 'Jessie Fauset: Genre and the Masking of the Subject'. In *Conjuring: Black Women, Fiction, and Literary Tradition*. Eds M. Pryse and H.J. Spiller. Bloomington, Ind., 1986.

Sylvander, C.W. 'Jessie Redmon Fauset'. *Dictionary of Literary Biography* 52 (1987), 76–85.

Bibliography and reference

Perry, Margaret. 'Jessie Fauset' (An Annotated Bibliography). In *The Harlem Renaissance: An Annotated Bibliography and Commentary*. New York, 1982, 77–82.

Eva Figes

Articles

Conradi, Peter. 'Eva Figes'. *Dictionary of Literary Biography* 14 (1982), 298–302.

Kenyon, Olga. 'Eva Figes'. *Women Novelists Today*. Brighton, 1988, 129–43.

Palmer, Paulina. *Contemporary Women's Fiction*. Hemel Hempstead, 1989.

Rimmer, Alison. 'Eva Figes'. *Dictionary of British Women Writers*. Ed. J. Todd. London, 1989, 250–1.

Roe, Sue. Review. *Literary Review* (1981), 13.

Zelda Fitzgerald

Books

Cooper, D.M. 'Form and Function: The Writing Style of Zelda'. Ph.D. University of Delaware, 1979.

Hardwick, Elizabeth. *Seduction and Betrayal: Women and Literature*. New York, 1970.

Hartnett, K.V. *Zelda Fitzgerald*. New York, 1991.

Mellow, J.R. *Invented Lives: F. Scott and Zelda Fitzgerald*. New York, 1984.

Milford, N.W. *Zelda*. New York, 1971.

Piper, Dan H. *F. Scott Fitzgerald: A Critical Portrait*. London, 1965.

Articles

Aaron, Daniel. 'The Legend of the Golden Couple'. *Virginia Quarterly Review* 48 (1972), 157–60.

Anderson, Nancy. 'Zelda Sayre Fitzgerald'. *Dictionary of Literary Biography* 84 (1985), 262–79.

Anderson, W.R. 'The Short Fiction of Zelda'. *Fitzgerald/Hemingway Annual* (1977), 19–42.

Anon. 'Putting Zelda Back Centre of Stage'. *Times Literary Supplement* (1 January 1971), 8.

Anon. 'The Far Side of Zelda Fitzgerald'. *Esquire* 62 (1964), 158–9.

Clemens, A.V. 'Zelda Fitzgerald: An Unromantic Revision'. *Dalhousie Review* 62 (1982), 196–211.

Fitzgerald, Zelda. 'Tribute to F. Scott Fitzgerald'. *Fitzgerald/Hemingway Annual* (1974), 9–10.

Going, W.T. 'Two Alabama Writers: Zelda Scott Fitzgerald and Sara Haardt Mencken'. *Alabama Review* 23 (1970), 3–29.

Gordon, Mary. 'Introduction'. In *Zelda Fitzgerald: The Collected Writings*. New York, 1991.

Hamblen, A.A. 'The Fitzgeralds' Coming of Age'. *University Review* (1968), 157–60.

Littleton, Taylor. 'A Letter from Zelda Fitzgerald'. *Fitzgerald/Hemingway Annual* (1974), 3–6.

Milford, Nancy. 'The Golden Dreams of Zelda Fitzgerald'. *Harper's Magazine* 238 (1969), 46–53.

Nanney, Lisa. '*Save Me the Waltz* as Southern Novel and *Kunstler-roman*'. In *The Female Tradition in Southern Literature*. Ed. C.S. Manning. Urbana, 1993, 220–32.

Petry, A.G. 'Women's Work: The Case of Zelda'. *Literature Interpretation Theory* 1 (1989), 69–83.

Samuels, C.T. 'A Woman's Place'. *New Republic* 162 (27 June 1970), 24–7.

Schorer, Mark. 'Zelda; or What's in a Name?'. *Atlantic* 226 (1970), 104–6.

Tavener-Courbin, J. 'Art as Women's Response and Search: *Save Me the Waltz*'. *Southern Literary Journal* 11 (1979), 22–42.

Wagner, L.W. '*Save Me the Waltz*: An Assessment in Craft'. *Journal of Narrative Technique* 12 (1982), 201–9.

Wood, M.E. '*Save Me the Waltz* as Asylum Autobiography'. *Tulsa Studies in Women's Literature* 11 (1992), 247–64.

Bibliography and reference

Bruccoli, M.K. *F. Scott Fitzgerald: A Descriptive Bibliography*. Pittsburg, 1988. Includes a complete list of Zelda's publications.

Janet Frame

Books

Australian and New Zealand Studies in Canada. Special issue 5 (1991).

Bennett, Bruce, ed. *A Sense of Exile: Essays in the Literature of the Asia-Pacific Region.* Nedlands, Western Australia, 1988.

Dalziel, Margaret. *Janet Frame.* Wellington, 1980.

Delbaere-Garant, Jeanne, ed. *Bird, Hawk, Bogie: Essays on Janet Frame.* Sydney, 1978.

Delbaere-Garant, Jeanne, ed. *The Ring of Fire: Essays on Janet Frame.* Sydney, 1992.

Dhawan, R.K. and Tonetto, W., eds. *New Zealand Literature Today.* New Delhi, 1993.

Evans, Patrick. *An Inward Sun.* Wellington, 1971.

Evans, Patrick. *Janet Frame.* Boston, 1977.

Penny, J.D. *I Have What I Gave: The Fiction of Janet Frame.* Wellington, 1992.

Stead, C.K., ed. *In the Glass Case. Essays on New Zealand Literature.* Auckland, 1981.

Williams, Mark. *Leaving the Highway: Six Contemporary New Zealand Novelists.* Auckland, 1990.

Articles

Ash, Susan. 'The Female Artist as Hero'. *Journal of New Zealand Literature* 6 (1988), 170–89.

Ash, Susan. 'The Narrow Frame: Unleashing (Im)Possibilities'. *Australian and New Zealand Studies in Canada* 5 (1991), 1–15.

Brown, Ruth. '*Owls Do Cry*: Portrait of New Zealand?'. *Landfall* 44 (1990), 350–8.

Brown, Ruth. 'The Unravelling of a Mad Myth'. *Women's Studies Journal* 7 (1991), 66–74.

Delbaere-Garant, Jeanne. 'Janet Frame and the Magic of Words'. In *Essays on Contemporary Post-Colonial Fiction.* Eds H. Bock and A. Wertheim. Ismaning, 1986, 311–31.

Evans, Patrick. 'The Autobiographical Parables of Frame'. *Modern Fiction Studies* 27 (1981), 31–40.

Evans, Patrick. 'Living and Writing in the Maniototo'. *SPAN* 18 (1984), 76–88.

Hankin, Cherry. 'Language as Theme in *Owls Do Cry*'. *Landfall* 28 (1974), 91–110.

Henke, Suzette. 'A Portrait of the Artist as a Young Woman: Frame's Autobiographies'. *SPAN* 31 (1991), 85–94.

Huggan, Graham. 'Resisting the Map as Metaphor'. *Kunapipi* 11 (1989), 5–15.

Jones, Laurence. 'The Personal Vision of *Owls Do Cry*'. *Landfall* 24 (1970), 280–96.

Jones, Laurence. 'One Story, Two Ways of Telling, Three Perspectives'. *Ariel* 16 (1985), 127–50.

Lawn, Jennifer. 'The Many Voices of *Owls Do Cry*: A Bakhtinian Approach'. *Journal of New Zealand Literature* 8 (1990), 87–105.

MacLennan, Carol. 'Dichotomous Values in the Novels of Frame'. *Journal of Commonwealth Literature* 22 (1987), 179–89.

MacLennan, Carol. 'Conformity and Deviance in Frame'. *Journal of New Zealand Literature* 6 (1988), 190–201.

MacNaughton, Howard. 'Fraying the Edge of an Alphabet'. *SPAN* 36 (1993), 131–43.

Mercer, Gina. 'Exploring the "Secret Caves of Language": Frame's Poetry'. *Meanjin* 44 (1985), 384–90.

New, W.H. 'The Frame Story World of Janet Frame'. *Essays on Canadian Writing* 29 (1984), 175–91.

O'Sullivan, Vincent. 'Exiles of the Mind: The Fiction of Janet Frame'. In *The Ring of Fire.* Ed. J. Delbaere. Sydney, 1992, 24–30.

Rhodes, H.W. 'Preludes and Parables: A Reading of Frame's Novels'. *Landfall* 26 (1972), 135–46.

Smith, Shona. 'Still Repressing: Reviewers and *Daughter Buffalo*'. *Untold* 8 (1987), 38–41.

Stein, K.F. 'The Dark Laughter of Frame'. *Pacific Quarterly* 9 (1985), 41–7.

Miles Franklin

Books

Barnard, Marjorie. *Miles Franklin: The Story of a Famous Australian.* Melbourne, 1967; reissued St Lucia Queensland, 1988, with a foreword by Jill Roe.

Coleman, Verna. *Her Unknown Brilliant Career.* London and Sydney, 1981.

Duncan, Roy. *On Dearborn Street.* St Lucia, Queensland, 1982.

Ferrier, Carole, ed. *Gender, Politics, and Fiction: Twentieth Century Australian Women's Novels.* St Lucia, Queensland, 1985.

Jurak, Mirko, ed. *Australian Papers.* Ljubljana, 1983.

Kessler-Harris, A., ed. *Faith of a (Woman) Writer.* Westport, Conn., 1988.

Matthew, Ray. *Miles Franklin.* Melbourne, 1963.

Modjeska, D. *Exiles at Home: Australian Women Writers 1925–1945.* London and Sydney, 1981.

Roderick, Colin. *Miles Franklin: Her Brilliant Career.* Adelaide, 1982.

Walker, S. *Who Is She?: Images of Women in Australian Fiction.* St Lucia, Queensland, 1983.

Articles

Bird, Delys. 'Towards an Aesthetics of Australian Women's Fiction'. *Australian Literary Studies* 11 (1983), 171–81.

Gingell, Susan. 'Delineating the Difference: An Approach to Miles Franklin's *My Brilliant Career*'. *Australian and New Zealand Studies in Canada* 3 (1990), 43–55.

Green, G.V. 'Overturning the Doll's House'. *CRUX* 17 (1983), 47–59.

Hooton, Joy 'Franklin's *Childhood at Brindabella* and *My Brilliant Career*'. *Meanjin* 46 (1987), 58–66.

Matthew, Brian. 'Directions in Recent Fiction'. *Island* 33 (1986).

Roe, Jill. 'Miles Franklin and Australian Identity'. *Hecate* 17 (1991), 67–73.

Roe, Jill. '"Syllabascape": Language and Landscape'. *SPAN* 32 (1991), 24–31.

Rutherford, Anna. 'Miles Franklin: The Outside Track'. In *Multiple Worlds, Multiple Words*. Eds H. Maes-Jelinek et al. Liège, 1988, 239–56.

Sircar, Sanjay. 'Franklin's *Bring the Monkey*'. *Clues* 15 (1994), 15–37.

Strauss, J. 'Portrait of the Artist as a Young Woman'. *Australian Canadian Studies* 8 (1991), 41–55.

Sutherland, Bruce. 'Stella Miles Franklin's American Years'. *Meanjin* 24 (1965).

Thomas, Glen. 'The Critical Reception of Miles Franklin'. *LING* 20 (1993), 78–82.

Webby, E. 'Introduction'. In *My Brilliant Career*. By Miles Franklin. London, 1990.

Webby, E. 'Introduction'. In *My Career Goes Bung*. By Miles Franklin. London, 1990.

Mary E. Wilkins Freeman

Books

Carpenter, L. and Kolmar, W.K. *Haunting the House of Fiction*. Knoxville, Tenn., 1991.

Donovan, Josephine. *New England Local Colour Literature*. New York, 1983.

Foster, Edward. *Mary E. Wilkins Freeman*. New York, 1956.

Hamblem, Abigail A. *The New England Art of Mary E. Wilkins Freeman*. Amherst, Mass., 1966.

Meese, E.A. *Crossing and the Double-Cross: The Practice of Feminist Criticism*. Chapel Hill, N.C., 1986.

Pattee, F.L. *The Development of the American Short Story*. New York, 1923.

Reichardt, M.R. *A Web of Relationship: Women in Wilkins Freeman*. Jackson, Miss., 1992.

Romines, Ann. *The Home Plot*. Amherst, Mass., 1992.

Westbrook, Perry D. *Mary Wilkins Freeman*. New York, 1967; rev. Boston, 1988.

Articles

Blum, V.L. 'Freeman and the Taste of Necessity'. *American Literature* 65 (1993), 69–94.

Cutter, M.J. 'Frontiers of Language: Engendering Discourse'. *American Literature* 63 (1991), 279–91.

Gardner, Kate. 'The Subversion of Genre in Wilkins Freeman'. *New England Quarterly* 65 (1992), 447–68.

Johnson, Norma. 'Artist and Audience in Three Wilkins Freeman Stories'. *Colby Quarterly* 29 (1993), 43–56.

Koppelman, S. 'About *Two Friends*'. *American Literary Realism* 21 (1988), 43–57.

McElrath, Joseph E. 'The Artistry of Mary E. Wilkins Freeman's "The Revolt"'. *Studies in Short Fiction* 17 (1980).

Orr, Elaine. 'Reading Negotiation and Negotiated Reading'. *CEA Critic* 53 (1991), 49–65.

Pryse, Marjorie. 'An Uncloistered "New England Nun"'. *Studies in Short Fiction* 20 (1983), 289–95.

Quina, J.H. 'Character Types in the Fiction of Mary Wilkins Freeman'. *Colby Library Quarterly* 7 (1971), 432–9.

Richard, Mary R. 'Mary Wilkins Freeman: One Hundred Years of Criticism'. *Legacy* 4 (1987), 31–44.

Sherman, Sarah W. 'The Great Goddess in New England: Mary Wilkins Freeman's "Christmas Jenny"'. *Studies in Short Fiction* 17 (1980).

Terrie, Philip G. 'Rituals of Meaning in *The Country of the Pointed Firs*'. *Colby Library Quarterly* 23 (1987), 16–25.

Toth, S.A. 'Defiant Light: A Positive View of Mary Wilkins Freeman'. *New England Quarterly* 46 (1973), 82–93.

Warner, Sylvia Townsend. 'Item: One Empty House'. *New Yorker* 42 (1966), 131–8.

Bibliography and reference

Eppard, Philip and Reichard, Mary. 'A Checklist of Uncollected Short Fiction by Mary Wilkins Freeman'. *American Literary Realism* 23 (1990), 70–4.

Mavis Gallant

Books

Beshner, N.K. *The Light of Imagination: Mavis Gallant's Fiction*. Vancouver, 1988.

Canadian Fiction Magazine. Special issue 28 (1978).

Delbaere, Jeanne, ed. *Multiple Voices*. Sydney, 1990.

Essays on Canadian Writing. Special issue 42 (1990).

Howells, C.A. and Hunter, L., eds. *Narrative Strategies in Canadian Literature: Feminism and Post-Colonialism*. Milton Keynes and Philadelphia, 1991.

Hutcheon, Linda, ed. *Double Talking*. Toronto, 1992.

Keith, W.J. *A Sense of Style: Studies in the Art of Fiction in English-Speaking Canada*. Downsview, Ontario, 1989.

Kiefer, J.K. *Reading Mavis Gallant*. Toronto, 1989.
Merler, Grazia. *Mavis Gallant: Narrative Patterns and Devices*. Ottawa, 1978.
Neuman, S. and Kambourell, S., eds. *A Mazing Space: Writing Canadian Women Writing*. Edmonton, 1986.
Nischik, R. and Korte, B., eds. *Modes of Narrative*. Wurzburg, 1990.
Smythe, Karen. *Figuring Grief: Gallant, Munro, and the Poetics of Elegy*. Montreal, 1992.

Articles
Alexander, Flora. 'Quebec Storytellers: Mavis Gallant's Narrators in their Settings'. *British Journal of Canadian Studies* 6 (1991), 304–12.
Clement, Lesley. 'Artistry in Gallant's *Green Water, Green Sky*'. *Canadian Literature* 129 (1991), 57–73.
Clement, Lesley. 'Mavis Gallant's Apprenticeship Stories, 1944–50: Breaking the Frame'. *English Studies in Canada* 18 (1992), 317–34.
Godard, Barbara. 'Modalities of the Edge. Towards a Semiotics of Irony: The Case of Mavis Gallant'. *Essays on Canadian Writing* 42 (1990), 72–101.
Hancock, Geoff. 'An Interview with Mavis Gallant'. *Canadian Fiction Magazine* 28 (1978), 18–67.
Hatch, Ronald. 'Gallant and the Creation of Consciousness'. In *Present Tense*. Ed. J. Moss. Toronto, 1985, 45–78.
Irvine, Lorna. 'Mavis Gallant's Fiction'. *Colby Quarterly* 29 (1993), 119–25.
Keefer, J.K. 'Bridges and Chasms: Multiculturism'. *World Literature Written in English* 31 (1991), 100–11.
Keith, W.J. 'Creating Fictional Worlds of Wonder'. In *Canadian Literature in English*. London and New York, 1985.
Rooke, Constance. 'Waiting for a Final Explanation: Mavis Gallant's *Irina*'. In *Fear of the Open Heart: Essays on Contemporary Canadian Writing*. Toronto, 1989, 27–53.
Schaub, Danielle. 'Mavis Gallant's Perception of Canadian Culture'. *Critique* 34 (1992), 33–46.
Schaub, Danielle. 'Structural Patterns of Alienation and Disjunction'. *Canadian Literature* 136 (1993), 45–57.
Stevens, Peter. 'Perils of Compassion'. *Canadian Literature* 56 (1973), 61–70.
Sturgess, Charlotte. 'Mavis Gallant's *In Transit* – Stories from the Border'. *British Journal of Canadian Studies* 6 (1991), 313–18.

Bibliography and reference
Malcolm, D. 'An Annotated Bibliography of Works by and about Mavis Gallant'. *Essays on Canadian Writing* 6 (1977), 32–52.

Jane Gardam

Articles
Craig, Patricia. 'Jane Gardam'. *Dictionary of Literary Biography* 14 (1983), 342–8.
McLeod, Marion. 'On the Borders'. *New Zealand Listener* (19 September 1992), 50–1.
Perkins, Agnes. 'A Comparison of Recent British and American Realistic Fiction'. *Proceedings of the Sixth Annual Conference on the Children's Literature Association*. Villanova, 1980, 155–64.
Purton, Valerie. 'Jane Gardam'. *Dictionary of British Women Writers*. Ed. Janet Todd. London, 1989, 262–4.

Martha Gellhorn

Books
Baker, Carlos. *Ernest Hemingway: A Life Story*. New York, 1969.
Matthews, T.S. *O My America! Notes on a Trip*. New York, 1962.
Orsagh, Jacqueline. 'A Critical Biography of Martha Gellhorn'. Ph.D., Michigan State University, 1978.
Rollyson, Carl. *Nothing Ever Happens to the Brave: The Story of Martha Gellhorn*. New York, 1990.

Articles
Orsagh, J. 'Martha Gellhorn'. *Dictionary of Literary Biography, Yearbook 1982*. Detroit, 1983, 244–50.

Charlotte Perkins Gilman

Books
Ammons, Elizabeth. *Conflicting Stories*. New York and Oxford, 1991.
Carpenter, L. and Kolmar, W.K., eds. *Haunting and House of Fiction*. Knoxville, Tenn., 1991.
Erskine, T.L. and Richards, C.L., eds. *Charlotte Perkins Gilman, 'The Yellow Wallpaper'*. New Brunswick, N.J., 1993.
Girgus, S.B. *Desire and the Political Unconscious*. Basingstoke, 1990.
Hill, Mark A. *Charlotte Perkins Gilman: The Making of Radical Feminism 1860–1896*. Philadelphia, 1980.
Horner, A. and Zlosnik, S. *Landscapes of Desire*. Hemel Hempstead, 1990.
Karpinski, J.B., ed. *Critical Essays on Charlotte Perkins Gilman*. New York, 1992.
Lane, Ann J. *To Herland and Beyond: The Life and Work of Charlotte Perkins Gilman*. New York, 1990.
Winkler, Barbara S. *Victorian Daughters: The Lives and Feminism of Gilman and Schreiner*. Ann Arbor, 1980.

Articles

Baden, Julia. 'Realism in Jewett, Freeman, and Gilman'. In *American Realism: New Essays*. Ed. E.J. Sundquist. Baltimore, 1982, 176–98.

Bak, J.S. 'Foucauldian Panopticism in "The Yellow Wallpaper"'. *Studies in Short Fiction* 31 (1994), 39–46.

Degler, Carl. 'Charlotte Perkins Gilman on the Theory and Practice of Feminism'. *American Quarterly* 8 (1956), 21–39.

Dimock, W.C. 'Feminism, New Historicism and the Reader'. In *Readers in History*. Ed. J.L. Machor. Baltimore, 1993, 85–106.

Gordon, R.B. 'Interior Decoration in Poe and Gilman'. *Literature Interpretation Theory* 3 (1991), 85–99.

Haney-Peritz, J. 'Another Look at "The Yellow Wallpaper"'. *Women's Studies* 12/13 (1986), 113–28.

Herndl, D.P. 'The Writing Cure'. *National Women's Studies Association Journal* 1 (1988), 52–74.

Hill, Mary A. 'Gilman: A Feminist's Struggle with Womanhood'. *Massachusetts Review* 21 (1980), 503–26.

Hume, B.A. 'Gilman's Interminable Grotesque'. *Studies in Short Fiction* 28 (1991), 477–84.

Johnston, Georgie. 'Gilman's Prewriting Irigaray'. *Women's Studies* 21 (1992), 75–86.

Knight, Denise. 'The Reincarnation of Jane'. *Women's Studies* 20 (1992), 287–302.

MacPite, Loralee. 'Environment as Psychopathological Symbolism in "The Yellow Wallpaper"'. *American Literary Realism* 8 (1975), 286–8.

Nies, Judith. 'Charlotte Perkins Gilman'. In *Seven Women: Portraits from the American Radical Tradition*. New York, 1977.

Peyser, T.G. 'Gilman's *Herland*'. *Studies in American Fiction* 20 (1992), 1–16.

Shumaker, Conrad. '"The Yellow Wallpaper"'. *American Literature* 57 (1985).

Shumaker, Conrad. 'Realism, Reform and the Audience'. *Arizona Quarterly* 47 (1991), 81–93.

Siegfried, C.H. 'Classical American Philosophy's Invisible Women'. *Canadian Review of American Studies* (1992), 83–116.

Treichler, Paula A. 'Escaping the Sentence: Diagnosis and Discourse in "The Yellow Wallpaper"'. *Tulsa Studies in Women's Literature* 3 (1984), 61–77.

Wiesenthal, C.S. 'The Language of Madness in "The Yellow Wallpaper"'. *Wascana Review* 25 (1990), 1–7.

Wilson, D.P. 'The Terrain of *Herland*'. *Women's Studies* 12/13 (1986), 271–92.

Bibliography and reference

Scharnhorst, Gary. *Charlotte Perkins Gilman: A Bibliography*. Metuchen, N.J., 1985.

Ellen Glasgow

Books

Ammons, Elizabeth. *Conflicting Stories*. Oxford and New York, 1991.

Auchincloss, Louis. *Ellen Glasgow*. Minneapolis, 1964.

Cabell, James B. *As I Remember It*. New York, 1955.

Dekker, George. *The American Historical Romance*. Cambridge, 1987.

Donovan, Josephine. *After the Fall: The Demeter–Persephone Myth in Wharton, Cather, and Glasgow*. University Park, Pa., 1989.

Ellen Glasgow Newsletter (1974– , semi-annually).

Fleishimam, F. *American Novelists Revisited*. Boston, 1982.

Godbold, Stanley, Jr. *Ellen Glasgow and the Woman Within*. Baton Rouge, La., 1972.

Inge, M. Thomas, ed. *Ellen Glasgow. Centennial Essays*. Charlottesville, Va., 1976.

McDowell, F.P.W. *Ellen Glasgow and the Ironic Art of Fiction*. Madison, 1960.

Manning, C.S., ed. *The Female Tradition in Southern Literature*. Urbana, Ill., 1993.

Mississippi Quarterly. Special sections 31 (1977–8) and 32 (1979).

Parent, Monique. *Ellen Glasgow: Romancière*. Paris, 1962.

Raper, J.R. *The Fiction of Ellen Glasgow, 1916–45*. Baton Rouge, La., 1980.

Richards, M.K. *Ellen Glasgow's Development as a Novelist*. The Hague, 1971.

Rouse, Blair. *Ellen Glasgow*. New York, 1962.

Santas, Joan Foster. *Ellen Glasgow's American Dream*. Charlottesville, Va., 1965.

Saunders, C.E. *Writing the Margins*. Cambridge, Mass., 1987.

Scura, D.M., ed. *Ellen Glasgow: The Contemporary Reviews*. Cambridge, 1992.

Thiebaux, Marcelle. *Ellen Glasgow*. New York, 1982.

Wagner, Linda. *Ellen Glasgow: Beyond Convention*. Austin, Tex., 1982.

Young, T.D., ed. *Modern American Fiction: Form and Function*. Baton Rouge, La., 1989.

Articles

These do not include those in the *Ellen Glasgow Newsletter*.

Bunselmeyer, J.E. 'Glasgow's "Flexible" Style'. *Centennial Review* 28 (1984), 112–28.

Day, Douglas. 'Ellen Glasgow's Letters to the Saxtons'. *American Literature* 35 (1963), 230–6.

Duke, Maurice. 'Cabell's and Glasgow's Richmond: The Intellectual Background of the City'. *Mississippi Quarterly* 27 (1974), 375–92.

Goodman, S. 'Competing Visions of Freud in Glasgow and Wharton'. *Colby Library Quarterly* 25 (1989), 218–26.

Gudd, L.J. et al. 'The Forgotten Decades of Southern Writing, 1890–1920'. *Mississippi Quarterly* 21 (1968), 275–90.

Harrison, Beth. 'Glasgow's Revision of Southern Pastoral'. *South Atlantic Review* 55 (1990), 47–70.

Heald, W.F. 'Ellen Glasgow and the Grotesque'. *Mississippi Quarterly* 18 (1964), 7–11.

MacDonald, E.E. 'The Glasgow–Cabell Entente'. *American Literature* 41 (1969), 76–91.

McDowell, F.P.W. 'Glasgow and the Art of the Novel'. *Philological Quarterly* 30 (1951), 328–47.

Rainwater, C. 'Narration as Pragmatism in *Barren Ground*'. *American Literature* 63 (1991), 664–82.

Steel, O.L. 'Gertrude Stein and Ellen Glasgow: Memoir of a Meeting'. *American Literature* 33 (1961), 76–7.

Walker, Nancy. 'Ellen Glasgow and American Naturalism'. *Southern Quarterly* 23/4 (1985).

Winniford, Lee. 'Glasgow's *Barren Ground*'. *Journal of Narrative Technique* 24 (1994), 141–52.

Wittenberg, J.B. 'The Critical Fortunes of *Barren Ground*'. *Mississippi Quarterly* 32 (1979), 591–609.

Bibliography and reference
Ellen Glasgow: Newsletter. 'Bibliography Continued' 24 (1987), 10–11.

Susan Glaspell

Books
Andrews, Clarence. *A Literary History of Iowa.* Iowa City, 1972.

Makowsky, Veronica. *Susan Glaspell's Century of American Women.* New York, 1993.

Noe, Marcia. 'A Critical Biography of Susan Glaspell'. Ph.D., University of Iowa, 1976.

Waterman, A.E. *Susan Glaspell.* New York, 1966.

Articles
Alkalay-Gott, Karen. 'Jury of her Peers: The Importance of Trifles'. *Studies in Short Fiction* 21 (1984), 1–9.

Anderson, Margaret. 'Neither Drama Nor Life'. *Little Review* 5 (1919), 59–62.

Andrews, C. and Noe, M. 'Glaspell of Davenport'. *Iowan* 25 (1977), 46–53.

Bach, G.P. 'Susan Glaspell: Supplementary Notes'. *American Literary Realism* 5 (1972), 67–73.

Carpentier, M.C. 'Glaspell's Fiction'. *Twentieth Century Literature* 40 (1994), 92–113.

Crawford, B.J. 'Susan Glaspell'. *Palimpsest* 11 (1930), 517–21.

Fettersley, Judith. 'Reading about Reading'. In *Gender and Reading.* Eds E.A. Flynn et al. Baltimore, 1986, 147–64.

Hedges, Elaine. 'Glaspell's "A Jury of Her Peers" '. *Women's Studies* 12 (1986), 89–110.

Kolin, P.C. 'Therapists in *Suppressed Desires*'. *Notes on Contemporary Literature* 18 (1988), 2–3.

Larabee, Ann. 'Death in Delphi'. *Mid-American Review* 7 (1987), 93–106.

Lewisohn, Lewis. 'The Verge'. *Nation* 113 (1921), 708–9.

Lewisohn, Ludwig. 'Susan Glaspell'. *Nation* 111 (1920), 509–10.

Mustazza, Leonard. 'Generic Translation and Thematic Shift in Glaspell'. *Studies in Short Fiction* (1989), 489–96.

Noe, Marcia. 'Glaspell's Analysis of the Midwestern Character'. *Books at Iowa* 27 (1977), 3–14.

Noe, Marcia. 'A Romantic and Miraculous City'. *Western Illinois Regional Studies* 1 (1978), 176–98.

Waterman, A.E. 'Susan Glaspell (1882–1948)'. *American Literary Realism* 4 (1971), 183–91.

Waterman, A.E. 'Susan Glaspell'. *Dictionary of Literary Biography* 78 (1989), 198–204.

Bibliography and reference
Noe, Marcia. 'A Bibliography of Susan Glaspell'. *Books at Iowa* 27 (1977).

Nadine Gordimer

Books
Ariel. Special issue 19 (1988).

Bazin N.T. and Seymour, M.D., eds. *Conversations with Gordimer.* Jackson, Miss., 1990.

Bucknell Review. Special section 37 (1993).

Clingman, S.R., ed. *The Essential Gesture: Writing, Politics and Places.* Cape Town, 1988.

Cooke, John. *The Novels of Nadine Gordimer: Private Lives/Public Landscapes.* Baton Rouge, La., 1985.

Haugh, Robert F. *Nadine Gordimer.* New York, 1974.

Heywood, Christopher. *Nadine Gordimer.* Windsor, 1983.

Journal of the Short Story in English. Special issue 15 (1990).

King, Bruce, ed. *The Later Fiction of Nadine Gordimer.* New York, 1993.

Louvel, Liliane. *Nadine Gordimer.* Nancy, 1993.

Newman, Judie. *Nadine Gordimer.* London and New York, 1988.

Smith, Rowland, ed. *Critical Essays on Nadine Gordimer.* Boston, 1990.

Trump, Martin, ed. *Rendering Things Visible: Essays on South African Literary Culture*. Johannesburg and Athens, Ga., 1990.

Wade, Michael. *Nadine Gordimer*. London, 1978.

Articles

Bailey, Nancy. 'Living Without the Future: *July's People*'. *World Literature Written in English* 25 (1984), 215–24.

Barnouw, Dagmar. 'Gordimer: Dark Times, Interior Worlds, and the Obscurities of Difference'. *Contemporary Literature* 35 (1994), 252–80.

Bazin, N.T. 'Madness, Mysticism and Fantasy: Shifting Perspectives in the Novels of Lessing, Head, and Gordimer'. *Extrapolation* 33 (1992), 73–87.

Bazin, N.T. 'Sex, Politics, and Silent Black Women'. *Bucknell Review* 37 (1993), 30–45.

Donaghy, Mary. 'Double Exposure: Narrative Perspective in *A Guest of Honour*'. *Ariel* 19 (1988), 19–32.

Engle, Lars. 'The Political Uncanny: The Novels of Gordimer'. *Yale Journal of Criticism* 2 (1989), 101–27.

Githii, E.W. 'Gordimer's *Selected Stories*'. *Critique* 22 (1981), 45–54.

Glenn, Ian. 'Gordimer, Coetzee, and the Politics of Interpretation'. *South Atlantic Quarterly* 93 (1994), 11–32.

Green, Robert. 'From *The Lying Days* to *July's People*'. *Journal of Modern Literature* 14 (1988), 543–65.

Greenstein, Susan. 'Miranda's Story: Nadine Gordimer and the Literature of Empire'. *Novel* 18 (1985), 227–42.

Halil, Karen. 'Subjectivity in *Burger's Daughter*'. *Ariel* 25 (1994), 31–45.

Knipp, Thomas. 'Eros and Polis in Gordimer'. *Research in African Literatures* 24 (1993), 37–50.

Lazar, K.R. 'Gender and Politics in Gordimer's Novels'. *English in Africa* 19 (1992), 53–65.

Lazar, Karen. 'Gordimer's Leap into the 1990s'. *Journal of Southern African Studies* 18 (1992), 783–802.

Neill, Michael. 'Translating the Present: Language, Knowledge, and Identity in *July's People*'. *Journal of Commonwealth Literature* 25 (1990), 71–97.

Newman, Judie. 'Nadine Gordimer'. In *Post-War Literatures*. Eds H. Bertens et al. Houten and Groningen, 1992.

Rich, Paul. 'Tradition and Revolt in South African Fiction'. *Journal of Southern African Studies* 9 (1982), 54–73.

Trump, Martin. 'The Short Fiction of Nadine Gordimer'. *Research in African Literatures* 17 (1986), 341–69.

Wade, Michael. '*A Sport of Nature*'. In *The Later Fiction of Nadine Gordimer*. Ed. B. King. New York, 1993, 155–72.

Weinhouse, Linda. 'The Deconstruction of Victory: *A Sport of Nature*'. *Research in African Literatures* 21 (1990), 19–101.

Wheeler, K.M. 'Irony and the Politics of Style'. *Journal of the Short Story in English* 15 (1990), 75–91.

White, Jonathan. 'Politics and the Individual'. In *Recasting the World*. Ed. J. White. Baltimore, 1993, 208–40.

Yelin, Louise. '*A Sport of Nature* and British Literary Tradition'. In *Decolonizing Tradition*. Ed. K.R. Lawrence. Urbana, Ill., 1992, 191–211.

Patricia Grace

Books

Beaton, Peter. *The Healing Tongue*. 1989.

Kedgeley, Sue. *Our Own Country*. Auckland, 1989.

King, Michael, ed. *Tihe Mauri Ora*. Wellington, 1978.

New, W.H. *Dreams of Speech and Violence. The Art of the Short Story in Canadian and New Zealand Literature*. Toronto, 1987.

Roberts, Heather. *Where Did She Come From? New Zealand Women Novelists 1862–1987*. Wellington and London, 1989.

Articles

Anderson, Laurie. 'Maoriness and the Clash of Cultures in *Mutuwhenua*'. *World Literature Written in English* 26 (1986), 188–90.

Bardolph, Jacqueline. ' "A Way of Talking": A Way of Seeing'. *Commonwealth Essays and Studies* 12 (1990), 29–39.

Beston, J.B. 'The Fiction of Patricia Grace'. *Ariel* 15 (1984), 41–53.

Fuchs, Miriam. 'Grace's *Potiki*, A Case Study'. *SPAN* 36 (1993), 566–83; reprinted *Boundary 2* 21 (1994), 165–84.

Guerin, Louise. 'Patricia Grace'. *Listener* (15 March 1986).

Hughes, S.F.D. 'Pakeha and Maori'. *Modern Fiction Studies* 27 (1981), 13–29.

Kaa, Keri. 'Patricia Grace and Maori Fiction'. *Spiral* 5 (1982).

McGill, David. 'Patricia Grace'. *Listener* (11 October 1975).

McGaw, William. 'Another Foothold; Exile and Return in *Mutuwhenua*'. *Australian and New Zealand Studies in Canada* 6 (1991), 103–11.

Nunns, R. 'Doing Her Job: Patricia Grace's Fiction'. *Islands* 7 (1979), 416–21.

Pearson, Bill. 'Ihimaeri and Grace'. In *Critical Essays on the New Zealand Short Story*. Ed. C. Hankin. Auckland, 1982, 166–84.

Prentice, Christine. 'Storytelling in Munro and Grace'. *Australian Canadian Studies* 8 (1991), 27–40.

Simms, Norman. 'A Maori Literature in English, Part 1: Prose Fiction: Patricia Grace'. *Pacific Quarterly* 3 (1978), 186–99.

Tausky, Thomas. 'Interview'. *Australian and New Zealand Studies in Canada* 6 (1991), 90–102.

Watego, Cliff. 'Cultural Adaptation in the South Pacific Novel'. *World Literature Written in English* 23 (1984), 488–96.

Webby, Elizabeth. 'Amazing Grace: Patricia Grace's *Electric City* and *Potiki*'. *CRNLE Reviews Journal* 1 (1989), 72–6.

Radclyffe Hall

Books

Baker, M. *Our Three Selves*. London, 1985.

Brittain, Vera. *Radclyffe Hall: A Case of Obscenity*. London, 1968.

Brunt, R. and Coward, R., eds. *Feminism, Culture, and Politics*. London, 1982.

Cruikshank, M. *Lesbian Studies Present and Future*. New York, 1982.

Dickson, Lovat. *Radclyffe Hall at the Well of Loneliness: A Sapphic Chronicle*. London and Glasgow, 1975.

Duncker, Patricia. *Sisters and Strangers*, Oxford, 1992.

Feminist Review. Special issue 35 (1990).

Franks, Claudia S. *Beyond the Well of Loneliness: The Fiction of Radclyffe Hall*. Amersham, 1982.

Jay, K. and Glasgow, J., eds. *Lesbian Texts and Contexts*. New York, 1990.

O'Rourke, R. *Reflecting on 'The Well of Loneliness'*. London, 1989.

Radford, Jean, ed. *The Progress of Romance: The Politics of Popular Fiction*. London, 1986.

Troubridge, Lady Una. *The Life and Death of Radclyffe Hall*. London, 1961.

Articles

Rolley, Katrina. 'Cutting a Dash: The Dress of Radclyffe Hall and Una Troubridge'. *Feminist Review* 35 (1990), 54–66.

Stimpson, Catherine R. 'Zero Degree Deviancy: The Lesbian Novel in English'. *Critical Inquiry* 8 (1981).

Elizabeth Hardwick

Books

Axelrod, Stephen G. *Robert Lowell: Life and Art*. Princeton, N.J., 1978.

Articles

Branin, J.J. 'Elizabeth Hardwick'. *Dictionary of Literary Biography* 6. Detroit, 1980, 133–6.

Didion, Joan. 'Meditation on a Life'. *New York Times Book Review* (29 April 1979), 1, 60.

Du Plessix Gray, Francine. 'Elizabeth Hardwick: A Fresh Way of looking at Literature – and at Life'. (An Interview). *Vogue* 169 (1979), 202–3, 250.

Lamont, R.C. 'Off-Centre Spatiality of Women's Discourse'. In *Theory and Practice of Feminist Criticism*. Eds G. Mora et al. Ypsilanti, Mich., 1982, 138–55.

Locke, Richard. 'Conversation on a Book'. *New York Times Book Review* (29 April 1979), 1, 61–2.

Plimpton, George. 'Interview'. In *Writers at Work*, vol. 7, Harmondsworth, 1986, 123–48.

Rahv, Philip. 'The Editor Interviews Elizabeth Hardwick'. *Modern Occasions* 2 (1972), 159–67.

Rudikoff, Sanya. 'Heroines of Literature and Life'. *Hudson Review* 27 (1974–5), 615–19.

Shirley Hazzard

Books

Brissenden, Alan, ed. *Aspects of Australian Fiction*. Nedlands, 1990.

Danvers, Dennis. 'Romantic Ideas in the Fiction of Shirley Hazzard'. Ph.D., University of Texas at Arlington, 1984.

Ferrier, Carole, ed. *Gender, Politics and Fiction*. St Lucia, Queensland, 1985.

Geering, R.G. *Recent Fiction. Australian Writers Series*. Melbourne, 1974, with bibliography.

Singh, Kirpal, ed. *The Writer's Sense of the Past. Essays on Southeast Asian and Australasian Literature*. Singapore, 1987.

Texas Studies in Language and Literature. Special issue on Hazard, Ozick and Redmond 25 (1983).

Articles

Baym, Nina. 'Artifice and Romance in Hazzard's Fiction'. *Texas Studies in Language and Literature* 25 (1983), 222–48.

Bird, Delys. 'Text Production and Reception – Hazzard's *Transit of Venus*'. *Westerly* 30 (1985), 39–51.

Capone, Giovanna. 'Shirley Hazzard: Transit and the Bay at Noon'. *Australian Literary Studies* 13 (1987), 172–83.

Colmer, John. 'Pattern and Preoccupations of Love: The Novels of Hazzard'. *Meanjin* 29 (1970), 461–7.

Colmer, John. 'The Transit of Venus'. *Journal of Commonwealth Literature* 19 (1984), 10–21.

Danvers, Dennis. 'Interview'. *Antipodes* 1 (1987), 40–3.

Kavanagh, P. 'Interview'. *Southerly* 45 (1985), 209–19, and see vol. 43 (1983).

Levy, Bronwen. 'The Reviewing Reception of *The Transit of Venus*'. In C. Ferrier, ed. *Gender, Politics and Fiction*. St Lucia, Queensland, 1985, 179–99.

Mattei, A.G. 'The Novel as "Work in Progress"'. *Australian Literary Studies* 15 (1991), 117–22.

Moon, E.G.B. 'Indispensable Humanity in *The Transit Of Venus*'. *Southerly* 45 (1985), 94–108.

Neri, A. '[Hazzard's Heroines in Italy]'. *Westerly* 28 (1983), 37–42.

Neri, A. '[The Fiction of Shirley Hazzard]'. *Journal of Commonwealth Literature* 26 (1991).

Olubas, B. 'Rewriting the Past: Exploration and Discovery in *The Transit of Venus*'. *Australian Literary Studies* 15 (1992), 155–64.

Priessnitz, Horst. 'Shirley Hazzard: Glimpses of Paradise'. In *International Literature in English*. Ed. R. Ross. Chicago and London, 1991, 335–50.

Rainwater, C. and Sheick, W.J. 'An Interview with Hazzard'. *Texas Studies in Literature and Language* 25 (1983), 213–21.

Sellick, R. 'Shirley Hazzard: Dislocation and Continuity'. *Australian Literary Studies* 9 (1979), 182–8.

Twidale, K.M. 'Discontinuous Narrative and Aspects of Love in Hazzard's Short Stories'. *Journal of Commonwealth Literature* 26 (1991), 101–16.

Wieland, James. 'Antipodean Eyes: Ways of Seeing in *The Transit of Venus*'. *Kunapipi* 5 (1983), 36–49.

Bibliography and reference

Beston, J.B. 'A Bibliography of Shirley Hazzard'. *World Literature Written in English* 20 (1981), 236–54.

Sheick, W.J. 'A Bibliography of Writings by Shirley Hazzard'. *Texas Studies in Language and Literature* 25 (1983), 249–53.

Bessie Head

Books

Abrahams, Cecil, ed. *The Tragic Life: Bessie Head and Literature in Southern Africa*. Trenton, N.J., 1990.

Barnett, Ursula A. *A Vision of Order*. Amherst, Mass., 1983.

Brown, L.W. *Women Writers in Black Africa*. Westport, Conn., 1981.

Davies, C.B. and Graves, A.A. *Ngambika: Studies of Women in African Literature*. Trenton, N.J., 1986.

Gérard, A.S., ed. *European-Language Writing in Sub-Saharan Africa*. Budapest, 1986.

Heywood, C., ed. *Aspects of South African Literature*. London, 1976.

Jones, E.D., ed. *Women in African Literature Today*. Trenton, N.J., 1987.

Larson, C.R. *The Emergence of African Fiction*. London, 1978; rev. from Bloomington, Ind., 1972.

MacKenzie, Craig. *Bessie Head. An Introduction*. Grahamstown, 1989.

MacKenzie, D. and Clayton, D., eds. *Between the Lines: Interviews with Bessie Head, Sheila Roberts, Ellen Kuzwayo, Miriam Tlali*. Grahamstown, 1989.

Massa, D., ed. *Individual and Community in Commonwealth Literature*. Msida, 1979.

Mphahlele, E. *The African Image*. London, 1973.

Nasta, Susheila. *Motherlands*. London, 1991.

Nichols, Lee. *Conversations with African Writers*. Washington, D.C., 1981.

Taiwo, O. *Female Novelists of Modern Africa*. London and New York, 1984.

Wisker, Gina, ed. *Black Women's Writing*. New York and Basingstoke, 1993.

Articles

Abrahams, C.A. 'The Context of Bessie Head's Fiction'. *ACLALS Bulletin* (1985).

Achufusi, G.I. 'Conceptions of Ideal Womanhood: The Example of Head and Ogot'. *Neohelicon* 19 (1992), 87–101.

Bazin, N.T. 'Weight of Custom, Signs of Change: Feminism in the Literature of African Women'. *World Literature Written in English* 25 (1985).

Bazin, N.T. 'Madness, Mysticism and Fantasy: Shifting Perspectives in the Novels of Lessing, Head, and Gordimer'. *Extrapolation* 33 (1992), 73–87.

Beard, L.S. 'Bessie Head's *A Question of Power*'. *Colby Library Quarterly* (1979).

Beard, L.S. 'Bessie Head's Syncretic Fictions'. *Modern Fiction Studies* 37 (1991), 575–89.

Chetin, Sara. 'Myth, Exile, and the Female Condition: Bessie Head's *The Collector of Treasures*. *Journal of Commonwealth Literature* 24 (1989), 114–37.

Clayton, Cherry. '"A World Elsewhere": Bessie Head as Historian'. *English in Africa* 15 (1988), 55–69.

De Smidt, Lorna. 'Where Rain is Paramount: Bessie Head'. *Africa Now* 7 (1981), 102–9.

Eilersen, G.S. 'Social and Political Commitment in Bessie Head's *A Bewitched Crossroad*'. *Critique* 33 (1991), 43–52.

Elder, A.A. 'Bessie Head: New Considerations, Continuing Questions'. *Callaloo* 16 (1993), 277–84.

Evasdaughter, E.N. 'Bessie Head's *A Question of Power*'. *Research in African Literatures* 20 (1989), 72–83.

Harrow, K.W. 'Head's *Collector of Treasures*'. *Callaloo* 16 (1993), 169–79.

Head, Bessie. 'Some Notes on Novel Writing'. *New Classic* 5 (1978), 30–3.

Johnson, Joyce. 'Bessie Head and the Oral Tradition: The Structure of *Maru*'. *Wasafiri* 5 (1985).

Johnson, Joyce. 'Metaphor, Myth, and Meaning in Bessie Head's *A Question of Power*'. *World Literature Written in English* 25 (1985), 198–211.

Johnson, Joyce. 'A Novelist at the Crossroads: Bessie Head's *A Bewitched Crossroad*'. *Kunapipi* 11/12 (1990), 126–32; and see *Kunapipi* 8 (1986), 56–69.

Lionnet, Françoise. 'Geographies of Pain'. *Callaloo* 16 (1993), 132–52.

MacKenzie, Craig. 'From Oral Tradition to Literary Form: The Short Stories of Bessie Head'. In *Catching Winged Words*. Eds E. Sienaert and N. Bell. Durban, 1988, 256–68.

MacKenzie, Craig. 'Allegiance and Alienation in the Novels of Bessie Head'. In *Essays on African Writing*. Ed. A. Gurnah. Oxford, 1993, 111–25.

Matsikidze, Isabella. 'A Poetics of Head's Fiction'. *Bucknell Review* 37 (1993), 123–32.

Peek, Andrew. 'Bessie Head and the African Novel'. *SPAN* 21 (1985), 121–36.

Peek, Andrew. 'Interview'. *New Left Review* 124 (1985), 150–4.

Petersen, K.H. 'Unpopular Opinions: Some African Women Writers'. *Kunapipi* 7/8 (1985).

Rooney, C. 'A Preface for Bessie Head and A.A. Aidoo'. In *Diverse Voices*. Ed. H.D. Jump. Hemel Hempstead, 1991, 214–46.

Sample, Maxine. 'Landscape and Spatial Metaphor'. *Studies in Short Fiction* 28 (1991), 311–19.

Severac, Alain. 'Beyond Identity: Bessie Head's Spiritual Quest in *Maru*'. *Commonwealth Essays and Studies* 14 (1991), 58–64.

Tucker, Margaret. '"A Nice-Time Girl" Strikes Back: An Essay on Bessie Head's *A Question of Power*'. *Research in African Literatures* 21 (1988), 170–81.

Vissel, Robin. '"We Bear the World and We Make It": Bessie Head and Olive Schreiner'. *Research in African Literatures* 23 (1990), 115–24.

Wilhelm, Cherry. 'Bessie Head: The Face of Africa'. *English in Africa* 10 (1983), 1–13.

Bibliography and reference

Gardner, S. and Scott, R. *Bessie Head: A Bibliography*. Grahamstown, 1986.

Winifred Holtby

Books

Brittain, Vera. *Testament of Friendship*. London, 1940, 1980.

Crosland, Margaret. *Beyond the Lighthouse*. London, 1981.

Kennard, J.E. *Vera Brittain and Winifred Holtby: A Working Partnership*. Hanover, N.H., 1989.

Leonardi, S.J. *Dangerous By Degrees: Women at Oxford and the Somerville College Novelists*. New Brunswick, N.J., 1989.

Miles, Rosalind. *The Female Form: Women Writers and the Conquest of the Novel*. London, 1987.

Monteith, M. *Women's Writing: A Challenge to Theory*. Hemel Hempstead, 1986.

White, E.E.M. *Winifred Holtby as I Knew Her*. London, 1938.

Articles

Cooper, Lettice. 'Introduction'. In *South Riding*. By Winifred Holtby. London, 1988.

Couzens, Tim. 'Keeping the Runway Clear'. *English Academy Review* 4 (1987), 38–52.

Satz, Martha. 'Winifred Holtby'. *Dictionary of British Women Writers*. Ed. J. Todd. London, 1989, 332–40.

Bibliography and reference

Handley-Taylor, G., ed. *Winifred Holtby: A Concise and Selected Bibliography with Some Letters*. Foreword by Vera Brittain, 1955.

Keri Hulme

Books

Jones, Lawrence. *Barbed Wire and Mirrors: Essays on New Zealand Prose*. Dunedin, 1987.

Kedgeley, Sue. *Our Own Country*. Auckland, 1989.

Ricketts, Harry. *Talking About Ourselves*. Wellington, 1986.

Stead, C.K. *Answering to the Language: Essays on Modern Writers*. Auckland, 1989.

Williams, Mark. *Leaving the Highway: Six Contemporary New Zealand Novelists*. Auckland, 1990.

Articles

Ash, S. '*The Bone People* after *Te Kaihau*'. *World Literature Written in English* 29 (1989), 123–35.

Benediktsson, T.E. 'The Reawakening of the Gods: Realism and the Supernatural in Silko and Hulme'. *Critique* 33 (1992), 121–31.

Dale, Judith. 'Connections and Disconnections in *The Bone People*'. In *Women's Studies Association of New Zealand*. Eds C. Philipson and H. Raskin. Auckland, 1985, 34–43.

Dale, Judith. 'The Bone People: [Not] Having it Both Ways'. Landfall 39 (1985), 413–28.

During, Simon. 'Postmodernism or Postcolonialism?'. Landfall 39 (1985), 366–80.

Fee, Margery. 'Why C.K. Stead Didn't like Hulme's The Bone People: Who Can Write as Other?' Australian and New Zealand Studies in Canada 1 (1989), 11–32.

Gaffney, Carmel. 'Making the Net Whole: Design in Hulme's The Bone People'. Southerly 46 (1986), 293–302.

Hall, Sandi. 'Interview'. Broadsheet 121 (1984), 16–21.

Heim, Otto and Zimmermann, Anne. 'Hu(l)man Medi(t)ations'. Australian and New Zealand Studies in Canada 8 (1992), 106–35.

Maxwell, A. 'Reading The Bone People'. Antic 3 (1987), 23–43.

Mita, Merata. 'Keri Hulme'. Republican (November 1984).

O'Brien, Susie. 'Raising Silent Voices'. SPAN 30 (1990), 79–91.

Prentice, Chris. 'Rewriting their Stories, Renaming Themselves'. SPAN 23 (1986), 68–80.

Smith, Shona. 'Keri Hulme: Breaking Ground'. Untold 2 (1984), 44–9.

Smith, Shona. 'Interview'. Untold 4 (1985), 26–34.

Stead, C.K. 'Keri Hulme's The Bone People'. Ariel 16 (1985), 101–8.

Talmor, Sasha. 'A Kiwi Tale of Love and Violence'. Durham University Journal 83 (1991), 93–8.

Webby, Elizabeth. 'Spiralling to Success'. Meanjin 44 (1985), 14–23.

Zora Neale Hurston

Books

Awkard, M., ed. New Essays on 'Their Eyes Were Watching God'. Cambridge, 1990.

Baker, H.A. The Workings of the Spirit. The Poetics of Afro-American Women's Writing. Chicago, 1991.

Bloom, Harold, ed. Zora Neale Hurston's 'Their Eyes Were Watching God'. New York, 1987.

Braxton, J.M. and McLaughlin, A.N., eds. Wild Women in the Whirlwind. New Brunswick, N.J. and London, 1990.

Christian, Barbara. Black Women Novelists: The Development of a Tradition 1892–1976. London, 1980.

Dearborn, M.V. Pocahontas's Daughters. New York, 1986.

Fulbrook, Kate. Free Women. Hemel Hempstead, 1990.

Hemenway, R.E. Zora Neale Hurston: A Literary Biography. 1977; reprinted London, 1986.

Holloway, K.F.C. The Character of the Word: The Texts of Zora Neale Hurston. New York and London, 1987.

Howard, Lillie. Zora Neale Hurston. Boston, 1980.

McKissack, Patricia and Frederick. Zora Neale Hurston: Writer and Storyteller. Hillside, N.J., 1992.

Turner, D.T. In a Minor Chord: Three Afro-American Writers and their Search for Identity. Carbondale and Edwardsville, Ill., 1971.

Walker, Alice. In Search of Our Mother's Gardens. London, 1984.

Washington, Mary H. Invented Lives: Narratives of Black Women 1860–1960. Garden City, N.Y., 1987.

Articles

Boi, Paola. 'A "Signifying" Reading of Hurston'. In Women and War. Eds M. Dietrich et al. New York, 1990, 107–25.

Dalgarno, E. 'Ethnography and the Creative Process in Their Eyes Were Watching God'. American Literature 64 (1992), 519–41.

Jarrett, Mary. 'The Idea of Audience in Hurston and Walker'. Journal of the Short Story in English 12 (1989), 33–44.

King, Sigrid. 'Naming and Power in Their Eyes Were Watching God'. Black American Literature Forum 24 (1990), 683–96.

McKay, Nellie. 'Race, Gender, and Cultural Context in Dust Tracks on a Road'. In Life/Lines: Theorizing Women's Autobiography. Ed. B. Brodzki. Ithaca, N.Y., 1988, 175–88.

Robey, Judith. 'Generic Strategies in Dust Tracks on A Road'. Black American Literature Forum 24 (1990), 667–82.

Walker, Alice. 'In Search of Hurston'. Ms 3 (1975), 74–90.

Wall, C.A. 'Mules and Men: Strategies of Narration'. Black American Literature Forum 23 (1989), 661–80.

Zaidinan, L.M. 'Zora Neale Hurston'. Dictionary of Literary Biography 86 (1989), 159–71.

Bibliography and reference

Newson, A.S. Hurston: Reference Guide. Boston, 1987.

Rachel Ingalls

Books

Landis, K.M. 'The Rhetoric of Madness'. Ph.D., University of Southern California, 1993.

Articles

Cowart, David. 'Fantasy and Reality in *Mrs. Caliban*'. *Critique* 30 (1989), 77–83.

McCall, W.W. 'A Note on *Mrs. Caliban*'. *Notes on Contemporary Literature* 18 (1988), 4–6.

Macdonald, Alan. 'Rewriting Hemingway: Rachel Ingalls's *Binstead's Safari*'. *Critique* 34 (1993), 165–70.

Rubenstein, R. 'Animal Idylls'. *Literature Interpretation Theory* 4 (1993), 123–35.

Upton, Lee. 'Mourning Monsters: Deception and Transformation in Rachel Ingalls's Fiction'. *Critique* 33 (1991), 53–61.

Sarah Orne Jewett

Books

Ammons, Elizabeth. *Conflicting Stories*. New York, 1991.

Auchincloss, Louis. *Pioneers and Caretakers: A Study of Nine American Women Novelists*. Minneapolis, 1961.

Cary, Richard. *Sarah Orne Jewett*. New York, 1962.

Cary, Richard, ed. *Appreciation of Sarah Orne Jewett*. New York, 1973.

Colby Library Quarterly. Special issue 22 (1986).

Dekker, George. *The American Historical Romance*. Cambridge, 1987.

Donovan, Josephine. *Sarah Orne Jewett*. New York, 1980.

Frost, John E. *Sarah Orne Jewett*. Kitty Point, Maine, 1960.

Matthiesen, F.O. *Sarah Orne Jewett*. Gloucester, Mass., 1929, 1965.

Nagel, G.L., ed. *Critical Essays on Sarah Orne Jewett*. Boston, 1984.

Roman, Margaret. *Sarah Orne Jewett*. Tuscaloosa, Ala., 1992.

Romines, Ann. *The Home Plot: Women, Writing and Domestic Ritual*. Amherst, Mass., 1992.

Sherman, S.W. *Sarah Orne Jewett*. Hanover, N.H., 1989.

Sundquist, E.J., ed. *American Realism: New Essays*. Baltimore, 1982.

Thorpe, Margaret F. *Sarah Orne Jewett*. Minneapolis, 1966.

Westbrook, Perry. *Acres of Flint: Sarah Orne Jewett and Her Contemporaries*. Metuchen, N.J., and London, 1981.

Wolfe, S.J. and Penelope, J., eds. *Sexual Practice, Textual Theory*. Cambridge, Mass., 1993.

Articles

For early articles, see Cary, 1962.

Ammons, E. 'The Female Geography of *The Country of the Pointed Firs*'. *Studies in the Literary Imagination* 16 (1983), 83–92.

Apthorpe, E.S. 'Revisioning Creativity: Cather, Chopin, Jewett'. *Legacy* 9 (1992), 1–22.

Atkinson, M. 'The Necessary Extravagance of S.O. Jewett'. *Studies in Short Fiction* 19 (1982), 71–4.

Bell, P.K. 'Kate Chopin and Sarah Orne Jewett'. *Partisan Review* 55 (1988), 238–51.

Bender, Bert. 'To Calm and Uplift "Against the Dark": Sarah Orne Jewett's Lyric Narratives'. *Colby Library Quarterly* 11 (1975), 219–29.

Cary, Richard. 'The Rise, Decline, and Rise of Sarah Orne Jewett'. *Colby Library Quarterly* 9 (1972), 650–63.

Church, Joseph. 'Transgressive Daughters in *Deephaven*'. *Essays in Literature* 20 (1993), 231–50.

Donovan, J. 'A Woman's Vision of Transcendence'. *Massachusetts Review* 21 (1980), 365–80.

Horn, R.L. 'The Power of Jewett's *Deephaven*'. *Colby Library Quarterly* 9 (1972), 617–31.

Kelchner, H. 'Unstable Narrative Voice in "A White Heron"'. *Colby Quarterly* 28 (1992), 85–92.

Oakes, Karen. 'Reflections on Jewett, Gender, and Genre'. *Colby Library Quarterly* 26 (1990), 152–60.

Stevenson, C.B. 'The Double Consciousness of the Narrator in Sarah Orne Jewett's Fiction'. *Colby Library Quarterly* 11 (1975), 1–12.

Strain, M.M. 'Dialogized Voices in Jewett'. *Colby Library Quarterly* 30 (1994), 131–45.

Subbaraman, S. 'Rites of Passage in Jewett's *The Country of the Pointed Firs*'. *Centennial Review* 33 (1989), 60–74.

Wittenberg, J.B. '*Deephaven*: Jewett's Exploratory Metafiction'. *Studies in American Fiction* 19 (1991), 153–63.

Woodress, James. 'Sarah Orne Jewett and Willa Cather: Anti-Realists'. *Emmerson Society Quarterly* 5 (1973), 477–88.

Bibliography and reference

Nagel, Gwen L. *Sarah Orne Jewett. A Reference Guide*. Boston 1978. And see the 'Update' in *American Literary Realism* 17 (1984), 228–63.

Weber, Clara C. and Carl J. *A Bibliography of the Published Writings of Sarah Orne Jewett*. Waterville, Maine, 1949.

Ruth Prawer Jhabvala

Books

Acheson, James. *The British and Irish Novel since 1960*. Basingstoke, 1991.

Agarwal, R.G. *Ruth Prawer Jhabvala*. New York, 1990.

Bevan, D., ed. *Literature and Exile*. Amsterdam, 1990.

Christ, Carol. *Diving Deep and Surfacing: Women Writers on Spiritual Quest*. Boston, 1980.

Dhawan, R.K. and Kerr, D., eds. *Australian Literature Today*. New Delhi, 1993.

Gooneratne, Jasmine. *Silence, Exile and Cunning: The Fiction of Ruth Prawer Jhabvala*. New Delhi, 1983.

Gupta, G.S.B., ed. *Studies in Indian Fiction in English*. Gulbarga, 1987.

Mukherjee, M. *The Twice-Born Fiction: Themes and Techniques of the Indian Novel in English*. London and New Delhi, 1971.

Nasta, Susheila, ed. *Motherlands*. London, 1991.

Pradhan, N.S. *Major Indian Novels: An Evaluation*. Atlantic Highlands, N.J., 1986.

Saxena, O.P. and Solanki, R. *Geography of Jhabvala's Novels*. New Delhi, 1986.

Shahane, V.A. *Ruth Prawer Jhabvala*. New Delhi, 1976.

Sucher, Laurie. *The Fiction of Ruth Prawer Jhabvala: The Politics of Passion*. Basingtoke, 1989.

Wiley, M. and Bona, D. *Inside Oscar*. New York, 1993.

Williams, H.M. *The Fiction of Ruth Prawer Jhabvala*. Calcutta, 1973.

Articles

Abel, E. '(E)Merging Identities: The Dynamics of Female Friendships'. *Signs* 6 (1981), 413–35.

Belliappa, Meena. 'A Study of Jhabvala's Fiction'. *Writers Workshop Miscellany* 43 (1971), 24–40.

Cronin, Richard. 'The Hill of Devi and *Heat and Dust*'. *Essays in Criticism* 36 (1986), 142–59.

Dudt, C. 'Jhabvala's Fiction'. In *Faith of a Woman Writer*. Eds A. Kessler-Harris and W. McBrien. New York, 1988, 159–64.

Gooneratne, Y. 'Ruth Prawer Jhabvala'. *In Essays on Contemporary Post-Colonial Fiction*. Eds H. Bock and A. Wertheim. Munich, 1986.

Lenta, Margaret. 'Narrators and Realism: 1902 and 1975'. *Ariel* 20 (1989), 19–36.

Newman, Judie. 'Postcolonial Gothic'. *Modern Fiction Studies* 40 (1994), 85–100.

Shepherd, Ron. 'The Need to Suffer'. *Commonwealth Review* 2 (1990–1), 196–203.

Singh, Ram Sewak. 'Ironic Vision of A Social Realist: Ruth Prawer Jhabvala'. In *The Indian Novel in English: A Critical Study*. New Delhi, 1977, 149–63.

Summerfield, Henry. 'Ruth Prawer Jhabvala Confronts the Irrational'. *Ariel* 17 (1986), 85–101.

de Souza, E. 'The Novels of Jhabvala'. *World Literature in English* 17 (1978), 219–24.

Weintraub, Bernard. 'The Artistry of Ruth Prawer Jhabvala'. *New York Times Magazine* (11 September 1983), 106–14.

Williams, H.M. 'R.K. Narayan and Jhabvala; Two Interpretations of Modern India'. *Literature East and West* 16 (1972), 1136–54.

Williams, Haydn. 'Mad Seekers, Doomed Lovers and Cemeteries in India'. *New Literature Review* 15 (1988), 11–20.

Bibliography and reference

Crane, R.J. 'Jhabvala: A Checklist of Primary and Secondary Sources'. *Journal of Commonwealth Literature* 20 (1985), 171–203.

Jennifer Johnston

Books

Barfoot, C.C. and D'haen, T., eds. *The Clash of Ireland: Literary Contrasts and Connections*. Amsterdam, 1989.

Dawe, G. and Longley, E., eds. *Across a Roaring Hill. The Protestant Imagination in Modern Ireland*. Belfast, 1985.

Imhof, R., ed. *Contemporary Irish Novelists*. Tübingen, 1990.

Johnson, T. and Cairns, D., eds. *Gender in Irish Writing*. Milton Keynes, 1991.

Rauchbauer, Otto, ed. *Ancestral Voices: The Big House in Anglo-Irish Literature*. Dublin and New York, 1992.

Sekine, M., ed. *Irish Writers and Society at Large*. Gerrard's Cross, 1985.

Staley, Thomas F., ed. *Twentieth Century Women Novelists*. London, 1982.

Articles

Connelly, Joseph. 'Legend and Lyric as Structure in the Selected Fiction of Jennifer Johnston'. *Eire–Ireland* 21 (1986), 119–24.

Gatrell, Simon. 'Jennifer Johnston'. In *Post-War Literatures*. Eds H. Bertens et al. Houten and Groningen, 1988.

Imhof, Rudiger. 'The Small World of Johnston's Fiction'. *Etudes Irelandaises* 10 (1985), 129–44.

Keannealy, M. 'Questions and Answers with Jennifer Johnston'. *Irish Literary Supplement* (Autumn 1984).

Lanters, Jose. 'Johnston's Divided Ireland'. *Dutch Quarterly Review of Anglo-American Letters* 18 (1988), 228–41.

McMahon, Sean. 'Anglo-Irish Attitudes: The Novels of Jennifer Johnston'. *Eire–Ireland* 10 (1975), 137–41.

Spacks, Patricia. Review of *How Many Miles to Babylon?*. *Yale Review* 64 (1975), 583–94.

SELECT BIBLIOGRAPHY

Elizabeth Jolley

Books

Bird, Delys and Walker, Brenda, eds. *Elizabeth Jolley: New Critical Essays*. North Ryde, New South Wales, 1991.

Gilbert, Pam. *Coming Out from Under: Contemporary Australian Women Writers*. North Sydney, 1988.

Lurie, Caroline, ed. *Central Mischief: Elizabeth Jolley on Writing, her Past, and Herself.* Ringwood, Victoria, 1992.

Westerly. 'A Symposium on Elizabeth Jolley'. 31 (1986).

Articles

These do not include special issues.

Carr, Julie. 'The Dancing Body'. *Westerly* 39 (1994) 75–80.

Ellison, J. 'Interview'. In *Rooms of Their Own*. Harmondsworth, 1986, 471–81.

Ferrier Elizabeth. 'From Pleasure Domes to Bark Huts'. *Australian Literary Studies* 13 (1987), 40–53.

Gillette, Sue. 'The Incestuous Father in *The Well*'. *Journal of Australian Lesbian Feminist Studies* 1 (1991), 69–79.

Gillette, Sue. '*The Well*: Beyond Representation'. *Westerly* 37 (1992) 33–41.

Goldsworthy, Kerryn. 'Voices in Time'. *Australian Literary Studies* 12 (1986), 471–81.

Howells, C.A. 'In Search of Lost Mothers'. *Ariel* 19 (1988), 57–70.

Jones, Dorothy. 'The Goddess, the Artist, and the Spinster'. *Westerly* 29 (1984), 77–88.

Kavanagh, Paul. 'Conversation'. *Southerly* 49 (1989), 438–51.

Kirkby, Joan. 'The Call of the Mother in Jolley'. *SPAN* 26–7 (1988), 46–63.

Kirkby, Joan. 'The Spinster and the Missing Mother in Jolley'. In *Old Maids to Radical Spinsters*. Ed. L.L. Doan. Urbana, Ill., 1991, 234–58.

Livett, Jennifer. 'Against the Grain'. *SPAN* 36 (1993), 211–19.

Manning, G.L. 'Nursing Home as Microcosm'. *Ariel E* 18 (1987), 27–43.

Riemer, Andrew. 'Between Two Worlds: An Approach to Jolley'. *Southerly* 43 (1983).

Riemer, Andrew. 'Displaced Persons: Jolley's Fiction'. *Westerly* 31 (1986), 64–79.

Salzman, Paul. 'Jolley: Fiction and Desire'. *Meridian* (1986).

Trigg, Stephanie. 'Interview'. *Scripsi 4* (1986), 245–64.

Webby, Elizabeth. 'The Uses of Fiction'. *SPAN* 21 (1985), 29–37.

Wimmer, Adi. 'Dualism and the Austrian Connection'. *Southerly* 52 (1992), 44–55.

Gayl Jones

Books

Beckles, F.N. *Twenty Black Women*. Baltimore, 1978.

Bell, P., Parker, B.J. and Guy-Sheftall, B., eds. *Sturdy Black Bridges: Visions of Black Women in Literature*. Garden City, N.Y., 1979.

Braxton, J.M. and McLaughlin, A.N., eds. *Wild Women in the Whirlwind*. New Brunswick, N.J., and London, 1990.

Byerman, K.E. *Fingering the Jagged Grain*. Athens, Ga., 1985.

Callaloo. Special section 5 (1982), 31–111.

Davis, M.W., ed. *Contributions of Black Women to America*. Vol. 1. Columbia, S.C., 1982.

Dearborn, M.V. *Pocahontas's Daughters*. New York, 1986.

Evans, Mari. *Black Women Writers*. London, 1985.

Flora, J.M. and Bain, R., eds. *Contemporary Fiction Writers of the South*. Westport, Conn, 1993.

Harper, M.S. and Stepto, R.B., eds. *Chant of Saints*. Urbana, Ill., 1979.

Koenen, Anne. *Zeitgenossische Afro-amerikanische Frauenliteratur: Morrison, Bambara, und Jones*. Frankfurt and New York, 1985.

Robinson, Sally. *Engendering the Subject*. Albany, N.Y., 1991.

Russell, Sandi. *Render Me My Song*. London, 1990.

Tate, Claudia, ed. *Black Women Writers at Work*. New York, 1983.

Weever, Jacqueline de. *Mythmaking and Metaphor in Black Women's Fiction*. Basingstoke, 1991.

Wilt, Judith. *Abortion, Choice and Contemporary Fiction*. Chicago, 1990.

Articles

Ash, Susan. 'Race, Gender and the Female Traveller'. *SPAN* 36 (1993), 347–56.

Bell, R.P. 'Gayl Jones: A Voice in the Whirlwind'. *Studia Africana* 1 (1977), 99–107.

Byerman, K.E. 'Black Vortex: The Gothic Structure of *Eva's Man*'. *MELUS* 7 (1980), 93–101.

Byerman, K.E. 'Intense Behaviours: The Use of the Grotesque'. *College Language Association Journal* 25 (1982), 447–57.

Harris, Janice. '*Corregidora*'. *Frontiers* 5 (1980), 1–5.

Harris, Trudier. 'A Spiritual Journey: *Song for Anninho*'. *Callaloo* 5 (1982), 105–11.

Hyman, Rebecca. 'Women as Figures of Exchange in Jones' *Corregidora*'. *Xanadu* 14 (1991), 40–51.

Kester, G.T. 'The Forbidden Fruit and Female Disorderly Eating'. In *Disorderly Eaters*. Eds L.R.

Furst and P.W. Graham. University Park, Pa., 1992, 231–40.

Lee, V.G. 'The Use of Folktalk in Novels by Black Women Writers'. *College Language Association Journal* 23 (1980), 266–72.

Lionnet, Françoise. 'Geographies of Pain'. *Callaloo* 16 (1993), 132–52.

Pettis, Joyce. 'Literary (Re)Vision and Transformation in *Corregidora*'. *College English* 52 (1990), 787–99.

Rowell, C.H. 'Interview'. *Callaloo* 5 (1982), 32–53.

Tate, Claudia. '*Corregidora*: Ursa's Blues Medley'. *Black American Literature Forum* 13 (1979), 139–41.

Updike, John. 'Eva and Eleanor and Everywoman'. *New Yorker* (9 August, 1976), 74–7.

Ward, J.W. 'Escape from Turblem: The Fiction of Gayl Jones'. *Callaloo* 5 (1982), 95–104.

Bibliography and reference

Glikin, Ronda. 'Gayl Jones' (A Primary and Secondary Bibliography). In *Black American Women in Literature*. Jefferson, N.C., and London, 1989, 89–91.

Weixlmann, Joe. 'A Gayl Jones Bibliography'. *Callaloo* 7 (1984), 119–31.

Anna Kavan

Books

Albinski, N.M. *Women's Utopias in British and American Fiction*. London, 1988.

Aldiss, B. with D. Wingrove. *Billion Year Spree: The True History of Science Fiction*. London, 1973, 1986.

Callard, David. *The Case of Anna Kavan: A Biography*. London, 1992.

Centing, R., ed. *Under the Sign of Pisces: Anaïs Nin and her Circle*. Journal, 1970–86.

Crosland, Margaret. *Beyond the Lighthouse*. London, 1981.

Dorr, Priscilla. 'Anna Kavan: A Critical Introduction'. Ph.D., University of Tulsa, 1988.

Nin, Anaïs. *The Novel of the Future*. New York, 1968.

Stuhlmann, Gunther, ed. *Anaïs: An International Journal*. Los Angeles, 1983.

Articles

Bryne, Janet. 'Moving toward Entropy: Anna Kavan's Science Fiction Mentality'. *Extrapolation* 23 (1982), 5–11.

Davies, Rhys. 'Anna Kavan'. *Books and Bookmen* (June 1978), 7–10.

Egremont, Max. 'The Twilight of Anna Kavan'. *Books and Bookmen* (June 1978), 43–4.

MacCarthy, Desmond. 'On Reading Fiction: *I am Lazarus* by Anna Kavan'. *New Statesman* (1946).

Moraes, Dom. 'Anna Kavan'. *Nova* (September 1967), 45.

Muir, Edward. 'Among the Lost: *A Scarcity of Love* by Anna Kavan'. *Sunday Times* (22 June 1956).

Owen, Peter. 'Publishing Anna Kavan'. *Anaïs: An International Journal* 3 (1985), 75–6.

Stuhlmann, Günther. 'Anna Kavan Revisited'. *Anaïs: An International Journal* 3 (1985), 55–62.

Molly Keane

Books

Chamberlain, Mary, ed. *Writing Lives: Conversations between Women Writers*. London, 1988.

Dawe, G. and Longley, E., eds. *Across a Roaring Hill: The Protestant Imagination in Modern Ireland*. Belfast, 1985.

Guppy, Shusha. *Looking Back: A Panoramic View of a Literary Age*. Latham, N.Y., 1991.

Higginson, S.H. *British and American Sporting Authors*. 1949.

Sekine, Masaru. *Irish Writers and Society at Large*. Gerrards Cross, 1986.

Articles

O'Toole, B. 'Molly Keane'. In *Across the Roaring Hill: The Protestant Imagination in Modern Ireland*. Eds G. Dawe and E. Longley. Belfast, 1985.

A.L. Kennedy

No bibliography has been found for this author.

Susan Kenney

No bibliography has been found for this author.

Jamaica Kincaid

Books

Butcher, Maggier, ed. *Tibisiri: Caribbean Writers and Critics*. Mundelstrup, 1989.

Cudjoe, Selwyn, ed. *Caribbean Women Writers*. Ithaca, N.Y., 1990.

Nasta, Susheila, ed. *Motherlands*. London, 1991.

Simmons, Diane. *Jamaica Kincaid*. New York, 1994.

Articles

Bonetti, Kay. 'Interview'. *Missouri Review* 15 (1992), 124–42.

Cousineau, Diane. 'Women and Autobiography'. *Caliban* 21 (1994), 97–105.

Covi, Giovanna. 'Kincaid: A Review Essay'. *Caribana* 1 (1990), 93–103.

Dilger, G. 'Interview'. *Wasafiri* 16 (1992), 21–5.

Donnell, Alison. 'Kincaid's Fiction'. *Women: A Cultural Review* 4 (1993), 18–26.

Dutton, Wendy. 'Kincaid's Fiction'. *World Literature Today* 63 (1989), 406–10.

Ferguson, Moira. 'Lucy and the Mark of the Colonizer'. *Modern Fiction Studies* 39 (1993), 237–59.

Ferguson, Moira. 'Interview'. *Kenyon Review* 16 (1994), 163–88.

Gilkes, Michael. 'The Madonna Pool: Woman as "Muse of Identity"'. *Journal of West Indian Literature* 1 (1987), 1–19.

Ismond, Patricia. 'Jamaica Kincaid: "First They Must be Children"'. *World Literature Written in English* 28 (1988), 336–41.

James, Louis. 'Reflections and the Bottom of the River'. *Wasafiri* 9 (1988), 15–17.

Kincaid, Jamaica. 'On Seeing England for the First Time'. *Transition* 51 (1991).

Mangum, Bryant. 'Jamaica Kincaid'. In *Fifty Caribbean Writers*. Ed. D.C. Dance. Westport, Conn., 1986.

Murdoch, H.A. 'Cultural Identity in *Annie John*'. *Callaloo* 13 (1990), 325–40.

Natov, Roni. 'Kincaid's Pre-Oedipal Narrative'. *Children's Literature* 18 (1990), 1–16.

Ramchand, K. 'Jamaica Kincaid'. In *Encyclopedia of Post-Colonial Literatures in English*. Eds E. Benson and L.W. Conolly. London and New York, 1994, 771–2.

Rubin, M.L. 'Adolescence and Autobiographical Fiction: Teaching *Annie John*'. *Wasafiri* 8 (1988), 11–14.

Tapping, Craig. 'Children and History in the Caribbean Novel'. *Kunapipi* 11 (1989), 51–9.

Tiffin, Helen. 'Decolonization and Audience'. *SPAN* 30 (1990), 27–38.

Tiffin, Helen. 'The Female Body in Brodber and Kincaid'. *Callaloo* 16 (1993), 909–21.

Ty, Eleanor. 'Identity and Sexuality in Kogawa and Kincaid'. *International Fiction Review* 20 (1993), 120–6.

Vorda, Allan. 'Interview'. *Mississippi Review* 1–2 (1991), 7–26.

Maxine Hong Kingston

Books

Amirthanayagam, G., ed. *Asian and Western Writers in Dialogue*. London, 1982.

Asian Women United of California, eds. *Making Waves: An Anthology of Writings By and About Asian American Women*. Boston, 1989.

Cheung, King-Kok. *Articulate Silences: Yamamoto, Kingston, and Kogawa*. Ithaca, N.Y., 1993.

Clarke, Graham, ed. *The New American Writing: Essays on American Literature Since 1970*. London, 1990.

Culley, Margo, ed. *American Women's Autobiography*. Madison, Wis., 1992.

Larson, Wendy. *Literary Authority and the Modern Chinese Writer*. Durham, N.C., 1991.

Lim, S. Geok-lin, ed. *Approaches to Teaching Maxine Hong Kingston's 'The Woman Warrior'*. New York, 1990.

Lim, S. Geok-lin, ed. *Reading the Literatures of Asian America*. Philadelphia, 1992.

Ling, Amy. *Between Worlds: Women Writers of Chinese Ancestry*. New York, 1990.

Minh-ha, T.T. *Women, Native, Other*. Bloomington, Ind., 1989.

Wong, S.C. *Reading Asian American Literature*. Princeton, N.J., 1993.

Articles

Bacchilega, Cristina. 'Feminine Voices Inscribing Saurraute's *Childhood* and Kingston's *The Woman Warrior*'. *Textual Practice* 6 (1992), 101–18.

Banez, L.G. 'Talk Story: Kingston's *Tripmaster Monkey*'. *Likha* 11 (1989–90), 17–24.

Cheung, K.K. '"Don't Tell": Imposed Silences in *The Color Purple* and *The Woman Warrior*'. *PMLA* 103 (1988), 162–74.

Couser, G.T. 'Maxine Hong Kingston: The Auto/Biographer as Ghost-Writer'. In *Biography East and West*. Ed. C. Ramelb. Honolulu, 1990, 231–7.

Deeney, J.J. 'Transformation in *Tripmaster Monkey* and K.H. Hwang's *Butterfly*'. *MELUS* 18 (1993–4), 21–39.

Frye, J.S. '*The Woman Warrior*: Claiming Narrative Power, Recreating Female Selfhood'. In *The Faith of a (Woman) Writer*. Eds. A. Kessler-Harris and W. McBrien. New York, 1988, 293–301.

Furth, I. 'Kingston's *Tripmaster Monkey*'. *Modern Fiction Studies* 40 (1994), 33–49.

Juhasz, Suzanne. 'Maxine Hong Kingston: Narrative Technique and Female Identity'. In *Contemporary American Women Writers*. Eds C. Rainwater and W.J. Scheik. Lexington, Ky., 1985, 173–89.

Koss, N. 'Cultural Identity in *Tripmaster Monkey*'. *Fu Jen Studies* 26 (1993), 24–50.

Li, D.L. 'Cross-Cultural Significations in *The Woman Warrior*'. *Criticism* 30 (1988), 497–515.

Li, D.L. 'China Men: Kingston and the American Canon'. *Acta Linguistica Hafniensia* 2 (1990), 482–502.

Lim, S. Geok-lin. 'Assaying the Gold: Or, Contesting the Ground of Asian American Literature'. *New Literary History* 24 (1993), 147–69.

Madson, D.L. '(Dis)figuration: The Body as Icon in the Writings of Kingston'. *Yearbook of English Studies* 24 (1994), 237–50.

Neubauer, C.E. 'Photography and Other Sources of Information in *China Men*'. *MELUS* 10 (1983), 17–36.

Pfaff, Timothy. 'Talk with Mrs. Kingston'. *New York Times Book Review* (15 June 1988), 25–6.

Rabine, L.W. 'No Lost Paradise: Social Gender and Symbolic Gender in the Writings of Kingston'. *Signs* 12 (1987), 471–92.

Rabinowitz, P. 'Conversation'. *Michigan Quarterly Review* 26 (1987), 177–87.

Schueller, M.J. 'Theorizing Ethnicity and Subjectivity'. *Genders* 15 (1992), 72–85.

Schueller, M.J. 'Questioning Race and Gender Definitions: Dialogic Subversions in *The Woman Warrior*'. *Criticism* 30 (1989), 421–37.

Wang, A.S. 'Kingston's Reclaiming of America'. *South Dakota Review* 26 (1988), 18–29.

Wang, V.C. 'Rape, Madness, and Silence: Breakdown and Recovery in Kingston's *Woman Warrior*'. *South Dakota Review* 28 (1990), 137–44.

Wong, S.C. 'Necessity and Extravagance in Kingston's *The Woman Warrior*: Art and the Ethnic Experience'. *MELUS* 15 (1988), 4–26.

Wong, S.C. 'Autobiography: Kingston and the Chinese American Autobiographical Controversy'. In *Multicultural Autobiography*. Ed. J.R. Payne, Knoxville, Tenn., 1992, 248–79.

Wong, S.C. 'Ethnic Subject, Ethnic Sign. Some Works of Chinese American Fiction'. *Yearbook of English Studies* 24 (1994), 251–62.

Margaret Laurence

Books

Buss, H.M. *Mother and Daughter Relationships in the Manawaki Works of Margaret Laurence*. Victoria, 1985.

Canadian Women's Studies. Special issue 8 (1987).

Davis, Geoffrey, ed. *Crisis and Creativity in the New Literatures in English: Canada*. Atlanta, Ga., 1990.

Delbaere, Jeanne, ed. *Multiple Voices; Recent Canadian Fiction*. Sydney, 1990.

Etudes Canadiennes. Special issue 11 (1981).

Gunnars, Kristjana, ed. *Crossing the River: Essays in Honor of Margaret Laurence*. Winnipeg, 1988.

Howells, C.A. and Hunter, L., eds. *Narrative Strategies in Canadian Literature*. Buckingham and Philadelphia, 1991.

Kertzer, J.M. *'That House in Manawaki': Margaret Laurence's 'A Bird in That House'*. Toronto, 1992.

Journal of Canadian Studies. Special issue 13 (1978).

Morley, Patricia. *Margaret Laurence*. Boston, 1981.

Morley, Patricia. *Margaret Laurence. The Long Journey Home*. Montreal, 1991 (rev. edn).

New, William, ed. *Margaret Laurence. The Writer and Her Critics*. Toronto, 1977.

Nicholson, Colin, ed. *Critical Approaches in the Fiction of Margaret Laurence*. London, 1990.

Sparrow, Fiona. *Into Africa with Margaret Laurence*. Toronto, 1992.

Stovel, Nora. *Rachel's Children: Laurence's 'A Jest of God'*. Toronto, 1992.

Stovel, Nora. *Margaret Laurence: The Fire-Dwellers*. Toronto, 1993.

Thomas, Clara. *Margaret Laurence*. Toronto, 1969.

Thompson, Elizabeth. *The Pioneer Woman: A Canadian Character Type*. Montreal, 1991.

Verduyn, Christl, ed. *Margaret Laurence: An Appreciation*. Peterborough, Ontario, 1988.

Warwick, Susan. *Margaret Laurence: 'The Diviners'*. Toronto, 1993.

Woodcock, George, ed. *A Place to Stand On: Essays by and About Margaret Laurence*. Edmonton, 1983.

Articles

Bailey, Nancy. 'Margaret Laurence, Carl Jung and the Manawaki Women'. *Studies in Canadian Literature* 2 (1977), 306–21.

Blodgett, Harriet. 'The Real Lives of Margaret Laurence's Women'. *Critique* 23 (1981).

Grace, Sherrill. 'Crossing Jordan: Time and Memory in the Fiction of Margaret Laurence'. *World Literature Written in English* 16 (1977), 328–39.

Hehner, Barbara. 'River of Now and Then: Margaret Laurence's Narratives'. *Canadian Literature* 74 (1977), 40–57.

Howells, C.A. 'In Search of Lost Mothers: Laurence and Elizabeth Jolley'. *Ariel* 19 (1988), 57–70.

Kearns, Judy. 'Rachel and Social Determinism: A Feminist Reading of *A Jest of God*'. *Journal of Canadian Fiction* 27 (1980).

Potvin, Elisabeth. '"A Mystery at the Core of Life": Laurence and Women's Spirituality'. *Canadian Literature* 128 (1991), 25–38.

Rooke, Constance. 'A Feminist Reading of *The Stone Angel*'. *Canadian Literature* 93 (1982), 26–41.

Salick, Roydon. 'Rampant with Memory: Theme and Technique in Laurence'. *Commonwealth Essays and Studies* 14 (1992), 98–105.

Scott, S.S. 'Margaret Laurence's *A Bird in That House*'. *Journal of the Short Story in English* 12 (1989), 87–105.

Thomas, Clara. 'Margaret, Morag, and the Scottish Ancestors'. *British Journal of Canadian Studies* 7 (1992), 19–101.

Warwick, Susan J. 'Margaret Laurence; An Annotated Bibliography'. In *The Annotated Bibliography of Canada's Major Authors*. Downsview, Ontario, 1979.

Harper Lee

Books

Johnson, Claudia D. *'To Kill a Mockingbird': Threatening Boundaries*. New York, 1994.

Articles

Interview: 'Mocking Bird Call'. *Newsweek* 57 (9 January 1961), 83.

Altman, D.J. 'Harper Lee'. *Dictionary of Literary Biography* 6, 1980, 180–3.

Chappell, C.M. 'The Unity of *To Kill a Mockingbird*'. *Alabama Review* 42 (1989), 32–48.

Dave. R.A. *'To Kill a Mockingbird*: Harper Lee's Tragic Vision'. *Indian Studies in American Literature*. Eds M.K. Naik et al. Dharwar, 1974, 311–23.

Deitch, Joseph. 'Harper Lee: Novelist of the South'. *Christian Science Monitor* 3 (1961), 6.

Erisman, Fred. 'The Romantic Regionalism of Harper Lee'. *Alabama Review* 26 (1973), 122–36.

Erisman, Fred. 'Literature and Place'. *Journal of Regional Culture* 1 (1981), 144–53.

Going, W.T. 'Truman Capote: Harper Lee's Fictional Portrait of the Artist as an Alabama Child'. *Alabama Review* 42 (1989), 136–49.

Johnson, Claudia. 'The Secret Courts of Men's Hearts: Code and Law in Lee's *To Kill a Mockingbird*'. *Studies in American Fiction* 19 (1991), 129–39.

McDonald, W.U. 'Harper Lee's College Writings'. *American Notes and Queries* 6 (1968), 131–2.

May, Jill. 'Censors as Critics: *To Kill a Mockingbird* as Case Study'. In *Cross-Culturalism in Children's Literature*. Ed. R.A. Thompson. New York, 1988, 91–5.

Nicholson, Colin. 'Hollywood and Race: *To Kill a Mockingbird*'. In *Cinema and Fiction*. Eds J. Orr and C. Nicholson. Edinburgh, 1992, 151–9.

Shuster, E.H. 'Discovering Theme and Structure in the Novel'. *English Journal* 52 (1963), 506–11.

Vernon Lee

Books

Cecil, Lord David, ed. *Humanities*. London, 1953.

Colby, Vineta. *The Singular Anomaly: Women Novelists of the Nineteenth Century*. New York and London, 1970.

Edel, Leon. *Henry James: The Middle Years*. New York, 1962.

Gardner, Burdett. *The Lesbian Imagination: A Critical and Psychological Study of Vernon Lee*. New York, 1987.

Graham, Kenneth. *English Criticism of the Novel 1865–1900*. Oxford, 1965.

Gunn, Peter. *Vernon Lee, Violet Paget*. London and New York, 1964.

Lodge, David. *The Language of Fiction*. London, 1966.

Articles

Brooks, V.W. 'Notes on Vernon Lee'. *Forum* 45 (1911), 447–57.

Callabero, Carlo. 'On Lee, Wagner, and Music'. *Victorian Studies* 35 (1992), 385–408.

Cary, R. 'Vernon Lee's Vignettes'. *Colby Library Quarterly* 9 (1970), 179–99.

Christensen, P.G. 'Lee's Artist Parable'. *Lamar Journal* 15 (1989), 3–15.

Christensen, P.G. 'History in Lee's Ghost Story'. *Studies in the Humanities* 16 (1989), 33–43.

Edel, Leon. 'Henry James and Vernon Lee'. *PMLA* 69 (1954), 677–8.

Edelstein, Debra. 'Vernon Lee'. *Dictionary of Literary Biography* 57 (1987), 158–67.

Horace, G. 'The Romantic Inventions of Vernon Lee'. Introduction in *The Snake Lady*. By Vernon Lee. New York, 1954, 1–24.

Preston, H.W. 'Vernon Lee'. *Atlantic Monthly* 55 (1885), 219–27.

Robbins, Ruth. 'Vernon Lee: Decadent Woman?'. In *Fin de Siècle, Fin de Globe*. Ed. J. Stokes, Basingstoke and New York, 1992, 139–61.

Sinha, A. 'Vernon Lee'. *Journal of the Department of English* 17 (1981–2), 75–83.

Bibliography and reference

Mannochi, Phyllis. 'Vernon Lee: A Bibliography'. *English Literature in Transition* 26 (1983).

Markgraf, C. 'Vernon Lee: A Guide to Secondary Criticism'. *English Literature in Transition* 26 (1983), 268–73.

Ursula Le Guin

Books

Barr, M. and Smith, N.D., eds. *Women and Utopia*. Lanham, Md., 1983.

Bittner, James. *Approaches to the Fiction of Ursula K. Le Guin*. Ann Arbor and Epping, 1984.

Bloom, Harold, ed. *Ursula K. Le Guin*. New York, 1986.

Bloom, Harold, ed. *Ursula Le Guin's 'Left Hand of Darkness'*. New York, 1987.

Bucknall, B.J. *Ursula Le Guin*. New York, 1981.

Clareson, T.D., ed. *Voices for the Future*. Vol. 2. Bowling Green, Ohio, 1979.

Coyle, W., ed. *Aspects of Fantasy*. Westport, Conn., 1986.

Cummins, E. *Understanding Ursula K. Le Guin*. Columbia, S.C., 1990.

De Bolt, J.W., ed. *Ursula K. Le Guin: Voyager to Inner Lands and to Outer Space*. Port Washington, N.Y., 1979.

Extrapolation. Special issue 21 (1980).

Ketterer, David. *New Worlds for Old*. Bloomington, Ind., 1974.

Olander, J.D. and Greenberg, M.H. *Ursula Le Guin*. New York, 1979.

Palumbo, D., ed. *Erotic Universe. Sexuality and Fantastic Literature*. New York, 1986.

Rabkin, E.S. et al., eds. *No Place Else*. Carbondale, Ill., 1983.

Remington, T.J., ed. *Selected Proceedings for the 1978 Science Fiction Research Association National Conference*. Cedar Falls, Iowa, 1979.

Riley, D., ed. *Critical Encounters*. New York, 1978.

Science Fiction Studies. Special issue 2 (1975).

Selinger, B. *Ursula Le Guin and Identity in Contemporary Fiction*. Ann Arbor, 1988.

Slusser, G.E. *The Farthest Shores of Ursula K. Le Guin*. San Bernadino, Calif., 1976.

Slusser, G.E., ed. *Storm Warnings*. Carbondale, Ill., 1987.

Slusser, G.E. and Rabkin, E.S., eds. *Aliens: The Anthropology of Science Fiction*. Carbondale, Ill., 1987.

Spivak, Charlotte. *Ursula K. Le Guin*. Boston, 1984.

Yalom, Marilyn, ed. *Women Writers of the West Coast*. Santa Barbara, 1983.

Articles

These do not include those collected in books mentioned above.

Baggesen, Soren. 'Utopian and Dystopian Pessimism: Le Guin'. *Science Fiction Studies* 14 (1987), 34–43.

Barry, N. and Prescott, M. 'Beyond Words'. *Extrapolation* 33 (1992), 154–65.

Jose, Jim. 'Reflections on the Politics of Le Guin's Narrative Shifts'. *Studies in Science Fiction* 18 (1991), 180–97.

Bibliography and reference

Cogell, E.C. *Ursula K. Le Guin: A Primary and Secondary Bibliography*. Boston, 1983.

Rosamond Lehmann

Books

Atkins, John. *Six Novelists Look at Society*. London, 1977.

Day Lewis, Sean. *C. Day Lewis: An English Literary Life*. London, 1980.

Kaplan, S.J. *Feminine Consciousness in the Modern British Novel*. Chicago, 1975.

LeSturgeon, D.E. *Rosamond Lehmann*. New York, 1965.

Marcovic, Vida. *The Changing Face: Disintegration of Personality in the Twentieth Century British Novel, 1900–1950*. Carbondale, Ill., 1970.

Monteith, Moira, ed. *Women's Writing: A Challenge to Theory*. Hemel Hempstead, 1986.

Siegil, Ruth. *Rosamond Lehmann: A Thirties Writer*. New York, 1989.

Simons, Judy. *Rosamond Lehmann*. Basingstoke, 1992.

Tindall, G. *Rosamond Lehmann: An Appreciation*. London, 1965.

Articles

Blodgett, Harriet. 'The Feminism of Lehmann's Novels'. *University of Mississippi Studies in English* 10 (1992), 106–21.

Dangerfield, George. 'Rosamond Lehmann and the Perilous Enchantment of Things Past'. *Bookman* 76 (1933), 172–6.

Dorosz, W. 'Subjective Vision and Human Relationships in the Novels of Rosamond Lehmann'. *Studia Anglistica Uppsaliensa* 23 (1975).

Gindin, James. 'A Revaluation'. *Contemporary Literature* 15 (1974), 203–11.

Kaplan, S.J. 'Rosamond Lehmann's *The Ballad and the Source*: A Confrontation with "That Great Mother"'. *Twentieth Century Literature* 27 (1981), 127–45.

Kent, John P. 'Rosamond Lehmann'. *Dictionary of Literary Biography* 15 (1983), 269–74.

Pfaltz, Katharine. 'The Lehmann Woman'. *Etudes Britanniques Contemporaries* 1 (1992), 99–113.

Raven, Simon. 'The Game that Nobody Wins: The Novels of Rosamond Lehmann'. *London Magazine* 3 (1963), 61.

Warner, O. 'Rosamond Lehmann'. *Bookman* 87 (1934).

Bibliography and reference

Gustafson, M.T. 'Rosamond Lehmann: A Bibliography'. *Twentieth Century Literature* 4 (1959), 143–7.

Doris Lessing

Books

Armett, Lucie. *Where No Man Has Gone Before: Women and Science Fiction*. London, 1991.

Brewster, Dorothy. *Doris Lessing*. New York, 1965.

Chown, L.E. *Narrative Authority and Homeostasis in the Novels of Lessing and Carman Martin Gaite*. New York, 1990.

Clayton, Cherry, ed. *Women and Writing in South Africa*. Marshalltown, 1989.
Contemporary Literature. Special issue 14 (1973).
Doris Lessing Newsletter. 1979– .
Draine, Betsy. *Substance Under Pressure: Artistic Coherence and Evolving Form in the Novels of Doris Lessing*. Madison, Wis., 1983.
Gardiner, J.K. *Rhys, Stead, and Lessing and the Politics of Empathy*. Buckingham and Philadelphia, 1989.
Hayles, N.K. *Chaos Bound: Orderly Disorder in Contemporary Literature*. Ithaca, N.Y., 1990.
Hite, Molly. *The Other Side of the Story: Structures and Strategies in Contemporary Feminist Narratives*. Ithaca, N.Y., 1989.
Holmquist, Ingrid. *From Society to Nature: A Study of Doris Lessing's 'Children of Violence'*. Gothenburg, 1980.
Kaplan, Carey et al., eds. *Approaches to Teaching Lessing's 'The Golden Notebook'*. New York, 1989.
Kaplan, S.J. *Feminine Consciousness*. London, 1975.
King, Jeanett. *Doris Lessing*. London, 1989.
Knapp, Mona. *Doris Lessing*. New York, 1985.
Modern Fiction Studies. Special issue 21 (1975).
Pickering, Jean. *Understanding Lessing*. Columbia, S.C., 1990.
Roberta, Robin. *A New Species: Gender and Science in Science Fiction*. Urbana, Ill., 1993.
Robinson, Sally. *Engendering the Subject*. Albany, N.Y., 1991.
Rose, E.C. *The Tree Outside the Window: Doris Lessing's 'Children of Violence'*. Hanover, N.H., 1976.
Rubenstein, Roberta. *The Novelistic Vision of Doris Lessing*. Urbana, Ill., 1979.
Sage, Lorna. *Doris Lessing*. London, 1983.
Sage, Lorna. *Women in the House of Fiction*. Basingstoke, 1992.
Schleuter, Paul. *The Novels of Doris Lessing*. Carbondale, Ill., 1973.
Sprague, C. *Rereading Doris Lessing*. Chapel Hill, N.C., 1987.
Sprague, Claire, ed. *In Pursuit of Doris Lessing*. New York, 1990.
Steele, M.C. *Children of Violence and Rhodesia: A Study of Doris Lessing as Historical Observer*. Salisbury, 1974.
Taylor, Jenny, ed. *Notebooks, Memoirs, Archives: Rereading Doris Lessing*. London, 1982.
Thorpe, Michael. *Doris Lessing's Africa*. London, 1978.
Whittaker, Ruth. *Doris Lessing*. Basingstoke, 1988.

Articles
These do not include those in the *Doris Lessing Newsletter*.
Bazin, N.T. 'Madness, Mysticism, and Fantasy'. *Extrapolation* 33 (1992), 73–87.

Carrera Suarez, Isabel. 'Metalinguistic Features in Short Fiction by Lessing and Atwood'. In *Short Fiction in the New Literatures in English*. Ed. J. Bardolph. Nice, 1989, 159–64.
Harris, Jocelyn. 'Lessing's Beautiful Impossible Blueprints'. In *The British and Irish Novel since 1960*. Ed. J. Acheson. New York, 1991, 32–47.
Henke, Suzette. 'Lessing's *Golden Notebook*: A Paradox of Postmodern Play'. In *Rereading Modernism*. Ed. L. Rado. New York, 1994, 159–87.
Malekin, Peter. 'Relativity of Perception in *Briefing for a Descent into Hell*'. In *The Celebration of the Fantastic*. Eds D.E. Morse et al. Westport, Conn., 1992, 73–9.
Roberts, Sheila. 'Sites of Paranoia and Taboo'. *Research in African Literatures* 24 (1993), 73–85.
Whittaker, Ruth. 'Lessing and the Means of Change'. In *Plotting Change*. Ed. L. Anderson. London, 1990, 1–16.

Bibliography and reference
Seligman, Dee. *Doris Lessing: An Annotated Bibliography of Criticism*. Westport, Conn., and London, 1981.

Meridel Le Sueur
Books
Coiner, Constance. 'Pessimism of the Mind, Optimism of the Will: Literature of Resistance'. Ph.D., University of California, Los Angeles, 1987.
Duncan, Erika. *Unless Soul Clap Its Hands*. New York, 1984.
Gelfant, Blanche, H. *Women Writing in America. Voices in Collage*. Hanover, N.H., 1984.
Killeen, R.C. 'Meridel Le Sueur's Vision of Women'. Ph.D., University of Rhode Island, 1991.
Wagner-Martin, Linda. *The Modern American Novel 1914–1945*. New York, 1990.

Articles
Coiner, Constance. 'Literature of Resistance in Le Sueur and Olsen'. In *Left Politics and the Literary Profession*. Eds L.J. Davis and M.B. Mirabella. New York, 1990, 162–85.
Duncan, Erika. 'Writing and Surviving: A Portrait of Meridel Le Sueur'. *Book Forum* 6 (1982), 25–36.
Gelfant, B.H. 'Foreword'. In *North Star Country*. By Meridel Le Sueur. Minneapolis, 1984.
Gelfant, B.H. 'Language as Theft in Meridel Le Sueur'. In *Tradition and the Talents of Women*. Ed. F. Howe. Urbana, Ill., 1991, 183–210.
Graulich, Melody. 'Violence Against Women'. *Frontiers* 7 (1984), 14–20.
Hedges, Elaine. 'Introduction'. In *Ripening: Selected Works of Meridel Le Sueur 1927–1980*. Old Westbury, N.Y., 1982.

Hoy, N.J. 'Interview'. *Iowa Woman* 7 (1987), 14–22.

Maierhofer, Roberta. 'Meridel Le Sueur: A Female Voice of the Thirties'. In *Women in Search of Literary Space*. Eds G.M. Grabher and M. Devine. Tübingen, 1992, 150–62.

Oktenberg, Adrian. 'From the Bottom Up'. In *A Gift of Tongues*. Eds M. Harris and K. Aguero. Athens, Ga., 1987, 83–111.

Pratt, L.R. 'Afterword'. In *I Hear Men Talking and Other Stories*. By Meridel Le Sueur. Minneapolis, 1984.

Pratt, L.R. 'Women Writers in the Communist Party'. *Women's Studies* 14 (1988), 147–64.

Rabinowitz, Paula. 'Maternity as History in *The Girl*'. *Contemporary Literature* 29 (1988), 538–48.

Roberts, N.R. 'Radical Women Writers of the Thirties'. *Left Curve* 17 (1993), 85–93.

Scheuning, N.J.Y. 'Meridel Le Sueur: Toward a New Regionalism'. *Books at Iowa* 33 (1980).

Sipple, Susan. 'Witness/to/the Suffering of Women'. In *Feminism, Bakhtin, and the Dialogue*. Eds D.M. Bauer and S.J. McKinstrey. Albany, N.Y., 1991, 135–53.

Alison Lurie

Books

Aldridge, J.W. *The American Novel and the Way We Live Now*. Oxford, 1983.

Bevan, David, ed. *University Fiction*. Atlanta, Ga., 1990.

Costa, R.H. *Alison Lurie*. New York, 1992.

Pearlman, M. and Henderson, L., eds. *Inter/View*. Lexington, Ky., 1990.

Articles

Clarke, Graham. 'The Great Wrong Place'. In *The American City*. Ed. G. Clarke. New York, 1988, 124–45.

Helfand, M.S. 'The Dialectics of Self and Community in Alison Lurie'. *Perspectives on Contemporary Literature* 3 (1977), 65–70.

Jackson, David. 'Interview'. *Shenandoah* 31 (1980), 15–27.

Kruse, Horst. 'Extended Wars – Extended Metaphors'. *Literature in Wissenschaft und Unterricht* 25 (1992), 3–12.

Kruse, Horst. 'Museums and Manners: Alison Lurie'. *Anglia* 111 (1993), 410–38.

Lear, Liz. 'Interview'. *Key West Review* 1 (1988), 42–52.

Lohrey, Amanda. 'The Liberated Heroine'. *Meanjin* 38 (1979), 294–304.

Newman, Judie. 'Alison Lurie'. *Post-War Literatures*. Eds H. Bertens et al. Houten and Groningen, 1990.

Newman, Judie. 'The Revenge of the Trance Maiden: Alison Lurie and Intertextuality'. In *Plotting Change*. Ed. L. Anderson. London, 1990. 113–27.

Rogers, K.M. 'Alison Lurie: The Uses of Adultery'. In *American Women Writing Fiction*. Ed. M. Pearlman. Lexington, Ky., 1989, 116–28.

Satz, Martha. 'A Kind of Detachment: An Interview'. *Southwest Review* 71 (1986), 194–202.

Stark, John. 'Alison Lurie's Career'. *Hollins Critic* 26 (1989), 1–8.

Bibliography and reference

Newman, Judie. 'Alison Lurie: A Bibliography 1945–89'. *Bulletin of Bibliography* 49 (1992), 109–14.

Rose Macaulay

Books

Bensen, Alice, R. *Rose Macaulay*. New York, 1950.

Crosland, Margaret. *Beyond the Lighthouse*. London, 1981.

Emery, Jane. *Rose Macaulay: A Writer's Life*. London, 1991.

Passty, J.N. *Eros and Androgyny: The Legacy of Rose Macaulay*. London and Toronto, 1988.

Smith, Constance B. *Rose Macaulay: A Biography*. London, 1972.

Stewart, D. *The Ark of God: Studies in Five Modern Novelists*. London, 1961.

Articles

Bensen, Alice. 'Rose Macaulay'. *English Literature in Transition* 9 (1966).

Boxwell, D.A. 'Pacifism in Macaulay'. *Tulsa Studies in Women's Literature* 12 (1993), 85–101.

Coates, John. 'Metaphor and Meaning in *The Towers of Trebizond*'. *Durham University Journal* 80 (1987), 111–21.

Fromm, Gloria. 'Reinscribing the Years: Woolf, Macaulay and the Critics'. *Journal of Modern Literature* 13 (1986), 289–306.

Guerinot, J.V. 'The Pleasures of Rose Macaulay'. *Twentieth Century Literature* 33 (1987), 110–28.

Lassner, Phyllis. 'Reimagining the Arts of War: Bowen and Macaulay'. *Perspectives on Contemporary Literature* 14 (1988), 30–8.

Lockwood, W.J. 'Rose Macaulay'. In *Minor British Novelists*. Ed. C.A. Hoyt. Carbondale and Edwardsville, Ill., 1967.

Thomas, Sue. 'Rose Macaulay's Fiction of the 1920s'. *Durham University Journal* 55 (1994), 93–104.

Gerger, H.E. and Lauterbach, E.S. '[Rose Macaulay]'. *English Literature in Transition* 5 (1962).

Carson McCullers

Books

Bloom, Harold, ed. *Carson McCullers.* New York, 1986.

Carr, Virginia, S. *The Lonely Hunter: A Biography of Carson McCullers.* Garden City, N.Y., 1975; London, 1977.

Cook, Richard, M. *Carson McCullers.* New York, 1975.

Evans, Oliver. *Carson McCullers: Her Life and Work.* London, 1965.

Graver, L.S. *Carson McCullers.* Minneapolis, 1969.

McDowell, Margaret B. *Carson McCullers.* Boston, 1980.

Pembroke Magazine. Special section 20 (1988), 4–103.

Southern Quarterly. Special issue 25 (1987).

Westling, Louise. *The Fiction of Welty, McCullers, and O'Connor.* Athens, Ga., 1985.

Articles

Buchen, I.H. 'Divine Collusion: The Art of Carson McCullers'. *Dalhousie Review* 54 (1974), 529–41.

Dazey, M.A. 'Two Voices of One Narrator in *The Ballad of the Sad Café*'. *Southern Literary Journal* 17 (1985), 33–40.

Dienhart, J.M. 'Adverbials, Direct Objects, and the Style of McCullers'. In *The Twain Shall Meet.* Ed. J.E Nielson. Copenhagen, 1992, 121–34.

Emerson, Donald. 'The Ambiguities of *Clock Without Hands*'. *Wisconsin Studies in Contemporary Literature* 3 (1962), 15–28.

Gaillard, D.F. 'The Presence of the Narrator in Carson McCullers's *The Ballad of the Sad Café*.' *Mississippi Quarterly* 25 (1972), 419–27.

Kaham, Claire. 'Gothic Mirrors and Feminine Identity'. *Centennial Review* (1980).

Lubbens, Klaus. 'The Necessary Order: A Study of Theme and Structure in Carson McCullers's Fiction'. *Jahrbuch für Amerika Studies* 8 (1963), 187–204.

Matsudaira, Yoko. 'Some Transformations in *The Ballad of the Sad Café*'. *Shoin Literary Review* 20 (1986), 51–66. (See also 21 (1987), 53–66, and (1985), 69–85).

Paden, F.F. 'Autistic Gestures in *The Heart is a Lonely Hunter*'. *Modern Fiction Studies* 28 (1982), 453–63.

Phillips, R.S. 'The Gothic Architecture of *The Member of the Wedding*'. *Renascence* 16 (1964), 59–72.

Scott, Louise. 'An Existential Everyman'. *West Virginia Philological Papers* 27 (1981), 82–8.

Westling, Louise. 'McCullers' Amazon Nightmare'. *Modern Fiction Studies* 28 (1982), 465–73.

Bibliography and reference

Bixby, George. 'Carson McCullers: A Bibliographical Checklist'. *American Book Collectors* 5 (1984), 38–43.

Kiernan, R.F. *Porter and Carson McCullers: A Reference Guide.* Boston, 1976.

Shapiro, A., Bryer, J. and Field, K. *Carson McCullers. A Descriptive Listing and Annotated Bibliography of Criticism.* New York, 1980.

Katherine Mansfield

Books

Alpers, A. *Katherine Mansfield: A Biography.* New York, 1953.

Bardolph, J., ed. *Short Fiction in the New Literatures in English.* Nice, 1989.

Berkman, Sylvia. *Katherine Mansfield: A Critical Study.* London, 1952.

Dhawan, R.K. and Tonetto, W., eds. *New Zealand Literature Today.* New Delhi, 1993.

Fulbrook, Kate. *Katherine Mansfield.* Brighton, 1986.

Hankin, C.A. *Katherine Mansfield and her Confessional Stories.* London, 1983.

Hanson, Clare. *Short Stories and Short Fiction 1880–1980.* London, 1985.

Hanson, Clare and Gurr, A. *Katherine Mansfield.* London, 1981.

Kaplan, S.J. *Katherine Mansfield and the Origins of Modernist Fiction.* Ithaca, N.Y., 1991.

Koêbler, J.F. *Katherine Mansfield.* Boston, 1990.

Magalaner, Marvin. *The Fiction of Katherine Mansfield.* Urbana, Ill., 1971.

Meyers, Jeffrey. *Katherine Mansfield, a Biography.* London, 1978.

Modern Fiction Studies. Special issue 24 (1978).

Moore, Leslie. *Katherine Mansfield.* London, 1971.

Murray, Heather. *Double Lives: Women in the Stories of Katherine Mansfield.* Dunedin, 1990.

Nathan, R.B. *Katherine Mansfield.* New York, 1988.

Nathan, R.B., ed. *Critical Essays on Katherine Mansfield.* New York, 1993.

Ricketts, H., ed. *Worlds of Katherine Mansfield.* Palmerston North, 1991.

Robinson, Roger, ed. *Katherine Mansfield: In From the Margins.* Baton Rouge, La., 1994.

Rohnberger, M. *The Art of Katherine Mansfield.* Oklahoma City, 1977.

Sampietro, Luigi, ed. *Declarations of Cultural Independence in the English-Speaking World.* Novara, 1990.

Tomalin, Clare. *Katherine Mansfield: A Secret Life.* Harmondsworth, 1987.

Van Gunsteren, Julia. *Katherine Mansfield and Literary Impressionism.* Amsterdam, 1990.

Articles

Cather, Willa. 'Katherine Mansfield'. In *On Writing.* Ed. S. Tennant. New York, 1968, 105–21.

Laurie, A. 'Mansfield – A Lesbian Writer?'. *Women's Studies Journal* 4 (1988), 48–70.

Morrow, Patrick. 'Katherine Mansfield: The Idea of a Perfect Story'. In *International Literature in English: Essays on the Major Writers.* Ed. R.L. Ross. New York: 1990, 669–80.

Mortimore, A.K. 'Mansfield's "Bliss"'. *Narrative* 2 (1994), 41–52.

O'Sullivan, V. 'Introduction'. In *The Aloe.* By Katherine Mansfield. Manchester, 1983.

Stead, C.K. 'Introduction'. In *The Letters and Journals of Katherine Mansfield.* Harmondsworth, 1977.

Watson, John. 'The Intentional Fallacy Revisited'. *Journal of New Zealand Literature* 8 (1990), 49–65.

Welty, Eudora. 'Looking at Short Stories'. In *The Eye of the Story.* London, 1987, 85–106.

Bibliography and reference

Kirkpatrick, B.J. *A Bibliography of Katherine Mansfield.* Oxford, 1989.

Kamala Markandaya

Books

Abidi, S.Z.H. *Kamala Markandaya's 'Nectar in a Sieve': A Critical Study.* Bareilly, 1976.

Afzal-Khan, Fawzia. *Cultural Imperialism and the Indian-English Novel.* University Park, Pa., 1993.

Davis, G. and Maes-Jelinek, M., eds. *Crisis and Creativity in the New Literatures in English.* Amsterdam, 1990.

Gupta, G.S. Balarama, ed. *Studies in Indian Fiction in English.* Gulbarga, 1987.

Kirpal, Viney, ed. *The New Indian Novel in English: A Study of the 1980s.* New Delhi, 1990.

MacDermott, D. and Ballyn, S., eds. *A Passage to Somewhere Else.* New Delhi, 1986.

Nelson, Emmanuel, S., ed. *Reworlding: The Literature of the Indian Diaspora.* Westport, Conn., 1992.

Pathania, Usha. *Human Bonds and Bondage: The Fiction of Anita Desai and Kamala Markandaya.* New Delhi, 1992.

Pradan, N.S. *Major Indian Novels: An Evaluation.* Atlantic Highlands, N.J., 1986.

Prasad, Madhusudan. *Perspectives on Kamala Markandaya.* Ghaziabad, 1984.

Rao, K.S.N. 'The New Harvest: The Indian Novel in English in the Post-Independence Era, Women at Work: Kamala Markandaya'. Ph.D., Pennsylvania State University, 1968.

Srivastava, A.K., ed. *Alien Voices: Perspectives on Commonwealth Literature.* Lucknow, 1981.

Walsh, William. *Indian Literature in English.* London and New York, 1990.

Articles

Barbato, L.R. 'Time and Reconciliation in Markandaya'. *Ariel* 22 (1991), 7–15.

Chandrasekharan, K.R. 'East and West in Markandaya'. In *Critical Essays on Indian Writing.* Eds M.K. Naik et al. Dharwar, 1972, 309–30.

Dale, James. 'Sexual Politics in Markandaya. *World Literature Written in English* 21 (1982), 347–56.

De Manuel, M.L. 'Elements of Existentialism in Modern Asian Fiction'. *Likha* 11 (1989–90), 25–42.

Drum, Alice. 'Markandaya's Modern Quest Tale'. *World Literature Written in English* 22 (1983), 323–33.

Geetha, P. 'Images and Archetypes in Markandaya'. *Journal of Commonwealth Literature* 26 (1991), 169–78.

Harrex, S.C. 'A Sense of Identity: Markandaya'. *Journal of Commonwealth Literature* 6 (1971), 65–78.

Kumar, Prem. 'Conflict and Resolution in Markandaya'. *World Literature Today* 60 (1986), 22–7.

Kumar, Prem. 'Markandaya's Development as Novelist'. *International Fiction Review* 14 (1987), 84–8.

Moktali, L.R. 'Experiments with Language in Markandaya'. In *Experimentation With Language in Indian Writing in English.* Ed. S.K. Desai. Kohlapur, 1974, 129–41.

Nedeljkovic, Maryvonne. 'The Role of Women in Markandaya'. *Commonwealth Essays and Studies* 8 (1985), 31–44.

Rao, S.N. 'Markandaya: The Novelist as Craftsman'. *Indian Writing Today* 3 (1969), 32–40.

Rao, S.N. 'The Fiction of Markandaya'. *Literary Half-Yearly* 34 (1993), 51–62.

Schmidt-Grozinger, Dagmar. 'Problems of the Immigrant in Commonwealth Literature: Markandaya and Emecheta'. In *Tensions Between North and South.* Ed. E. Mettke. Würzburg, 1990.

Sethuraman, Ramchandran. 'Possession'. *Ariel* 23 (1992), 101–20.

Bibliography and reference

Rao, K.S.N. 'A Bibliography of Kamala Markandaya'. *World Literature Written in English* 20 (1981), 344–50.

SELECT BIBLIOGRAPHY

Paule Marshall

Books

Bruck, P. and Karrer, W. *The Afro-American Novel Since 1960*. Amsterdam, 1982.

Callaloo. Special issue 6 (1983).

Cartey, Wifred. *Whispers from the Caribbean. I Going Away. I Going Home*. Los Angeles, 1991.

Christian, Barbara. *Black Women Novelists: The Development of a Tradition 1892–1976*. Westport, Conn., 1980.

Christian, Barbara. *Black Feminist Criticism*. New York, 1985.

Cudjoe, S.R., ed. *Caribbean Women Writers*. Wellesley, Calaloux, 1990.

DeWeever, Jacqueline. *Mythmaking and Metaphor in Black Women's Fiction*. Basingstoke, 1991.

Evans, Mari, ed. *Black Women Writers: 1950–80*. New York, 1984.

Kubitschek, M.D. *Claiming the Heritage: African-American Novelists and History*. Jackson, Miss., and London, 1991.

Pryse, M. and Spillers, H.J., eds. *Conjuring: Black Women, Fiction, and Literary Tradition*. Bloomington, Ind., 1985.

Shaw, H.B. *Perspectives of Black Culture*. Bowling Green, Ohio, 1990.

Wall, Cheryl, ed. *Changing Our Own Words: Essays on Criticism, Theory, and Writing by Black Women*. Newark, N.J., 1989.

Wilentz, Gay. *Binding Cultures: Black Women Writers in Africa and the Diaspora*. Bloomington, Ind., 1992.

Willis, Susan. *Specifying: Black Women Writing the American Experience*. Madison, 1987.

Articles

Benston, Kimberly. 'Architectural Imagery and Unity in Paule Marshall's *Brown Girl, Brownstones*'. *Negro American Literature Forum* 9 (1975), 67–70.

Braithwaite, Edward. 'West Indian History and Society in the Art of Paule Marshall's Novel'. *Journal of Black Studies* 1 (1970), 225–38.

Brock, Sabine. 'Marshall's Placing of Female Generations'. *Callaloo* 10 (1987), 79–90.

Brown, L.W. 'The Rhythms of Power in Paule Marshall's Fiction'. *Novel* 7 (1974), 159–67.

Carby, H.V. 'Reinventing History/Imagining the Future'. *Black American Literature Forum* 23 (1989), 581–7.

Christian, Barbara. 'Ritualistic Process and the Structure of *Praisesong for the Widow*'. *Callaloo* 6 (1983), 74–84.

Christol, Helene. 'Paule Marshall's Bajan Women'.

In *Women and War: The Changing Status of American Women from the 1930s to the 1950s*. New York, 1990, 141–54.

Davis, C.B. 'Black Women's Journey into Self'. *Matatu* 1 (1987), 19–34.

DeLamotte, Eugenia. 'Women, Silence, History in *The Chosen Place, The Timeless People*'. *Callaloo* 16 (1993), 227–42.

Dennison, Dorothy. 'Early Short Fiction of Marshall'. *Callaloo* 6 (1983), 31–45.

Hawthorne, Evelyn. 'Ethnicity and Cultural Perspectives in Paule Marshall's Short Fiction'. *MELUS* 13 (1986), 37–48.

Kapai, Leela. 'Dominant Themes and Techniques in Paule Marshall's Fiction'. *College Language Association Journal* 16 (1972), 49–59.

Kubitschek, M.C. 'Marshall's Women on Quest'. *Black American Literature Forum* 21 (1987), 43–60.

Lindberg-Seyersted, Brita. 'New World Black Heritage in Paule Marshall'. *Studia Neophilologica* 64 (1992), 183–94.

Nazareth, Peter. 'Paule Marshall's Timeless People'. *New Letters* 40 (1973), 113–31.

Ogunyemi, C.O. ' "The Old Order Shall Pass": The Examples of "Flying Home" and "Barbados" '. *Studies in Short Fiction* 20 (1983), 23–32.

Pollard, Velma. 'Cultural Connections in *Praisesong for the Widow*'. *World Literature Written in English* 25 (1985), 285–98.

Reyes, Angelita. 'Politics and Metaphors of Materialism in Marshall and Morrison'. In *Politics and the Muse*. Ed. A.J. Sorkin. Bowling Green, Ohio, 1989, 179–205.

Schneider, Debborah. 'A Search for Selfhood: Paule Marshall's *Brown Girl, Brownstones*'. In *The Afro-American Novel since 1960*. Eds P. Bruck and W. Karrer. Amsterdam, 1982, 53–73.

Stoelting, W.L. 'Time Past and Present: The Search for Viable Links in *The Chosen Place, The Timeless People*'. *College Language Association Journal* 16 (1972), 60–71.

Washington, M.H. 'Afterword'. In *Brown Girl, Brownstones*. By Paule Marshall. London, 1982.

Wilentz, Gay. 'Marshall's Diasporic Vision'. *Obsidian II* 5 (1990), 1–21.

Bibliography and reference

Glikin, Ronda. 'Paule Marshall' (a bibliography of primary and secondary literature). In *Black American Women in Literature*. Jefferson, N.C., and London, 1989, 112–14.

Kulkarni, Harihar. 'Paule Marshall: A Bibliography'. *Callaloo* 16 (1993), 245–67.

Miriam Masoli (Tlali)

Books

Barnett, U.A. *A Vision of Order: A Study of Black South African Literature in English 1914–1980.* Amherst, Mass., 1983.

Clayton, Cherry, ed. *Women and Writing in South Africa. A Critical Anthology.* Marshalltown, 1989.

Mackenzie, C. and Clayton, C., eds. *Between the Lines: Interviews.* Grahamstown, 1989.

Watts, Jane. *Black Writers from South Africa: Toward a Discourse of Liberation.* Basingstoke, 1989.

Articles

Interview. *Argus* (17 July 1980), 10.

Alvarez-Pereyre, J. 'The Novels of Miriam Tlali'. *Matatu* 2 (1988), 111–24.

Bruner, C.H. 'There is No Time in South Africa Now for Fairy Stories'. *World Literature Today* 61 (1987), 410–14.

Davies, C.B. 'Finding Some Space: Black South African Women Writers'. *Current Bibliography on African Affairs* 19 (1987), 31–45.

Driver, Dorothy. 'Women as Mothers, Women as Writers'. In *Rendering Things Visible.* Ed. Martin Trump. Johannesburg, 1990, 225–55.

Lee, Denice. 'Interview'. *African Literature Association Bulletin* 17 (1981), 40–2.

Lenta, Margaret. 'Two Women and their Territories'. *Tulsa Studies in Women's Literature* 11 (1992), 103–11.

Lockett, Cecily. 'Miriam Masoli'. In *Encyclopedia of Post-Colonial Literatures in English.* Eds E. Benson and L.W. Conolly. London and New York, 1994, 1565–6.

Schipper, Mineke. 'Interview'. In *Unheard Words.* Ed. M. Schipper. London, 1985, 59–68.

Sole, Kelwyn. 'The Days of Power: Depiction of Politics and Community in Four Recent South African Novels'. *Research in African Literatures* 19 (1988), 65–88.

Bibliography and reference

Berriman, Brenda F. 'An Update: Bibliography of Twelve African Women Writers'. *Research in African Literatures* 19 (1988), 206–31.

Bobbie Ann Mason

Books

Flora, J.M. and Bain, R., eds. *Contemporary Fiction Writers of the South.* Westport, Conn., 1993.

Gainey, K.F.W. 'Subverting the Symbolic: The Semiotic Fictions of Tyler, Phillips, Mason, and Paley'. Ph.D., University of Tulsa, 1990.

Hobson, F. *The Southern Writer in the Postmodern World.* Athens, Ga., 1991.

Hornby, Nick. *Contemporary American Fiction.* London and New York, 1992.

Michigan Quarterly Review. Special issue 26 (1987).

Articles

Interview. *New York Times Book Review* (26 November 1989).

Interview. *Daily Telegraph* (4 December 1989).

Interview. *Contemporary Literature* 32 (1991), 449–70.

Amidon, Stephen. 'Bobbie Ann Mason'. *Literary Review* 31/2 (December 1989).

Brinkmeyer, R.H., Jr. 'Finding One's History: Bobbie Ann Mason and Contemporary Southern Literature'. *Southern Literary Journal* 19 (1987), 22–33.

Giannone, R. 'Mason and the Recovery of Mystery'. *Studies in Short Fiction* 27 (1990), 553–66.

Havens, Lila. 'Residents and Transients: An Interview with Bobbie Ann Mason'. *Crazyhorse* 29 (1985), 87–104.

Henning, Barbara. 'Minimalism and the American Dream'. *Modern Fiction Studies* 34 (1989), 689–98.

Hill, D.R. 'Food and Food Rituals in Mason'. *Southern Quarterly* 30 (1992), 81–9.

Hill, D.C. 'Interview'. *Southern Quarterly* 31 (1992), 85–118.

Morphew, G.O. 'Downhome Feminists in *Shiloh and Other Stories*'. *Southern Literary Journal* 21 (1990), 41–9.

Morrissey, T.J. 'Mason's *In Country*'. *Explicator* 50 (1991) 62–4.

Ryan, B.T. 'Decentered Authority in Mason's *In Country*'. *Critique* 31 (1990), 199–212.

Shomer, Enid. 'An Interview with Bobbie Ann Mason'. *Black Warrior Review* 12 (1986), 87–102.

Sloane, Kay. 'Bobbie Ann Mason'. In *Post-War Literatures.* Eds H. Bertens et al. Houten and Groningen, 1989.

Towers, Robert. 'American Graffiti'. *New York Review of Books* (16 December 1982), 38–40.

Wilhelm, A.E. 'Making Over or Making Off: The Problem of Identity in Mason's Short Fiction'. *Southern Literary Journal* 18 (1986), 76–82.

Wilhelm, A.E. 'Private Rituals: Coping with Change in the Fiction of Bobbie Ann Mason'. *Midwest Quarterly* 28 (1987), 271–82.

Winter, Marjorie. 'Popular and Corporate Culture in *In Country*'. *Literature Interpretation Theory* 4 (1993), 195–201.

Zverev, A. 'Prose of the 1980s: Three New Names'.

In *Language and Literature*. Ed. C.A. Blackshire-Belay. Westport, Conn., 1992, 272–83.

Toni Morrison

Books

Awkard, Michael. *Inspiriting Influences: Tradition, Revision, and Afro-American Women's Novels*. New York, 1989.

Baker, H.A. *The Workings of the Spirit: The Poetics of Afro-American Women's Writing*. Chicago and London, 1991.

Bjork, P.B. *The Novels of Morrison*. New York, 1994.

Bloom, Harold, ed. *Toni Morrison*. New York, 1990.

Bruck, P. and Karrer, W. *The Afro-American Novel since 1960*. Amsterdam, 1982.

Butler-Evans, E. *Race, Gender and Desire*. Philadelphia, 1989.

Byerman, K.E. *Fingering the Jagged Grain: Tradition and Form in Recent Black Fiction*. Athens, Ga., 1985.

Christian, Barbara. *Black Women Novelists*. Westport, Conn., 1980.

Christian, Barbara. *Black Feminist Criticism*. New York, 1985.

Evans, Mari. *Black Women Writers: Arguments and Interviews*. London and Sydney, 1985.

Gunter, H., ed. *History and Tradition in Afro-American Culture*. Frankfurt, 1984.

Harris, Trudier. *Fiction and Folklore: The Novels of Toni Morrison*. Knoxville, Tenn., 1991.

Heinze, Denise. *The Dilemma of 'Double Consciousness': Toni Morrison's Novels*. Athens, Ga., 1993.

Holloway, K. and Dematrakopoulos, S. *New Dimensions of Spirituality in the Novels of Toni Morrison*. Greenwood, Conn., 1987.

Hussey, Mark et al., eds. *Virginia Woolf: Emerging Perspectives*. New York, 1994 (several articles on Morrison and Woolf).

Jones, B.W. and Vinson, A.L. *The World of Toni Morrison: Explorations in Literary Criticism*. Dubuque, Iowa, 1985.

McKay, N.Y., ed. *Critical Essays on Toni Morrison*. Boston, 1988.

Modern Fiction Studies. Special double issue 39 (1993).

Otten, Terry. *The Crime of Innocence in the Fiction of Toni Morrison*. Columbia, Mo., 1989.

Pryse, M. and Spillers, H.J., eds. *Conjuring: Black Women, Fiction, and Literary Tradition*. Bloomington, Ind., 1985.

Rigney, B.H. *The Voices of Toni Morrison*. Columbus, Ohio, 1991.

Samuels, W.D. and Hudson-Weems, C. *Toni Morrison*. Boston, 1990.

Smith, Valerie. *Self-Discovery and Authority in Afro-American Narrative*. Cambridge, Mass., 1987.

Tate, Claudia, ed. *Black Women Writers at Work*. New York, 1983.

Whisker, Gina. *Black Women's Writing*. New York, 1993.

Willis, Susan. *Specifying: Black Women Writing the American Experience*. Madison, Wis., 1987.

Yaeger, Patricia, ed. *Refiguring the Father. New Feminist Readings of Patriarchy*. Carbondale, Ill., 1989.

Articles

Abel, Elizabeth. 'Black Writing: White Reading'. *Critical Inquiry* 19 (1993), 470–98.

Blake, S.L. 'Folklore and Community in *Song of Solomon*'. *MELUS* 7 (1980), 77–82.

Clark, Norris. 'Flying Black: Toni Morrison'. *Minority Voices* 4 (1980), 51–63.

Cummings, Kate. 'Reclaiming the Mother('s) Tongue: *Beloved, Ceremony, Mothers and Shadows*'. *College English* 52 (1990), 552–69.

Epstein, Grace. 'Dream Flight and Narrative Construction in Morrison'. In *The State of the Fantastic*. Ed. N. Ruccick. Westport, Conn., 1992.

Guth, Deborah. 'Beloved's Dialogue with Christianity'. *Journal of Narrative Technique* 24 (1994), 83–97.

Hoffarth-Zellow, M. 'Resolving the Paradox: An Interlinear Reading of *Sula*'. *Journal of Narrative Technique* 22 (1992), 114–27.

Lawrence, D. 'Fleshly Ghosts and Ghostly Flesh: The Word and the Body in *Beloved*'. *Studies in American Fiction* 19 (1991), 189–201.

Lepow, Lauren. 'Paradise Lost and Found: Dualism and Edenic Myth in *Tar Baby*'. *Contemporary Literature* 28 (1987), 364–77.

Ogunyemi, C.O. 'Order and Disorder in Toni Morrison's *The Bluest Eye*'. *Critique* 19 (1977), 112–20.

Rodriques, E. 'The Telling of *Beloved*'. *Journal of Narrative Technique* 21 (1991), 153–69.

Royster, Philip. 'Milkman Flying: The Scapegoat Transcended in Morrison's *Song of Solomon*'. *CLA Journal* 24 (1981), 419–40.

Rushdy, A.H.A. 'Daughters Signifying History'. *American Literature* 64 (1992), 567–97.

Samuels, Wilfrid. 'Liminality and the Search for Self in Morrison's *Song of Solomon*'. *Minority Voices* 5 (1981), 59–68.

Scarpa, Guilia. 'Narrative Possibilities at Play in *Beloved*'. *MELUS* 17 (1991–2), 91–103.

Tonegawa, Maki. 'Morrison's Exploration of the Relational Self in *Sula* and *Beloved*'. *Studies in American Literature* 29 (1992), 91–106.

III SECONDARY CRITICISM ON INDIVIDUAL AUTHORS

Bibliography and reference

Middleton, D.L. *Toni Morrison: An Annotated Bibliography*. New York, 1987.

Mix, Debbie. 'Toni Morrison: A Selected Bibliography'. *Modern Fiction Studies* 39 (1993), 795–817.

Alice Munro

Books

Besner, N.K. *Introducing Alice Munro's 'Lives of Girls and Women'*, Toronto, 1990.

Carrington, Ildiko de Papp. *Controlling the Uncontrollable: The Fiction of Alice Munro*. DeKalb, Ill., 1989.

Carscallen, James. *The Other Country: Patterns in the Writings of Alice Munro*. Toronto, 1993.

D'haen, Theo and Bertens, Hans, eds. *Postmodern Fiction in Canada*. Amsterdam, 1992.

Gibson, Graeme, ed. *Eleven Canadian Novelists* (Interviews). Toronto, 1973.

Howells, C.A. and Hunter, L., eds. *Narrative Strategies in Canadian Literature: Feminism and Postcolonialism*. Buckingham and Philadelphia, 1991.

Keith, W.S. *A Sense of Style. Studies in the Art of Fiction*. Downsview, Ontario, 1989.

MacKendrick, L.K., ed. *Some Other Reality*. Toronto, 1993.

MacKendrick, L.K. ed. *Probable Fictions: Alice Munro's Narrative Acts*. Downsview, Ontario, 1983.

Martin, W. *Alice Munro: Paradox and Parallel*. Edmonton, 1987.

Miller, Judith, ed. *The Art of Alice Munro: Saying the Unsayable*. Waterloo, Ontario, 1984.

Nischik, R.M. and Korte, B., eds. *Modes of Narrative*. Würzburg, 1990.

Rasporich, B.J. *Dance of the Sexes: Art and Gender in the Fiction of Alice Munro*. Edmonton, 1990.

Redekip, Magdalene. *Mothers and Other Clowns. The Stories of Alice Munro*. London, and New York, 1992.

Ross, C.S. *Alice Munro: A Double Life*. Toronto, 1992.

Articles

Carrington, Ildiko de Papp. 'What's in a Title?'. *Studies in Short Fiction* 30 (1993), 555–64.

Gadpaille, M. 'Alice Munro'. In *The Canadian Short Story: Perspectives on Canadian Culture*. Toronto, 1988, 567–81.

Houston, Pam. 'The Making of Metonymic Meaning in Munro'. *Kenyon Review* 14 (1992), 79–92.

Hoy, Helen. '"Dull, Simple, Amazing and Unfathomable": Paradox and Double Vision in Alice

Munro's Fiction'. *Studies in Canadian Literature* 5 (1980), 100–15.

Mayberry, K.J. '"Every Last Thing Everlasting": Alice Munro and the Limits of Narrative'. *Studies in Short Fiction* 29 (1992), 531–46.

Struthers, J.R. 'Alice Munro and the American South'. In *The Canadian Novel Here and Now*. Ed. J. Moss. Toronto, 1983, 121–33.

Thacker, Robert. 'Alice Munro's Willa Cather'. *Canadian Literature* 134 (1992), 42–57.

Ventura, Heliane. 'Munro's "Boys and Girls"'. *Commonwealth Essays and Studies* 15 (1992), 80–7.

York, Lorraine. '"Gulfs" and "Connections": The Fiction of Munro'. *Essays in Canadian Writing* 35 (1987), 135–46.

Iris Murdoch

Books

Arnold, D.S. *Liminal Readings*. New York, 1993.

Baldanza, Frank. *Iris Murdoch*. Boston, 1974.

Bock, H. and Wertherim, A., eds. *Essays on the Contemporary British Novel*. Munich, 1986.

Bradbury, Malcolm. *Possibilities: Essays on the State of the Novel*. London, 1973.

Byatt, A.S. *Degrees of Freedom: The Novels of Iris Murdoch*. London and New York, 1965.

Byatt, A.S. *Iris Murdoch*. London, 1976.

Conradi, Peter. *Iris Murdoch*. Brighton, 1987.

Dipple, Elizabeth. *Iris Murdoch: Work for the Spirit*. Chicago, 1982.

Gerstenberger, Donna. *Iris Murdoch*. Lewisburg and London, 1975.

Johnson, Deborah. *Iris Murdoch*. Brighton, 1987.

Kermode, Frank. *Modern Essays*. London, 1971.

Mettler, D.D. *Sound and Sense in Iris Murdoch*. New York, 1991.

Modern Fiction Studies. Special issue 15 (1969).

Rabinowitz, Rubin. *Iris Murdoch*. New York, 1968.

Todd, Richard. *Iris Murdoch*. London and New York, 1984.

Todd, Richard. *Encounters with Iris Murdoch*. Amsterdam, 1988.

Wolff, Peter. *The Undisciplined Heart: Iris Murdoch and her Novels*. Columbia, Mo., 1966.

Articles

Leavis, C.R. 'The Anti-Artist'. *Punjab University Research Bulletin* 21 (1990), 53–7.

Meyers, Jeffrey. 'Interviews'. *Denver Quarterly* 26 (1991), 102–11.

Phillips, Diane. 'Murdoch and the Legacy of the Great Nineteenth Century Novelists'. *Caliban* 27 (1990), 73–81.

Sturrock, John. 'Reading Murdoch'. *Salmagundi* 80 (1988), 144–60.

403

Todd, Richard. 'Iris Murdoch'. In *Post-War Literatures in English*. Eds H. Bertens et al. Houten and Groningen, 1988– .

Vahali, D.O. 'Murdoch's *The Black Prince*'. *Punjab University Research Bulletin* 21 (1990), 53–7.

Bibliography and reference

Bove, C.E. *A Character Index and Guide to the Fiction of Iris Murdoch*. London, 1986.

Fletcher, John. *Iris Murdoch. A Descriptive Primary and Annotated Secondary Bibliography*. New York, 1990.

Gloria Naylor

Books

Awkard, Michael. *Inspiring Influences: Tradition, Revision, and Afro-American Women's Novels*. New York, 1991.

Braxton, J.M. and McLaughlin, A.N., eds. *Wild Women in the Whirlwind*. New Brunswick, N.J., and London, 1990.

Byerman, K.E. *Fingering the Jagged Grain*. Athens, Ga., 1985.

Christian, Barbara. *Black Feminist Criticism*. New York, 1985.

Pearlman, M. and Henderson, K.U., eds. *Inter/View*. Lexington, Ky., 1990.

Smith, V., Baechler, L. and Litz, A.W., eds. *African American Writers*. New York, 1991.

Wilt, Judith. *Abortion, Choice, and Contemporary Fiction*. Chicago, 1990.

Articles

Andrews, L.R. 'Black Sisterhood in Naylor's Novels'. *College Language Association Journal* 33 (1989), 1–25.

Christian, Barbara. 'The Theme of Lesbianism in Lorde, Naylor, Shange, Walker'. *Feminist Issues* 5 (1985), 3–20.

Clayton, Jay. 'The Narrative Turn in Recent Minority Fiction'. *American Literary History* 2 (1990), 375–93.

Fraser, Celeste. 'Stealing B(l)ack Voices'. *Critical Matrix* 5 (1989), 65–88.

Gates, H.L., Jr. 'Significant Others'. *Contemporary Literature* 29 (1988), 606–23.

Homans, Margaret. 'Recent Feminist Fiction and the Classical Underworld'. *Contemporary Literature* 29 (1988), 369–402.

Inoue, Kazuko. 'Gloria Naylor's Narrative'. *Language and Culture* 18 (1990), 157–76.

Kardux, Joke. 'Gloria Naylor'. In *Post-War Literatures*. Eds H. Bertens et al. Houten and Groningen, 1994.

Kelly, L.D. 'Dream Sequence in *The Women of Brewster Place*'. *Notes on Contemporary Literature* 21 (1991), 9–10.

Matus, J.L. 'Dream, Deferral, and Closure in *The Women of Brewster Place*'. *Black American Literature Forum* 24 (1990), 49–64.

Meisenhelder, Susan. '"The Whole Picture" in *Mama Day*'. *African American Review* 27 (1993), 405–19.

Montgomery, M.L. 'The Fathomless Dream: Gloria Naylor's Use of the Descent Motif in *The Women of Brewster Place*'. *College Language Association Journal* 26 (1992), 1–11.

Palumbo, Kathryn. 'The Uses of Female Imagery in Naylor's *The Women of Brewster Place*'. *Notes on Contemporary Literature* 15 (1985), 6–7.

Sandiford, K.A. 'Gothic and Intertextual Constructions in *Linden Hills*'. *Arizona Quarterly* 47 (1991), 117–39.

Saunder, J.R. 'Naylor's First Three Novels'. *Hollins Critic* 27 (1990), 1–11.

Tanner, L.E. 'Reading Rape: *Sanctuary* and *The Women of Brewster Place*'. *American Literature* 62 (1990), 559–82.

Toombs, C.P. 'Food and Identity in *Linden Hills*'. *College Language Association Journal* 37 (1993), 1–18.

Tucker, Lindsey. 'Recovering the Conjure Women'. *African American Review* 28 (1994), 173–88.

Ward, C.C. 'Gloria Naylor's *Linden Hills*'. *Contemporary Literature* 28 (1987), 67–81.

Wells, Linda et al. 'The Role of Mentor in *Women of Brewster Place* and *Praise Song for the Widow*'. *Exploration in Ethnic Studies* 13 (1990), 41–60.

Bibliography and reference

Glikin, Ronda. 'Gloria Naylor' (a short bibliography of primary and secondary literature). In *Black American Women in Literature*. Jefferson, N.C., and London, 1989, 133–4.

Frances Newman

Books

Abbott, E.R. 'Purple Prejudices: The Critical Writings of Frances Newman'. Ph.D., Vanderbilt University, 1993.

Cabell, James Branch. *Some of Us*. New York, 1921.

Duggan, M.M. '"The Gold-Fish Bowl": Miss Newman's Five-Finger Exercise'. Ph.D., University of South Carolina, 1986.

Seidel, Kathryn L. *The Southern Belle in the American Novel*. Tampa, 1985.

Wade, B.A. 'Frances Newman: Southern Feminist and Literary Experimenter of the 1920s'. Ph.D., University of Washington, 1989.

Articles

Abbott, Reginald. 'A Southern Lady Still'. *Southern Quarterly* 27 (1989), 49–70.

Abbott, Reginald. 'A Note on Ellen Glasgow and Frances Newman'. *Ellen Glasgow Newsletter* 31 (1993), 5, 8–9, 11.

Drake, Robert. 'Frances Newman: Fabulist of Decadence'. *Georgia Review* 14 (1960), 389–98.

Gallo, Louis. 'Frances Newman'. *Dictionary of Literary Biography: Yearbook 1980*. Detroit, 1981, 276–9.

Gallo, Louis. 'Notes on Some Recently Found Lost American Fiction'. *Missouri Review* 4 (1981), 91–8.

Mayfield, Chris. 'A Return Visit: Frances Newman'. *Southern Exposure* 6 (1978), 104–5.

Anaïs Nin

Books

Benstock, Shari. *Women of the Left Bank: Paris, 1900–1940*. Austin, Tex., 1986.

Deduck, P.A. *Realism, Reality and the Fictional Theories of Alain Robbe-Grillet and Anaïs Nin*. Washington, D.C., 1982.

Evans, Oliver. *Anaïs Nin*. Carbondale, Ill., 1968.

Franklin, Benjamin and Schneider, Duane. *Anaïs Nin*. Athens, Ohio, 1979.

Harm, Valerie, ed. *Celebration with Anaïs Nin*. Riverside, Conn., 1973.

Hinz, E.J. *The Mirror and the Garden: Realism and Reality in the Writings of Anaïs Nin*. Columbus, Ohio, 1971.

Knapp, Bettina. *Anaïs Nin*. New York, 1978.

Mosaic. Special issue 11 (1978).

Paine, Sylvia. *Beckett, Nabokov and Nin: Motives and Modernism*. Port Washington, N.Y., 1981.

Pine, R. *The Dandy and the Herald*. Basingstoke, 1988.

Salber, Linde. *Anaïs Nin*. Hamburg, 1992.

Scholar, Nancy. *Anaïs Nin*. Boston, 1984.

Spencer, Sharon. *Collage of Dreams: The Writings of Anaïs Nin*. New York, 1981.

Spencer, Sharon, ed. *Anaïs, Art and Artists*. Greenwood, Fla., 1986.

Stuhlmann, Gunther, ed. *Anaïs: An International Journal*. Los Angeles, 1985.

Under the Sign of Pisces: Anaïs Nin and her Circle. 1970–81.

Zaller, Robert, ed. *A Casebook on Anaïs Nin*. New York, 1974.

Articles

These do not include articles in *Anaïs: An International Journal* 1983– .

Anderson, Margaret. 'Critical Approaches to Anaïs Nin'. *Canadian Review of American Studies* 10 (1979), 255–65.

Brennan, Karen. 'Anaïs Nin: Author(iz)ing the Erotic Body'. *Genders* 14 (1992), 66–86.

Hinz, E.J. 'Recent Nin Criticism: Who's on First'. *Canadian Review of American Studies* 13 (1982).

Kuntz, P.G. 'Art as Public Dreams: The Practice and Theory of Anaïs Nin'. *Journal of Aesthetics and Art Criticism* 32 (1974), 525–37.

Spencer, Sharon. 'Anaïs Nin's "Feminine" Writing'. In *Breaking the Sequence*. Eds E.G. Friedman and M. Fuchs. Princeton, N.J., 1989, 161–73.

Studies in the Twentieth Century 1 (1968) has several articles on Nin, but is not a special issue.

Bibliography and reference

Cutting, R.M. 'Anaïs Nin: A Reference Guide', 1978, updated yearly by R.R. Centing in the journal *Under the Sign of Pisces: Anaïs Nin and her Circle*, 1970–81.

Edna O'Brien

Books

Dunn, Nell, ed. *Talking to Women*. London, 1965.

Eckley, Grace. *Edna O'Brien*. Lewisburg, Pa., 1974.

Staley, Thomas, ed. *Twentieth Century Women Novelists*. London, 1982.

Articles

Carpenter, Lynette. 'The Novels of Edna O'Brien'. In *Essays on the Contemporary British Novel*. Eds H. Bock and A. Wertheim. Munich, 1986, 263–81.

Carricker, Kitti. 'O'Brien's "The Doll"'. *Notes on Modern Irish Literature* 1 (1989), 6–13.

Hargreaves, Tamsin. 'Women's Consciousness and Identity in Four Irish Women Novelists'. In *Cultural Contexts and Literary Idioms in Contemporary Irish Literature*. Ed. M. Kenneally. Gerrard's Cross, 1988.

Harmon, Maurice. 'Generations Apart: 1925–75'. In *The Irish Novel in Our Time*. Eds P. Rafroidi and M. Harmon. Villeneuve-d'Ascq, 1975, 49–65.

Haule, J.M. 'Tough Luck: The Unfortunate Birth of Edna O'Brien'. *Colby Library Quarterly* 23 (1987), 216–24.

McMahon, Sean. 'A Sex By Themselves: An Interim Report on the Novels of Edna O'Brien'. *Eire–Ireland* 2 (1977), 79–87.

O'Brien, Peggy. 'An Assessment of Edna O'Brien'. *Massachusetts Review* 28 (1987), 474–88.

O'Hara, Kiera. 'Love Objects'. *Studies in Short Fiction* 30 (1993), 317–25.

Pelan, Rebecca. 'Edna O'Brien's "Stage-Irish"

Persona'. *Canadian Journal of Irish Studies* 19 (1993), 67–78.

Plimpton, George. 'Interview'. In *Writers at Work*, vol. 7. Harmondsworth, 1986, 241–66.

Popot, Raymond. 'Edna O'Brien's Paradise Lost'. In *The Irish Novel in Our Time*. Eds P. Rafroidi and M. Harmon. Villeneuve-d'Ascq, 1975, 255–86.

Salmon, Mary. 'Edna O'Brien'. In *Contemporary Irish Novelists*. Ed. R. Imhof. Tübingen, 1990.

Snow, Lotus. '"That Trenchant Childhood Route": Quest in Edna O'Brien's Novels'. *Eire–Ireland* 14 (1979), 74–83.

Kate O'Brien

Books

Crosland, M. *Beyond the Lighthouse*. London, 1981.

Dalsimer, A.M. *Kate O'Brien: A Critical Study*. Boston, 1990.

Hildebidle, John, ed. *Five Irish Writers*. Cambridge, Mass., 1989.

Hoehn, Matthew A., ed. *Catholic Authors: Contemporary Biographical Sketches 1930–47*. Newark, N.J., 1952.

Jeffares, A.N. *Anglo-Irish Literature*. London, 1982.

Lawrence, Margaret. *The School of Femininity*. New York, 1936.

Reynolds, Lorna. *Kate O'Brien: A Literary Portrait*. Gerrards Cross, 1987.

Rivollan, A. *Littérature irlandaise contemporaine*. 1939.

Ryan, J. 'The Role of Women in the Irish Novels of Kate O'Brien'. Ph.D., Trinity College, Dublin, 1989.

Walshe, Eibhear, ed. *Ordinary People Dancing* (essays on Kate O'Brien). Cork, 1993.

Articles

Closter, Susan Vander. 'Kate O'Brien'. *Dictionary of Literary Biography* 15, Detroit, 1983, 389–96.

Jordan, L. 'Kate O'Brien: A Passionate Talent'. *Hibernia* (30 August 1974).

Kiely, Benedict. 'The Novels of Kate O'Brien'. *Hollin's Critic* 29 (1992), 1–11.

Lawrence, Margaret. 'Matriarchs'. In *The School of Femininity*. New York, 1936, 243–7.

Madden, Deirdre. 'Postscript'. In *The Ante-Room*. By Kate O'Brien. London, 1989.

Quielo, Rose. 'The Hysteric in *Mary Lavelle*'. *Eire–Ireland* 25 (1990), 46–57.

Reynolds, Lorna. 'The Image of Spain in the Novels of Kate O'Brien'. In *Literary Interrelations*. Eds W. Zach and H. Kosok. Tübingen, 1987, 181–8.

Ryan, J. 'Women in the Novels of Kate O'Brien: The Mellick Novels'. In *Studies in Anglo-Irish Literature*. Ed. H. Kosok. Bonn, 1982.

Ryan, Joan. 'Class and Creed in Kate O'Brien'. In *The Irish Writer and the City*. Ed. M. Harmon. Totowa, N.J., 1983, 125–35.

Tryphonopoulos, D.P. 'Kate O'Brien'. In *Dictionary of British Women Writers*. Ed. J. Todd. London, 1989, 508–10.

Flannery O'Connor

Books

Asals, Frederick. *Flannery O'Connor: The Imagination of Extremity*. Athens, Ga., 1982.

Asals, Frederick. *Flannery O'Connor: 'A Good Man is Hard to Find'*. New York, 1993.

Baumgaertner, J.P. *Flannery O'Connor: A Proper Scaring*. Wheaton, Ill., 1988.

Brinkmeyer, Robert. *The Art and Vision of Flannery O'Connor*. Baton Rouge, La., 1989.

Desmond, J.F. *Risen Sons: Flannery O'Connor's Vision of History*. Athens, Ga., 1988.

Di Renzo, Anthony. *American Gargoyles: O'Connor and the Medieval Grotesque*. Carbondale, Ill., 1993.

Feeley, Kathleen. *Flannery O'Connor: Voice of the Peacock*. New Brunswick, N.J., 1972.

Fickett, Harold and Gilbert, Douglas. *Flannery O'Connor: Images of Grace*. Grand Rapids, Mich., 1986.

Flannery O'Connor Bulletin. 1973– .

Freedman, M.J. and Lawson, L.A., eds. *The Added Dimension: The Art and Mind of Flannery O'Connor*. New York, 1966.

Gentry, M.B. *Flannery O'Connor's Religion of the Grotesque*. Jackson, Miss., 1986.

Giannone, Richard. *Flannery O'Connor and the Mysteries of Love*. Chicago, 1989.

Hyman, S.E. *Flannery O'Connor*. Minneapolis, 1966.

Kessler, Edward. *Flannery O'Connor and the Language of Apocalypse*. Princeton, N.J., 1986.

Manning, C.J., ed. *The Female Tradition in Southern Literature*. Urbana, Ill., 1993.

Martin, C.W. *The True Country: Themes in the Fiction of Flannery O'Connor*. Nashville, 1969.

Orvell, Miles. *Flannery O'Connor: An Introduction*. Jackson, Miss., 1991.

Paulson, S.M. *Flannery O'Connor: A Study of the Short Fiction*. Boston, 1988.

Ragen, B.A. *A Wreck on the Road to Damascus: Innocence, Guilt, and Conversion in Flannery O'Connor*. Chicago, 1989.

Schloss, Carol. *Flannery O'Connor's Dark Comedies*. Baton Rouge, La., 1980.

Studies in the Literary Imagination. Special issue 20 (1987).

Westarp, K.H. and Gretlund, J.N., eds. *Realist of*

Distances: Flannery O'Connor Revisited. Aarhus, 1987.

Young, T.D., ed. *Modern American Fiction: Form and Function*. Baton Rouge, La., 1990.

Articles

Those in the *O'Connor Bulletin* are not usually listed here.

Blackwell, Louise. 'Humor and Irony in the Works of O'Connor'. *Ranam* 4 (1971), 61–8.

Butler, Robert. 'Visions of Southern Life and Religion in O'Connor'. *College Language Association Journal* 36 (1993), 349–70.

Burns, Margie. 'A Good Rose is Hard to Find'. In *Image and Ideology in Post-Modern Discourse*. Eds D.B. Downing and S. Bazargan. Albany, N.Y., 1991, 105–23.

Burns, S.L. 'O'Connor and the Critics: An Overview'. *Mississippi Quarterly* 27 (1974), 483–95.

Clasby N.T. 'O'Connor as Visionary Artist'. *Studies in Short Fiction* 28 (1991), 509–20.

Gordon, Sarah. 'Milledgeville: The Perils of Place as Text'. *Flannery O'Connor Bulletin* 20 (1991), 73–87.

Gregory, Donald. 'Enoch Emery: Ironic Doublings in *Wise Blood*'. *Flannery O'Connor Bulletin* 4 (1975), 52–64.

Hardy, D.E. 'Free Indirect Discourse, Irony, and Empathy in "Revelation"'. *Language and Literature* 16 (1991), 37–53.

Katz, Claire. 'Flannery O'Connor's Rage of Vision'. *American Literature* 46 (1974), 54–67.

McDowell, F.P.W. 'Toward the Luminous and the Numinous: The Art of Flannery O'Connor'. *Southern Review* 9 (1973), 998–1013.

Mellard, J.M. 'O'Connor's Others: Freud, Lacan, and the Unconscious'. *American Literature* 60 (1989), 625–43.

Nielsen, Erik. 'The Hidden Strut of *Wise Blood*'. *New Orleans Review* 19 (1992), 91–7.

Reuman, A.E. 'Revolting Fictions'. *Papers on Language and Literature* 29 (1993), 197–214.

Roos, John. 'The Political in O'Connor'. *Studies in Short Fiction* 29 (1992), 161–79.

Satterfield, Ben. '*Wise Blood*, Artistic Anemia, and the Hemorrhaging of O'Connor Criticism'. *Studies in American Fiction* 17 (1989), 33–50.

Shinn, T.V. 'Flannery O'Connor and the Violence of Grace'. *Contemporary Literature* 9 (1968), 58–73.

Wilson, C.Y. 'Family as Affliction, Family as Premise in *The Violent Bear it Away*'. *Studies in the Literary Imagination* 20 (1987), 77–86.

Wyatt, B.N. 'The Domestic Dynamics of *Everything that Rises Must Converge*'. *Twentieth Century Literature* 38 (1992), 66–88.

Bibliography and reference

Farmer, D.R. *Flannery O'Connor: A Descriptive Bibliography*. New York, 1981.

Golden, Robert and Sullivan, Mary. *Flannery O'Connor and Caroline Gordon: A Reference Guide*. Boston, 1977.

Tillie Olsen

Books

Bak, H. and Piket, V., eds. *Looking Outward: American Fiction in the 1930s and 1940s*. European University Press, 1990.

Duncan, Erika. *Unless Soul Clap its Hands*. New York, 1984.

Frye, Joanna. *Tillie Olsen*. New York, 1991.

Martin, Abigail. *Tillie Olsen*. Boise, 1984.

Orr, M.E.N. *Tillie Olsen and a Feminist Spiritual Vision*. Chicago, 1987.

Pearlman, Mickey and Werlock, A.H.P. *Tillie Olsen*. Boston, 1991.

Yalon, L. and Pearlman, M., eds. *Women Writers of the West Coast*. Santa Barbara, 1983.

Articles

Aarons, Victoria. 'The Outsider Within: Women in Contemporary Jewish-American Fiction'. *Contemporary Literature* 28 (1987), 378–93.

Catalupo, Barbara. 'Olsen's Visceral Voice in *Yonnondio*'. *Studies in American Jewish Fiction* 11 (1992), 128–38.

Clayton, John. 'Tillie Olsen and the Fiction of Jewish Americans'. *Response: A Contemporary Jewish Review* 46 (1984), 60–6.

Coiner, Constance. 'Literature of Resistance in Le Sueur and Olsen'. In *Left Politics and the Literary Profession*. Eds L.J. Davis and M.B. Mirabella. New York, 1990, 162–85.

Coiner, Constance. 'A Bakhtianian Reading of *Tell Me a Riddle*'. *Feminist Studies* 18 (1992), 257–81.

Culver, Sara. 'Eva in *Tell Me a Riddle*'. *Midwestern Miscellany* 10 (1932), 38–48.

DeForest, Mary. 'Mazie in *Yonnondio*'. In *The Anna Book*. Ed. M. Pearlman. Westport, Conn., 1992, 113–22.

Duncan, Erika. 'Coming of Age in the Thirties: A Portrait of Tillie Olsen'. *Book Forum* 6 (1982), 207–22.

Frye, J.S. 'I Stand Here Ironing: Motherhood as Experience and Metaphor'. *Studies in Short Fiction* 18 (1981), 287–92.

Gelfant, B.H. 'Olsen's "Requa"'. *Studies in American Fiction* 12 (1984), 61–9.

Jacobs, Naomi. 'Earth, Air, Fire, and Water'. *Studies in Short Fiction* 23 (1986), 401–6.

Kamel, Rose. 'Olsen's Autobiographical Fiction'. *MELUS* 12 (1985), 55–72.

Kaplan, Cora. 'Introduction'. In *Tell Me a Riddle.* By Tillie Olsen. London, 1980.

Kaplan, Cora. 'Introduction'. In *Yonnondio: From the Thirties.* By Tillie Olsen. London, 1980.

Lyons, Bonnie. 'Olsen: The Writer as Jewish Woman'. *Studies in American Jewish Literature* 5 (1986), 89–102.

O'Connor, W.V. 'The Short Stories of Tillie Olsen'. *Studies in Short Fiction* 1 (1964), 21–5.

Orr, Elaine. '*Yonnondio* and Call it Sleep'. *Studies in American Fiction* 21 (1993), 209–23.

Park-Fuller, L. 'Interview'. *Literature in Performance* 4 (1983), 75–7.

Rosenfelt, Deborah. 'From the Thirties: Tillie Olsen and the Radical Tradition'. *Feminist Studies* 7 (1981), 371–406.

Sage, Lorna. 'Tillie Olsen'. In *Women in the House of Fiction*. Basingstoke, 1992, 60–6.

Wolfe, Kathy. 'The Impressionist Fiction of Olsen'. *Midwestern Miscellany* 21 (1993), 57–67.

Bibliography and reference

Craft, B.W. 'A Bibliography of Reviews and Criticism, 1934–91'. *Bulletin of Bibliography* 50 (1993), 189–205.

Cynthia Ozick

Books

Bloom, Harold, ed. *Cynthia Ozick*. New York, 1986.

Dipple, Elizabeth. *The Unresolvable Plot: Reading Contemporary Fiction*. New York and London, 1988.

Friedman, L.S. *Understanding Cynthia Ozick*. Columbia, S.C., 1991.

Kauvar, E.M. *Cynthia Ozick's Fiction*. Bloomington, Ind., 1993.

Kielsky, V.E. *Inevitable Exiles: Cynthia Ozick's View of the Precariousness of Jewish Existence in a Gentile Society*. New York, 1989.

Liron, Naomi. 'Cynthia Ozick: The Self-Subverting Artist'. Ph.D., University of California, Berkeley, 1987.

Logsdon, L. and Mayer, C.W. *Since Flannery O'Connor*. Macomb, Ill., 1987.

Studies in American Jewish Literature. Special issue 6 (1987), includes a bibliography, 145–61.

Texas Studies in Literature and Language. Special issue on Ozick, Hazzard and Redmon 25 (1983).

Articles

These do not include those in special issues.

Aarons, Victoria. 'The Outsider Within'. *Contemporary Literature* 28 (1987), 378–93.

Borchers, Hans. 'The Difficulty of Imagining Germany'. In *Germany and German Thought in American Literature and Cultural Criticism*. Ed. P. Freese. Essen, 1990.

Brown, Erella. 'The Ozick–Bloom Controversy'. *Studies in American Jewish Literature* 11 (1992), 62–82.

Burstein, J.H. 'Ozick and Transgressions of Art'. *American Literature* 59 (1987), 85–101.

Cohen, S.B. 'The Fiction-Writer as Essayist'. *Judaism* 39 (1990), 276–81.

Cole, Diane. 'Cynthia Ozick'. *Dictionary of Literary Biography* 28 (1984), 213–25.

Finkelstein, Norman. 'The Struggle for Historicity in Ozick'. *Literature Interpretation Theory* 1 (1990), 291–302.

Fishman, S.B. 'Imagining Ourselves: *The Messiah of Stockholm*'. *Studies in American Jewish Literature* 9 (1990), 84–92.

Friedman, L.S. 'A Postcolonial Jew: Ozick'. *SPAN* 36 (1993), 436–43.

Greenstein, Michael. 'Ozick's Aesthetics'. *Studies in American Jewish Literature* 8 (1989), 50–65.

Greenstein, Michael. 'Ozick, Roth, and Postmodernism'. *Studies in American Jewish Literature* 10 (1991), 54–64.

Harap, Louis. 'The Religious Art of Ozick'. *Judaism* 33 (1984), 353–63.

Kauvar, E.M. 'Interview'. *Contemporary Literature* 34 (1993), 359–94.

Klingenstein, Susanne. 'Destructive Intimacy'. *Studies in American Jewish Literature* 11 (1992), 162–73.

Klingenstein, Susanne. 'Visits to Germany in Recent Jewish-American Fiction'. *Contemporary Literature* 34 (1993), 538–70.

Krupnik, Mark. 'Ozick as the Jewish T.S. Eliot'. *Soundings* 74 (1991), 351–68.

Meyers, Judith. 'Double Otherness: "Rosa"'. In *Selected Essays from the International Conference on the Outsider*. Ed. J.M. Crafton. Carrollton, Ga., 1990, 141–51.

New, Elisa. 'Ozick's Timing'. *Prooftexts* 9 (1989), 288–94.

Pifer, Ellen. 'Ozick: Invention and Orthodoxy'. In *Contemporary American Women Writers*. Eds C. Rainwater and W.J. Scheik. Lexington, Ky., 1985, 89–116.

Pinksker, Sanford. 'Jewish American Literature: How Roth and Ozick Reimagine their Significant Dead'. *Modern Fiction Studies* 34 (1989), 223–34.

Plimpton, George. 'Interview'. In *Writers at Work*, vol. 8. Harmondsworth, 1988.

Rose, Elizabeth. 'Ozick's Liturgical Postmodernism'. *Studies in American Jewish Literature* 9 (1990), 93–107.

Scrafford, Barbara. 'Nature's Silent Scream: A Commentary on "The Shawl"'. *Criticism* 31 (1989), 11–15.

Sokoloff, N.B. 'Interpretation: *Cannibal Galaxy*'. *Prooftexts* 6 (1986), 239–57.

Strandberg, Victor. 'The Art of Ozick'. *Texas Studies in Literature and Language* 25 (1983), 266–312.

Grace Paley

Books

Anderson, Linda. *Plotting Change*. London, 1990.

Arcana, Judith. *Grace Paley's Life and Stories*. Urbana, Ill., 1993.

Delta. Special issue 14 (1982).

Eckstein, Barbara. *The Language of Fiction in a World of Pain: Reading Politics as Paradox*. Philadelphia, 1990.

Klinkowitz, Jerome. *Structuring the Void: The Struggle for Subject in Contemporary American Fiction*. Durham, N.C., 1991.

Mickelson, Anne Z. *Reaching Out: Sensitivity and Order in Recent American Fiction by Women*. Metuchen, N.J., 1979.

Taylor, Jacqueline. *Grace Paley: Illuminating the Dark Lives*. Austin, Tex., 1990.

Articles

Aarons, Victoria. 'The Outsider Within: Women in Contemporary American Jewish Fiction'. *Contemporary Literature* 28 (1987), 378–93.

Aarons, Victoria. 'A Perfect Marginality'. *Studies in Short Fiction* 27 (1990), 35–43.

Aarons, Victoria. 'Talking Lives: Storytelling and Renewal in Paley'. *Studies in American Jewish Literature* 9 (1990), 20–35.

Baba, Minako. 'Paley's Short Stories'. *Studies in American Jewish Literature* 7 (1988), 40–54.

Batt, N. and Rocard, M. 'Interview'. *Caliban* 25 (1988), 119–37.

Baumgartner, Murray. 'Urban Rites and Civic Premises'. *Contemporary Literature* 34 (1993), 395–424.

Byatt, A.S. 'Introduction'. In *Enormous Changes at the Last Minute*. By Grace Paley. London, 1979.

Clayton, John. 'Grace Paley and Tillie Olsen'. *Response: A Contemporary Jewish Review* 46 (1984), 37–52.

Coppula, K.A. 'Not for Literary Reasons: The Fiction of Paley'. *Mid-American Review* 7 (1986), 63–72.

Criswell, J.S. 'Ozick and Paley'. In *Since Flannery O'Connor*. Eds L. Logsdon and C.W. Mayer. Macomb, Ill., 1987, 93–100.

Cronin, G.L. 'Resistance, Subversion, and Survival

in Paley'. *Studies in American Jewish Fiction* 11 (1992), 140–9.

Fredericksen, Brooke. 'Home is Where the Text is'. *Studies in American Jewish Fiction* 11 (1992), 36–44.

Gelfant, B.H. 'Grace Paley: Fragments for a Portrait in Collage'. *New England Review* 3 (1980), 276–93.

Greiner, Hoke. 'The Question of Chronology in Paley's "Two Short Sad Stories"'. *Studies in Short Fiction* 29 (1992), 583–6.

Eckstein, Barbara. 'Paley's Community'. In *Politics and the Muse*. Ed. A.J. Sorkin. Bowling Green, Iowa, 1989, 124–41.

Janssen, Marian. 'Grace Paley'. In *Post-War Literatures*. Eds H. Bertens et al. Houten and Groningen, 1991.

Kamel, Rose. 'To Aggravate the Conscience: Grace Paley's Loud Voice'. *Journal of Ethnic Studies* 11 (1983), 29–49.

Kaplan, Cora. 'Grace Paley'. In *Writing Lives: Conversations Between Women Writers*. Ed. M. Chamberlain. London, 1988, 181–90.

Lidoff, Joan. 'Clearing her Throat: An Interview with Grace Paley'. *Shenandoah* 32 (1981), 3–26.

Lyons, Bonnie. 'Paley's Jewish Miniatures'. *Studies in American Jewish Fiction* 8 (1989), 26–33.

Mandel, Dena. 'Paley's Sturdy American Jewess'. *Studies in American Jewish Fiction* 3 (1983), 85–98.

Marchant, P. and Ingersoll, E. 'A Conversation with Paley'. *Massachusetts Review* 26 (1985), 606–14.

Meyer, Adam. 'Faith and the Black Thing'. *Studies in Short Fiction* 31 (1994), 79–89.

Perry, Ruth. 'Grace Paley'. Interview. In *Women Writers Writing*. Ed. J. Todd. New York, 1983, 35–46.

Schleifer, Ronald. 'Grace Paley: Chaste Compactness'. In *Contemporary American Women Writers: Narrative Strategies*. Eds C. Rainwater and W.J. Scheik. Lexington. Ky., 1985, 31–49.

Sorkin, Adam. '"What Are We, Animals?": Paley's World of Talk and Laughter'. *Studies in American Jewish Literature* 2 (1982), 144–54.

Taylor, Jacqueline. 'Documenting Romance Knowledge: Two Narrative Techniques in Paley's Fiction'. *Southern Speech Communications Journal* 53 (1987), 65–79.

Taylor, Jacqueline. 'Paley on Storytelling and Story Hearing'. *Literature in Performance* 7 (1987), 46–58.

Wilde, Alan. 'Grace Paley's World-Inventing Words'. In *Middle Grounds: Studies in Contemporary American Fiction*. Philadelphia, 1987, 173–87.

Bibliography and reference

Hoffmann, Ulrich and Gerlach, Philipp. 'Grace Paley: A Bibliography'. *Tulsa Studies in Women's Literature* 8 (1989), 339–54.

Dorothy Parker

Books

Drennan, R.E., ed. *The Algonquin Wits*. New York, 1968.

Frewin, Leslie. *The Late Mrs Dorothy Parker*. New York, 1986.

Gaines, J.R. *Wit's End: The Algonquin Round Table*. New York, 1977.

Guiles, F.L. *Hanging on in Paradise*. New York, 1975.

Hendrickson, R. *American Literary Anecdotes*. 1986.

Keats, John. *You Might as Well Live: The Life and Times of Dorothy Parker*. New York, 1970; London, 1971.

Kinney, A.F. *Dorothy Parker*. Boston, 1978.

Masson, T.L. *Our American Humorists*. New York, 1922.

Meade, Marion. *Dorothy Parker: What Fresh Hell is This? A Biography*. New York, 1988.

Woolcott, A. *While Rome Burns*. New York, 1934.

Yates, N.W. *The American Humorist*. Ames, Iowa, 1964.

Articles

Brown, J.M. 'High Spirits in the Twenties'. *Horizon* 4 (1962), 33–41.

Bunker, S.L. 'I am Outraged Womanhood'. *Regionalism and the Female Imagination* 4 (1978), 25–34.

Capron, M. 'Dorothy Parker'. *Paris Review* 4 (1956), 72–87.

Cooper, W. 'Whatever You Think Dorothy Parker Was Like, She Wasn't'. *Esquire* 70 (1968), 56–7, 110–14.

Cowley, Malcolm, ed. 'Interview'. In *Writers at Work*, vol. 1. London, 1962, 63–74.

Freibert, L.M. 'Dorothy Parker'. *Dictionary of Literary Biography* 86 (1989), 223–33.

Gill, Brendan. 'Introduction'. In *The Collected Dorothy Parker*. London, 1973.

Hellman, Lillian. 'Dorothy Parker'. In *An Unfinished Woman*. Boston, 1969, 212–28.

Horden, Marvyn. 'Parker: An American Centenary'. *Contemporary Review* 263 (1993), 320–1.

Kinney, A.F. 'Parker's Letters to A. Woolcott'. *Massachusetts Review* 30 (1989), 487–515.

MacDermott, Kathy. 'Light Humor'. *Studies in Popular Culture* 10 (1987), 37–53.

Maurois, André. 'Ecrivains américains'. *Revue de Paris* 54 (1947), 9–24.

Miller, Nina. 'Making Love Modern: Dorothy Parker and her Public'. *American Literature* 64 (1992), 763–84.

Toth, Emily. 'Parker, Erica Jong, and New Feminist Humor'. *Regionalism and the Female Imagination* 3 (1977), 70–85.

Treichler, P. 'Verbal Subversions in Dorothy Parker'. *Language and Style* 13 (1980), 46–61.

Van Doren, Mark. 'Dorothy Parker'. *English Journal* 23 (1934), 535–43.

Julia M. Peterkin

Books

Landess, Thomas. *Julia Peterkin*. New York, 1976.

Thompson, H.D., Jr. 'Minerva Finds a Voice: The Early Career of Julia Peterkin'. Ph.D., 1988. *Dissertation Abstracts International* 48 (1988), 2339–40.

Articles

Bennett, Isadora. 'Lang Syne's Miss'. *Bookman* 69 (1929), 357–66.

Cheney, Brainard. 'Can Julia Peterkin's "Genius" Be Revived for Today's Black Myth-Making?'. *Sewanee Review* 80 (1972), 173–9.

Clark, Emily. 'Julia Peterkin'. In *Innocence Abroad*. New York, 1931, 213–31.

Durham, Frank. 'The Reputed Demises of Uncle Tom; or, the Treatment of the Negro in Fiction by White Southern Authors in the 1920s'. *Southern Literary Journal* 2 (1970), 26–50.

Goldstein, P. 'Peterkin's *Scarlet Sister Mary*: A Forgotten Novel'. *Southern Studies* 22 (1983), 138–45.

Law, R.A. 'Mrs Peterkin's Negroes'. *Southwestern Review* 14 (1929), 455–61.

Peterkin, Julia. 'What I Believe'. *Forum* 84 (1930), 48–52.

Polk, Noel. 'Peterkin's *Green Thursday*'. In *South Carolina Women Writers*. Ed. J.B. Meriweather. Spartanburg, S.C., 1979, 177–90.

Sessions, W.A. 'The Land Called Chicora'. *Southern Review* 19 (1983), 736–48.

Shealy, Ann. 'Peterkin: A Souvenir'. In *The Passionate Mind*. Philadelphia, 1976, 31–54.

Williams, S.M. 'Peterkin's Black Voices'. *Publications of the Arkansas Philological Association* 15 (1989), 144–53.

Yates, Irene. 'Conjures and Cures in the Novels of Julia Peterkin'. *Southern Folklore Quarterly* 10 (1946), 137–49.

Ann Petry

Books

Braxton, J.M. and McLaughlin, A.N., eds. *Wild Women in the Whirlwind*. London and New Brunswick, N.J., 1990.

Christina, Barbara. *Black Women Novelists: The Development of a Tradition 1892–1976*. Westport, Conn., and London, 1980.

De Jongh, J. *Vicious Modernism: Black Harlem and the Literary Imagination*. Cambridge, 1990.

Isaacs, Diane. 'Ann Petry's Life and Art'. Ph.D. 1982.

Pryse, M. and Spiller, H.J., eds. *Conjuring: Black Women, Fiction, and the Literary Tradition*. Bloomington, Ind., 1985.

Watson, Carole M. *Prologue: The Novels of Black American Women, 1891–1965*. Westport, Conn., and London, 1985.

Willis, Susan. *Specifying: Black Women Writing the American Experience*. Madison, 1986.

Articles

Adams, G.R. 'Riot as Ritual: Ann Petry's "In Darkness and Confusion"'. *Negro American Literature Forum* 6 (1972), 54–60.

Clarke, Keith. 'Petry and the Art of Subversion'. *African American Review* 26 (1992), 495–505.

Greene, M. 'Interview with Ann Petry'. *Opportunity* 24 (1946), 78–9.

Ivy, J.W. 'Ann Petry Talks about her First Novel'. *Crisis* 53 (1946), 43–6.

Jaskowski, H. 'Power Unequal to Man: The Significance of Conjure in Works by Five Afro-American Authors'. *Southern Folklore Quarterly* 38 (1974), 91–108.

McKay, N.V. 'Ann Petry's *The Street*'. In *Women and War*. Eds M. Diedrich and D. Fischer-Horning. New York, 1990, 127–40.

Madden, David. 'Ann Petry: "The Witness"'. *Studies in Black Literature* 6 (1975), 24–8.

O'Brien, John. 'Ann Petry'. In *Interviews With Black Writers*. New York, 1973, 153–63.

Shinn, T.J. 'Women in the Novels of Ann Petry'. *Critique* 16 (1974), 110–20.

Washington, G.J. 'Petry's Short Fiction'. *College Language Association Journal* 30 (1986), 14–29.

Weir, Sybil. '*The Narrows*'. *Studies in American Fiction* 15 (1987), 81–93.

Wilson, M.K. 'Interview'. *MELUS* 15 (1988), 71–84.

Bibliography and reference

Hill, James Lee. 'Bibliography of the Works of Chester Hines, Ann Petry, and Frank Yerby'. *Black Books Bulletin* 3 (1975), 60–72.

Levin, H.A. *Ann Petry: A Bio-Bibliography*. New York, 1993.

Jayne Anne Phillips

Books

Flora, J.M. and Bain, R., eds. *Contemporary Fiction Writers of the South*. Westport, Conn., 1993.

Gainey, K.F.W. 'Subverting the Symbolic: The Semiotic Fictions of Tyler, Phillips, Mason, and Paley'. Ph.D., University of Tulsa, 1991.

Hornby, Nick. *Contemporary American Fiction*. London and New York, 1992.

Manning, C.S., ed. *The Female Tradition in Southern Literature*. Urbana, Ill., 1993.

Pearlman, Mickey, ed. *American Women Writing Fiction*. Lexington, Ky., 1989.

Articles

Adams, Michael. 'Jayne Anne Phillips'. *Dictionary of Literary Biography, Yearbook 1980*, 297–300.

Baker, J.N. 'Interview'. *Newsweek* 94 (1979), 116–18.

Douglass, T.E. 'Jayne Anne Phillips'. *Appalachian Journal* 21 (1994), 182–9.

Gainey, K.F.W. '*Machine Dreams*: Leo Marx, Technology and Landscape'. *Journal of the American Studies Association of Texas* 21 (1990), 75–84.

Squier, S.M. 'Fetal Voices'. *Tulsa Studies in Women's Literature* 10 (1991), 170–80.

Zverev, A. 'Prose of the 1980s: Three New Names'. In *Language and Literature*. Ed. C.A. Blackshire-Belay. Westport, Conn., 1992, 272–83.

Bibliography and reference

Capper, N. 'Jayne Anne Phillips: An Annotated Primary and Secondary Bibliography 1976–1989'. *Bulletin of Bibliography* 47 (1990), 177–85.

Katherine Anne Porter

Books

Auchincloss, L. *Pioneers and Caretakers*. Minneapolis, 1965.

Baumgartner, Paul R. *Katherine Anne Porter*. New York, 1969.

Bloom, Harold, ed. *Katherine Anne Porter*. New York, 1986.

Brinkmeyer, R.H. *Porter's Artistic Development*. Baton Rouge, La., 1993.

Carr, V.S. *Porter: 'Flowering Judas'*. New Brunswick, N.J., 1993.

Core, G. and Hartley, L., eds. *Katherine Anne Porter: A Critical Symposium*. Athens, Ga., 1969.

Demouy, Jane K. *Katherine Anne Porter's Women: The Eye of her Fiction*. Austin, Tex., 1983.

Emmons, Winifred S. *Katherine Anne Porter: The Regional Stories*. Austin, Tex., 1967.

Givner, Joan. *Katherine Anne Porter: A Life*. New York, 1982, 1991.

Hartley, L. and Core, G., eds. *Porter: A Collection of Critical Essays*. Englewood Cliffs, N.J., 1969.

Hendrick, W. and G. *Katherine Anne Porter*. Boston, 1987.

Liberman, M.M. *Katherine Anne Porter's Fiction*. Detroit, 1971.

Machann, C. and Clark, W.B., eds. *Porter and Texas*. College Station, Tex., 1990.

Manning, C.S., ed. *The Female Tradition in Southern Literature*. Urbana, Ill., 1993.

Mooney, Harry J. *The Fiction and Criticism of Katherine Anne Porter*. Pittsburg, 1962.

Unrue, D.H. *Truth and Vision in Porter's Fiction*. Athens, Ga., 1985.

Unrue, D.H. *Understanding Porter*. Columbia, S.C., 1988.

Walsh, T.F. *Porter and Mexico: The Illusion of Eden*. Austin, Tex., 1992.

Warren, Robert Penn, ed. *Katherine Anne Porter: A Collection of Critical Essays*. Englewood Cliffs, N.J., 1979.

Welty, Eudora. *The Eye of the Story*. New York, 1978.

West, Ray. *Katherine Anne Porter*. Minneapolis, 1963.

Westcott, Glenn. *Images of Truth*. New York, 1962.

Articles

Baker, H. 'The Upward Path: Notes on the Work of Katherine Anne Porter'. *Southern Review* 4 (1968), 1–19.

Baldeshwiler, Eileen. 'Structured Patterns in Porter's Fiction'. *South Dakota Review* 11 (1973), 45–53.

Cheatham, G. 'Death and Repetition in Porter's Miranda Stories'. *American Literature* 61 (1989), 610–24.

Erdem, E. 'The New Woman in Porter's Fiction'. In *Women and War*. Eds M. Dierrich et al. New York, 1990, 51–67.

Gross, Beverly. 'The Poetic Narrative: "Flowering Judas"'. *Style* 2 (1968), 129–39.

Hartley, Lodwick. 'Katherine Anne Porter'. *Southern Literary Journal* 6 (1974), 139–50.

Howell, Elmo. 'Katherine Anne Porter as a Southern Writer'. *South Carolina Review* 4 (1971), 5–15.

Jones, S.W. 'Reading the Endings in "Old Mortality"'. *Southern Quarterly* 31 (1993), 29–44.

Liberman, M.M. 'The Responsibility of the Novelist: The Critical Reception of *Ship of Fools*'. *Criticism* 8 (1966), 377–88.

Pierce, Marvin. 'Point of View: Katherine Anne Porter's "Noon Wine"'. *Ohio University Review* 3 (1961), 95–113.

Walsh, T.F. 'The Making of *Flowering Judas*'. *Journal of Modern Literature* 12 (1985), 109–30.

Warren, Robert Penn. 'Porter (Irony with a Center)'. *Kenyon Review* 4 (1942), 29–42.

Welty, Eudora. 'My Introduction to Porter'. *Georgia Review* 44 (1990), 13–27.

Young, Vernon A. 'The Art of Katherine Anne Porter'. *New Mexico Quarterly* 15 (1945), 326–41.

Bibliography and reference

Hilt, K. and Alvarez, R.H. *Katherine Anne Porter: An Annotated Bibliography*. New York, London, 1990.

Kiernan, Robert. *Porter and Carson McCullers: A Reference Guide*. Boston, 1976.

Waldrip, Louise and Bauer, S.A., eds. *A Bibliography of the Works of Katherine Anne Porter*. Metuchen, N.J., 1969.

Katharine Susannah Prichard

Books

Beasley, J. *The Rage for Life: The Work of Katharine Susannah Prichard*. Sydney, 1964.

Drake-Brockman, H. *Katharine Susannah Prichard*. Melbourne, 1967.

Ferrier, C., ed. *Gender, Politics, and Fiction*. St Lucia, Queensland, 1985.

Grieve, N. and Grimshaw, P., eds. *Australian Women*. Melbourne, 1981.

Hay, J. and Walker, B., eds. *Prichard Centenary Essays*. Nedlands, 1984.

Modjeska, D. *Exiles at Home*. London and Sydney, 1981.

Overland. Special issue on Prichard 12 (1959).

Throssel, Ric. *Wild Weeds and Wind Flowers: The Life and Letters of Katharine Susannah Prichard*. Sydney, 1975.

Walker, Shirley, ed. *Who Is She?*. New York, 1983.

Articles

Brady, Veronica. 'Prichard and the Tyranny of History'. *Westerly* 26 (1981), 65–71.

Burchill, Sandra. 'The Early Years of K.S. Prichard: The Growth of her Political Consciousness'. *Westerly* 33 (1988), 89–100.

Eldershaw, M. Barnard. 'Two Women Novelists: H.H. Richardson and K.S. Prichard'. In *The Literature of Australia*. Ed. G. Dutton. Harmondsworth, 1964, 1–41.

Heseltine, H.P. 'A Historical Evaluation of K.S. Prichard'. *Hecate* 4 (1978).

Hewett, Dorothy. 'Excess of Love: The Irreconcilable in K.S. Prichard'. *Overland* 43 (1969).

Holburn, Muir. '[Prichard]'. *Meanjin* 10 (1951).

Hope, A.D. 'The Great Australian Mirage: K.S. Prichard'. In *Native Comparisons*. Sydney, 1974.

Lindsay, Jack. '[The Novels of Prichard]'. *Meanjin* 20 (1961), 366–87.

Malos, Ellen. 'J. Lindsay's Essay on K.S. Prichard'. *Meanjin* 22 (1963).

Malos, Ellen. 'Some Major Themes in Prichard's Novels'. *Australian Literary Studies* 1 (1963), 32–41.

Modjeska, Dorothy. 'Introduction'. In *Coonardoo*. By Katharine Susannah Prichard. Sydney, 1990.

Nile, R. 'The Making of a Really Modern Witch'. *Working Papers in Australian Studies* 56 (1990).

Palmer, Aileen. 'Notes on the Creative Writing of Katharine Susannah Prichard'. *Overland* 12 (1959), 29–33, and see 12 (1958), 25–31.

Sadleir, Richard. 'Prichard: A Critical Evaluation'. *Westerly* 3 (1961), 31–5.

Sutherland, Jane. '[Women in the Novels of K.S. Prichard]'. *Hecate* 4 (1978).

Thomas, Sue. 'Interracial Encounters in Prichard's *Coonardoo*'. *World Literature Written in English* 27 (1987), 234–44.

Throssel, Ric. 'Introduction'. In *Intimate Strangers*. By Katharine Susannah Prichard. Sydney, 1990.

Throssel, Ric. 'K.S. Prichard: A Reluctant Daughter of Mark Twain'. *Antipodes* (1989), 89–93.

Wilkes, G.A. 'The Novels of Prichard'. *Southerly* 14 (1953), 220–31.

Bibliography and reference
Anderson, Hugh. 'K.S. Prichard: A Checklist'. *Biblionews* 12 (1959).

Barbara Pym

Books
Ackley, K.A. *The Novels of Barbara Pym*. New York, 1989.

Barbara Pym Newsletter 1986– .

Benet, Diana. *Something to Love: Barbara Pym's Novels*. Columbia, Mo., 1986.

Burkhart, Charles. *The Pleasure of Miss Pym*. Austin, Tex., 1987.

Cooley, Mason. *The Comic Art of Barbara Pym*. New York, 1990.

Cotsell, Michael. *Barbara Pym*. New York, 1989.

Holt, Hazel. *A Lot to Ask: A Life of Barbara Pym*. Basingstoke, 1990.

Liddell, Robert. *Mind at Ease: Barbara Pym and Her Novels*. London, 1989.

Long, R.E. *Barbara Pym*. New York, 1986.

Rossen, Janice. *The World of Barbara Pym*. New York, 1987.

Rossen, Janice, ed. *Independent Women: The Function of Gender in the Novels of Barbara Pym*. New York, 1988.

Salwak, Dale, ed. *The Life and Work of Barbara Pym*. Iowa City, 1987.

Wyatt-Brown, A.M. *Barbara Pym: A Critical Biography*. Columbia, Mo., 1992.

Articles
Doan, L.L. 'Pym's Singular Interest: The Self as Spinster'. In *Old Maids to Radical Spinsters*. Ed. L.L. Doan. Urbana, Ill., 1991, 139–54.

Keener, F.M. 'Barbara Pym Herself and Jane Austen'. *Twentieth Century Literature* 31 (1985), 89–110.

Larkin, Philip. 'The World of Barbara Pym'. *Times Literary Supplement* 11 (1977), 260.

Saar, D.A. 'Irony in the Early Novels of Pym'. *West Virginia University Philological Papers* 33 (1987), 68–75.

Thomas, Francis-Noël. 'Barbara Pym'. In *Post-War Literatures*. Eds H. Bertens et al. Houten and Groningen, 1992.

Bibliography and reference
Myers, M.H. 'A Supplement to a Further List of Secondary Sources'. *Bulletin of Bibliography* 49 (1992), 81–2 (and see previous years).

Ann Quin

Books
Gordon, Giles, ed. *Beyond the Words: Eleven Writers in Search of a New Fiction*. London, 1975.

Sewell, Brocard. *Like Black Swans. Some People and Themes*. Padstow, 1982.

White, John J. *Mythology in the Modern Novel: A Study of Prefigurative Techniques*. Princeton, N.J., 1971.

Articles
Mackrell, Judith. 'Ann Quin'. *Dictionary of Literary Biography* 14 (1983), 608–14.

Stevick, Philip. 'Voices in the Head: Style and Consciousness in the Fiction of Ann Quin'. In *Breaking the Sequence*. Eds E.G. Friedman and M. Fuchs. Princeton, N.J., 1989, 231–9.

Jean Rhys

Books
Angier, Carole. *Jean Rhys*. London, 1990.

Davidson, A.E. *Jean Rhys*. New York, 1985.

Emery, M.L. *Jean Rhys at 'World's End'*. Austin, Tex., 1990.

Frickey, P.M. *Critical Perspectives on Jean Rhys*. Washington, D.C., 1990.

Gardiner, Judith. *Rhys, Stead, Lessing, and the Politics of Empathy*. Bloomington, Ind., 1989.

Gregg, Marie. *Jean Rhys' Historical Imagination*. Chapel Hill, N.C., 1995.

Harrison, N.R. *Jean Rhys and the Novel as Women's Text*. Chapel Hill, N.C., 1988.

Hemmerechts, K. *A Structural Analysis of Rhys' Novels*. New York, 1987.

Hite, Molly. *The Other Side of the Story*. Ithaca, N.Y., 1989.

Howells, C.A. *Jean Rhys*. Hemel Hempstead, 1991.

James, Louis. *Jean Rhys*. London, 1978.

Jean Rhys Review 1988– .

Kloepfer, D.K. *The Unspeakable Mother: Forbidden Discourse in Rhys and H.D.* Ithaca, N.Y., 1989.

Le Gallez, Paula. *The Rhys Woman*. Basingstoke, 1990.

Nebeker, Helen. *Jean Rhys: Woman in Passage*. Montreal, 1981.

O'Connor, Teresa F. *Jean Rhys. The West Indian Fictions*. New York and London, 1986.

Review of Contemporary Fiction. Special issue 5 (1985).

Staley, Thomas. *Jean Rhys: A Critical Study*. Austin, Tex., 1979.

Wolfe, Peter. *Jean Rhys*. Boston, 1980.

Articles

Abel, Elizabeth. 'Women and Schizophrenia: The Fiction of Jean Rhys'. *Contemporary Literature* 20 (1979), 155–77.

Alvarez, A. 'The Best Living English Novelist'. *New York Times Book Review* (17 March 1974), 6–7.

Bender, T.K. 'Jean Rhys and the Genius of Impressions'. In *The Female Novelist in Twentieth-Century Britain*. Ed. J.I. Biles. Athens, Ga., 1978, 43–54.

Curtis, Jan. 'Rhys' *Voyage in the Dark*: A Reassessment'. *Journal of Commonwealth Literature* 22 (1987), 144–58.

Draine, Betsy. 'Chronotype and Intertext: The Case of *Quartet*'. In *Influence and Intertextuality*. Eds J. Clayton and E. Rothstein. Madison, Wis., 1991, 318–37.

Friedman, E.G. 'Breaking the Master Narrative: Jean Rhys' *Wide Sargasso Sea*'. In *Breaking the Sequence*. Eds E.G. Friedman and M. Fuchs. Princeton, N.J., 1989, 117–28.

Mellown, Elgin W. 'Characters and Themes in the Novels of Jean Rhys'. *Contemporary Women Novelists*. Ed. P.M. Spacks. Englewood Cliffs, N.J., 1977, 118–36.

Roe, Sue. '"The Shadow of Light": The Symbolic Underworld of Jean Rhys'. *Women Reading Women's Writing*. Ed. S. Roe. Brighton, 1987, 229–64.

Staley, Thomas. 'The Emergence of a Form: Style and Consciousness in Jean Rhys' *Quartet*'. *Twentieth Century Literature* 24 (1978), 203–24.

Webb, Ruth. '*Wide Sargasso Sea*: The Manuscripts'. *British Library Journal* 14 (1988), 165–77.

West, Rebecca. 'Jean Rhys'. *Sunday Times* 5626 (8 February 1931), 10.

Wheeler, Kathleen M. 'Style as Characterization in Jean Rhys' Novels'. In *'Modernist' Women Writers and Narrative Art*. Basingstoke, 1994, 99–120.

Wyndham, Francis. 'Introduction to Jean Rhys'. *London Magazine* 7 (1960), 115–18.

Wyndham, Francis. 'Introduction'. In *Wide Sargasso Sea*. By Jean Rhys. London, 1966.

Bibliography and reference

Mellown, Elgin W. *Jean Rhys: A Descriptive and Annotated Bibliography of Works and Criticism*. New York and London, 1984.

Dorothy Richardson

Books

Blake, C.R. *Dorothy M. Richardson*. Ann Arbor, Mich., 1960.

Bronfen, E. *Der literarische Raum*. Niemeyer, 1986.

Edel, Leon. *The Modern Psychological Novel 1900–1950*. New York, 1955.

Fromm, Gloria G. *Dorothy Richardson: A Biography*. Urbana, Ill., 1977.

Gregory, Horace. *Dorothy Richardson: An Adventure in Self-Discovery*. New York, 1967.

Hanscombe, Gillian E. *The Art of Life: Dorothy Richardson and the Development of Feminine Consciousness*. London, 1982; Athens, Ohio, 1983.

Hanscombe, G.E. and Smyers, V. *Writing for their Lives: The Modernist Women 1910–1940*. London, 1987.

Humphrey, Robert. *Stream of Consciousness in the Modern Novel*. Berkeley, Calif., 1965.

Kaplan, S.J. *Feminine Consciousness in the Modern British Novel*. Urbana, Ill., 1975.

Labovitz, Esther. *The Myth of the Heroine*. New York, 1986.

Miles, Rosalind. *The Female Form: Women Writers and the Conquest of the Novel*. London and New York, 1987.

Monteith, Moira, ed. *Women's Writing: A Challenge to Theory*. Brighton, 1986.

Nischik, R.M. et al., eds. *Modes of Narrative*. Würzburg, 1990.

Powys, John Cooper. *Dorothy M. Richardson*. London, 1931.

Radford, Jean. *Dorothy Richardson*. London and Bloomington, 1991.

Rado, Lisa, ed. *Rereading Modernism*. New York, 1994.

Rosenberg, John. *Dorothy Richardson: The Genius they Forgot: A Critical Biography*. New York, 1973.

Stanley, Thomas F. *Dorothy Richardson*. Boston, 1976.

Articles

Ellman, Mary. 'Dorothy Richardson's Pilgrimage'. *New Republic* 157 (1967).

Fernihough, Anne. 'Dorothy Richardson'. In *Dictionary of British Women Writers*. Ed. J. Todd. London, 1989, 563–6.

Friedman, E.G. 'Utterly Other Discourse: The Anticanon of Experimental Women Writers from Dorothy Richardson to Christine Brooke-Rose'. *Modern Fiction Studies* 34 (1988), 353–70.

Fromm, Gloria. 'Richardson & Co.'. *Library Chronicle of the University of Texas* 23 (1993), 50–69.

Fulbrook, Kate. 'Dorothy Richardson, et al.: Varieties of Modernism'. In *Free Women*. Hemel Hempstead, 1990, 113–40.

Glikin, Gloria. 'The Personal Pilgrimage'. *PMLA* 78 (1963), 586–600.

Hanscombe, Gillian. 'Dorothy Richardson versus the Novvle'. In *Breaking the Sequence: Women's Experimental Fiction*. Eds E.G. Friedman and M. Fuchs. Princeton, N.J., 1989.

Heath, Stephen. 'Writing for Silence: Richardson and the Novel'. In *Teaching the Text*. Eds S. Kappeler and N. Bryson. London, 1983.

Kemp, Sandra. 'Feminism, Fiction, and Modernism'. *Critical Quarterly* 32 (1990), 99–118.

Maisel, E.M. 'Dorothy M. Richardson's *Pilgrimage*'. *Canadian Forum* 19 (1939), 89–92.

Podmeks, Elizabeth. 'Richardson's *Pilgrimage*'. *Frontiers* 14 (1994), 67–94.

Rose, Shirley. 'The Unmoving Centre: Consciousness in Richardson's *Pilgrimage*'. *Contemporary Literature* 10 (1969), 366–82.

Schuyler, Sarah. 'Double-Dealing Fictions'. *Genders* 9 (1990), 75–92.

Sinclair, May. 'The Novels of Dorothy Richardson'. *Egoist* (1918), 57–9.

Sinclair, May. 'The Novels of Dorothy Richardson'. *Little Review* 4 (1918), 3–11.

Würzbach, N. 'Dorothy Richardson's *Pilgrimage*: Constructivist Narrative'. In *Modes of Narrative*. Eds R.M. Nischik et al. Würzburg, 1990.

Bibliography and reference

Glikin, Gloria. 'Checklist of Writings by Dorothy M. Richardson'. *English Literature in Transition* 8 (1965), 1–11.

Henry Handel Richardson

Books

Buckley, Vincent. *Henry Handel Richardson*. Melbourne, 1961.

Clarke, Axel. *Henry Handel Richardson: Fiction in the Making*. New York and London, 1990.

Elliott, William D. *Henry Handel Richardson*. Boston, 1975.

Green, Dorothy. *Ulysses Bound: Richardson and her Fiction*. Canberra, 1973.

Kramer, Leonie. *A Companion to 'Australia Felix'*. Melbourne, 1962.

Kramer, Leonie. *Henry Handel Richardson*. Melbourne, 1967.

Kramer (Gibson), Leonie. *Richardson and Some of Her Sources*. Melbourne, 1954.

McLeod, Karen. *Henry Handel Richardson. A Critical Study*. Cambridge, 1985.

Nichols, J.R. *Art and Irony: The Tragic Vision of Henry Handel Richardson*. Washington, D.C., 1982.

Palmer, Nettie. *Henry Handel Richardson: A Study*. Sydney and London, 1950.

Purdie, E. and O.M. Roncoroni, eds. *Henry Handel Richardson: Some Personal Impressions*. Sydney, 1957.

Singh, Kirpal, ed. *The Writer's Sense of the Past*. Singapore, 1987.

Zwicky, Fay. *The Lyre in the Pawnshop. Essays on Literature and Survival 1974–1984*. Nedlands, Western Australia, 1986.

Articles

Arkin, Marian. 'A Reading Strategy for Richardson's Fiction'. *World Literature Written in English* 30 (1990), 120–30.

Bird, Delys. 'Woman-as-Artist/Woman-as-Mother'. *Australian and New Zealand Studies in Canada* 7 (1992), 10–19.

Butcher, Margaret K. 'From *Maurice Guest* to *Martha Quest*: The Female *Bildungsroman* in Commonwealth Literature'. *World Literature Written in English* 22 (1982).

Dyson, Mandy. 'Form and the Feminine in *The Getting of Wisdom*'. *LING* 20 (1993), 83–8.

Franklin, Carol. '"Germany" in the Work of Four Antipodean Women Writers'. *Kunapipi* 12 (1990), 56–69.

Franklin, Carol. 'H.H. Richardson's "Two Hanged Women"'. *Kunapipi* 14 (1992), 41–52.

Green, Dorothy. 'The Tradition of Social Responsibility in the Australian Novel: Richardson and Murphy'. *Literary Criticism* 15 (1980).
Pratt, Catherine. 'Gender and Narrative in *Mahony*'. *Australian Literary Studies* 16 (1993), 152–60.

Bibliography and reference
Howells, Gay. *Henry Handel Richardson 1870–1946: A Bibliography*. Canberra, 1970.

Michèle Roberts

Books
Duncker, Patricia. *Sisters and Strangers*. Oxford, 1992.
Palmer, Paulina. *Contemporary Women's Fiction*. Hemel Hempstead, 1989.

Articles
Duncker, Patricia. 'Writing and Roaring: In Search of the Truly Political Feminist Novel'. *Trouble and Strife* 6 (1985).
Roberts, Michèle. 'Questions and Answers'. In *On Gender and Writing*. Ed. M. Wandor. London, 1983, 62–8.
Roberts, Michèle. 'Write, She Said'. In *The Progress of Romance. The Politics of Popular Fiction*. Ed. J. Radford. London and New York, 1986.

Joanna Russ

Books
Albinski, N.M. *Women's Utopias in British and American Fiction*. London, 1988.
Armitt, Lucie, ed. *Where No Man Has Gone Before: Women and Science Fiction*. London and New York, 1991.
Barr, M. *Future Females*. Bowling Green, Ohio, 1981.
Barr, M. and Smith, N.D., eds. *Women and Utopia*. Lanham, Md., 1983.
King, Betty. *Women of the Future: The Female Main Character in Science Fiction*. Metuchen, N.J., and London, 1984.
Lefanu, S., ed. *In the Chinks of the World*. London, 1988.
Moyland, Tom. *Demand the Impossible: Science Fiction and the Utopian Imagination*. London, 1986.
Munt, Sally, ed. *New Lesbian Criticism*. New York, 1992.
Palumbo, D., ed. *Erotic Universe*. New York, 1986.
Rosinskyu, N.M. *Feminist Futures: Contemporary Women's Speculative Fiction*. Ann Arbor, Mich., 1984.
Shinn, Thelma. *Worlds Within Women: Myth in*

Fantastic Literature by Women. Westport, Conn., 1986.
Weedman, J.B., ed. *Women Worldwalkers: New Dimensions of Science Fiction and Fantasy*. Lubbock, Tex., 1985.
Wolfe, S.J. et al., eds. *Sexual Practice, Textual Theory*. Cambridge, Mass., 1993.

Articles
Byrne, Deirdre. 'The Postmodernization of Gender: Russ's *Extraordinary People*'. *UNISA English Studies* 30 (1992), 47–52.
Gardiner, J.K. 'Empathic Ways of Reading'. *Feminist Studies* 20 (1994), 84–111.
Garland, Barbara. 'Joanna Russ'. *Dictionary of Literary Biography* 8 (1981), 88–93.
Montgomerie, Les. Reviews of Various Novels. In *Interzone* 25 (1988).
Murphy, P.D. 'Russ's Who We Are About to . . .'. In *State of the Fantastic*. Ed. N. Ruddick, Westport, Conn., 1992.
Rosinsky, N.M. 'A Female Man? The Medusan Humour of Russ'. *Extrapolation* 23 (1982), 31–6.
Spector, Judith. 'The Functions of Sexuality in the Science Fiction of Russ, Piercy, and Le Guin'. In *Erotic Universe: Sexuality and Fantastic Literature*. Ed. D. Palumbo. Westport, Conn., 1986, 197–207.
Spencer, K.L. 'The Fiction of Russ'. *Science Fiction Studies* 17 (1990), 167–86.

Bibliography and reference
A bibliography can be found in *Facts on File*.

Olive Schreiner

Books
Beeton, Ridley. *Facets of Olive Schreiner*. Craighall, 1987.
Berkman, Joyce. *Olive Schreiner; Feminism on the Frontier*. St Albans, 1979.
Berkman, Joyce. *The Healing Imagination of Olive Schreiner*. Amherst, Mass., 1989.
Buchanan-Gould, Vera. *Not Without Honour: The Life and Writings of Olive Schreiner*. London, 1948.
Clayton, Cherry, ed. *Olive Schreiner*. Johannesburg, 1983.
Colby, V. *The Singular Anomaly: Women Novelists of the Nineteenth Century*. New York and London, 1970.
Cronwright-Schreiner, S.C. *The Life of Olive Schreiner*. London, 1924.
First, Ruth and Scott, Ann. *Olive Schreiner*. London, 1980.

Friedlander, Zelda. *Until the Heart Changes: A Garland for Olive Schreiner*. Cape Town, 1967.

Harmel, Michael. *Olive Schreiner*. Cape Town, 1955.

Hobman, D.L., *Olive Schreiner; Her Friends and Times*. London, 1915.

Horton, S.R. *Difficult Women, Artful Lives: Olive Schreiner and Isak Dinesen*. Baltimore and London, 1995.

Meintjes, Johannes. *Olive Schreiner*. Johannesburg, 1965.

Monsman, Gerald. *Olive Schreiner's Fiction*. New Brunswick, N.J., 1991.

Schoeman, Karel. *Olive Schreiner: A Woman in South Africa*. Johannesburg, 1991.

Showalter, Elaine. *A Literature of Their Own: British Women Novelists from Brontë to Lessing*. London, 1982.

Ward, David. *Chronicles of Darkness*. London, 1989.

Articles

Barsby, C. 'Schreiner: Towards a Redefinition of Culture'. *Pretexts* 1 (1989), 18–39.

Chrisman, L. 'Allegory, Feminist Thought, and the *Dreams*'. *Prose Studies* 13 (1990), 126–50.

Clayton, C. 'Women Writers and the Law of the Father'. *English Academy Review* 7 (1990), 99–117.

Holloway, Myles. 'Thematic and Structural Organization in *The Story of an African Farm*'. *English in Africa* 15 (1989), 77–89.

Jacobson, Dan. 'Introduction'. In *The Story of an African Farm*. By Olive Schreiner. Harmondsworth, 1979.

Lefew, P.A. 'Schopenhauerian Pessimism in *The Story*'. *English Literature in Transition* 37 (1994), 303–16.

Lessing, Doris. 'Introduction'. In *The Story of an African Farm*. By Olive Schreiner. London, 1987.

Monsman, Gerald. 'Patterns of Narration and Characterization in Schreiner's *The Story of an African Farm*'. *English Literature in Transition* 30 (1987), 253–70.

Monsman, Gerald. 'Schreiner's Allegorical Vision'. *Victorian Review* 18 (1992), 49–62.

Bibliography and reference

Beeton, Ridley. *Schreiner: A Short Guide to her Writings*. Cape Town, 1974.

Davis, Roslyn. *Olive Schreiner 1920–1971: A Bibliography*. 1972.

Leslie Marmon Silko

Books

Allen, P.G., ed. *Studies in American Indian Literature*. New York, 1983.

American Indian Quarterly. Special issue 5 (1979).

D'Haen, T. and Barfoot, C., eds. *Shades of Empire: Studies in Colonial and Post Colonial Literatures*. Amsterdam and Atlanta, Ga., 1993.

Halperin, Daniel, ed. *Antaeus on Nature*. London, 1989.

Larson, C.A. *American Indian Fiction*. Albuquerque, N.Mex., 1978.

Lincoln, Kenneth. *Native American Renaissance*. Berkeley, Calif., 1983.

Mogen, D., Busby, M. and Bryant, P., eds. *The Frontier Experience and the American Dream*. College Station, Tex., 1990.

Murray, David. *Forked Tongue: Speech, Writing, and Representation in North American Indian Texts*. London, 1991.

Nischik, R.M. and Korte, B., eds. *Modes of Narrative*. Würzburg, 1990.

Seyersted, Per. *Leslie Marmon Silko*. Boise, Idaho, 1980.

Sollers, Werner, ed. *The Invention of Ethnicity*. New York, 1989.

Velie, A.R. *Four American Indian Literary Masters: Momaday, Welch, Silko, and Vizenor*. Norman, Okla., 1982.

Vizenor, Gerald, ed. *Narrative Chance: Postmodern Discourse on Native American Indian Literatures*. Albuquerque, N.Mex., 1989.

Articles

Bell, R.C. 'Circular Design in *Ceremony*'. *American Indian Quarterly* 5 (1979), 47–62.

Benediktsson, T.E. 'The Reawakening of the Gods: Realism and the Supernatural in Silko and Hulme'. *Critique* 33 (1992), 121–31.

Blicksilver, Edith. 'Traditionalism versus Modernity: Silko on American Indian Women'. *Southwest Review* 64 (1979), 149–60.

Blumenthal, Susan. '*Ceremony*'. *American Indian Quarterly* 14 (1990), 367–77.

Castillo, S.P. 'Postmodernism, Native American Literature, and the Real: The Silko–Erdrich Controversy'. *Massachusetts Review* 32 (1991), 285–94.

Castillo, S.P. 'The Construction of Gender and Ethnicity in the Texts of L.M. Silko and L. Erdrich'. *Yearbook of English Studies*. Ed. A. Gurr. London, 1994, 228–36.

Coltelli, Laura. 'Interview'. In *Winged Words: American Indian Writers Speak*. Lincoln, Nebr., 1990, 135–53.

Danielson, Linda. '*Storyteller*: Grandmother's Spider Web'. *Journal of the Southwest* 30 (1988), 325–55.

Dasenbrock, R.W. 'Forms of Biculturalism in Southwestern Literature'. *Genre* 21 (1988), 307–19.

Evasdaughter, E.N. 'Silko's *Ceremony:* Healing Ethnic Hatred'. *MELUS* 15 (1988), 83–95.

Freese, Peter. 'Silko's *Ceremony'*. *Amerikastudien* 37 (1992), 613–45.

Hirsch, B.A. 'The Telling which Continues: Oral Tradition and the Written Word in Silko's *Storyteller'*. *American Indian Quarterly* 12 (1988), 1–26.

Hoilman Dennis. '"A World Made of Stories": An Interpretation of Silko's *Ceremony'*. *South Dakota Review* 17 (1979), 54–66.

Jahner, Elaine. 'An Act of Attention: Event Structure in *Ceremony'*. *American Indian Quarterly* 5 (1979), 37–46.

Jahner, Elaine. 'Interview'. *Book Forum* 5 (1981), 383–8.

Lorentz, P.H. 'The Other Story of Silko's *Storyteller'*. *South Central Review* 8 (1991), 59–75.

McFarland, R.E. 'Silko's Story of Stories'. *Journal of Contemporary Literature* 4 (1979).

Nelson, R.M. 'Place and Vision: The Function of Landscape in *Ceremony'*. *Journal of the Southwest* 30 (1988), 281–316.

Ruoff, A.L. 'Ritual and Renewal in Silko'. *MELUS* 5 (1979), 2–17.

Rupert, James. 'Story Telling: The Fiction of Silko'. *Journal of Ethnic Studies* 9 (1981).

Rupert, James. 'The Reader's Lessons in *Ceremony'*. *American Quarterly* 44 (1988), 78–85.

Seyersted, Per. 'Interview'. *American Studies in Scandinavia* 13 (1981), 17–33.

Slowick, Mary. 'Henry James, Meet Spider Woman: A Study of Narrative Form in Silko's *Ceremony'*. *North Dakota Quarterly* 57 (1989), 104–20.

Swan, Edith. 'Healing via the Sunrise Cycle in Silko's *Ceremony'*. *American Indian Quarterly* 12 (1988), 313–28.

Swan Edith. 'Laguna Symbolic Geography and Silko's *Ceremony'*. *American Indian Quarterly* 12 (1988), 229–49.

Bibliography and reference

Colonnese, T. and Owens, L. 'Leslie Marmon Silko'. In *American Indian Novelists: An Annotated Critical Bibliography*. New York and London, 1985, 80–99.

May Sinclair

Books

Boll, Theophilus E.M. *Miss May Sinclair: Novelist*. Rutherford, N.J., 1973.

Brewster, D. and Burrell, A. *Dead Reckoning in Fiction*. New York, 1924.

Bullett, Gerald. *Modern English Fiction*. London, 1926.

Chevalley, Abel. *The Modern English Novel.* Trans. B.R. Redman. New York, 1930.

Hanscombe, Gillian and Smyers, Virginia L. *Writing for their Lives: The Modernist Women 1910–1940*. London, 1987.

Johnson, R. Brimley. *Some Contemporary Novelists (Women)*. London, 1920.

Kaplan, Sidney Janet. *Feminine Consciousness in the Modern British Novel*. Urbana, Ill., 1975.

Myers, Walter L. *The Later Realism*. Chicago, 1927.

Stevenson, Lionel. *The History of the English Novel.* Vol. 11: *Yesterday and Today*. New York, 1967.

Zegger, H.D. *May Sinclair*. Boston, 1976.

Articles

Gillespie, Diane F. 'May Sinclair and the Stream of Consciousness'. *English Literature in Transition* 21 (1978).

Harris, J.H. 'Three Marriage Novels by Sinclair'. *Papers in Language and Literature* 29 (1993), 436–58.

Kemp, Sandra. 'Feminism, Fiction, and Modernism'. *Critical Quarterly* 32 (1990), 99–118.

Mumford, L.M. 'May Sinclair'. In *Arms and the Woman*. Eds H.M. Cooper et al. Chapel Hill, 1989, 168–83.

Neff, R.K. 'May Sinclair's Uncanny Stories'. *English Literature in Transition* 26 (1983), 187–91.

Neff, R.K. '"New Mysticism" in the Writings of May Sinclair and T.S. Eliot'. *Twentieth Century Literature* 26 (1979).

Stark, S. 'Overcoming Butlerian Obstacles: May Sinclair'. *Women's Studies* 21 (1992), 265–83.

Bibliography and reference

Boll, T.E.M. 'On the May Sinclair Collection'. *The University of Pennsylvania Chronicle* 27 (1961).

Boll, T.E.M. 'May Sinclair: A Checklist'. *Bulletin of the New York Public Library* 74 (1970), 459–67.

Robb, K. 'An Annotated Bibliography of Writing About May Sinclair'. *English Literature in Transition* 16 (1973), 177–231.

Taylor, C.Y. 'A Study of May Sinclair – Woman and Writer, 1863–1946 – with an Annotated Bibliography'. Ph.D., Washington State University, 1969.

Elizabeth Smart

Books

Barker, George. *The Dead Seagull*. New York, 1950.

Burridge, Christine, ed. *Autobiographies*. Vancouver, 1987.

Sage, Lorna. *Women in the House of Fiction*. Basingstoke, 1992.

Sullivan, Rosemary. *By Heart: Elizabeth Smart: A Life*. London, 1991.

Articles

Goddard, John. 'An Appetite for Life'. *Books in Canada* 11 (1982), 8.

Horne, Dee. 'Smart's Novel-Journal'. *Studies in Canadian Literature* 16 (1991), 128–46.

Lobdell, David. 'Eros in the Age of Anxiety: Elizabeth Smart and Louise Maheux-Forcier'. *Essays in Canadian Writing* 40 (1990), 57–79.

Oliver, M.B. 'Elizabeth Smart: Recognition'. *Essays on Canadian Writing* 12 (1978), 106–33.

Sullivan, Rosemary. 'Romantic Obsession'. *Island* 56 (1993), 9–15.

Van Wart, Alice. *'By Grand Central Station I Sat Down and Wept:* The Novel as a Poem'. *Studies in Canadian Literature* 11 (1986), 38–51.

Van Wart, Alice. 'Elizabeth Smart: A Reconsideration'. *Brick: A Journal of Reviews* 33 (1988) 51.

Van Wart, Alice. 'Life out of Art: Smart's Early Journals'. In *Essays on Life Writing*. Ed. M. Kadar. Toronto, 1992, 21–7.

Pauline Smith

Books

Clayton, Cherry, ed. *Women and Writing in South Africa*. Marshalltown, 1989.

Coetzee, J.M. *White Writing: On the Culture of Letters in South Africa*. New Haven, 1988.

Driver, Dorothy, ed. *Pauline Smith*. Johannesburg, 1983.

Haresnape, G. *Pauline Smith*. New York, 1969.

Articles

Clayton, C. 'Women Writers and the Law of the Father'. *English Academy Review* 7 (1990), 99–117.

Cosser, M. 'Free Indirect Discourse in Pauline Smith's "The Pain"'. *English in Africa* 19 (1992), 85–100.

Driver, Dorothy. 'Pauline Smith: A Gentler Music of Her Own'. *Research in African Literature* 15 (1984), 45–71.

Eglington, Charles. '"Quaintness" in Pauline Smith'. *English Studies in Africa* 3 (1960), 48–56.

Gardiner, Michael. 'Critical Responses and Smith'. *Theoria* 60 (1983), 1–12.

Haresnape, Geoffrey. 'Pauline Smith and the Place of her Inspiration'. *English Studies in Africa* 6 (1963), 70–6.

Hooper, M. 'The Renunciation of Vice in *The Schoolmaster'. English Studies in Africa* 34 (1991), 21–6.

Periera, Ernest. 'Pauline Smith: A Centenary Tribute'. *English Academy Review* (November 1982), 12–17.

Ravenscroft, Arthur. 'Pauline Smith'. *Review of English Literature* 4 (1963), 55–67.

Roberts, Sheila. 'A Confined World: A Rereading of Pauline Smith'. *World Literature Written in English* 24 (1984), 232–8.

Sarvan, C.P. 'Pauline Smith: A Gentle Rebel'. *World Literature Written in English* 24 (1984).

Scheub, Harold. 'Smith and the Oral Tradition'. *English in Africa* 8 (1981), 1–11.

Smith, Pauline. 'Why and How I Became an Author'. *English Studies in Africa* 6 (1963), 149–53.

Stopforth, L.M.D. 'Short Stories of Pauline Smith: A Critical Survey'. *University College of the Western Cape Annals* 4 (1967), 1–37.

Stevie Smith

Books

Barbera, Jack, and McBrien, William. *A Biography of Stevie Smith*. London and New York, 1986.

Kay, Dick, ed. *Ivy and Stevie*. (Interviews). London, 1971.

Montefiore, Jan. *Feminism and Poetry*. London, 1987.

Orr, Peter, ed. *The Poet Speaks* (Interview). London, 1966.

Severin, Laura. *Stevie Smith's Resistant Poetics*. Madison, Wis., 1997.

Spalding, Frances. *Stevie Smith: A Critical Biography*. London, 1988.

Sternlicht, Sanford. *Stevie Smith*. Boston, 1990.

Sternlicht, Sanford. *In Search of Stevie Smith*. Syracuse, 1991.

Wheeler, K.M. *'Modernist' Women Writers and Narrative Art*. Basingstoke, 1994.

Articles

Bedient, Calvin. 'Stevie Smith'. In *Eight Contemporary Poets*. London, 1974.

Enright, D.J. 'Did Nobody Teach You?'. *Encounter* (1971), 53–7.

Holmes, Liz. 'Stevie Smith: An Appreciation'. In *Still the Frame Holds*. Eds S. Roberts et al. San Bernadino, Calif., 1993, 59–68.

Lassner, Phyllis. 'Storm Jameson, Smith, and the Fate of Europe's Jews'. In *Visions of War*. Ed. M.A. Schofield. Bowling Green, Ohio, 1992, 181–90.

Lawson, Elizabeth. 'Stevie Smith and Metaphors of Disengagement'. *Sydney Studies in English* 9 (1983–4), 94–106.

Nemesvari, Richard. 'Language and Fictional Form in *Novel on Yellow Paper'. Dalhousie Review* 71 (1991), 26–37.

Severin, Laura. 'Recovering the Serious Antics of Stevie Smith's Novels'. *Twentieth Century Literature* 40 (1994), 461–76.

Stevenson, Sheryl. 'Stevie Smith's Voices'. *Contemporary Literature* 33 (1992), 24–45.

Storey, Mark. 'Why Stevie Smith Matters'. *Critical Quarterly* 21 (1979), 31–40.

Upton, Lee. 'Stevie Smith and the Anxiety of Intimacy'. *CEA Critic* 53 (1991), 22–31.

Watts, Janet. 'Introduction'. In *The Holiday*. By Stevie Smith. London, 1979.

Watts, Janet. 'Introduction'. In *Novel on Yellow Paper*. By Stevie Smith. London, 1980.

Watts, Janet. 'Introduction'. In *Over the Frontier*. By Stevie Smith. London, 1980.

Bibliography and reference

Barbera, Jack et al. *Stevie Smith: A Bibliography*. Westport, Conn., 1987.

Susan Sontag

Books

Bruss, Elizabeth. *Beautiful Theories: The Spectacle of Discourse in Contemporary Criticism*. Baltimore, 1982.

Pestino, J.F. 'The Reader/Writer Affair'. Ph.D., Pennsylvania State University, 1986.

Sayres, Sohnya. *Susan Sontag: The Elegiac Modernist*. New York and London, 1990.

Showalter, Elaine, ed. *Modern American Women Writers*. New York, 1991.

Articles

Bawer, Bruce. 'That Sontag Woman'. *New Criterion* 11 (1992), 30–7.

Behar, Jack. 'Against the Self'. *Hudson Review* 19 (1966), 347–52.

Bellamy, J.D. 'Susan Sontag'. In *The New Fiction*. Chicago, 1974, 113–29.

Boyers, Robert. 'On Susan Sontag and the New Sensibility'. *Salmagundi* 1 (1966), 27–32.

Boyers, Robert. Interview: 'Women, the Arts, and the Politics of Culture'. *Salmagundi* 31–2 (1975), 29–48.

Branham, R.J. 'Speaking Itself: Sontag's Town Hall Address'. *Quarterly Journal of Speech* 75 (1989), 259–76.

Brooke-Rose, Christine. 'Eximplosions'. *Genre* 14 (1981), 9–21.

Brouwers, Ton. 'Susan Sontag'. In *Post-War Literatures*. Eds H. Bertens et al. Houten and Groningen, 1994.

Cott, Jonathan. 'Susan Sontag: The Rolling Stone Interview'. *Rolling Stone* (4 October 1979), 46–53.

Esonwanne, Uzoma. 'Feminist Theory and Discussion of Colonialism'. In *Reimagining Women*. Ed. S. Newman. Toronto, 1993, 233–55.

Frank, Marcie. 'Sontag's Writing and Gay Cultures'. In *Camp Grounds*. Ed. D. Bergman. Amherst, Mass., 1993, 173–84.

Houston, Gary. 'Susan Sontag'. *Michigan Quarterly Review* 9 (1970), 272–5.

Jeffords, Susan. 'Susan Sontag'. *Dictionary of Literary Biography* 67 (1988), 268–75.

Kavolis, Vytautas. 'The Social Psychology of Avant-Garde Cultures'. *Studies in the Twentieth Century* 6 (1970), 13–34.

Kennedy, Liam. 'Precocious Archaeology: Susan Sontag'. *Journal of American Studies* 24 (1990) 23–39.

Louvre, Alf. 'The Reluctant Historians'. *Prose Studies* 9 (1986), 47–61.

Marx, Leo. 'Susan Sontag's "New Left Pastoralism"'. *Triquarterly* 23–4 (1972), 552–75 (republished in *Essays on Literature, Technology, and Culture in the United States*. New York, 1988).

Miller, D.A. 'Susan Sontag's Urbanity'. *October* 49 (1989), 91–101.

Munk, Erika. 'Interview'. *Theatre* 24 (1993), 31–6.

Nelson, Cary. 'Soliciting Self-Knowledge: The Rhetoric of Susan Sontag'. *Critical Inquiry* 6 (198), 707–26.

Phillips, William. 'Radical Styles'. *Partisan Review* 36 (1969), 388–400.

Ross, Andrew. 'Uses of Camp'. *Yale Review* 2 (1988), 1–24.

Roudiez, L.S. 'Sontag: Against the Ideological Grain'. *World Literature Today* 57 (1983), 219–23.

Rubin, L.D. 'Susan Sontag and the Camp Followers'. *Sewanee Review* 82 (1974), 503–10.

Sayres, Sohnya. 'Sontag and the Practice of Modernism'. *American Literary History* 1 (1989), 593–611.

Tanner, Tony. 'Space Odyssey'. *Partisan Review* 35 (1968), 446–51.

Taylor, Benjamin. 'A Centered Voice: Susan Sontag's Short Fiction'. *Georgia Review* 34 (1980), 907–16.

Wiseman, Susan. 'Femininity and the Intellectual in Sontag and Cixous'. In *The Body and The Text*. Eds H. Wilcox et al. New York and Hemel Hempstead, 1990.

Muriel Spark

Books

Bold, Alan. *Muriel Spark: An Odd Capacity for Vision*. London and Totowa, N.J., 1984.

Bold, Alan. *Muriel Spark*. London and New York, 1986.

Bradbury, M. and Perkins, D., eds. *The Contemporary English Novel*. London, 1979.

Dipple, Elizabeth. *The Unresolvable Plot: Reading Contemporary Fiction.* London, 1988.

Doan, L.L., ed. *Old Maids to Radical Spinsters.* Urbana, Ill., 1991.

Edgecombe, R.A. *Vocation and Identity in Muriel Spark.* Columbia, Mo., 1990.

Fokkema, D.W., ed. *Approaching Postmodernism.* Amsterdam, 1986.

Hynes, Joseph. *The Art of the Real: Muriel Spark's Novels.* Teaneck, N.J., London, and Toronto, 1988.

Kermode, Frank. *Modern Essays.* London, 1971.

Little, Judy. *Faith, Comedy, and the Woman Writer: Woolf, Spark, and Feminism.* Lincoln, Nebr., 1983.

Lodge, David. *The Novelist at the Crossroads and Other Essays on Fiction and Criticism.* London, 1971.

Malkoff, Karl. *Muriel Spark.* New York and London, 1968.

Massie, Allan. *Muriel Spark.* Edinburgh, 1979.

Page, Norman. *Muriel Spark.* Basingstoke, 1990.

Randisi, J.L. *On Her Way Rejoicing: The Fiction of Muriel Spark.* Washington, D.C., 1991.

Richmond, V.B. *Muriel Spark.* New York, 1985.

Sproxton, Judy. *The Women of Muriel Spark.* London, 1992.

Stubbs, Patricia. *Muriel Spark.* Harlow, 1973.

Wallace, G. and Stevenson, R., eds. *The Scottish Novel since the Seventies.* Edinburgh, 1993.

Whittaker, Ruth. *The Faith and Fiction of Muriel Spark.* London, 1982.

Articles

Black, Elizabeth. 'The Nature of Fictional Discourse: A Case Study'. *Applied Linguistics* 10 (1989), 281–93.

Bower, A.L. 'The Narrative Structure of Spark's *The Prime of Miss Jean Brodie*'. *Midwest Quarterly* 31 (1990), 488–98.

Devoize, J. and Vallette, P. 'Interview'. *Journal of the Short Story in English* 13 (1989), 11–22.

Glavin, John. 'Spark's "Unknowing" Fiction'. *Women's Studies* 15 (1988), 221–41.

Hynes, Joseph. 'Spark and the Oxymoronic Vision'. In *British Women Writers: Narrative Strategies.* Ed. R.E. Hosmer. New York, 1993, 161–87.

Kimball, S.L. 'International Garble: Irony in the Communication of Spark'. *West Virginia University Philological Papers* 33 (1987), 86–91.

Leonard, John. 'Spark's Parabolic Technique'. *Studies in the Literary Imagination* 18 (1985), 65–77.

Little, Judy. 'Spark's Grammers of Assent'. In *The British and Irish Novel Since 1960.* Ed. J. Acheson. New York, 1991, 1–16.

Manning, G.F. 'Sunsets and Sunrises: Nursing

Home as Microcosm in *Memento Mori* and *Mr Scobie's Riddle*'. *Ariel E* 18 (1987), 27–43.

Parrinder, Patrick. 'Spark and her Critics'. *Critical Quarterly* 25 (1983), 23–31.

Rankin, Ian. 'Surface and Structure: *The Driver's Seat*'. *Journal of Narrative Technique* 15 (1985), 146–55.

Richmond, V.B. 'Chaucer's Religiosity and Muriel Spark'. *Modern Language Quarterly* 51 (1990), 427–45.

Robb, D.S. 'Spark's *Prime of Miss Jean Brodie*'. *Scotnotes* 7 (1992), 1–57.

Rowe, M.M. 'Muriel Spark and the Angel of the Body'. *Critique* 28 (1987), 167–76.

Schiff, Steven. 'Muriel Spark Between the Lines'. *New Yorker* (24 May 1993), 36–43.

Stevenson, Sherly. '"Poetry Deleted", Parody Added'. *Ariel* 24 (1993), 71–85.

Todd, Richard. 'The Crystalline Novels of Muriel Spark'. In *Essays on the Contemporary British Novel.* Eds H. Bock and A. Wertherim. Munich, 1993, 175–92.

Elizabeth Spencer

Books

Inge, Tonette B., ed. *Southern Women Writers: The New Generation.* Tuscaloosa, Ala., 1990.

Prenshaw, P.W., ed. *Conversations with Elizabeth Spencer.* Jackson, Miss., 1991.

Roberts, T.L. 'Ties that Bind: The Fiction of Elizabeth Spencer'. Ph.D., University of North Carolina, 1991.

Articles

Anderson, Hilton. 'Elizabeth Spencer's Two Italian Novellas'. *Notes on Mississippi Writers* 13 (1981), 18–35.

Anderson, Hilton. 'Elizabeth Spencer's Portraits of New Orleans'. *Xavier Review* 8 (1988), 47–52.

Broadwell, E.P. and Hoag, R.W. 'Conversation'. *Southern Review* 18 (1982), 111–30.

Bunting, C.T. 'In That Time and at That Place: The Literary World of Elizabeth Spencer'. *Mississippi Quarterly* 28 (1975), 435–60.

Burger, N.K. 'Elizabeth Spencer's Three Mississippi Novels'. *South Atlantic Quarterly* 63 (1964), 351–62.

Cole, H.M. 'Elizabeth Spencer at Sycamore Fair'. *Notes on Mississippi Writers* 7 (1974), 81–6.

Cole, H.M. 'Windsor in Spencer and Welty: A Real and an Imaginary Landscape'. *Notes on Mississippi Writers* 7 (1974), 2–11.

Evoy, Karen. 'Marilee: A Permanent Landscape of the Heart'. *Mississippi Quarterly* 36 (1983), 569–73.

Haley, Josephine. 'An Interview with Elizabeth Spencer'. *Notes on Mississippi Writers* 1 (1968), 42–53.

Poore, C. A Review of *Ship Island*. *New York Times* (26 December 1968).

Prenshaw, P.W. 'Elizabeth Spencer' *Dictionary of Literary Biography* 6 (1980), 320–7.

Prenshaw, P.W. 'The Heroines of Elizabeth Spencer's Fiction'. *Southern Quarterly* 22 (1983), 13–31.

Pugh, D.G. 'The Voice at the Back Door: Elizabeth Spencer Looks into Mississippi'. In *The Fifties: Fiction, Poetry, and Drama*. Ed. W.C. French. Deland, Fla., 1970, 291–304.

Roberts, Terry. 'This Crooked Narrow Way'. *Mississippi Quarterly* 46 (1992–3), 61–75.

Winchell, M.R. 'The Achievement of Elizabeth Spencer'. *Sewanee Review* 97 (1989), 580–6.

Bibliography and reference

Barge, Laura. 'An Elizabeth Spencer Checklist, 1948–76'. *Mississippi Quarterly* 29 (1976), 569–90.

Lewis, C.E. 'An Elizabeth Spencer Checklist'. *Mississippi Quarterly* 47 (1994), 241–62.

Jean Stafford

Books

Ackley, K.A. ed. *Women and Violence in Literature*. New York, 1990.

Auchincloss, Louis. *Pioneers and Caretakers: A Study of Nine American Women Novelists*. Minneapolis, 1961.

Goodman, C.M. *Jean Stafford: The Savage Heart*. Austin, Tex., 1990.

Hulbert, Ann. *The Art and Life of Jean Stafford*. Amherst, Mass., 1992.

Roberts, David. *Jean Stafford: A Biography*. London, 1988.

Stauffer, H.W., ed. *Women and Western American Literature*. Troy, N.Y., 1982.

Articles

Bawer, Bruce. 'Stafford's Triumph'. *New Criterion* 7 (1988), 61–77.

Burns, S.L. 'Counterpoint in Jean Stafford's *The Mountain Lion*'. *Critique* 9 (1967), 2–32.

Greiner, C.F. 'Stafford's Traveling through the Dark: A Discussion of Style'. *English Journal* (1966), 1015–18, 1048.

Hassan, I.H. 'Jean Stafford: No Expense of Style and the Scope of Sensibility'. *Western Review* 19 (1955), 185–203.

Leary, William. 'Jean Stafford: The Wound and the Bow'. *Sewanee Review* 98 (1990), 333–49.

Ryan, Maureen. 'Stafford and the New Journalism' *Kenyon Review* 16 (1994), 104–19.

Vickery, O.W. 'Jean Stafford and the Ironic Vision'. *South Atlantic Quarterly* 61 (1962), 484–91.

Vickery, O.W. 'The Novels of Jean Stafford'. *Critique* 5 (1962), 14–26.

White, Barbara. 'Stafford's *The Mountain Lion*'. *Essays in Literature* 9 (1982), 194–210.

Bibliography and reference

Avila, Wanda. *Stafford: A Comprehensive Bibliography*. New York, 1983.

Christina Stead

Books

Brydon, Diane. *Christina Stead*. Basingstoke, 1987.

Clancy, Laurie. *Christina Stead's 'The Man Who Loved Children' and 'For Love Alone'*. Melbourne, 1981.

Eldershaw, M. Barnard. *Essays in Australian Fiction*. Melbourne, 1938.

Gardiner, J.K. *Rhys, Stead, Lessing, and the Politics of Empathy*. Bloomington, Ind., 1989.

Geering, R.G. *Christina Stead*. Melbourne and New York, 1969.

Lidoff, J. *Christina Stead*. New York, 1983.

Rowley, Hazel. *Christina Stead: A Biography*. Port Melbourne, Victoria, 1993.

Sage, Lorna. *Women in the House of Fiction. Post-War Women Novelists*. Basingstoke, 1992.

Sheridan, Susan. *Christina Stead*. Hemel Hempstead, 1988.

Southerly. Special issue on Stead 23 (1962).

Southerly. Special issue on Stead 38 (1978).

Southerly. Special issue on Stead 44 (1984).

Southerly. Special issue on Stead 53 (1993).

Williams, Chris. *A Life of Letters*. London, 1989.

World Literature Written in English. Special issue on Stead 32 (1992).

Articles

Calisher, Hortense. 'Stead'. *Yale Review* 76 (1987), 169–77.

Carter, Angela. 'Unhappy Families'. *London Review of Books* (16 September–6 October 1982), 11–13.

Draine, Betsy. 'Ever "Unread": *The Man Who Loved Children*'. *Contemporary Literature* 31 (1990), 470–541.

Kiernan, Suzanne. '"Ugly by Design": The Fiction of Stead'. *Modern Fiction Studies* 34 (1988), 185–202.

Muncaster, Tina. 'The Pleasures of Text and Table: *I'm Dying Laughing*'. *Southerly* 53 (1993), 106–15.

Richlin, Amy. 'The Artist as Classicist in Stead and Others'. *Tulsa Studies in Women's Literature* 11 (1992), 265–87.

Rowley, Hazel. '"Dramatic Truth" and "Process Verbal" in *The Man Who Loved Children*'. *Contemporary Literature* 31 (1990), 499–511.

Tracy, Lorna. 'The Virtue of the Story: *The Salzburg Tales*'. *Stand* 23 (1982), 48–53.

West, Rebecca. 'Christina Stead: A Tribute'. *Stand* 23 (1982), 31–3.

Yelin, Louise. 'A Reception Study of *The Man Who Loved Children*' *Contemporary Literature* 31 (1990), 472–98.

Yelin, Louise. 'Stead's *For Love Alone* and the Writing of Exile'. *Yale French Studies* (1993), 183–203.

Bibliography and reference

Ehrhardt, Marianne. 'Christina Stead: A Checklist'. *Australian Literary Studies* 9 (1980), 508–35.

Gertrude Stein

Books

Benstock, Shari. *Women of the Left Bank. Paris, 1900–1940*. Austin, Tex. 1986.

Berry, E.E. *Curved Thought and Textual Wandering: Stein's Postmodernism*. Ann Arbor, 1992.

Bridgeman, Richard. *Gertrude Stein in Pieces*. New York and Oxford, 1970.

Brinnin, J.M. *The Third Rose: Gertrude Stein and her World*. Boston, 1959.

Broe, M.L. and Ingram, A., eds. *Women's Writing in Exile*. Chapel Hill, 1989.

Bush, Clive. *Halfway to Revolution: Investigation and Crisis in the Work of Henry Adams, William James and Gertrude Stein*. New Haven, 1991.

De Koven, Marianne. *A Different Language: Gertrude Stein's Experimental Writings*. Madison, 1983.

Delta English Studies. Special issue 10 (1980).

Fifer, Elizabeth. *Rescued Readings: A Reconstruction of Stein's Difficult Texts*. Detroit, 1992.

Hobhouse, Janet. *Everybody Who Was Anybody: A Biography of Gertrude Stein*. New York, 1975.

Hoffman, M.J. *The Development of Abstractionism in the Writings of Gertrude Stein*. Philadelphia, 1965.

Hoffman, M.J. *Gertrude Stein*. New York, 1976.

Hoffman, M.J., ed. *Critical Essays on Gertrude Stein*. Boston, 1986.

Jump, H.D., ed. *Diverse Voices: Essays on Twentieth Century Women Writers in English*. Hemel Hempstead, 1991.

Kellner, Bruce, ed. *A Gertrude Stein Companion*. New York, 1988.

Lost Generation Journal. Special issue 2 (1974).

Mellow, J.R. *Charmed Circle: Gertrude Stein and Company*. New York, 1975.

Neuman, S. and Nadel, I.B., eds. *Gertrude Stein and the Making of Literature*. London, 1988.

Perelman, Bob. *The Trouble with Genius: Reading Pound, Joyce, Stein, and Zukofsky*. Berkeley, Calif., 1994.

Rogers, W.G. *When This You See, Remember Me: Gertrude Stein in Person*. New York, 1948.

Ruddick, Lisa. *Reading Gertrude Stein. Body, Text, Gnosis*. Ithaca, N.Y., 1990.

Schmitz, Neil. *Of Huck and Alice: Humorous Writings in American Literature*. Minneapolis, 1983.

Simon, Linda. *The Biography of Alice B. Toklas*. Garden City, N.J., 1977.

Souhami, Diana. *Gertrude and Alice*. London, 1991.

Toklas, Alice B. *What is Remembered*. New York, 1963.

Twentieth Century Literature. Special issue 24 (1978).

Walker, J.L. *The Making of a Modernist: Gertrude Stein from 'Three Lives' to 'Tender Buttons'*. Amherst, Mass., 1984.

Articles

Antin, David. 'Some Questions about Modernism'. *Occident* 8 (1974), 7–38.

Bloom, Lynn Z. 'Gertrude is Alice is Everybody: Innovation and Point of View in Stein's Autobiographies'. *Twentieth Century Literature* 24 (1978), 81–93.

Dydo, Ulla E. 'Must Horses Drink; or "Any Language is Funny if You Don't Understand It"'. *Tulsa Studies in Women's Literature* 4 (1985), 272–80.

Gotjohn, Robert. 'Stein and the Prose Long Poem'. *Genre* 24 (1991), 173–89.

Gubar, Susan. 'Blessings in Disguise: Cross Dressing as Re-Dressing for Female Modernists'. *Massachusetts Review* 22 (1981), 477–508.

Johnston, Gloria. 'Reading Anna Backwards'. *Studies in the Literary Imagination* 25 (1992), 31–7.

Murphy, M.S. '*Tender Buttons*'. *Contemporary Literature* 32 (1991), 383–402.

Nevola, Helene. '"Double Negation": Stein and Kristeva'. *Antithesis* 5 (1992), 111–21.

Porter, Katherine Anne. 'Gertrude Stein: A Self-Portrait'. In *Collected Essays and Occasional Writings of Katherine Anne Porter*. New York, 1973.

Stimpson, C.R. 'The Mind, the Body, and Gertrude Stein'. *Critical Inquiry* 3 (1977), 491–506.

Stimpson, C.R. 'Are the Differences Spreading? Feminist Criticism and Postmodernism'. *English Studies in Canada* 14 (1989), 364–82.

Van Dyke, Carolynne. 'Bits of Information and Tender Feeling'. *Texas Studies in Language and Literature* 35 (1993), 168–97.

Wilson, Edmund. 'Gertrude Stein Old and Young'. In *The Shores of Light: A Literary Chronicle of the Twenties and Thirties*. New York, 1952.

Bibliography and reference
White, R.L. *Gertrude Stein and Alice B. Toklas: A Reference Guide*. Boston, 1984.
Wilson, R.A. *Gertrude Stein: A Bibliography*. New York, 1974.

Amy Tan

Books
Asian Women United of California, eds. *Making Waves: An Anthology of Writings by and about Asian American Women*. Boston, 1989.
Clarke, Graham, ed. *The New American Writing: Essays on American Literature Since 1970*. London, 1990.
Lee, A.R., ed. *A Permanent Etcetera: Cross Cultural Perspectives on Post-War America*. London, 1993.
Lim, S.G. et al., eds. *The Forbidden Stitch: An Asian American Women's Anthology*. Corvallis, Oreg. 1989.
Lim, S.G. and Ling, A., eds. *Reading the Literatures of Asian America*. Philadelphia, 1992.
Ling, Amy. *Between Worlds: Women Writers of Chinese Ancestry*. New York, 1990.
Minh-ha, T.T. *Women, Native, Other*. Bloomington, Ind., 1989.
Pearlman, M. and Henderson, K.U., eds. *Inter/Views*. Lexington, Ky., 1990.
Wong, S.C. *Reading Asian-American Literature*. Princeton, N.J., 1993.

Articles
Boters, Babs. 'Amy Tan'. In *Post-War Literatures*. Eds H. Bertens et al. Houten and Groningen, 1994.
Heung, Maria. 'Daughter-Text/Mother-Text: Matrilineage in Tan's *Joy Luck Club*'. *Feminist Studies* 19 (1993), 597–616.
Kepner, Susan. 'Imagine This: The Amazing Adventure of Amy Tan'. *San Francisco Focus* (May 1989), 58–60 and 160–2.
Lee, A.R. 'Eat a Bowl of Tea: Asian America'. *Yearbook of English Studies* 24 (1994), 263–80.
Lim, S.G. 'Assaying the Gold: Or, Contesting the Ground of Asian American Literature'. *New Literary History* 24 (1993), 147–69.
Lowe, Lisa. 'Heterogeneity, Hybridity, Multiplicity: Marking Asian-American Differences'. *Diaspora* 1 (1991), 24–44.
Schueller, M.J. 'Theorizing Ethnicity and Subjectivity'. *Genders* 15 (1992), 72–85.
Shear, Walter. 'Generation Differences and the Diaspora in *The Joy Luck Club*'. *Critique* 34 (1993), 193–9.
Tan, Amy. 'The Language of Discretion'. In *The State of the Language*. Eds C. Ricks and L. Michaels. Berkeley, Calif., 1990, 25–32.

Bibliography and reference
Cheung, King K. and Yogi, Stan, eds. *Asian American Literature: An Annotated Bibliography*. New York, 1988.

Emma Tennant

Books
Alexander, Flora. *Contemporary Women Novelists*. London, 1989.
Haffenden, John. *Novelists in Interview*. London, 1985.
Kenyon, Olga. *Women Writers Talk*. Oxford, 1989.
Malzahn, M. *Aspects of Identity*. Frankfurt, 1984.
Palmer, Paulina. *Contemporary Women's Fiction*. Hemel Hempstead, 1989.

Articles
Anderson, Carol. 'Listening to Women Talk'. In *The Scottish Novel since the Seventies: New Visions*. Eds Gavin Wallace and R. Stevenson. Edinburgh, 1993.
Babinec, L.S. 'Emma Tennant'. In *Post-War Literatures*. Eds H. Bertens et al. Houten and Groningen, 1992.
Hughes, G.H. '*The Confessions of a Justified Sinner* and *The Bad Sister*'. *Newsletter of the James Hogg Society* 1 (1982), 14–16.
'Indiana, Gary'. 'Novel 2: Emma Tennant's Higher Powers'. *Village Voice Literary Supplement* 95 (1991), 14–16.
Lambert, G.L. 'Emma Tennant'. *Dictionary of Literary Biography* 14 (1983), 708–15.

Kylie Tennant

Books
Blaber, Ronald and Gilman, Marion. *Roguery: The Picaresque Tradition in Australian, Canadian and Indian Fiction*. Springwood, New South Wales, 1990.
Dick, Margaret. *The Novels of Kylie Tennant*. Adelaide, 1966.
Dutton, Geoffrey. *The Literature of Australia*. Harmondsworth, 1976.

Articles
Auchterlonie, D. '[The Novels of Kylie Tennant]'. *Meanjin* 12 (1953).
Clancy, Laurie. 'Fathers and Lovers'. *Australia Literary Studies* 10 (1982), 459–67.

Goldsworthy, Kerryn. 'Introduction'. In *Ride on Stranger*. By Kylie Tennant. Sydney, 1990.

Jones, Dorothy. '[Kylie Tennant]'. *World Literature Written in English* 24 (1984).

Matthews, Brian. 'Orwell, Tennant, and Others'. *Westerly* 26 (1981), 65–72.

Moore, T.I. 'Tragic-Comedies of Kylie Tennant'. *Southerly* 1 (1957).

Pearce, Sharyn. 'Changing Places: Working-Class Women in the Fiction of the Depression'. *Westerly* 31 (1986).

Pons, Xavier. '*The Battlers:* Kylie Tennant and the Australian Tradition'. *Australian Literary Studies* 6 (1974).

Salzman, Paul. 'Working the Self'. *Meanjin* 46 (1987), 513–24.

Rose Tremain

Articles

Bogels, Theo. 'Rose Tremain'. In *Post-War Literatures*. Eds H. Bertens et al. Houten and Groningen, 1994.

Edwards, Simon. 'Rose Tremain'. *Dictionary of Literary Biography* 14 (1983), 721–3.

Eyres, Harry. 'Interview'. *The Times* (25 September 1989).

Fitzgerald, Penelope. 'Time's Wounding Arrow'. *Times Literary Supplement* (4 September 1992).

Kermode, Frank. 'Wannabee'. *London Review of Books* (8 October 1992), 14.

Walsh, John. 'Interview'. *Sunday Times* (30 August 1992).

Anne Tyler

Books

Evans, Elizabeth. *Anne Tyler*. New York, 1993.

Gullette, M.M. *Safe At Last in the Middle Years: The Invention of the Midlife Progress Novel*. Berkeley, Calif., 1988.

Hornby, Nick. *Contemporary American Fiction*. London and New York, 1992.

Linton, Karin. *The Temporal Horizon: A Study of the Theme of Time in Anne Tyler's Major Novels*. Uppsala, 1989.

Nesanovich, Stella. 'The Individual and the Family: A Critical Introduction to the Novels of Anne Tyler'. Ph.D., Baton Rouge, La., 1979.

Petry, Alice Hall. *Understanding Anne Tyler*. Columbia, S.C., 1990.

Petry, Alice Hall, ed. *Critical Essays on Anne Tyler*. New York, 1992.

Southern Quarterly. Special issue 31 (1992).

Stephens, C.R., ed. *The Fiction of Anne Tyler*. Jackson, Miss., 1990.

Voelker, J.C. *Art and the Accidental in Anne Tyler*. London and Columbia, Mo., 1989.

Articles

Almond, B.R. 'The Accidental Therapist'. *Literature and Psychology* 38 (1992), 84–104.

Betts, Doris. 'The Fiction of Anne Tyler'. *Southern Quarterly* 12 (1983), 23–38.

Bowers, Bradley. 'Tyler's Insiders'. *Mississippi Quarterly* 42 (1988–9), 47–56.

Cunningham, Henry. 'An Accidental Tourist's Best Friend'. *Writing on Contemporary Literature* 23 (1993), 10–12.

Dvoak, A.G. 'Cooking as Mission and Ministry'. *Southern Quarterly* 30 (1992), 90–8.

Eckard, P.G. 'Family and Community in *Dinner at the Homesick Restaurant*'. *Southern Literary Journal* 22 (1980), 33–44.

Gibson, M.E. 'Family as Fate: The Novels of Anne Tyler'. *Southern Literary Journal* 15 (1983), 47–58.

Gilbert, Susan. 'Anne Tyler'. In *Southern Women Writers: The New Generation*. Ed. T.B. Inge. Tuscaloosa, Ala. 1990.

Jones, Anne. 'Home at Last and Homesick Again'. *Hollins Critic* 23 (1986), 1–14.

Lamb, Wendy. 'Interview'. *Iowa Journal of Literary Studies* 3 (1981), 59–64.

Petry, A.H. 'The Black Norm in Tyler's Novels'. *Southern Quarterly* 31 (1992), 7–13.

Robertson, M.F. 'Anne Tyler: Medusa Points and Contact Points'. In *Contemporary American Women Writers*. Eds C. Rainwater and W.J. Sheick. Lexington, Ky., 1985, 119–52.

Ross-Bryant, Lynn. 'Anne Tyler's *Searching for Caleb*'. *Soundings* 73 (1990), 191–207.

Shelton, F.W. 'The Necessary Balance: Distance and Sympathy in the Novels of Anne Tyler'. *Southern Review* 20 (1984), 851–60.

Verhoeven, Wil. 'Anne Tyler'. In *Post-War Literatures*. Eds H. Bertens et al. Houten and Groningen, 1990.

Willrich, P.R. 'Watching Through Windows: A Perspective on Anne Tyler'. *Virginia Quarterly* 68 (1992), 497–516.

Bibliography and reference

Gardiner, E. and Rainwater, C. 'A Bibliography'. In *Contemporary American Women Writers*. Eds C. Rainwater and W.J. Sheick. Lexington, Ky., 1985, 142–52.

Alice Walker

Books

Bloom, Harold, ed. *Alice Walker*. New York, 1989.

Brack, P. and Karrer, W., eds. *The Afro-American Novel since 1960*. Amsterdam, 1982.

SELECT BIBLIOGRAPHY

Braxton, J.M. and McLaughlin, A.N., eds. *Wild Women in the Whirlwind.* New Brunswick, N.J., and London, 1990.

Butler-Evans, E. *Race, Gender, and Desire.* Philadelphia, 1989.

Christian, Barbara. *Black Women Novelists.* Westport, Conn., and London, 1980.

Christian, Barbara. *Black Feminist Criticism.* New York, 1985.

Evans, Mari, ed. *Black Women Writers 1950–1980: A Critical Evaluation.* Garden City, N.Y., and London, 1984.

Gates, H.L. *The Signifying Monkey.* New York, 1988.

Goldsmith, E. *Writing the Female Voice: Essays on Epistolary Literature.* London, 1989.

Hernton, C.C. *The Sexual Mountain and Black Women Writers.* New York, 1987.

Russell, Sandi. *Render Me My Song.* London, 1990.

Strout, Cushing. *Making American Tradition: Visions and Revisions from Ben Franklin to Alice Walker.* New Brunswick, N.J., 1990.

Tate, Claudia, ed. *Black Women Writers at Work.* New York, 1983.

Walker, Melissa. *Down from the Mountaintop.* New Haven, 1991.

Weever, Jacqueline de. *Mythmaking and Metaphor in Black Women's Fiction.* Basingstoke, 1991.

Winchell, D.H. *Alice Walker.* New York, 1992.

Wisker, Gina, ed. *Black Women's Writing.* Basingstoke, 1993.

Articles

Abbandonato, Linda. 'Subversive Sexuality and the Rewriting of the Heroine's Story in *The Color Purple*'. *PMLA* 106 (1991), 1106–15.

Anderson, Jace. 'Rewriting Race: Subverting Language'. *A/B Auto/biography Studies* 8 (1993), 33–50.

Cheung, King-Kok. 'Don't Tell: Imposed Silences in *The Color Purple* and *The Woman Warrior*'. *PMLA* 102 (1988), 162–74.

Christophe, M.A. '*The Color Purple:* An Existential Novel'. *College Language Association Journal* 36 (1993), 280–90.

Digby, Joan. 'From Walker to Spielberg'. In *Novel Images.* Ed. P. Reynolds. London, 1993, 157–74.

Fifer, E. 'The Dialect and Letters of *The Color Purple*'. In *Contemporary American Women Writers.* Eds C. Rainwater and W.J. Sheick. Lexington, Ky., 1985, 165–88.

Hall, Christin. 'Art, Action, and Ancestors: *Meridian*'. In *Black Women Writers.* Ed. G. Wisker. New York, 1993, 96–110.

Hite, Molly. 'Two Modern Black Romances'. *Novel* 22 (1989), 257–73.

Jamison-Hall, A. 'She's Just too Womanish for

Them'. In *Censored Books: Critical Viewpoints.* Eds N.J. Karolides et al. Metuchen, N.J., 1993, 191–200.

Jones, S.W. 'Dismantling Stereotypes'. In *The Female Tradition in Southern Literature.* Urbana, Ill., 1993, 140–57.

Juncker, Clara. 'Black Magic: Woman(ist) as Artist in *The Temple of My Familiar*'. *American Studies in Scandinavia* 24 (1992), 37–49.

Lewis, T.W. 'Moral Mapping and Spiritual Guidance in *The Color Purple*'. *Soundings* 73 (1990), 483–91.

Light, Alison. 'The Fear of the Happy Ending: *The Color Purple*'. *Essays and Studies* 40 (1987), 103–17.

McDowell, Deborah. 'The Self in Bloom: Alice Walker's *Meridian*'. *College Language Association Journal* 24 (1981), 262–75.

Nadel, Alan. 'Reading the Body'. *Modern Fiction Studies* 34 (1988), 55–68.

Stein, K.F. '*Meridian*: Alice Walker's Critique of Revolution'. *Black American Literature Forum* 20 (1986), 129–41.

Tucker, Lindsey. 'Alice Walker's *The Color Purple*'. *Black American Literature Forum* 22 (1988), 81–95.

Wall, Wendy. 'Lettered Bodies and Corporeal Texts in *The Color Purple*'. *Studies in American Fiction* 16 (1988), 83–97.

Weisenburger, S.C. 'Errant Narrative and *The Color Purple*'. *Journal of Narrative Technique* 18 (1989), 257–75.

Bibliography and reference

Glikin, Ronda. 'Alice Walker' (a bibliography of primary and secondary literature). In *Black American Women in Literature 1976–87.* Jefferson, N.C., and London, 1989, 162–72.

Pratt, L.H. and D.D. *Alice Walker: An Annotated Bibliography 1968–86.* Westport, Conn., 1988.

Margaret Walker

Books

Braxton, J.M. and McLaughlin, A.N., eds. *Wild Women in the Whirlwind.* New Brunswick, N.J., and London, 1990.

Christian, Barbara. *Black Women Novelists: The Development of a Tradition 1892–1976.* Westport, Conn., and London, 1980.

Evans, Mari, ed. *Black Women Writers 1950–1980: A Critical Evaluation.* Garden City, N.Y., 1984.

Giovanni, Nikki and Walker, Margaret. *A Poetic Equation Conversation between Giovanni and Walker.* Washington, D.C., 1974.

Gwin, M.C. *Black and White Women of the Old South.* Knoxville, Tenn., 1985.

Hannighausen, L. et al., eds. *Rewriting the South.* Tübingen, 1993.

Jones, J.G., ed. *Mississippi Writers Talking II.* 2 vols. Jackson, Miss., 1986.

Pryse, M. and Spillers, H.J., eds. *Conjuring.* Bloomington, Ind., 1985.

Tate, Claudia, ed. *Black Women Writers at Work.* New York, 1983; Harpenden, 1985.

Walker, Alice. *In Search of Our Mothers' Gardens.* New York, 1983.

Walker, Margaret. *How I Wrote 'Jubilee'.* New York, 1990.

Willis, Susan. *Specifying: Black Women Writing the American Experience.* Madison, 1986.

Articles

Baraki, Amiri. 'Interview'. In *The Black Nation.* Oakland, Calif., 1982.

Bonnetti, Kay. 'Interview'. *Missouri Review* 15 (1992), 112–31.

Collier, Eugenia. 'Fields Watered with Blood: Myth and Ritual in the Poetry of Margaret Walker'. In *Black Women Writers: Arguments and Interviews.* Ed. Mari Evans. London, 1983, 499–510.

Graham, Maryerra. 'Interview'. *African American Review* 27 (1993), 279–86.

McDowell, Margaret. 'The Black Woman as Artist and Critic'. *Kentucky Review* 7 (1987), 19–41.

Miller, R.B. 'The "Etched Flame" of Walker'. *Tennessee Studies in Literature* 26 (1981), 157–72.

Pettis, Joyce. 'Walker: Black Women Writers of the South'. In *Southern Women Writers: The New Generation.* Ed. T.B. Inge. Tuscaloosa, Ala. 1990, 9–19.

Spears, J.E. 'Black Folk Element in *Jubilee'. Mississippi Folklore Register* 14 (1980), 13–19.

Traylor, Eleanor. 'Music Theme: The Blues Mode in the Works of Margaret Walker'. In *Black Women Writers 1950–1980: A Critical Evaluation.* Ed. M. Evans. Garden City, N.Y., 1984, 511–25.

Traylor, Eleanor. 'Walker's Poem of the Century'. *Callaloo* 10 (1987), 570–95.

Sylvia Townsend Warner

Books

Ackland, V. *For Sylvia: An Honest Account.* New York and London, 1985.

Atkins, John. *Six Novelists Look at Society.* London, 1977.

Bristow, Joseph, ed. *Sexual Sameness: Textual Differences in Lesbian and Gay Writing.* London, 1992.

Harman, C. *Sylvia Townsend Warner: A Biography.* London, 1989.

Kime, Bonnie, ed. *The Gender of Modernism.* Bloomington, Ind., 1990.

Mulford, W. *This Narrow Place: Sylvia Townsend Warner and Valentine Ackland: Life, Letters, and Politics 1930–51.* London, 1988.

Squier, S., ed. *Women Writers and the City.* Knoxville, Tenn., 1984.

Articles

Baldwin, Dean. 'The Stories of Warner'. *Crazyhorse* 31 (1986), 71–80.

Brothers, Barbara. 'Warner and the Spanish Civil War'. In *Women Writers in Exile.* Eds M. Broe and A. Ingram. Chapel Hill, N.C., 1989, 349–68.

Brothers, Barbara. '*Lolly Willowes* as Female "Bildungsroman"'. In *Old Maids to Radical Spinsters.* Ed. Laura Doan. Champaign, Ill., 1991, 195–212.

Caserio, R.L. 'Celibate Sisters-in-Revolution: Towards Reading S.T. Warner'. In *Engendering Men.* Eds J.A. Boone and M. Cadden. New York and London, 1990, 254–74.

Castle, Terry. 'Warner and the Counterplot of Lesbian Fiction'. *Textual Practice* 4 (1990), 213–35.

Davidson, Peter. 'Sylvia Townsend Warner'. In *Post-War Literatures.* Eds H. Bertens et al. Houten and Groningen, 1988– .

Harman, Clare. 'Introduction'. In *Summer Will Show.* By Sylvia Townsend Warner. London, 1987.

Joyce, Elizabeth. 'Sylvia Townsend Warner'. In *Dictionary of British Women Writers.* Ed. J. Todd. London, 1989, 692–5.

Mitchell, J.L. 'In Another Country. Sylvia Townsend Warner at Large'. In *Writers of the Old School.* Eds R.M. Colt and J. Rossen. Basingstoke, 1992.

Montefiore, Janet. 'Listening to Minna: Feminism and the Politics of Reading'. *Paragraph* 14 (1991), 197–216.

Morgan, Louise. 'Interview'. In *Writers at Work.* London, 1931, 27–35.

Fay Weldon

Books

Alexander, Flora. *Contemporary Women Novelists.* London, 1989.

Kenyon, Olga. *Women Novelists Today. A Survey of English Writing in the Seventies and Eighties.* Brighton, 1988.

Palmer, Paulina. *Contemporary Women's Fiction.* Hemel Hempstead, 1989.

Sage, Lorna. *Women in the House of Fiction.* Basingstoke, 1992.

Wandor, Michelene, ed. *On Gender and Writing*. London, 1983.

Zeman, Anthea. *Presumptuous Girls: Women and Their World in the Serious Woman's Novel*. London, 1977.

Articles

Anderson, Carol. 'Fay Weldon'. In *Post-War Literatures*. Eds H. Bertens et al. Houten and Groningen, 1989.

Blodgett, H. 'Fay Weldon'. *Dictionary of Literary Biography* 14 (1982), 750–9.

Brookner, Anita. 'The Return of the Earth Mother'. *Times Literary Supplement* (22 February 1980), 202.

Ford, Betsy. 'Belladonna Speaks'. *West Virginia University Philological Papers* 38 (1992), 322–33.

Griffin, Gabriele. 'Fay Weldon'. In *Dictionary of British Women Writers*. Ed. J. Todd. London, 1989, 704–5.

Herbert, A.M. 'Rewriting the Feminine Script'. *Critical Matrix* 7 (1993), 21–40.

Krouse, A.N. 'Feminism and Art in Fay Weldon's Novels'. *Critique* 20 (1978), 5–20.

Smith, P.J. 'Weldon's *The Life and Loves of a She-Devil*'. *Explicator* 51 (1993), 255–7.

Wilde, Alan. 'Weldon and the Limits of Poststructuralist Criticism'. *Contemporary Literature* 29 (1988), 403–19.

Eudora Welty

Books

Appel, A., Jr. *Season of Dreams: The Fiction of Eudora Welty*. Baton Rouge, La., 1965.

Binding, Paul. *Separate Country*. Jackson, Miss., 1988.

Bryant, J.A., Jr. *Eudora Welty*. Minneapolis, 1968.

Delta Review. Special issue on Welty 14 (1977).

Carson, B.H. *Eudora Welty*. Troy, N.Y., 1992.

Desmond, John, ed. *A Still Moment: Essays on the Art of Eudora Welty*. Metuchen, N.J., and London, 1978.

Dollarhide, L. and Abadie, A.J. *Eudora Welty: A Form of Thanks*. Jackson, Miss., 1979.

Eudora Welty Newsletter 1977– .

Evans, Elizabeth. *Eudora Welty*. New York, 1981.

Gray, Richard. *The Literature of Memory*. Baltimore, 1977.

Gray, Richard. *Writing the South*. Cambridge, 1986.

Kreyling, Michael. *Eudora Welty's Achievement of Order*. Baton Rouge, La., 1980.

Prenshaw, P.W., ed. *Eudora Welty: Critical Essays*. Jackson, Miss., 1979.

Prenshaw, P.W., ed. *Conversations with Eudora Welty*. Jackson, Miss., 1984.

Romines, Ann. *The Home Plot*. Amherst, Mass., 1992.

Rubin, L.R., Jr. *Writers of the Modern South*. Seattle, 1963.

Schmidt, Peter. *The Heart of the Story. Eudora Welty's Short Fiction*. Jackson, Miss., 1991.

Southern Literary Journal. Special issue 26 (1993).

Southern Quarterly. Special issue 32 (1993).

Trowand, Dawn, ed. *Eudora Welty*. Kent, Ohio, 1990.

Vande Kieft, R.M. *Eudora Welty*. Boston, 1962.

Westling, Louise. *Eudora Welty*. Basingstoke, 1989.

Articles

These do not include articles in the *Eudora Welty Newsletter*.

Bass, E.E. 'The Languages of *Losing Battles*'. *Studies in American Fiction* 21 (1993), 67–82.

Carson, B.H. 'Eudora Welty's Dance with Darkness'. *Southern Literary Journal* 20 (1988), 51–68.

Glenn, S.M. 'In and Out of the Circle: The Individual and the Clan in Welty's *Delta Wedding*'. *Southern Literary Journal* 22 (1989), 50–60.

Marrs, Suzanne. 'Memory and Imagination in Delta Wedding'. *Southern Literary Journal* 25 (1993), 79–91.

Mortimer, Gail L. 'Image and Myth in Eudora Welty's *The Optimist's Daughter*'. *American Literature* 62 (1990), 617–33.

Orr, Elaine. 'Welty's "A Worn Path"'. *South Atlantic Review* 57 (1992), 57–72.

Pepperdene, M.W. '"When Our Separate Journeys Converge": Notes on *The Optimist's Daughter*'. *Mississippi Quarterly* 41 (1989), 147–60.

Peterman, G.D. '*A Curtain of Green*: Welty's Suspicious Beginning'. *Mississippi Quarterly* 46 (1992–3), 91–114.

Pollack, Harriet. 'On Welty's Use of Allusion'. *Southern Quarterly* 29 (1990), 5–31.

Walker, Ellen and Seaman, Gerda. '*The Robber Bridegroom* as Capitalist Fable'. *Southern Quarterly* 26 (1988), 57–68.

Walter, James. 'Place Dissolved in Grace'. *Southern Literary Journal* 20 (1989), 35–53.

Woolf, Sarah. 'Interview with Eudora Welty'. *Southern Review* 26 (1990), 81–8.

Bibliography and reference

McHaney, P.A. 'A Checklist of Welty Scholarships, 1992–3'. *Eudora Welty Newsletter* 17 (1993), 10–15.

Polk, Noel. *Welty: A Bibliography of the Work*. Jackson, Miss., 1994.

Swearingen, Bethany. *Eudora Welty: A Critical Bibliography*. Jackson, Miss., 1984.

Jessamyn West

Books

Farmer, Ann. D. *Jessamyn West,* Boise, Idaho, 1982, 208–16.

Shivers, Alfred S. *Jessamyn West. A Biography.* New York, 1972.

Articles

Anderson, D.D. 'The Way it Was: West's *The Witch-Diggers'. Society for the Study of Midwestern Literature Newsletter* 13 (1983), 38–46.

Bakerman, J.S. 'Daughters and Jessamyn West'. *Midwestern Miscellany* 10 (1982), 49–58.

Carpenter, F.I. 'The Adolescent in American Fiction'. *English Journal* 46 (1957), 313–19.

Chapman, Jennifer. 'Jessamyn West'. In *Women Writers of the West.* Ed. M. Yalom. Santa Barbara, Calif., 1983, 81–90.

Crider, Bill. 'Jessamyn West'. *Dictionary of Literary Biography* 6 (1980), 362–6, and see *Dictionary of Literary Biography Yearbook 1984.*

Flanagen, J.T. 'The Fiction of Jessamyn West'. *Indiana Magazine of History* 67 (1971), 299–316.

Flanagen, J.T. 'Folklore in Five Middle-Western Novelists'. *Great Lanes Review* 1 (1975), 43–57.

Graham, Lee. 'An Interview with Jessamyn West'. *Writer's Digest* 47 (1967), 24–7.

Katope, C.G. 'West's "Love, Death, and the Ladies' Drill Team"'. *Explicator* 23 (1964), 27.

Rout, K.K. 'The Social Morality of *The Massacre at Fall Creek'. Society for the Study of Midwestern Literature Newsletter* 13 (1983), 1–11.

Shivers, Alfred S. 'Jessamyn West'. *Indiana Magazine of History* 67 (1971), 299–316.

Rebecca West

Books

Deakin, Motley F. *Rebecca West.* Boston, 1980.

Glendinning, Victoria. *Rebecca West: A Life.* London, 1987.

Orel, Harold. *The Literary Achievement of Rebecca West.* Basingstoke, 1986.

Ray, Gordon N. *H.G. Wells and Rebecca West.* New Haven, 1974.

Weldon, Fay. *Rebecca West.* Harmondsworth, 1985.

Wolfe, Peter. *Rebecca West: Artist and Thinker.* Carbondale and Edwardsville, Ill., 1971.

Articles

Adamson, Jane. 'States of Soul, Styles of Mind: Rebecca West's *The Fountain Overflows'. Critical Review* 32 (1992), 114–41.

Norton, Ann. 'Rebecca West's Ironic Heroine: Beauty as Tragedy in *The Judge'. English Literature in Transition* 34 (1991), 295–308.

Ray, Philip E. '*The Judge* Reexamined'. *English Literature in Transition* 31 (1988), 297–307.

Scott, B.K. 'The Strange Necessity of Rebecca West'. In *Women Reading Women's Writing.* Ed. Sue Roe. Brighton, 1987, 265–86.

Scott, B.K. 'Rebecca West as Feminist Modernist'. *Twentieth Century Literature* 34 (1991), 169–91.

Spender, Dale. 'Rebecca West'. In *Dictionary of British Women Writers.* Ed. J. Todd. London, 1989, 707–11.

Bibliography and reference

Hutchinson, G.E. 'A Preliminary List of the Writings of Rebecca West 1912–1951'. Updated by M.F. Deakin. *Bulletin of Bibliography* (1982).

Packer, J.G. *Rebecca West: An Annotated Bibliography.* New York and London, 1991.

Edith Wharton

Books

Ammons, Elizabeth. *Edith Wharton's Argument with America.* Athens, Ga., 1980.

Auchincloss, Louis. *Edith Wharton.* Minneapolis, 1971.

Bell, Millicent. *Edith Wharton and Henry James.* New York, 1965.

Bendixen, A. and Zilversmit, A., eds. *Edith Wharton.* New York and London, 1992.

Benstock, Shari, ed. *Edith Wharton: The House of Edith.* New York, 1993.

Benstock, Shari. *A Biography of Edith Wharton.* New York, 1994.

Edith Wharton Review 1983– .

Erlich, G.C. *The Sexual Education of Edith Wharton.* Berkeley, Calif., 1992.

Fryer, Judith. *Felicitous Space: The Imaginative Structures of Wharton and Cather.* Chapel Hill, N.C., 1986.

Fulbrook, Kate. *Free Women: Ethics and Aesthetics in Twentieth Century Women's Fiction.* Hemel Hempstead, 1990.

Goodman, Susan. *Edith Wharton's Women: Friends and Rivals.* Hanover, N.H., 1990.

Goodman, Susan. *Wharton's Inner Circle.* Austin, Tex., 1994.

Goodwyn, Janet. *Edith Wharton: A Traveller in the Land of Letters.* Basingstoke and New York, 1990.

Hadley, K.M. *Edith Wharton's Narrative Strategies.* New York, 1993.

Howe, Irving, ed. *Edith Wharton: A Collection of Critical Essays.* Englewood Cliffs, N.J., 1962.

Joslin, Katherine. *Edith Wharton.* Basingstoke, 1991.

Joslin, K. and Price, A., eds. *Essays on Wharton in Europe.* New York, 1993.

Lawson. R.H. *Edith Wharton*. New York, 1977.

Lewis, R.W.B. *Edith Wharton: A Biography*. London and New York, 1975.

Lyde, M.L. *Edith Wharton: Convention and Morality*. Norman, Okla., 1959.

McDowell, Margaret B. *Edith Wharton*. Boston, 1976.

Nevius, Blake. *Edith Wharton: A Study of Her Fiction*. Berkeley, Calif., 1961.

Raphael, Lev. *Edith Wharton's Neglected Fiction*. Basingstoke, 1991.

Springer, Marlene. *Ethan Frome: A Nightmare of Need*. New York, 1993.

Tuttleton, J.W. et al., eds. *Edith Wharton: The Contemporary Reviews*. Cambridge and New York, 1992.

Vita-Finzi, P. *Edith Wharton and the Art of Fiction*. London, 1990.

Walton, Geoffrey. *Edith Wharton: A Critical Interpretation*. Rutherford, N.J., 1970.

Wershaven, Carol. *The Female Intruder in the Novels of Edith Wharton*. Rutherford and London, 1982.

Wolff, Cynthia Griffin. *A Feast of Words: The Triumph of Edith Wharton*. New York and Oxford, 1977.

Articles

Ammons, Elizabeth. 'The Business of Marriage in *The Custom of the Country*'. *Criticism* 16 (1974), 326–38.

Benert, A.L. 'The Geography of Gender in *The House of Mirth*'. *Studies in the Novel* 22 (1990), 26–42.

Dupree, Ellen. 'Jamming the Machinery: Mimesis in *The Custom of the Country*'. *American Literary Realism* 22 (1990), 5–16.

French, Marilyn. 'Introduction'. In *Roman Fever and Other Stories*. By Edith Wharton. London, 1983.

Gooder, Jean. 'Unlocking Edith Wharton'. *Cambridge Quarterly* 15 (1980), 33–52.

Hadley, K.M. 'Ironic Structure and Untold Stories in *The Age of Innocence*'. *Studies in the Novel* 23 (1991), 262–72.

Kato, N. 'The Doubling in Wharton's Postwar Fictions'. *Studies in American Literature* 28 (1991), 53–76.

McDowell, Margaret B. 'Edith Wharton's Feminism'. *Contemporary Literature* 15 (1974), 521–38.

Olin-Ammentorp, J. 'Wharton's Challenge to Feminist Criticism'. *Studies in American Fiction* 16 (1988), 237–44.

Phelps, Donald. 'Edith Wharton and the Invisible'. *Prose* 7 (1973), 227–45.

Tuttleton, J.W. 'Edith Wharton: Form and the Epistemology of Artistic Creation'. *Criticism* 10 (1968), 334–51.

Tuttleton, J.W. 'Mocking Fate: Romantic Idealism in *The Reef*'. *Studies in the Novel* 19 (1987), 459–74.

Wheeler, K.M. 'The Attack on Realism: Edith Wharton's *In Morocco* and "Roman Fever"'. In *'Modernist' Women Writers and Narrative Art*. Basingstoke, 1994, 77–97.

Woolf, Cynthia G. 'Lily Bart and the Beautiful Death'. *American Literature* 46 (1974), 16–40.

Bibliography and reference

Garrison, Stephen. *Edith Wharton: A Descriptive Bibliography*. Pittsburg, 1990.

Lauer, K.O. and Murray, M.P. *Edith Wharton: An Annotated Secondary Bibliography*. New York, 1990.

Springer, Marlene. *Edith Wharton and Kate Chopin: A Reference Guide*. Boston, 1976 (updated in *Resources for American Literary Studies* 14 (1984), 85–111).

Jeanette Winterson

Books

Duncker, Patricia. *Sisters and Strangers: An Introduction to Contemporary Feminist Fiction*. Oxford, 1992.

Munt, Sally, ed. *New Lesbian Criticism. Literary and Cultural Readings*. New York, 1992.

Rossum-Guyon, F. Van, ed. *Femmes Frauen Women*. Amsterdam, 1990.

Sellars, S. et al., eds. *Feminist Criticism: Theory and Practice*. Hemel Hempstead, 1991.

Articles

Anshaw, Carol. 'Into the Mystic: Winterson's Fable Manners'. *Village Voice Literary Supplement 1986* (1990), 16–17.

Hinds, Hilary. 'Reaching Audiences Other Lesbian Texts Cannot Reach'. In *New Lesbian Criticism*. Ed. S. Munt. Hemel Hempstead, 1992.

Klein, Y.M. 'Myth and Community in Recent Lesbian Autobiographical Fiction'. In *Lesbian Texts and Contexts*. Eds K. Jay and J. Glasgow. New York, 1990.

Lainsbury, G.P. 'The Problem of the "Introduction" to *Oranges are Not the Only Fruit*'. *Notes on Contemporary Literature* 22 (1992), 2–3.

Virginia Woolf

Books

Bazin, N.T. *Virginia Woolf and the Androgynous Vision*. New Brunswick, N.J., 1973.

Beja, Morris, ed. *Critical Essays on Virginia Woolf.* Boston, 1985.

Bell, Quentin. *Virginia Woolf: A Biography.* New York and London, 1972.

Bennett, Joan. *Virginia Woolf: Her Art as a Novelist.* Cambridge, 1964.

Bowlby, Rachel. *Virginia Woolf: Feminist Destinations.* Oxford, 1988.

Bulletin of the New York Public Library. Special issue 80 (1977).

Caughie, P.L. *Virginia Woolf and Postmodernism.* Chicago, 1991.

Clements, Patricia and Grundy, Isabel, eds. *Virginia Woolf: New Critical Essays.* New York, 1983.

DiBattista, Maria. *Virginia Woolf's Major Novels.* New Haven, 1980.

Fleishman, Avrom. *Virginia Woolf: A Critical Reading.* Baltimore, 1975.

Foster, E.M. *Virginia Woolf.* London and New York, 1942.

Freedman, Ralph, ed. *Virginia Woolf: Revaluation and Continuity.* Berkeley, Calif., 1980.

Gordon, Lyndall. *Virginia Woolf: A Writer's Life.* Oxford, 1984.

King, James. *Virginia Woolf.* London, 1994.

Lee, Hermione. *The Novels of Virginia Woolf.* London, 1977.

Majuridan, Robin and McLaurin, Allen, eds. *Virginia Woolf: The Critical Heritage.* London, 1975.

Marcus, Jane, ed. *New Feminist Essays on Virginia Woolf.* Lincoln, Nebr., 1981.

Marcus, Jane. *Virginia Woolf and the Languages of Patriarchy.* Bloomington, Ind., 1984.

Minow-Pinkney, Makiko. *Virginia Woolf and the Problem of the Subject.* Brighton, 1987.

Rose, Phyllis. *A Life of Virginia Woolf.* Oxford, 1978.

Sprague, Clair, ed. *Virginia Woolf: A Collection of Critical Essays.* Englewood Cliffs, N.J., 1971.

Squier, S.M. *Virginia Woolf and London.* Chapel Hill, N.C., 1985.

Articles

Beer, Gillian. 'The Body of the People in Virginia Woolf'. In *Women Reading Women's Writing.* Ed. Sue Roe. Brighton, 1987.

Cohn, Ruby. 'Art in *To the Lighthouse'*. *Modern Fiction Studies* 8 (1962), 127–36.

DeSalvo, Louise. 'Virginia Woolf's Revisions for the 1920 *Voyage Out'*. *Bulletin of Research in the Humanities* Woolf Issue 2 (1979) 338–66.

Eisenberg, Nora. 'Virginia Woolf's Last Words on Words'. In *New Feminist Essays on Virginia Woolf.* Ed. J. Marcus. Lincoln, Nebr., 1981, 256–66.

Fussell, B.H. 'Woolf's Peculiar Comic World: *Between the Acts'*. In *Virginia Woolf: Revaluation*

and Continuity. Ed. Ralph Freedman. Berkeley, Calif., 1980, 263–83.

Hoffman, C.C. 'The Manuscript Revision of *Mrs Dalloway'*. *Modern Fiction Studies* 14 (1968), 171–86.

Kamuf, Peggy. 'Interruptions in *A Room of One's Own'*. *Novel* 16 (1982), 5–18.

MacNeillie, Andrew. 'Introductions'. In *The Collected Essays of Virginia Woolf.* 4 vols. Ed. A. MacNeillie. London, 1986–94.

May, Keith. 'The Symbol of "Painting" in *To the Lighthouse'*. *Review of English Literature* 8 (1967), 91–8.

Moore, Madeline. 'Virginia Woolf's *The Years,* and Years of Adverse Male Reviewers'. *Women's Studies* 4 (1977), 147–63.

Silver, Brenda. 'Virginia Woolf and the Concept of Community'. *Women's Studies* 4 (1977), 291–8.

Bibliography and reference

Kirkpatrick, B.J. *A Bibliography of Virginia Woolf.* Oxford, 1980, 3rd edn.

Anzia Yezierska

Books

Ammons, Elizabeth. *Conflicting Stories.* New York and Oxford, 1991.

Dearborn, M.V. *Love in the Promised Land.* New York, 1988.

Fried, L. et al., eds. *A Handbook of American Jewish Literature.* Westport, Conn., 1988.

Henriksen, L.L. and Boydston, J.A. *Anzia Yezierska: A Writer's Life.* New Brunswick, N.J., 1988.

Neidle, C.S. *America's Immigrant Women.* New York, 1976.

Schofield, M.A., ed. *Cooking By the Book.* Bowling Green, Ohio, 1989.

Shoen, Carol B. *Anzia Yezierska.* Boston, 1982.

Articles

Babbette, I. 'Daughters of Loneliness: Yezierska'. *Studies in American Jewish Literature* 1 (1975), 1–10.

Dearborn, M.V. 'Yezierska and the Making of an Ethnic American Self'. In *The Invention of Ethnicity.* Ed. W. Sollers. New York, 1989.

Drucken, S.A. 'Dialect in Jewish-American Writing'. *Yiddish* 6 (1987), 99–113.

Ferraro, T.S. 'Yezierska's *Bread Givers'*. *South Atlantic Quarterly* 89 (1990), 547–81.

Golub, Ellen. 'The Fiction of Yezierska'. *Studies in American Jewish Literature* 3 (1983), 51–61.

Goodman, Charlotte. 'Anzia Yezierska'. *Dictionary of Literary Biography* 28 (1984), 332–5.

Henriksen, L.L. 'Introduction'. In *Red Ribbon On a White Horse: My Story.* By Anzia Yezierska. London, 1987.

SELECT BIBLIOGRAPHY

Hindus, M. 'The Art of Anna Yezierska'. *Chicago Jewish Forum* (1966–7).

Kesslen-Harris, Alice. 'Introduction'. In *Bread Givers*. By Anzia Yezierska. New York, 1975.

Kesslen-Harris, Alice. 'Introduction'. In *The Open Cage. An Anzia Yezierska Collection*. New York, 1979.

Krut, Riva. 'Introduction'. In *Hungry Hearts and Other Stories*. By Anzia Yezierska. London, 1987.

Regenbaum, Shelly. 'Art, Gender, and the Jewish Tradition in Yezierska and Potok'. *Studies in American Jewish Literature* 7 (1988), 55–66.

Marguerite Young

Books

Duncan, Erika. *Unless Soul Clap Its Hands*. New York, 1984.

Friedman, E.G. and Fuchs, M., eds. *Review of Contemporary Fiction: Kathy Acker, Christine Brooke-Rose and Marguerite Young*. Special issue, 8 (1989).

Newquist, Roy. *Conversation*. New York, 1967.

Nin, Anaïs. *The Novel of the Future*. New York, 1968.

Ruas, C. *Conversations with American Writers*. New York, 1985.

Articles

Bergonzi, Bernard. 'Queen for a Day'. *New York Review of Books* 25 (November 1965), 34–5.

Byatt, Antonia S. 'The Obsession with Amorphous Mankind: Marguerite Young's Strange Best-Seller'. *Encounter* 27 (1966), 63–9.

Duncan, Erika. 'A Reminiscence with Marguerite Young'. *Book* Forum 3 (1975), 426–35.

Durand, Regis. 'La fabrique de la fiction: lecture du roman de Marguerite Young'. *Caliban* 12 (1975), 45–60.

Fuchs, Miriam. 'Marguerite Young's *Miss MacIntosh, My Darling*: Liquescence as Form'. In *Breaking the Sequence*. Eds E.G. Friedman and M. Fuchs. Princeton, N.J., 1989, 188–98.

Gardner, John. Review of *Miss MacIntosh, My Darling*. *Southern Review* 3 (1967), 459–62.

Goyer, William. 'Marguerite Young'. *New York Times Book Review* (12 September 1965).

McEvilly, Wayne. 'The Philosopher without Answers: A Look at Metaphysics and Marguerite Young'. *Studies in the Twentieth Century* 3 (1969), 73–81.

Nin, Anaïs. 'Introduction'. In *Miss MacIntosh, My Darling*. By Marguerite Young. 1979.

Shaviro, S. 'Lost Chords and Interrupted Births: Marguerite Young's Exorbitant Vision'. *Critique* 31 (1990), 213–22.

Index

Note: main entries are in **bold** type.

INDEX

writing, 7, 8, 17–18, 34–5, 42, 51, 61, 76, 81, 105–6, 110, 121–3, 125, 142, 154, 167–9, 170–1, 193, 198–9, 215–17, 219–24, 230, 231, 232–4, 238–40, 245, 268, 291–3, 297–8, 302–3, 312, 313, 320
Wylie, Elinor, 340
Wynter, Sylvia, 331

Yeats, W.B., 30, 62, 307, 313
Yezierska, Anzia, 18, **61–2**, 84

Young, E.H., 333
Young, Florence E. Mills, 325
Young, Marguerite, 77, 128, 135, 136, 151, 154, **161–4**, 187, 206, 207, 218–19, 220, 232, 251, 271, 292, 293, 311
Yu, Ovidia, 330

Zola, Émile, 13, 107, 234
Zwi, Rose, 324